INTERNET 101

INTERNET 101

A Beginner's Guide to the Internet and the World Wide Web

Wendy G. Lehnert

UNIVERSITY OF MASSACHUSETTS, AMHERST

▲ ADDISON-WESLEY

An imprint of Addison Wesley Longman, Inc.

Reading, Massachusetts • Harlow, England • Menlo Park, California

Berkeley, California • Don Mills, Ontario • Sydney • Bonn • Amsterdam • Tokyo • Mexico City

ACQUISITIONS EDITOR:	Susan Hartman
ASSISTANT EDITOR:	Julie Dunn
PRODUCTION EDITOR:	Patricia A. O. Unubun
DESIGN EDITOR:	Alwyn R. Velásquez
MANUFACTURING COORDINATOR:	Judy Sullivan
COVER ILLUSTRATION:	Susan Cyr
TEXT DESIGN:	John Reinhardt
COMPOSITOR:	Sally Simpson
COPYEDITOR:	Laura K. Michaels
PROOFREADER:	Diane Freed

Access the latest information about Addison-Wesley books at our World Wide Web site:
http://www.awl.com/cseng

Many of the designations used by manufacturers and sellers to distinguish their products are claimed as trademarks. Where those designations appear in this book, and Addison-Wesley was aware of a trademark claim, the designations have been printed in caps or initial caps.

Library of Congress Cataloging-in-Publication Data

Lehnert. Wendy G.
   Internet 101 : a beginner's guide to the Internet and the WWW /
Wendy G. Lehnert
     p. cm.
   Includes index.
   ISBN 0-201-32553-5
   1. Internet (Computer network)—Handbooks, manuals, etc. 2. World
Wide Web (Information retrieval system)—Handbooks, manuals, etc.
I. Title.
TK5105.875.I57L465 1998
004.67'8—dc21
                               97-34600
                               CIP

Reprinted with corrections, March 1998.

6 7 8 9 10 MA 010099

For Mark, Michael, Kate, and Annelise

Preface

Preface

This book is more than just a book about the Internet. It is part of an integrated package (or coursepack) that includes Web pages for both students and teachers. The Internet 101 coursepack is designed primarily for undergraduates who have little or no computer experience and who want to use the Internet. In its entirety, this text is appropriate for a 3-credit college-level course on the Internet. Alternatively, selected chapters can be integrated into a general computer literacy curriculum or an introduction to computer science course. It can be used as the basis for a workshop on the Internet, independent course projects, self-instruction, or personal reference. The text covers all the basic Internet applications of interest to a non-technical audience, and also includes optional topics appropriate for an honors section or computer science majors. Its only prerequisite is some prior exposure to some computer application (such as a word processor, spreadsheet, or educational software). However, no specific knowledge of a particular computer platform is required.

The Internet requires skills and know-how that can only be acquired through online experience. This book takes a hands-on approach right from the start, and encourages a systematic exploration of the Internet. Anyone who reads this book and works through a sampling of the exercises will become proficient in the use of the Internet.

Using the Internet 101 Web Pages

The best way to learn about the Internet is by spending time on the Internet, but that time must be spent intelligently. The Internet 101 Web pages accompany each chapter as a timely source of supplemental readings, related topics, and software resources. Students and teachers alike can use these pages to pursue a subject in greater depth, and anyone can use them as a source of reliable pointers to high-quality Internet resources. Through the integration of the book with a Web site, the Internet becomes an extension of the book, where problems and exercises can be pursued without any need for extensive lists of bookmarks or notes based on the text. Why retype a lengthy URL from a printed page when you can launch a Web browser and click a link? The book provides important background and explanations that are essential for Internet mastery, while the Web pages streamline the process of transforming instruction into action, encouraging the crucial hands-on experimentation that leads to true Internet mastery. Additional online resources are also available specifically for teachers (see "Notes to the Teacher" below).

Why the Iguana?

The green iguana is a fitting symbol for everything that is unique and wonderful about the Internet. Iguanas are surprisingly popular in the United States as pets, especially among college students and the 20-or-30-something crowd. Unfortunately, there is much published misinformation available to a prospective iguana owner when it comes to simple matters such as what constitutes a healthy diet or how an iguana should be housed. Luckily for the iguana, many iguana enthusiasts are active on the Internet and talking to each other. Questions from beginners are being answered in great detail by herpetologists and experienced iguana owners. Thanks to the Internet, this native inhabitant of tropical rain forests now thrives in Arizona, Alaska, and all kinds of intemperate regions. The iguana community is not a place you will find on any map, but it is alive and well on the Internet!

Meeting the Challenges

One can argue that there are already more than enough books about the Internet. That's certainly what I thought in 1995 when I set out to design a course on the subject. It's true that many books have been written, but precious few are textbooks written by experienced teachers. I've tried to teach from the available books. At first I inflicted a 1300-page reference book on my students. The next year I tried out a 200-page book that contained only the minimal basics. In both cases, I found myself preparing extensive notes for my students in order to give them what they really needed to know. The shortcomings of many Internet books are readily recognized by anyone who has taught this material. The major difficulties are (1) material and pointers that are out of date, (2) the inclusion of too many low-level details about platform-dependent software, and (3) a failure to convey anything about the history and real-world implications of the Internet. The Internet 101 coursepack has been designed to address each of these problem areas, as described below.

The Currency Solution

The Internet is a moving target. Servers that were popular two years ago are no longer maintained or used by as many people today. The most popular Web browsers are enhanced and re-released at least once a year. The best Web search engines redesign their interfaces and expand their services in an effort to stay competitive. Any Internet book that was written more than a year ago invariably contains outdated material. The currency problem applies to both Internet software and Internet resources, both of which are at the heart of any introduction to the Internet. Many books about the Internet have been written with no regard for the problem of maintaining currency.

For example, many Internet books contain lengthy compilations of useful Internet addresses (URLs). Unfortunately, URLs have a half-life of about 6-12 months. This means that of any collection of URLs that are operational today, at least half of the URLs are likely to produce a "404 Not Found" error a year from now. A book that contains an obsolete URL and does not explain how to find the new URL for the same material or other comparable resources is not teaching essential Internet skills. Readers are being handed a proverbial fish when they really need to learn how to catch their own.

This book does not contain extensive lists of URLs. I have tried to keep the number of URLs down to a minimum because of their short lives. However, I realize that a small collection of high-quality Web pointers are invaluable to a beginner. So whenever it is appropriate to provide the reader with pointers to a select collection of Web pages, I have included these URLs in the text itself. But the better place to look for specific URLs is at the Internet 101 Web site:

```
http://www.awl.com/cseng/titles/0-201-32553-5/
```

URLs found at this site will be updated as needed to minimize the frustration of pursuing outdated pointers. I will also post updates to the Internet 101 text on this site, in the event that material in print becomes outdated. Information that is inherently unstable is best managed on a Web site where addresses and descriptions can be readily updated. Only the most stable information about the Internet belongs in a book. This book was organized from the start with an associated Web site in mind in order to conquer the currency problem.

The Platform Dependence Solution

Too many Internet books are mired in the technical details of specific software that is irrelevant for a large number of otherwise potential readers. If a book assumes a Macintosh platform, no one will read it but Macintosh users. Likewise for PCs and UNIX workstations. Shopping around for a platform-dependent text does not always solve the problem, because a reader really wants a book that covers a specific collection of software: the software that is available to the reader. Platform-specific books typically fail to include all the software readers need to know, even though the book addresses the right platform. For example, if a book assumes a UNIX platform, its author can select from three popular text editors (pico, vi, and emacs), two popular mail clients (elm and pine), and many possible newsreaders (readnews, vnews, rn, trn, xrn, and tin). If a book covers only one option from each category, it will invariably miss the mark for many potential readers.

A few books attempt to deal with this by taking the opposite tack: They try to cover all of the most popular software on one or more hardware platforms in an effort to maximize their readership. But this comprehensive approach necessarily results in a hefty, encyclopedic-type reference book.

It is an egregious error to give students the impression that computers and the Internet demand substantial software mastery. It is better to describe a minimal kernel of essential software features and then move on to other matters. Most all Web browsers have the same navigational capabilities and preference options, just as most text editors support paragraph formatting and grab-and-drop. By concentrating on generic software descriptions rather than specific command sets, this book stresses the more stable functionality of Internet applications while avoiding the less stable details of specific interfaces and applications. On the other hand, command list summaries do come in handy and beginners benefit greatly from software demonstrations.

To solve the platform dependence problem, I have placed software-specific material on the Internet 101 Web pages. There you will find pointers to software introductions, command summary sheets, and additional software-related material for Macintosh, Windows, and UNIX platforms. By keeping this information online, I avoid burdening the reader with irrelevant pages of text. It is easier to skip an irrelevant link on a Web page than 200 pages of irrelevant material in a printed book.

In a classroom environment, teachers can duplicate brief command summary handouts and instruction sheets to cover whatever software is supported by their own computer facilities. Many schools have an Information Technology Office or a Computer Support Service that routinely distribute software overviews to students and staff for quick reference. Software summaries and command sheets are also available on the Internet 101 Web pages. If you ever change your software or your computer platform, you won't need a new book. You'll just need new software summaries.

The Big Picture Solution

When an Internet book is preoccupied with low-level details, it can't place the Internet in the larger context of its historical roots, social impact, and legal ramifications. Chapter 2 presents basic Internet concepts in an historical framework to set the stage for everything that follows. In addition, each chapter that introduces a new application explains a little about its origins and motivation.

Students can absorb the whats and the hows more readily when they are combined with some whys and whens.

Moreover, no one should claim to understand the Internet without having first explored the most important social issues that perplex lawyers, politicians, publishers, and telecommunication analysts (to name a few). Chapter 13 describes seven illegal activities facilitated by the Internet, and discusses the major social issues associated with the Internet. Readers will also find short digressions addressing the real-world side of the Internet throughout all of the chapters. In my experience, students enjoy anecdotes based on real events, and concrete examples make general concepts more memorable for everyone.

Special Features of This Book

Visual icons have been used throughout this textbook to highlight specific kinds of information. Each icon signals an information category, alerting the reader to information that may be of practical value, pedagogical import or that is a real-world example of something described in the text. Six different icons are used:

The Internet 101 Web Pages
Under this icon at the start of each chapter is a short list of related content on the Internet 101 Web pages. These lists are meant to be more suggestive than comprehensive to give the reader a taste of what is available online.

Helpful Hints
Experience in the classroom has taught me to anticipate specific traps into which students frequently fall. Under this icon the reader will find helpful advice about these most common beginner pitfalls.

Heads-Up Warnings
When it is appropriate to warn the reader about a potentially regrettable scenario, it is highlighted with this icon. Everyone likes to avoid disasters and embarassment, and a fearful neophyte may eschew hands-on exploration in an effort to prevent serious mistakes. But armed with an understanding of the most commonly encountered mistakes and technical difficulties, beginners can venture forth on the Internet without fear.

Useful Jargon and Definitions
All books about the Internet must explain a certain amount of technical jargon in order to prepare readers for life online. Many relevant definitions and

explanations have been distributed throughout this text, introduced in the context of a specific motivating application. Important concepts and jargon are also emphasized with this icon for easy reference.

Software Checklists

Under this icon, readers will find essential software features highlighted in software checklists. These checklists describe generic software features that are common to all application packages of the same genre. If you have software documentation for a specific application, and a software checklist, you can test your mastery of the software by working through the checklist. If you can do everything on the checklists for a specific application, you have the software mastery needed to put that application to work for you.

The First E-mail Message

Real-World and the Internet

Real-world anecdotes and interesting facts about the Internet can be found throughout this book under this icon. Concrete examples of general concepts may be included in these digressions to illustrate the Internet in action or a specific class of Internet phenomena. Concrete examples can make an abstract concept easier to grasp and remember. They also lighten up the reading.

The Index

The index for this text was designed by me with beginners and casual readers in mind. Entries like "newbies: classic mistakes", and "e-mail: missing" will help readers zero in on practical information that might otherwise be difficult to find.

A Note to the Student

It has been my experience that students find this material thoroughly enjoyable and easy to learn. This book is designed to give you all the basics needed for full Internet mastery in a few months. If you set out to cover a chapter a week, you should be able to complete the software checklists, problems, and exercises that are designed to give you first-hand experience with the Internet. Take advantage of the Internet 101 Web pages and do as many exercises as you can.

If you are not enrolled in a class and wish to use this book for self-study, Chapter 1 and Appendix A will show you how to obtain Internet access from scratch. Chapter 2 lays out some foundational concepts that will be referenced throughout the remainder of the text. Once you are off the ground, you can visit specific chapters in any order you wish as your interests dictate (see "Internet Topics and Chapter Selection").

The Internet offers educational resources, social enrichment, professional advantage, and entertainment. Efforts to commercialize the Web have undoubtedly contributed to a picture of the Internet as a bountiful landscape which can be traversed and harvested with minimal effort. But mastering the command set for a Web browser does not constitute Internet mastery. The Web is indeed a potential gold mine, but its treasures are not easily found without informed search strategies and some knowledge of the Internet in general. True Internet mastery is not difficult to achieve, but it does require some effort. This book was written to make that effort fruitful, so that the Internet will be an enjoyable and worthwhile addition to your life.

A Note to the Teacher

An instructor's manual is available on the Internet 101 Web pages with a sample course syllabus, suggested homework assignments, answers to all of the problems and exercises, and general advice about the logistics of managing online homework collection and other matters. If you have never taught a course about the Internet before, a special section covers tips and advice that I have acquired from first-hand experience. Some of this information is publically available and some (e.g. answers to exercises) is available only to registered course instructors. Please contact your Addison-Wesley representative for information about accessing this manual or send e-mail to aw.cse@aw.com.

Internet Topics and Chapter Selection

It is standard practice to organize Internet books around individual software applications. This text follows suit, but emphasizes additional material in the context of each software application. A brief synopsis of the topics will give you a feel for the material beyond the software, and where to find it.

E-mail and Mailing Lists

Many people who rely on the Internet in work environments have discovered that working with the Internet can be very time-consuming. With more and more people using e-mail for business communications, it is important to go beyond the commands for reading, deleting, and writing e-mail messages. Automated filters and mail routing can be used to separate urgent messages from messages that can be ignored. But there are additional techniques for minimizing the time spent with e-mail. Chapter 3 begins with the basics of e-mail and goes on to outline 14 strategies for effective e-mail management. Chapter 4 covers mailing lists, including techniques for handling the extremely heavy volumes of e-mail (e.g. 100 messages a day) associated with highly active mailing lists.

Finding Things on the World Wide Web

According to one survey, 84% of Internet users are not satisfied with their ability to find things on the Web. For every book that talks about what to do after a Web search engine returns 80,000 so-called hits, there are 30 more that merely offer pointers to additional search engines. As a result, too many people are under the impression that it is impossible to find information on the Internet. With so many books about the Internet, it is remarkable how few discuss the skills and tricks that make the difference between success and failure with a Web search engine. Effective keyword searches should be a central component of any syllabus dedicated to the Internet. This book includes two self-contained chapters (5 and 7) devoted to the Web and how to find things on the Web. You will not find long lists of URLs in these chapters but you will find an introduction to keyword search engines, subject trees, and clearinghouses. In addition, Chapter 7 presents a systematic approach to keyword searches based on a simple taxonomy of the questions behind the queries.

Gopher resources are in decline, but students will invariably stumble across Gopher menus with their Web browser. Chapter 6 answers the question "Why do these Web pages all look alike, and why do they keep mentioning Veronica?" Gopher is also pedagogically interesting as the answer to the question, "What would the Web look like if it had no graphics and no hypertext?" A comparison of Gopher space and the Web makes it easier to appreciate those unique elements of the Web that make it such a compelling communication medium.

Usenet Newsgroups

The Usenet newsgroups are a favorite haunt for those who enjoy channel surfing through 20,000 ongoing conversations. But the true legacy of Usenet lies in the tradition of FAQ files as a repository of reliable information. FAQs are also a striking example of the "gift economy" of the Internet. Usenet raises additional issues as well. The problem of Usenet spam motivates an examination of Netiquette, free speech, censorship, self-regulation, and legislative intervention. The existence of searchable Usenet archives raises questions of privacy and whether anything on the Internet can be truly private. Chapter 8 covers the operation of news readers and resources for finding newsgroups along with the larger issues that go hand-in-hand with Usenet.

Software on the Internet

Students are often eager to exploit the software resources of the Internet, but they should know more than the basics of FTP before they download executables onto a home computer. Chapter 9 covers FTP, the practical ins and outs of file formats and file utilities, and clearinghouses for reputable shareware and freeware. Computer viruses and virus detection software are covered, including the new class of macro viruses which are an increasingly common problem for people who use mail attachments.

Online Communities

Public Telnet servers are another example of an Internet application which is gradually being absorbed by the Web. However, Telnet servers and their tradition of registered members shows how online privileges can be tied to community standards for acceptable online behavior. This model of community membership provides an interesting counterpoint for the anarchy of Usenet. Telnet servers also gave rise to MUDs and IRC, which are interesting playgrounds for gender bending, general role playing, and the curious phenomenon of TinySex. Chapter 10 covers all of this as well as Freenets and community networks. Other chapters that cover communication vehicles for online communities include Chapter 4 (on mailing lists) and Chapter 8 (on the Usenet newsgroups).

Web Page Construction

Many students are drawn to the Internet because they want to construct a home page on the Web. Basic HTML is not difficult and students are pleasantly surprised to see how quickly they can bring up their own Web pages. The last section of Chapter 5 and all of Chapter 11 constitute a short workshop on Web page construction: text formatting, absolute links, named links, relative links, directory path names, the alignment of inline graphics, text/graphics alignment, GIF and JPEG images, transparent GIFs, interlaced GIFs, clickable graphics, thumbnail sketches, tables, frames, and useful items for a Webmaster's toolbox. I stop short of anything involving real programming (CGI and Java), but Web page construction may prove to be an entry point into computer programming for students who would otherwise have no interest in the subject.

Encryption on the Internet

Chapter 12 offers an optional foray into digital encryption with an emphasis on practical PGP. Double-key cryptography is explained along with the mechanics of encrypted files, clear signed documents, signature verification, and public key validation. If you skip this material it won't be missed, but students tend to find it interesting. Chapter 12 lays out the basics of PGP along with the saga of Phil Zimmermann and the difficulties of legislative efforts to control strong encryption on the Internet. An optional (extra credit) PGP assignment at the end of the semester is a great way to wrap things up on a fun note.

Chapter Selection

This book was written for students enrolled in a course devoted to the Internet, as well as students in computer literacy courses or other courses where the Internet is only part of the curriculum. Because each chapter is largely self-contained, an instructor has a lot of flexibility in the selection of reading assignments and exercises. There is more than enough material here to fill a 15-week semester, and optional sections can be omitted to fit trimester or quarter schedules. Here are some suggested curriculum options:

For a course devoted to the Internet:
All chapters 1-13, omitting selected optional sections as needed

For an Internet unit in a computer literacy course:
Chapters 1, 2, 3, 5, 8, and 13

For an Internet unit in an introductory computer science course:
Chapters 2, 5, 9, 12, and 13

For a workshop or independent project on the World Wide Web:
Chapters 5, 7, 11, and 13 including all optional sections

For an online research course aimed at students in journalism, legal studies, or other specialities in the humanities:
Chapters 1, 2, 3, 4, 5, 7, and 8

Selected readings from chapters 2 and 13 can be scattered throughout a syllabus in order to balance hands-on activities with the "big picture." Some material can be regarded as optional and may be reserved for an honors section or extra credit. In the table of contents, optional material has been marked (*) for easy identification.

Acknowledgments

Many people helped make this book possible. First and foremost, I am indebted to Professor David Stemple, Dean Linda Slakey, and the computer science faculty at the University of Massachusetts for encouraging me to develop an undergraduate course on the Internet, especially Professor Barbara Lerner who took it over for one semester while I was writing this book. This book grew out of my lecture notes for CmpSci 191 at the University of Massachusetts at Amherst during 1995-96. Many enthusiastic undergraduate assistants have made CmpSci 191 possible since 1995: Ben DeLong, Lee Weiner, Kevin Gallant, Sanjay Patel, Eric Frietag, Sara Yaffe, Mert Cambol, and Jason Levisse. I am also fortunate to have had access to the expertise of an excellent technical support staff: Steve Cook (Director of the Computer Science Computing Facility at UMass-Amherst), Valerie Caro, Ole Craig, John Greene, Ethan Haslett, Terrie Kellogg, Michael Kieras, Glenn Loud, Sanjay Patel, Gary Rehorka, Jane Ricard, Paul A. Sihvonen-Binder, and Rob Wise. In addition, my lab manager, David Fisher, deserves special thanks for all the e-mail conversations at 6 am and for keeping me operational no matter what. Additional assistance was provided by Professors Rick Adrion (on Internet history), Jim Kurose (on networking concepts), and Ethan Katsh (on the First Amendment). Any errors that may have found their way onto these pages are undoubtedly my doing and must be attributed only to me.

I am also indebted to Fitchburg State College for providing me with reliable Internet access from my home. I am most grateful to Rodney Gaudet and Roy Hall for the professional courtesies they have extended to me. Others who have enriched my own experiences with the Internet include Phil Agre, Jon Aseltine, Roger Cappallo, Larry Hunter, Ellen Riloff, and John Ting. Other people and organizations have kindly allowed me to use various Internet-related materials throughout the book, including David Albert, Michael Betts, Wade Blomgren, Adam Boettiger, Rolf Braun, Marian Briones, Vint Cerf, Patrick D. Crispen, Helen Doerr, Adam C. Engst, Aaron Flin, Jay Garcia, Anu Garg, Iain Lea, Austin Meredith, Adam Miller, Mark Moraes, John Pike, Steve Sample, Leo G. Simonetta, Daniel Sleator, Ceylon Stowell, Argonne National Laboratory, Business Week, CNET Inc., Digital Equipment Corp., Excite, Inc., Infoseek Corp., MicroMUSE Operations Council, Microsoft Corp., the National Fraud Information Center, Netscape Comunications Corp., Pretty Good Privacy, Inc., QUALCOMM Inc., and Sleator Games, Inc.

I am grateful beyond words for Priscilla Coe's excellent administrative support. With Priscilla in my corner I can tackle large all-consuming projects without fear. And speaking of fear, the data recovery services of Ontrack Computer Systems, Inc. rescued half of this manuscript from digital oblivion when a catastrophic hard drive failure ate all my laptop's files.

Many thanks go to everyone at Addison-Wesley who supported me in this endeavor. My editor, Susan Hartman, encouraged me and guided me from the beginning. Assistant editor Julie Dunn provided considerable assistance with copyright permissions. Production editor Patricia Unubun reworked all of my graphics and managed the production process and design editor Alwyn Velásquez designed the cover of the book and guided the interior designer through the design stages. My copy editor, Laura Michaels, caught countless problems with my exposition as well as my sentences. I am very impressed with her diligent efforts. In addition, many reviewers provided timely feedback and valuable suggestions: Bruce Char (Drexel University), H. E. Dunsmore (Purdue University), Dennis Foreman (Binghamton University), Henry L. Jackson (Austin Community College), Floyd LeCureux (California State University at Sacramento), Mark Leone (Indiana University), Kimberly Pollack (City College of San Francisco), Kris Rudin (Eastern Washington University), Stu Smith (University of Massachusetts at Lowell), and James Ward (University of Wyoming). This book benefited greatly from their comments. Thank you one and all.

Finally, I want to thank my husband, Mark Snyder, who has always supported me in every way, and my children, Michael, Kate, and Annelise, for tearing me away from the computer from time to time. All my distractions should be so delightful.

Wendy Lehnert

Contents

Optional sections/chapters are marked (*)

CHAPTER 13 Social Issues   **457**

INTERNET 101

First Things First

Great works are performed, not by strength, but perseverance.

- SAMUEL JOHNSON

THE INTERNET 101 WEB PAGES

- Timely Updates on ISPs
- Online Access Innovations
- Downloading the Most Popular Web Browsers
- Moving Files across a Modem

Getting Started

1.1

Before you can do anything online, you must have access to the Internet. Students at colleges and universities can usually obtain an educational account. Check whether your school has an Office of Information Technology or a Computer Services Office that maintains educational accounts for students. If you do not have access to an educational computing facility, you will need to look for a commercial **Internet Service Provider (ISP)**, a company that provides access to the Internet. Some considerations associated with ISPs are discussed in Appendix A. Either kind of service provider (an educational facility or an ISP) should be able to help you with everything you need for Internet access. When you work from an educational computing lab, all the necessary software will be in place and ready to go. If you want to use your own personal computer (PC) for Internet access, you will need to install some special software on your computer. Working from a computer lab is the easier option, but it won't give you the convenience of Internet access from home.

If you are not setting up a home computer for Internet access at this time, you can skip the rest of this section and go directly to Section 1.2.

Your service provider can give you recommendations for preferred system configurations, including memory requirements. They will also set up a personal userid and password for you and give you a special telephone number that you will need to connect your computer to the Internet. Software installation can be handled a number of ways. Most service providers will assist you with obtaining and installing the software you need. Many provide conveniently bundled software with step-by-step instructions for installation and start-up. If you are not very experienced with computers, let your service provider guide you, and follow their recommendations. Most of their users are beginners, and it is their job to get all of their users up and running as quickly and easily as possible.

If you have an IBM-compatible or a Macintosh and you want to explore the Internet from your home, here's what you need to do:

1. Select an ISP (or educational facility) for Internet access.
2. Check memory recommendations; upgrade your memory if needed.
3. Make sure you have at least a 28.8Kbps modem.
4. Obtain your service provider's dial-up telephone number.
5. Obtain your service provider's numeric IP address.
6. Obtain your login ID (username) and password.
7. Obtain instructions for installing Internet software on your computer.
8. Follow the software installation instructions.

If you cannot obtain local Internet access, you can subscribe to a national service provider and let them set you up. **America Online (AOL)** is the most popular of the national services. You will find advertisements for other national service providers in magazines and on television. *These services do not always provide full Internet access. However, they will give you their own version of Internet-based services and they are often the easiest option for people who are inexperienced with computers.*

The national service providers used to be more expensive than local ISPs, but competition has forced down their pricing. The most competitive services now offer unlimited access for a fixed monthly rate. Try to avoid any services that charge you by the hour for your connect time and watch

When the Modem Pool Has a Melt-Down

In December 1996, AOL announced it would provide unlimited Internet access for a flat monthly rate of $19.95. Their subscriber base quickly swelled from 6 million to 8 million. The new flat-rate billing system also encouraged AOL subscribers to dial in more often and stay connected for longer periods of time. By January 1997, AOL was facing lawsuits from frustrated customers who couldn't connect to their AOL accounts. The AOL modem pool was not large enough to support all of the AOL customers and their demands for more connect time. AOL promised to add more modems and expected to have 400,000 modems in place by June 1997.

Each customer connection ties up one modem, so 400,000 modems would allow only 5% of the 8 million AOL subscribers to be online at any one time. Most ISPs can connect between 5 to 10% of their subscribers at a given time, and even the best ISPs are set up to cover no more than 14% of their customers at once. (For comparison's sake, your local phone company is probably engineered to handle about 14% of their total customers at any one time as well.) Smaller ISPs who experience these types of "growing pains" are often forced out of business because they can't keep up with a rapidly expanding customer base. AOL's problems received national attention, but their modem crisis was typical of the problems experienced by many growing ISPs.

out for any extra charges, which can add up quickly. A national service provider gives you special interface software that works only with their service. These interfaces are designed to get you up and running as quickly and painlessly as possible.

What Is Full Internet Access?

How do you know if a service provides "full" Internet access? Here's a simple checklist of the Internet applications that define full access:

1. The World Wide Web (the Web)
2. Usenet newsgroups
3. E-mail
4. Telnet
5. FTP

Don't worry if you have no idea what these things are right now. That's why you're reading this book.

As a final option, you can also purchase commercial Internet software from a software retailer. These packages generally contain an e-mail interface, a graphical Web browser, a newsgroup reader, Telnet and FTP utilities, and a configuration utility to help you set up everything. Most of these packages integrate all of the software inside an easy-to-use interface, and they support full Internet access through a local ISP. The idea is to get you on to the Internet quickly and painlessly (albeit for a price).

Some Commercial Internet Set-Up Software

If your local ISP is not able to get you up and running, you might want to investigate commercial all-purpose navigation packages. Quality varies from product to product though, so read some software reviews or get a recommendation from a satisfied user before you lay down your money.

> EXPLORE Internet
> IBM Internet Connection for Windows
> Internet Anywhere
> Internet Chameleon
> Internet in a Box
> Netscape Navigator Personal Edition
> SuperHighway Access

In addition to these navigation packages, there are also some special-purpose interfaces for the Internet. For example, if you play chess, you can purchase a chess interface so that you can play chess with people all over the world via the Internet. These special-purpose interfaces are very good, but read Chapter 10 before you spend money on a commercial interface.

Note that much of the software you can buy commercially is also available for free on the Internet. For example, Netscape Navigator is available for free as long as you are using it for educational or nonprofit purposes. If you use it at work, it is free for a 90-day trial period; after that, you pay a licensing fee. Once you have learned how to download software from the Internet, you can experiment with different Web browsers and decide which one you like best. But to get started, just follow the recommendations of your service provider.

If you are buying a new computer to connect to the Internet, pay attention to how fast the CPU is, how much memory you're getting (both RAM memory and hard drive capacity), and how fast the modem is. In general, you want to get the fastest hardware and the most memory that you can afford. The following section offers some specific guidelines to keep in mind.

A Friend in Need . . .

Ask a friend or relative for advice about local ISPs. Anyone who uses an ISP will be happy to share their war stories. If someone helps you install your Internet software, repay their kindness with a favor in return. People who work with computers frequently ask one another for help. If you try to go it alone, everything will be harder and take longer.

HINT

The CPU

The CPU is analogous to a car engine: Fast, powerful CPUs make fast, powerful computers. A Pentium-based PC will give you enough horsepower for the Internet. A 486-based PC won't be quite as zippy, but it is adequate. If you are looking at Macs, check out the PowerPC line and look into the newer companies marketing Mac clones. Almost any home computer manufactured after 1996 has enough horsepower for the Internet.

RAM Memory

You need 16MB if you want to run Windows 95, and that's a minimal configuration for new machines (in 1997). If you expect to get involved with Web page design and computer graphics, you'll want at least 32MB of RAM.

The Hard Drive

A 1GB hard drive is standard on even a low-end PC these days. You can get by with less, but if you expect to install a lot of applications, you'll see how quickly a smaller hard drive fills up. Today's larger hard drives are designed to store memory-intensive applications and graphics. If you don't need many applications and you aren't planning to work with graphics, you can manage with less storage; as little as 120MB could get you going in a pinch. However, you won't be happy in such cramped living quarters for very long. Get the biggest hard drive you can afford, but be prepared to settle for 540MB if you are bargain hunting.

Beyond Bits and Bytes

The smallest unit of computer memory is a bit. A **bit** is basically an on/off switch and is usually described as a 1 or a 0. A **byte** is a pattern of 8 bits. A byte is the amount of memory needed to encode an alphanumeric character such as A–Z or 0–9. Additional units of memory are defined by powers of 2:

Continued on Next Page

Continued from Previous Page

1 **kilobyte** (1K) = 1,024 bytes
($1,024 = 2^{10}$)

1 **megabyte** (1MB) = 1,024K = 1,048,576 bytes
($1,048,576 = 2^{20}$)

1 **gigabyte** (1GB) = 1,024MB = 1,073,741,824 bytes
($1,073,741,824 = 2^{30}$)

Pages of text are usually described in terms of kilobytes. This chapter contains about 44 kilobytes (44K) of text. Megabytes are the units most often used to describe computer memory and disk storage capacities. Most PCs today contain between 8 and 32MB of RAM. Today's hard drives are measured in hundreds of megabytes, sometimes even in gigabytes.

Text files are relatively undemanding as far as storage requirements go. The complete works of Shakespeare consume roughly 5MB. On the other hand, a single copy of Netscape Navigator requires 18MB. Graphics and video clips also consume a lot of memory. A few photographs can eat up an entire megabyte, and a 1-minute video requires nearly 100MB. No matter how much memory you have, you'll want more.

The Modem

These days a 28.8Kbps modem is commonly used to connect a home computer to the Internet, although you can go up to 56Kbps on a regular phone line. 28.8K refers to the speed of the modem as measured in bits per second (bps). If you intend to spend lot of time on the Web, don't settle for less than 28.8K. If you expect to spend most of your time reading e-mail, you can get by with a 14.4K modem. You can use a 14.4K modem for Web browsing, but it will be pretty pokey. For example, it takes about 40 minutes to download Netscape Navigator using a 14.4K modem. It doesn't really matter if the modem is internal (installed inside your computer) or external (sitting outside on top of your desk). If your desk is cramped for space, you have reason to prefer an internal modem. The functionality, however, is the same in either case.

MODEM PROBLEMS?

If your modem frequently disconnects you, the problem might be your service provider, or it might be something else. For example, if you have call waiting on your phone line, turn it off when you go online. If call waiting isn't the problem, you may have some touchy hardware on your end. A flakey modem or faulty modem connection could be the problem. The cable that runs between your modem and your phone jack can become damaged, yet show no signs of wear. A damaged cable may appear to be working insofar as you can establish your connection, but frequent disconnections can occur due to signal degradation. If you are losing your connection on a regular basis, try replacing your modem cable. To prevent cable problems, keep the cable where it won't get stepped on. Also note that some service providers automatically disconnect customers if no activity is detected for some time. Check to see if your service provider has such a policy.

What about a Mac?

If you prefer a Macintosh computer, any of the newer models are fine for Internet access. A PowerPC is an excellent choice. You should have a machine that runs System 7.5 (or above). The only drawback with a Mac is that many ISPs are PC-oriented and may not have staff who can provide good Mac support. If you are worried about this, investigate your service provider options and ask about Mac support before you invest in a Mac. Adequate technical support from your service provider is very important when you are just getting started.

Accessing the World Wide Web

1.2

The Web is the premier Internet application. It is the application that made the Internet accessible to children, senior citizens, and everyone in between. The most remarkable thing about the Web is how easy it is to work with. Once you have a Web browser installed and working, the basic mechanics of the browser are very simple. Learn a few navigational commands, and you are off and running.

The Web consists of graphics and **hypertext.** Hypertext is a little hard to describe in words, but it is easy to grasp in practice. Think of hypertext as footnotes run amuck. When you are reading text and you see a superscript indicating a footnote, either you can choose to ignore the footnote and keep reading or you can interrupt the main flow of ideas and digress for a moment into the footnote. Traditional text can have as many footnotes as the author sees fit to include, but no one inserts a footnote inside another footnote.

Footnotes are limited to a linear progression of comments that relate to the main text.

In hypertext, the notion of a footnote is generalized. Not only can you nest footnotes inside footnotes, but now footnotes can point to anything, including entire documents written by other authors. Whenever a new document is added to the Web, it becomes available to anyone who wants to identify it as a potential digression from their own document. There is no hierarchy that makes one document more important than any other, and digressions to other documents often lead to rich collections of related information. Hypertext enables associations across multiple authors that sometimes resemble collective authorship but without the overhead of a coordinated effort. A pointer from a main text to a related document is called a **link.** The terms **hyperlink**, **hot link**, **button**, **hot button**, and **pointer** are also used. Hyperlinks on a Web page may be underlined, appear in boldface, or be displayed in a different color (usually blue) so you can easily see them. Different browsers use different display conventions. Figure 1.1 shows a Web document of interest to Netscape Navigator users.

A **Web page** is a single text document in the Web. A single Web page can contain any number of words. When a page is long, you can scroll it. Most Web browsers allow you to scroll up and down by pointing to arrows on a scroll bar that runs vertically along the right-hand side of the document. If a Web page contains no links of its own to other Web pages, it is effectively a dead end. Most documents on the World Wide Web contain links to additional Web pages. You can traverse a link by clicking it with your mouse.

The process of reading Web pages and traversing links to more Web pages is called **browsing**, or **surfing**. You can browse Web pages casually for entertainment, or you can browse with a serious goal in mind. But either way, you are browsing when you don't know beforehand exactly where a link is going to take you. Browsing is an exploratory process. It comes naturally to people because it is a lot like daydreaming. You simply go where your interests lead you.

It is possible to traverse a lot of links in a few minutes of browsing time. This may make it confusing when the time comes to back up and return to the document you left 20 links ago. Fortunately, all Web browsers make it easy to get back to where you started, even if you can't remember where that was. Each time you traverse a link from one document to another, your browser updates a **history list** of the documents you've visited. If you need to go back, you can ask the browser to pop up its history list. In this way, you can always retrace your steps just as if you had left bread crumbs along the way. The **Back button** lets you retrace your hyperlinks one step at a time. You can also visit the history list and see links to all the documents that you've

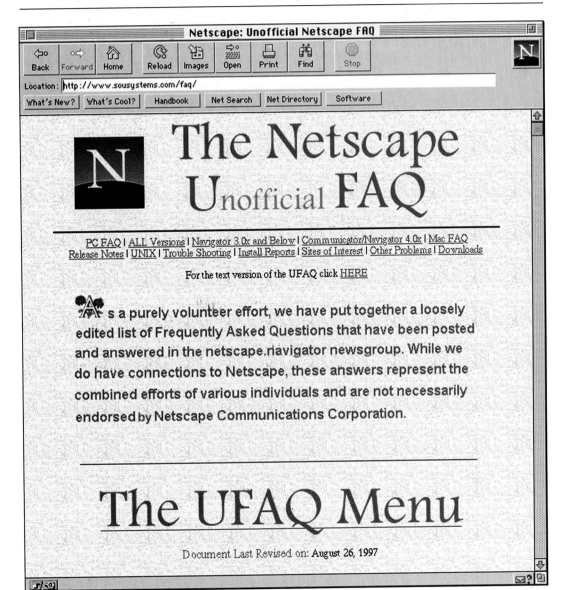

FIG. 1.1

Viewing a Web Page
with Netscape
Navigator

put on hold. This is useful in case you want retrace a lot of links in one quick mouse click. The history list is useful when you've wandered far from familiar territory and you just want to get back to an earlier starting point without having to revisit each page you've seen along the way. Figure 1.2 shows the History command on a pull-down Menu.

Each time you start up your Web browser, you start from the same **default Web page**. This might be the home page for your ISP, a home page at your

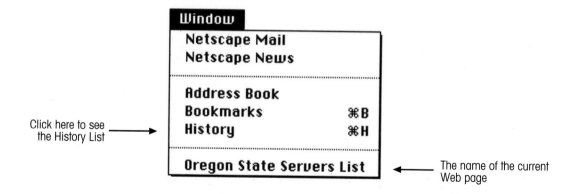

Click here to see
the History List

The name of the current
Web page

FIG. 1.2

The History Command
in Netscape Navigator

school, or a home page associated with your specific Web browser. Your default Web page can be reset if you prefer a different starting point. You can pick any Web page that gives you useful links to places you tend to visit each time you get on the Web.

When you are done using your browser, make sure you know the proper procedure for shutting it down. With graphical Web browsers, pull down the File menu and click Quit. ***If you are dialing in over a phone line, you need to both exit the browser software and also shut down the phone line connection.*** Check with your service provider for the correct shut-down instructions that apply to your set-up. For example, on a Mac running freePPP, you close the phone connection from a button on a ConfigPPP window. If you do not close the ConfigPPP connection, it remains open and you are still connected to your service provider even though your Web browser has been turned off and you aren't doing anything online. Figure 1.3 shows what the ConfigPPP window looks like.

IF YOU DIAL IN, LEAVING THE WEB TAKES TWO STEPS

Leaving the Web is a two-step process. You need to (1) exit your Web browser, and (2) shut down your phone connection correctly. If you are paying for connect time, those charges are based on the amount of time that your phone line connection is open, regardless of whether you are using it. Even if you don't pay connect time charges, an open connection ties up one of your service provider's modems so that no one else can use it. The proper shut-down procedure depends on the software you are using, so follow your service provider's instructions for terminating a dial-up session. If you are uncertain of the correct procedure, ask a technical support person for help.

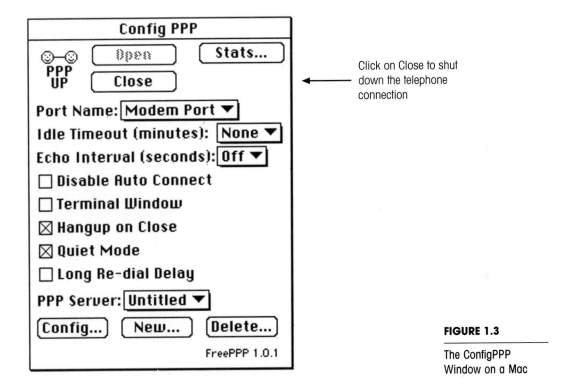

Click on Close to shut
down the telephone
connection

FIGURE 1.3

The ConfigPPP
Window on a Mac

Each Web page has a unique address called a **Uniform Resource Locator
(URL)**, which allows you to go directly to that page no matter where you are
currently positioned on the Web. All Web browsers let you link directly to a
URL. In Netscape, there is a text box marked Location: in which you can
type in a URL. Just click the text box, type the URL, and hit Enter or Return.

Little Tricks Can Make a Big Difference

URLs are popping up all over these days. You can find them in newspapers, magazines, books, and even on television. Unfortunately,
many URLs are long and hard to remember. Even when you have
one sitting in front of you, you may find it difficult to type it accurately,
and it takes only one typing error for the URL to be rendered useless.

When you find a URL online, you can always hand it off to your
Web browser with a powerful technique called **grab-and-drop**:

1. Use the left mouse button (if there is more than one button) to
   highlight the URL you want to grab.

Continued on Next Page

> *Continued from Previous Page*
>
> 2. Copy the URL.
> 3. Reposition the insertion point where you want the grabbed URL to appear.
> 4. Drop the URL.
>
> Depending on your platform, steps (2) and (3) may require different commands.
> On a Mac, you do this:
>
> 2. Copy it by pressing ⌘-c.
> 3. Drop it by pressing ⌘-v.
>
> If you're working with MS Windows, do this:
>
> 2. Copy it by pressing Ctrl-Insert.
> 3. Drop it by pressing Shift-Insert.
>
> And in a UNIX X-Windows environment:
>
> 2. Releasing the left mouse button copies the URL.
> 3. Drop it by clicking the middle mouse button.
>
> Grab-and-drop can save you a lot of time in many situations. Make sure you know how grab-and-drop works on your particular machine and look for opportunities to use it. If you can't find any documentation for it, try looking under cut-and-paste or pick-and-put. They all refer to the same operation.

Many people are think the Web is the same as the Internet. This is not true, but the confusion is understandable. The Web is just one software application that utilizes the Internet. Indeed, it is a recent newcomer to the Internet, but it is the one application that integrates resources from other Internet applications as well. Older resources, such as Gopher menus and FTP directories, are easy to access with a Web browser. This contributes to some confusion about where the Web stops and everything else begins. In addition, software designers have created Web browsers that offer their users more than the Web. For example, Netscape Navigator gives you a mail reader and a news reader, as well as a Web browser. All of this software integration creates confusion about where the Web ends and the rest of the Internet begins.

Because a Web browser can support many Internet activities in addition to Web browsing, it is an excellent starting point for Internet exploration. The most popular Web browsers have all evolved toward easy integrated Internet access designed to handle the most commonly used Internet operations. Even though the Web is not the same as the Internet, many users will find that all their Internet needs can be adequately addressed by the right Web browser.

It's important to get online and start using your Web browser as soon as possible. If you read ahead without getting online, you may find some of the material harder to grasp. Here is a checklist of activities that will get you off on the right foot. Note that steps 1, 2, and 14 apply only if you are accessing the Internet from your home computer.

1. Obtain the recommended software and installation instructions from your service provider.
2. Install the software as directed.
3. Fire up your Web browser and see if you can complete the connection to your service provider.
4. The default Web page that you'll see probably belongs to your service provider. Read it.
5. Use grab and drop to pick up the URL of your default Web page and record it in a text file (you need to run a text editor for this).
6. Make sure you know how to scroll up and down a long Web page.
7. Make sure you know how to recognize and traverse a hyperlink.
8. Find the Back button so that you can retrace your hyperlink movements one at a time.
9. Explore some links from your default Web page. Get a feeling for the pages you can get to from there.
10. Locate the history list and try it out.
11. Visit the Internet 101 Web pages at
    `http://www.awl.com/cseng/titles/0-201-32553-5/`
12. Explore the Web pages and see what's there.
13. Exit your Web browser.
14. Close your telephone connection.

If you have trouble with any of these steps, get help from a friend, your teacher, teaching assistant, or technical support staff. Once you can access the Web, take some time to explore until you feel at home with your browser. Once you're on the Web, you have gotten past a big hurdle. Everything is more fun once you're online.

1.3 Mastering Complicated Software

Computers are supposed to make people more productive. Unfortunately, gross productivity (on a national scale) appears to have declined since the advent of the PC. The result is the so-called **productivity paradox**.

Commercial software is plentiful and the best products are easy to use from day one. But not all software is easy to learn. Sometimes, the difficulty lies in the complexity of the software. Sometimes, the problem is poor documentation. Whatever the reason, the productivity paradox is at least partially due to the difficulty of mastering complicated software. Moreover, you may have to "master" the same software several times as upgrades and replacements take their toll.

Given enough time and motivation, anyone can master any given software package. But the time required may be considerable. The real trick is to master the software you need and still have a life. The secret is simple. The secret is . . . (psst) . . . don't learn anything you don't have to learn.

Every complicated piece of software has enough features, options, and capabilities to fill a book. This book is usually called a user's manual. If you believe it is necessary to learn and remember everything in a user's manual, you are doomed. What you really want to do is learn just enough to be minimally operational. In time, you will need to figure out which additional features might make you more efficient or more effective. But you need to strengthen your mastery only on an as-needed basis, as you gain more experience with the software and can better assess its potential impact on you.

Creeping Featurism	In 1992, Microsoft WORD 2.0c contained 311 commands. The 1997 version, WORD97, contains 1,033 commands. There are undoubtedly some useful features in the 1997 version that weren't in the earlier version, but most users probably don't need to learn 722 new commands. The trick is to figure out which new commands you really need so you can ignore the rest.

If you have a user's manual or an online tutorial, you can probably become minimally operational after scanning a well-written introduction. The better the documentation, the easier this is. Don't try to memorize everything. If you need to remember something that's important, just keep looking it up until it finally sticks. Put stick-it notes or paper clips on the pages that you refer to the most. If something is really important, you'll remember it eventually.

As soon as you can stumble along in any manner whatsoever, congratulate yourself on a job well done and consider it finished. In time, you will become impatient because you are sure there must be a better way to do something, or you will become curious about more-powerful features. That's the time to go back and learn a little more. It helps to be in touch with other users who can tell you what they've learned and point you in the right directions. If you don't know anyone who can act as your guide, you'll find communities of users on the Internet (see Chapters 4 and 8) who ask questions and discuss their experiences with the more-popular software packages.

The Wisdom of Hanging Back

Never be the first on your block to try out brand new software. Always talk to someone else who has tried it first. The first release of something new is sometimes buggy and often difficult to master. It is always better to let others suffer through a first release. By hanging back, you can hear what other people have to say about the software before you make your move. You might decide it's not worth it. And if cost is a factor, you will always benefit, because retail prices for software usually drop after a product has been available for a year or so. If you really want to be on the cutting edge, expect to get skewered every so often.

HINT

The minimal mastery strategy for software works well in the sense that it puts your software where it belongs: in the background. You may never master all of the features, and you may never become optimally efficient. But you will be productive, and you will be able to concentrate on things that are more important than the software you are using. It's really just a question of getting your priorities straight. The only people who need to make software their top priority are professional programmers. They are paid to be experts about the software they use. For the rest of us, it's enough to muddle along with less than total software mastery.

There is, however, one situation that is particularly frustrating with respect to software mastery (or mini-mastery). If you use your software only sporadically, you may find it difficult to remember commands and details. There is usually a lot to remember. Constant use is the best way to keep that knowledge fresh and operational. If you don't use a piece of software for a long time, you'll probably have to relearn a lot of commands. There is no clever solution to this problem, unless you can structure your work in a way that keeps you in touch with your software on a regular basis. Don't let your software skills slip away from lack of use.

This book demonstrates throughout the power of minimal software mastery. It does not attempt to teach you everything there is to know, but it does introduce you to the basics you need to be operational. There is no need to drop out of the real world in order to enjoy the Internet.

1.4 A Game Plan for Online Exploration

The key to making the Internet fun is to make it personal. You need to find online resources that address your personal interests. Since only you can identify your most passionate interests, you will have to customize your online explorations yourself. This is easy to do, but you will have to spend some time exploring on your own.

Picking Three Target Topics

It may take a day or two for you to identify three good target topics for your Internet explorations. Just remember to pick things that truly interest you. Don't pick a topic just because you think it should interest you. To find good topics, ask yourself how you spend your leisure time or what sorts of books you like to look at when you go into a bookstore. Here are some possible topics to help you get your juices flowing:

bike trails in the United States	travel in Europe
investigative journalism	civil rights
a favorite TV show	UFOs
a favorite rock group	conspiracy theories
a favorite author	quilting and fabric arts
vegetarian cooking	Magic Card tournaments
chocolate desserts	recreational running
violent weather	alternative medicine
careers in advertising	ethnic restaurants
the stock market	environmental lawsuits
political scandals	Monty Python movies
college basketball	tropical fish

You can start right now by identifying three topics that interest you. These could be academic interests, professional interests, or an interest relating to a hobby or leisure-time activity. Pick anything you want, as long as it is a topic of genuine interest for you. It could be a topic that you already know a lot about, or it could be a new interest area about which you would like to learn more. Try to pick topics that you will enjoy returning to as you explore different aspects of the Internet. Each time you read about a new tool or software application, you should see if you can find some new Internet resources that pertain to your three target topics.

You will discover that some topics are easier to locate on the Internet than others, and you will learn how to search for information at different levels, ranging from the most specific topics to more general categories. Finding the right level of description can make the difference between success and failure on the Internet. Get a spiral notebook and take notes whenever you work on your three target topics. If you keep a record of your online explorations, you will learn more from the experience, and you can develop a bibliography of resources worth keeping.

Pick your three target topics now and plan to spend some time each week with them. You might change your mind and decide to replace one later, but try to pick three topics that you know you'll enjoy.

Getting Help Online   ◀ 1.5

Getting help online is the first big hurdle to overcome when going online. But it won't be your last. Each time you experiment with a new piece of software, you may need help getting started. The Internet itself is a good place to get help, but you have to know where to go for help and how to ask for it. Chapters 4 and 8 discuss public forums, where people can look for help with their software problems. The Internet opens up a world of expertise, once you learn how to participate in public discussion groups. This information is of no use to you at the start, when you're struggling just to get online. But once you're over that initial hurdle, you can tap into dozens of discussion groups that are relevant to your particular interests and software problems.

The Internet grew out of a community of researchers and scientists who routinely answered questions for one another and offered helpful pointers and insights to anyone who asked. This culture of intellectual generosity is still out there, and it continues to operate in all areas associated with computing. The beauty of the medium is that it encourages newcomers to jump into a dialog without prior introduction. You don't have to gain admission to a public discussion group by posting your credentials or applying for membership. The group is open to the general public. These groups are powerful resources for those who utilize them.

Most people who need help with software prefer to seek out technical support personnel for a private conversation. If you have access to tech support people who can take care of you in a timely manner, that's a good strategy. However, please read Appendix C before you ask technical support staff for help. If you cannot obtain responsive technical support, you need to find other solutions. In that case, it pays to set pride aside and ask strangers for help so that you can get on with your work.

Coping with Technical Problems

Everyone has technical problems. You are not alone.

Everyone needs technical help once in a while, even people with PhDs.

No one will think you are stupid if you ask for help.

No one will laugh at you if you ask for help.

Sometimes people can help even if they aren't experts.

If you ask for help nicely, total strangers often come to the rescue.

People are sometimes happy to help out even if it's not their job.

Don't pretend you know it all. That's the worst thing you can do.

Once you break the ice and speak up in public, it's easier to do it again.

If you are a student taking a course about the Internet, there is probably a mailing list just for your class. If you are an ISP subscriber, there is probably a newsgroup for everyone who subscribes to that particular ISP. These local discussion groups can be a very useful source of information for all sorts of computer-related questions and problems. Even in a discussion group limited to fellow students, you will often find people who know enough to help you. Sometimes it's hard to get things rolling in a newly formed discussion group (e.g., a course-related group), but groups that are ongoing normally have a daily flow of conversation involving many participants who read the posts regularly. There are global discussion groups dedicated to specific pieces of software. They are good places to go with both beginning and more-sophisticated questions. Chapter 4, which covers mailing lists, and Chapter 8, which deals with Usenet newsgroups, show you what you need to know to participate in these public dialogs.

Many people are uncomfortable with the idea of posting questions in a public forum and receiving answers from total strangers. Most of us grew up in classrooms in which teachers and books were authoritative sources of information. We were cautioned not to believe everything we read, and we learned to respect the authority of professionals for the really important decisions in our lives. How then, can it make sense to cast aside concerns for credibility and embrace the advice of people who could be charlatans? How can you trust the information you get? What if someone gives you bad information with malicious intent? Who can you trust online?

While these concerns are legitimate, it is fairly easy to protect yourself from incorrect information and malicious advice. A public discussion is monitored by all of those who participate in it. If someone says something in public that is wrong, others will step in to set the record straight. When you get advice in a public forum and no one contradicts it within a day or two, it is probably legitimate information. If someone replies to you privately, wait to see if others give you the same advice. When two people independently agree on a course of action, it is likely to be the right advice.

In some discussion groups, there can be a lot of disagreement among the experts. But the realm of publicly available software is relatively straightforward. Most questions have definitive answers, and when there is more than one way of doing something, most people will agree on the relative merits of each solution. Chances are the most common misinformation you'll find are statements of the form "You can't do that," when in fact you can. But if that's the worst thing someone tells you, you are no worse off than you were beforehand. Public forums about computers and software are normally safe, reliable places to get answers to your technical questions.

When Smart People Act Stupid

The only stupid question is the one you didn't ask.

HINT

Note that I am not telling you to go to a stranger for heart surgery. When a problem entails serious risks, it makes sense to search for expertise you can trust. Although some software problems are associated with risks, most problems encountered by a beginner are thoroughly mundane. Asking for help with these problems is analogous to asking a stranger for the correct time. You shouldn't think twice about it. But if you sense potential danger, then proceed with caution. Don't open up your computer and start pulling wires. Use your good judgment and back off from any advice that assumes more technical expertise than you possess.

Networking Concepts and Facts

2

> "God help us.
> We're in the hands
> of engineers."
>
> - FROM *JURASSIC PARK*
>   (THE MOVIE)

THE INTERNET 101 WEB PAGES

- Internet Operation and History

What Is the Internet?

2.1

The Internet is a global assemblage consisting of over 19 million computers in rapid intercommunication. The communication links consist of regular telephone lines, digital cables, optical fiber, and satellite transmissions. There is no central authority in charge of everything, and an estimated 50 million people are active users.

The Internet can be described in terms of the hardware infrastructure that supports it, the demographics of the people who populate it, and the software that facilitates it. Although it is natural to think of the Internet in terms of computers and communication links between computers, the real force that shapes the Internet are the people who use it. Until the early 1990s, the Internet was used by scientists and academics pursuing long-distance collaborations and scholarly research. Computer science students and professional programmers also used the Internet for more casual communications and have been responsible for much of the enabling software. In 1994, widespread distribution of a graphical browser for the Web triggered an explosive interest in the Internet on the part of mainstream America. Commercial service providers quickly materialized and offered Internet access to anyone who had a PC and a telephone line.

The Internet wasn't discussed by the popular press much before 1990. However, its origins date to 1970 when four computers—one each at the Stanford Research Institute, the University of California at Los Angeles, the University of California at Santa Barbara, and the University of Utah at Salt Lake City—were first hooked up to each other over phone lines. Twenty years of concerted effort by computer scientists and engineers has since created an all-purpose global network for high-speed digital communications. This same 20-year period also witnessed the creation and commercialization of PCs, which made it possible for anyone to hop on the Internet from the convenience of their own home. No one in 1970 could have imagined the Internet of today. There was never a master plan in place to guide all of the contributing technologies.

Famous Computer Visionaries	"I think there is a world market for maybe five computers." - Thomas Watson, Chairman of IBM (1943) "There is no reason anyone would want a computer in their home." - Ken Olson, Chairman/Founder of DEC (1977)

Although there was no grand plan in mind, a sense of limitless possibilities attracted a generation of scientists and technicians to the field of computer science, where innovation is a way of life and nothing stands still for very long. In 1983, there were 562 computers on the Internet. By 1993, that number had grown to over 1.2 million; in 1996, the number exceeded 12 million. In 1983, the Internet was a computer science experiment used primarily by scientists. By 1993, the Internet had attained the status of a global infrastructure with pressing implications for the business world and telecommunications industries. The number of computers on the Internet has doubled every 12–14 months for the last 15 years. Everyone thought the Internet was gigantic in 1992. But the number of computers on the Internet in 1992 accounted for less than 10% of the 1996 computer count. Technical innovation supported this extraordinary growth rate, and there has been a lot of work behind the scenes to keep everything operational. Figure 2.1 shows the growth rate of computers on the Internet.

One critical component underlying today's Internet is the software that supports network communications. In the Internet's early days, network

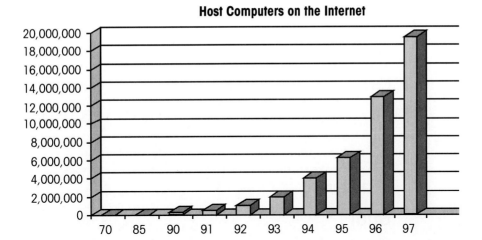

software was not particularly friendly. The only people who used it were computer scientists, and they didn't care about user-friendly interfaces. The software they designed was somewhat difficult to use, although it served its intended user community very well. Telnet was created in 1969 and the File Transfer Protocol (FTP) was first used in 1971. Both Telnet and FTP are still in use, but they were designed long before anyone had begun to think about point-and-click user interfaces.

Although the Web is the fastest-growing segment of the Internet, the most popular software application on the Internet has always been e-mail. More people have access to e-mail than to the Web, and e-mail messages are gradually replacing traditional mail correspondence and telephone conversations for a new generation of workers and private citizens. The Internet delivered more mail messages than the United States Postal Service for the first time in 1995. E-mail software now sports user-friendly interfaces, and Internet communication via e-mail is a snap. But there are still some rules of the road worth learning and some important concepts all educated users should know.

Other popular communication applications that have evolved with the Internet include Usenet newsgroups, Gophers, Internet Relay Chat, and MUDs. Each application is different and addresses different kinds of information needs.

FIG. 2.1

Growth of the Internet

Usenet Newsgroups

Usenet newsgroups allow strangers to exchange e-mail-like messages in a public forum open to millions of onlookers. Usenet dialogs are broadcast to the public via 20,000 different online newsgroups out of 500,000 distribution sites with conversational updates rolling around ten times an hour, 24 hours a day, seven days a week. Anyone can join in on any of the Usenet conversations at any time.

Gopher

Gopher resources are generated by institutions rather than by random individuals. The information found in Gopher space is therefore relatively stable and reliable since the reputation of an institution is at stake. Gopher menus can reference other Gopher menus as well as directories of text documents. As a massive collection of interlinked menus, Gopherspace is similar to the Web. If the Web hadn't materialized, Gopher might have evolved in Web-like directions itself.

Chat

Chat channels enable typed conversations between two or more people in either a public or private manner. Online chat is a favorite haunt for teenagers and young adults, especially when conversations are embedded in a simulated environment in which participants can move in and out of virtual locations (e.g., the "kitchen," "sauna," or "TV room"). Friendships are often made on chat channels, and romance has been known to blossom from random chat channel encounters.

The Web

Of all of the available Internet applications, only the Web was designed for hypertext and multimedia. The intuitive appeal of Web pages and Web browsers has made the Web an easy place for newcomers to get started online. Anyone can add their own pages to the Web. This makes the Web an entertaining mix of information and imagination.

Each Internet application appeals to different segments of the Internet community. Understanding the Internet amounts to understanding all of its online habitats and their information resources.

Who Uses the Internet?	The average Internet user is 35 years old with an annual household income of $60,000. 56% of all Internet users hold a college degree, 69% are male, and 46% are married.
	- Georgia Tech Research Corp., 1996 WWW User Survey

The demographics of the Internet have changed just as the Internet has changed. The greatest changes have taken place since 1990, when the general public began to climb aboard. For example, according to one 1994 survey, only

5% of Internet users were female. By 1996, that percentage had grown to 31%, and by 1997, to 42%. Demographic profiles of Internet users are of great interest to the business community, and user surveys are frequently conducted.

Protocols and Other Jargon   2.2

Computer scientists tend to speak in acronyms. The only other segment of society that uses acronyms so freely is probably the U. S. military. One can only wonder whether all of the Department of Defense funding behind computer science research left its stamp on the field in the form of this affinity for acronyms. For whatever reasons, acronyms are a fact of life in computer circles, and the Internet is no exception. Acronyms are ubiquitous on the Internet, but you don't need a degree in computer science to get past the jargon.

Many Internet acronyms involve a P. For example, there's SLIP, PPP, TCP, IP, FTP, SMTP, and HTTP. In addition, the P always occupies the last position in each of these acronyms. All of them stand for the word "protocol." Whenever you see a P at the end of a computer acronym, chances are excellent it stands for "protocol."

In diplomatic circles, the term **protocol** refers to ceremonies and etiquette observed by heads of state. In computer circles, the term has a similar meaning. That is, it refers to formalities and conventions observed by computers during cross-computer communication. For computers to share data, each computer must use the same data transfer rules; otherwise, there will be no communication. In the days of the telegraph, Morse Code was a communication protocol used by telegraph operators. Later on, ham radio operators established their own communication protocol. Each new communication medium requires its own communication protocol. Internetworked computers are no exception.

The more machines that share the same protocol, the more powerful the resulting communication medium. Protocols on the Internet are universally recognized. This widespread adoption of common protocols is a key ingredient for global communication. The **Internet Protocol** (**IP**) is the cornerstone for all Internet communications. In fact, you can tell if a specific computer is part of the Internet by asking for its **IP address**. Each computer on the Internet has a unique IP number that operates as its Internet address. When it is said that there were more than 12 million computers on the Internet in 1996, that figure is based on the number of IP addresses in use that year.

You will probably come across more references to **TCP/IP** than to IP by itself. **TCP**, or the **Transmission Control Protocol**, works closely with IP in order to prepare packets of data before an Internet data transfer. TCP also interprets those same packets at the receiving end after the transfer. All computers that communicate on the Internet run TCP/IP, and TCP/IP software is available for all computer platforms. It is the common language for network communication that has prevented the Internet from becoming a hopeless Tower of Babel.

Additional protocols are used on top of IP to support specific software applications. For example, the **File Transfer Protocol** (**FTP**) was designed in 1971 to move files from one computer to another**.** The **Simple Mail Transfer Protocol** (**SMTP**) was designed in 1982 to support e-mail communications. The **Hypertext Transfer Protocol** (**HTTP**) was designed in 1990 so that Web browsers could read documents on the Web. Major software innovations for Internet communication generally require new communication protocols. Casual Internet users don't need to understand these protocols because they are only of interest to software designers. But protocol acronyms are often used to name the software applications they support, so the jargon becomes mainstream even if the technical underpinnings are not. (We're lucky the term "e-mail" was embraced before SMTP had a chance to take root.)

The **Point-to-Point Protocol** (**PPP**) and the **Serial Line Internet Protocol** (**SLIP**) are terms you will encounter if you need to set up access to the Internet over a telephone line through a commercial ISP. These protocols are used when a computer communicates with the Internet over a serial transmission line (such as an analog telephone line) and the user wants to run a graphical Web browser such as Netscape. ISPs offer PPP or SLIP accounts to users who want to view graphics on the Internet. Both protocols support graphical Web browsers, and there is no reason for an end user to prefer one over the other. When your home computer is connected to a PPP or SLIP account, it transmits and receives data over a phone line using the TCP/IP protocol. PPP and SLIP accounts assign a reserved IP number to your home computer each time you connect, thereby making your machine a bona fide part of the Internet.

If you become heavily involved with the Internet, you will want to learn about **Integrated Services Digital Network** (**ISDN**) phone lines and T1 lines. These are high-speed digital lines typically used by institutional sites because the cost of these services is too steep for casual users (although ISDN lines are becoming less expensive and can be cost-effective for certain types of home-based users).

The Internet moves data across a variety of communication lines. When you download an image stored on a computer 3,000 miles away, that image may move along an Internet backbone connection, such as an FDDI line, at the rate of 100 million bps. That same image may move within a local area network across an ethernet connection at a rate of 10 million bps. But by the time it gets to the "driveway" leading up to your home computer, it can't travel any faster than your modem allows. If you have a 9.6K modem, its top

Network Transmission Speeds

28.8 kbps modem	28,800 bps
ISDN (1 channel)	64,000 bps
T-1 line (24 channels)	1,500,000 bps
Ethernet	10,000,000 bps
T-3 line (672 channels)	45,000,000 bps
FDDI (optical fiber)	100,000,000 bps
ATM (optical fiber)	660,000,000 bps
Wideband ATM (optical fiber)	1,000,000,000 bps

speed across the modem is 9,600 bps. Computer modems and analog phone lines are data bottlenecks that limit data transfer to end users. Most of the time you spend waiting for data is the time it takes to cross that "last mile" to your PC.

Analog phone lines were designed for voice communication, not digital data. So it is not surprising that we are limited by technological bottlenecks along that last mile. Cable-based communication is an improvement over analog phone lines, and the telecommunications industry is trying to establish new standards for data transmission into private homes.

> **How Reliable Are Computer Networks?**
>
> The SABRE network handles 25% of the world's airline reservations, 20% of the world's hotel reservations, and 30% of the U. S. car rentals. This private computer network handles thousands of messages each second and is accessed 150 million times a day by users in 71 nations. Based in Tulsa, Oklahoma, the SABRE system generally responds to queries in under 1 second with 99.96% reliability during prime time usage periods. This system also averages 200,000 fare changes each day in its airline database, so reliable data updates are a crucial aspect of SABRE's operation. This is especially true during an "airfare war," when there can be as many as 1.5 million fare changes each day and the peak message rate can climb as high as 4,652 messages per second.

Computer networks have created pressing needs for technological innovation and scientific advancement. Most of this work is done in universities and commercial laboratories throughout the United States. According to the Internet Patent News Service, 3,966 patents were issued during the first half of 1996; of those, 919 were awarded for network software innovations. All of this progress is being eagerly embraced by the telecommunications industry and the business community. In 1991, U. S. businesses spent more money on computer and communications equipment than on industrial, mining, farm, and manufacturing equipment combined. All of the major newspapers now have their own columnists who write reviews for computer software and hardware. The world is scrambling to keep up with computer technologies that promise to shape our lives in ways no one can foresee. The United States leads the world in computer networking technology.

2.3 Host Machines and Host Names

A computer that has been assigned an IP address is called a **host machine**. Each IP address consists of four integers separated by periods. For example, one host machine at the University of Massachusetts in Amherst has the IP address 128.119.40.195. Just as zip codes embody geographical information that can be read from left to right, IP addresses can also be read from left to right, although the information these addresses reveal is associated with computer networks rather than geographical locations. The leftmost number represents the largest division within the Internet, and the rightmost number represents a specific host machine. A machine at Yale University (76 miles from Amherst or 150 milliseconds via the Internet) has the IP address 130.132.21.136, and a host machine at MIT (72 miles from Amherst, or 70 milliseconds via the Internet) has the IP address 18.92.0.3.

If you know the userid of someone who has an account on a specific host machine, you can send e-mail to them using a mailing address that consists only of that person's userid and the IP address of his or her host machine. For example, I have an account on 128.119.41.229, where my userid is lehnert, so you could send mail to me at `lehnert@128.119.41.229` (or perhaps `lehnert@[128.119.41.229]`, depending on your software).

My userid and the host machine's IP address make this a unique Internet e-mail address. While IP addresses are fine for computer communications, long strings of numbers are not easy for people to remember. To make life easier for people, most host machines have a symbolic name as well as a numeric address. The addresses of the three machines mentioned previously are a bit easier to remember when given in their symbolic equivalents:

128.119.40.195	`freya.cs.umass.edu`
130.132.21.136	`yalevm.ycc.yale.edu`
18.92.0.3	`mitvma.mit.edu`

Symbolic host names are always converted to their IP addresses for the purposes of network communications. The **Domain Name Service** (**DNS**) is responsible for mapping symbolic names to their numeric equivalents, and symbolic host names are often called **DNS names** or **DNS addresses**. DNS names follow certain naming conventions that may help you remember host names more easily. The leftmost segment of a DNS name refers to the name of a specific host machine. For example, "freya," "yalevm," and "mitvma" are all names of machines. The middle segment(s) refers to institutional sites. For example, "cs" = a Computer Science Department, "umass" = the University of Massachusetts, "ycc" = Yale Computing Center, "yale" = Yale University, and "mit" = the Massachusetts Institute of Technology. The final segment is a generic domain name (e.g., "edu" always refers to an educational site). Once you've learned some institutional acronyms, you'll be able to recognize and unravel at least some of the more commonly encountered host addresses on your own. The segment of a DNS name following the host machine's name is called the **domain name**.

Host Names and Domain Names

Each DNS host address has a host name followed by a domain name. Here are some examples:

DNS Address	Host Name	Domain Name
`freya.cs.umass.edu`	`freya`	`cs.umass.edu`
`yalevm.yale.edu`	`yalevm`	`yale.edu`
`mitvma.mit.edu`	`mitvma`	`mit.edu`

People also talk about **high-level domain names** (which are also called "domain names," just to confuse things) when they refer to the final suffix in the full domain name. A high-level domain name identifies the type of site where the host machine resides. The "edu" suffix indicates that the host is part of an educational site. Following are some common high-level domain name suffixes:

com	A commercial organization
edu	An educational site in the United States
gov	A government agency in the United States
mil	A military site in the United States
net	A network site
org	A nonprofit organization

Continued on Next Page

Continued from Previous Page

Following are some high-level domain name suffixes that identify geographical locations by country (this is only a partial list):

au	Australia
ca	Canada
de	Germany
dk	Denmark
es	Spain
fr	France
gb	Great Britain
hk	Hong Kong
hu	Hungary
ie	Ireland
il	Israel
lk	Sri Lanka

Although each host machine has a unique IP address, some hosts have more than one symbolic address. Machines are often assigned an **alias** (an alternative name). There is no limit to the number of aliases a host can have. For example, `yalevm.ycc.yale.edu` is also recognized by the names `yalevm.cis.yale.edu` and `yalevm.yale.edu`. These host names all share the same numeric IP address, so we know they all refer to the same machine.

No one polices the aliases that a machine can use or the selection of DNS names beyond making sure that each DNS address is unique. Anyone can register a host machine under any name they want as long as no one else has claimed it first. This means that you should be cautious when making assumptions based on a host machine's DNS name. For example, `dole96.org` sure looked like a credible host name for the official Dole Presidential Campaign, but it was actually used by a counterfeit operation posting a satiric Web page. Also, before the world caught on to "digital homesteading," a number of enterprising programmers registered their machines under names like `nyc.com` and `mcdonalds.com`. They were betting that large corporations would eventually find it worth their while to purchase the rights to these domain names. So when you see a suggestive Internet address, just remember that anyone can claim any DNS name on a first-come, first-serve basis. If something you find on the Internet smells fishy, it probably is.

Internet Architecture and Packet Switching

On the Internet, not all computers are equal. Some Internet hosts play a special role in the architecture of the Internet and are fully dedicated to Internet communications. To understand the different roles played by these Internet facilitators, you must first understand how data is moved across the Internet—by **packet switching**.

To understand packet switching, you will find it helpful to understand some of the communication goals that packet switching achieves. When the Department of Defense sponsored the original network research that led to the Internet, they wanted a robust network that could withstand regional power blackouts or other partial failures. To achieve robust communication, it was important to design a transmission protocol that could readily find new routes to a given destination if a preferred route was not available. Network designers decided that **dynamic routing** should be the standard means of moving data across the network. Dynamic routing means routes for data are always selected at the time of transmission, after taking current network conditions into consideration.

It was also important to distribute route-selection capabilities throughout the network so that there could be no key site that was responsible for the operation of the entire network. Suppose a network was designed **hierarchically** so that all transmissions moved through a central routing site. If something happened to that central routing site, the entire network would fail. Any hierarchical organization would create critical sites that, if they failed, could compromise robust communication. So the Internet was designed **heterarchically** (see Figure 2.2). Instead of one central routing site, there are a large number of routing sites distributed all over the network. The hosts that decide how to route transmissions across the Internet are called **routers**. The Internet contains thousands of routers.

Dynamic heterarchical routing is what makes the Internet work, and the key idea that holds it all together is packet switching. All data is moved across the Internet in units called **packets**. Traffic on the Internet is often measured by counting the number of packets transmitted during a given time period. Each packet finds its own pathway to its intended destination, and once there, it may be reunited with other packets to complete the original transmission. Packets come in different sizes, but the average is about 15K.

To see how packet switching works, suppose you need to move a large file from New York to San Francisco. The software sending the file first breaks it up into packets. A 50K file may be broken up into three or four packets. Each

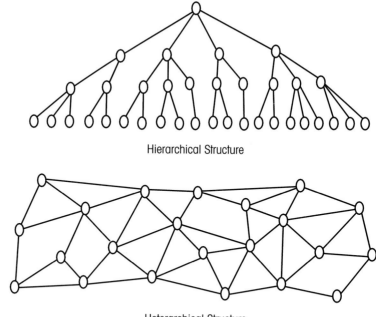

Hierarchical Structure

FIG. 2.2

Heterarchical Structure

packet is stamped with the IP address of its destination, as well as the IP address of the originating host. Additional instructions describe the size of the original transmission and where each specific packet should be positioned when the original transmission is reassembled in San Francisco. Each packet is then sent out onto the Internet to find its way to the destination address. The packets do not have to travel together; they may even follow different pathways across the country. The packets are first handed to a router, which looks at the destination address and decides where to send the packets next. The router at that location then sends each packet on the next leg of its journey to another intermediate destination. The packets make their way across the Internet in this piecemeal fashion, with intermediate destinations being assigned as they go. Different routers are responsible for each leg of the journey. If a preferred pathway is temporarily unavailable or overloaded, the router will pick another.

Eventually, all of the packets arrive at their destination in San Francisco, where they must be reassembled into the original file. Each packet is first checked to see if it has arrived intact. If a transmission error has corrupted one of the packets, a request to resend that packet is sent to the originating host. Packet switching minimizes network load because it is not necessary to resend complete files; individual packets are resent only as needed. When all of the packets check out, they are reassembled and handed to the destination host as a complete file. See Figure 2.3.

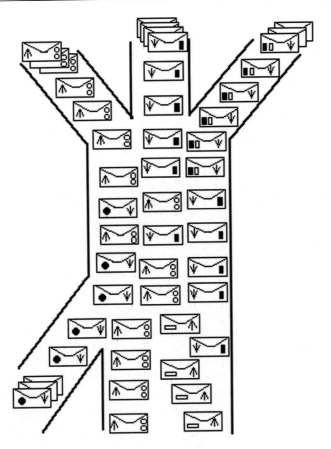

FIG. 2.3

Packet Switching

All of this activity at the packet level is hidden from the end user, although evidence of packet switching can sometimes be seen when you know what to look for. For example, some Web browsers display a byte count during each file download so that you can see how much progress has been made. These byte counts stand still every so often; if you watch closely, you might see the same numbers over and over again. Each byte count shows you how the Web pages have been divided into packets.

TCP/IP is the standard packet switching protocol used by Internet hosts. At the sending end, TCP divides files into individual packets and IP stamps each packet with host addresses. At the receiving end, IP collects all of the packets associated with a single transmission and TCP reassembles them into the original file. Computers of all types running different operating systems and using different network technologies can all run TCP/IP. This universal standard was adopted by the Internet in 1974. It is one reason why the Internet operates as effectively as it does, in spite of its dramatic growth over the last two decades. Figure 2.4 shows how much the Internet has grown in terms of packet traffic.

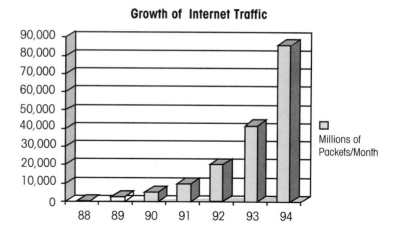

FIG. 2.4

Packet Count Growth

Packet switching enables multiple packets to share a single transmission channel with a minimal amount of delay for each packet. Greater **bandwidth** in a communication channel means that more packets can be handled simultaneously on that channel. The backbone portions of the Internet are designed to handle the heaviest traffic loads, so they incorporate the highest possible bandwidth levels.

Internet communication channels are very different from the **dedicated lines** that are used for telephone calls. When a telephone connection is established between two locations, a dedicated channel is reserved for that one connection. As long as the connection is maintained, that channel cannot be used by anyone else. The great advantage to dedicated lines is the speed with which communication takes place. When a transmission line doesn't have to be shared, the transmission is guaranteed to move at maximal speed. Delays associated with dedicated lines occur when a transmission can't be assigned to a dedicated line right away. When there aren't enough dedicated lines to go around, some transmissions will have to wait and will be completely locked out until some resources free up. Whenever you get a "trunk busy signal," you have been locked out of the phone system because too many phone calls are competing for a limited number of dedicated lines. With packet switching, no one ever gets completely locked out. However, everyone will experience slower communications when the available bandwidth is saturated.

When we talk about "The Internet," it sounds as if we are talking about one large computer network. In fact, the Internet is really a collection of more than 50,000 smaller networks. There is no one network holding everything together, but there is a seamless communication protocol across the smaller networks so that they can all talk to one another. Each one subscribes to the TCP/IP packet switching protocol. This standardization creates the appearance of a single unified network. The Internet is really a collection of local area networks (LANs), wide area networks (WANs), high-speed backbones operated by long distance telephone companies, and thousands of on/off ramps that connect everyone to the backbone.

Special host machines called **gateways** are used to handle communications across network boundaries. Access to specific networks must be mediated by the gateways to that network. Hence, bottlenecks can occur at popular gateways, much like rush hour traffic patterns on major thoroughfares. Gateways and routers are two critical components of the Internet.

On August 7, 1996, 6 million AOL customers were unable to access the Internet because AOL had recently loaded new software onto its network routers. This software contained incorrect routing information. As a result, AOL couldn't route packets on or off its gateway hosts. AOL service was interrupted for 19 hours while technicians worked to identify and fix the problem. During this period, the rest of the Internet continued to operate as usual, but anyone who relied on an AOL account for Internet access was frozen out.

The 1996 AOL failure was the largest service provider failure to date, but smaller failures happen from time to time when problems with software or hardware disrupt network communications. Difficulties with gateways and routers can temporarily disconnect isolated segments of the Internet, but there has never been a hardware failure that knocked out the whole Internet. The Internet has been successful in its original quest for robust communication.

The Importance of Network Routers

Who Is in Charge?   ◀ 2.5

Questions about Internet management and maintenance are downright perplexing. Who is paying for all this? Who fixes it when it breaks? Who is responsible for keeping everything in working order? Who decides when and how to upgrade the infrastructure? Who makes important decisions about the future of the Internet?

As explained in the last section, the Internet is composed of thousands of smaller networks that are independent of one another. These smaller networks are managed by corporations, universities, and government agencies and are often incompatible in the sense that they employ different hardware platforms and different network technologies. The glue that holds it all together at the technical level is TCP/IP. But what holds it all together administratively? How can something this complicated operate in the absence of a central authority or administrative body?

Communities of technicians and programmers have always pushed the Internet forward in the spirit of a grand experiment. As a result, many forces have influenced different aspects of the Internet along the way. The computer scientists who developed the TCP/IP protocol made their specifications public so that TCP/IP could be readily implemented on any hardware platform. Although most of the original funding for the Internet came from the Department of Defense, most of the scientists who made technological contributions were university researchers who openly published their work and distributed it freely. Anyone with access to the Internet could access technical documentation describing the Internet. This made it easy for computer science graduate students and professional programmers to jump in and influence the technological evolution of the Internet. Anyone with a good idea could speak up, and the best ideas were nurtured by the community as a whole. No one was pressured to pursue an inferior approach because of corporate decrees or pressure from management. Scientists and programmers were free to champion their best ideas on the basis of technical merit. This atmosphere of open experimentation and communication was crucial for the fast-paced evolution of the Internet, and it established important cultural norms for Internet access and usage. It also spawned an egalitarian culture in which everyone has a voice and superior content tends to win. The rapid cross-pollination of ideas came to characterize Internet communications and shape the Internet in ways that even the original Internet visionaries never anticipated.

Within this participatory culture, a number of organizations have been created to address problems and issues specific to the Internet. The main group that oversees the continuing evolution of the Internet is the **Internet Society** (**ISOC**), an umbrella organization that oversees a number of focus groups, including the following:

- Internet Architecture Board (IAB)
- Internet Engineering Task Force (IETF)
- Internet Assigned Number Authority (IANA)
- Internet Engineering Steering Group (IESG)
- Internet Research Task Force (IRTF)
- K-12 Committee
- Disaster Assistance Committee
- Internet Operations Forum

ISOC has no official sanction or governmental power, but it operates as a central resource for people who want to participate in the ongoing evolution of the Internet. Several other nonprofit organizations also operate as technology watchdogs and resource centers (see Chapter 13), so there is a lot of oversight coming from many different directions.

The Internet's high-speed backbone is a key component of the Internet, and different organizations have assumed responsibility for maintenance of the backbone. During the 1970s, research sites funded by the Advanced Research Projects Agency (ARPA) were given access to the **ARPAnet**. In the late 1970s, the National Science Foundation (NSF) joined forces with ARPA to create a network that would be more widely available to computer scientists all over the United States. NSF subsequently gave birth to **CSnet** in 1979. CSnet began to level the playing field between the computer science "haves" (those with ARPAnet access) and "have nots" (those without ARPAnet access). However, the ARPAnet and CSnet were not connected to one another until 1982, when a gateway was established between them. This joining of ARPAnet and CSnet demonstrated the viability of a network of networks. The term **Internet** was then adopted as a shorthand for "internetworked communication."

In 1983, more networks began to expand and establish their own user communities. The City University of New York created **Bitnet (Because It's Time Network)**. In San Francisco, **FidoNet** connected **FidoBBS (Bulletin Board Systems)** across the nation so that users of local bulletin boards could exchange messages via e-mail and discussion groups. In 1983, the Department of Defense further enhanced the credibility of TCP/IP by switching all of its military networks to the TCP/IP protocol. By then, TCP/IP software was included in all UNIX software distributions out of the University of California at Berkeley. UNIX was the operating system of choice for computer scientists, so the inclusion of TCP/IP as a part of UNIX set the stage for the next phase of Internet expansion. With new networks being created independently, and most of these networks running UNIX with TCP/IP, all of the pieces were in place for massive internetworked communication.

In 1985, NSF assumed a leadership role in networking and obtained funding from Congress to join one hundred additional universities to the Internet. This goal required some innovations in networking technology, and NSF began by connecting five supercomputer sites in a new network called **NSFnet**. In keeping with a long-term goal of connecting every computer and engineering researcher to the Internet, NSF poured a lot of funding into the expansion of NSFnet, which required a new high-speed backbone to support larger numbers of users. In 1987, NSF reviewed proposals for the new NSFnet backbone. Funding was awarded to a proposal jointly submitted by IBM (a computer manufacturer), MCI (a long-distance telephone company), and MERIT (an organization that maintained an educational network in

Michigan). In 1988, the new NSFnet backbone was in place; NSF's old CSnet would be overtaken by NSFnet within 3 years. By that time (the end of 1991), it was apparent that the NSFnet backbone would soon reach its maximal capacity.

It was also apparent that the federal government could no longer afford to subsidize the Internet. It was time for private industry to shoulder some of the costs associated with the Internet backbone. So the three firms responsible for the earlier NSFnet backbone (IBM, MCI, and MERIT) created a nonprofit company called **Advanced Networks and Services (ANS)**. In 1992, ANS built a new Internet backbone, **ANSnet**, with 30 times the bandwidth of the old NSFnet backbone. ANSnet is the current backbone for the Internet and the first backbone maintained by a private company rather than the federal government.

The commercialization of the Internet is often said to have begun with the adoption of ANSnet, but an earlier step toward commercialization occurred in 1990 when the Federal Networking Council changed their Internet membership policy. Prior to 1990, any organization requesting access to Internet resources (most notably access to the backbone) had to be sponsored by a government agency. In 1990, the Federal Networking Council dropped this requirement so that any organization could apply for Internet access without governmental justification. This opened the door for commercial interests and stimulated a new round of extraordinary Internet growth.

Although there are some federally sponsored organizations that monitor specific aspects of the Internet, there is no single agency that oversees everything associated with the Internet. The **Federal Communications Commission (FCC)** does not have any authority over the Internet per se, but it does regulate the billing practices of telephone companies. The FCC does not allow phone companies to bill people for digital communications differently than they do for voice communications. To do otherwise could have a major impact on usage patterns. So, in this sense, the FCC has some control over the Internet indirectly through the telephone companies. When questions arise about how to bill people for their Internet access over telephone lines, the FCC must balance the public good against the legitimate costs incurred by telephone companies. Policy changes on the part of the FCC could have profound implications for equitable Internet access on the part of the American public.

Regulating Internet Access Costs

In February of 1997, the following notice was put out on the Internet:

"Many local telephone companies have filed a proposal with the FCC [The United States' Federal Communications Commission] to impose per minute charges for Internet service. They contend that use of Internet has or will hinder the operation of the telephone network."

Patrick Douglas Crispen asked the FCC for a verification and reported:

"First, some local telephone companies have indeed asked the FCC to allow them to assess a per minute access charge on the telephone lines used by Internet Service Providers. Local telephone companies currently charge long-distance carriers (like AT&T and MCI) an interstate access charge for the long-distance traffic that travels over their local lines, and the local telephone companies would like to see this charge extended to include the high-speed lines that your local Internet Service Provider uses to access the Internet.

In December, the FCC rejected the telephone companies' request and tentatively concluded "that the existing pricing structure for information services should remain in place." In other words, the FCC has tentatively concluded that Internet service providers should *NOT* be subject to the interstate access charges that local telephone companies currently assess on long-distance carriers."

- The Internet Tourbus, 2/13/97

Although it is natural to think about government control in high places, most of the people who exert control over the Internet operate over smaller spheres of influence. For example, mailing lists and Usenet newsgroups are often monitored by individuals who have taken it upon themselves to set standards of conduct and acceptable behavior. While it is difficult to exclude an offender from a Usenet newsgroup, it is easy to exclude someone from a mailing list. Similarly, many chat channels are continuously monitored for participants who violate the channel's standards with respect to language and content. Hundreds, perhaps thousands, of self-appointed guardians monitor specific locales on the Internet in an effort to maintain acceptable standards of online behavior. A person who does not conform to the standards of a given site can be denied access to the site.

Self-appointed "net police" are generally protective of free speech and do not censor content unless a site is specifically designed for children. However, the preservation of relevance and concerns for the good of the community must be balanced against individual rights in order to encourage productive communications. Since the commercialization of the Internet, there has been an alarming rise in the amount of unsolicited junk mail on the Internet. Without some rules of conduct, the Internet could degenerate into a sorry place that is both repellent to adults and inappropriate for children. Most people recognize this and are happy to accept the authority of self-appointed monitors as needed. When no one steps in to take charge of an unruly minority, rude behavior on the part of a few immature individuals can kill off an otherwise thriving community.

There are no officials with absolute authority over the Internet, but there are a large number of people who assume authority over small pieces of the Internet in order to protect the peaceful operation of specific sites. No one is in charge, and everyone is in charge. As long as self-regulating behavior can be relied upon to contain disruptive behavior, ad-hoc authority will continue to work. If nothing else, we are witnessing a sociological experiment on a grand scale.

A lack of central authority doesn't have to be a recipe for anarchy, but it does make the Internet susceptible to scam artists and thrill-seeking teenagers. If you cross paths with an unscrupulous miscreant on the Internet, you might get hurt. By educating yourself about the Internet, you can reduce the likelihood of problems online, although there is always some small chance that you will stumble across a new and creative example of Internet abuse.

Although new forms of Internet abuse can't be anticipated, users can be warned about traps and zaps as soon as they are discovered. With this in mind, abuse-monitoring sites have been created to keep wary Internet users on guard.

Digital Scam Artists

On February 4, 1997, the National Fraud Information Center posted the following warning about a Web site that was responsible for unexpected and expensive phone bills for a number of Web surfers using dial-up Internet connections:

"Consumers who visited a pornographic website (www.sexygirls.com) last month got a big surprise on their phone bills. After a few teaser pictures, [the] surfer was told he/she needed to download a special program to view the archived images. That program was actually a viewer with an entire communications suite hidden deep inside (a non-self propagating Trojan Horse). The program disconnected [the] user from his/her ISPs, shut off the volume on the modem if it was computer controlled, and dialed a number in Moldova — a small, former republic of the Soviet Union wedged in between Ukraine and Romania. All the while the consumer was on the website, and even if he/she then browsed other sites on the World Wide Web, the Internet access was being provided through the Moldova number, resulting in huge international phone charges!"

- quote from http://www.fraud.org/february97.htm

The peculiarities of this Web site attracted the interest of law enforcement agencies, and authorities took action on February 19, 1997, to halt its operation:

"The Federal Trade Commission today won a court order to shut down "free adult entertainment" Internet sites that it alleges illegally billed Net surfers hundreds of thousands of dollars. ... CNET reported that at least two pornographic Web sites— "sexygirls.com" and "erotic2000.com"— used the program to make international calls. Along with "sexygirls.com," which was inaccessible earlier this month, the FTC is targeting "beavis-butthead.com" and "1adult.com.""

- quote from `http://news.com/News/Item/0,4,8077,00.html`

Here are some things you can do to stay informed and protect yourself from potentially harmful Internet experiences:

1. Visit the CNET Web site `http://news.com/` and click "The Net." This is a reliable information source for all kinds of news pertaining to the Internet.

2. Read the Internet Fraud feature at the National Fraud Information Center `http://www.fraud.org/report.htm` for periodic reports.

3. If you don't have the time to monitor these sites every day, trust someone else to do it for you and let them pass on the most important news. The Internet Tourbus mailing list is a good news service that describes major Internet scams as they arise. Chapter 4 explains how to subscribe to the Internet Tourbus.

4. Be extremely careful about executable files available on the Internet. The Moldavan scam couldn't hurt you if you refused to download and run their so-called viewer file. The most harmful Internet incidents involve executable files that you move onto your home computer. Chapter 9 discusses safeguards you should take before you download any executable files.

Some people have compared the Internet to the lawless Old West where behavior was rarely regulated. While this pioneer metaphor does describe the novelty and excitement of the Internet, it is prudent to remember that behavior on the Internet is still subject to all sorts of laws that require compliance both on and off the Internet. Chapter 13 summarizes some of the more commonly violated laws. In the meantime, remember that if something is illegal off the Internet, it is also going to be illegal on the Internet.

2.6 The Client/Server Software Model

Many different software applications enable communication on the Internet. E-mail readers, Web browsers, Gopher, Usenet newsgroups, and multi-user telnet sites are all examples of popular Internet applications. This book describes these in some detail. They are all different, yet they all share a basic software design element. They are all examples of the **client/server software model**, which is the basic design for all Internet applications.

In the client/server model, one host computer plays the role of the server and one or more other hosts play the role of the client. The server acts as a resource for all of its clients and provides a service for those clients. It typically interacts with multiple clients at one time; heavily utilized servers are sometimes overwhelmed by client requests. For example, a Web server houses publicly accessible Web pages. A Web browser plays the role of the client, and many Web browsers (many clients) can view the Web pages on the Web server simultaneously. In the same way, Gopher files are housed on a Gopher server, which makes them publicly available to any hosts that run Gopher clients. In a client/server interaction, client software interacts with server software so that the total computing load is shared by both the client's host machine and the server's host machine. Clients and servers are designed to form a seamless computing environment so that the end user may have no idea exactly which machine is performing which operations. See Figure 2.5. Indeed, the exact division of labor is irrelevant to the end user, who is free to concentrate on other matters.

Sometimes a proprietary piece of software is made available to the public through the client/server model. For example, a keyword search engine for the Web may reside on a server that can be accessed on demand by a large number of remote clients. This means that many people can use the server's software without having to install copies of that software on their own host machines.

The client/server model is a very powerful framework for sharing computational resources over a computer network. Popular servers require dedicated machines that are reserved exclusively for server interactions. By making the computational power of a host available for public use, a software designer can maximize the number of users (who may also be paying customers), while retaining maximal control over the software. The client/server model is a de facto standard for network-oriented computing, and client/server terminology is encountered all over the Internet. For example, you might be instructed to download and install your own client software in order to access a specific server. Sometimes, a number of competing clients are available to you, and you have to decide which to use.

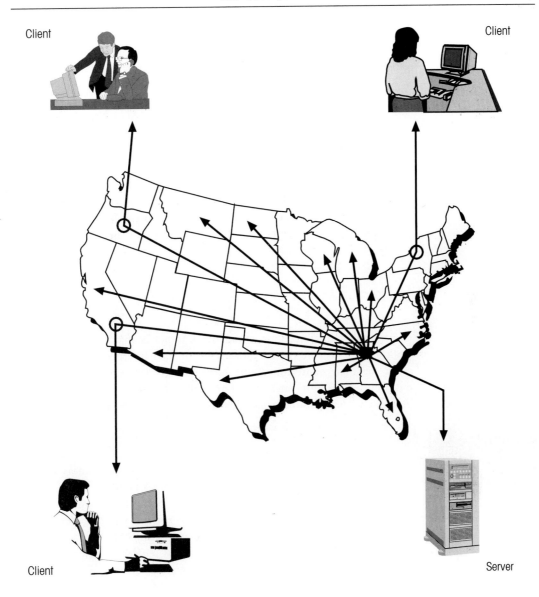

FIG. 2.5

Clients and Servers

When client software runs on a PC or Mac platform, you are expected to obtain the software and install it yourself. But if you are working on a time-sharing machine, it is best to check with technical support personnel to see if the client has already been installed on your host in some publicly accessible area. If it's not already available, tech support may want to install it themselves in a public directory so that others can use it, too. In a time-sharing environment, in which multiple users have accounts on a single host machine, it makes sense to install a client software package once and make that one copy available to everyone on that host. Otherwise, dozens of users might each install their own private copies of the same software. This is both an inefficient use of storage space and an unreasonable bit of overhead for all of the individual users who must spend time installing software on their own. Lynx, Netscape, and Mosaic are all examples of Web browsers that run in time-sharing environments, in which they should be installed by tech support.

Most people who use the Internet work with client software. Even if you use the Internet heavily and incorporate it into your professional activities, you will probably never need to install your own server software. The people who install and operate server packages are usually professional programmers or people with a background in computer science. So if you ever stumble across documentation for server software, chances are it is something you can safely ignore.

2.7 Who Pays for Everything?

One popular misconception about the Internet is that everything is free. College students who pay no direct costs for their Internet access can be forgiven for their confusion about such matters. ISP subscribers who pay monthly subscription rates and phone bills are aware of *those* costs but are probably ignorant about other costs associated with the Internet.

Boon or Bust for the Baby Bells?	Tired of telephone companies' complaints that Internet usage is overwhelming their network capacity, the Internet Access Coalition has released findings contending that Net usage is, in reality, a bonanza for the Bells. The study found that local carriers received a total of $1.4 billion in 1995 in revenues resulting from the installation of second lines in homes, while spending only $245 million to beef up their networks for the additional usage. A Bell Atlantic spokesman says the real problem is that the telcos have no idea when a line will be used for data rather than voice, and thus tied up longer. Both sides agree that the ultimate solution is higher capacity networks.
	- *Business Week*, 2/17/97

To help you get some idea about the actual costs involved, it helps to look at the costs incurred by NSF when it was in charge of the Internet. As a government agency, NSF was required to account for all of the money it spent on the Internet. NSF maintained the backbone (NSFnet) for the Internet before it was handed off to long distance phone companies in 1992. NSFnet ceased operation in April 1995 and was thought to handle about 10% of the total U. S. usage before it shut down.

At that time, NSF was spending about $20 million a year to keep NSFnet going. This amount covered basic connectivity costs, but it did not include the cost of creating and maintaining servers, application software, individual machines, or individual user accounts. Also, remember that Internet usage has been doubling every year since 1994, so the expenses in 1994 are not a good indicator of comparable expenses today.

If NSFnet was handling 10% of the total load, then the infrastructure costs for the full Internet must have been around $200 million a year in 1994. Once again, this does not cover software or personnel costs, which are extremely hard to estimate, but very big. The Clinton Administration has estimated that the National Information Infrastructure represents a $500 billion investment over the next 20 years. This figure presumably includes all manner of resource development costs above and beyond the care and feeding of the basic infrastructure.

Cost recovery for the Internet's backbone relies on monthly subscription fees and **flat-rate pricing**. Institutions pay for the strength of the bandwidth given to them, regardless of their actual bandwidth consumption. Each institution has to estimate its projected usage in order to obtain adequate bandwidth while trying to avoid overpayments for excess bandwidth. When everyone pays the same amount regardless of actual use, the heavy bandwidth consumers pay less for more and the light bandwidth consumers pay more for less. In a flat-rate pricing system, light users subsidize heavy users.

Flat-rate pricing was adopted by NSF in order to encourage exploration and experimentation. Flat rates encouraged students and researchers to try out the Internet and participate in its evolution. University students have always benefited from this cost recovery strategy. As long as a university could afford some amount of bandwidth, there was generally enough to go around. This was especially true during the 1980's and early 1990's when most of the people on the Internet were scientists, programmers, and graduate students.

Who are the heavy users, and who are the light users? Connect time doesn't always correlate with bandwidth consumption, so you can't go by the amount of time someone spends online. In general, heavy users are downloading lots of graphics and videos (e.g., a Netscape user). Light users are text consumers (e.g., someone who handles a lot of e-mail). The fast-rising popularity of the Web, therefore, represents a significant increase in bandwidth consumption that is not adequately represented by the increasing host machine counts alone.

Every so often, someone predicts the demise of the Internet. They say the Internet is growing at remarkable rates and was never designed to support the heavy traffic patterns of many users and their ever-increasing bandwidth demands. It seems that the Internet is bound to break down sooner or later;

it's just a matter of time. Interestingly, these predictions have not yet materialized. But the concerns are sound. So just how close are we to saturating the capacity of the Internet?

Toward the end of NSFnet in 1994, the average traffic loads on NSFnet were operating at 5% of the available capacity. But average use is not the important measure. Peak usage is the real test of a network's adequacy, and peak traffic loads tend to run at ten times the average traffic load. Traffic on the Internet tends to be "bursty." That is, there are long periods with little or no activity interspersed with short bursts of heavy traffic. Those short bursts are what strains the network. So you need to look at peak traffic rates to see how close we are to a serious mismatch of resources and demand.

The peak traffic load in 1994 was about 10 x 5% = 50% of the available capacity. Internet traffic has doubled each year since 1994, so the peak load in 1995 was 10 x 10% = 100%, and no one wants to see it climb higher than 100% peak usage. By the same reasoning, saturation should have been surpassed in 1996 with 10 x 20% = 200%, or double the capacity of the Internet. Indeed, many users complained about very pokey Web browsers during busy periods (e.g., the lunch hour). But there was no general breakdown of the Internet.

The Internet and its users are in a delicate balancing act. When the Internet begins to reach saturation, people experience slower and slower response times. If a user is used to faster response times and has come to expect a relatively speedy response rate, these periodic slow-downs will be stressful. Some users will become frustrated and go away. Some may go away and never return. This adjustment on the part of the user population frees up Internet capacity and improves response times for the remaining users. One could argue that the Internet is unlikely to exceed capacity because some segment of the user population can always be counted on to go away, thus resulting in a correction in any overloads. This turnover scenario makes it difficult to measure demand as a function of actual Internet traffic. Also, there is no data on user turnover rates, so it is very hard to know if the Internet is approaching a steady state in spite of other metrics that reflect continued growth.

Many Internet facts and figures are actually only estimates and educated guesses. We can count the actual number of Internet hosts because they are all assigned IP numbers by the DNS Registry at InterNIC. It is much harder to determine how many people are using the Internet because there is no way to know how many people are using all of the host machines. Some hosts are personal workstations with only one user, while others are time-sharing systems with dozens of registered users. No one collects data on exactly where all of the CPU cycles are going. Further, user surveys are always limited to some very small fraction of the total user population. So there are many seemingly simple questions about the Internet that have no verifiable answers.

Where Does All the Bandwidth Go?

Most people don't have a good sense of which activities stress the Internet. Here are some examples of bandwidth consumption that illustrate how big the differences are between text and graphics:

A 700-page novel (just the text)	1 MB
A collegiate dictionary	5 MB
The complete works of Shakespeare	5 MB
A few days of a single newsfeed	5 MB
1 large GIF image (uncompressed)	.5 MB
1 large GIF image (compressed)	.1 MB
A 13-second movie	> 4 MB

The average Internet user currently consumes about 1MB per month, or 25 pages of text per day. This is equivalent to 2–4 GIF images each month or 3 seconds of a compressed movie.

In time, the Internet will most likely move toward a **usage-based** pricing scheme. Although flat-rate pricing does encourage people to experiment and learn freely, it does not sensitize users to their own bandwidth consumption patterns. Under usage-based pricing, the following will likely occur:

- Users will become acquainted with the true costs of their actions.
- Congested resources will be allocated in accordance with priorities.
- Services can be allocated according to usage (e.g., e-mail is not as urgent as video conferencing).

One model for usage-based pricing is **smart market pricing**. In this system, each packet goes out with a priority bid. Packets are queued according to their bids, and the price of a packet transmission is determined by the highest bid packet *that you bump*. Because price is based on actions taken rather than stated priorities, costs stay low as long as there is no congestion. But when the Internet is congested, costs go up for anyone who places a high priority on their packets.

Although smart market pricing sounds like a good plan, there are some thorny difficulties:

1. Clients should be billed for packets sent by servers.
2. Accounting costs must be minimized.
3. Poorly designed pricing will reduce usage.

4. Poorly designed pricing will interfere with technological innovation.

5. Provisions must be made for socially equitable access.

As for software/server costs, there are a variety of models already in place. It is difficult to know which of these strategies will prove successful:

- Commercial advertising online
- Commercial pay-per-view access
- Commercial subscription access
- Government subsidies/grants

It is also important to understand the pervasive role of open access on the Internet. The **gift economy of the Internet** refers to all of the educational Web sites and mailing lists and informational hosts that benefit the public at no charge and with no expectations of cost recovery. The gift economy is a natural outgrowth of the university environments that gave birth to the Internet in the 1970s and 1980s. Information is distributed freely and openly by universities, and the Internet was viewed as a powerful communication medium that would enhance scholarly communications in this tradition.

Computer science departments have supported the gift economy by freely sharing the software they develop. Much of the software available on the Internet today was written by computer science students and is freely distributed. People with expertise in other fields have followed suit and created informational sites as an alternative to traditional publication channels. Indeed, a large percentage of technical papers published by university scientists are now available online, in the form of either electronically distributed journals or publications placed online by authors.

This tradition of the gift economy has set a tone for open and free communication on the Internet. Commercial interests looking for ways to turn a profit on the Internet must compete with the gift economy. If one hundred major newspapers are distributing online editions free of charge, how many people will be willing to pay a subscription charge for an online newspaper? Indeed, Internet surveys indicate that over 60% of Internet users refuse to pay for online resources beyond general access charges.

The Gift Economy and Chess

In January 1995, the Internet Chess Server (ICS) removed itself from the gift economy of the Internet. ICS had previously allowed chess players to register on the ICS server free of charge, and scores of programmers had made chess-related software available to this community free of charge. Then ICS turned itself into a club, the Internet Chess Club (ICC), and asked everyone to pay $50 a year for the privilege of being registered on the

ICC server. Within one or two weeks of the ICS/ICC transformation, the same programmers who had supported ICS brought up a new chess server, the Free Internet Chess Server (FICS), effectively recreating ICS under a new name. FICS was virtually indistinguishable from the old ICS and it was free, just as ICS had been previously.

Interestingly, ICC and FICS are both thriving today. Some people believe the fee charged by ICC attracts a more serious group of chess players, so they are happy to pay to be included in that group. Others are satisfied with FICS and enjoy those resources free of charge. It seems that commercialism and the gift economy can coexist on the Internet as long as underlying data and computer programs are not proprietary.

The gift economy has made the Internet a colorful and free-wheeling environment in which anyone can publish a novel, anyone can promote a cause, and anyone can organize a virtual community. If the Internet were to evolve into a totally commercial enterprise, sites without adequate market appeal would disappear and mainstream tastes would begin to dominate. The gift economy must be preserved if we cherish choice and diversity as much as we value convenience and mass markets.

Bandwidth and Asynchronous Communication

2.8

Online communication takes a little getting used to. The off-line world is dominated by two-way, real-time communication. When two people converse over lunch, the conversation operates in two directions, with responses to questions and comments occurring right away. In computer circles, a two-way communication mediated by shared signals for starting and stopping is called **synchronous** communication. Synchronous communication is the natural modality of human conversation, and conversational skills have evolved to facilitate fluid verbal interactions. We use body language, eye contact, and vocal intonations to pick up on conversational signals that enable smooth transitions back and forth between multiple speakers. We are annoyed when someone dominates the conversation, and we notice when someone is shy or reluctant to participate in a conversation. A typical speaker/listener takes advantage of many nonlinguistic cues in order to participate in conversations effectively.

Face-to-face conversations benefit from a **high-bandwidth** communication channel. A lot of information flows across multiple modalities: body language, hand gestures, vocal intonations, linguistic styles, and timing all convey information. We are normally not conscious of all of the subtle signals present during a conversation, but we quickly become more appreciative of what's missing when we shift into any conversational medium that has restricted bandwidth. For example, participants in a telephone conversation lose all of the visual cues associated with body language and hand gestures. Telephone conversations can be a little awkward when the participants have not learned to adapt to this restriction. People who do not know each other very well often go through a period of adjustment during which they learn to compensate for lost bandwidth. Even people who are normally comfortable on telephones experience some awkwardness during conference calls when a large number of people are on the line and no one knows how to signal the group for permission to speak. This problem can be solved only by a conference call facilitator, who takes charge of the group, spells out the goals of the meeting, and makes sure everyone gets an opportunity to speak.

Bandwidth Benchmarks

It is important to have some feel for the relative bandwidth demands of different data types. Here are a some useful bandwidth benchmarks:

Plain text	44 bits/word
Telephone-quality audio	21,000 bits/word
Stereo CD	466,000 bits/word
Network-quality video	100,000,000 bits/sec
Video conferencing	400,000,000 bits/sec

When real-time video is added to real-time audio, we recover most of the bandwidth lost in a telephone call, but even here we see how very sensitive we are to delicately timed visual cues. Software like CU-CMe and RealVideo allow Internet users with properly equipped hosts to converse with others through a video channel. In theory, this should supply us with all of the visual cues needed to conduct a smooth conversation, but in practice, the video quality is often too primitive—images can be jerky and stroboscopic. When an image received is not perfectly in sync with its audio, the resulting mismatch between sight and sound is enough to undermine most conversational signals.

In written communication, a completely new set of conventions must be adopted to facilitate two-way communication. Many people have bemoaned the lost art of letter writing, as telephones became the long-distance communication medium of choice. Why write a letter if you can make a phone call? Given a choice, most of us opt for the phone call; few people exchange personal letters anymore. Letters seem especially awkward to modern sensibilities because there is nothing fluid about a two-way interaction that transpires over a period of days. It may take a week for the answer to a question to materialize, and questions sometimes "cross" in the mail because of the lag time between sending and receiving. Communication via letters is two-way, but it is not synchronous communication.

When a communication exchange does not rely on shared signals for starting and stopping, it is called **asynchronous** communication. Asynchronous communications online are characterized by longer waits for responses. There is the sense that it pays to say as much as you can at each opportunity because it's going to be a while before you get another chance to speak. Asynchronous communication requires a moderate amount of forethought and organization.

One of the great ironies of the Internet is that it has forced millions of people to return to the fine art of asynchronous written communication. The most popular application on the Internet is e-mail, which is an asynchronous communication medium. E-mail messages are delivered in a matter of seconds, but there is no guarantee that an intended recipient will be ready and waiting to reply as soon as your message is received. Some amount of time is likely to pass before a full e-mail interaction can be completed, so it pays to say what you need to say intelligibly. If you ask for something that requires clarification, your correspondent may have to come back to you and request more information before answering your original question. Time delays are often annoying, so it pays to write carefully during online interactions.

If you work with a community of people who all communicate online, e-mail can easily supplant phone calls and "snail mail" as the communication medium of choice. In time, everyone develops useful skills for efficient e-mail communication, but these skills invariably benefit from practice and experience. For example, if you are asking someone to help you with a problem, you need to describe the problem concisely. If your problem is urgent, you don't want to lose time going back and forth with an excessive number of questions and answers. Software technicians who rely on one another for technical assistance are well-practiced at the fine art of asking for help online, but newcomers need to hone their e-mail communication skills if they hope to get timely assistance.

The skills associated with efficient e-mail communication are grounded in common sense, but some simple guidelines may save substantial time and effort. It pays to think about what you are saying and how you are saying it.

2.9 Where to Learn More

There are some excellent books that describe the history, architecture, and inner workings of the Internet in much more detail than can be given here. If you want to learn more, the following books are highly recommended. All were written for a general audience and assume no technical background in computer science.

The Internet Book: Everything You Need to Know about Computer Networking and How the Internet Works, by Douglas E. Comer. Prentice Hall, Englewood Cliffs, NJ, 1995. (312 pages)

This highly readable book takes you behind the scenes of your favorite Internet applications. If you've been using the Internet a while and you're curious about how things really work, this book will give you intelligible descriptions.

The Internet 1997 Unleashed, by Jill Ellsworth and Billy Baron (Eds.). Sams.net Publishing, Indianapolis, IN, 1996. (1,269 pages)

This is a comprehensive guide to the Internet that includes some interesting chapters describing the Internet and its history.

Netizens: On the History and Impact of Usenet and the Internet, by Michael Hauben and Ronda Hauben. IEEE Computer Press, 1997. (384 pages)

This is a detailed and fascinating resource on Internet history, rich with quotations and anecdotes from the people behind the scenes. Notable chapters are dedicated to the history of ARPAnet and the Usenet newsgroups, while other chapters emphasize the social implications of the Internet. It is also available on the Web at

```
http://www.columbia.edu/~hauben/netbook/
```

Where Wizards Stay Up Late, by Katie Hafner and Matthew Lyon. Simon and Shuster, New York, NY, 1996. (304 pages)

This describes the birth of the Internet. Technical issues are explained well, and the major players are fleshed out with personalities and private lives. This is a very entertaining perspective on the Internet's historical roots and evolution.

The following books offer different perspectives on the Internet. You will appreciate this material more after you have spent some time on the Internet and you are ready to reflect on your experiences.

Being Digital, by Nicholas Negroponte. Vintage Books (Random House), New York, NY, 1995. (255 pages)

Professor Negroponte is the Founding Director of the Media Lab at the Massachusetts Institute of Technology. His book covers the future of computers and computer networks in a way that everyone can understand. He is less interested in the Internet of today than in the computer technologies of tomorrow. The Media Lab at MIT is inventing the future, and this book will give you glimpse of what's coming.

City of Bits: Space, Place, and the Infobahn, by William J. Mitchell. MIT Press, Cambridge, MA, 1995. (225 pages)

William Mitchell is Professor of Architecture and Media Arts and Sciences and Dean of the School of Architecture and Planning at the Massachusetts Institute of Technology. This is a thoughtful book that places the Internet in a historical perspective by examining the concepts of community, public and private spaces, and the political and economic consequences of communication technologies.

Digital Literacy, by Paul Gilster. John Wiley & Sons, New York, NY, 1997. (276 pages)

This book shows how the author has integrated the Internet into his professional and personal life, while successfully surmounting the challenges of information overload and online time management.

The Next 50 Years: Special Anniversary Issue. Communications of the Association of Computing Machinery. February 1997, Vol. 40, No, 2.

This is a collection of articles by over forty computer scientists and technologists invited to speculate about the future of computing. The articles are short, more speculative than technical, and highly informative. Look here for visions of the future.

PROBLEMS AND EXERCISES

1. How many computers were hooked up in the first long-distance network experiment in 1970?

2. How many networks make up the Internet?

3. How can you tell if a computer is part of the Internet?

4. Explain how packet switching works. How big is a typical packet? What protocols set the standard for packet switching?

5. What are the two main parts of a DNS name?

6. Explain the roles of routers and gateways on the Internet.

7. Why is a heterarchical network architecture better than a hierarchical architecture for the Internet?

8. Where is the greatest bandwidth bottleneck for a home computer on the Internet?

9. Who ran the backbone for the Internet before 1992? What is the name of the current backbone?

10. What kind of data consumes the most bandwidth?

11. If someone has the e-mail address `smith@france.ett.com`, do you think that person lives in France? Explain why or why not.

12. How does the Federal Communications Commission exert control over the Internet?

13. Explain the difference between synchronous and asynchronous communication.

14. What is the relationship between peak network traffic and average traffic loads?

15. Is a Web browser a client or a server?

16. What three organizations are responsible for the backbone of the Internet today?

17. Name two milestones that marked the commercialization of the Internet. When did they occur?

18. What is flat rate pricing and why did NSF adopt it? Explain how light bandwidth consumers subsidize heavy bandwidth consumers under flat rate pricing.

19. Explain how smart market pricing would regulate costs as a function of network traffic.

20. What is the gift economy of the Internet? How did it start?

Working with E-mail   3

> "Somewhere along the line our conception of what a computer is began to change fundamentally . . . .Their real role is to construct cyberspace—a new kind of place for human interactions and transactions."
>
> - WILLIAM J. MITCHELL

THE INTERNET 101 WEB PAGES

- Command Sets for Specific Mail Programs
- Some Mail-Related URLs
- How to Find People on the Internet

E-mail: The Prototypical Online Experience   3.1

E-mail is the most popular activity on the Internet. At least 75% of everyone with access to the Internet uses e-mail. E-mail has been around for over 25 years, from the earliest days of the original ARPAnet. Because e-mail is based on text files, it does not require powerful computers or high-speed Internet connections. Users who do not have access to state-of-the-art computers can still participate in e-mail dialogs.

Access to e-mail can keep you in touch with coworkers in your local work environment, friends and relatives in faraway places, and online communities of people who share common professional or recreational interests. Timely information can be distributed to a large number of readers via e-mail, and countless newsletters are distributed to subscribers all over the world. Although e-mail communication is asynchronous, people can exchange multiple messages in a matter of minutes. E-mail communications either can be one-on-one or can extend to a large number of recipients, thereby making it both a private and a public communication medium.

The First E-mail Message

Ray Tomlinson sent the first e-mail message across the ARPAnet in 1971. No one documented the event because it didn't seem very important at the time. The first presidential e-mail message was sent by Bill Clinton on March 2, 1993. We honor dubious achievements by important people because so many of our real achievements slip by unnoticed. Chances are no one noticed when you sent your first e-mail message either. The truly significant events in life take place quietly, without fanfare, so we mark their furtive passage by celebrating random nonevents, like birthdays.

Although e-mail is a relatively simple Internet application, its greatest strength is that so many people use it now and even more people will use it in the future. When you reach the point at which you can say that a large percentage of the people you need to talk to are reading e-mail daily, you'll experience e-mail at its best. By then, e-mail will probably be part of your daily routine, too.

This chapter and Chapter 4 explore the practical know-how of e-mail communication. No one can claim to be "Internet literate" without first having a good working knowledge of e-mail tools and management.

An Hour a Day

Corporate e-mail is very popular with company communicators spending an average of 1.19 hours a day using it.

- NUA Internet Surveys: 1996 Review of the Year

Anatomy of an E-mail Message   ◄ 3.2

An e-mail message is very similar to an office memo. It has the following properties:

Is usually fairly short.

Usually addresses a single topic.

Relies on plain text (no graphics or fancy fonts, and so on).

Is usually written in an informal style.

Might be a reply to a previous message.

Can be sent to one person or many people.

Can be passed along to lots of other people.

Is often timely.

May some day come back to haunt you.

Although these are typical features of e-mail messages, the technology does not prohibit other uses for e-mail. You could send an entire book manuscript to someone via e-mail (although there are better ways to send large documents). You can send files through e-mail that are not text files (e.g., a photograph). You can hold a private conversation with someone else about all sorts of highly personal matters, despite the fact that e-mail is not secure or truly private (but see Chapter 12 for more about privacy safeguards).

Each e-mail message contains two parts: a **message header** and a **message body**. The header contains addressing information, such as who the message is from and who the message is being sent to, the time the message was sent, and a subject header describing the contents of the message. Here is a sample e-mail message:

```
Date: Fri, 14 Feb 1997 06:31:34 -0500 (EST)
From: DRBMC986@aol.com
To: jas@wideworld.stt.com
Subject: Summer Soccer Program

We need a volunteer to coordinate a summer program for
our soccer players. Responsibilities include contacting
parents, collecting money, writing checks. Basically it is
an administrative job that needs to be done by a volunteer.

Please reply to me if you are willing to take this on.

Dave Brown
```

The first four lines of the message are part of the message header; the rest is the message body. When you create an e-mail message, some parts of the header are entered by you, specifically the **To:** field and the **Subject:** field. Other parts of the header will be filled in for you. The **From:** field and the **Date:** field are always filled in automatically. In fact, the only part of the message that absolutely *must* be filled in is the **To:** field. You can leave **Subject:** blank. You can even leave the message body empty and still have a perfectly legal e-mail message. But if you leave the **To:** field unfilled, your message will have no place to go.

When you fill in the **To:** field, you must specify a valid e-mail address. A valid e-mail address consists of a userid and a host address separated by the @ character. If there are any typographical errors in the address, your message will be returned to you along with an error message. Note, however, that a typographical error might send your mail to a legitimate address, although not the one you intended. In that case, no error message will alert you. If the accidental recipient does not respond, you will have no reason to believe anything went wrong. So be careful when you complete the **To:** field.

Following are some examples of valid e-mail addresses:

Userid	Host Address	E-mail Address
ajones	apple.orchard.com	ajones@apple.orchard.com
deadbug	antfarm.net	deadbug@antfarm.net
kgranite	context.wccm.org	kgranite@context.wccm.org

If you don't know the address of the person you want to contact, you will have to track it down. There are many online directories that may be useful in this situation (see the Internet 101 Web pages for directory pointers). If you think you know the address, it might be worth a guess, but only if you are prepared for the possibility of the mail getting to the wrong person. Some userids are not particularly formulaic. For example, if you know Dave Brown is an AOL subscriber, you will have only the host address, aol.com. It would be impossible to guess at a userid like DRBMC986.

Alias Shortcuts for E-mail Addresses

If you send a lot of e-mail to the same person, most mail software will let you refer to that person's full e-mail address by using a shortcut abbreviation. Check your software for an alias or nickname feature. This is especially useful when you have to look up an address over and over again or when an address is very long and tedious to type.

The use of an alias will also save you from typographical errors and addressing errors. You can use the alias feature to create an address book for all your frequently used addresses. Then all you have to remember is the alias for each person in your address book. A system of first names followed by a last initial is easy to remember. If the names of two people collide using this system, you can enter their full last names. Whatever system you use, keep your alias entries systematic and easy to remember.

Whenever you pass text strings to a computer program, it is helpful to know if the program you are using is case-sensitive. **Case-sensitivity** means that uppercase and lowercase characters are distinct and cannot be substituted for one another. When software is not case-sensitive, you can freely substitute uppercase characters for lowercase characters and vice versa. Without case sensitivity, the following e-mail addresses are all equivalent:

```
DRBMC@aol.com

drbmc@aol.com

DrBmc@AOL.com

DrBMC@AOL.COM
```

When dealing with case-sensitive software, your chances of a typographical error are greater because you may use the wrong case for one of the characters; any such error will render your input unrecognizable. Happily, e-mail addresses are normally handled by software that is not case-sensitive. Host names, site names, and domain names are normally all lowercase, so if you don't know what case to use, use lowercase throughout. It is unusual to find userids in uppercase, but you might find some userids in mixed case characters. With luck, the software used to deliver your mail will not be case-sensitive and mail messages won't bounce if you don't get the case right. Some Internet software can be much fussier about case (e.g., addresses for Web pages), but e-mail messages tend to get where they need to go despite case errors.

Another Addressing Shortcut

HINT

Sometimes you will find yourself in a LAN that contains a group of computers used by people in a specific department or local work environment. If your computer account resides in a LAN, you may

Continued on Next Page

Continued from Previous Page

be able to send e-mail to other people working on the same LAN by specifying only their userid and omitting the host name. If you aren't sure who's on the LAN and who isn't, you can always try the userid alone and see if it works. A LAN may support accounts for hundreds of users. Some LANs are set up to allow this shortcut and some are not. But the userid shortcut always works for two users who have accounts on the same host machine. In that case, abbreviated addresses are always recognized. You never need to type the host's domain name if it is the same as your own host machine's.

Although you normally type in two or three header fields when you send e-mail, the actual header used by your mail software is a bit more involved. In the previous example, only a short version of the full mail header is displayed. The full version looks something like this (from a different message):

```
From clark_school-approval@europe.stt.com Sun Feb 23 19:06:35 1997
Received: from freya.cs.umass.edu (freya.cs.umass.edu [128.119.40.195])
 by thidwick.cs.umass.edu (8.7.6/8.7.3) with ESMTP id TAA07678 for
 <lehnert@thidwick.cs.umass.edu>; Sun, 23 Feb 1997 19:06:34 -0500
Received: from europe.stt.com (europe.stt.com [199.174.62.20])
    by freya.cs.umass.edu (8.7.6/8.6.9) with ESMTP id TAA01268 for
    <lehnert@cs.umass.edu>; Sun, 23 Feb 1997 19:06:33 -0500
Received: by europe.stt.com (8.7.5/BZS-8-1.0)
    id TAA24271; Sun, 23 Feb 1997 19:04:34 -0500 (EST)
    X-Authentication-Warning: europe.stt.com: daemon set sender to
    clark_school-approval using -f
Received: from wideworld.stt.com by europe.stt.com (8.7.5/BZS-8-1.0)
    id TAA24267; Sun, 23 Feb 1997 19:04:33 -0500 (EST)
Received: from localhost by wideworld.std.com (5.65c/Spike-2.0)
    id AA21689; Sun, 23 Feb 1997 19:04:32 -0500
Date: Sun, 23 Feb 1997 19:04:32 -0500 (EST)
From: John A Smith <jas@wideworld.stt.com>
To: mailing-list Clark_School <Clark_School@wideworld.stt.com>
Subject: Contract is Done (fwd)
Message-Id: <Pine.SGI.3.93.970223190420.21029A-
           100000@wideworld.stt.com>
Mime-Version: 1.0
Content-Type: TEXT/PLAIN; charset=US-ASCII
Sender: clark_school-approval@wideworld.stt.com
Precedence: list
Reply-To: clark_school@europe.stt.com
```

The header in this message contains routing information and additional time stamps that indicate when the message was received by different hosts along the way (see all of the different **Received:** fields). Most users don't need to see all of this information, so most mailers hide it from the user, although it should always be available on request. Each e-mail message is stored with its complete header. There are times when it may be useful to see the full version.

Each e-mail message you receive is stored in a plain text file. The full header appears at the top of the file; the message body follows. Your mail program is responsible for scanning this file and deciding how much of it you probably want to see. Note that the full header is never deleted from the original message file. Don't confuse a mail message with the way that mail message is being displayed. There may be more to your mail than meets the eye.

Other address fields are available to use when you send an e-mail message. The most commonly used optional field is the **Cc: (Carbon copy)** field. When you put an e-mail address in this field, a copy of your message is sent to that person. Some people always **Cc:** to themselves so they can have a copy of all of the messages they send out. This is called a "self-Cc:". Some mailers give you a switch you can set to make self-Cc: copies automatically. If a message is primarily intended for one person, but it is useful for five other people to see it as well, use the **Cc:** field for the other five addresses. However, if your message is intended for more than one person and they are all equally important as recipients, you can put multiple addresses in the **To:** field.

How to Create a Distribution List

If you send mail to the same group of people on a regular basis (maybe you are all members of the same committee), you can use the alias feature to create a mail distribution list. Just create a new alias. When you enter the e-mail address, give your mailer a list of e-mail addresses, separated by blanks or commas. A distribution list alias will save you from a lot of tedious typing and typographical errors.

HINT

When a message is sent with a **Cc:** entry, recipients will see that field in your message header. If you want to keep a **Cc:** entry secret (perhaps someone has asked you to hold their e-mail address in confidence), then you can use the **Bcc: (Blind carbon copy)** field instead of the usual carbon copy field. The contents of a **Bcc:** field are not revealed to any of the message recipients.

What to Expect from Your Mail Program

3.3

There are many different **mail programs** (also called **mailers**), and they are all very similar in their operation and features. This makes it possible to describe a generic mailer that will apply to almost any mailer you will encounter. Once you've seen one mail program, you'll know what to expect from the next one. This means that you don't have to worry too much about which mailer to adopt. Moreover, if you ever need to switch mail programs, you won't have to relearn everything from scratch. A few basic commands are enough to make you operational. If you are used to some special features, you should be able to find equivalent commands in your new mailer.

All mail programs will enable you to do the following:

- Send a message that you have written yourself
- Read any message that has been sent to you
- Reply to any message that has been sent to you
- Forward a mail message to a third party
- Save or delete mail messages sent to you
- Scan the **Subject:** and **From:** fields for all your new mail

A good mail program also supports other features, such as these:

- The ability to sort mail and save it in different locations
- The ability to tag unread mail messages for easy identification
- Address aliases or nicknames
- A reply option that allows you to edit the original message
- A customizable mail filter that sorts mail before you see it
- Automatic signature file inclusion

If you are working on a PC or a Mac and you have Internet access through an ISP or university account, the Eudora mail program is a popular option. It includes many advanced features as well as an intuitive interface. On a UNIX platform, the elm and pine mail programs are very popular. A good mail program will remind you of the most commonly used commands via convenient buttons and pull-down menus or a few command descriptions at the bottom of the screen. Even if you can't remember all of the details of your particular program, it should be easy to look up something in the online documentation.

Many Web browsers now include their own integrated e-mail package. A national service such as AOL provides its own mailer to subscribers. However, feel free to experiment with different mail programs. If you find yourself spending an hour or more each day on e-mail, it makes sense to shop around and find the program that best meets your personal needs. Talk to friends about their mailers and their mailers' favorite features. After using a mail program regularly for a few weeks, you'll be better able to evaluate the features of different programs and decide which is best for you.

Which Mail Program?

If you can't spell, look for a mailer with a spelling checker. If you expect to handle a lot of e-mail, look for a mailer that supports automated filtering and routing. For some users, a single crucial feature may be enough to decide the issue. For example, the mailer that comes with Netscape Navigator is integrated with the Netscape Web browser. If someone sends you a URL in a mail message, the Netscape mailer will recognize it as a hot link, underline it for you in your message display, and make it an operational hot link that you can click if you want to visit the Web page right then and there. For people who get a lot of Web pointers in their mail, this might be the most wonderful feature in the world. For people who never see URLs in their e-mail, it won't matter. Only you can decide what features matter to you.

HINT

Before you embark on your first mail program, now is a good time to remember what was said in Chapter 1 about complicated software. That is, you don't need to master all of the available commands right away (or maybe ever). You need only a partial mastery of all of the available features in order to function. Plan to refine and expand your mastery later and don't feel intimidated by all of the commands you don't understand.

Viewing Your Inbox   ◀ 3.4

The first thing people normally do when they fire up their mailer is to check for new mail. When new mail arrives it is stored in your inbox. The **inbox** is very much like a mailbox, in which new mail waits for you to retrieve it. Many mailers take you directly to this mailbox as soon as you start them. Others may require you to load the inbox in order to see your new mail.

Once you have gotten into your inbox, you will see a display that lists each piece of mail with a single line for each mail message. This line displays the **Subject:** header and the **From:** header so that you can see what each message is about and who sent it to you. Most displays also show the date of arrival for each message. Here is a sample inbox display from the elm mail program:

```
      1    Feb 19 Patrick Douglas Cr (253)   TOURBUS - 20 FEBRUARY 1997
      2    Feb 19 Bill Curtis          (39)   Undergrad Jobs with CIIR
N     3    Feb 19 Bob Rankin           (44)   FLASH: Du Jour Address
N     4    Feb 19 Bob Rankin          (121)   TOURBUS 18 Feb 1997 - More Fun
      5    Feb 11 top5@lists.zdnet.c  (146)   Top5 - 2/12/97 - Signs Your Dog Has
      6    Feb 3  mtz@student.umass.   (29)   Comp Sci 191a
      7    Feb 1  mtz@student.umass.  (137)   Fwd: FW: PLEASE SEND THIS ON!!!
O     8    Jan 23 To webmaster@zocal   (31)   500 Server Error
O     9    Jan 15 Terrie Kellogg   A3  (40)   EDLAB   cleanup scheduled for Friday
     10    Jan 9  L-Soft list server   (53)   Subscription probe for TOURBUS -
```

Each message in this sample inbox has a number that allows you to refer to specific messages by using keyboard commands. The code "N" indicates the message is new since the last time the mailbox was visited and has not been read during this visit. The code "O" indicates the message is old (it was present during a previous visit to the inbox) and has never been read. A message listed without a code next to it means that message has already been read. All messages are sorted by their dates, with the most recently received messages at the head of the list. In this sample inbox, messages #1 and #2 have already been read, messages #3 and #4 are new and have not been read, and messages #8 and #9 are old and have never been read. Judging from their dates, #8 and #9 have been ignored for a long time, perhaps because they are not thought to be very important.

The entry after the date tells who sent the message. Some of these entries are actual e-mail addresses; others are names of people (e.g., "Bob Rankin") or software (e.g., "L-Soft list server"). Whenever you send mail, your **From:** field is filled with both your e-mail address and an alias for yourself, if one has been made available to your mailer. Your mailer may give you an opportunity to enter your full name at some point. If it does, whatever you give it will be added to your **From:** field whenever you send mail and then used by other mail programs designed to display full names in addition to or in place of e-mail addresses. You can specify any alias that you want. Most people just enter their real names.

The mailbox display shows you a short form of each mail message's header, limited to whatever fits on a single line. In the previous display, some of the **From:** and **Subject:** entries have been truncated. The mailer did this to keep each message displayed on a single line. Remember this when you write your own subject headers. That is, you can give a mail message a long subject header, but only the first few words will show in the recipient's inbox.

Between the **From:** field and the **Subject:** field, elm displays a number in parentheses. This is the number of lines in the mail message. It gives you a quick feel for how long it may take to read a given message. Someone in a hurry who is trying to get through a lot of mail may skip over the longest messages to avoid getting bogged down. Long messages are often set aside until there is more time to read them.

> "Shortly after I joined the Commission in May 1994, my then-six-year-old son, David, visited me in my office while I was deleting e-mail. He announced, "Mom, there's a faster way to do that," and with two keystrokes, it was all gone."
>
> - Susan Ness,
> Commissioner of the Federal Communications Commission

Generation Gaps

Sometimes, there are more messages in your inbox than your screen display can contain in one window. In that case, you will be able to page or scroll to the next block of messages and move back and forth across different segments of your inbox. Make sure to view all of the headers in your inbox so that you can get the full picture of what's in there. In a keyboard interface, you should be able to find commands for paging forward and backward. In a point-and-click interface, you can move forward and backward by using the vertical scroll bar on the right side of the window. If you know the number of a particular message that you want to see, usually you can type that number, press Return, and be taken directly to that message.

Now is a good time to make sure you know how to exit your mail program. There will be times when all you want to do is quickly scan your mail headers and then leave. You will probably have two options for exiting your mailer: a normal exit and a quick exit. The **normal exit** saves any changes you may have made during your visit. The **quick exit** leaves your mail unchanged regardless of what you've done to it. See if you can find these two different Exit commands for your mailer. If you are using a point-and-click interface, you may have only one Exit command, but after selecting it, you then can pick a normal exit or a quick exit in a dialog box. The dialog boxes do not exactly give you a *fast* quick exit, but at least you'll be able to exit the mailer, leaving your mailbox unchanged. Don't worry if you don't understand the difference between a normal exit and a quick exit right now. It will make more sense after you've seen more mail operations.

Study your mail program's documentation and make sure you know how to do the following:

1. View your inbox and identify all your new mail.
2. Know how to distinguish read messages from unread messages.
3. Navigate multiple pages in a large inbox (both forward and backward).
4. Exit your mail program (Can you find two separate Exit commands?).

3.5

Viewing Individual Mail Messages

When you view your inbox, you see only a short header for each mail message. To see the message body for a given message, you must first select that message. If you have a point-and-click interface, select a message by pointing to it and clicking it. A double-click opens the message so that you can view its message body. If you have a keyboard interface, you can select a message by entering its message number or navigate your way to the message using up and down keyboard commands. These navigational commands could be your arrow keys or the keys K (for up) and J (for down). Once the proper message has been selected, pressing Return or Enter will likely open the message. Whenever you view a nonempty inbox, some message will always be selected. The selected message is often identified by highlighting. In some older mail programs, a special character (often >) to the left of the header is sometimes used. Most mailers expect you to select and open specific mail messages one at a time.

Once you have opened a mail message, you will see a screen display that contains an abbreviated version of the message header followed by the message body. If the message body is very long, it may not fit inside a single screen display, so you'll need a command that advances you to the next page in order to view the complete message. Your mailer will let you navigate both forward and backward through a message body. In a point-and-click interface, you can move up and down using the vertical scroll bar on the right border of the window.

When you are done reading your mail message, you will want to leave that message and return to the display of mail headers. In a point-and-click interface, look for a Close button. Other mailers may offer a keyboard command. Watch the bottom of the screen for a helpful reminder about how to exit a mail message.

All mail programs have a lot of options you can set, along with many advanced commands that might be useful to you. Start by learning the settings and commands you need in order to complete the e-mail checklists in this chapter. Whenever you need to learn a new command, check your online help facility first. In a keyboard interface, you can reach help by typing H or ?. In a point-and-click interface, there is probably a menu command Help.

Study your mail program's documentation and make sure you know how to do the following:

1. Select a specific message in your inbox.
2. Open up a single mail message in order to view its message body.
3. Page forward and backward through a long message body.
4. Exit a mail message display and return to the inbox.
5. Display the long version of a message header.

E-MAIL CHECKLIST #2

Sending a New Mail Message

3.6

Once you know someone's e-mail address, you are ready to send a mail message. If you want to experiment without any risk of embarrassment, try sending a test message to yourself before you send a message to someone else. Just put your own userid in the **To:** field; the mail will be sent to you. All mailers have a command that puts you in a mode for creating and sending your own mail messages. In a point-and-click interface, you may find a New Message command in a pull-down menu. If you have a keyboard interface, the command may be "m" (for "mail").

After issuing the command for starting a new message, you will be put into a mode for constructing an e-mail message. You'll be given an opportunity to enter the **To:** header, the **Subject:** header, and the optional **Cc:** header. The **From:** header will be filled in for you automatically. In a point-and-click interface, you will probably be given a window display in which all of these items can be filled by moving your mouse around and clicking the field you want to complete. In other interfaces, you will move through a sequence of prompts for each header field. If you don't want to put something in a given field, just press Return or Enter to leave it blank. The only header field that can't be left blank is the **To:** field.

In most mailers, a blank window is reserved for the message body. Just type your message in and edit it as needed, and you're ready to send the message. Some mail programs will give you their own built-in text editor for entering your message body. Almost any text editor will suffice for writing e-mail. Other mailers, especially those found on UNIX platforms, will give you the ability to hook up any text editor you prefer. The specification of an external text editor is normally set under an Options or Preferences menu. For users who have strong feelings about the editor they use, the ability to write e-mail using their favorite text editor is a non-negotiable requirement. This issue is usually more important for people who are working with a keyboard interface rather than a point-and-click interface. Once you've learned a dozen keyboard navigation commands for one text editor, you probably don't want to learn a whole new set of keyboard navigation commands for another editor. For people using point-and-click interfaces, the adjustment is much less traumatic. You may prefer the look and feel of a specific text editor, but if you need to write your mail message under a slightly different interface, it's not likely to be a big deal. All point-and-click interfaces are designed to make the most basic operations highly intuitive, and editing an e-mail message is not likely to require much beyond the most basic editing commands.

Getting Plugged

HINT

Software that lets you pick and choose other software components is usually more sophisticated than software that doesn't. User-controlled software options are called plug-ins. Plug-ins let you customize your computing environment just the way you want it. Many plug-ins are initialized with some default setting, so you may not know a plug-in is in place unless you poke around in the options settings. When you are experienced enough to care, you will watch for plug-in options wherever it is possible for two applications to interact with each other. For example, the Netscape mail program lets you view hyperlinks inside mail messages with Netscape, but the Eudora mailer lets you plug-in any Web browser you want for the same purpose.

One thing a good mail editor should do for you is monitor the length of each line you type and make sure you don't create lines that exceed 72 characters. If you have a full-fledged text editor hooked into your mail program, you can set the margins yourself to make sure you don't exceed the 72-character limit. Text lines that are too long will not display well in your recipient's mailbox. People reading your mail may see "raggy text"—text that wraps around to the next line and then abruptly halts after an inch or two, only to continue on the next line where it wraps around again, and then halts, and so on and so on. Raggy text is very difficult to read and will annoy people trying to read your mail. Some mail programs do not incorporate any defaults about line length, so this is something you may need to check yourself. You may also want to set yourself a limit of 65 characters per line just to be safe. Lines no greater than 65 characters will always break correctly even if your message is forwarded to a third party or included in an e-mail reply. If you can't set any margins to control your line length, then you have to remember to monitor it yourself each time you compose a new e-mail message. ***Even if the message body looks readable to you, your recipient may see a different display.*** Different mailers can display your message differently, and you have no control over someone else's mailer. A 72-character limit (or less) is the only way to make sure you aren't subjecting your recipients to raggy unreadable text.

Plain ASCII Text

E-mail messages cannot contain text with different fonts, special effects like italics or boldface, or fancy formatting involving tables or flowing columns. If you have mastered a sophisticated word processor or desktop publishing program, don't hope to put its more-powerful features into your e-mail messages. Mail programs are designed to read **plain text** files, or, to be slightly more technical, **plain ASCII text** files. You can use all of the visible characters on your keyboard, both lowercase and uppercase, but you cannot incorporate control characters or other commands that may be meaningful to a word processor. When it comes to e-mail, you have to keep it simple. You can manually indent paragraphs with blank spaces, but that's about as fancy as you can get. Don't even try to use tab characters.

When you evaluate the editor that comes with your mail program, keep in mind that all you really need are navigational controls so that you can edit your text and correct typographical errors. A spelling checker is a very nice feature to have for your e-mail, especially if you are spelling-impaired. If you ever need to send someone a text document that contains graphics or that must be viewed with sophisticated formatting in place, then you will need to reformat your non-ASCII text file as an encoded ASCII file. An ASCII encoding utility is described at the end of this chapter.

Enter the text for your message body, read it over to make sure it says what you think it says, and prepare to send your message. In a point-and-click interface, there is probably a Send button. In other interfaces, you will first need to exit the editor (using the Exit command for whatever editor you are using), after which you will be given an opportunity to either send the message, edit the message body again, or edit the message headers. All mailers will also give you an opportunity to scrap the whole thing if you decide you don't want to send it after all. However, if you decide to torpedo your message, you must do it *before* you issue the Send command. Once you've told your mailer to send a message, that's that. There is no way to recall a message once it's been sent.

As soon as you have mastered the basics of sending a mail message, it's time to put two more goodies in your bag of tricks. Earlier in this chapter, the alias feature was described as a shortcut device for long or difficult-to-remember e-mail addresses. Now is a good time to start an address book that you can update regularly as needed. Find the **alias** or **nickname** command for your mailer and set up an alias for someone you know you'll be writing to often. The next time you send e-mail to this person, use that person's alias instead of the full e-mail name. This is a powerful feature that can save you a lot of time.

Another time-saver is the use of **signature files** (or **sig files**). People who send a lot of e-mail have signature files that they append to the end of their message bodies. These signature files identify the sender in some appropriate way. For business communications, a signature file should contain the person's name, title, organization, mailing address, phone number, fax number, and e-mail address. For casual e-mail, a name, e-mail address, and favorite quotation can add a little personality into an e-mail message. The signature file personalizes your e-mail and saves you from the tedious task of having to retype the same signature lines each time you compose a mail message.

Signature Files

You can say a lot about yourself with a clever sig file. Just don't try to say everything. Figure 3.1 shows some inspirational examples. Some of them break the 4-line rule, but they are so good you have to forgive their creators. If you read through the rest of this chapter carefully, you'll find out what the third line of the first signature says.

Some mailers automatically add your sig file to the end of your message body, while others add it only on command. Some mailers also let you set up multiple sig files to allow you to convey different online personas. You might

```
--
▓▓▓▓▓▓▓▓▓ EMT-P, K5ZC, PP-ASEL | Never ascribe to malice that which can
▓▓▓▓▓▓▓@oac.hsc.uth.tmc.edu    | adequately be explained by stupidity.
   "begin 666 foo B22!C86XG="!B96QI979E('E0=2!D96-09&5D('1H:7,A"@ ` end"
                   -- ▓▓▓▓▓▓▓▓▓▓▓
```

```
___*___   ▓▓▓▓▓▓▓▓▓▓▓▓▓ - Westendallee 100 d, D-1000 Berlin 19 - +4930-▓▓▓▓▓
=======   E-mail to ▓▓▓▓▓▓@heaven7.{in-berlin.de|sub.org}|cloud9.in-berlin.de}
|||  |||  -------------------------------------------------------------------
|||  |||  ------ Everybody wants to go to heaven, but nobody wants to die ------
```

```
  _/|_
 /o   \/:--|--|------------------------------------------------------------|
 \_~_/\:--| ▓▓▓▓▓▓▓▓▓▓▓▓▓▓ / ▓▓▓▓▓▓▓.mdata.fi, in Espoo, Finland  |
          | "I won't have a battle of wits with an unarmed opponent." |
          |------------------------------------------------------------|
```

```
+---------------------------------------+--------------------------------+
| ▓▓▓▓▓▓▓▓▓▓▓▓▓                         |      Unite Mixte BULL Imag     |
| e-mail : ▓▓▓▓▓▓@aaricia.imag.fr       | ZI de Mayencin - 2,rue Vignate -|
+---------------------------------------+                                |
| Children are hereditary;              | ▓▓▓▓▓▓ieres - France           |
| if your parents didn't have any,      |                                |
| neither will you.                     | tel : (33)▓▓▓▓.48.47           |
|                                       | fax : (33)▓▓▓▓.76.15           |
+---------------------------------------+--------------------------------+
```

```
Regards,
Alan
                        |-----------------------|
\   Internet:           | ▓▓▓▓▓▓▓▓▓▓▓▓          |---------------------------\
 \    ▓▓▓▓@den.mmc.com  | ▓▓▓▓▓▓▓▓▓▓▓XTech Ops  |  Std disclaimers apply.  /
  )Voice:               | P.O. Box ▓▓▓ M/S 5422 |                          <
 /   303-▓▓▓▓▓▓▓        | Denver, CO 80201-0179 USA| (But you knew that!)  \
/_____)  |-----------------------|  <_____\
```

FIG. 3.1

Stylish Signature Files

want to stick to a straightforward signature until you've been online for a while and seen a lot of example signatures.

Keep in mind that some people will be seeing your signature over and over again. An unobtrusive sig file wears well after repeated exposures. Extremely lengthy signatures become annoying after a few encounters. As a general rule, keep your sig file no more than four lines long. If you use all of the available horizontal space, you can pack a lot of information into those four lines.

Message Body Do's and Don't's

There are some standard mistakes that beginners often make with their e-mail. Since you are reading this book, there is no reason for you to make these newbie mistakes:

1. Limit each line to no more than 72 characters. 65 characters is safer.

2. Keep your sig file short and sweet. As a general rule, use no more than four lines for your sig file.

3. Reread the complete message body before you send your mail. Make sure it says what you think it says and catch any errors before you send it off. Careless errors can be embarrassing, especially if the message goes out to many people. Be extra careful when people are relying on you for accurate information.

It is often useful to import text from an existing file for inclusion in an e-mail message body. If the text fragment is small, it is easy to do this with grab-and-drop. For longer pieces of text, you might find it more convenient to read the file into your message body using an editor command. All good text editors have a command that allows you to insert one text file inside another. The command may be called Read, Readfile, or Insert. If your e-mail editor has menu bars, look for an Insert menu with a File command. Text insertion comes in handy when you want to set up stock replies to frequently encountered requests or situations. You can create what amounts to a form letter in a file and then, when you need to send it to someone, insert it into your message body, tweak it here and there as needed, and you're done. A need for form letters is most often found in work environments, but you may find them useful for certain casual communications as well.

Practice sending lots of e-mail to a friend until you feel comfortable and confident about your mail software. Once you get the hang of it, the mechanics of sending e-mail will become second nature and you can concentrate on your content. Remember: *On the Internet, you are what you type.* A message that is filled with misspelled words and ungrammatical sentences says a lot about the sender. The quality of your writing is particularly important when you are writing people who have no contact with you outside of e-mail. Some people take creative liberties with e-mail and devise their own quirky writing styles. This may be appropriate in some contexts, but it is not likely to be appreciated in the business world. Think about who you are writing to, how busy they are, how well you know them, and what the point of your message is. Each message you send takes a little time away from the person reading it. Try not to waste anyone's time and think carefully about what you write. The rules of e-mail Netiquette are discussed in more detail later in the chapter.

Study your mail program's documentation and make sure you know how to do the following:

1. Set up an alias or nickname for someone.
2. Start up a new message you want to send.
3. Enter the message headers and message body.
4. Change the message headers and message body as often as needed.
5. Torpedo a message after you've written it and before you send it.
6. Run the spelling checker if you have one.
7. Set up a sig file if your mailer supports it.
8. Insert text from a file into a message body.
9. Send a message after you've completed the message body.

Sometimes a host machine that you want to contact will be down or unreachable for some time. When this happens, all mail sent to that server will be "bounced" back to the sending servers. This is not an unusual circumstance, and most mail servers are set up to automatically resend bounced messages periodically in an effort to get through. You will be informed of such situations with a notification that looks like this:

```
Date: Tue, 11 Mar 1997 14:14:31 -0500
From: Mail Delivery Subsystem <MAILER-DAEMON>
Subject: Warning: could not send message for past 4 hours
To: lehnert


          *******************************************
       **        THIS IS A WARNING MESSAGE ONLY      **
       **    YOU DO NOT NEED TO RESEND YOUR MESSAGE  **
          *******************************************


The original message was received at Tue, 11 Mar 1997 09:27:34 -0500
from lehnert@localhost

    —- The following addresses have delivery notifications —-
Wayne_Frost@siginc.com   (transient failure)
```

```
    —- Transcript of session follows —-
451 Wayne_Frost@siginc.com... siginc.com: Name server
timeout
Warning: message still undelivered after 4 hours
Will keep trying until message is 5 days old
```

Note the instructions at the head of this message: ***You do not need to resend your message.*** Your mail server will keep trying to resend your message for you. If it cannot succeed after trying for five days, then it gives up. Most hosts experiencing temporary difficulties are restored to service within a day or two, so five days should be more than enough time to get the mail through. You will be informed if your server failed to get through after five days.

Delivery notification warnings are good to see when the message in question is very important or urgent. In that case, you should follow up with a fax or a phone call. Also, be assured that when you receive no such delivery notification, your mail has been successfully picked up by the receiving host. You cannot know if your intended recipient has read the message, but at least you know that the message made it to the inbox.

3.7 ▶ Replying To and Forwarding E-mail Messages

Many e-mail conversations begin when someone replies to a message. One-on-one discussions can be conducted in a series of replies to previous messages, and conversations involving a large group of people can also be conducted using the Reply command.

Before you send any replies to anyone, first make sure you know the difference between two variations on the Reply command. There is a **sender-only reply** and a **group reply**. In the first case, your message is sent only to the original author of the current message. In the second case, your message is sent to the original author, plus everyone included in the **To:** field and everyone included in the **Cc:** and **Bcc:** fields. The first type of reply is private, while the second type may be very public. There are times when you want to use a group reply, but the sender-only reply is used more often. With a point-and-click interface, the sender-only Reply command should be easy to find either on a button or in a pull-down menu. If you have a keyboard interface, the sender-only command is probably "r," but it might be "R." ***Make sure you know which is which before you send any replies.***

Mail's Reply Trap

The UNIX Mail utility is an older mail program that was written long before the phrase "user friendly" came into being. UNIX users who need to use Mail and who aren't very familiar with it inevitably get caught in the Mail program's diabolical reply trap. In the Mail utility, there is an "r" command that replies to a message. Lowercase characters are normally used for UNIX commands; UNIX users rarely use uppercase commands. So it seems logical that "r" would be reserved for the most commonly invoked Reply command, the sender-only reply. Alas, if you use "r" inside the Mail program, you'll send out a group reply. If you want to restrict your reply to the sender only, you have to use the "R" command, a thoroughly unnatural command key for UNIX users.

Many otherwise computer-savvy individuals have mistakenly used "r" when they meant to use "R." It doesn't always matter which is used (there may be no group to include), but when it does, the mistake can be very embarrassing. At worst, it is the sort of thing that can harm a career (suppose you happen to bad-mouth someone who gets to read your message). You will probably never need to use the Mail program, but if you do, be extra careful with your replies.

One of the most useful features used with mail replies is the inclusion of the original mail message in your message body. All of the better mail programs give you the option of either including the original message you are replying to in your message body or starting from scratch with an empty message body. If you include the original message in your reply, you don't have to preserve it in its entirety. Just keep the parts you need to make your reply coherent and use your editor to delete anything that does not need to be seen again. This courtesy is especially important if a large number of people are going to receive your reply. No one wants to scroll through a long message if they've already read it once and don't need to read it again.

Each mailer uses a convention for distinguishing the text of an original message from the text you add in your own reply. Indentations with the > character to the left of each line are used by some mail programs, as shown in this example:

```
>  When do you want to have dinner tonight?

How about 7?

>  I have an early meeting tomorrow so I can't stay out late
>  tonight. We'll have to find some other night for a movie.

OK. We can talk about that over dinner.
```

A reply to a reply includes two levels of indentation, a reply to that will show three levels, and so on. You can make a dialog more readable by using blank lines to separate different speakers. Use your editor freely.

E-mail Reply Do's and Don't's

Here are some more newbie mistakes to avoid:

1. Know which command is the sender-only reply and which is the group reply. If you use the group reply for a message intended for the original sender only, you might embarrass yourself by broadcasting something unintentionally.

2. If you get into a lengthy dialog with someone, take the time to replace the subject header when the original subject header no longer describes the topic of your conversation. It is easy to keep the original subject header, but after a few back-and-forths, your mailbox might end up holding a lot of messages with the same subject header. If you ever need to go back to one of these messages to find something, you won't know where to look.

3. If you find yourself responding emotionally to a piece of e-mail, it is usually wise to cool off a bit before replying, especially if you feel angry. Take some time to think about what you want to say before responding to something out of anger. Your feelings may be justified, but give yourself 24 hours to cool off anyway.

4. Be selective when you include text from the original message in your reply. Don't duplicate the original message in its entirety unless it is absolutely necessary.

When you reply to a mail message, your mailer may or may not include your sig file automatically. There may be a preference setting to control this if you know which default you would like to have. It makes sense to forego a sig file if all of your e-mail replies go to people who already know you. Friends and colleagues don't need to see your signature over and over again. In fact, a lot of old-timers who have been using e-mail since the beginning tend to not use sig files at all because they grew up in an e-mail culture in which they sent messages only to people they knew. Signature files make more sense when your mail is going to people who don't know who you are.

Forwarding e-mail is just like replying to e-mail, except that you send the message to a third party. Most mailers will give you an opportunity to edit the message body when you forward a mail message. This is appropriate when you want to insert your own comments. Although there is nothing to stop you from forwarding anything to anyone, be aware that you may be dealing with sensitive information or information given to you in confidence. If you betray a confidence, you can hurt someone who trusted you, and you can make yourself look untrustworthy in the process. ***Just because a piece of software makes something easy to do doesn't necessarily make it a good idea.***

Study your mail program's documentation and make sure you know how to do the following:

1. Send a reply only to the original author of the current message.
2. Send a group reply to everyone associated with the current message.
3. Include the text of the current message in your reply.
4. Reply using a blank message body (no old text included).
5. Change the subject header for your reply.
6. Forward a message to a third party with or without your own comments.

E-MAIL CHECKLIST #4

E-mail Netiquette   ◄ 3.8

Netiquette is all about respect. Good Netiquette ensures that you show respect for people you don't know and whom you may never get to know all that well in spite of long-standing, online conversations. It is especially important because the Internet encourages interactive communication between strangers on a truly grand scale, a scale that we never experience in other public forums in which the reality of physical distance limits our reach and binds us to familiar communities.

Whenever you send e-mail, remember a few Netiquette guidelines:

- Keep your messages short and to the point.
- Watch your grammar and spelling.
- Be careful with humor. Avoid sarcasm.
- Use uppercase words very sparingly. UPPERCASE TEXT YELLS AT PEOPLE.
- Never leave your **Subject:** header blank.
- Include your e-mail address in the message body (e.g., in your sig file).

If you are new to e-mail, you have not yet experienced its mixed blessings. Some people deal with a hundred e-mail messages every day. They are understandably annoyed by any message that wastes their time, especially if the message was written by someone who does not use good Netiquette.

Online conversations are not the same as face-to-face conversations or even telephone conversations. When you talk online there are no body language cues or vocal intonations. If you are inexperienced with online dialogs, you may not realize how important and useful all of this "unspoken" communication is. For example, you will find that a lot of good-intentioned humor falls flat on the Internet. Or worse, it may be completely misinterpreted and end up making someone feel hurt or angry. If you are in the habit of speaking with sarcasm, temper that tendency until you have a very good feeling for how your words are coming across to people. What you intend is not always what others see.

Some people use a whole vocabulary of **emoticons** to express themselves—combinations of characters that represent emotions. For example, the most commonly seen emoticon is the **smilee**, shown as :-). While a smilee may seem unnecessarily cute and perhaps a little annoying if you aren't used to it :-(, smilees are actually useful. It explicitly tells a reader when something is being said in jest or when something shouldn't be taken seriously. Emoticons allow people to insert some personality into their writing without fear of being misinterpreted. Messages with smilees are written by people who are trying to make sure that no one misunderstands the spirit of their words. I don't think I have ever seen someone take offense at a statement punctuated by a smilee. It's the equivalent of a smile and a wink or a friendly laugh accompanied by a pat on the back. It works well among people who don't know each other all that well. ;-)

If you do find yourself in an emotional exchange, it is usually a good idea to cool down before you respond. Angry e-mail messages are called **flames** and people who write them are **flaming**. Flaming is not polite, and if you ever get flamed, you may feel hurt or downright abused. The Internet seems to encourage some people to indulge their pent-up rage by subjecting innocent bystanders to verbal abuse. When two people trade flames, you have a **flame war.** This behavior seems to be peculiar to the Internet; it would probably not take place in a face-to-face interaction. Flames can be strangely contagious. It seems that heat has a way of generating more heat unless someone is willing to cool off and break the cycle. If a message makes you angry, wait 24 hours before responding. That's usually enough time for the heat to dissipate. You may have misinterpreted what was said (it may not have been intended the way you read it), or there may be no misinterpretation, but a flame war may not be worth the elevated blood pressure. Sometimes the best reply is no reply.

If you value your relationship with someone, be especially careful about emotionally charged e-mail. If you are communicating with someone you work with, do your best to avoid online misunderstandings or unintentional slights. People can read all sorts of things into e-mail. For example, "Gee, that reply was awfully short, I must not matter very much to her." Or, "How come it took so long for him to answer me? Doesn't he know how important this is?" It is easy to damage a relationship with careless e-mail exchanges. Even worse, you may not even realize that damage has been done. If you care about good working relationships, you can't be too careful with your online communications. If you're angry or upset about something, resolve to deal with it face-to-face. E-mail is not a suitable medium for everything.

HANDLE WITH CARE

Your Mail Inbox and Mail Folders

3.9

Your inbox is not the only place to keep incoming e-mail and to save old messages. In fact, you have many options to help you keep your e-mail nicely organized. You may want to keep a record of all of your e-mail interactions, both incoming and outgoing, with a particular individual. Perhaps you may want to keep all of the messages about a specific topic in one place. Just as you can file hard-copy correspondence in a file cabinet, you can use a system of electronic **mail folders** for storing your e-mail.

You can create as many mail folders as you want and move mail from one folder to another whenever you want. Most mail programs start you off with a **default mail folder** that is set up for you automatically. One mailer may call it your **inbox** and another, **received**, but the purpose of this default folder is always the same: This is where you can store newly received mail quickly and easily. When you exit your mail program, does it always ask you if you want to store your mail in some special place? If so, that's your default mail folder. You may have wondered about this query. Why bother moving it from the original inbox? What's the point?

To understand the point of the default mail folder, you need to understand a little more about how e-mail works. Here's a quick look under the hood: When a mail message is sent to you, it goes to the host machine specified by your e-mail address. The mail is then stored in a private inbox where all of your incoming e-mail is collected and held indefinitely. See Figure 3.2.

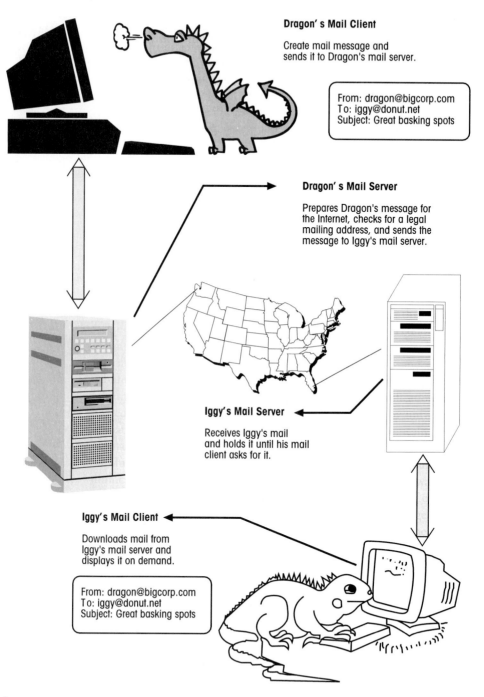

Dragon's Mail Client

Create mail message and
sends it to Dragon's mail server.

From: dragon@bigcorp.com
To: iggy@donut.net
Subject: Great basking spots

Dragon's Mail Server

Prepares Dragon's message for
the Internet, checks for a legal
mailing address, and sends the
message to Iggy's mail server.

Iggy's Mail Server

Receives Iggy's mail
and holds it until his mail
client asks for it.

Iggy's Mail Client

Downloads mail from
Iggy's mail server and
displays it on demand.

From: dragon@bigcorp.com
To: iggy@donut.net
Subject: Great basking spots

FIG. 3.2

E-mail Clients and Servers

To move mail out of your inbox, you must save it in another location. That's what mail folders are for. When you exit your mail program, you can tell it to save everything in your default folder, and it will transfer all of the messages from your inbox to your default mail folder. This is a good idea. ***You should get into the habit of making this default folder transfer whenever you leave your mail program.***

Transferring mail to a mail folder is good for your inbox and good for you. If you let all of your e-mail pile up in your inbox, you are taking up space needed for incoming mail. After a few weeks or months of letting your mail pile up, this could be a lot of space. More important, there could be a hundred other users doing the same thing, so before you know it, the inboxes run out of storage. If that were allowed to happen, new mail would not be deliverable and everyone's e-mail communications would come to a grinding halt. Moving mail from an inbox is also good for you because it puts your mail where you can organize it the way you want.

If you don't handle a lot of e-mail, if you delete most of your messages right after you read them, and if you then find that you can delete the rest of your e-mail a few weeks later, then you don't need an involved mail filing system. Your default mail folder is all you'll ever need for effective mail management.

The first key to good mail management is to delete everything you don't absolutely need to save. Your mail messages are never deleted without your consent; you must explicitly delete messages. To delete a message, select it and type D (or ⌘-D or alt-D, depending on your platform). This will mark your message for deletion. Mail messages marked for deletion are not immediately eliminated. They are deleted when you exit your mail program, or when you move to a different mail folder. Even then, your mail program may ask you to confirm that you really want to delete the items marked for deletion. This confirmation check is often something you can control in a preference setting. Once you confirm and then exit your inbox, the deletion takes place. You can't undo a Delete command once it has been executed, but you can change your mind at any time before then. If a message has been marked for deletion, you can always select it and undelete it if you have second thoughts. Check your documentation for information about your mailer's Undelete command.

Is It Really Gone Forever?

Colonel Oliver North (who was known in the 1980's for "Irangate") learned about e-mail the hard way when he thought that hitting the Delete key was equivalent to sending his (potentially incriminating) e-mail to a paper shredder. With computers, the destruction of a file is never quite so simple. A mail message may or may not go away forever when you delete

Continued on Next Page

Continued from Previous Page

it. A message deleted from your inbox probably is gone forever. A message deleted from a mail folder may be recoverable from system backups; whether it is depends on how long the mail sat in the folder and how often system backups are conducted. In any case, other computers can always harbor copies of a mail message (e.g., the sender might have a copy or the sender's host might have a backup of the original message). So it is very difficult to know when a mail message is honestly and truly gone forever.

Computer files are notoriously difficult to secure, and incriminating e-mail is accepted as admissible evidence in court cases. If you are concerned about the privacy of your online communications, read Chapter 12 for an introduction to privacy in digital environments.

Your inbox and your default mail folder are two places in which to keep your mail messages. Think of your inbox as short-term temporary storage and your default mail folder as permanent storage. Transfers from the inbox to the default folder are easily accomplished when you exit your mail program. Most mailers will ask you if you want to move messages into the default folder. If you answer yes, everything will be transferred automatically.

WHERE DID ALL MY MAIL GO?

It is very distressing to fire up your mail program, expecting to find a mailbox full of all of the messages you read yesterday, only to discover a mailbox that is empty or almost empty. Where did all of the old messages go? Are they gone forever? If you didn't explicitly delete them, messages that "mysteriously" disappear from your inbox have probably been saved in your default mail folder. To see them again, you just need to view your default mail folder.

Most mail programs make it easy to transfer mail from the inbox to the default mail folder, so you may have accidentally made the transfer without realizing it. However, you cannot transfer mail messages back to your inbox once they have been removed from the inbox. Besides, there is no good reason to move anything back into your inbox, since that space is reserved for new incoming mail.

To see the contents of your default mail folder, you have to change mail folders. Look for a Change Folder command. When you summon the Change Folder command, you need to specify the name of a specific mail folder. In the case of your default mail folder, there is often a shortcut. Make sure you know how to move back and forth between your inbox and your default mail folder in your mail program. Find out if there are any shortcuts for these two operations.

Mailboxes in Eudora

The Eudora mail program is a very popular mailer that operates on PC and Mac platforms. In Eudora, mail folders are called mailboxes, but the underlying concept is the same. However, Eudora users never view the contents of their inbox directly. Instead of an inbox, Eudora uses a mailbox called In that is actually Eudora's default mail folder. When Eudora starts up, it makes a POP (Post Office Protocol) connection to a mail server and immediately copies all of the mail found in the user's inbox. These copies are then stored in the In mailbox on the user's PC. All mail management with Eudora starts with the In mailbox. Under its default settings, Eudora deletes messages from the server's inbox as soon as they have been transferred to the In mailbox. This is the only way to keep the inbox from growing indefinitely, since Eudora users have no direct control over their inbox. See Figure 3.3.

If you find that your default mail folder is getting too big, it's time to create more mail folders. All mailers support **user-defined mail folders**. People who handle a lot of e-mail can't live without them. You should be able to create new folders using a **Save** or **Transfer** command. Select a message you want to move to a new folder and issue the Save command. When you are prompted to specify a mail folder, assign the new folder a name. In one step,

FIG. 3.3

Eudora's Default Mail Folder: The In Mailbox

```
 ⌂  File  Edit  Mailbox  Message  Transfer  Special  Window
```

		Who	Date	K	Subject
		Ralph A. ✕✕✕✕✕✕	9/20/96	4	Re: GIGO law in action
		Lou ✕✕✕✕✕✕	9/20/96	2	Re: GIGO law in action
		Don ✕✕✕✕✕	9/20/96	2	KY Workshop--number bases
•		Margaret's group	9/20/96	2	Problems in training preservice elementary education major
•		Jackie ✕✕✕✕✕	9/20/96	2	Re: Math Forum workshop at Western Kentucky University
•		Jack ✕✕✕✕✕	9/20/96	2	Re: Problems in training preservice elementary education m
		Tad ✕✕✕✕✕✕✕	9/20/96	3	Re: KY Workshop--number bases
•		Henry ✕✕✕✕✕	9/20/96	3	NSF PROGRAM DIRECTOR VACANCY ANNOUNCEMENT
		Ed ✕✕✕✕✕✕	9/20/96	2	Re: KY Workshop--number bases
		Don ✕✕✕✕✕✕	9/20/96	2	Domain and range
		KIDSPHERE Mailing	9/20/96	2	Satellite Tracking Information

867/2663K/955K

the new mail folder will be created and the message saved there. If you already have a user-defined mail folder, you move messages into it in the same way.

Some mailers support hierarchical structures for organizing old mail messages. See Figure 3.4. For example, if you are running a project involving three subprojects, you might want a folder at the top level that contains three additional folders. As Figure 3.4 shows, a professor who needs to track professional activities for an annual personnel evaluation could have a folder at the top level called "Tenure" with three separate mailboxes inside it called "Teaching," "Research," and "Service." Not all mail programs support hierarchical mail folders. Eudora does. From the Mailbox pull-down menu, select New. A dialog box asks if you want to create a mail folder; check the option. Note that when Eudora refers to a "mail folder," it means a parent in a hierarchy of mailboxes. It reserves the term "mailbox" for the places in which you can store mail. In Eudora's world, "mailboxes" are really files and "mail folders" are file directories. Also, mail messages are always stored in mailboxes, and the mailboxes themselves can be stored in mail folders, if you want to create a hierarchy of mailboxes. While Eudora's terminology is consistent with the Mac operating system's folder/file terminology, it is not consistent with the way some other platforms use the term "mail folder." (Under UNIX, for example, a mail folder is always a file because UNIX mailers do not support a hierarchical mail organization.) Try not to let the terminology confuse you. The concepts are more important, and the concepts are always the same.

WHAT DID I CALL IT?

If you create a lot of mail folders, you will probably forget the names of some of them. All mail programs have some way of displaying all of your mail folders in case you need to be reminded of them. In a keyboard-oriented interface, you may get a complete list by using a wildcard string designator. In pine, the command L lists all existing folders. In Eudora, user-defined mailboxes are all listed under the Transfer menu.

How Are Mail Folders Stored?

Each mail folder is simply a text file that has been saved in a subdirectory set aside exclusively for mail storage. On a UNIX account, look for a subdirectory called "Mail" or "mail" under your home directory. Your mail program appends new messages to the specified folder whenever you tell it to save a message in a mail folder. These folders consume memory in your available storage space. If

Continued on Next Page

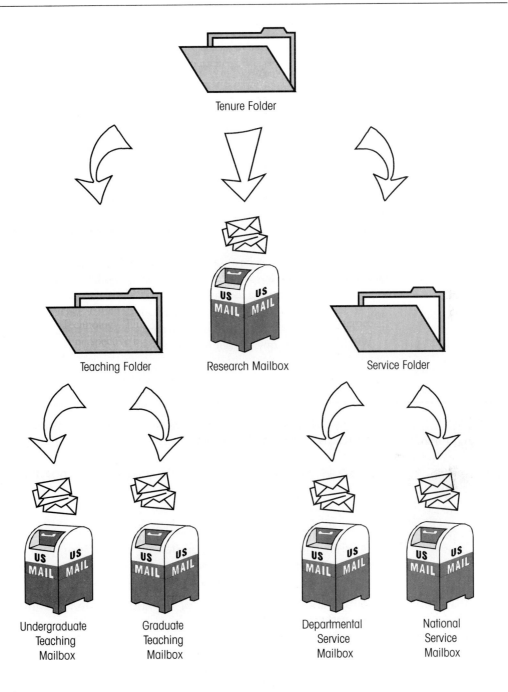

FIG. 3.4

Hierarchical Mail Folders

Continued from Previous Page

you are handling your mail remotely on a home computer using Eudora, all of your mailboxes are stored on your home computer. Wherever they are, each mail repository is just a plain ASCII text file. However, it is not wise to open these files with a text editor because you might inadvertently alter header formatting or change the file in some way that makes it unreadable to your mailer. If you ever want to move some mail folders from one computer to another or from one computer account to another, just transfer the desired text files. It is easy to take your mail with you wherever you go.

Once a mail message has been saved to a mail folder, it doesn't have to stay there forever. It can always be deleted or moved to another mail folder at any time. When you transfer a message from one folder to another, your mailer will mark the original copy for deletion. You can undelete it if you want multiple copies of the same message in different mail folders, but it's usually enough to have one copy of each mail message.

E-MAIL CHECKLIST #5

Study your mail program's documentation and make sure you know how to do the following:

1. Move mail from your inbox to your default mail folder (what is its name?).
2. Mark a specific mail message for deletion.
3. Undelete a mail message marked for deletion.
4. View the contents of your default mail folder (use the Change Folder command).
5. Move back to your inbox from your default mail folder.
6. Use shortcut commands for moving between the inbox and the default mail folder.
7. Create a new mail folder and save a message in it.
8. Move to any existing mail folder.
9. Move a message from one folder to another.
10. Save a mail message to a file (look for a Save command).

Fourteen Mail Management Tips and Tricks

If you receive fewer than ten e-mail messages a week, you can probably skip this section. Come back later when you need it.

If you use e-mail at work, you may be getting dozens of messages each day. This is when you need to think about mail management. Alternatively, you may use e-mail only for personal purposes, but you are paying an ISP connect-time charges, so you need to minimize the amount of time you spend handling your e-mail online. As more and more people use e-mail, e-mail is increasingly used as an alternative to telephone calls and correspondence sent via the U. S. Postal Service ("snail mail"). If you have ever played phone tag with someone, you are ripe for the e-mail revolution. Shifting to e-mail can be advantageous in many ways, but it is also easy to feel overwhelmed by the number of messages that start to pour in.

Computer professionals have been using e-mail for a long time and have already made the big shift from telephone calls and snail mail. Within this user community, everyone checks their e-mail at least once a day. Some people monitor it more or less continuously throughout the day (and in some cases, on an almost 24-hour basis). The prospect of not reading e-mail for an entire week is nearly unthinkable, although a few spouses do manage to tear their mates away for e-mail-free vacations. For some people, a full day away from their mailbox translates into two or more solid hours of e-mail catch-up when they return. No wonder e-mail is so compelling. It's time-consuming when you keep up with it. It's even more time-consuming when you don't.

Here are some good ideas that will help you keep your head above the e-mail water line. The first two are standard tricks. The rest are usually acquired after years of experience.

E-mail Tip #1: Use the Alias Feature.

If you know someone you expect to write to again, create an alias for that person. Your system doesn't care how many aliases (or nicknames) you create, so there's no need to be stingy with them. E-mail addresses are difficult to remember and can be very difficult to track down. If you maintain an online adddress book with formulaic alias names (e.g., first initial/last name), you will always be able to write to anyone as long as you can remember his or her name.

E-mail Tip #2: Use Signature Files.

Signature files are a convenient way to tell people who you are when you write to people who don't know you. A short sig file is a courtesy to your readers and is fast becoming a Netiquette norm. Just adhere to the four-line limit and avoid highly charged quotations unless you want to make a very strong impression. If you both work and play online, design one sig file for work and a different one for play.

Be creative with your e-mail management strategies. If you think of a good idea, try it out. However, be cautious when trying something for the first time. Some ideas that sound good in theory can flop in practice. The following tip shows how a seemingly good idea can fail for subtle reasons.

E-mail Tip #3: The To-do List Trap.

Some people find it useful to organize their work into lists of things to do. Maybe one to-do list is enough, or you may want multiple lists. If you have a lot of projects, you may get involved with lots of lists. Then you have to worry about organizing all your to-do lists. It's very tempting to create mail folders for mail associated with requests, promises, and reminders of things to do. Try this if you want, but be aware of a hidden danger: If you create a "to-do" folder, it is very easy to forget about it and never look at it. If you don't get into the habit of reviewing your "to-do" folder every day, you might find it easy to ignore, especially if the items in it are not urgent. Handwritten to-do lists are usually displayed in prominent places so that you can't miss them. But mail folders are much more unobtrusive. You have to constantly remind yourself that they're there. To-do lists turn out to be totally useless if you never look at them.

Just as there is no universal filing system that works well for everyone, there is no universal system for mail folders that works well for everyone. You may have to experiment with different filing systems before you find one that works well for you. You may also have to experiment with different deletion strategies. How long should you keep a message around before it's safe to delete it? Some messages clearly must be kept for a while; others are easy to delete immediately. Then there are messages in a "gray area" that might be useful to have on hand somewhere down the road, but how long should you let them stick around? Those are the ones that will bloat your default mail folder if you can't find appropriate homes for them elsewhere. You could always designate a special folder just for those gray-area messages. But that folder will expand indefinitely if you have no method for trimming it from time to time. To keep life simple, you might decide just to delete the gray-area messages and suffer the consequences. Try this and see if you can get away with it. But if you think there's got to be a better way, tips #4 and #5 offer two alternatives.

E-mail Tip #4: Keep a Rotating Temp Folder of Nearly Fixed Length.

This strategy allows you to keep things around for a while, but not forever, and it doesn't require much effort on your part. Turn your default mail folder into a rotating queue. The most recently added messages will shuffle their way down through the queue. When they get close to the end, they'll be deleted. Since mail messages are normally sorted by date when they are inserted into a mail folder, it is easy to identify the oldest messages—they are always at the bottom of the folder. So whenever the folder gets to be too big (one hundred messages? five hundred messages?), you delete the last specified number of messages in order to pare the folder to some fixed length. It never actually stays at a fixed length, but you keep pulling it back to some target length when it gets out of hand. If you can find a fixed length that seems to work well, this is a good strategy. The key is to make the paring operation fast and mindless. You don't want to be reading old e-mail in order to figure out where to start deleting old messages. If you find yourself reading all of your old e-mail whenever it's time to delete it, then this method isn't working for you.

E-mail Tip #5: Keep a Folder for Each Month of the Year.

Let your gray-area messages pile up in your default mail folder until the end of the month and then move all of them into a folder named for that month. This will allow you to hang onto a large number of mail messages (a whole year's worth if you really think you need that much), while preventing your default mail folder from getting too big. If you ever need to look for an old message, you can probably remember roughly when it arrived, so monthly archives should make it reasonably easy to find something. After you've used this system for a full year, you can either add to the old file (and go for a two-year archive) or delete the year-old mail archive before adding to it again. Most people don't need to hang onto all of their gray-area mail for more than a year.

Now that you know of some ways to manage large amounts of e-mail, the following tips will help you find old messages if you ever need to search for a specific message in a mail folder containing a few hundred mail messages. Most mailers support a keyword search capability. This will save you a lot of time whenever you need to retrieve old messages. Learn about the search capability of your mailer and use it to find old messages in large mail folders.

E-mail Tip #6: Header Searches and Body Searches.

If you are trying to find an old mail message and you can think of an identifying keyword in its message header, locate that message with a message header search instead of manually scrolling through a large mail folder. For example, if you know you have only one message from Fay Ray, try searching for it with the string "Fay Ray." If you are in the same mail folder as the Fay Ray message, the header search will succeed.

Sometimes, it's hard to come up with good keywords that work on message headers. You may have better luck with a message body search. This search will look for your search string inside all of the message bodies in the current mail folder. For example, if only one message mentions the Empire State Building, a search for "Empire State Building" will take you where you want to go. Keyword searches are much faster than visual inspection and manual scrolling when you have mail folders containing hundreds of messages. Figure 3.5 shows the use of Eudora's Find command.

FIG. 3.5

Eudora's Special Menu
Find Command

Once you've had to hunt through a large mail folder for a specific message, you will better appreciate the importance of informative subject headers. Keep this in mind when you create your own subject headers, not just for the

Find

Find: algebra   [Find]

Options: ☐ Whole word   ☐ Match case

Starting: [◄] [◄◄] [◄] [In:mark snyder,8/24/9...orld algebra problem] [►] [►►] [Choose...]

☒ Summaries only   [Search "In"]   [Search "Eudora Fo...] [Search To End]

sake of your recipients, but for your own sake, too. Many of your own subject headers will come back to your inbox with a **Re:** tag ("In reference to"). *Try to use subject headers that might be helpful during a keyword search.*

E-mail Tip #7: Don't Recycle the Same Subject Header Over and Over Again.

When two people engage in a protracted e-mail discussion, it is usually done by clicking the Reply command and automatically inheriting the old subject header at each turn. The Reply command is efficient and it encourages fast responses, but it is not a good idea to recycle the same subject header ad infinitum. What if one of you needs to go back and find something that was said during the dialog? How much fun is it to track down the desired message from among ten possible messages with identical subject headers? A subject header that was appropriate at the beginning of a dialog is usually off-topic after a few e-mail interactions. It is a good idea to update these subject headers from time to time. You don't need to update it on every reply. But it is useful to watch for how many times you've recycled an old subject header. After two or three replies, it's probably time to use a new subject header.

If you have a lot of mail that you manually route into different mail folders, you may be able to automate at least some of that sorting and routing. For example, maybe you keep a mail folder where you store everything that comes from a specific individual. Many mail programs have routing capabilities that will move new mail into appropriate folders automatically, before you've even seen it. For example, if you always mail a copy of your own messages to yourself, you might want to file all of them in one place for your own records. If you set up a routing rule that watches for mail from you, you can have all of those copies go into a mail folder automatically and you will never see them unless you open up that particular folder. Everything you send to yourself will be there if you ever need something, but you won't have to deal with any of it cluttering up your inbox.

E-mail Tip #8: Use Automated Routing When Possible.

Check your mailer to see if it supports automatic mail routing. It may also be called "mail filtering." Customizing rules for routing your mail

Continued on Next Page

> *Continued from Previous Page*
>
> based on keyword patterns in the mail headers enables you to reduce the amount of mail you need to scan each day. You should be able to sort a lot of mail on the basis of the **From:** header or the **Subject:** header. If you do set up automatic mail routing, remember that you will never see any of the routed mail unless you open up the receiving mail folders and look for it. This can be a dangerous situation, somewhat like the "to-do list" trap. Automatic routers make it easy to get incoming mail out of the way. But you have to remember to look at it periodically, or you will never see it. Be very careful with mail routing, or you might miss some important and urgent messages.

Once in a while, you'll send mail to someone and within a minute or two you'll get back an automated reply explaining that the recipient is away and will not be able to read your mail until he or she returns. This is done with an **autoreply** utility (usually on a UNIX host). If you access the Internet through an ISP, they may or may not offer an autoreply service to their subscribers. Check with tech support to find out about the availability of this utility.

E-mail Tip #9: An Autoreply May Be Helpful When You Go Away.

If you are going to be away from your e-mail for at least a week, you may want to make sure everyone who tries to contact you knows you are away. A truly helpful autoreply message will tell people when you expect to return. However, you should not use an autoreply message under certain circumstances:

- Do not use it if you are gone for only a few days.
- Do not use it if you are subscribed to any mailing lists (see Chapter 4).
- Do not use it if you expect to read your e-mail while you are gone or if your e-mail is primarily recreational rather than work-related.

If you ever find yourself typing the general message body over and over again, you could put that text in a file so that you can just read it in the next time you need it. For example, you may find it appropriate to maintain several different sig files to support all of your different online personas. If your mailer supports only one sig file, you can still use other sig files by manually inserting them. If you field a lot of queries from lots of people who often ask the same questions, you may be able to write a generic response for these situations that can be recycled with a minimum amount of tuning.

E-mail Tip #10: Recycle Text for Routine Message Bodies.

Whenever you find yourself saying the same thing over and over again, you can save time by creating a generic file that can be quickly inserted into your message body. If you can generate a response or part of a response on the basis of a generic reply, don't hesitate to do so. You can also create a customized response by starting with a generic file and then tweaking it as needed for a given situation. Because it's so easy to edit text files, nothing you send out needs to read like a form letter if you don't want it to. But if a form letter is adequate and appropriate, inserting a generic file makes it easy to generate a stock reply.

While I'm on the topic of saving time, suppose you're paying connect-time charges for your Internet access. Most ISP's charge flat monthly rates, but you might be stuck with one that doesn't. Or someday, you might have to dial into your Internet host long distance (a horrible prospect, but it could happen). To minimize your connect time, use a mailer that allows you to handle your mail remotely. Eudora makes it easy to do this. To handle mail remotely with Eudora, follow these steps (from inside Eudora):

1. Connect to your POP mail server.
2. Transfer all of the inbox messages to your In mailbox.
3. Disconnect from the mail server.
4. Read your e-mail, write replies, write new messages, file mail in mailboxes, create new mailboxes, search for old mail, forward e-mail, and so on.
5. Connect to your POP mail server.
6. Send all of the new messages you just wrote.
7. Disconnect from the mail server.

The most time-consuming activity here is step 4, and this takes place while you are not connected to your ISP. When you write a mail message with Eudora, you don't send it with a Send command. Eudora uses a Queue command instead. When you click the Queue button, Eudora moves your message into a special mailbox called Out. Each time you connect to your mail server, Eudora checks the Out mailbox to see if it has anything in it. If it finds something there, Eudora asks you if you want to send those messages. If you say yes, that's when your outgoing mail gets sent. Eudora also has a Send Queued Messages command (under the File menu). You use it when you are in the middle of a session and you want to send some new mail. Eudora is designed to minimize your connect time. This is kind to the Internet and kind to your ISP, and, if connect-time charges apply, it can be quite kind to your wallet. On the downside, you have to watch your disk quota because all Eudora mailboxes are stored on your PC's hard drive. But text files do not consume tremendous amounts of memory. You could probably store all of your e-mail for a year or more without exhausting your hard drive.

Effective e-mail management is all about time management. Remember that your time is valuable and the availability of your e-mail address to a lot of people does not in any way obligate you to answer every question or comment that make its way into your inbox. E-mail is less intrusive than a phone call because you don't have to read it until you want to. On the other hand, it feels a bit more personal than hard-copy correspondence, perhaps because of the immediacy with which messages can be sent back and forth. You may feel that everyone who sends you a message deserves an answer or at least an immediate acknowledgment. Sometimes they do. But don't fall into the trap of replying to everyone all of the time.

E-mail Tip #11: Manage Your E-mail Off-line Whenever Possible.

When Internet access is at a premium, you can help to ease the crunch by handling your e-mail off-line via a POP mail server. If you are a heavy mail user and you do a lot of e-mail from your home, you are a good candidate for Eudora or other mailers that support off-line e-mail management. Even if you aren't paying for connect time charges, it is good to work off-line during peak usage periods in order to free up Internet resources for other people. E-mail does not require constant Internet interaction the way other applications like Web browsers do. If you don't have to be online, disconnect and work off-line.

E-mail Tip #12: You Don't Have to Respond to Everything.

Your e-mail address will eventually become available to a lot of people you don't know. Some of these people may contact you with unsolicited information or with queries that may not be your job to answer. If you are in a work situation in which it is appropriate to forward a query to someone else, then you have a legitimate right to pass mail on without further comment. Exercise your good judgment in these situations. Perhaps you want to reply to something that comes in from left field because it interests you. But if you find yourself pressed for time and you discover yourself talking to perfect strangers about things that you aren't being paid to discuss, you need to get serious and ignore more of your mail. At the very least, forward legitimate queries to other people if you aren't the appropriate respondent.

Many people unthinkingly fall into work habits for no good reason other than the fact that some piece of technology seems to encourage it. Word processors make it possible to revise documents quickly and easily, so a lot of people spend too much time twiddling text. Voice mail makes it possible to leave the telephone unattended, so too many telephones go unanswered too much of the time. E-mail allows people to send responses back and forth easily and quickly, but that doesn't mean you always have to reply to your e-mail as fast as possible. Reserve the right to reply when you are good and ready. Keep this in mind and slow down whenever a thoughtful response is prudent.

E-mail Tip #13: Don't Always Reply Right Away.

Because the technology makes it possible to reply to a message immediately, you may feel compelled to keep up the pace. But it's not always in your best interests to reply to all of your e-mail as soon as possible. Some queries are mundane, and there's no harm in answering them right away. Others may require some thought. If you see one of the latter, it is usually wise to let it sit for a day. Give yourself some time to mull it over. There are many queries that might get answered one way right away and somewhat differently a day later. If a query is not absolutely urgent, there's no harm in waiting a day or two to reply. Don't feel rushed just because you're working with technology that makes fast responses possible.

There was a time when middle managers had secretaries who routed incoming mail and screened incoming phone calls. As we move into a world increasingly connected by e-mail, more of us are on the "front lines" with respect to incoming communications. We are responsible for more outgoing communications as well. In many offices, the secretary who used to transcribe dictation and answer the phone has been replaced by e-mail. More and more managers must now fend for themselves. The following final tip relates to general time management, which is always a critical challenge for people who work extensively with computers

E-mail Tip #14: Be Aware of How Much Time You Spend On E-mail.

If you are a heavy e-mail user, either for business or pleasure, it is important to be realistic about how much time you spend on e-mail. Monitor yourself for a couple of weeks and track the amount of time you spend each day reading and answering your e-mail. If you think it's getting out of hand, think hard about what you're doing and see if you can cut it back. It's easy to feel that any amount of time with e-mail is time well spent, especially if you enjoy your daily e-mail routine. But be careful to make sure the rest of your job (and life) is not suffering. E-mail can become very time-consuming. It may be taking you away from other things that are more important.

When you are new to the Internet, you may find yourself very excited about the possibilities it opens up and all of the new resources that are suddenly available to you. This initial excitement is appropriate. You need to take some time to explore the Internet in order to better understand how it may be valuable to you. But don't give your life over to it just because it's easy to spend a lot of time on the Internet. Other less novel aspects of your life are still important and deserve your attention, too. Try to keep things in perspective if you feel like the Internet is beginning to take over your life. The Internet can become addictive for some individuals. If need be, put a time limit on the Internet, just as you put limits on everything else you do.

How to Get Around the ASCII Text Barrier

E-mail is normally used for sending simple messages in plain text. As long as what you have to say can be communicated with a plain ASCII text file, e-mail will serve you well. However, there are times when you want to transfer a document that contains special formatting or graphics. In this case, you probably need FTP (described in Chapter 9). But for occasional use, e-mail can be made to do the job under two conditions: (1) You are willing to put a little more effort into sending the mail message, and (2) your recipient is prepared to deal with incoming e-mail that requires special handling.

The ASCII text barrier gets in the way when you want to transfer a document created by a word processor. Word processing files are usually saved as binary files rather than ASCII text files. Most word processors will give you a number of formatting options when you save a file; one of these will convert your document into an ASCII-based text format. For example, Microsoft Word can translate its documents into an **RTF (Rich Text Format)** file. This is an ASCII text file that contains all of the information Word needs to reconstruct the formatting and fonts that were used to construct the original Word document. An RTF file can be inserted into a message body and sent as a regular e-mail message, as long as the person receiving the file knows what to do with it. If your recipient uses Microsoft Word, then they can save the mail message to a file, strip off any message headers that aren't part of the RTF message body, and then open it with Word. This is one way that people can get around the ASCII text barrier.

Some mailers will not accept files that contain more than 1,000 lines or 50,000 characters. Other mailers will break up large messages into pieces and display each piece in a separate mail message. If you need to send a very large file, it may be a good idea to break it up yourself in a way that will make it easy to handle or reassemble at the receiving end.

E-MAIL AND BIG FILES

Another way to move non-ASCII files through e-mail is via attachments. A **mail attachment** is an ASCII-encoded version of a binary file that is generated for you by your mail program. To use attachments, both you and your recipient must use a mailer that handles attachments. This used to be a bit of a restriction. Most popular mailers all support attachments now, however, so the use of attachments is becoming more common. A standard format is used for e-mail attachments: **Multipurpose Internet Mail Extensions (MIME).** So, a reference to a MIME attachment is just a technical way of referring to a mail attachment.

Sending an attachment in Eudora is simple. You create a normal mail message with the usual header and an appropriate message body. Then before you send the message, go to the Message menu and click Attach Document. This puts you in a dialog window in which you can specify the file you want to include as an attachment. Select the desired file and click the Attach button; the file is attached. An **Attachments:** header will appear in your outgoing mail message with a reference to the file that you've attached to your message. Once your attachment is in place, send your message as usual.

When you are on the receiving end of an attachment, the attachment is automatically placed in an attachments folder unless you have specified a different folder for attachments. If you receive a lot of mail with attachments, Eudora lets you set up appropriate plug-ins for viewing graphics, spreadsheets, and word processing documents (you need the application that generated the attachment unless its format is recognized by other applications). Once the right plug-ins are set up, Eudora can automatically interpret attachments for you without further direction from you. This is about as painless as it gets.

E-MAIL AND VIRUSES

You will periodically see warnings on the Internet about e-mail messages carrying computer viruses. The most famous one is the "Good Times" virus warning, but there are many others. They typically tell you to never read anything with a specific subject header (like "Good Times"). These warnings are all hoaxes. You cannot get a computer virus from reading a plain text mail message. However, mail messages containing mail attachments are another story. Mail attachments can carry viruses, and reading a mail attachment can cause a computer virus to swing into action.

If you are reading mail on a UNIX host, don't worry about mail attachments. But if you are reading your e-mail on a PC or a Mac via a POP mail server (such as Eudora), then you need to be careful about mail attachments. You should either (1) refuse to read any mail attachments or (2) obtain a good (up-to-date) virus scanner and run it on all attachments *before* you read them. If the scanner detects no viruses in an attachment, the attachment is likely safe to read.

Mail attachments are problematic because they are not always just data files. Some mail attachments contain executable code in the form of macros. That's where a virus can be inserted.

Macros for word processors and spreadsheets were a leading cause of computer viruses in 1996. According to the National Computer Security Association, macro viruses associated with Word documents accounted for about half of all of the reported infections in 1996. A user can pass on a macro virus without realizing it, so it is not enough to trust the person who sends you the attachment. Macro viruses will be discussed in more detail in Chapter 9 .

Attachments make e-mail more versatile. However, their use is a fairly recent innovation, so you should be familiar with the techniques that people used before attachments were available to everyone. UNIX users have long had access to a tool called **uuencode**, which turns a binary file into an ASCII-based version suitable for e-mail transfers. If someone in a UNIX environment wants to send an executable file or a graphics file to another UNIX user, it is easy to create a uuencoded version that can then be sent via e-mail. Once received, the uuencoded file can be handed to a tool called **uudecode**, which unravels the encoded file and returns it to its original binary format.

You may see uuencoded files from time to time on the Internet. They often appear in Usenet newsgroups when someone wants to post a graphics file. Figure 3.6 shows an example of some uuencoded text. Someone might send one to your inbox someday. You can always recognize a uuencoded file by the way it begins. The string "begin 666 . . ." followed by a lot of random characters always signals a uuencoded file. One was shown in the example sig files given earlier in the chapter and is shown in Figure 3.6.

The uuencoded part is of the sig file in the figure is

```
"begin 666 foo
B22!C86XG="”!B96QI979E(‘EO=2!D96-O9&5D(‘1H: 7,A”@ ` end”
```

To see what this fragment means, you have to run it through uudecode. All platforms have versions of uuencode and uudecode these days, so you don't need a UNIX account in order to unscramble these things. Most uuencoded files are considerably longer than this sample one, so not much is expected from the small sample fragment given here. Unencoded, it reads like this:

```
“I can’t believe you decoded this!”
```

FIG. 3.6

Uuencoded Text (a short sample)

```
--
XXXXXXXXXX EMT-P, K5ZC, PP-ASEL | Never ascribe to malice that which can
XXXXXX@oac.hsc.uth.tmc.edu       | adequately be explained by stupidity.
   "begin 666 foo B22!C86XG="”!B96QI979E(‘EO=2!D96-O9&5D(‘1H: 7,A”@ ` end”
              -- XXXXXXXXXXXXX
```

Typical geek humor. By the way, if you want to decode this yourself, be aware that the string may have to be broken into three lines in order to be readable by uudecode. Reformat it to look like this:

```
"begin 666 foo
B22!C86XG=";!B96QI979E('EO=2!D96-09&5D('1H:7,A"@ `
end"
```

After running this through uudecode, look for the output in a file named `foo`.

3.12 ▶ Internet Abuse

Sooner or later, everyone who uses e-mail encounters instances of Internet abuse. It is important to understand what constitutes Internet abuse so that you don't inadvertently contribute to it yourself. It is also good to know how to respond to it when it happens to you. The most common form of net abuse via e-mail involves unsolicited messages. These are typically commercial advertisements. But they can also be political calls for action, religious sermons, philosophical manifestos, or the incoherent ravings of someone with a mental problem.

If you are affiliated with a commercial interest, *never* broadcast product announcements or advertisements via e-mail. This is called **spamming** and is a classic form of Internet abuse. However, it is all right, for example, to compile a list of friends and acquaintances and then tell them that you've changed jobs and now have a new Internet address. But don't try to sell anything at the same time. You can tell people what your new company does. You can even include a URL pointer to a corporate Web page. But keep the chest-thumping to a minimum lest anyone think you are plugging your new employer.

| Why Is It Called Spam? | The term "spam" comes from a Monty Python sketch involving a man and a waitress in a cafe. The man asks the waitress what they have for breakfast, and she embarks on a long list of possibilities: "Well, there's egg and bacon; egg sausage and bacon; egg and spam; egg bacon and spam; egg bacon sausage and spam; spam bacon sausage and spam; spam egg spam spam bacon and spam; spam sausage spam spam bacon spam tomato and spam…" Right about here some Vikings at another table (remember this is Monty Phython) start to chant, "Spam spam spam spam…" and the waitress continues with the Vikings chanting in the background: "spam spam spam egg and spam; spam spam spam spam spam spam baked beans spam spam spam…" The relentless uncontrollable repetition in this sketch captured the tedious and annoying experience of junk mail in a single word: spam. |

If you get spammed, don't bother going back to the offending party for retaliation. Do *not* try to reply to the original sender directly. An angry reply to the sender will have no effect whatsoever. If you try sending hundreds or thousands of e-mail messages to the reply address in the hope of causing disk quota overloads, you might injure an innocent party. Chances are that that account was terminated or abandoned right after the spamming event (the people who do these things are no fools) and all that e-mail could bounce right back to you. Alternatively, the account in question may have been broken into by the spammer, in which case you will only be victimizing another victim. It is also relatively easy to forge a mail header, so the information in a **From:** slot may be totally fictitious (in which, case your e-mail bounces back to you again). Mailing hundreds of messages to a single e-mail address is called **mail bombing**. Mail bombing is just another form of Internet abuse, no matter how justified it seems. There are legitimate things you can do in response to Internet abuse, but retaliation with more Internet abuse is not one of them.

If you are spammed, you can bring the offense to the attention of appropriate system administrators. This is easy to do, it doesn't take a lot of time, and it helps technical support people track down the mail spammer. Inspect the **From:** header in the offending mail message and identify the host name of the address found there. To contact the system administrators for that host, send mail to the **postmaster** at that address. Here's an example, a spam message that came to me a while ago:

```
Date: Sun, 8 Dec 1996 03:55:03 -0500
Subject: Search for Paradise


_____ -

Forwarded message:
Subj:    Search for Paradise
Date:    96-12-08 03:41:25 EST

From:    ChrisM 11
To:      ChrisM 11


     This is to inform you about the new adult game that
VCS Magazine rated "The best game of '96" and gave an
"Outstanding ****" (4 stars).  "The Search for Paradise is
no doubt one of the greatest XXX Adult games available."
```

This message continued on for some time, concluding with instructions for how to order the game. This mail was sent shortly after midnight on a Sunday morning. A lot of spammers deliberately strike at that time because it gives them the greatest head start for a clean getaway. Sunday mornings are usually periods of low Internet traffic. Most recipients of this spam wouldn't see it for at least 12 hours, maybe even up to 24 hours. This delay gives the mail spammer time to erase his tracks.

To see the full address of the sender, examine the full message header, which in this case identifies the originating address as ChrisM11@aol.com. This is an AOL account. So you would send a note about this incident to `postmaster@aol.com`. All Internet hosts have an account named "postmaster" that is read by technical support staff. The postmaster is responsible for fielding complaints about e-mail associated with the host machine.

Where's the Right Administrator?

If you are having trouble contacting a postmaster, you can send your complaint to a special server designed to handle reports of Internet abuse. Send your complaint to (domain name)@abuse. networks.net. Your message will be forward to all of the abuse contacts for that domain. For example, gnn.com@abuse.networks. net is converted to gnnadvisor@gnn.com and abuse@aol.net, both of which are GNN's abuse contacts. See http://www. abuse.net for more information about this service.

Sometimes mail headers are doctored so that you can't know for sure if the account the spamming came from is the actual originating account. If the spammer is very sophisticated, you're looking at a false lead. But there is more information in the full message header that may be useful to technical support folks who want to track this down. So when you contact the postmaster, forward a copy of the spamming message along with the full mail header. This will give tech support all of the information they need to track down the offending party.

Whenever I forward a mail spam to a postmaster, I include a form letter at the head of my message to explain what's going on. I keep this in a file so that I can grab it and insert it into a mail message quickly and easily whenever I need it (this is an example of E-mail Tip #10). Here is the letter:

```
Dear Administrator,

The following message was sent to me by a mail spammer.
Please take action w.r.t. the offending account to
ensure that no additional Internet abuse can originate
from this site.

Thank You,
Professor Wendy G. Lehnert
Department of Computer Science
University of Massachusetts
Amherst, MA 01003
lehnert@cs.umass.edu
==============================================================
```

I also append the full message headers and the message body from the spamming message. You can write a similar message for these situations yourself. You don't need an official title to report instances of Internet abuse. ***Everyone has a right to complain about unsolicited e-mail.***

When you write to a postmaster, you may either receive no reply, an autoreply form letter, or a personal reply. When I wrote to the postmaster at AOL, I got a generic autoreply message:

```
Date: Sun, 8 Dec 1996 12:33:54 -0500 (EST)

To: lehnert@thidwick.cs.umass.edu
Old-Subject: Re: Notification of Spamming Activity
Precedence: junk
X-Loop: pmd@aol.net
Reply-To: postmaster@aol.com
Subject: Postmaster Mail Receipt Notification

Dear Internet Correspondent:

Thanks for writing to us with your question, concern or
comment. You are receiving this automatically-generated
message to acknowledge that your mail has been received.
To keep from further consuming bandwidth and mailbox
space, you will only receive this message once a month
(per account).

Our goal is to process all mail sent to
postmaster@aol.com within 24 hours of receipt, and when
possible to personally follow up on mail we've received.
However, during times of high volume, staff outages and
similar situations, we may not be able to meet this
goal. We hope that you will understand that under these
conditions, replies may be delayed or omitted. We will
only do this when it is necessary, and your patience
and understanding is greatly appreciated. Due to the
large number of reports we receive regarding USENET
abuse, not all complaint/reports can be responded to
personally.
```

This message continued with additional information for people in different situations, much like a written version of a voice mail recording. Eventually, a human being will see my actual message, but in the meantime, I feel reassured that my complaint was sent to the right place and (I hope) that the recipient is staffed to deal with it. In any case, that's as much as I normally ever do when I get spammed. By my reporting the spamming to the appropriate authorities, actions can be taken to prevent the same person from trying it again. If this mail really did come from an AOL account and AOL can determine that the owner of the account was responsible for it, that account will be shut down and the person responsible for it will (I assume) be blacklisted from AOL.

In this particular case, the AOL postmaster followed up with a second reply a few days later:

```
X-Authentication-Warning: zipcode: pmd7 owned process doing -bs
Date: Fri, 13 Dec 1996 13:25:54 -0500 (EST)
X-Sender: pmd7@zipcode.atg.aol.com
To: Mike Truman <pmd7@aol.net>
Subject: Got the spam...

Hello,
    You don't have to reply to this, but thought I'd
send an E-mail to thank you for sending the large and
rather nasty junk E-mail that was sent from our site.
We've taken measures to stop the person responsible
for this from doing it again. If in the future you
receive mail of this nature just send it directly to
postmaster@aol.com and we'll take care of it.

Thanks.

Have a good one,
* * * * * * * * * * * * * * * * * * * * * * * * * * * * * * * * * * * * * * * * * * * * * * * * * *
Michael Truman                  pmd7@aol.net
Assistant PostMaster            postmaster@aol.com
America Online, Inc.
PostMaster Services Team
* * * * * * * * * * * * * * * * * * * * * * * * * * * * * * * * * * * * * * * * * * * * * * * * * *
```

You don't always get a follow-up like this, and indeed, this is quite possibly another form letter as well. But this type of response gives the recipients of spam the sense that someone is doing their job and that it is worthwhile to report mail spammers. At least you don't have to feel totally helpless in the face of unwanted junk mail.

If you are new to the Internet, you won't see much mail spamming right away. After you've been online awhile, you will begin to see spam from time to time. How much you get depends on how visible your own e-mail address is, who has collected it, who has sold it, and who has bought it.

Since the Internet is not policed by any legal authority, only customs and conventions associated with Internet abuse can be described; the abuse can't be defined in strict terms. There are clear-cut cases of Internet abuse, and there are some borderline areas that will strike some people, but not everyone, as a form of abuse. Here's an example of the latter. Suppose you send a very short message to a very large list of "acquaintances" announcing your move to a new company. The message includes a corporate URL in the message body but nothing remotely personal about you as anyone more than a corporate contact. If this goes out to people who don't recognize your name, it is probably Internet abuse. An even trickier example is the case of sig files. What if you insert a brief plug for your freelance services in your sig file just in case someone might be interested? If the sig file is no more than four lines, chances are no one will object. However, some people might consider even that to be tacky.

All of these prohibitions apply primarily to commercial interests, although politics and religion are not far behind. No one wants to get unsolicited e-mail about a favorite political cause (no matter how worthy) or one's latest transcendental experience (no matter how profound). If you study a few hundred sig files, you will find that most Netizens stick to innocuous quotations or opinionated proclamations of a purely technical nature. Responsible people try to err on the side of caution when it comes to Internet abuse.

For a more detailed discussion of Internet abuse, consult the relevant Web sites listed on the Internet 101 Web pages.

PROBLEMS AND EXERCISES

1. If you send e-mail to someone on your own host, how can you abbreviate their e-mail address?

2. Can you forward old mail to someone a year after you received it? Five years?

3. What is the difference between a carbon copy and a blind carbon copy?

4. Explain how your inbox differs from your mail folders.

5. Why is it a bad idea to let mail pile up in your inbox?

6. If you mark for deletion a mail message in a mail folder and then you change to another mail folder, has the mail message been deleted or is it still there?

7. Explain the difference between a normal exit and a quick exit from your mailer.

8. Why is it a bad idea to be sarcastic in an e-mail message?

9. Describe two ways that you could send a graphics file to someone via e-mail.

10. To what e-mail address should you complain if you are spammed by someone with the address bozo@freeway.com?

11. If you exit your mail program when there are one hundred unread messages in your inbox and the next time you read your mail, the inbox contains only 20 messages, what probably happened?

12. [**Hands On**] Where does your computer store your mail folders? Try to determine how much memory they are consuming.

13. Is it possible for someone to forge the return address on an e-mail message?

14. Explain the difference between the single Reply command and the group Reply command.

15. Is there a limit to the number of messages you can put in a mail folder?

16. If someone sends you a file that looks like gibberish, what should you do?

17. If a mail message gets bounced by the recipient's mail server, should you resend the message?

18. What is a POP connection, and when would you want one?

19. How can you add a sig file to your mail if your mailer doesn't support sig files?

20. What is the maximal number of characters per line that belong in a message body? Why should you avoid longer lines?

Mailing Lists and E-mail Archives

4

"Never doubt that a small group of thoughtful, committed citizens can change the world, indeed, it's the only thing that ever has."

- MARGARET MEADE

THE INTERNET 101 WEB PAGES

- An E-mail Archive Search Challenge
- List-Related Resources
- Spam-Related Resources
- Dealing with Bitnet Addresses for Mailing Lists
- A UNIX Interface for Faster Archive Searches

What Is a Mailing List?

4.1

A mailing list is a forum in which a group of people can share information with each other using e-mail. Some mailing lists are small and are used by only a handful of people, while others have thousands of subscribers. Some have restricted membership and so are not open to the general public, while others are open to anyone who wants to join. Some mailing lists are **moderated mailing lists**, that is, the owner of the list posts all of the messages to the list and approves any suggested posts offered by list subscribers. These lists typically operate as a broadcast medium: One person talks to the list, and everyone else listens. Other mailing lists are fully **interactive mailing lists**: Anyone can post a message to the list at any time without prior approval.

On the Internet, one doesn't need to justify the existence of a mailing list by pointing to a large number of subscribers. Most mailing lists are maintained by servers that carry on many other computing tasks in addition to the operation of the mailing list. Smaller mailing lists can be easily maintained as background jobs that run when nothing else is competing for machine cycles. As such, a mailing list on an Internet host represents a negligible computing load for the host machine. Mailing lists normally operate on the basis of plain ASCII text, so they do not consume a great deal of bandwidth. Plus, automated list management minimizes the need for human supervision in the daily operation of most mailing lists. Internet mailing lists are therefore one of the most cost-effective resources available online. Maintaining a successful mailing list requires only minimal computer time, minimal network bandwidth, and minimal human intervention.

| The AWAD List | A good example of a moderated mailing list is A.Word.A.Day (AWAD). Subscribers to this list receive one message from the list each day. The message contains an interesting word, its dictionary definition, and a quotation using the word. It's a painless way to expand your vocabulary or test your command of the English language. As of June 1997, AWAD was being sent out to over 76,000 people in more than 115 countries. For more information about AWAD, see `http://www.wordsmith.org/awad/`. |

A mailing list with thousands of subscribers is usually a moderated mailing list. An openly interactive list with that many subscribers would flood everyone's mailbox. Most UNIX hosts can maintain a mailing list for a few hundred subscribers without any visible loss of computing cycles. This makes it easy for computer professionals to create mailing lists for all sorts of topics in the spirit of the gift economy. But even a powerful UNIX workstation will begin to feel some strain when the number of subscribers to a mailing list nears 100,000. As a result, many mailing lists "top out" at around 80,000 subscribers, at which point the mailing list is terminated and an alternative broadcast medium is sought. In most of these cases, the mailing list is replaced by a Web site, which is better equipped to handle thousands of visitors on a daily basis.

Although a Web site is sometimes an alternative to a very large mailing list, mailing lists are different from Web sites in some important ways. Material from a mailing list lands in your mailbox, where it demands attention. You can delete a mail message without reading it, but you are always prompted to take some action with your mail. When a message arrives in your mailbox, you are reminded that there is new information on hand that might interest you. A Web site is inherently passive and requires an active effort on your part. Only you can remember to visit a Web site. It's easy to forget about a Web site, but it's much harder to ignore e-mail that's consuming your storage space.

Push and Pull

As the Internet becomes more commercialized, more is being said about **push technology** and **pull technology**. A Web browser is an example of a pull technology because you have to direct the browser to Web locations and pull those Web pages back to your host on demand. A push technology shoves information at you whether or not you asked for it. A mailing list is an example of a push technology. With pull technology, information consumers have more control over the information flow. With push technology, information providers have more control over the distribution of their information. The client/server model accommodates both types of technologies, and Internet users can decide for themselves which they prefer.

An interactive mailing list is a good way to meet people who share your interests, especially when your interests are off the beaten track. Many online relationships begin on a mailing list. However, the vast majority of mailing list subscribers tend to lurk and read posts to the list without ever posting their own. It has been estimated that only 10% of the subscribers on an interactive mailing list ever post a message to that list. There is usually a vocal minority responsible for most of the talking, while everyone else lurks and listens. So if you like to keep a low profile, you'll feel right at home lurking on a mailing list.

Subscribing to Mailing Lists 4.2

Before you can receive messages from a mailing list, you first must subscribe to the list. Most lists are maintained automatically by server software. A list manager may watch over the list and intervene as needed when someone gets out of hand, but the normal operations of accepting new subscribers and removing the addresses of people who want to leave the list are typically handled by a computer program.

There are a number of software packages designed to maintain mailing lists, and as a subscriber, you don't have to know much about them. In fact, you don't even have to know their names. But it helps to know that there are a few different ones out there and that each uses its own command sets. A summary of common mailing list commands is given in Appendix D.

A computer that operates a mailing list is sometimes called a **listserv** (mailing *list serv*er). This is also the name of a very popular mailing list software package. Confusion between a specific piece of software and a computer running the software is very common in Internet jargon. The term "server" is used in reference to both a server software package and a computer that runs the server software package. It's a little sloppy to mix the two, but it's also fairly harmless. In this book, I attempt to avoid pedantic language by using the term "listserv" in accordance with its sloppy conventional usage, despite its being technically incorrect.

Regardless of which software is managing a given mailing list, there are always two e-mail addresses associated with each interactive mailing list: **list command** and **list distribution**. You use the list command address to send a command to the listserv and the list distribution address to post a message to everyone on the list. The classic hallmark of a mailing list newbie is ignorance of or confusion about these two addresses. Newbies typically forget that there are two addresses, so they often send the wrong kind of e-mail to the wrong address.

The terms "list command address" and "list distribution address" are not standard jargon. They are used here because they are more suggestive than some of the other terms used by other books and Internet guides. For example, you will see the terms "listserv address" and "list address" used instead. Don't be confused. There are only two e-mail addresses associated with each interactive mailing list, and each always performs the same functions regardless of what they are called.

EMBARRASSING NEWBIE BLOOPERS

If you remember only one thing about mailing lists, remember that there are two addresses for each interactive mailing list and be clear about when each one is used. When the time comes to unsubscribe from a list, make sure you send the Unsubscribe command to the list command address. ***Do not send an Unsubscribe command to the list distribution address; everyone on the list will have to see it.*** This is very annoying for list subscribers who pay for their e-mail on a per-message basis. Plus, it won't get you off the list. When you subscribe to a mailing list, you will receive a welcome message that contains important information, including (1) the list command address, (2) the list distribution address, and (3) instructions on how to subscribe or unsubscribe from the list. ***Always save the welcome message for each mailing list to which you subscribe.*** With a little foresight and a little effort, you can avoid embarrassing yourself before hundreds, possibly thousands, of list subscribers worldwide.

A moderated mailing list has no list distribution address, so you do not need to worry about two addresses with a moderated list. You also don't need to worry about inadvertently sending mail to some list distribution address by mistake. The only people who are allowed to post messages to an interactive mailing list are list subscribers. No one else can send mail to a distribution address and have it distributed to a mailing list.

Different mailing list software packages have different command conventions for accepting new subscribers and removing old subscribers. Subscription updates are the most important functions performed by a mailing list. However, there are other commands for users who want additional information about the mailing list. You need to read the welcome message for each mailing list in order to acquaint yourself with the operation and capabilities of different mailing lists. They are not all the same.

The original **listserv mailing list** software is still very popular and may still be the most common mailing list software in use. So we will explain the commands used to **subscribe** and **unsubscribe** to listserv mailing lists.

If a mailing list is maintained by a listserv, you subscribe by sending an e-mail message to the listserv address with a message body of the form

```
subscribe name-of-list your-first-name your-last-name
```

You make appropriate substitutions for the items in italics. Listservs are not case-sensitive, but you should enter your name in mixed case when you subscribe to the mailing list. Sending this message automatically makes you a new subscriber. Most of the time, you'll get a fast autoreply— an acknowledgment or welcome message—within minutes. However, if a server for a mailing list is not online 24 hours a day, a reply might take up to a day or so.

To unsubscribe, send the listserv address a message body of the form:

```
unsubscribe name-of-list
```

For example, suppose I wanted to subscribe to an interactive list for discussion related to golden retrievers. The name of the list is *golden*, and the list command address is `listserv@hobbes.ucsd.edu`. To subscribe to this list, I would send a message to `listserv@hobbes.ucsd.edu` with a message body that says

```
subscribe golden Wendy Lehnert
```

To post a message to the golden list, I would send the message to the list distribution address, `golden@hobbes.ucsd.edu`. When I want to unsubscribe, I would send my Unsubscribe command to the list command address, `listserv@hobbes.ucsd.edu`. Only golden list subscribers can post messages to the golden list, and only list subscribers can receive list messages as they are posted.

How Many Messages Will You Get?

It is difficult to know in advance exactly how much traffic a list will bring to your mailbox. Some lists are barely alive, while others are highly active. A popular list will fill your mailbox with lots of reading material every day. For example, the golden list generated over 19,700 messages between August 1995 and August 1996. That's a daily average of 50 or more messages. All of these messages, if saved, would consume more than 31MB of storage. By the end of 1996, more than 1,800 subscribers were reading this list. While this is one of the more active lists, there are others with even more traffic. For example, a mailing list devoted to Windows 95 handled about one hundred messages a day during 1996.

It is fine to try out a list for a short time in order to see if it is something you like or need. You can always subscribe to a list for a few days or weeks, never post a message yourself, and then unsubscribe. No one will care. ***Just remember to save the welcome message so that you'll know how to unsubscribe.***

MULTIPLE ACCOUNTS AND MAILING LISTS

When you subscribe to a mailing list, the list records your e-mail address and expects to see that address whenever you interact with the list. If you have access to multiple host machines, you will not be able to post a message to a list you have subscribed to if you send it from a different host than the one used when you first subscribed. You also must issue your Unsubscribe command from the same machine you used when you first subscribed. If you ever need to close down a computer account on one machine or you want to shift your daily operations from one machine to another, make sure you unsubscribe from all active mailing lists on the old machine first. Then (re)subscribe to all of them from your new host machine. Do not expect a mailing list to recognize you if you try to contact it from different host machines.

Whenever you interact with a computer program, be careful to type your commands correctly. No human ever sees your listserv commands; they will be either accepted and processed or rejected with an error message. If you write a command in the **Subject:** header instead of the message body, the listserv will not see the command. If you mangle the syntax of a Subscribe or Unsubscribe command (e.g., you list your name first followed by the name of the list), the listserv will not be able to process the command. Remember that you are dealing with a computer program and that computer programs tend to be rather unforgiving about their expectations. Computers are very good at multiplying two 20-digit numbers, but they're not very smart when it comes to figuring out what you want if you mess up on command syntax.

Some Great Mailing Lists

There are many good lists that can help you master the Internet and keep you up to date on Internet-related news. Here are four that will keep you well informed without overwhelming your mailbox:

"The Internet Tourbus" is a weekly (more or less) newsletter that profiles specific Internet resources and offers Internet news of general interest. Written with light humor and a personal touch, the "Tourbus" is a friendly addition to your mailbox. To subscribe, send an e-mail message to `listserv@listserv.aol.com` and include in the body of the message the command

```
subscribe tourbus <firstname> <lastname>
```

"Net Surfers Digest" is a monthly newsletter with profiles of interesting Web sites and short articles addressing timely Internet news. To subscribe, send an e-mail message to `nsdigest-request@netsurf.com` and include in the body of the message the command

```
subscribe nsdigest-text
```

"The Scout Report" is a weekly newsletter describing new and newly discovered Web sites of interest to educators and researchers. For information on subscribing to "The Scout Report," send an mail message to `listserv@internic.net` and in the body of the message type the command

```
info scout-report
```

"The Red Rock Eaters News Service" distributes items written by technologists discussing policy, politics, and sociological issues related to the Internet. Expect 5–10 messages each week. To subscribe, send an e-mail message to `rre-request@Weber.ucsd.edu` and in the **Subject:** header type the command

```
subscribe <firstname> <lastname>
```

4.3 ▶ Managing Mailing List Traffic in Your Mailbox

If you subscribe to several mailing lists and your inbox is getting flooded with too much mail, here are three effective strategies for managing the messages and keeping them from interfering with work-related e-mail or personal e-mail of a more urgent nature:

1. Use a digest option to subscribe to the digest version of a mailing list.
2. Use a mail filter to automatically route messages received from mailing lists into separate mail folders.
3. Temporarily turn off some list subscriptions during your busiest periods.

Use the Digest Option

Most mailing lists offer a **digest option** that is very useful when a list generates a great deal of traffic. With the digest version of a list, the listserv collects some number of messages before sending them out to you. Then when the messages are sent, they are bundled into a single mail message with a list of the contents that contains all of the **Subject:** headers included in the current digest. All messages are included, and you see all of the full message bodies. A highly active list may send out two digests a day. A less active list may send out two or three a week. If you do not need to see everything that is posted to a list as soon as possible, you lose nothing by subscribing to the digest version of a mailing list. The digest will put one mail message in your inbox rather than 10, 20, or more separate messages. This makes it easier to manage your inbox and see mail that is not associated with mailing lists.

The digest version of a list is often managed as a second mailing list that has its own name and its own Subscribe/Unsubscribe commands. On a listserv list, you can change from the regular list to the digest version by using the digest command

```
set name-of-list mail digest
```

For example, for the golden list:

```
set golden mail digest
```

When you first subscribe to a new list, check the welcome message to see if it mentions a digest option. If so, then it should include instructions for switching to the digest. You may need to unsubscribe to the regular version of the list and then subscribe to a separate digest version. Note that if you subscribe to a list digest, you can still post messages to the list just like a subscriber to the regular list.

There are two small disadvantages associated with list digests. First, you won't receive all of the messages as quickly as you would otherwise. If you are subscribing to a list for extremely timely information, you may find the delays associated with a digest unacceptable. Second, it is harder to separate out individual messages if you want to save one and delete the rest. If you don't save very many messages, this occasional inconvenience is probably tolerable. But if you save, for example, half of all of the messages that come through, it may be better to stay away from the digest and opt for a mail filter (described shortly). If you could go either way, it is better to subscribe to the digest because it decreases the load on the Internet and eases the load on the listserv's host machine.

Use a Mail Filter

If a list does not offer a digest option, you can still control the amount of mail in your inbox by setting up an automated **mail filter** that routes all of the messages from a mailing list into a mail folder reserved just for that list. For example, messages from the golden list can be recognized by a filter rule for the elm mail program that looks like this:

```
if from contains "golden@hobbes.ucsd.edu" then
save /usr/ren/nlp/lehnert/Mail/golden
```

This routes incoming mail from the golden list to a mail folder on my UNIX account called "golden." With a filter like this in place, no mail from the golden list will ever appear in my inbox. As soon as mail from the golden list arrives, it is routed to the golden mail folder, where it waits for me to get around to it.

Eudora Pro 3.1 supports automated mail routing. To set up a similar rule using Eudora, a user would do the following (see Figure 4.1):

1. From the Mailbox menu, click New. Name the new mailbox golden. Do *not* check Make It a Folder.

2. From the Special menu, click Filters.

3. Click NEW in the far lower-left corner. Then check the "Incoming" box under Match:.

4. Click the Header button and use the arrow button to select **From:**. You will also see a box that says Contains. Leave that box alone. It's fine as it is.

Match:

☒ Incoming   ☐ Outgoing   ☐ Manual

Header: | From: | ▼ |

| contains | | golden@hobbes.ucsd.edu |

| ignore |

Header: | | ⌄ |

| contains | | |

Actions:

| Transfer To | | golden |

FIG. 4.1

Creating a Filter Rule
in Eudora

5. In the box to the right of Contains, type `golden@hobbes.ucsd.edu`.

6. Move down the screen to where it says Actions. You can program up to five actions that Eudora will perform whenever it sees a message with the specified **From:** heading. In this case, program it to automatically transfer all such messages into the golden folder.

7. In the first box under Actions, click where it says "none" and then select Transfer To.

8. Click the box next to Transfer To and use the Transfer menu to select the golden folder.

9. Save this filter rule by going to the File menu and clicking Save.

| OUT OF SIGHT, OUT OF MIND | If you set up a filter rule that routes mail from a mailing list into a mail folder, be careful not to forget about the folder. Remember that all mail folders occupy memory. A very active mailing list can consume as much as 1MB every week or two. If you are collecting mail for one of these lists and never deleting any of it, you can eat up a lot of memory without realizing it. Automated mail routing is wonderful, but it also makes a lot of incoming mail invisible to you. Be careful to monitor any mail folders receiving automatically routed mail. |

Turn Off Some Subscriptions during Busy Periods

If you route a mailing list to a mail folder and then discover you don't have the time to keep up with it, you are probably just too busy for the list. You may discover that you don't get around to reading it regularly, you tend to forget about it, and you don't really miss it very much. When this happens, it makes sense to unsubscribe for a while. You can always go back to the list later when you have more time on your hands or when your interest in the list returns. For example, if you know that you will be interested in the list again as soon as you finish a time-consuming project, then you can temporarily halt mail from a mailing list by sending a **Suspend command** to the listserv, as follows:

```
set name-of-list nomail
(or else try: set name-of-list mail postpone)
```

This should be sent to the listserv address in the message body. When you are ready to resume the list, send the **Unsuspend command**:

```
set name-of-list mail
```

Most listservs will recognize either "nomail" or "mail postpone." The Suspend command is very useful if you intend to go on a vacation and you want to use an autoreply utility to announce your absence. However, *you should never use an autoreply message while you are actively subscribed to a mailing list.*

If you are active on any mailing lists, do not set up an autoreply. Each time a mail message comes in from your mailing list, the autoreply software will send a message to the list address; this creates problems for the list administrator. You are likely to receive a reprimand from the list administrator, and you will probably be removed from the list in order to stop the flow of autoreply mail. With a heavily used list, your autoreply utility will be sending mail to the listserv dozens of times a day, so the list administrator is totally justified in taking any steps needed to shut you down. You can still use an autoreply message if you want. Just be careful to unsubscribe or temporarily suspend yourself from all of

DO NOT ANNOY
YOUR LIST
ADMINISTRATOR

Continued on Next Page

Continued from Previous Page

your active mailing lists before you set up an autoreply. You probably don't want list messages piling up while you're gone anyway. All those unread messages will just overwhelm you when you
get back and need to handle more pressing matters.

There are many other useful commands that can be used with listservs in
addition to the usual Subscribe, Unsubscribe, Suspend, and Unsuspend commands. Some of these are reviewed in the next section.

4.4 ▶ Some Useful Listserv Commands

Here are other commands you may find helpful:

- To receive copies of your own messages

  When you subscribe to your first mailing list and post your first message to the list, you may never see your own message. If no one responds
  to your message, you may wonder if it made it onto the list or if you
  made some sort of a mistake when you sent it. Many listservs are deliberately set up so that list members do not receive their own posts. If you
  want a copy of your own posts to the list, send an e-mail message to the
  listserv whose body contains this command:

  ```
  set name-of-list repro (or try: set name-of-list ack)
  ```

  If you decide later that you no longer want to see your own messages,
  then issue this command:

  ```
  set name-of-list norepro
  ```

- To unsubscribe to all of your mailing lists

  If you ever want to unsubscribe to all your mailing lists, a listserv network
  will try to help you out with a universal Unsubscribe command. Send

  ```
  unsubscribe   *   (   netwide
  ```

  to a listserv address. The command will be forwarded to hundreds of
  listserv hosts in an effort to find all of your active listserv subscriptions.

As helpful as this may be, there are two ways that this universal command can fail. First, not all of your mailing lists may be managed by listserv software; this command doesn't affect any list that is not a listserv mailing list. Second, if you subscribed to a list from a different host machine, your subscription can be terminated only by a command issued from that machine. If you maintain multiple computer accounts, it is probably a good idea to keep all of your mailing lists on a single host so as to minimize confusion.

- To obtain a listing of all list subscribers

  With a listserv mailing list, it is sometimes possible to get a listing of all of the current list subscribers. Try sending the **Review command**:

  ```
  review name-of-list
  ```

  If the list administrator wants to protect the privacy of list subscribers, the Review command may be disabled.

- To find out which commands work for a list

  Each list administrator can enable or disable specific listserv commands, so different lists may or may not respond to specific listserv commands. If you are having difficulties with any commands, try asking the listserv itself for a list of commands that should work. Do this by issuing the **Info command**:

  ```
  info name-of-list
  ```

- To protect your privacy

  If you are trying to keep a low profile and would rather not have anyone know that you are a member of a specific mailing list, you can take steps to protect your privacy by issuing the **Conceal command**:

  ```
  set name-of-list conceal
  ```

  which can always be reversed with the **Noconceal** command:

  ```
  set name-of-list noconceal
  ```

When your name is concealed, it will not be sent to anyone who requests a list of all of the subscribers. Some mailing lists address sensitive topics. Those membership lists should be handled with discretion. For example, if you are coping with a serious disease, you might not want that to be public knowledge. In such cases, one might expect the list administrator to take appropriate steps to protect the privacy of list members. But it is always wise to check using an Info command if you are concerned. In general, you should not assume that your Internet activities are private or protected from snoops. You can take steps to protect your privacy on the Internet, but no one can guarantee that privacy.

Keep in mind that some mailing lists are handled by other types of list software and they will not respond to the same commands that work on a listserv mailing list. Look for online documentation to find out which commands are available for each mailing list to which you subscribe.

4.5 ▶ E-mail Netiquette

When you subscribe to a mailing list, you must remember that each message you post goes out to a large number of people you don't know. They may not share your values, your beliefs, your sense of humor, or your neophyte sense of accomplishment. The Internet is a global communication vehicle; you never know who's out there reading what you type. The Internet population is *not* a homogeneous group of people from one country or one socioeconomic class. The Internet is truly a global medium, and we must remember how far-reaching our communications can be. Some lists are friendly and forgiving about minor transgressions in courtesy and Netiquette. Others are policed by individuals who take a hard line on what's appropriate.

With a few rules of the road in hand, you can safely get out there and explore. If you find a mailing list that interests you, go ahead and subscribe to it. You can conceal your identity if you are very worried about preserving your privacy. Then no one will ever know you're there unless you post a message to the list.

WATCH AND LEARN	When you first subscribe to a new mailing list, it is wise to **lurk before** you leap. This means you should plan just to read messages for a while before you post any of your own. By lurking quietly in the background, you can learn how the list is used, what topics are appropriate, and what might provoke angry reactions from other list members. Don't feel compelled to jump right in the first day you're on a new list. Watch and learn before you say something you might regret.

A lot of conversational threads start publicly on a mailing list and then shift to a private conversation via personal e-mail. For example, when you first introduce yourself as a new list member, there are often a few friendly souls who reply to you and say something to make you feel welcome.

Sometimes these replies are posted to everyone on the list and sometimes they come back as private e-mail. If you decide to pursue a conversation with one other person, it is usually a good idea to continue it privately unless you think you are saying something that is of general interest to the entire list. This is a good way to make new online friends, if you are looking for "pen pals." In fact, a lot of private e-mail relationships are spawned by brief exchanges on a mailing list. ***Always include your full e-mail address in the message body of each post you send to a mailing list.*** Some list subscribers may be working with a mailer that does not display your return address in their message headers. If you are going to post messages to a mailing list, you should make it easy for people to reply to you privately.

It is also good Netiquette to give people your real name when you post messages to a mailing list. There have been cases of fictitious personas operating as participants on mailing lists; this practice is generally frowned on. It is easy enough to misrepresent yourself online and get away with it, but most people feel doing this is highly unethical. People tend to take their online contacts at face value and often form caring relationships with e-mail correspondents. If you write to someone for an extended period of time and then find out that the person you thought you knew is a total fiction, the experience can be very unsettling. Deliberate misrepresentation is disrespectful of those who are honest about their real identities. There are some chat environments in which identity-bending and role-playing are accepted as standard practice (see Chapter 10), but mailing lists operate under a different set of (unspoken) rules.

You will find that on a mailing list, some people talk publicly, while others interact only privately. If you subscribe to a list on which you see a lot of people posting questions, but not many people posting answers, it may be that replies are being sent out privately. There's no way of knowing how responsive list members are in their private communications until you post a question yourself.

When you decide to post a message to a mailing list, here are some Netiquette guidelines to remember:

- Keep it short.
- Make sure your topic is relevant to the list.
- Send personal messages to individuals, not to the whole list.
- Keep facts and opinions clearly separated.
- Try to avoid insulting anyone.
- Include your full (real) name in your signature.
- Include your full e-mail address with your signature.
- Do not include any mail attachments.
- Do not set up an autoreply if you are active on any mailing lists.

And when you move or change your ISP, always remember to unsubscribe yourself from all mailing lists before terminating an account.

If you are thinking of posting a message to a mailing list and you are uncertain about its relevance to the list, it is best to err on the side of caution and not post it. Many beginners pass along information that is off-topic but believed to be of great general interest. If you find yourself thinking, *"**Surely everybody would want to know about this even though it's not relevant to the list . . .",** **please resist the impulse to post.**

In the box that follows is an excerpt from the welcome message for the golden list, written by Wade Blomgren, the owner of the golden list. His guidelines are very clear about what to avoid when you post to the list.

Do Not Post Irrelevant Material to a Mailing List	Do not EVER post any sort of "security alert" or "Internet virus" or "kid wants postcards/business cards" or "student/Santa wants email messages" or "save the Internet or Sesame Street from Congress or the FCC" or "send email to get books donated to sick kids" or pyramid scheme or political plea/warning of any kind or graphics file of any kind or vt100 escape sequence "greeting cards" or commercial solicitation or any (ANY) other kind of off topic "forward this to everyone you know" spam or chain letter or good luck letter or joke collection or top 10 list or joke you just heard to this list. Nearly all such items are either provably bogus or long since expired (in the case of alerts or pleas), or incompatible with the many and varied computer systems your fellow subscribers are using, and the remainder, if any, just plain DON'T BELONG HERE no matter how funny or important you may think they are. Mail me privately to discuss any post that might even SLIGHTLY violate this rule, before you post it. I will decide if any such message is appropriate for this list. If you don't check first you risk immediate and permanent termination of your subscription, possibly a formal complaint to your system administrator, and definitely a lifetime flea curse on your dwelling.

These guidelines are relevant for all mailing lists, unless their stated topic explicitly includes one of the prohibited items. List administrators can impose whatever behavioral codes they see fit, and they can always enforce these codes by removing violators from the list.

When a dialog gets rolling and the content is humorous, you'll find lots of **Netspeak acronyms** laced throughout the messages. These are often there to convey an emotional undertone. You may see a cryptic LOL or ROFL in response to something punctuated with a smilee. LOL stands for "I laughed out loud." ROFL means "I'm rolling on the floor laughing."

Other abbreviations are used to soften statements that everyone might not agree with. IMO means "in my opinion." An even more cautious caveat is IMHO ("in my humble opinion"). These terms make it clear that the writer is not trying to assume authority or trying to step on someone whose opinions might differ.

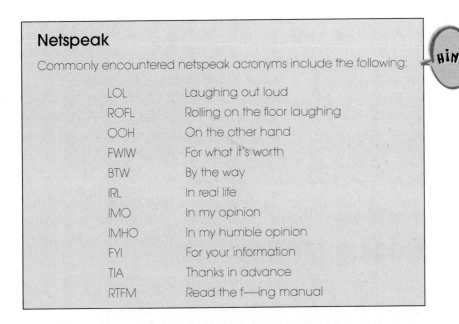

Netspeak

Commonly encountered netspeak acronyms include the following:

HINT

LOL	Laughing out loud
ROFL	Rolling on the floor laughing
OOH	On the other hand
FWIW	For what it's worth
BTW	By the way
IRL	In real life
IMO	In my opinion
IMHO	In my humble opinion
FYI	For your information
TIA	Thanks in advance
RTFM	Read the f—ing manual

If you participate in a list on which your words might be misinterpreted, try to be sensitive to the ambiguities of written dialog and use emoticons and Netspeak where appropriate. Online communication is different from the verbal communication medium we're all used to. It may look easy enough, but it takes some time to catch on.

Another important aspect of Netiquette is simply to be educated about the Internet. If you were going to visit a foreign country, you would probably want to learn something about the place beforehand. You would look at a map and maybe try to learn a little of the language. Unfortunately, too many newcomers to the Internet are not sensitive to the fact that they are also visiting a kind of foreign land with its own cultural mores.

In particular, many newcomers don't taken the time to learn about the gift economy. This kind of ignorance has resulted in some unfortunate misunderstandings. For example, in 1995 a list administrator in Texas found himself dealing with too many ignorant list subscribers. A run-in with an AOL user was the last straw. The AOLer was paying to download e-mail on a per message basis and was very annoyed because some of the posts to this particular mailing list were off-topic. Miffed about paying for irrelevant posts, the AOLer complained to the list administrator and demanded better list management. The AOL subscriber didn't understand where the AOL service stopped and the rest of the Internet began. He was under the impression that everything on the Internet was run by AOL staff as part of AOL's services. Since he was paying AOL for access to the mailing list, he assumed the list administrator was responsible for delivering relevant content. So if he wasn't getting his money's worth, the list administrator must be at fault. But the list in question was part of the gift economy. The list administrator was not compensated for his time or trouble, and he resented the fact that he was suddenly expected to explain himself to irate AOL subscribers. He didn't have a lot of time for the list, and he couldn't afford to deal with people making unreasonable demands on his time. In the end, the mailing list, after more than a decade of operation, was shut down amidst many hard feelings. If you detect a certain disdain for AOLers on the part of some old Netheads, stories like this one are behind much of the animosity.

4.6 Finding Mailing Lists

Suppose we're designing a new curriculum for a math course that uses a computer lab. We want to know what sorts of graphing software other teachers are using, and if possible, which software packages are best. We would like to find some teachers on the Internet who can give advice based on their own experiences.

There are probably around 20,000 active mailing lists open to the public. No one knows exactly how many because there is no single master list of all of the mailing lists. But some databases do keep a partial list of active mailing lists, and these databases can be searched. Some mailing list databases are on the Web (see the Internet 101 Web pages), and most can be queried via e-mail. For the graphing software problem, we'll go to a large listserv database called LIST. This database is good for academically oriented mailing lists, so it's a reasonable place to find math teachers.

We start by looking for mailing lists where math teachers talk to each other. We need to conduct a keyword search using the LIST database, so we could search with either "teacher" or "mathematics." A mailing list for teachers in general won't have the kind of narrow focus we need, so we start our search with "mathematics."

We can conduct our search remotely by sending a command to a listserv that maintains the LIST database. In fact, most listservs will reply to a LIST database query. If one server is down, we can always find another that will respond. Here are a few servers to try:

```
listserv@ubvm.cc.buffalo.edu    (New York)
listserv@smtpgate.uvm.edu        (Vermont)
listserv@uafsysb.uark.edu        (Arkansas)
listserv@listserv.kent.edu       (Ohio)
listserv@ulkyvm.louisville.edu   (Kentucky)
listserv@uicvm.uic.edu           (Illinois)
listserv@vm1.nodak.edu           (North Dakota)
listserv@ualvm.ua.edu            (Alabama)
listserv@listserv.rice.edu       (Texas)
listserv@cmsa.berkeley.edu       (California)
listserv@listserv.net            (Sweden)
```

Note: Don't feel you have to use one of these servers just because they are listed here. There are over 250 listserv hosts throughout the world. Try to find a listserv that is as geographically close to you as possible. You'll see addresses for more listservs as we move through our example. Just keep your eye out for one close to you, and in the meantime, use one of the ones listed here.

To conduct our search, we send a mail message containing a **List Global command** to a listserv address. Any listserv address will work, and since the command is a listserv command, uppercase/lowercase variations don't matter. But we do need to supply an appropriate keyword, otherwise the listserv might send us a list of its entire database. The LIST database contains over 13,000 mailing lists, so the complete output file would be over 40,000 lines long and require over 1.3MB of storage. ***Never send a List Global command without a keyword.***

The command we send requires no **Subject:** header, but in the message body we type

```
list global math
```

The e-mail response from the server yields a directory of 52 mailing lists about mathematics. Some of these are for researchers; others are for teachers. The ones marked "closed" are not open to the general public. But there are a lot of public lists. It's difficult to know which is the best to pursue. We may need to investigate a few of them. Note that it is important to try different keywords when you conduct these keyword searches. The keyword "mathematics" will give you a different list than the keyword "math." With experience, you will learn how to think of keywords that produce good results.

Whenever you send a request to a listserv for information, you will get back two separate messages from the listserv. One contains the information you want, like the directory of 52 lists obtained in the example. The other looks like billing information. Here's an example of the latter that came back from `listserv@uicvm.uic.edu` in response to the command `list global uic`. This particular search returns all of the mailing lists maintained at the University of Illinois at Chicago:

```
> list global uic
File "LISTSERV LISTS" has been mailed to you under separate
cover.

Summary of resource utilization
───────────────────────────
   CPU time:        0.220 sec      Device I/O:      22
   Overhead CPU:    0.021 sec      Paging I/O:       7
   CPU model:       3090           DASD model:    3390
```

This isn't really a charge for services rendered. It is a gentle reminder that we have used the computing resources of someone else's machine and that these services have been extended to us as a courtesy. If you are conducting a lot of searches on a listserv, it is good Netiquette to conduct these explorations during off hours as a courtesy to the other users of the server.

Finding a Listserv Host Near You

One way to find a server near you is to conduct a list global search. Try conducting a search using the name of your state or city as a keyword. This may uncover some regional lists housed on machines near you. Try it and see what comes back.

If you want to submit multiple searches to a listserv at once, just add additional lines to your message body:

```
list global math
list global mathematics
list global spreadsheets
```

Each search must be based on a single keyword, but you can request multiple searches with a single mail message. Doing this is a little kinder to the server as well as your own mailbox because it generates fewer CPU resource messages. If you put multiple keywords on a single command line, the listserv will conduct a phrase match. For example, the command `list global applied math` narrows our search down to mailing lists with descriptions that contain the phrase "applied math" (any case combinations will match).

Now back to our graphing software problem. From the collection of 52 mailing lists sent to us, a few seem particularly promising:

```
PRECALC     PRECALC@IPFWVMB.BITNET
            Precalc/Development Math Curriculum Teaching
                Methods, Research

QMSTE-L     QMSTE-L@QUCDN.QUEENSU.CA
            Mathematics, Science, and Technology Education
                Group

SMETDIAL    SMETDIAL@VM.TEMPLE.EDU
            SMETDIAL - Science/ Math/ Engineering/
                Technology Dialog

SNYMAP-L    SNYMAP-L@SNYCENVM.BITNET
            SUNY Mathematics Alert Program Discussion list

SUSIG       SUSIG@MIAMIU.MUOHIO.EDU
            Teaching in the Mathematical Sciences with
                Spreadsheets

TEACHMAT    TEACHMAT@LISTSERV.UIC.EDU
            Methods of Teaching Mathematics

TROLL-L     TROLL-L@CESNET.CZ
            Information technologies in mathematics
                (closed)

WVMS-L      WVMS-L@WVNVM.WVNET.EDU
            NASA Classroom of the Future: WV Mathematics
                and Science List
```

Some of these are for researchers, while others are for teachers. Any list marked "closed" is not open to the general public. It's hard to know which list is the best one to look at, so we will need to investigate of few of them. To keep this discussion short, we'll pick some good ones first. In real life, you may not be so lucky, but don't give up if some of your lists don't pan out.

Our first job is to learn which of these lists have searchable archives. We do this by contacting the different listservs and asking each for a list of the searchable archives it maintains. While this might sound tedious, it's often fun to see what is being archived at various sites. You might stumble across some surprising lists this way. For example, the listserv at Miami University in Ohio (`listserv@miamiu.muohio.edu`) maintains a large number of interesting archives. As luck would have it, the SUSIG list mentioned in our List Global output is not among them, so we can forget about SUSIG. Not all mailing lists maintain public archives, so it is good to cast your net wide and expect to check a number of different listservs.

Let's start by checking on the listserv for the SMETDIAL list. This host is located at Temple University. We can reach it at the list command address `listserv@vm.temple.edu`.

Note that you can always construct the correct list command address by putting "listserv" in front of the domain name for the list distribution address. For example, if the list distribution address is `teachmat@uicvm.uic.edu`, then the list command address is `listserv@uicvm.uic.edu`. If the distribution address is `precalc@vmb.ipfw.indiana.edu`, then the command address is `listserv@vmb.ipfw.indiana.edu` (this happens to be an alternative address for the PRECALC list shown previously).

Note also that ***all listserv database queries must go to a list command address. If you send a listserv query to an address that does not start with "listserv," your query will fail.*** All listservs are addressed in the same way (thank goodness). So, to check on SMETDIAL we go to the listserv at Temple and ask it what mail archives it maintains. This is done by sending mail to `listserv@vm.temple.edu` with a **Database List command** in the message body:

```
database list
```

When the Temple listserv replies, we get back a long list of all of the available archives housed at Temple University:

```
ACMET-L    Archives of "Academic Metal Crafts discussion"
ADM-NEWS   Archives of "Temple OCIS Admin Systems News"
ADM-SYS    Archives of "Temple OCIS Admin Systems Internal News"
AYUDANET   Archives of "Bitnet/Internet Help Resource (Spanish)"
BITEARN    Information on all BITNET nodes
CTCIV      Archives of "Court Technology Conference IV"
CULTUR-L   Archives of "Cultural differences in curriculum discussion"
DENTST-L   Archives of "Discussion list for dental students"
E_INVEST   Archives of "eINVEST - Electronic Journal of Investing"
GRADLAW    Archives of "Communications Law course"
HELP-NET   Archives of "Bitnet/Internet Help Resource"
J411       Archives of "Journalism 411 discussion"
MACCHAT    Archives of "The Mac*Chat Newsletter"
MEDIAWEB   Archives of "Film/Video Web sites discussion"
MLCOPER    Archives of "MLC Operations Sub Committee"
MLCTECH    Archives of "MLC Technology Sub Committee"
NASH       Archives of "The NASH newsletter"
NEWOWLS    Archives of "Listserv for new Temple students"
PEERS      Information on all the LISTSERV servers in the network
PHOTOTUJ   Archives of "Photojournalism discussion"
RELGSA     Archives of "TU Religion GSA discussion"
SLTLT-L    Archives of "Second Language Teaching & Learning Tech Discussion"
SMETDIAL   Archives of "SMETDIAL - Science/ Math/ Engineering/ Technology"
SPA-L      Archives of "Sponsored Projects Admin Discussion"
```

```
SPORTPSY   Archives of "Exercise and Sports Psychology"
SPORTSOC   Archives of "Sociological aspects of sports discussion"
SUGGEST    Archives of "Temple's mainframe discussion"
SUPERINT   Archives of "The Supervision Interest Network"
TEMPLELC   Archives of "Temple Learning Communities Instructors"
THUC-L     Archives of "Thucydides discussion"
TU-INTL    Archives of "Temple University International Students"
TUDOR-L    Archives of "Temple University Dept. of Religion Discussion"
VEGAN-L    Archives of "Vegan Discussion Group"
VISCOM     Archives of "Visual Communications Discussion"
```

We don't really need to see all of this. We just want to know if SMETDIAL is on the list. A quick inspection shows that it is one of the archived lists on the Temple listserv. So this is a good result. Next, we search the SMETDIAL archive.

Before we continue our search, you need to know one more thing. The LIST database contains thousands of mailing lists and is very useful. However, it does not represent a comprehensive collection of all of the public mailing lists on the Internet. So if you are interested in a topic that does not materialize after a list global search, don't despair. You may just need to poke around in some other mailing list databases. Some mailing lists are mentioned only in FAQ files or in periodic posts to Usenet newsgroups. Sometimes, you find out about a mailing list from a Web page. There are even mailing lists that do nothing but announce new mailing lists. You may be able to locate archives of these lists that you can search using the techniques described in this chapter.

If you want to search for listserv mailing lists on the Web, visit the **CataList** site. This site includes a searchable catalog of listserv lists (`http://www.lsoft.com/lists/listref.html`). CataList shows which lists have more than 10,000 subscribers and which lists have more than 1,000 subscribers, so you can see which lists are seriously active. It also lets you conduct keyword searches for specific lists. CataList is part of the official listserv software site. It's an interesting site to visit if you are looking for another window on the world of listserv mailing lists.

Another mail server where you can conduct a keyword search for mailing lists is **Liszt-by-Mail** at `liszter@bluemarble.net`. Just send an e-mail with a message body of the form

```
search <keyword>
```

You will get back a directory of matched items via e-mail. Liszt-by-Mail maintains a larger database than LIST because it contains other types of mailing lists (majordomo, listproc, smartlist, and so on) as well as listserv lists. A search with the keyword "math" at Liszt-by-Mail produced 218 matches (as opposed to 52 with the LIST database). You can also visit the Liszt-by-Mail Web site at `http://liszt.bluemarble.net/`, which claims to index 71,618 mailing lists (some large number of these are probably private lists). This Web site also lets you browse mailing list descriptions indexed by broad subject areas. These are fun to explore if you are casting about for new interests.

4.7 ▶ Searching E-mail Archives

To search a mailing list archive, you send the listserv a **Search command**. Each Search command must be of the form:

```
search <list-of-keywords> in <name-of-list>
```

This query goes in the message body and is sent to the appropriate listserv command address (for the host that houses the archive). While many command addresses can be used for list global queries, an archive search must always be directed to the listserv that houses the archive. There is normally only one listserv that maintains the active archive for a given mailing list.

In our graphing software example, we would replace *<list-of-keywords>* with "graphing software" and replace *<name-of-list>* with "smetdial" (remember, case never matters to a listserv). Once we've made these substitutions in the generic template, we can send the query:

```
search "graphing software" in smetdial
```

The listserv will then return a list of pointers to all of the e-mail messages posted in the SMETDIAL archives that contain the phrase "graphing software." For each hit, the listserv shows the **Subject:** header of the mail message found so that we can decide whether to retrieve that message. Some archives also list the line of text from the mail message that contains our keyword or key phrase.

You never know if you are going to find too many hits or too few. Sometimes you come up empty-handed. When the SMETDIAL listserv responds to our search query, it comes back with this response:

```
> search  graphing software  in  smetdial
-> No hit.

> index
-> No hit in previous search, nothing to list.
```

This means that no messages in the SMETDIAL archive contain the phrase "graphing software." The archive may still be useful to us; perhaps our search was too narrow to create useful hits. So we should relax the search some in order to see what's in this archive.

Experience will teach you how to conduct keyword searches at the right level of specificity. A large archive will return hundreds of hits if a search is too wide, while the same search on a smaller archive may return only a few hits. When you are tapping an unfamiliar resource, you are wise to assume that it is very big and to use narrow searches rather than broad searches. Getting back more information than you can handle can be just as useless as getting back no information at all.

ALWAYS ASSUME IT'S BIG

In the case of SMETDIAL, a subsequent search on "graphing" also comes back empty. At this point, we might wonder just what's in this archive, if anything. So let's throw caution to the wind and conduct a search using the single keyword "software." This would normally be very foolhardy, but in the case of SMETDIAL, we receive only three hits:

```
> search   software   in   smetdial
-> Database SMETDIAL, 3 hits.

> index
Item # Date        Time    Recs  Subject
──────  ──── ───── ───── ────
000003 96/03/27 17:10  585   The Ways We Communicate On-line: A Survey
000005 96/04/05 07:18  591   The Ways We Communicate On-line: A Survey
000007 96/07/29 00:48  152   ANNOUNCEMENT> Summer Make the Link ...
```

The item number (Item #) to the left of each entry shows the entry's position in the stream of all indexed messages for this particular archive. Here, the item numbers are very revealing because they are all so low. Looking at the dates for the messages listed, we can see that although the list was started on or before March 1996, only seven messages had been posted to the list by the end of July 1996. This indicates that the list is barely alive, so it is not likely to produce anything useful no matter what keywords we try.

Since SMETDIAL wasn't very successful, let's move to another archive. This time we'll try the PRECALC list. The address for the PRECALC listserv is given as `precalc@ipfwvmb.bitnet`, which is a Bitnet address. Some mail servers do not know how to handle Bitnet addresses, so we may need to massage the address a little in order to establish communication with the Bitnet server. If we aren't sure what our own mail server does with Bitnet addresses, we can always try the usual distribution list → command list formula to see if a message addressed to `listserv@ipfwvmb.bitnet` goes through. If it doesn't, then we can route our mail to a **Bitnet gateway** that will take care of it for us. For more information about Bitnet addresses and routing mail to Bitnet gateways, see the Internet 101 Web pages.

In fact, my own UNIX host at UMass doesn't know how to handle Bitnet addresses, so I have to construct an address that routes my mail to a Bitnet gateway. Any Bitnet gateway will know how to handle a Bitnet address. For me, the closest Bitnet gateway is probably at MIT, so I can send my query to `listserv%ipfwvmb.bitnet@mitvma.mit.edu`.

As before, we start by sending a Database List command to the PRECALC listserv to determine if it maintains an archive for the PRECALC mailing list. Once an archive is confirmed, we again try the keyword search for "graphing software." This time we substitute PRECALC for ⟨*name-of-list*⟩ in the query template:

```
search "graphing software" in precalc
```

Remember that the listname is not case-sensitive, so it doesn't matter whether we capitalize it. This time, we get a response from the PRECALC listserv that looks a little more hopeful:

```
> search graphing software in precalc
-> Database PRECALC, 2 hits.

> index
Item #  Date      Time    Recs  Subject
_____  ____      ____    ____  _____
000091  96/02/14  19:48   35    good graphing software
000092  96/02/15  16:21   9     Re: good graphing software
```

There aren't many messages here, but they look relevant. If we relax our search a bit, we might find more good hits. But let's find out exactly what these messages say first. To see a mail message that we want to view in its entirety, we note its item number so that we can ask for it by item number.

All we have so far are two pointers to actual mail messages. These two look promising, so we send the listserv another query designed to retrieve the complete e-mail messages that interests us. To retrieve the full text of specific messages in an e-mail archive, use the Getpost command:

```
getpost <name-of-list> <item1> <item2> ...
```

We need to specify the name of mailing list, as well as the item numbers of any posts we want to retrieve. In our case, we send:

```
getpost precalc 91 92
```

Note that it is not necessary to include any leading zeros in the message indices. Now the listserv returns the requested posts and we can see the original e-mail messages in their entirety:

```
>>> Item number 91, dated 96/02/14 19:48:34 — ALL
Date:            Wed, 14 Feb 1996 19:48:34 -0500
Reply-To:        "Precalc/Development Math Curriculum Teaching Methods,
                 Research" <PRECALC@VMB.IPFW.INDIANA.EDU>
Sender:          "Precalc/Development Math Curriculum Teaching Methods,
                 Research" <PRECALC@VMB.IPFW.INDIANA.EDU>
From:            "XXXXXXXXXXXXXX" <XXXXXXX@XXXXXXXXXXX>
Subject:         good graphing software
```

Hello,

I am looking for some "good" graphing software (preferably multi-platform, but at least for a Mac). Some of the available software that I have looked at include: f(g) scholar, best grapher, master grapher, function probe, and nucalc. Only f(g) scholar and function probe seem to have any serious capability of handling data tables. (I am excluding Excel from this list just because of the complexity of use and that it doesn't support standard algebraic notation.)

Is anyone aware of other software packages for graphing functions that support the use of data tables? If so, let me know and if there's interest I'll summarize and re-post to the list!

XXXX XXXXX

XXXXXXXXXXXXXX
Assistant Professor
Mathematics & Mathematics Education
XXXXXXXXXX
XXXXXXXXXX
XXXXXXXXXXXXX

```
Phone:    XXX-XXX-XXXX
Email:    XXXXXXX@XXXXXXXXXXX
Fax:      XXX-XXX-XXXX
```

```
>>> Item number 92, dated 96/02/15 16:21:41 — ALL
Date:            Thu, 15 Feb 1996 16:21:41 -0500
Reply-To:        "Precalc/Development Math Curriculum Teaching Methods,
                 Research" <PRECALC@VMB.IPFW.INDIANA.EDU>
Sender:          "Precalc/Development Math Curriculum Teaching Methods,
                 Research" <PRECALC@VMB.IPFW.INDIANA.EDU>
From:            "XXXXXXXXXXXXXX" <XXXXXXX53@XXXXXXXX>
Subject:         Re: good graphing software
```

Have you tried Theorist from Maple? Much easier than Mathematica.

This is exactly the sort of dialog we were hoping to see. We could now follow up with a personal note to the authors of these messages in order to pursue things on a more personal level. Or we could try to plunder PRECALC for more information by conducting additional keyword searches. And, of course, we could always try our luck with another archive.

When you are just starting out, it makes sense to explore a lot of archives. With experience, you will develop a feel for the so-called "curve of diminishing returns" that tells you when enough is enough. Try to develop a feel for where you are on the curve of diminishing returns. If you spend too much time reaping too few benefits, you are not spending your time wisely. See Figure 4.2.

Keep in mind that the Search and Getpost commands apply only to listserv archives. You may find an archive that is maintained by some other type of mailing list software, in which case different commands will apply. Always look for online documentation and follow any instructions you can find.

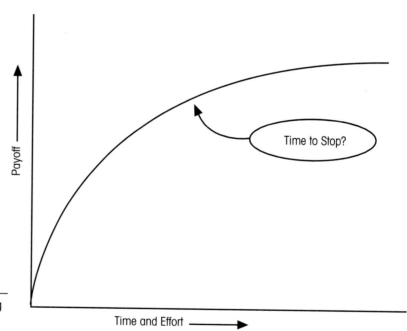

FIG. 4.2

The Curve of Diminishing Returns

Retrieving E-mail Notebook Archives

The keyword search described in the last section can be very useful if you are looking for posts about a particular item and you can identify some useful keywords that index relevant messages effectively. Another way to tap into old e-mail is through the use of **weekly mail notebooks**. For example, suppose a specific event occurred on a particular date and you want to review all of the e-mail posted to a list concerning that news item. If you know the exact date, you can retrieve all of the messages sent to the list on that day and after.

   To retrieve a weekly notebook for a list, start by asking the list for an index of all of the available notebook files. Send an **Index command** to the list command address:

```
index <name-of-list>
```

When we send this to the server for the PRECALC list, we receive a file that starts out like this:

```
*
*    NOTEBOOK archives for the list
*    (Weekly notebook)
*

   PRECALC LOG9507A    ALL OWN V    77   365 95/07/05 16:16:35 Started on
                                    Sat, 1 Jul 1995 16:30:26 -0700
   PRECALC LOG9507B    ALL OWN V    7781 95/07/10 15:12:18 Started on
                                    Thu, 6 Jul 1995 10:46:14 -0700
   PRECALC LOG9507C    ALL OWN V    78167 95/07/20 00:43:23 Started on
                                    Tue, 18 Jul 1995 01:41:12 -0400
```

These are the first three entries in a long list of notebook files. By examining the dates, we can decide which ones to retrieve. If we want to get the notebook for the first week of July 1995, for example, we ask for it with the command

```
get precalc LOG9507A
```

In general, you can retrieve a notebook file with the **Get command**:

```
get name-of-list <filename>
```

where `filename` is the name of the log file found in the notebook index. All of these commands must go to the command address for the list in question.

Sometimes you may find it useful to start an archive search on the basis of keywords and then complete the search by retrieving notebook files to cover the periods for which posts containing your keywords were found. A follow-up with notebook files will allow you to see entire conversational threads and the surrounding context for specific messages. Sometimes the best results can be obtained through the use of both keyword and notebook searches.

4.9 ▶ More Internet Abuse

After you subscribe to a few mailing lists, you may notice that you start getting spammed more often. Sometimes a spam message makes it onto the list itself through a security hole. Most of the time, it comes to your e-mail address directly. Sometimes list subscribers will spam a mailing list out of ignorance because they just saw a virus warning (usually a bogus one) or a call for action and they thought they should pass it on. Just make sure you don't add to the problem by forwarding any spam yourself.

Before commercial interests moved onto the Internet, Netizens were extremely sensitive to anything that smacked of commercial advertising. Even today, people are reluctant to endorse specific products or discuss products by name. Some lists maintain separate secondary mailing lists dedicated to product announcements and product discussions. In this way, list participants can decide for themselves if they want to see these messages.

Since the commercialization of the Internet, there has been a marked increase in commercial spamming by people who do not respect Netiquette. Advocates for commercial interests argue that the Internet has to change and that the original Internet culture is no longer appropriate for the Internet of today. Proponents for the opposing view argue that e-mail is in peril because of the time it can take to sift through massive quantities of junk mail. Others argue that spam is a privacy violation and laws should be created to stop the practice before the Internet degenerates into a digital nightmare of unrestrained commercialism. Whatever happens, the problem of spamming is bound to get worse before it gets better, so it is important for people to voice their opposition to spamming.

Chapter 3 showed how to register a complaint when you get spammed. It is a good idea to notify appropriate administrators. However, you can take other steps to protect yourself from the annoyance and distraction of spam. When you start to get spammed on a daily or almost-daily basis, you will probably feel ready for strategic warfare. To save yourself from too much aggravation, you can wage a preemptive strike against spam.

Whenever technology creates new problems, we naturally look to technology to solve those same problems. In the world of software, strikes and counter-strikes follow one another like night and day. In fact, you've already been introduced to a software weapon that will help you keep your inbox clear of junk—automated mail routing, which can help you control heavy e-mail traffic (see E-mail Tip #8 in Chapter 3). Automated routing can also work to identify likely spam messages in order to yank them out of your inbox and away from your view.

If you have a mailer that supports automated routing, you can set up filter rules that watch for spam on the basis of both **Subject:** fields, **From:** fields, and message bodies. To set up some spam filter rules, first create a mail folder in which you can save all of the possible spam. Then write some rules to save suspected spam in the spam folder. It is important to save these messages rather than just delete them because you can't be 100% certain that all of the mail picked up by the filter rules will be spam. You should periodically scan the mail that gets routed into your spam folder to make sure something legitimate didn't get picked up by mistake.

You can make up your own rules based on text strings that you think will work. You can also collect domain names from spam messages that escape your filter in order to lock out anything that comes from one of these domains in the future. Filter rules based on domain names are moderately risky because one spamming incident from a specific domain does not mean that that ISP condones spamming or that all users in that domain are mail spammers. This is why you have to check your spam folder on a regular basis in case something legitimate gets caught in the filter. If you find that a specific filter rule is responsible for a lot of poor routing decisions, you might want to remove that filter rule.

If you would rather not take the time to create your own filters, you can create a spam filter based on published lists of domain names that have been associated with spamming activity. Adam Boettiger is the moderator for the I-Advertising Digest, a moderated discussion on Internet advertising, marketing, and online commerce (see `http://www.exposure-usa.com/i-advertising`). He has posted his own filter rules for anyone who wants to try a ready-made spam filter. Visit Adam's anti-spam Web site at `http://www.exposure-usa.com/email/spam.html` to see his most current list of filter rules and more timely information about the fight against spam. A spam filter is a good way to reduce the amount of garbage you have to handle each day. And it just might save your sanity when the spam gets out of hand.

A large number of commercial spam messages can be picked up with a handful of keyword filters. The following rules (adapted from Boettiger's filter) are good spam detectors:

```
Subject Contains: !!!
Body Contains: $$
```

```
Body Contains:  !!!
Body Contains:  OPPORTUNITY
Body Contains:  FREE
Body Contains:  MONEY
```

Note that filters based on domain names are inherently dangerous because legitimate users can also subscribe to most of these ISPs. ***The inclusion of a domain name in a spam filter does not mean that the associated ISP necessarily condones or encourages spamming practices.*** It just means that spam activities have been traced to the site; spamming from that site may (or may not) happen again.

Just How Good Is a Spam Filter?	It takes some time to create a set of filter rules like the ones suggested by Adam Boettiger. Is it worth the effort? To find out, I took Boettiger's rules and applied them to 76 recent spam messages from my own inbox. Of the 76 messages, 44 (58%) were caught by the filter.

It takes some time to create a set of filter rules like the ones suggested by Adam Boettiger. Is it worth the effort? To find out, I took Boettiger's rules and applied them to 76 recent spam messages from my own inbox. Of the 76 messages, 44 (58%) were caught by the filter.

Interestingly, only 23 of my 76 messages were trapped by Boettiger's domain rules, even though he listed 150 domains. An examination of the **From:** headers showed that my 76 messages came from 61 unique domain names. Using my own spam sampling, I could add 36 new domains to Boettiger's list. 15 additional messages were trapped by the single rule "Body Contains: !!!".

Boettiger reports that his filter traps 98% of his spam, so it appears that optimal filtering requires customized filter rules based on collected spam samples and safe keyword candidates. Offending domains undoubtedly shift over time, so even a very effective filter will probably lose its effectiveness if it is never updated with new domain rules.

If spam is driving you crazy, set up a spam filter and see how it does. You'll feel better when you see large hunks of spam getting sucked out of your inbox.

There are additional strategies for dealing with spam if you want to recruit more software for your cause. For example, a program called "Spam Hater" can help you if you run Windows. See the Internet 101 Web pages for a pointer to Spam Hater. Those pages also include other Web pointers related to spam and spam control.

Spam is a problem that has aroused the ire and passion of many Netizens. You may find it reassuring to see how many people are working to eliminate spam from the Internet.

If you want to experiment with spam filters, be careful to monitor the spam that you trap in case some legitimate messages get caught in the filter. A filter based on "FREE" in the message body may trap a lot of spam, but how many legitimate messages will also get picked up by that same rule? For some people, this particular rule may work well, while for others it might be a disaster. People need to tune their own filters, since everyone reads different kinds of e-mail.

WATCH YOUR SPAM FOLDER!

PROBLEMS AND EXERCISES

Because the more active e-mail archives "turn over" their messages every six months or so, exercises designed around e-mail archives tend to become obsolete in a matter of months. This is one time when it makes sense to maintain some exercises online so that they can be kept current for you. There are nevertheless many questions that do not rely on specific e-mail archives that can change over time; the problems included here reflect that. You will find additional problems in the Internet 101 Web Pages.

1. Explain why there are two e-mail addresses for each mailing list. What type of messages should be sent to each one?

2. Explain how to subscribe to the listserv ducks@high.water.net. Does the Subscribe command go into the subject header or the message body? What exactly is the Subscribe command? Where should it be sent?

3. Describe two ways to keep the messages from a high-volume mailing list from cluttering your inbox.

4. What does "lurk before you leap" mean? Why is it a good idea to lurk before you leap?

5. If you hear about a scary new virus on the Internet, should you post a message about it on all of your mailing lists? Explain.

6. How can you protect your privacy when you subscribe to a listserv?

7. Roughly what percentage of all subscribers are likely to be active participants on any given mailing list?

8. If someone posts a question on a mailing list and nobody replies, does that mean no one on the list knows the answer? Explain.

9. Why should you always save the welcome message you receive when you first subscribe to a mailing list?

10. Explain how to find out if a listserv has a searchable public archive.

The following exercises refer to the game plan for online exploration from Chapter 1.

11. **[Hands On]** For each of the three target topics that you selected for yourself in Chapter 1, try to find at least one relevant mailing list. Subscribe to one mailing list for each topic and monitor the amount of mail that comes to you from each list for a few days. Switch to the digest option for any list that is generating more than five messages a day.

12. **[Hands On]** If any list that you found in Exercise 11 is inactive or does not address the topic you had in mind, unsubscribe from it and see if you can find a better list.

13. **[Hands On]** For each list, try to retrieve a listing of all of the list's subscribers. How many subscribers are on each of your lists?

14. **[Hands On]** Examine any e-mail addresses you see on posted list messages on your three lists and watch for addresses from other countries. How many different countries can you identify in the space of a week? Is one of your lists more internationally active than the others?

15. **[Hands On]** See if you can download a weekly notebook from one of your lists. Compare the amount of traffic on the list now to the amount of traffic on it a year ago.

16. **[Hands On]** Do any of your lists maintain searchable archives? Make up a question and see if you can answer it on the basis of keyword searches. Were you able to find an answer? How many keywords did you try? How many messages from the archive did you read?

17. **[Hands On]** Experiment with variations on your keywords and see how this affects your search results. Can you narrow your search (reduce the number of hits) and expand it (increase the number of hits) by manipulating your keywords?

18. **[Hands On]** After monitoring one of your lists for a week or so, post a message. Depending on the nature of the list, this could be an introductory message or a request for information. How many people respond to your message? How many responses are sent to you personally, and how many are sent to the list as a whole?

19. **[Hands On]** After monitoring your three lists for a week or two, see if any of the lists have shown you instances of Internet abuse. Have you been spammed yet? Have you seen any flame wars? Have you seen a list administrator intervene or make any announcements?

20. **[Hands On]** Have you exchanged any personal e-mail with someone you met on one of your mailing lists? If so, do you think you've found a friend, or is it unlikely that the two of you will exchange e-mail again? Can you make any generalizations about the people who are subscribed to your three lists? Do there seem to be any clear differences in these user populations?

THE WORLD WIDE WEB

5

"Chance is always powerful. Let your hook be always cast; in the pool where you least expect it, there will be a fish."

- OVID

THE INTERNET 101 WEB PAGES

- An Internet Hunt
- Web Browsers Online
- Web Search Engines
- Of General Interest
- Scholarship on the Web
- How to Cite Online Resources
- How to Learn More HTML

Hypertext and Multimedia

5.1

If the Internet corresponds to the invention of the wheel, then the Web must be a Corvette Stingray. More than anything else, the Web was responsible for bringing the Internet out of the laboratory and into the living room. At its best, the Web combines everything that is near and dear to American sensibilities: a novel technology; flashy, creative graphics; millions of places to visit; a frontier mentality; breathtaking speed for a price; information designed for short attention spans; and more than a few get-rich-quick schemes. The Web captured the imagination of the media, spawned excitement within the educational establishment, and encouraged middle-class families to get online. Channel surfers turned into Web surfers, and inexpensive Internet access became a real estate commodity.

Some of the dust has started to settle, and reasonable questions are being asked about the true value of the Web. No one would deny that the Web has been hyped and that people need to be realistic about what it really offers. The Web may seem miraculous, but so did radio and television when they first appeared. The Web is a lot like radio and television insofar as it is yet another communication medium. In fact, it is a curious blend of television's graphical broadcast capabilities with the interactiveness of the telephone. Relatively few people can create a TV show, but almost anyone can create a Web page that can be viewed by millions of people. The Web challenges the publishing establishment by making it possible for almost anyone to be a publisher. This encourages unbridled innovation, but it also creates an overwhelming morass of material devoid of quality control. Anyone who wants to use the Web as serious source of quality information must learn to watch for indicators of responsible scholarship and reporting. Quality information sources are plentiful on the Web and the very best resources are readily identifiable.

People who thought their home computer was limited to the offerings of commercial software manufacturers were suddenly able to access commercial services, online news, an alternative to prime-time television, a vast array of educational materials, and free high-quality software. A remarkable array of resources are out there on the Internet. The Web simply makes it easier to check them out.

Many things had to converge in order for the Web to materialize. When all of the key components fell into place around 1994, the Web assumed a life of its own:

- Powerful, inexpensive computers
- Widespread access to the Internet
- An easy-to-learn language (HTML)
- The combination of HTML and graphics
- Easy-to-use and readily available Web browsers
- Attention from the mass media

If any one of these had been absent, the Web would never have taken off the way it did. Interestingly, it was more of a grassroots phenomenon than a carefully planned innovation. The Web took both computer scientists and commercial software designers by surprise. It was a technological firestorm that

In April 1996, the Internet Archive Project (`http://www.archive.org/`) took a "snapshot" of the Web by saving copies of all of the publicly available Web pages, including video and audio segments. The complete collection takes up about 1.5 terabytes (TB) of storage. Note: (1TB = 1,024GB = 1,048,576MB = 1,073,741,824K= 1,099,511,627,776 bytes).

The Library of Congress has been estimated to contain about 20TB of text, although it is difficult to say exactly because these holdings are not online.

The Internet Archive Project is possible in part because of falling costs associated with digital storage devices. It costs about $200 to store 1GB of data on a hard drive but only about $20 to store 1GB on magnetic tape. Most of the Internet Archive Project is being stored on tape.

How Big Is the Web?

roared into existence without the benefit of marketing studies, commercial development, or carefully orchestrated research.

The concept of **hypertext** can be traced to an *Atlantic Monthly* article written in 1945 by Vannevar Bush entitled "As We May Think." The term "hypertext" was never used by Bush, but he described a vision for computer/human interaction that relied on associative connections and rich digital resources that could be easily distributed and retrieved. The actual term was first coined by Theodore H. Nelson in 1965. His description of the term is quite consistent with its realization in the Web. In particular, Nelson envisioned a world in which computer technology would give everyone comprehensive access to information worldwide.

Hypertext was used prior to the creation of the Web. A program called **HyperCard** was distributed for free by Apple Computer with all of its Macintosh computers starting in 1987. HyperCard users with little or no programming background could create "stacks" of cards that could be navigated by clicking buttons. Everyone was impressed by the ease with which richly linked resources could be created by a person with a minimal computer background. In addition, clip art and photographs could be easily added to HyperCard stacks in order to make them visually attractive. Many educational resources were created using HyperCard, and well-designed HyperCard stacks gave everyone a sense of just how engaging a point-and-click environment could be.

Meanwhile, on the DOS platform, millions of Windows users saw hypertext help systems in software designed by Microsoft. Taking online help one step beyond the traditional printed user's manual, Microsoft incorporated associative links to related topics by embedding hyperlinks in the text of its help pages. This made it easier to navigate relevant segments of text with a minimal amount of thrashing through text.

As useful as Hypercard and the Microsoft help systems were, they were essentially static. A stack was a closed system containing all of the links it would ever have. Similarly, each help system was bounded by the topics deemed relevant for the software application. The potential power of hypertext could not be fully realized until multiple hypertext documents generated by different authors could be linked to one another in a dynamically evolving environment.

The inclusion of multiple documents was first seen in CD-ROM products like the Microsoft Bookshelf, which bundled a number of desktop library resources into a single CD-ROM. Interconnecting hot button links were inserted to make navigation across multiple resources relatively effortless. The vast storage capacity of CD-ROMs made it possible to include graphics, video, and sound clips as well, thereby creating the first **multimedia applications** for home computers. But even these massive resource compilations were constrained by the design decisions of the CD-ROM manufacturers. No matter how much material was included, each CD-ROM was a static resource. It was always the same each time you looked at it.

All of these hypertext applications were known to computer users in the 1980s, and the stage was set for the development of the Web. All that was missing was network connectivity across many computers. That connectivity was already in place in the form of a rapidly expanding Internet community. But no one had yet pulled it all together. The first person to add network connectivity to hypertext was Tim Berners-Lee, a researcher at the European Particle Physics Laboratory (CERN). In 1989, Berners-Lee wrote a proposal for a hypertext system that would make it easy for physicists to share research ideas and results despite the geographical distances that separated them.

A very primitive text-based Web browser was written by Berners-Lee in 1990. A **text-based Web browser** displays text and text-based hyperlinks, but does not display any graphics. By 1991, the Berners-Lee browser was being used extensively by researchers at CERN and word of network-based hypertext began to spread. By early 1993, fifty Web servers were operating and programmers were talking about how to add graphics to the Web. A **graphical Web browser** displays graphics as well as text, and the National Center for Supercomputing Applications (NCSA) in Champaign, Illinois, released the first graphical browser, MOSAIC, designed by Marc Andreesen. Mosaic was released in April of 1993, and the Web became synonymous with Mosaic (people used to talk about Mosaic pages instead of Web pages). By the end of 1993, the number of Web servers exceeded 500.

In 1994 the media began to talk about the potential of the Web and entrepreneurs took notice. Marc Andreesen left NCSA to take part in a commercial venture, the Mosaic Communications Corporation, which later became Netscape Communications Corporation.

Once hyptertext authors could connect their creations to each other via a computer network, the world of hypertext took on a new dynamic dimension, as pointers to new resources could be easily incorporated into old resources. The Web began to evolve in an organic fashion. Its rapid development was also encouraged by the user-friendly feel of Web browsers like Mosaic and Navigator and the relatively minimal overhead associated with simple Web page design. Most people who saw the Web could appreciate its potential. Further, anyone who wanted to add something to the Web could do so without learning a programming language. It was new, it was easy, and it was fun. It was the "killer app" (killer application) that no one saw coming.

The Web is an inherently democratic medium, exploding with free-wheeling content that stimulates innovative experiments in communication. It is viewed as a challenge to traditional broadcast media by some people, and a threat by others. For commercial publishers, it raises some thorny questions regarding copyright law. However, many educators are entranced by the potential they see in wired classrooms. In addition, many people have discovered how entertaining it can be to surf the Web in search of quirky and unexpected bits of "infotainment."

Some of the fallout from the Web is less than wonderful. Security problems have prompted large corporations to build bullet-proof "firewalls" around their in-house intranets. People operating in less secure environments have been stung from time to time by malicious programmers who know how to exploit the weaknesses of a given Web browser or a poorly protected Web server. Even the powerhouse software giant Microsoft couldn't build a Web browser that was immune to security problems. This general lack of security has also made the public understandably wary of online credit card transactions.

For the people who would like to use the Web as a serious information resource, the openly democratic nature of the Web undermines the credibility of everything out there. When anyone can publish a work and distribute it as freely as anyone else, there are no editors on hand to squelch information that is unreliable, questionable, or downright misleading. It may be intoxicating to have fast and easy access to millions of documents on thousands of topics, but what good is any of it if you can't distinguish fact from fiction?

To make the Web an effective research tool for students, business people, and professionals, new skills are needed that go beyond the point-and-click mastery of a particular Web browser. Responsible information consumers need to assess the reliability of their online sources. While this is true for everything on the Internet, it is especially true of the Web.

In the traditional world of printed matter, we expect publishers to strive for high standards with respect to reliable information. Fiction is always identifiable as fiction, even when it mixes in facts based on real people or historical events. We have, therefore, become complacent with the traditional print media. Editors are paid to detect fraudulent materials and protect us from falsehoods and misinformation. We trust editors to do their job well, and we take their presence for granted. It is therefore a bit jarring and annoying to discover that no one is out there to protect us from bad information on the Web.

Some people have thrown up their hands and declared the Web useless because it offers so much questionable material and, in some cases, outright garbage. They claim that if you are truly serious about researching a topic, your local library is still your best bet. If the Web offered us nothing more than the contents of newspapers and special interest magazines and books, all mixed up with less credible materials, then you might indeed wonder if ease of access justifies all of the extra work you must now go through in order to assess reliability.

In fact, there is more to the Web than the online versions of traditional print materials. There are thousands of experts who post fascinating pages based on years of experience and hard-won expertise. Some of these people are wholly legitimate and can be trusted. Moreover, many would never publish a book or even write a short article for a magazine, but they are writing their own Web pages. It would be a shame to reject their wisdom just because you need to exercise caution. You also can find lecture notes for college courses and lovingly assembled resource pages on everything from the health problems of dachshunds to sheet music emporia for musicians. Science fiction fans can find spirited discussions of their favorite authors, and new mothers can look for advice on solving all kinds of parenting problems (including whether to let children surf the Web).

Many organizations post timely information that would never be circulated in any other way because of the costs associated with printing, mailing, and maintaining membership lists. Special interest groups on the Web can get their information out to a much wider audience, including casual Web surfers, than would be possible through any other medium. Professional print newsletters are generally produced by at least one full-time employee who is paid to lay out a newsletter, push it through production, and get it mailed out to subscribers on a regular basis. With the Web, it is possible for a computer-literate person to create a newsletter complete with photographs and clip art and get it online in the space of a few hours. Many online newsletters are created by students, house-bound parents, and hobbyists working in their spare time just for the fun of it.

The Web is remarkable in many ways, but the single most remarkable feature of the Web is its open-ended hypertext. Even traditionally conceived documents assume a new dimension when pointers to related materials are inserted into the text. A richly linked document can become the basis for an educational adventure that is effortless and efficient (if one can only maintain focus and stay on topic). So don't be too quick to reject the unique offerings of the Web just because navigating it requires caution.

It is wonderful to find a leading-edge technology that is so inclusive and open to the participation of so many people. It is also horribly frustrating to waste time wading through questionable material in an effort to find a resource that can be trusted. All URLs may be created equal, but some documents are more valuable than others. The associative interconnectivity of the Web allows the sheep and the wolves to coexist in close proximity, and there are no trusty sheepdogs in sight.

There are, nevertheless, some good strategies you can use to navigate the Web and cope with what you find. It takes more than knowing the basic navigational commands of a Web browser to become a truly intelligent Web user, but the little extra effort to learn how will pay off. You just need to understand that there's more to this business of Web navigation than a few point-and-click buttons on a slick-looking Web browser. New environments demand new ways of thinking. The Web is pressuring its first generation of digital explorers to adjust to a new medium that no classroom ever prepared them for. Whenever new territories are being explored, it is impossible to say what tomorrow may bring. You could stumble onto a gold mine or get stuck in a swamp. Either way, you're a pioneer.

Web Browser Tips and Tricks   ◀ 5.2

For many people, a Web browser and a mail program are all they need to tap the resources of the Internet. Recognizing a need for "one-stop shopping," software designers have made Web browsers that can do more than just browse the Web. For example, Navigator and Microsoft Internet Explorer™ both have added mail programs and news readers to their software packages.

In this chapter, only Web-specific browser features are considered. But even within the Web, there is a convergence of Internet protocols that gives the Web a "one-stop shopping" feel all its own. From some Web pages, you can send e-mail (at least to the author of the page). Also, there are hypertext links that start up Telnet sessions, take you into Gopher space, and enable FTP file transfers. What used to require five separate software clients can now be accomplished with a single Web browser. This is why a Web address is called a Uniform Resource Locator (URL). URLs are truly universal because they allow you to visit Internet resources that predate the Web and that rely on older protocols.

Universal Resource Locators

Most addresses on the Web begin with the prefix http:// (Hypertext Transfer Protocol). This protocol is reserved for hypertext files located on Web servers. But you can also visit files on different types of servers. Here are some of the other URLs you will run into on the Web:

gopher://	Pointer to a Gopher resource
ftp://	Pointer to an FTP site
telnet://	Pointer to a Telnet server
news:	Pointer to your local news server

The news: URL doesn't include the double slashes because it points to whatever news server is available on your host machine or the host machine into which you are dialing. When you configure your Web browser, you can tell it which news server to contact whenever it sees a news: URL. All of the other URLs refer to absolute addresses that are the same for everyone. One other URL prefix you might see is https://, which refers to a "secure" Web server. With all of these different protocols available on the Web, a URL really is a universal address.

This convergence of previously disjoint Internet protocols on the Web is one reason why many people say the Web is swallowing up the rest of the Internet. If you can go anywhere you need to go from inside the Web, why bother with other clients? Much of the Web's appeal lies in its ability to unify and simplify a multitude of older client/server capabilities.

Although Web browsers are very easy to use without much instruction, some useful tricks will make your browsing activities more efficient and less time-consuming:

- Change your default home page.
- Use the Find command.
- Use your history list.
- Use bookmarks.
- Abort a download if you get stuck.
- Reset your memory cache.
- Reload Web pages for updates.
- Turn off graphics.
- 404 Not Found (But don't give up).
- Avoid peak hours.

These tips are discussed in the following sections.

Change Your Default Home Page

Each browser is configured to visit a default home page every time you start up. There is an excellent chance that the default home page set up for you is not the best one for you. An alternative might be a Web page that contains lots of links to places you like to visit each time you get on the Web.

To change your default home page in Navigator, follow these steps:

1. From the Options menu, click General Preferences.
2. Click the Appearance tab and then click Home Page Location.
3. Click the Home Page Location text button and type in the URL you want to use.
4. Close the dialog box by clicking OK.

Internet Explorer has a similar setting that you can reach from the Edit menu and clicking Options. To reset the default home page for Internet Explorer, you have to be visiting the page you want at the time you change the setting.

Use the Find Command

If you know exactly where you want to go, you can often use the Find command to take you there immediately. Most browsers have a keyword search command that lets you enter a text string and go directly to the first instance of that string on the current Web page. There may also be a Find Next command that takes you to the next occurrence of that same string. The Find command can also be useful on long Web pages when you are interested in a specific topic and want to read only about that topic. Use the Find command whenever possible.

Use Your History List

If you really want to save time on the Web, you should master some navigational tricks associated with hyperlinks. For example, it is easy to wander off down a path of links on some digression that takes you deeper and deeper into a region of the Web that is not really relevant to your original topic. Eventually, you decide to get back to business and you need to retrace a lot of links back to some page you were on 10 or 20 minutes ago (possibly an hour ago, if you have no sense of time). You can do this by hitting the Back button a dozen times. Or, you can look at your **history list**. All Web browsers have a History command that will take you to a display of all of the pages you've visited. Consult this list and click an address to go back to an earlier page. Experiment with your history page and get into the habit of using it whenever you need to retrace a lot of steps. It might save you from getting distracted all over again on your way home.

Use Bookmarks

If you spend much time on the Web, you'll likely find many Web pages you'll want to revisit regularly. You could start a listing of their URLs and some notes about each one. Or, you can take advantage of your browser's **bookmark file**. In this file, you store pointers to the sites that you want to revisit. You can add a URL to your bookmark file whenever you are viewing the page or a pointer to the page you want to save. To set up a bookmark file in Navigator, do this:

1. Visit the page you want to mark.
2. From the Bookmark menu, click Add Bookmark (or just type Command-D).

Your bookmark file will display each entry using a name for each URL. Once a bookmark has been added to the bookmark file, you simply click the bookmark entry whenever you want to return to that particular URL. You also can edit these names as you wish. To edit a particular bookmark entry in Navigator, do this:

1. From the Windows menu, click Bookmarks.
2. Highlight the bookmark entry.
3. From the Item menu, click Edit Bookmark. You will see a window that tells you the name of the bookmark, its URL, when you added it to your bookmark file, and when you last visited it.
4. You can add a more detailed description of the site or change its name from inside this window.

The only problem with a bookmark file is that it can grow very quickly and get out of control. Your browser will allow you to delete bookmark entries, but you have to take the time to periodically review your bookmark file and weed out obsolete entries that are no longer being used. A good browser will also let you organize your bookmark entries in a hierarchy so that you can categorize your bookmarks for easier reference. To do this in Navigator, you would:

1. From the Bookmark window, click Item/Insert Folder. A dialog window opens.
2. In the dialog, name the new folder. The name will be inserted at the top level of your bookmark list.

You can then place bookmarks in the folder or put the folder itself inside another folder with drag-and-drop operations inside the bookmark window.

If you collect a lot of bookmarks, your Bookmark window will become an extensive URL directory. Keep it well organized and don't hesitate to prune it as your information needs change.

It is tempting to save in your bookmark file everything that could ever be of interest to you. However, doing this will result in an unwieldy bookmark file. A Web page deserves to be in your bookmark file only if you really do intend to visit the page frequently. If a pointer is good to save but you expect it to be useful only for infrequent visits, then it is better to store it elsewhere.

ADD BOOKMARKS WITH CARE

Abort a Download If You Get Stuck

Sometimes, you click a link and your browser appears to get stuck during the download. This can happen for a number of reasons, and it happens with all browsers. If your browser has a status line showing how much progress has been made with the download, you will sometimes see it freeze and appear to be dead. Check your browser for a command that aborts downloads. In Navigator, this is the Stop button. In the Internet Explorer, look for a button containing a page with a red X. With some browsers, issuing this abort command mysteriously makes the page appear (as if it had been waiting for you to ask). With Navigator, the page will sometimes pop up for you if you click the same link again right after aborting.

Reset Your Memory Cache

Have you noticed that it usually takes a long time to download a page the first time you visit it, but then subsequent visits to the same page happen very fast? This is because of the **memory cache**. A memory cache is a reserved block of memory that is dedicated to a specific function. In this case, the memory cache is set up to store Web pages. Whenever you view a Web page for the first time, it is downloaded from the server specified by the URL. The files that make up the page are then stored locally, in the memory cache, just in case you decide to visit the page again later. Many Web pages are visited more than once (for example, whenever you use the Back command), so it makes sense to store the page locally. If you later ask to see a page that is present in the memory cache, your browser will pull up the local copy instead of returning to the server to retrieve the same page. The cache will store as many pages as it can. Older pages—those downloaded earlier in the session—are erased to make space for newer ones—those downloaded later in the session. The longer a page has been in the cache without being accessed, the more likely it is to be erased so that a newer page can be saved.

All Web browsers are designed to take advantage of a memory cache, and you can optimize this feature for your particular machine. The default cache size for Navigator is 5MB. If you are on a time-sharing machine, make sure your cache disk does not exceed your memory quota. You will want to reduce the disk quota if your total memory quota is 5MB. If you are working on a home computer, you can increase or decrease your disk cache depending on the size of your hard drive. In Navigator, do this:

1. From the Options menu, click Network Preferences. A window will pop up with information about your disk cache.

2. Increase or decrease the disk cache by clicking on the up or down arrow.

If you revisit many pages that contain hefty graphics, a large disk cache will save you from having to download these more than once.

Reload Web Pages for Updates

Because Web pages can be stored locally, you may want to turn off the memory cache feature, or at least override it, for specific files. For example, suppose you are viewing a page that is updated every 5 minutes with new sports results. If you go back to the page that was stored in your memory cache, you will see the original version of the page without any updates. You can override the local version of the page by clicking the **Reload command**. This command tells your browser to go back to the original URL address and download the current version of the page, even though an older version may be present in the memory cache.

Whenever a page is subject to change, you need to make sure you are viewing the most recent version of the page. All browsers give you a Reload command for handling these situations.

Turn Off Graphics

When the Web gets pokey, you'll find that the pages with lots of graphics are always the slowest to load. This is because graphics files are relatively large and consume a fair amount of bandwidth. If you don't have a fast modem or enough memory on your machine or if the Internet is very busy, you may find yourself waiting too often for some Web pages. This is no fun if you are used to faster performance or if you are simply in a hurry. One way you can speed things up is by trading the graphics for faster downloads. Sometimes you don't need to see the graphics. They may be purely cosmetic. Or you may have already seen a page a hundred times and the graphics are no longer important to you.

All the graphical browsers have a switch to turn off graphics. Each page will then be displayed with a placeholder to indicate where a graphic would have been. Because your browser never requested the graphic's file, you don't have to wait for that graphic to appear. In Navigator, go to the Options menu and toggle the AutoLoad Images command off. In Internet Explorer, go to the Edit menu, click Options, and then click the Web Content tab. Look for a box marked Show pictures, and click it to turn pictures on and off (an X turns them on and a blank turns them off). If you've turned off all the graphics and you decide that you must see a specific image, click its placeholder to download and display that one file. Most browsers support image downloads-on-demand in this way.

404 Not Found (But Don't Give Up)

From time to time, everyone sees this error message: 404 Not Found. It means that the requested URL was not found on the specified server. This might mean that the page has been completely removed from the server, in which case you can't download it. Or the page may have been moved, in which case you might be able to find it at its new location (if you know that new location). Sometimes authors rearrange their files and file directories; this can result in obsolete URLs. But there are some tricks you can try before you give up all hope of ever seeing the lost page.

Suppose you try linking to `http://www.unv.edu/lib/launcch/oct96n.htm` and you get the 404 Not Found error message. Start by examining the URL to see if the Web page might be accessible from a related Web page. Following is a diagram of a URL. The first segment gives the name of the Web server. The last segment is the name of the file in which the page resides. Everything in between are names of folders or subdirectories.

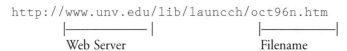

```
http://www.unv.edu/lib/launcch/oct96n.htm
        |—————— |          |————————|
         Web Server               Filename
```

If this link used to be operational, you don't have to worry about the possibility of typographical errors. Otherwise, it might be worth trying the URL with `launch` instead of `launcch` just in case there's a typographical error in your typed URL.

Assuming there are no errors in the URL, try to backtrack to a related Web page. Sometimes a home page or page index can be found by going to a subdirectory. In this case, there are two subdirectories to try: the subdirectory `lib` and the subdirectory `launcch` that sits under `lib`. To visit these, try these URLs:

```
http://www.unv.edu/lib/
http://www.unv.edu/lib/launcch/
```

One of these may give you a link or a path to the old Web page. This often works in a large institutional site or one that houses many Web pages. Large Web sites are periodically reorganized into new subdirectories and then old URLs become obsolete. When all else fails, see if the server has a Web page at the root address:

```
http://www.unv.edu/
```

If the site still exists, there should be a high-level home page at this address that can point you in the right direction.

Avoid Peak Hours

Just as we all try to avoid the rush hours on major highways, it is wise to avoid peak usage periods on the Internet as well. The heaviest usage periods are generally during the middle of the day on weekdays. Many people do recreational browsing from their workplace during the lunch hour. Try to hit the Web early in the morning or late at night. You'll be surprised how much faster your response times can be. To experience the Internet at its fastest, surf on Sunday mornings.

Study your Web browser's documentation and make sure you know how to do the following:

1. Change your default home page.

2. Search a Web page for a keyword.

3. View your history list and use it for navigation.

4. Add a URL to your bookmark file.

5. Remove a URL from your bookmark file.

6. Abort a download if you get stuck.

7. Find the default settings for your memory cache.

8. Change your memory cache settings (as needed).

9. Turn off graphics.

10. Copy a Web page to a file on your hard drive.

Finding Things on the Web   5.3

Once you've mastered the basics of Web navigation, you can start to put the Web to work for you. This is where some people become frustrated because the wealth of material on the Web makes it difficult to find exactly what they want. Indeed, you may never know for sure if what you want is really out there because it may be so difficult to find. How do you go about finding information on the Web? When should you give up and stop wasting your time? Can you know beforehand what's out there?

These are the questions that separate satisfied users from disgruntled quitters. This text covers the tools and the strategies you need, but you will need to invest some time learning and using them to make them pay off. Experience with the Web is a big factor; you may feel frustrated in the beginning. Be patient. You'll find that it all becomes easier with time and experience.

Once you get going, you will find that there are many directions to explore and many skills to acquire. See Figure 5.1. There are two major tools for locating information on the Web: **search engines** and **subject trees**. These are discussed shortly. In bookstores you can also find published directories of URLs that may or may not be useful, depending on your specific needs. You will need to learn how to sharpen your browsing activities to make your explorations more productive and exercise some self-discipline in order to keep your time online focused. You will discover the power of serendipity on the Web and how to exploit human contacts for quality resources. I show you how later in this chapter.

You also will learn to mine mailing lists and other Internet resources for good Web pointers, and you will learn how to find **clearinghouses**, where considerable effort has already been put into collecting lots of pointers to reliable information. This, too, is covered in this chapter.

Last but not least, you will discover that time and patience are essential ingredients when it comes to the Web. You can often find exactly what you want, but it might not happen in time for an urgent deadline. Always give yourself as much time as possible when you hunt for treasures on the Web. It takes a little effort and patience to find the best of the Web, but anyone can learn to be an effective Web researcher. As usual, you will learn most effectively when you work with materials that interest you. So throughout this chapter, you should work with your three target topics (from Chapter 1).

FIG. 5.1

There Are Many
Directions to Explore
on the Web

5.4 ▶ Search Engines

For many people, searching the Web is synonymous with using a **search engine**. If you have ever used an online card catalog to locate a book in a library, then you have some idea what to expect from the Web search engines, although search engines give you more search options and search features. Keyword search systems work best when you can tell them exactly what you are looking for. They tend to produce mixed results when you are shooting in the dark. Nevertheless, they are powerful tools that can locate resources you might never find in any other way. There are dozens of search engines for the Web, including AltaVista, Infoseek, HotBot and WebCrawler.

Software programs called **spiders** scan the Web periodically, collecting URLs. Starting with a list of "seed" URLs, these programs watch for hyperlinks to other URLs and add any new URLs not previously seen to their master list of all URLs. Each new URL is then visited in order to scan it for more URLs. Then each of those URLs is visited, and so forth and so on. Spiders collect Web pages for search engines, and the search engines send spiders out onto the Web in an effort to keep current. Each page is indexed for keyword retrieval. The results are added to massive databases of Web page indices from which you can get a fast response when you run a keyword search.

There are several search engines open to the general public. Experiment with them to get a feel for their strengths and weaknesses. As a beginner, you might be attracted to an engine that has an easy-to-use interface. Once you gain more experience, you can learn to use some special features that will help you conduct more effective searches. You will discover that not all search engines support the same search options, and you may prefer one search engine because of its special features. If you do a lot of searches, you might discover that some searches work better with one set of search options while other searches work better with a different set of search options. It takes a lot of experience to hook up specific search problems with the search engines that are most likely to give you the best results. Professional researchers always run more than one search and use multiple search engines to see if different results come back.

To use a search engine, you must first construct a **search query**. Most search engines work by matching keywords in the query against a database of Web page indices. For example, say you want to find a description of an ACLU lawsuit that you remember hearing about. You would want to use any information that you can remember in the query. Suppose the lawsuit involved a high school student in Washington state who got into trouble at school for publishing a satirical home page about the school. The ACLU supported the student on the grounds that the student's civil rights were violated when his school took punitive action. If this is all you know, you can create a query based on relevant keywords, such as the following:

ACLU high school student web page satire Washington civil rights

Search engines are generally incapable of finding the best possible document for any given query, so they are designed to retrieve a number of possible documents in order to increase the chance of finding at least one good one. A document returned in response to a query is called a **hit**, and some search engines will produce thousands of hits for a single query. You then must review the hits to find the ones that appear to be good, that is, on target, rather than bad or off base. With a large number of hits, the search engine presents hits in ranked order, based on criteria such as how many keywords were successfully matched against each document.

More Signal, Less Noise

A **false hit** is a hit that doesn't address the question you're trying to answer. All Web search engines generate a lot of false hits. A false hit isn't really an error on the part of the search engine, since the search engine is only doing exactly what it was programmed to do. One could instead argue that each false hit is really an error on the part of the user who made the query. If the user had generated a better query, the number of false hits may have been smaller.

Unfortunately, it is usually impossible to eliminate all false hits during a keyword search. The term "**noise**" is often used to describe the rate of false hits: the more false hits, the more noise. You want to increase the signal and reduce the noise when you conduct a keyword Web search. If the hit you want is number 5,872 in a ranked list of 7,329 documents, the search has succeeded in some technical sense, but probably not in any practical sense. When too much noise overwhelms a large list of hits, there is no reasonable way to zero in on whatever good hits may be present.

Many people think up two or three keywords, hand them to a search engine, and then feel disappointed when nothing relevant pops up in the first ten hits. Search engines are easy to use in the sense that anyone can think up a couple of keywords. If you want to get good results, however, you will probably have to work a little harder. Chapter 7 talks about some powerful search features that are supported by many search engines. These features are often all you need to get better search results. For now, here are some guidelines to remember when you need to come up with effective keywords for a search query:

- Five to ten keywords are better than one or two.
- Names of specific people or places can help narrow the query.
- Enter keywords in lowercase throughout unless they are proper names.
- Proper names should have the first letter capitalized.
- Include the name of an organization that might post the information you want.
- Use specific nouns that are relevant to your topic.
- Include alternative spellings or abbreviations for important names.
- Play around with variations on your query.
- If one keyword seems to be leading you astray, remove it or replace it.

One of the easier keyword search engines for beginners is Webcrawler. Go to Webcrawler at `http://Webcrawler.com/` and spend some time exploring your three target topics by entering some queries and examining the resulting hits. For each of your three topics, answer the following questions:

1. Is it easy to identify good and bad hits on the basis of the document summaries? When can you feel confident about a document on the basis of its summary?

2. Can you see why false hits are being returned? Can you explain why the search engine thought they might be good?

3. Is it easy to alter your query in order to improve your hits? Do you get better results by removing terms? Adding new terms? Replacing old terms? Give an example of a query that you were able to modify to improve your hits.

4. Which of your topics seemed easiest to search? Can you explain what made it easy?

5. Were you able to locate relevant documents for each topic? If not, was it because you couldn't find any hits or because you couldn't eliminate false hits?

While a keyword search engine can be quick and easy, it is not always the best search tool available for a given problem. *A keyword search is likely to work best if you use keywords that aren't in irrelevant documents.* For example, if in the ACLU lawsuit example given earlier you could remember the name of the student and the name of the high school, you could form a much better query for a keyword search. When the best query you can think up returns too many false hits, it is sometimes better to abandon the keyword approach and try something else.

Subject Trees 5.5

Another popular search strategy is to use a **subject tree**, or a **directory**. A subject tree is a hierarchically organized collection of categories and subcategories that can be browsed to locate specific information. Subject trees are really browsing aids because they require some exploration, but they are designed to get you where you need to go. The most popular subject tree on the Web is probably Yahoo!, which is constantly being updated and expanded.

When using a subject tree, always start from the root of the tree and branch out to more specific topics after selecting appropriate options at each decision point. For example, in the ACLU example, you know that the case involved the Internet, so you might move through a tree that lets you branch through the category headers, like this:

Internet → activism → civil rights → watchdog organizations → ACLU

Then, from the ACLU home page, you might be able to locate a description of the case in question.

A good subject tree will make it easy for you to get where you want to go without having to go back and try alternative categories. Subject trees are also advantageous in another way—they index only documents that have been checked by reviewers and accepted as legitimate sources of information. Something found in a subject tree is relatively trustworthy. Subject trees may not cover every topic under the sun, but if the information you seek is more mainstream than esoteric, a subject tree will often give you your fastest pathway to it.

Subject trees are far from perfect, however. It is difficult to design a comprehensive hierarchy in a way that seems perfectly intuitive to everyone who uses it. Different subject trees use different categories and organizational hierarchies. There is no single best hierarchy, but some are better than others. This means that some trees may be easier to navigate than others.

Another difficulty with subject trees is that storing everything that is relevant to a single topic under a single location is often impossible. For example, if you are interested in weaving, should you look under art, textiles, or crafts? Depending on exactly what you want to know, you might find relevant documents under all of these subcategories. This makes it difficult to know when you have exhausted the possibilities of the subject tree. As with all browsing activities, some creative thinking often helps.

For example, suppose you want to find resources for professional dog trainers. You want to find some recommendations for books or online documents that are useful to people who train dogs for obedience trials and conduct obedience classes for dog owners. Logically, you might think about categories associated with career development, since you want to find out what the pros know. But career development as a topic is too broad and might never narrow down to each of the different types of careers. Even if you found a career category that attempted to list them all, what are the chances of finding professional dog trainers in a list of career options?

To find information associated with dog training, you need to think less hierarchically and more associatively (see Figure 5.2). Perhaps information for professional dog trainers is too narrow. Maybe you would do better to broaden this topic to the more general one of dog training. Then you could ask who is likely to be interested in dog training in general. It seems obvious that most people who care about training dogs are people who own dogs. So

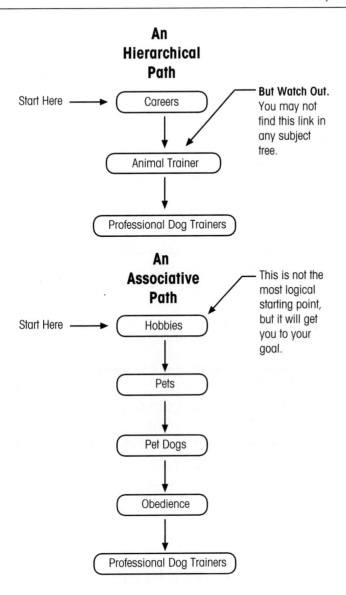

**An
Hierarchical
Path**

Start Here ⟶ (Careers)

But Watch Out. You may not find this link in any subject tree.

(Animal Trainer)

(Professional Dog Trainers)

**An
Associative
Path**

Start Here ⟶ (Hobbies)

This is not the most logical starting point, but it will get you to your goal.

(Pets)

(Pet Dogs)

(Obedience)

(Professional Dog Trainers)

FIG. 5.2

Associative Pathways and Hierarchical Pathways

now you are on the topic of dog ownership. Where should you look for information related to dog ownership? Well, most people who own dogs aren't professional trainers or breeders. They are simply people who own a dog as a pet. Information about pets is likely to be found under recreational activities or hobbies. Once you tap into this segment of a tree and locate resources specific to dogs, you are on your way. Resources about training and obedience trials will link to other resources that are more appropriate for someone with professional interests as well.

Working with subject tree traversals is an art as much as a science. The earliest branching decisions you make are crucial; they may not always take you where you want to go. Here are some general tips for conducting an effective subject tree search:

- If one path doesn't work, back up to the root and try again.
- If your ultimate interest is very narrow, consider a broader topic.
- Look for different perspectives on your topic.
- Ask yourself what sorts of people are most likely to care about your topic.
- Look for ways to approach a topic "from the side" rather than head on.

SUBJECT TREE CHECKLIST

One of the most popular subject trees is **Yahoo!** (Yet Another Hierarchical Officious Oracle). Go to Yahoo! at `http://www.yahoo.com/` and spend some time exploring it for information about your three target topics. For each of your three topics, answer the following questions:

1. How many different paths can you find that take you to relevant documents?
2. Do the different paths take you to different documents or the same ones?
3. Did you find exactly what you wanted or only something more general?

5.6 ▷ Calculated Serendipity

Serendipity is the faculty of making fortunate discoveries by accident. It is nothing to sneeze at on the Internet. You will sometimes stumble across wonderful resources when you are looking for something else. It is also possible to discover extraordinarily useful Web sites when you are just surfing for entertainment. It pays always to keep your eyes open and be on the watch for valuable URLs. They often pop up when you least expect them. These pleasant surprises are the result of serendipity. You can't count on serendipity to be there when you need it, so you have to grab it when it happens.

Site Reviews

The forces of serendipity cannot be controlled, but they can be helped along from time to time. One way to encourage serendipitous discovery is to spend some time scanning site reviews on a regular basis. There are many online newsletters that periodically produce lists of recommended Web sites. It doesn't take long to scan a mail message describing a few noteworthy Web sites, and you might learn about something that interests you. Most newsletters specialize in a broad topic of some general interest, such as education or media-related topics, so you can select a newsletter that meshes with your general interests. The people who assemble these site reviews are careful to include only sites that merit serious attention, so some amount of quality control is applied to the sites that get reviewed.

A good Web site newsletter is worth whatever time it takes to read it once a week or once a month. You shouldn't feel compelled to monitor every newsletter you can find, but one or two that mesh well with your interests are a very good time investment. Many are available as point-broadcast mailing lists. Others are distributed over the Web. Chapter 4 explained how to subscribe to two general Web site newsletters: the "Netsurfer Digest" and "The Scout Report." Keep your eyes open, and you will probably be able to find additional site reviews that address your personal interests.

Friends, Colleagues, and Strangers

Just because the Internet is a computer technology, you shouldn't overlook the human element when it comes to fortuitous discoveries. If you know people who are active on the Internet, ask them for their favorite sites and resources. People on the Internet are usually happy to talk about their experiences and help other people with useful pointers. If you talk to people who share your interests, you increase the chances of discovering sites that are valuable to you. Always ask for pointers to sites on a particular topic, since it is easy for people to reply to a request that is focused. Don't ask people for their favorite Web sites in general. The result is likely to be a very long list.

Bookmark Files

Someday celebrity profiles will include bookmark URLs. For example, ". . . Sean's favorite recreations are wind surfing, homemade chili, and cozy evenings at home with a good video. His bookmark file includes . . . ." Indeed, you can learn a lot by looking at someone's bookmark file, especially if they are experienced with the Web and careful not to let their bookmarks get out of hand. If you know someone well, you might ask for a copy of his or her bookmark file.

However, asking to see someone's bookmark file is a little forward and should probably be reserved for close acquaintances. A bookmark file can tell a lot about a person. If someone uses the Web for personal as well as professional interests, he or she might not be comfortable revealing that much personal information. One way to acknowledge this potential problem is to request a copy of the file minus any pointers that are too personal or sensitive. A good friend would probably be happy to edit his or her bookmark file for you. However, it does take some time and thought. So this is not a reasonable request to make of a stranger or someone who might feel inconvenienced by such a request.

Lost Car Keys

This is an old joke with an important moral. A drunk drops his car keys near his car and then walks halfway down the block to look for them under a street light. When asked why he's looking for his keys so far from where he lost them, he replies, "Because the light is so much better over here."

This resembles how a lot of people conduct their Web searches. They find one tool they like (often the only one they know), and then they use it all of the time regardless of whether it's the best tool for their current purposes. If you find yourself using the same search engine all of the time, or the same subject tree, remember the drunk and the street light. It may pay to try out new tools.

Search Engines and Subject Trees

All Web searches involve an element of luck. You can't control your luck, but you can enhance your chances for success by using appropriate search tools. As you become more experienced, you'll find that some search tools are better at handling certain types of queries. Some reasons for this are covered in Chapter 7. For now, here are some of the important differences between search engines and subject trees to help you decide which might be better for certain types of information:

	Subject Trees	Search Engines
Quality of URLs	Human reviewers.	No quality control.
Breadth of coverage	There can be gaps.	Spiders try to find everything.
Amount of noise	Not a problem.	Can be a big problem.
Ease of use	No study needed.	Advanced features need to be studied.
Commercial ads allowed?	None or isolated as such.	Yes, mixed in with everything else.
Obsolete links	Few or none.	Sometimes many.
Stability of results	Very stable.	Less stable.

The differences between subject trees and search engines can be important for certain types of queries. For example, suppose you want to find home pages written by rock climbing enthusiasts. You aren't really looking for the answer to a particular question, and you aren't looking for information on a specific topic. You just want to peruse some Web pages written by rock climbers. In that case, it is unlikely that a subject tree can help you. You will probably do better with a search engine and a query such as "rock climbing."

Now suppose you want to find demographic data from the 1990 U. S. Census. This is official information of great general interest. It is exactly the sort of thing that a good subject tree should contain. If you can maneuver yourself into the right categories and subcategories, you should be able to find the information quickly. Could a search engine get you there as fast? Let's see.

The WebCrawler search engine has set up a page that displays the keywords of 28 random searches being submitted to WebCrawler by real users in real time. The display is automatically updated every 15 seconds for most browsers, or you can always update the display manually with the Reload command. These queries are not censored (parental discretion advised). Visit the WebCrawler Search Ticker at `http://webcrawler.com/cgi-bin/SearchTicker`

Other People's Keywords

Here are the top 12 hits returned by a simple WebCrawler search with just a few keywords:

United States Census Bureau 1990

1. Data Sources—U. S. Government Sites
2. `http://www.ncjrs.org/txtfiles/crimepol.txt`
3. Cool Data Page
4. REI Profile of Northeast Ohio
5. Geography Division Map Gallery
6. basic sources of economic statistics
7. Vital U. S. Statistics and Facts home page
8. Kearl's Guide to the Sociology of the Family
9. CGRER NetSurfing: Maps and References Review
10. Statistical Sources
11. `http://www.census.gov/genealogy/names/nam_meth.txt`
12. `talk.politics.guns` Official Pro-Gun FAQ 1/2

Judging from the titles, it seems that the best bets are hits (1), (7), and (10). Starting with (1) Data Sources—U. S. Government Sites, you can path through a succession of hyperlinks like this:

General → United States Census Bureau → Topics in Text

which will take you to a page named **topics in text: Census Bureau** containing the following hyperlinks:

- **News**
- **Search**
- **Access Tools**
- **CenStats - CenStore**
- **Subjects A-Z**
- **Just for Fun**
- **About the Census**
- **User Manual**
- **New on the Site**
- **Pop Clock**
- **Economic Clock**

You can explore these links and presumably find whatever you need. Following the **Access Tools** link leads you to a link called **1990 Census Lookup** and to a search engine that operates specifically on 1990 census data. You may also want to look at some of the other links on the **topics in text: Census Bureau** page. You also might want to go back to the WebCrawler hits and check out (7) and (10) just to see what they look like. Maybe they are good resource pages to bookmark if this is a topic that we care about in general.

   Here's what this search could like in a subject tree. The following is a path of links that you could follow from the Yahoo! home page:

Government → Agencies → Census Bureau → 1990 U.S.Census LOOKUP

This path will take you to the same specialized search engine in fewer hops and with fewer opportunities for distraction along the way (see Figure 5.3). It also offers fewer opportunities for serendipitous discovery. If you want to find something straightforward as quickly as possible, a subject tree is probably your best search tool. If you want to explore and allow yourself to be distracted, a search engine will give you lots of interesting paths to investigate.

   Note: These examples were minimized to show the shortest possible pathways available. It is always easy to take a wrong turn and start down a path that takes you further away from your goal. There are perhaps more opportunities for wrong turns when you start with a search engine. Subject trees, however, are not always so easy to navigate either.

Clear-Cut or Open-Ended Questions?

What you want to investigate may also be a factor in selecting a search tool. If you have a very specific question with a clear-cut sort of answer, a subject tree will probably suffice. But if your question is vague or open-ended, you probably want to spend more time exploring lots of relevant resources in order to get a broader sense of all of the available information. In that case, a search engine may be more effective at pointing you in lots of potentially useful directions.

There are also times when it pays to use both a search engine and a subject tree. This is always the case if you are conducting a fairly comprehensive investigation of a topic that has many perspectives. It never hurts to gather as many resources as you can.

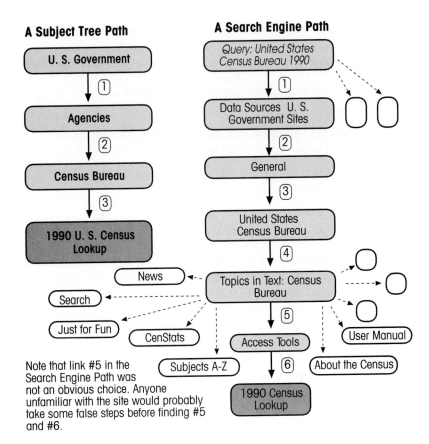

Note that link #5 in the Search Engine Path was not an obvious choice. Anyone unfamiliar with the site would probably take some false steps before finding #5 and #6.

FIG. 5.3

Search Engines and Subject Trees

Keyword Searches in Subject Trees

Most major subject trees now incorporate a keyword search option that operates in conjunction with the subject tree. You can conduct a keyword search for items in the subject tree from the root level, or you can descend a particular branch and conduct a keyword search that is limited to that branch. A keyword search from the root of a subject tree is a very powerful tool if you are having trouble navigating a subject tree or you suspect that relevant information may be located in several different branches.

Figure 5.4 shows the home page for Yahoo!. The box to the left of the **Search** hyperlink is where you enter a keyword query. Any hits that Yahoo! returns will come from the Yahoo! subject tree. For example, suppose you conduct a keyword search at the top level of Yahoo! using the query "census data 1990." Here's what is returned:

Found 0 Category and 4 Site Matches for census data 1990.

Yahoo! Site Matches (1 – 4 of 4)

Social Science: Data Collections

** <u>1990 Census Data Locator</u> (University of Michigan Documents Center)
- Determine appropriate Census questionnaire and level of
geography to identify possible printed reports, CD-ROMS, magnetic
tapes, or Internet connections containing the desired data.

* <u>1990 Census LOOKUP</u>

* <u>1990 Census of Population and Housing</u>—includes statistics on
STF3, STF1, income, labor, social, housing.

Government: Executive Branch: Departments and Agencies:
Department of Commerce: Census Bureau

* <u>1990 Census Data Lookup</u>

These four links, marked by the asterisks, are all on target. Yahoo! shows where each is located in the subject tree. Three came from the Social Sciences branch of the tree and one came from the Government branch (where you learn that the Census Bureau is part of the Executive Branch). In this example, matches were found to specific Web sites rather than to subject tree categories. A different query (e.g., "Census Bureau") would return hits associated with the general category of the U. S. Census Bureau but not the specific sites returned from the query "census data 1990." Sometimes, it is very useful to play around with variations on your keyword query in order to find everything in the subject tree that might be useful to you.

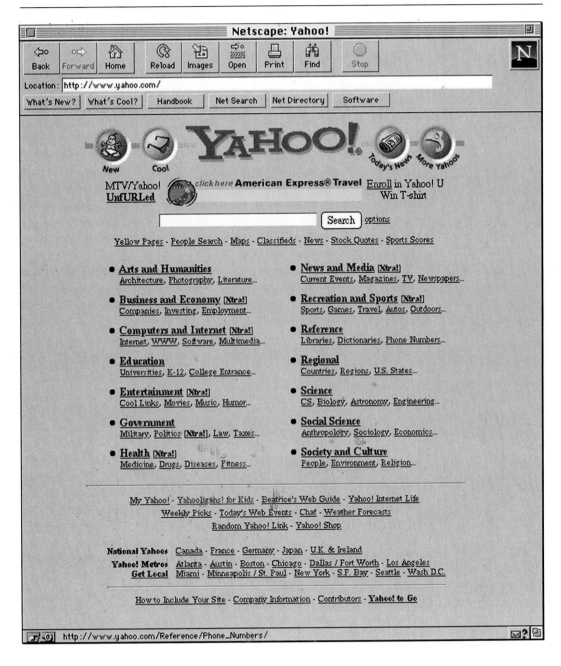

A thorough keyword search on a subject tree is a good way to make sure that you are getting the best that the subject tree has to offer.

FIG. 5.4

The Yahoo! Home Page

5.7 Clearinghouses

A **clearinghouse** is a large collection of resources or documents on a given topic. On the Internet, some publicly available clearinghouses have been created by researchers who were subsidized by federal funding. Others are compiled by commercial interests and may be available only to paid subscribers. A few are compiled by librarians, teachers, or random individuals. Some have all of their documents available online, while others have indices and bibliographies online, but the actual documents are available only in hard-copy form. Be on the lookout for clearinghouses that address your interests. Each is organized differently and supports its own search tools, so you have to learn about each on a case-by-case basis.

A relevant clearinghouse is a powerful research tool because it is both comprehensive in scope and maintains high standards for document quality. The existence of a good clearinghouse means that 90% of the hard work has already been done for you. All you have to do is work your way through the offerings to the specific information you want.

Here is a sampling of some general and special-purpose clearinghouses:

East View Publications

http://www.eastview.com/

Features publications from Russia, the CIS, and Central Europe.

The Electronic Newsstand

http://www.enews.com/

Has links to more than 3,000 magazines, with a search engine for titles and full-text articles.

ERIC—Clearinghouse on Elementary and Early Childhood Education

http://ericps.ed.uiuc.edu/

Focuses on the areas of child development, the education and care of children from birth through early adolescence, the teaching of young children, and parenting and family life.

Galt Shareware Site

http://www.galttech.com

A good software clearinghouse designed for beginners.

Improv Page

`http://sunee.uwaterloo.ca/~broehl/improv/index.html`

Focuses on improvisational theater.

National Security Website

`http://www.nationalsecurity.org/`

Features links to publications, policy experts, and Web sites on a wide spectrum of national security issues. Good for reporters, researchers, and concerned Americans.

Ready Reference Using the Internet

`http://k12.oit.umass.edu/rref.html`

A large list of links arranged by subject heading. Compiled by Ellen Berne.

The Riley Guide

`http://www.dbm.com/jobguide/`

A comprehensive guide and resource clearinghouse for online job searches. Compiled by Margaret Riley.

The Running Network

`http://www.runningnetwork.com/`

Covers major regional and specialized running magazines in the United States.

Statesearch

`http://www.nasire.org/ss/index.html`

Focuses on state government information on the Internet.

Virus Information

`http://csrc.ncsl.nist.gov/virus/`

Contains information about computer viruses. From the Computer Security Resource Clearinghouse.

There are hundreds of online clearinghouses. If you want to conduct some serious research, always check first to see if a relevant clearinghouse can help you. How do you find a clearinghouse when you need one? One possibility is the **Argus Clearinghouse** (`http://www.clearinghouse.net/`). This is basically a clearinghouse of clearinghouses, complete with its own search engine. You can also go into any general subject tree for the Web and conduct a keyword search that includes the term "clearinghouse." For example, in response to the simple query "clearinghouse," the Yahoo! subject tree returns 277 hits.

You may also find some comprehensive resource pages that have not been identified with the keyword "clearinghouse." To locate these, ask yourself what organizations are involved with your topic of interest. Ask yourself: Who cares about these issues? Is there a nonprofit group or coalition that might track relevant resources? If you can find such an organization, you may be able to benefit from the work of a professional Internet researcher who has spent a lot more time than you can tracking down relevant resources.

If your activities on the Web tend to be focused in one direction, you might want to set your default home page to an appropriate clearinghouse page. Always take the time to investigate pointers to clearinghouses that might be useful to you. Clearinghouse pointers are good bookmark entries because they give you fast access to a lot of links via a single URL.

5.8 ▶ Assessing Web Page Credibility

If you want to use the Internet as a source for legitimate research, you need to develop a critical eye for high-quality information. If you are not cautious in your use of online resources, you may inadvertently disseminate misinformation and, in the process, damage your own credibility. There are legitimate sources on the Web that can be trusted, but there are also many dubious information sources. You must learn to evaluate all online information before you reference it or use it in your own projects.

Your evaluation should focus on the content of the Web page. Don't be influenced by a page's cosmetic "look and feel." Beautiful graphics and carefully constructed text formatting means the author cares about the attractiveness of the page, but that by itself does not guarantee the information's credibility. If the graphics do not contribute to the actual content of the page, you might find it helpful to turn them off in order to better concentrate on the written content.

The Internet is a content-neutral medium: It distributes falsehoods and fantasies as easily as facts and truth. It encourages people to produce pages on everything under the sun, and the line between fact and fiction can be twisted in many subtle ways. A delusional author may report wishful thinking or hallucinogenic experiences as fact. If the departure from reality is subtle and believable, it may be impossible to assess credibility with absolute certainty. Conspiracy theories thrive on the Internet because conspiracy buffs can easily hook up with one another and find strength in numbers. Always use common sense when it comes to assessing credibility on the Web. If the topic you are researching involves conspiracy theories or controversial political scandals, everything you find should be treated with extreme caution.

A good content evaluation can be completed with the help of a credibility checklist. Many checklist criteria apply to the evaluation of traditional print documents, but others are specific to Web documents. Several useful checklists for Web page assessment are available (see the Internet 101 Web pages for pointers to online articles). The following sections discuss some of the most commonly mentioned criteria that can be used to assess Web page credibility.

Authorship Credibility

Any page that does not identify its author is useless for research purposes. The author's name should be clearly identified, and additional information about the author should be available in the current document or from hyperlinks in the document. The author's institutional affiliation and job title should be available, along with a phone number and complete mailing address. Look for a short professional biography on an associated Web page.

An author's e-mail address that ends in `.gov` or `.edu` is evidence of a legitimate institutional affiliation, but remember that college students and staff members all have `.edu` addresses, too. The author should make it clear whether he or she is the original author of the material in question. Look for a copyright statement. If there is some doubt about that statement or if there is no statement, contact the author to double-check the material's originality. A legitimate author is normally happy to verify authorship.

Try to verify that the author is who he or she claims to be. If someone is identified as a biology professor at Home State University, go to the home page for Home State University and look for a list of the faculty in the Biology Department, or look for a general University directory. Most universities and colleges maintain a faculty/staff directory on the Web. Corporate environments may or may not have online employee directories, but a phone call to corporate headquarters will tell you if someone is legitimate.

Author credibility is normally not a concern if the work in question has been published by a respected journal or magazine or if you have located in a journal or magazine a published citation to the work in question. You can double-check anything that claims to be published by going to the publication's home page and locating a table of contents that contains the article in question. This will protect you from the possibility of a fraudulent publication claim. It is increasingly common for magazines and journals to maintain Web sites, where you can see at least a table of contents, if not entire articles.

After you've verified the identity of an author, ask yourself if the author is qualified to write on the topic. A university professor may not be expert in an area that is not related to his or her professional specialty. If you aren't sure, look for additional evidence of scholarly activities in the given area. A single isolated paper is more questionable than a dozen papers in the same area. If the author has published other papers in the area, but the article in question has not been published, a certain amount of credibility can be inherited from the other publications. But the title "professor" does not automatically confer expertise in all areas, so always do a background check on the author.

When the author is a reporter or writer for a news organization, it is best to verify reported facts independently. If the article mentions a published source for its information, go to that original source document and check it yourself. If no additional sources are cited, look for independent corroborating reports.

Accurate Writing and Documentation

If an article is poorly written and has grammatical errors and misspellings, it may be sloppy with regard to content as well. Serious writing takes time and effort. If you sense that the article was written casually and quickly, it is probably not a good source. Does the author reference other sources? Are these complete citations? If they are hyperlinks to other online sources, are the links operational and up-to-date? An accurate information source will be careful to provide correct attributions where needed and include disclaimers when information or conclusions are questionable.

If the resource has been published, is the online version identical to the print version or is it a shorter version? Some magazines publish partial versions of their printed articles. The Web site should make it clear whether you have a complete or partial version of the full article.

Objectivity

If the author of an article is affiliated with a commercial entity, be very careful to separate informational content from advertising. This is not always easy. Some pages are carefully designed to make it clear where the institutional promotion stops and the objective information starts. If no effort has been made to do this and the article is unpublished, then you should be concerned about its objectivity.

Scientists working in private industry publish their legitimate research in order to establish credibility within the scientific establishment. It is harder to evaluate the objectivity of writers outside the scientific establishment, but articles in respected publications are good indicators of objective writing.

Many authors provide information online as a public service. These articles are sometimes affiliated with some sort of a nonprofit organization, and objectivity can be a problem if the organization has its own political agenda. If you cite information distributed by an advocacy group, do your own fact checking with independent sources and try to corroborate the information.

Stability of Web Pages

The Web is a dynamic medium with new information popping up every day. Pages also disappear every day. You can't know if a page will still be on the Web next year or even next month. This is a problem when doing scholarly research. But there are indications of page stability. Here are a few guidelines that can help you assess this stability:

1. Is the page dated? When was it last revised?
2. Is it part of a larger site that has other dated materials?
3. Do other Web sites reference the work at this address?
4. Is the page part of an institutional resource?

If you reference an online source, always be careful to reference the original URL rather than a copy at a mirror site. If a work is heavily referenced, it may appear at multiple Web sites. The original site will usually be associated with the author or the author's home institution, and this is presumably the most stable site.

No matter how hard you try to select stable Web pages, it is impossible to know how long a Web page will either be available or be available at its current URL. Sometimes an author needs to rearrange a Web site, especially if it is growing. This means that old URLs may become obsolete, but the pages are still available under new URLs. One study found that the lifetime of the average URL is only 75 days. Presumably, this average is low because of a large number of experimental pages created by newcomers to the Web that have since ceased to exist, as well as Web pages that have moved to new URLs. Regardless, 75 days is a sobering statistic.

Fraudulent Web Pages

It is easy to bring up a Web site in another person's name in order to misrepresent that individual, although this is unlikely within the academic community. Bogus Web sites for political candidates were found during the 1996 presidential campaign, and bogus home pages are often created as parodies of the real thing. However, the possibility of a more maliciously crafted Web page is a real concern and should be considered if you find material that is blatantly offbeat, contradictory, or surprising in any way.

When the integrity of online material is a serious concern, an author can use PGP (see Chapter 12) to authenticate a Web page. However, this technique is not well-known outside the computer science community and is unlikely to be encountered outside of the technical computer science literature.

5.9

Constructing Your Own Home Page

Most people can walk, but only a few can dance the tango. The same applies to Web pages. Almost anyone can work up a home page, but it takes a professional to create a Web page that takes your breath away. This section will teach you how to walk, but it's not going to turn you into a professional Web page designer. The goal is to show you the minimum you need to know to create a readable Web page. If you want to learn more, you can start by reading Chapter 11 and consult other books and online resources.

To create a home page, you need to learn **HTML** (the HyperText Markup Language), which is used to create files that are readable by Web browsers. You also need an environment in which you can edit text files. This could be your favorite word processor on your home computer.

Further, you need access to a Web server on which you can post your Web page files. Most Web servers are UNIX hosts on which individuals are given personal accounts that include a limited disk quota to hold personal Web pages (5MB or 10MB are common allocations on ISP Web servers). You will need to know enough UNIX to create your Web pages under UNIX or to transfer Web pages created on a home computer over to your UNIX account. Chapter 9 describes how clients transfer files between Internet hosts. Dealing with UNIX need not be a big stumbling block, and you should be able to get recommendations from the technical support personnel who support your Web server. You don't need to know very much about UNIX in order to post a Web page on a UNIX host.

HTML Editors, Assistants, and Construction Kits

You can write Web pages with any text editor or word processor, but there are also special HTML editors designed to speed the process of Web page creation. These editors typically give you a point-and-click interface, whereby frequently used HTML commands can be inserted into the file with a single mouse click rather than a dozen keystrokes. Some Web browsers contain their own HTML editors and will preview your page for you so that you can see how it will appear on the Web.

You can also find software that leads you through the process of designing a Web page one step at a time. For example, Netscape Navigator Gold contains the Netscape Page Wizard, which works with you to create a first-pass Web page. If you need to refine the page beyond the capabilities of the Wizard, you can use the Netscape Page Editor to pick up where the Wizard leaves off. Although it is very limited, the Netscape Page Wizard demonstrates how a simple set of HTML elements (including graphics) can be assembled into an attractive Web page. Start the Wizard by clicking New Document on the File menu and then select the From Wizard option.

There are also Web page construction kits which you can use to build prefabricated Web pages from HTML templates. Each template is designed for a particular genre (e.g., a personal home page or a small business advertisement). All you do is select a template and add the content. If you need to bring up a simple Web page fast, the right template can do 90% of the work for you.

Special HTML editors, interactive assistants, and construction kits are all instructional for beginners. Try out some of these tools and find out how easy it is to get off the ground with HTML.

You don't need to know much HTML in order to post a simple Web page. This text covers the basics and then suggests some useful strategies for additional self-study. Don't expect to learn all about HTML before you put a Web page online. You can learn what you need for the page you want to create and forget about the rest. Only a professional should worry about knowing everything there is to know. Many Web pages are forever "works in progress." It is easy to start with a simple page and then embellish it as you learn more. The most advanced HTML features are associated with graphics and special effects, so if you are primarily interested in posting text, you can post a textual Web page very easily.

A Sample Web Page

A Web page is just a text file. However, it is a text file that contains HTML tags in addition to the text that appears when the page is viewed with a Web browser. You can start a Web page by writing all of the visible text first (this takes no knowledge of HTML) and then inserting the HTML tags later. You can edit your Web page using any text editor or word processor, as long as the file is saved as plain ASCII text.

A well-designed Web page normally consists of three parts:

1. Head
2. Body
3. Graphics

The head is reserved for the title of the document, as well as some optional data that I won't go into. Every Web page should have a title, which will be displayed in the title bar of a Web browser. The title is also important to some search engines, which may weigh keywords found in a title more heavily than other keywords.

HINT

Viewing Local Files with a Web Browser

If you are creating a Web page on a home computer, you can view your own pages locally by using the Open File command. From the File menu, click Open File. Then use the directory dialog box to highlight the file you want to view and click Open to load the file. Your file will appear in the browser's display window.

A Web page is built with **HTML elements**, and each element is associated with an **HTML tag** or pair of tags. For example, the title of a Web page is an HTML element, and it is created with a pair of **tags** that mark the beginning of the title and the end of the title—<TITLE> and </TITLE>:

```
<TITLE> How to Build a Tree House </TITLE>
```

Angle brackets < > are always used to signal an HTML tag. Any HTML tag without a forwards slash (/) marks the beginning of an HTML element, and any HTML tag with a forwards slash marks the end of an HTML element. You don't have to put all of the HTML commands in uppercase, but it is advised. Doing so makes the HTML commands stand out so that you can see them easily when you edit your document.

The body of a Web page is identified by another pair of tags that mark the beginning of the body and the end of the body—<BODY> and </BODY>:

```
<BODY>
If you want to build a tree house,
you need a tree, some good lumber, and a few tools.
A construction plan is also a good idea, but some people
think they can wing it.
</BODY>
```

With this head and body, you can now assemble a simple Web page by enclosing the head and the body inside an HTML element with the tag pair —<HTML> and </HTML>. The HTML element is used to mark the start and end of a Web page. In fact, Web browsers are very forgiving about deviations from this structure. A web browser will try to display any plain text file it can open, even if it contains no HTML elements. However, a random text file

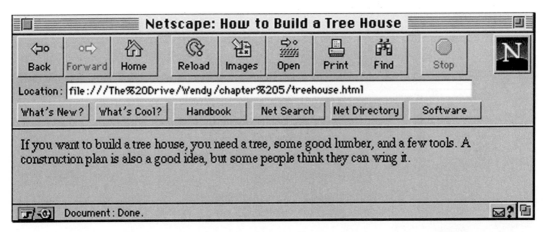

Netscape: How to Build a Tree House

Back | Forward | Home | Reload | Images | Open | Print | Find | Stop

Location: file:///The%20Drive/Wendy/chapter%205/treehouse.html

What's New? | What's Cool? | Handbook | Net Search | Net Directory | Software

If you want to build a tree house, you need a tree, some good lumber, and a few tools. A construction plan is also a good idea, but some people think they can wing it.

Document: Done.

FIG. 5.5

Example Web Page

will not be very readable without HTML formatting. If you do use the head and body elements, make sure the head precedes the body, and make sure the title goes inside the head:

```
<HTML>
<HEAD>
<TITLE> How to Build a Tree House </TITLE>
</HEAD>
<BODY>
If you want to build a tree house,
you need a tree, some good lumber, and a few tools.
A construction plan is also a good idea, but some people
think they can wing it.
</BODY>
</HTML>
```

When this page is viewed through a Web browser, the text in the body will be automatically justified. That is, line breaks or indentations will not be preserved (unless you insert special HTML tags to keep them intact). Also note that the title will not appear on the page per se, although it may be displayed in a title bar at the top of the page. Different browsers do different things with the title of a Web page. Figure 5.5 shows how the example HTML file will be displayed by Netscape Navigator.

Filenames for Web Pages

HINT

Always include in the name of your Web page file the extension .html. This makes it easy to recognize Web page files when you are viewing a directory of files, and it is a convention used by all Web page designers. If you create your Web pages on a PC where a file extension can contain only three characters, use the extension .htm.

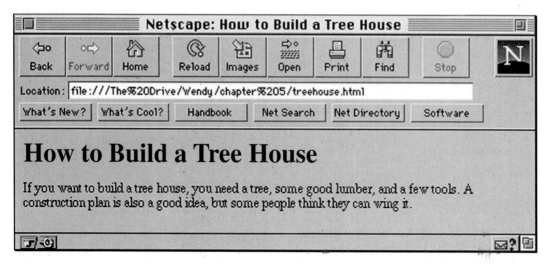

How to Build a Tree House

If you want to build a tree house, you need a tree, some good lumber, and a few tools. A construction plan is also a good idea, but some people think they can wing it.

FIG. 5.6

The Example Web Page with a Heading Added

Most people want to see a visible title on their Web page, so a heading needs to be added to the body of the page. Web page headers can be created in different sizes. You can use an <H1> tag, which will produce the largest possible header, <H2> to produce the next largest header, all of the way down to <H6>, which is a very small header. Suppose you add a header element to the example HTML file:

```
<HTML>
<HEAD>
<TITLE> How to Build a Tree House </TITLE>
</HEAD>
<BODY>
<H1> How to Build a Tree House </H1>
If you want to build a tree house,
you need a tree, some good lumber, and a few tools.
A construction plan is also a good idea, but some people
think they can wing it.
</BODY>
</HTML>
```

Figure 5.6 shows the results.

HTML ERRORS

If your Web page won't display properly when viewed through a Web browser, there is probably an HTML error in the file. Check all of the HTML elements that require a pair of start/end tags and make sure both tags are present and don't have any typographical errors. These are the most common HTML errors. Viewing your file periodically as you create it will make it easier to track down HTML errors. If you create a large file and look at it only when you are done, it may be difficult to locate errors.

The heading is left-justified because no other formatting was specified for it. To center the heading, you add an alignment attribute to the heading element—ALIGN=CENTER. You also can add some more text. A paragraph tag—<P>— is used to separate paragraphs by a blank line. Paragraph tags are single tags rather than paired tags; that is, an end tag is not required, so you can mark only the beginning of a paragraph.

```
<HTML>
<HEAD>
<TITLE> How to Build a Tree House </TITLE>
</HEAD>
<BODY>
<H1 ALIGN=CENTER> How to Build a Tree House </H1>
<P> If you want to build a tree house,
you need a tree, some good lumber, and a few tools.
A construction plan is also a good idea, but some people
think they can wing it.
<P> Make sure the tree is large enough to support the
extra weight. Sometimes a stand of two or three trees
works nicely. If you distribute the weight over two or
three trees, smaller trees can be considered.
</BODY>
</HTML>
```

If you prefer, place the paragraph tags on their own lines. This can make the HTML document is easier to read and won't change the resulting Web page display:

```
<HTML>
<HEAD>
<TITLE> How to Build a Tree House </TITLE>
</HEAD>
<BODY>
<H1 ALIGN=CENTER> How to Build a Tree House </H1>
<P>
If you want to build a tree house,
you need a tree, some good lumber, and a few tools.
A construction plan is also a good idea, but some people
think they can wing it.
<P>
Make sure the tree is large enough to support the extra
weight. Sometimes a stand of two or three trees works
nicely. If you distribute the weight over two or three
trees, smaller trees can be considered.
</BODY>
</HTML>
```

In either case, the new Web page now looks like Figure 5.7.

Notice how the new alignment attribute inside the heading element centers the heading.

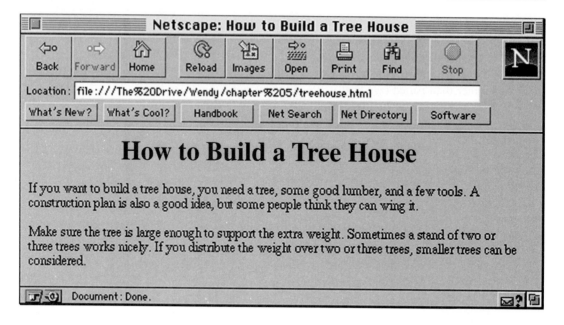

FIG. 5.7

Example Web Page
with Two Paragraphs

There are many formatting commands that control the appearance of your text. For example, you could set up a bulleted list. You would use the <UL> and </UL> (Unordered List) pair of tags to mark the start and end of the list and the <LI> (List Item) tag to indicate each bulleted item:

```
<HTML>
<HEAD>
<TITLE> How to Build a Tree House </TITLE>
</HEAD>
<BODY>
<H1 ALIGN=CENTER> How to Build a Tree House </H1>
<P> If you want to build a tree house,
you need:
<P>
<UL>
<LI>a tree
<LI>some good lumber
<LI>a few tools
</UL>
<P> A construction plan is also a good idea, but some
people think they can wing it.
<P> Make sure the tree is large enough to support the
extra weight. Sometimes a stand of two or three trees
works nicely. If you distribute the weight over two or
three trees, smaller trees can be considered.
</BODY>
</HTML>
```

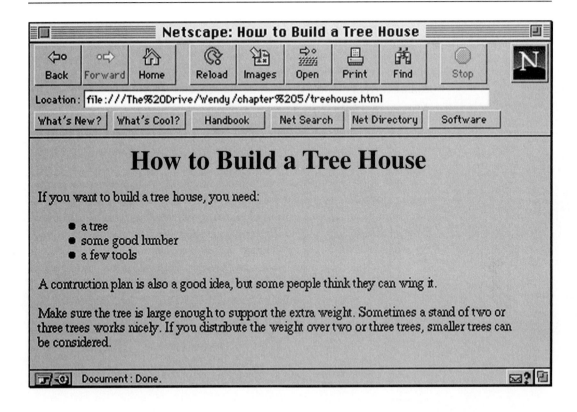

Figure 5.8 shows the result.

FIG. 5.8

Example Web Page
with a Bulleted List

How to Learn More

You can learn more HTML elements by looking at the HTML files for existing Web pages. If you see something you like on the Web, you can use your browser's Source command to view the underlying HTML file. Copy the tags you see in the file in order to duplicate text formatting or other Web page elements in your own Web pages. The HTML version of any Web page can be viewed in this way and can even be saved to a file if you want to save the HTML version instead of the more readable original Web page. Existing Web pages can be very instructive, and learning from examples is a painless way to master HTML.

Creating Hypertext Links

Using only a few formatting commands, you can create a simple Web page of text. It won't be hypertext, however, until you add some links. The most common types of links are absolute, named, and relative.

Absolute Links

Suppose you want to add a hyperlink to a page written by a different author and located on a different Web server. This is an **absolute link**, and it requires the other page's URL.

To set up an absolute link, you mark a **label** that will operate as the hyperlink on your Web page. The label could be a segment of text embedded in a paragraph or an item in a bulleted list. You decide what the label should be. Going back to the example Web page, suppose you had a pointer to a page on which someone has catalogued tree house plans. The page's URL is `http://www.treehouse.com/construct/plans.html`. You would insert a hyperlink in the Web page by using a pair of **anchor** tags—<A> and </A>—with a hypertext reference attribute (HREF) inside the anchor element. This is shown in boldface in the following example:

```
<HTML>
<HEAD>
<TITLE> How to Build a Tree House </TITLE>
</HEAD>
<BODY>
<H1 ALIGN=CENTER> How to Build a Tree House </H1>
<P>
If you want to build a tree house,
you need a tree, some good lumber, and a few tools.
A <A
HREF="http://www.treehouse.com/construct/plans.html">
construction plan</A> is also a good idea, but some
people think they can wing it.
<P> Make sure the tree is large enough to support the
extra weight. Sometimes a stand of two or three trees
works nicely. If you distribute the weight over two or
three trees, smaller trees can be considered.
</BODY>
</HTML>
```

The text associated with the new hyperlink will appear on your pages as boldfaced or underscored or colored, depending on the Web browser that displays the page. Figure 5.9 shows the result.

That's all there is to it. If the URL is current, and you insert it into your HTML file accurately, it should be operational. Always check each link you

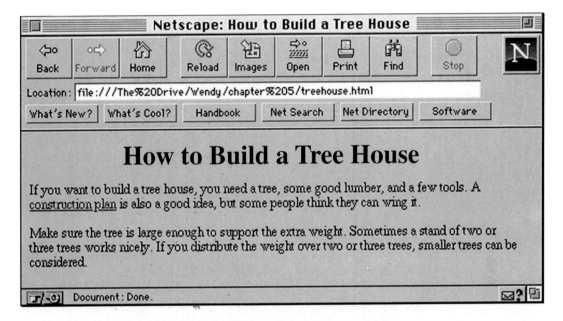

How to Build a Tree House

If you want to build a tree house, you need a tree, some good lumber, and a few tools. A construction plan is also a good idea, but some people think they can wing it.

Make sure the tree is large enough to support the extra weight. Sometimes a stand of two or three trees works nicely. If you distribute the weight over two or three trees, smaller trees can be considered.

add to a Web page to make sure it is a working link. Readers get frustrated by links that don't work. You should do your best to keep your Web page in good operational condition. **Web page maintenance** is the process of periodically checking your Web pages to make sure all links still work. A link that worked today may not work tomorrow if the author of the other document has renamed the file or made other changes. It is not enough to know that a hyperlink was working at the time of its creation. Ongoing maintenance is needed to ensure a fully operational Web page next week, next month, and next year. This is one of the hidden costs associated with the Web. It is fun to create new Web pages, but most people find it fairly tedious to maintain them.

FIG. 5.9

Example Web Page with an Absolute Link

After you update your Web page, always check the new version to ensure it properly displays and operates. Watch out for the following scenario:

1. You view one of your Web pages, and you find a problem with one of the links.
2. You replace the faulty link with an updated link.

Continued on Next Page

CHECKING YOUR WEB PAGES

Continued from Previous Page

3. You view the new Web page to check it, but the problem is still there.

Make sure you are really viewing the newly updated HTML file. If the Web page is being retrieved from a disk cache, you are seeing the original file instead of the updated one. Use the Reload command to see the new file before you conclude that your update isn't working.

Named Links

A hyperlink that points to another location *in the same document* is a **named link**. Setting up a named link takes a little more work than setting up an absolute link because you have to mark the target location as well as the hyperlink that points to that location. This is done with a **name** tag.

Here's how it would work if the example Web page were longer and it contained different sections in which various subtopics were discussed in some detail. Suppose it included a bulleted list up front that operated as a table of contents. Then each item on the list would be a named link to a section found later in the same document. The HTML source would look like this (new material is boldfaced):

```
<HTML>
<HEAD>
<TITLE> How to Build a Tree House </TITLE>
</HEAD>
<BODY>
<H1 ALIGN=CENTER> How to Build a Tree House </H1>
<P> If you want to build a tree house,
you need:
<P>
<UL>
<LI><A HREF="#tree">a tree</A><BR>
<LI><A HREF="#lumber">some good lumber</A><BR>
<LI><A HREF="#tools">a few tools</A><BR>
</UL>
<P> A construction plan is also a good idea, but some
people think they can wing it.
<A NAME="tree"><H3>A Tree</H3></A>
<P> Make sure the tree is large enough to support the
extra weight. Sometimes a stand of two or three trees
works nicely. If you distribute the weight over two or
three trees, smaller trees can be considered.
```

```
.
.
.
<A NAME="lumber"><H3>Some Good Lumber</H3></A>
.
.
.
<A NAME="tools"><H3>A Few Tools</H3></A>
.
.
.
</BODY>
</HTML>
```

Figure 5.10 shows the result.

A named link uses the same HREF attribute used by absolute links, but instead of specifying a URL, you specify a link name. You also insert a # character at the front of the link name; this indicates that the link is a named link. Each named link must be anchored to a location somewhere in the current document. These anchors must contain a NAME= attribute as shown in the above example with the named links `tree`, `lumber`, and `tools`.

FIG. 5.10

Example Web Page with a Named Link

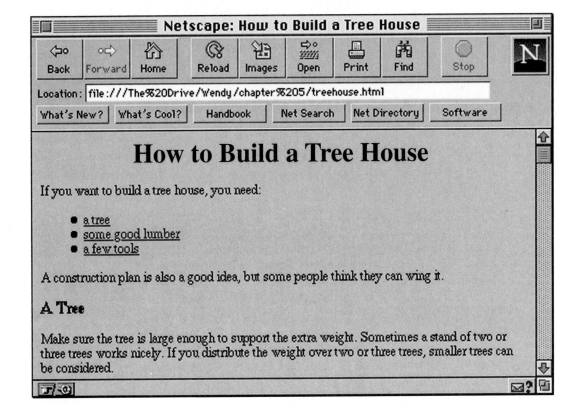

Named links help readers move through your text in a nonlinear fashion. If you supply hyperlinks from a table of contents, it is a good practice to insert named links at the end of each text section (not included in the previous example) that will take people back to the table of contents. Good hypertext design means anticipating all of the directions a user might want to go and making it easy to go there.

Relative Links

When you have multiple Web pages in the same directory on your Web server, you can insert links to your own pages without specifying the full URL (although the full URL will also work). Instead, you can use a shortcut address that consists of only the filename. This type of link is called a **relative link**. The simplest relative link is used when both the page in which the link is inserted and the file targeted by the link are in the same subdirectory. Here is an example:

```
<A HREF="booklist.html"> .... </A>
```

Relative links are often used by Web page authors who need to reference multiple pages from their own Web sites. Relative links address files by describing file addresses relative to the current subdirectory; each one is sensitive to the current location of its parent file. This means that you can't copy a relative link from someone else's Web page and expect it to work. Whenever you want to link to a web page by another author, use an absolute link.

Adding Graphics to Your Web Page

You insert a graphical image in your Web page by creating a pointer to a graphics file. Suppose you have a file named `logo.gif` that contains a company logo. To insert this logo into your Web page, use the IMG (image) element with a SRC (source) attribute:

```
<IMG SRC="logo.gif">
```

This example uses a relative link, so the `logo.gif` file must be in the same directory as the file containing the IMG element.

If you would like to have a clickable graphic that operates as a hyperlink, use an IMG element as the label for an anchor element containing a hypertext reference attribute:

```
<A HREF="mycompany.html"><IMG SRC="logo.gif"></A>
```

This turns the logo graphic into a pictoral label that can be clicked just like a text label.

Now that you know how to set up pointers to graphics files, you may be tempted to grab all sorts of graphical material to spice up your Web pages. If you have access to a flatbed scanner, you might want to use a picture from a magazine or a book. If you see a nice image on another Web page, you might want to make your own copy and use it in your own pages. Although computer technology makes doing this easy, any of these activities would probably break copyright laws. Chapter 13 discusses copyright violations and the application of copyright law to the Internet. In general, you need to secure the permission of a copyright holder before you use a published image. Learn about your responsibilities before you act on impulse. Ignorance of the law is never a good defense.

LEARN ABOUT COPYRIGHT RESTRICTIONS

Good Web Page Design

If you have spent much time on the Web, you have probably seen pages that are exemplary, as well as pages that are frustrating or disappointing in some way. When you create your own pages, try to avoid the mistakes you've seen others make. Copy the style and organizational layouts of pages that you admire.

If you create a small Web site, you may only need one page (one HTML file) and it may be obvious how to organize it. If you are creating a large Web site that has many pages, you need to think about the organization of your pages. Good pages incorporate basic principles of good design, good organization, and good writing. Here are some general suggestions:

- Design visually attractive layouts.
- Chose color combinations carefully (restraint works well).
- Ensure your graphics add to the content rather than distract from it.
- Use hyperlinks to emphasize hierarchical organizations.
- Add hyperlinks to related sites where appropriate.
- Uphold all of the traditional elements of good writing.

A large site needs to be planned in advance to have a good hierarchical structure. Some sites can be outlined and mapped out before the first Web page goes up. This is called **top-down** design. Other sites start out small and then expand in unanticipated ways over time. This is called **bottom-up** design. A top-down site will probably require less revision and reorganization than a bottom-up site, so it is best to go top-down if you possibly can. But this requires a strong sense of your ultimate Web site goals, and some Web sites are too dynamic for that. If you find yourself working bottom-up, be sensitive to the feel of your site to new visitors and expect to revise your pages from time to time for the sake of your readers.

Good Hypertext Design Principles

Hypertext should be readable as normal text and subject to all of the usual rules for good writing. In addition, links should be self-explanatory so that readers can quickly decide which to visit.

Keep the text as concise as possible to minimize scrolling by the user. Sometimes it is a good idea to limit each topic to a short page that can be viewed in its entirety without any scrolling. A richly linked collection of many short pages loses the linear organization of a traditional text, but it is convenient for someone in browsing mode. A reader controls the content of a hypertext document by choosing to traverse some links and not others. An effective hypertext author will create pages that read well no matter which pathways are followed. Here is a typical hypertext paragraph with hot links underlined. A reader can click whichever links look interesting and in any order:

The Internet is the best place to learn about the Internet. If you need *a brief definition of the Internet* or a *detailed description of the Internet*, many sites can help you out. You will also find many organizations associated with the Internet, including the *Electronic Frontier Foundation* and the *Internet Society*. There are also resource pages designed to help you find *Internet Service Providers* and copies of *graphical Web browsers*, as well as *tutorials for beginners* who want to learn more about the Internet.

Hypertext authors have less control over their creations than do authors of traditional text because readers can move through a hypertext document in many ways. Well-written hypertext will encourage this freedom on the part of the reader and ensure that each pathway through a Web site remains coherent.

Make sure you know how to do the following:

1. Create an HTML file on your home computer using a text or HTML editor.
2. Use your browser to view an HTML file stored on your home computer.
3. Download the HTML source version of a Web page and save it to a file.
4. Reload a revised HTML file (instead of reading a cached version).
5. Insert a graphics file.

PROBLEMS AND EXERCISES

1. How are Web pages collected for search engines?

2. Give three reasons why different keyword search engines may return different results in response to the same query.

3. Explain what a disk cache is. How would your browser behave differently if it didn't have one?

4. Explain two possible causes for the 404 Not Found error message.

5. How big is the Web? Is it larger than the Library of Congress?

6. Name four ways to find useful clearinghouses on the Web.

7. If a Web page author has a `.edu` e-mail address, what can you conclude?

8. Name five ways in which subject trees differ from search engines.

9. When is it time to delete items from your bookmark list?

10. Describe two situations in which you would need to use the Reload command.

11. If a Web page is found in a subject tree, can you trust its content?

12. If a Web page is found on a server named `www.NewYorkTimes.com`, what can you conclude?

13. Name four factors that contributed to the dramatic growth of the Web in 1994.

14. If you want to explore an open-ended specific topic, discuss the pros and cons of search engines versus subject trees.

15. **[Hands On]** How many Web pages does your Web browser store on its history page?

16. **[Hands On]** Explain how to save the HTML version of a Web page to a file on your hard drive. (The answer depends on which browser you use.)

17. **[Hands On]** Look at an online HTML guide and find out how to mark a body of text so that it will appear exactly as you type it in your HTML file (without text justification).

18. Explain the difference between top-down and bottom-up Web site development.

19. What is Web page maintenance?

20. If you click a link that looks like `<A HREF="#tree">A Tree</A>`, will your browser download a new file?

Note: The following exercises describe things you can do with your three target topics (see Chapter 1):

21. **[Hands On]** For each of your three target topics, search for relevant information using a keyword search engine. Experiment with different keyword combinations and different search engines. Is one search engine giving you better results for all three topics? Are different search engines better for different topics? Does one search engine find hits that the others miss?

22. **[Hands On]** For each of your three target topics, search for relevant resources using the Yahoo! subject tree. Start by examining through the subject tree to see if you can find all of the relevant subcategories. Then use the keyword search facility to see if you missed anything. Convince yourself that you have located all of the relevant resources available to you on Yahoo!.

23. **[Hands On]** Compare the resources you found in Problem 21 with the resources you found in Problem 22. Did you find different sites using different tools? Was one tool better for all three topics? Were different tools better for different topics? Did you see differences in the quality of the sites found? What conclusions would you draw from these explorations?

24. **[Hands On]** Try to find some clearinghouses for each of your three target topics. How credible are the resources mentioned by these clearinghouses?

25. **[Hands On]** Compare the results of your efforts for Problem 24 with the results found for Problems 21 and 22. Can you draw any general conclusions? Which tools were easy to use? Which tools gave you the fastest results? Which tools gave you the best quality results? Did all three tools produce many of the same resources? How would you characterize the differences you saw?

Gophers and Veronica

6

"Why should I
bother with made-
up games when
there are so many
real ones going
on?"

- KURT VONNEGUT, JR.

THE INTERNET 101 WEB PAGES

- Gopher Updates

Gophers and Gopher Space

6.1

Gopher is a client-server application that is very similar to Web browsers and Web servers. There are **Gopher clients** and **Gopher servers**. The documents that can be viewed with a Gopher client comprise **Gopher space.** The first Gopher was created in 1991 at the University of Minnesota as a campus information resource. The idea was to set up a central server on which each department could post, update, and control its own announcements, news, and text documents. At the same time, a Gopher user could move easily from department to department and even from one Gopher server to other inter-connected Gopher servers.

Although Gophers and Web browsers were developed independently and roughly simultaneously, many universities set up Gopher servers first in order to broadcast campus directories and other campus information. Most educational and government institutions developed extensive Gopher resources before they began to craft home pages for the Web. In this sense, Gophers set the stage for Web browsers.

Why Gopher?

Minnesota is known as the Gopher State. The reasons why are not clear. Maybe since the Granite State and the Sunshine State were already taken, there just wasn't much left. In any case, the Minnesota basketball team is called the Golden Gophers, so gophers are firmly ensconced in the Minnesota mindset. When a group of programmers at the University of Minnesota came up with a powerful and easy-to-use client/server software package, the image of an energetic little creature gleefully carrying packets back and forth across a computer network must have been a collective hallucination. As a result, the University of Minnesota became well known (at least in computer circles) as the "Mother of All Gophers" (or "Mother Gopher"). Countless Gophers all over the world maintain pointers back to mom as a way of saying thanks.

If you have done much Web browsing, you may have visited Gopher space without realizing it. Addresses in Gopher space can be accessed with a Web browser by using a URL prefaced by `gopher://` instead of the usual `http://`. So you can click a hyperlink on a Web page and enter Gopher space without fanfare. Since you can navigate Gopher space with a Web browser, there is no great need for you to run a Gopher client. Just point your Web browser to a Gopher address and use all of your familiar browser commands. However, although the Web can take you into Gopher space, you can't follow a pointer out of Gopher space back into the Web. Gophers can point only to other Gophers. So when you want to get back to the Web, you will have to backtrack or jump to a Web page URL.

While the Web contains pages of hypertext, Gopher space contains **menus**. Each menu contains clickable titles that link you to other locations. When you click a menu title, you usually go to either another menu or a text document. Each Gopher server maintains a hierarchy of Gopher menus, and you navigate them in much the same way that you navigate Web pages. One main menu functions as the starting-off point. This is the **root menu**, or the **Gopher root.** From a root menu, you can navigate to any other Gopher menu on that server. Most Gopher servers are highly interconnected via menu titles that point to other Gopher servers as well as to their own menus. So an excursion starting at one Gopher root can take you to any number of other Gopher servers in a seamless fashion, in the same way that Web browsing carries you from one Web server to another Web server.

If you are a university student, your school may have an institutional Gopher where you can find useful information about your university community. As your first excursion into Gopher space, you will visit a university Gopher.

Gopher Addresses

You will often see addresses for Gophers that look like host names. For example, the root Gopher for the University of Southern California is `cwis.usc.edu`. Someone might tell you to "point your Gopher to `cwis.usc.edu`." This is analogous to pointing a Web browser to a URL. Gopher clients are designed to accept host names as Gopher addresses. For a Web browser to interpret a host name as a Gopher address, turn the host name into a URL by adding the prefix `gopher://`. So `cwis.usc.edu` becomes `gopher://cwis.usc.edu`.

Start by pointing your Web browser to the Mother Gopher at the University of Minnesota, located at `gopher://gopher.micro.umn.edu/1` (remember that this URL uses a Gopher protocol rather than the usual http protocol, so don't preface this address with `http://`). If you have trouble connecting to the Mother Gopher, try Kent State University at `gopher://gopher.kent.edu` instead.

If you connect to the Mother Gopher, you will see the menu for the root Gopher:

```
Gopher Menu

(DIR)  Information About Gopher
(DIR)  Computer Information
(DIR)  Discussion Groups
(DIR)  Fun & Games
(DIR)  Internet file server (ftp) sites
(DIR)  Libraries
(DIR)  News
(DIR)  Other Gopher and Information Servers
(DIR)  Phone Books
 (?)     Search Gopher Titles at the University of Minnesota
 (?)     Search lots of places at the University of Minnesota
(DIR)  University of Minnesota Campus Information
```

Your page display may not look exactly like this, but you will see a screen of text with a list of menu items. Most root Gophers have a menu item called "Other Gophers" or something similarly worded. On this particular menu, it is called "Other Gopher and Information Servers." This link is your pathway to all of the other Gopher servers in Gopher space. To follow the link, click it. Next, you'll see a new menu:

```
Other Gopher and Information Servers

(DIR) All the Gopher Servers in the World
 (?)     Search All the Gopher Servers in the World
(DIR) Search titles in Gopherspace using veronica
(DIR) Africa
(DIR) Asia
(DIR) Europe
(DIR) International Organizations
(DIR) Middle East
(DIR) North America
(DIR) Pacific
(DIR) Russia
(DIR) South America
(DIR) Terminal Based Information
(DIR) WAIS Based Information
(FILE) Gopher Server Registration
```

All Gopher menus are constructed from a fixed set of Gopher **item types** (or **selection types**). Each item listed on a Gopher menu must be one of the legal Gopher item types. There are about a dozen Gopher item types but a typical Gopher menu contains mostly items of the type *directory* (these items always point to other Gopher menus) and the type *file* (these items always point to ASCII text files). Gopher clients use various display conventions to help you recognize item types when you view items on a Gopher menu.

- Viewed with the lynx Web browser, directory-type items are marked (DIR), file-type items are marked (FILE), and an item marked with (?) is a keyword search engine.

- Viewed through a text-based Gopher client, directory-type items end in a forward slash /, file-type items end with a period, and <?> marks a keyword search engine.

- When viewed with Navigator, menu items are marked by selection type icons (see Figure 6.1).

Whatever display you have, there will be some annotation system to help you see where you're going before you go.

From the "Other Gopher and Information Services" menu, you can search for specific Gopher servers. "All the Gopher Servers in the World" gives a master list (organized alphabetically) that is fun to browse. Here is the first screen of the master list menu:

All the Gopher Servers in the World

(DIR) Search Gopherspace using Veronica
(DIR) The Online World resources handbook (de Presno)
(DIR) 1848 Information & Resources
(DIR) 187resist: Immigrant Rights in California
(DIR) 1994 California Voter Information
(DIR) 3k Associates Gopher Server
(DIR) 807-CITY Ontario Tourism Database
(DIR) AAAS (American Association for the Advancement of Science)
(DIR) AACE - Association for the Advancement of Computing in Education
(DIR) AACRAO National Office, Washington, DC
(DIR) AAMC - Association of American Medical Colleges
(DIR) AAMC - Association of American Medical Colleges
(DIR) AARNET
(DIR) AATF - American Association of Teachers of French
(DIR) ABRF - Association of Biomolecular Resource Facilities
(DIR) ACADEME THIS WEEK (Chronicle of Higher Education)
(DIR) ACE GOPHER (American Council on Education)

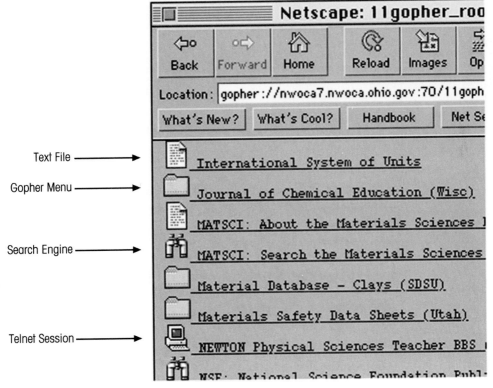

FIG. 6.1

Netscape's Selection Type Icons

There were 2,572 items on the master list of Gopher servers at the time of this writing. You might want to scroll through a few screens just to get a feel for what's there, but don't try to scroll through the whole list. The keyword search command will take you to a specific Gopher more efficiently than scrolling will. For example, if you search "University of Massachusetts," you'll land on the following display:

```
All the Gopher Servers in the World

(DIR)  University of Massachusetts Systemwide Administration
(DIR)  University of Massachusetts at Amherst
(DIR)  University of Massachusetts at Boston
(DIR)  University of Massachusetts at Boston Healey Library Gopher
(DIR)  University of Medicine and Dentistry of New Jersey
(DIR)  University of Miami Biomedical Gopher
(DIR)  University of Michigan ArchiGopher
(DIR)  University of Michigan CITI
(DIR)  University of Michigan College of Engineering Technology Transfer
(DIR)  University of Michigan Computing Club
(DIR)  University of Michigan Computing Club
(DIR)  University of Michigan GOpherBLUE Service
(DIR)  University of Michigan Libraries
(DIR)  University of Michigan Medical Center
(DIR)  University of Mining and Metallurgy, Cracow, (PL)
(DIR)  University of Minnesota
(DIR)  University of Minnesota - Duluth
(DIR)  University of Minnesota Alumni Association
(DIR)  University of Minnesota Plant Pathology Gopher
(DIR)  University of Minnesota Soil Science Gopher Information Service
```

If you can find your university on this list, you are one click away from the root Gopher for your school.

6.2   Campus-Wide Information Servers (CWIS)

If your school has a Gopher server, it almost certainly supports a **CWIS (Campus-Wide Information Server).** This is a directory of campus-specific information that is maintained by the Gopher server. Some of these directories are now housed on Web servers and may no longer be available from a Gopher server, but most campuses have a CWIS somewhere.

To illustrate, let's visit the CWIS at the University of Massachusetts (UMass) at Amherst. (You should try to visit the CWIS at your own university. All CWIS's are fairly similar.) The root Gopher for UMass looks like this:

```
              University of Massachusetts at Amherst

         UMass Amherst Campus-Wide Information System

         * * * * * * * * * * * * * * * *  NOTICE  * * * * * * * * * * * * * * * * * * *

         The information presented by this server is no longer
         being actively maintained. This server may be
         decommissioned shortly.  For current information,
         please refer to our campus Web server at
         http://www.umass.edu

         * * * * * * * * * * * * * * * * * * * * * * * * * * * * * * * * * * * * * * * * * * * *

(DIR) Course Catalogs/Descriptions
(DIR) Academic Department Information
(DIR) University Services
(DIR) Class Materials
(DIR) Hobbies, Special Interest Groups, and other Entertainment
(DIR) About the UMass Campus Wide Information Service (CWIS)
(DIR) Using Computers on Campus
(DIR) Research Information
(DIR) Libraries and Online Media
(DIR) Administrative Department Information
(DIR) More Gophers and Other Internet Services
(DIR) Telephone, Office, and Email Directories
(DIR) News, Jobs, and Other Timely Information
(DIR) About the University
(DIR) Student Organizations
```

Note the message at the top, which indicates that this particular Gopher may not be around much longer. To read about the CWIS at UMass, we could go to "About the UMass Campus Wide Information Service (CWIS)" and consult various documents that describe the facility. One document addresses CWIS policy. There, we find this statement:

> Any legitimate campus organization may provide information
> to be delivered by the CWIS and designate an "information
> provider." A legitimate campus organization might be a
> school, an administrative office, an academic department, or a
> registered student organization.

This indicates that CWIS is an institutional information resource that is restricted to official channels. This is standard CWIS policy, so information posted on a CWIS Gopher is authorized and relatively trustworthy. Each CWIS is a local resource, customized by its host campus, and hierarchically organized in a large tree of Gopher menus. Most CWIS systems interconnect with Gopher space at large, so you can always access CWIS systems for other campuses as well, no matter from which root Gopher you choose to start.

Let's visit the item titled "Telephone, Office, and Email Directories." This takes us to the Gopher menu:

```
Telephone, Office, and Email Directories

(FILE)    About the Directories
(DIR)     Local WHOIS directory server (search only on names)
(CSO)     Local CSO directory server (search on any field)
(FILE)    Emergency Numbers
(DIR)     Directory information from other institutions
```

There are two searchable directories: **WHOIS** and **CSO**. These are both directories for people on the UMass-Amherst campus. We don't really need both of them, and many CWIS sites won't give users a choice. WHOIS is an older directory system, and CSO is a little more powerful. Let's see if I can find my own entry using CSO. If we go to the CSO directory server, we see this:

```
Local CSO directory server (search on any field)

  This is a searchable index of a CSO database.

  Press the 's' key and enter search keywords.

  The keywords that you enter will allow you to search on
a person's name in  the database.
```

Following the instructions, I press "s" and am given a query prompt at the bottom of the screen:

```
Enter a database query:
```

At this prompt, I enter "lehnert," and a new screen appears:

```
CSO Search Results

name: Wendy G Lehnert

        email:  lehnert@cs.umass.edu
        title:  Director, Natural Language Lab
   department:  Computer Science
     building:  Lederle Grad Research Center
        phone:  (413) 545-3639
```

WHOIS allows searches only on names, but CSO allows you to locate an entry by searching any of the database fields. If you didn't know my name, but you knew my phone number or title, you could give CSO my phone number or title and find out who I am. This is especially useful when you have someone's e-mail address and you want to verify that they are who they say they are.

Even if a university doesn't have a Gopher-based WHOIS or CSO directory, you can look for one under their Web pages. If you find information in a WHOIS or CSO directory, you have legitimate information about a person's institutional affiliation. It might not be perfectly accurate (e.g., it might be outdated), but it would be difficult for someone to plant grossly inaccurate information in one of these databases. On the other hand, you shouldn't jump to conclusions if you can't find someone using WHOIS or CSO. Some campuses update these databases in a timely fashion, while others don't. Also, a data-entry typographical error in the name field might make it impossible to locate the entry. If it is very important to locate someone or verify their title, try an online CWIS directory. But follow up with a phone call if the directory comes up empty.

The Veronica Search Engine   6.3

As mentioned earlier, it is possible to find search engines in Gopher space. Many are specific to a particular database (e.g., WHOIS and CSO). But what if you want some general information and you have no idea what server it's on? Then you need to conduct a keyword search over all of Gopher space. The tool you used to do this is **Veronica**.

Finding Veronica

Veronica can be run from public Veronica servers at a number of Gopher sites. To find a Veronica server near you, start at a Gopher root close to home (e.g., a local university). *It is good to use resources nearby in order to minimize Internet traffic and to ensure the fastest possible client/server interactions.* From your root Gopher, look for a menu item that says "Other Services." For example, from the UMass Gopher, you can go to "More Gophers and Other Internet Services." This item leads to a menu that looks like this:

```
More Gophers and Other Internet Services

 (DIR) International Organizations Gophers
 (DIR) United States Commerce Business Daily and Federal Register
 (DIR) Terminal Based Information
 (DIR) FTP Gateways & Archie Searches
 (DIR) WAIS Based Information
  (?)  Gopher NEWS Archives at University of Minnesota
 (DIR) Search GopherSpace using Veronica
 (DIR) Five College Gophers
 (DIR) Other Local/Regional Gophers
 (DIR) Subject Categorized Resources
 (DIR) All Registered Gophers
 (DIR) University of Massachusetts Gophers
```

Here, you'll find a link to Veronica under "Search GopherSpace using Veronica." Following that link, you reach this menu:

```
Search GopherSpace using Veronica

  (?)  Find GOPHER DIRECTORIES by Title word(s) (via PSINet)
  (?)  Find GOPHER DIRECTORIES by Title word(s) (via UNAM)
(FILE) Frequently-Asked Questions (FAQ) about veronica - January 13, 1995
(FILE) How to Compose veronica Queries - June 23, 1994
 (DIR) More veronica: Software, Index-Control Protocol, HTML Pages
  (?)  Search GopherSpace by Title word(s) (via PSINet)
  (?)  Search GopherSpace by Title word(s) (via UNAM)
         Simplified veronica chooses server - pick a search type:
  (?)  Simplified veronica: Find Gopher MENUS only
  (?)  Simplified veronica: find ALL Gopher types
```

This is a menu of different Veronica servers and Veronica search options. Your menu will probably look different because each Gopher tries to point to servers close to home in order to keep response times as fast as possible. Once you are familiar with Veronica, you will understand how to navigate a Veronica menu no matter what Veronica menu you are using.

Two Types of Veronica Searches

There are two different Veronica search options based on two different databases of indices. While the Web offers dozens of available search engines, Gopher space offers only one search engine with two search options. Public Veronica servers are found at ten different Gopher sites, and they all run the same software. This means that *once you've conducted a search using one Veronica server, there is no reason to try again on a difference Veronica server.*

Most Veronica menus give you a choice of servers in case the first one you try doesn't connect. Sometimes these public servers are overloaded, so they'll refuse new requests from additional clients. If you have trouble connecting, try again when the servers are less congested.

Knowing that there are different Veronica servers and two Veronica search options, you can now hope to make sense of any Veronica menu. In the previous menu, you can choose from two servers: PSINet (in Maryland) and UNAM (in Mexico). It doesn't matter which one you use as long as you get a response. If you are very unlucky and neither PSINet or UNAM will connect, you can drop to the bottom of the menu and run a "Simplified veronica" search. In this case, the server decision is made for you automatically. Helpful software kicks in and runs down a list of possible Veronica servers until it finds one that responds. If you frequently experience difficulty when you try to connect to a Veronica server, look for a "Simplified veronica" link and add it to your bookmark file.

Veronica returns Gopher menu items harvested from all of Gopher space. Each Veronica server offers two search options:

1. **Menus-only**: Returns only menu items that point to other Gopher menus. When a Veronica menu title mentions "Directories" or "Menus," it is referring to the menus-only option.

2. **All-types**: Returns all possible menu items regardless of their item type. The hits from an all-types search can point to Gopher menus, text files, keyword search engines, and binary files, among others. When a Veronica title mentions "Gopherspace" or "All Gopher Types," it is referring to the all-types option.

In the case of PSINet, the two Veronica options look like:

```
(?) Find GOPHER DIRECTORIES by Title word(s) (via PSINet)
(?) Search GopherSpace by Title word(s) (via PSINet)
```

Figure 6.2 shows different ways of describing the two Veronica search spaces. Note that the two options are not always worded the same way, but any menu of Veronica options will always offer both search spaces for each of the Veronica servers that it lists. Once you know this, it is easier to figure out which is which.

FIG. 6.2

Two Veronica Search Options

If the menu title says:	then the search option is:
"find (or search) gopher directories"	menus-only
"find (or search) gopher menus"	menus-only
"find (or search) only gopher directories"	menus-only
"find (or search) only gopher menus"	menus-only
"search all of gopherspace"	all-types
"search gopherspace"	all-types
"find (or search) all gopher types"	all-types

On any given search, the menus-only option will normally return fewer hits than the all-types option. This is because the menus-only search space is a subset of the all-types search space. As a rule, it makes sense to try the menus-only option first. If you find hits among menu titles, those menus are likely to contain a lot of relevant pointers. You can find the most relevant Gopher subtrees this way. If a menus-only search doesn't return many hits, you can always move to the all-types option to find additional hits.

Note that Veronica never offers full-text indexing on text documents, so you must select keywords that are likely to appear in Gopher menus. Since menu entries are necessarily limited in length, shorter keywords are generally more successful than longer keywords. For example, using an acronym for an organization is often more successful than using the full name of the organization.

Veronica Queries

The simplest Veronica search is one in which you enter a single keyword. Let's try a search on "eff." EFF stands for the Electronic Frontier Foundation, a nonprofit organization that is concerned with civil rights on the Internet.

In this search, we'll use the menus-only option "Find GOPHER DIRECTORIES by Title word(s) (via PSINet)." This is the smaller of the two search spaces. We get back items containing both "eff" and "EFF." Veronica searches are not case-sensitive. Veronica indicates that there are 14,013 hits, but it lists only 200. Veronica defaults to 200 hits, but you can tell it to show you a different number of results. To see more or fewer than 200 hits, you add a **flag** after your keyword. A flag tells the search engine to override its default setting with a setting that you prefer. Flags are very helpful when you want to change the way Veronica operates. In this case, the flag you use is -m (for "maximum"), followed by the number of hits you want returned. For example, the query "eff -m300" will return the first 300 hits. The dash before the m is just a signal that marks the start of a flag.

EFF maintains an extensive Gopher, so we get back a lot of hits for our single keyword. To look for a specific resource on the EFF Gopher, we should enter a more specific query.

When Veronica is given more than one keyword, it looks for the conjunction of all of the keywords given. So a search on the query "eff guide" will return all of the hits that contain both the keywords "eff" and "guide." Veronica does not look for them as a phrase, and it does not care about the order of the terms. Hence, a search on the query "guide eff" will return the same hits as "eff guide" (but probably not in the same order). From the query "guide eff" and viewing the results with the lynx Web browser, we get back 140 hits, including these:

```
2.   EFF's Guide to the Internet v 3.1 (aka: The Big Dummy's Guide)/
3.   EFF's Guide to the Internet v 3.1 (aka: The Big Dummy's Guide)/
4.   EFF_Net_Guide/
5.   EFF_Net_Guide/
6.   EFF_Net_Guide/
7.   EFF's (Extended) Guide To The Internet/
8.   * Net Info (EFF's Guide to the Internet, FAQs, etc.)/
9.   EFF's Guide to the Internet (ex- Big Dummy's Guide)/
10.  EFF's Extended Guide to the Internet/
11.  EFF's "Big Dummy's Guide to the Internet"/
12.  * Net Info (EFF's Guide to the Internet, FAQs, etc.)/
13.  EFF's (Extended) Guide to the Internet /
14.  EFF's (Extended) Guide to the Internet /
15.  EFF's Guide to the Internet/
16.  eff-guide/
17.  eff-guide/
18.  EFF - The Big Dummy's Guide to Internet/
       .
       .
       .
109. EFF's Guide - ASCII, split to 1000 lines per file/
110. EFF's Net Guide - other versions (TeX/PS/Amiga/Mac/WWW/etc.)/
111. Hungarian Versions of EFF's Guide to the Internet/
112. EFF's Guide - ASCII, split to 1000 lines per file/
113. EFF's Net Guide - other versions (TeX/PS/Amiga/Mac/WWW/etc.)/
114. Hungarian Versions of EFF's Guide to the Internet/
115. EFF's Guide - ASCII, split to 1000 lines per file/
116. EFF_Net_Guide/
117. EFF's Net Guide - other versions (TeX/PS/Amiga/Mac/WWW/etc.)/
118. Hungarian Versions of EFF's Guide to the Internet/
119. EFF's Guide - ASCII, split to 1000 lines per file/
120. EFF's Net Guide - other versions (TeX/PS/Amiga/Mac/WWW/etc.)/
121. Hungarian Versions of EFF's Guide to the Internet/
122. EFF's Guide - ASCII, split to 1000 lines per file/
123. EFF's Guide    (ex-Big Dummy's )/
124. EFF's guide to the internet/
125. EFF's guide to the internet in chapters/
126. EFF's guide to the internet/
```

Note that each menu title ends in a slash (/). This means that all of the hits
are pointers to Gopher menus, as expected.

Note, too, that whenever you get many hits from Veronica, you will see a lot
of duplicate items. If you clicked ten identical menu titles from this list, you
would likely discover that they all lead to the same resource. So, there are fewer
unique resources here than the hit list might suggest. Veronica is showing you
all of the menu titles collected from all Gopher space that point to the same
place. For example, there are many pointers to ***EFF's Guide to the Internet***,
an online book that is well-known and very visible in Gopher space. So, while

there are 140 Veronica hits, there are really only a handful of different locations associated with the EFF Internet guide, and those refer to different versions of the same guide. When Veronica gives you a lot of hits, you might be getting a large number of relevant resources, but you may also just be seeing how visible a single item is to all of the different Gophers in Gopher space.

Links in Gopher space can die and become obsolete just like links on the Web, so you will probably encounter dead menu items from time to time. If you click a dead link, you will be told that the server is not available or the document was not found. If this happens with a link found by Veronica, then before you conclude that the resource is truly unavailable, try some duplicate links. Many Gopher documents are mirrored at multiple sites. If you can't find a document at one address, you might find it at another.

If you have a choice of links, always try to select a site close to home to speed your file transfers. This is especially important if you are looking at a very large set of documents such as an online book. You will find that many Gopher servers are located in Europe as well as the United States, so be aware of the distances you may be traversing. All Web browsers will let you view the URL for a hyperlink before you traverse that link. Navigator and Internet Explorer both have a text box at the bottom of the window that displays the URL for any link over which your mouse is positioned. Look at the domain name to see if you are venturing outside of your country or continent.

If you want to locate the closest possible server, you can conduct a Veronica search that collects all the host names for you in a single file. To scan all of the host names that go along with your Veronica hits, conduct your search using a -l (for "link") flag. For example, if you send the query "guide eff -l," you get back the following:

```
Gopher Menu

(FILE) *** The word "1" is too common a word and is not indexed ***
(FILE) *** Link info for guide eff -1 ***
 (DIR) EFF's Guide to the Internet (ex- Big Dummy's Guide)
 (DIR) EFF's Guide to the Internet v 3.1 (aka: The Big Dummy's Guide)
 (DIR) EFF's Guide to the Internet v 3.1 (aka: The Big Dummy's Guide)
 (DIR) EFF_Net_Guide
 (DIR) EFF_Net_Guide
 (DIR) EFF_Net_Guide
 (DIR) EFF's (Extended) Guide To The Internet
 (DIR) * Net Info (EFF's Guide to the Internet, FAQs, etc.)
 (DIR) EFF's Guide to the Internet (ex- Big Dummy's Guide)
 (DIR) EFF's Extended Guide to the Internet
 (DIR) EFF's "Big Dummy's Guide to the Internet"
 (DIR) * Net Info (EFF's Guide to the Internet, FAQs, etc.)
 (DIR) EFF's (Extended) Guide to the Internet
 (DIR) EFF's (Extended) Guide to the Internet
 (DIR) EFF's Guide to the Internet
```

All of the Gopher addresses associated with these hits have now been compiled for you and can be viewed by going to "Link info for guide eff -l." The first two entries in this file look like this:

```
Type=1
Name=EFF's Guide to the Internet (ex- Big Dummy's Guide)
Path=1/internet/what/EFF_Net_Guide
Host=Gopher.urz.uni-heidelberg.de
Port=70
#
Type=1
Name=EFF's Guide to the Internet v 3.1 (aka: The Big
Dummy's Guide)
Path=1/beginner/netguide
Host=lib-Gopher.lib.indiana.edu
Port=5000
#
```

This indicates that the first Gopher menu is located on a host in Germany (`.de`), while the second menu is on a host in Indiana (`indiana.edu`). Scanning this file further, you'll find hosts in Austria (`.at`), Spain (`.es`), Poland (`.pl`), the Netherlands (`.nl`), and Hungary (`.hu`), along with the original EFF Gopher at `Gopher.eff.org`.

Veronica Search Strategies

Do not expect to wrap up a Veronica search after just one query. Start with a broadly crafted query and then narrow it after you've seen what comes back. Play around with your keywords. Experiment with different synonyms and try a few different combinations of keywords. If you don't know exactly what keywords have been used in Gopher menus, you have to try a number of possibilities.

Logical Connectives

Veronica supports some advanced search features that sometimes can be very useful. For example, you can connect two keywords in a Veronica query with a **logical connective**:

eff AND guide
> —-> Returns titles containing both terms (same as "eff guide").

eff OR guide
> —-> Returns titles containing either term alone or both terms together.

eff NOT guide
> —-> Returns titles that contain "eff" but do not contain "guide."

You don't have to capitalize the connectives; Veronica will recognize them in either uppercase or lowercase. You never have to type AND in a simple query because Veronica assumes the connective AND whenever it sees two keywords without a connective. You will also find that the connective OR is only useful with highly infrequent keywords; most of the time, Veronica queries using OR return too many hits. Of the three logical connectives, only NOT is likely to be of much use.

Wildcard Extenders

Keyword search engines are not very intelligent. They have no understanding of the keywords they process, so they cannot know that anyone using the keyword "archive" would probably also want to match instances of "archives." Keywords that are nouns often lead to good hits in both their singluar and plural forms. But users find it tedious to constantly list all the morphological variants of a good keyword (e.g. `archive OR archives`). To make life a little easier on everyone, some search engines support **wildcard pattern matching**. The wildcard in a keyword is like a wildcard in a card game: it always matches everything.

For example, Veronica supports a form of wildcard pattern matching called a **wildcard extender**. The asterisk character (*) acts as the wildcard. For example, the query "`archive*`" returns all titles that contain "archive," "archived," or "archives."

A wildcard extender works only at the end of words. It is intended to give you flexibility with word endings. You cannot insert the wildcard asterisk at the beginning or in the middle of a word. However, having a wildcard that works at the end of words is still very useful because English has many verb forms and noun forms that share a common root and differ only in their suffixes.

| BEWARE OF WILD CARD EXTENDERS ON VERY SHORT KEYWORDS | Be careful if you use the wildcard extender on a very short word. You might be surprised at the large number of irrelevant matches that come back. For example, suppose you give Veronica the keyword `cat*` because you are interested in cats. In addition to "`cat`" **and** "`cats,`" you might also get hits on "`catalyst,`" "`catapult,`" "`catarac,`" "`Catawba,`" "`catbird,`" "`catch,`" "`catcher,`" "`catechism,`" "`categories,`" "`caterpillar,`" "`catfish,`" "`cathedral,`" "`Catherine,`" "`catheter,`" "`cathode,`" "`Catholic,`" **and** "`cattle.`" |

Learning More about Veronica

To learn more about Veronica search queries, take a look at "How to Compose veronica Queries—June 23, 1994." For some interesting facts about Veronica, consult "Frequently-Asked Questions (FAQ) about Veronica—January 13, 1995." Where are these documents? You can find them in Gopher space. Just use Veronica.

Jughead

As you move around in Gopher space, you may run into **Jughead.** Jughead is just Veronica operating on a smaller search space. While Veronica covers all of Gopher space in its search space, Jughead restricts its searches to a single Gopher server. Not all Gophers have a Jughead, but most of the largest ones do. When present, Jughead is usually found on the root Gopher menu.

Jughead is very useful when you know you once saw something on a particular Gopher, but you can't remember where it was. It is also helpful if you are having trouble finding things on a large Gopher. Jughead search queries can be cast more broadly than Veronica searches because Jughead indexes a smaller amount of material. Like Veronica, Jughead supports OR, AND, and NOT. If you put two keywords in a query with no connective, the connective AND is assumed, just as with Veronica. Jughead also is case-insensitive, like Veronica. All of the same rules that apply to Veronica apply to Jughead. However, you might find the OR connective more useful in Jughead because the number of hits associated with each keyword will be much smaller in Jughead's smaller search spaces. If you want to see some online documentation for Jughead, find a Gopher that supports Jughead and enter a query with the keyword `?help` in the first position.

Why Veronica? Why Jughead?

Some books say that Veronica stands for Very Easy Rodent Oriented Network Index to Computerized Archives. and Jughead stands for Jonzy's Universal Gopher Hierarchy Excavation And Display. But even a computer person would admit that the meanings behind these acronyms are suspiciously strained. In fact, the names Veronica and Jughead come from familiar characters in the old Archie comic strip. Now, any search engine would be proud to work the term "archive" into its name, so "Archie" (**Archive**) was an obvious name for a search engine. Unfortunately, "Archie" had already been snatched up by another Internet search tool (see Chapter 9).

Continued on Next Page

Continued from Previous Page

So when the search engine for Gopher space was created in 1992, it made sense to associate it with Archie by calling it Veronica (Archie's girlfriend). Then, when the site-specific version of Veronica came along in 1993, it was hard to resist the Archie and Veronica theme. The choice of Jughead might have been further encouraged by the fact that Jughead's last name in the comic strip was Jones, and Jughead (the software) was created by Rhett Jones. This also explains Jonzy.

6.4 Subject Trees

Just as the Web gives you a choice of search engines and subject trees, so does Gopher space. Any thorough Gopher hunt should include a visit to at least one or two good subject trees. Subject trees in Gopher space are very similar to their Web-based cousins. There is no one correct topic hierarchy, and some trees will be easier to navigate than others. On the other hand, human beings have created the subject trees, so there is some quality control in the resources that they reference.

Gopher-based subject trees differ from subject trees on the Web in one important way. When you follow a link out of a subject tree on the Web, you can tell that you've left the subject tree. The boundary line is obvious on the Web when you move from a menu-oriented Web page in the subject tree to a Web page that probably contains formatted text and may contain color graphics. But subject tree boundaries in Gopher space are less obvious. This is because all Gopher space is menu-based; one Gopher menu looks just like another Gopher menu. So you may not notice when you move from a menu on one server to a menu on a different server. Even so, if you move to a new server, you've left the original subject tree. To make things even more confusing, you could actually move from one subject tree to another. Keep this in mind when you explore subject trees in Gopher space. If you begin to feel very confused about the path you're following, check to see if you've left your original server.

Subject trees indexed by Jughead are easier to search. Not only will Jughead find relevant items that you might not have been able to find on your own, but you can trust Jughead to keep you within the bounds of the subject tree.

It is a good idea to familiarize yourself with two or three of the larger Gopher subject trees and consult them when you conduct searches in Gopher space. Make bookmarks for your favorites. Here are some good subject trees to explore:

University of Southern California Gopher Jewels

`gopher://cwis.usc.edu`

Follow the menu to: Other Gophers and Information Resources/
                           Gophers-Jewels/

(also at `http://galaxy.einet.net/GJ/`)

InfoSlug at the University of California at Santa Cruz

`gopher://scilibx.ucsc.edu`

PEG at the University of California at Irvine

`gopher://peg.cwis.uci.edu`

North Carolina State University

`gopher://dewey.lib.ncsu.edu`

(use Jughead with the query "study carrels" to reach the subject tree)

MountainNet's AMI Gopher

`gopher://gopher.mountain.net`

PSU Subject Shelf

`gopher://psulias.psu.edu`

U. S. Dept. of Education

`gopher://gopher.ed.gov`

National Weather Forecasts

`gopher://downwind.sprl.umich.edu`

Follow the menu to: Weather Text/
                           U. S. City Forecasts/

(indexed by state and city)

Sometimes it is easier to find things from a subject tree than from Veronica. This is often true when a resource is highly visible and has a large number of menu items pointing to it. Many Gophers have outdated or obsolete menu titles, and these will all show up as hits in a Veronica search. A subject tree is less likely to maintain an obsolete title, but if it does, there will be only one copy of it. Try finding Gopher Jewels from a Veronica search, and you'll see how many dysfunctional menu items are out there.

6.5 ▶ Gophers Tomorrow

As Internet software evolves and Internet demographics shift from academics to mainstream America and beyond, market forces and a form of Darwinian selection will shape the Internet's resources and usage. Some resources will thrive and prosper, while others will flounder and fade away. In the United States, the Web is clearly thriving and Gopher space is quietly fading away. Web spiders have overtaken the Gophers, and there is very little new material in Gopher space these days.

This outcome was inevitable, since there is nothing you can do with a Gopher that you can't do on the Web and there are lots of things you can do on the Web that you can't do with a Gopher. At one time, Web development and Gopher space expansion were running neck and neck. In late 1993, there were more than 500 Web servers and 700 Gopher servers. But in 1994, the mass media began to talk about the Web, and the momentum shifted from Gophers to the Web. By June 1995, there were roughly 9,000 Gopher servers but more than 23,000 Web servers. By June 1996, the number of Web servers had mushroomed to 230,000, leaving the Gophers far behind.

Graphics tipped the scale toward the Web. A Web page can incorporate both text and graphics, but a Gopher menu is limited to text. Although plain text is very practical and frequently adequate, people are visual creatures. A medium that offers graphics will always win out against one that doesn't when all other things are equal (witness the supremacy of television over radio).

Nevertheless, Gophers have some advantages that will be lost if and when the Web completely consumes Gopher space. First, Gophers were created by institutions for the sake of posting institutional information. Random individuals did not set up personal Gophers the way random individuals can now set up personal Web pages. This makes the Web more colorful and less predictable than Gopher space, but there is a price to be paid for the Web's open-ended membership policy.

Second, if your information needs are serious and require credible sources, Gophers are a relatively safe resource. No one worries about bogus Gophers claiming fraudulent affiliations. The people who compile Gopher resources are trusted to do their jobs well. With institutional reputations on the line, no one worries about irresponsible material or shoddy scholarship. Gopher space may not be as large as the Web, but it still contains a wealth of reliable information.

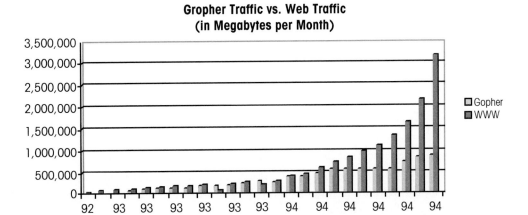

Gropher Traffic vs. Web Traffic
(in Megabytes per Month)

Many Gophers are still available, but they may be frozen in time, reflecting the state of the world circa 1994 or 1995. Many universities are planning to shut down their Gopher servers. In an era of cost cutting and downsizing, Gopher space and the Web were thrown into direct competition with one another, and the Web won. Some organizations still keep their Gophers up to date, but the trend away from Gophers seems clear, at least in the United States and Western Europe. The graph in Figure 6.3 compares Gopher traffic to Web traffic on the NSFnet backbone during the Web's first two years of development.

FIG. 6.3

Gopher Traffic versus Web Traffic

PROBLEMS AND EXERCISES

1. How can you tell if you've stumbled into a Gopher on the Web?
2. How can you create a hypertext link to a Gopher server from a Web page?
3. Explain how Gopher documents differ from Web documents with respect to the credibility and quality of content.
4. Are Veronica searches case-sensitive?
5. What is Jughead?
6. Explain the difference between WHOIS and CSO.
7. Will a Veronica search on the query "University Massachusetts" give you more hits or fewer hits than a Veronica search with the query "Massachusetts?" Explain.
8. Explain the difference between a menus-only search and an all-types Veronica search. Which one uses a larger search space?

9. Explain why 100 different Veronica hits might all point to the same document. Why does this seem to happen more with Veronica than with keyword search engines on the Web?

10. **[Hands On]** Use Veronica to locate all of the public Veronica servers in Gopher space (there are ten). In what countries are these servers located?

11. Explain how a "Simplified Veronica" search differs from other Veronica searches.

12. Name three item types that you will see in Gopher space.

13. **[Hands On]** *Let's Go Gopherin'* is a 35-lesson tutorial on Gopher. Use Veronica to find this tutorial. Who wrote this tutorial, and when was it first offered online?

14. **[Hands On]** Use a Gopher subject tree to find InterNIC (the Internet Network Information Center). Then try to find InterNIC using Veronica. Which way was faster?

15. Why are Gophers good for people with limited bandwidth or older computers?

16. **[Hands On]** The University of Nevada at Reno maintains a directory of Gopher resources at `gopher.scs.unr.edu`. Visit this site and explore it. Starting from this root Gopher, see if you can find (a) a large subject tree, (b) keyword search engines for three different directories of mailing lists, and (c) a fast path to the CSO directory at the University of Massachusetts. Note: Each of these things is only one or two menus away from the root Gopher at Reno.

17. **[Hands On]** Many University Extension Services maintain their own Gophers. Extension services typically contain regionally relevant information related to agriculture, home care, health, and diet. Their Gophers are a great place to find practical information about topics such as gardening and animal care. Different extension services focus on different topics, and they tend to reflect regional interests. Experiment with Veronica queries to get a list of extension service Gophers. Try to eliminate irrelevant hits by using the NOT connective. What do think your best query is?

18. How do Gopher menus differ from hypertext? Describe two differences.

19. Why have some sites stopped maintaining their Gopher servers?

20. **[Hands On]** Suppose you wanted to compile a list of host names for all of the Gophers that support Jughead. What Veronica query would give you this information? Try it. Roughly how many Jughead hosts did you find?

Search Strategies for the Web

> The ability to ask the right question is more than half the battle of finding the answer.
>
> - Thomas J. Watson

THE INTERNET 101 WEB PAGES

- Search Engines
- Meta Engines
- All-In-One Pages
- Specialized Search Engines
- Evaluations and Reviews

Order from Chaos 7.1

The Web opened up the Internet to the general public, generated a great deal of excitement, and created teenage Web surfers. But for people trying to integrate the Web into their work routines and professional activities, the Web is sometimes more monstrous than magical. High expectations for the Web quickly deflate in the face of disappointment, too often supplanted by frustration and disdain. User-friendly software is supposed to be easy to use, so when it fails to deliver, the software has failed. If we equate "easy" with "effortless," then disappointment is inevitable. If we hope to use the Web for serious information needs, then a little effort is in order. Learning just a few powerful strategies should be enough to make a difference. According to one user survey, 84% of the respondents said they did not feel satisfied with their ability to find information on the Web. This chapter should put you in the other 16%.

Anyone who has summoned a search engine and typed in a keyword knows the frustration of trying to take a drink from a fire hose. It may be mildly amusing to see that the search engine thinks there are 800,000 relevant documents out there that relate to a particular query, but most of us don't have time to look at more than 20 or 30 document summaries and perhaps 5 or 10 actual documents. The trick is to make those first 20 or 30 hits the ones you want to see.

If you expect to get what you want on the basis of the first keyword that comes to mind, you will certainly be disappointed. However, if you take the time to learn how to conduct a search on the Web, you can dramatically reduce your false hits without jeopardizing your best hits. An initial search that might bring in 800,000 documents can often be reduced to a few dozen hits in a matter of minutes. This chapter will show you how to analyze your information needs, create different types of queries, and select appropriate search engines. It explores specific search techniques and discusses their relative merits.

Since computer technology evolves rapidly, anything you read about search engines today will be out of date tomorrow. In 1995, Lycos was thought to be the most powerful search engine available to the public. By 1997, there were at least half a dozen better ones. This might make you feel discouraged, especially if you are thinking that everything you learn today is bound to be useless tomorrow. But all of the search engines available in 1997 were recognizable variants of search engines from 1995. Search engines in 2000 and beyond will likely be recognizable variants of those available in 1997. You just need to start somewhere.

Start by figuring out which of three types of questions you have:

1. **Voyager Questions**

   A Voyager question is an open-ended, exploratory question. You use it when you are generally curious about something and you just want to see what's out there. You may have some general expectations, but you are largely ignorant and willing to be educated. If the topic of interest is the solar system, you send out the Voyager to collect as much data as possible. That's the spirit in which Voyager questions are asked.

2. **Deep Thought Questions**

   A Deep Thought question is an open-ended question that is more specific than a Voyager question. In the *Hitchhiker's Guide to the Galaxy*, by Douglas Adams, a computer named Deep Thought sets out to find the meaning of life. This is a good example of an open-ended question. The search for an answer could go on for quite a while. Most people quit when they are too tired to continue or, in the case of Deep Thought, after 7.5 million years. Deep Thought questions are more specific than Voyager questions because they have a specific question to answer. But they are still open-ended because there may be many possible answers. Whenever you want to collect multiple information resources, multiple opinions, or multiple perspectives on an issue, you are asking a Deep Thought question.

3. **Joe Friday Questions**

   A Joe Friday question is a very specific question that has a simple answer. In the 1950s, Jack Webb played a police detective name Joe Friday on the television show "Dragnet." Joe Friday was a dry, business-like soul who was famous for the line, "Just the facts, ma'am. Just the facts." When you pose a Joe Friday question, you know the answer when you see it, and there's no point in looking any further once you have it. Questions that ask about names, dates, locations, and other verifiable facts are all Joe Friday questions.

Once you have categorized your question, you know more about what to expect during your Web search. No category is necessarily harder to work with than any other, as long as you know how to handle it. Before I launch into a discussion of what to do with each question type, let's look at some useful concepts that are used during the Web searches in this text. The next section introduces some basic information retrieval concepts and terminology. Then we will launch a few search expeditions and pull it all together with some concrete examples.

The Meaning of Life

In the *Hitchhiker's Guide to the Galaxy*, the computer Deep Thought worked for 7.5 million years to find the answer to "The Great Question, The Ultimate Question of Life, The Universe, and Everything." When Deep Thought is done, it returns the answer "Forty-two." Douglas Adams once explained in a Prodigy chat room that he used the number 42 because it was the funniest two-digit number he could think of. Adams probably also understood (but has never felt compelled to explain) that 42 is the quintessential Joe Friday answer, and it is mildly disconcerting to see a Joe Friday answer in response to a Deep Thought question. On the other hand, 42 is exactly what you would expect a computer to come up with because computers are so good at handling quantifiable data. By the way, the very real computer that triumphed over World Chess Champion Garry Kasparov in 1997 was named Deep Blue. And, believe it or not, Deep Blue's technological father was a chess computer named Deep Thought. Sometimes the truth is stranger than Douglas Adams (but not often).

7.2 ▶ Basic Information Retrieval Concepts

Information retrieval (IR) is the branch of computer science that deals with the problem of finding information in large text databases. Information retrieval has been around for decades, but general interest in IR heated up with the birth of the Web. A **Web search engine** is an IR system dressed up in a user-friendly interface. Beneath the interface is a computer program that has no understanding of natural language and no ability to comprehend your information needs. IR systems work by looking at the keywords in your input query and trying to locate documents that contain those same keywords.

A search engine **query** can be a single word, a grammatical sentence, or a group of words tossed together in random order. For most search engines, the grammatical construction of a query is irrelevant. The most important information lies in the specific words of the query. Words index the document database. The better the indexes, the more successful the query. It is your job to distinguish effective indexes from less effective ones whenever you compose a query. It is generally impossible to know beforehand which queries are best, so experimentation and feedback are keys to success. There is a system to the madness, but you will still need to feel your way through the process each time.

Fast response times from query engines are possible because all of the documents in a search engine's database have been indexed beforehand. Document indexing is managed behind the scenes by processes that have nothing to do with you or your search engine interactions. It goes on continually because new URLs need to be added to the database all of the time. The better engines also work to eliminate obsolete URLs from their databases as quickly as possible. So any Web database that you tap today is not likely to be the same one you will tap tomorrow. It won't be terribly different, but it will be different.

The Web is a big moving target, so Web search engines must create and update their document databases automatically. Humans cannot hope to examine each new Web page in order to identify good indexes for that page. Instead, Web spiders are constantly working to find new pages, identify indexes for each new page, and add these indexes to the engine's database.

Search Engine Indexing Methods

Some search engines document their text indexing methods online. Special online newsletters and subscription services are also dedicated to tracking this information and summarizing it for conscientious Webmasters who care about making their own Web pages as visible as possible. The indexing for any specific search engine is not described here in full detail. Rather, this section describes the most commonly encountered methods so that you will have some idea how it's done. Because search engines evolve over time, a change in indexing methods can result in a skewed database in which older documents are indexed using one method and newer documents using another. Online documentation sometimes describes the most current indexing method without any reference to previous methods. This makes it difficult to know if a search engine's database has been indexed consistently throughout.

For retrieval purposes, the most important question is whether a database is indexing most of its documents with selective text indexes or with full text indexes. The answer to this question has important implications for query design and search engine selection.

Selective Text Indexing

Selective text indexing operates on the premise that not all text is equal. The title of a document is very important, and the first paragraph is probably very important. On the Web, hyperlinks are also important. It follows that a good set of indexes can be created on the basis of those text components alone, and the rest of the document can be ignored. Each word in the title is therefore added to the database and associated with its parent URL. Similarly, each of the first, say, 100 or 200 words may be added to the database, along with each word that is part of a hyperlink. When the same word is found in a few thousand other Web page titles, all of those URLs are also indexed under that one word. Before you know it, a single word can index hundreds or thousands of Web pages.

Additional database entries are added in order to capture word adjacencies. These are needed to match exact phrases. The database is probably also organized in a way that makes it easy to find frequency counts for each URL index. These frequencies are often helpful in the ranking of retrieved documents.

Different text selection methods may be invoked. For example, an engine might index words found in bulleted lists or in text headers. HTML commands make it easy for a computer to identify selected text, and selected text is found by looking for specific HTML notations. If you knew exactly how a given search engine looked for its document indexes, you could design your Web pages with special attention to the text elements from which the keywords are selected. In addition to writing the text that is visible through a Web browser, a Web page author also can insert meta tags just for the Web spiders. These "hidden" notations are recognized and picked up as document indexes. By using meta tags, you can manually craft a list of keywords that are seen by spiders but invisible to browsers. In this way, you can influence the way a Web page is indexed in case the visible document does not provide adequate indexes on its own.

Full Text Indexing

Full text indexing allows no text to go to waste. All of the text in a document is scanned for indexing terms. It takes more time to index a document in this manner, and the resulting database will be bigger than one that uses selective text indexing. Until very recently, the computational load associated with full text indexing was too demanding for most search engines. But since 1995, the most powerful host machines have had enough memory and speed to make compiling a full text document database a viable option.

Although a full text database is thought to be more powerful than a selective text database, it seldom abandons the utility of selected text. Even in a full text database, some terms are still identifiable as selected text. So a full text database does not necessarily treat all words as equals. A term from the title or the first 50 words of the document can be indexed as such in order to weight it more heavily. So full text indexing can effectively maintain a selective text database alongside its full text database and therefore retain the functionality of two separate databases. There are times when it is advantageous to work with the smaller set of indexes associated with selected text.

Fudging with Full Text	Search engines that use full text indexing typically stop indexing very large documents after a certain point. If a Web page is bigger than 50K, anything after the first 50K is probably never indexed. This can be a problem for some very large archive files that contain hundreds of e-mail messages or Usenet articles.

Some Words Get Ignored

All search engines have a list of terms that they consistently ignore. For example, articles, conjunctions, and prepositions appear in too many documents to be of any use as document indexes. Also, some nouns (e.g., "people" and "Internet") are also ignored because they appear in too many documents. Alta Vista's Simple Search shows you which words in your query were ignored (it marks them "ignored:"). If a preposition or some other word is crucial for your query and your search engine is ignoring it, try to reword your query.

Document Rankings

In the world of information retrieval, few things are black and white. Documents can be strongly connected to a query or only mildly connected. A document that contains all of the query terms clears the qualifying hurdles with room to spare. But what about a document that contains only one query term? Should it be returned, too? What if a document contains multiple instances of the query's terms. Does that make it an even stronger hit?

Term counts and term frequency counts can reflect an intuitive sense of strong hits and weak hits, but it's hard to know how all of the hits should be ranked. If a term appears in the title of a document, is that better than seeing the same term a hundred times throughout the body of the document? However impossible it is to answer a question like this, these judgment calls must be made one way or another. ***As a rule, you shouldn't look past the first 20 or 30 items in a hit list no matter how long the list.*** So some method of ranking relevant documents is needed that puts the best possible candidates at the very top of the list. If a Web search engine does everything else right but gets its document rankings wrong, it will be totally useless.

Sometimes a search engine returns a highly ranked document that makes no sense and you can't understand why it was picked up. When this happens, the search engine may have been responding to hidden text on the Web page. HTML documents can contain text that is not displayed by Web browsers but is nevertheless used by search engines. In particular, a document may contain a list of keywords for retrieval purposes that are never displayed by the Web browsers. Similarly, document descriptions can also be used by a search engine when it describes the documents in its hit list. **Document keywords** and **document descriptions** are created with the META tag in HTML, as shown in these examples:

```
<META     name="description"
          content="Make your own environmentally-friendly
                   glass or windshield cleaner. It's
                   easy.">

<META     name="keywords"
          content="cleaning clean cleaners green
                   environment">
```

Most Web browsers look for a meta description when they display a brief document summary. When no meta description is available, a summary is made from the first few visible words in the document. Words in the meta keyword list can be heavily weighted as important document indexes, so a keyword list can influence the ranking of a document.

Fuzzy Queries

The most popular search engines offer a **simple query option** whereby users are encouraged to type in full sentences or questions describing their information needs. These queries are called **fuzzy queries** and they require nothing of the user but plain English. However, fuzzy query processing should not be confused with human sentence comprehension. You can enter ungrammatical sentences, incomplete sentence fragments, disjoint phrases, or nonsense words, and the search engine won't know the difference. All the search engine sees is a collection of words. When a user enters an English sentence for a fuzzy query, ignored words are removed from the query and documents are ranked on the basis of the surviving terms.

A fuzzy query is often a good starting point for a search session because it gives you a sense of how large your overall search space is going to be. A fuzzy query with a large number of terms will normally return many hits, possibly over 100,000 hits if the database is very large. This is not terribly helpful, but it does tell you that your query is not atypical. If a fuzzy query returns a small number of hits (fewer than 100), then you know you are dealing with a query that may be very challenging.

The 1,000 Document Limit	Although a search engine may tell you that it has found thousands of hits for your query, no search engine is prepared to deliver more than the top 1,000 hits on the ranked hit list. Chances are, you would never have discovered this if I hadn't told you. So don't feel too shortchanged.

Here is an example of a fuzzy query:

I need a chocolate mousse recipe for a dinner party of eight people

The surviving terms are likely to be "chocolate," "mousse," "recipe," "dinner," "party," and "eight." AltaVista returns about 50,000 hits on this query.

You can usually improve the hits at the top of the document rankings by marking **required terms** (+) and **prohibited terms** (-). Most search engines that offer a fuzzy query option also let you mark terms as required or prohibited. When a search engine sees these tags, it reduces its hit list by deleting all documents that contain any prohibited terms as well as all documents that fail to contain all of the required terms. Using the example above, a better query would be:

I need a +chocolate +mousse recipe for a dinner party of eight people

AltaVista returns about 5,000 hits for this query. That's still too many, but it shows that 90% of the hits from the original query must have been totally irrelevant. This second query is a big improvement, but it could still return a recipe for a vanilla mousse cake with chocolate frosting. False hits of this sort could be eliminated by enclosing "chocolate mousse" in double quotation marks instead of using two separate terms "chocolate" and "mousse," which might appear independently in two different parts of the document:

I need a "chocolate mousse" recipe for a dinner party of eight people

Most search engines support **exact phrase matching** and recognize quoted phrases in a query as a signal for exact phrase matching. Quoted phrases can be very useful in fuzzy queries, and they can be marked with + or – just like single-word terms.

Once you understand how fuzzy queries are handled, you can create queries by starting with an English sentence and then modifying it with phrases and extra terms as needed. For example, "dinner" and "party" are not likely to get you any closer to chocolate mousse recipes. In fact, these terms are probably counterproductive because they might lead to a narrative in which someone goes to a dinner party and eats chocolate mousse. On the other hand, you could try harder to capture the eight servings requirement:

+ "chocolate mousse" "eight people" "eight servings" "8 people" "8 servings"

AltaVista returns about 1,000 hits for this query, and the ones at the top of the list are all on target. Your best query is still a fuzzy query, but it wasn't the original English question. To narrow your search, you used exact phrase matching, a required term, and four phrase variations in an effort to zero in on a specific type of recipe. The process of moving from a broad query to a narrow query is called **successive query refinement**. See Figure 7.1.

How Numbers Are Handled

HINT

Some search engines don't index specific numbers, but they do replace numbers with a generic number marker so that numbers will match numbers (although not necessarily the same number). If you need to match a phrase containing a specific number, check first to see if your search engine includes specific numbers in its document indexes. Try a test query with a required number in it and see what comes back.

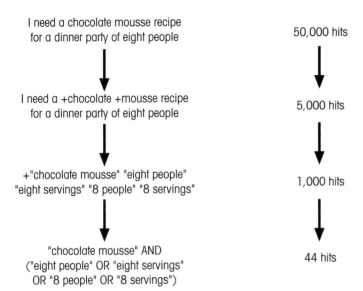

I need a chocolate mousse recipe
for a dinner party of eight people

50,000 hits

I need a +chocolate +mousse recipe
for a dinner party of eight people

5,000 hits

+"chocolate mousse" "eight people"
"eight servings" "8 people" "8 servings"

1,000 hits

"chocolate mousse" AND
("eight people" OR "eight servings"
OR "8 people" OR "8 servings")

44 hits

FIG. 7.1

Successive Query
Refinement

When working with a new query, start with a simple fuzzy query to see how many hits come back. Then narrow your query by marking required and prohibited terms wherever possible. Sometimes a quick inspection of highly ranked hits will suggest helpful prohibited terms that will serve to narrow your query. Refine your query in this manner until it brings back a manageable number of hits. When the document rankings are on your side, you don't need to narrow the query all the way down to a very small hit list. A hit list of 1,000 documents with 20 good ones right at the top is usually a signal to stop searching. Never judge a search result without a quick look at the top ten hits. Hit numbers alone tell you nothing (with the possible exception of zero hits).

Term Counts

HotBot and Alta Vista's Simple Search option show you term counts for each word in your query. These counts tell you how many times a term has been seen in the entire document database. This count is not necessarily equal to the number of documents that contain the term. This is because some documents probably contain the term more than once and each instance of the term is being counted. It is nevertheless useful to see how frequently some of your terms are found. If a query brings in too few hits, you can check these counts to see if one of your required terms was excessively restrictive. **To broaden a query to increase your hit count, look at your required terms and remove the required marker from the term with the smallest term count.** Required terms that occur with low frequency are very beneficial when they are on target, but they can lead to dead ends when they are a little off.

Sometimes the inclusion of a single required term will reduce your hits dramatically, even in a fuzzy query. For example, the query:

+"chocolate mousse" +"Julia Child" +servings

produces exactly six hits on AltaVista, and the first hit is a chocolate mousse recipe, adapted from Julia Child, that serves 6–8 people. Notice that it didn't take a very complicated query to reach this particular document: You simply needed to refine the query with a highly restrictive term (Julia Child). In fact, Alta Vista indexes 1,776 documents containing the term "Julia Child" and 1,965 documents containing "chocolate mousse." So neither of these terms are very restrictive by themselves. But when combined, they produce a very small intersection of documents that contain both phrases (see Figure 7.2).

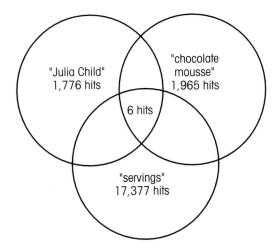

FIG. 7.2

Intersecting Terms in a
Fuzzy Query

Terms always must be considered in the context of the full query in order to assess their effectiveness in successive query refinement.

Where Can I Enter a Fuzzy Query?

Most search engines offer fuzzy queries as the first search option they show you. These are often called Simple Search options. If the interface encourages you to enter an English sentence or question, that's the fuzzy query option. Don't expect to find an input box labeled "fuzzy." Any search option that allows required (+) terms and/or prohibited (-) terms is a fuzzy query option. To enter a fuzzy query for HotBot, change the default setting "all of the words" to "any of the words."

Intelligent Concept Extraction

Some search engines offer a fuzzy query option that tries to identify underlying concepts in your query. For example, the phrase "senior citizens" refers to a concept that is semantically close to other words and phrases, such as "retired people," "grandparents," and "the elderly." Most search engines require the user to think of all of these variations in order to get full coverage from a query. A few search engines perform **intelligent concept extraction** that automatically augments your query with synonyms and related terms.

Intelligent concept extraction attempts to rewrite the original query in terms that capture its underlying concepts. If you are not confident that you can think of all of the different ways that a concept might be expressed, then this is a wonderful feature. On the other hand, if you have a very specific need and you don't want to see any variations on your terms, then you should bypass any search engines that use intelligent concept extraction.

If you are having trouble finding enough hits, you might try intelligent concept extraction to see if a broader interpretation of your needs can locate more documents. Documents will still be ranked with exact matches first, so you should easily see any documents containing your specific query terms. In addition, you may be surprised to see how many more relevant documents can be found when appropriate term substitutions are made.

Excite and Magellan are two search engines that utilize intelligent concept extraction. This feature will probably become more common as search engines try to be more helpful and intelligent.

Relevance Feedback

There are few situations in which you can hope to create the perfect query for a problem on the first try. Most people who work extensively with search engines toss out some exploratory queries before they try to craft the query they really want. Successive query refinement is one way to explore a search space and zero in on a good query. It requires the user to generate a sequence of queries that are increasingly more focused. Sometimes this works well, and sometimes it doesn't. So IR researchers have tried to automate much of the effort associated with successive query refinement. The most successful strategy for automated query refinement is called **relevance feedback**.

In a relevance feedback system, the user issues an initial query and then reviews some number of the resulting hits. If a hit is on target, the user marks it as a "good hit." If a hit is not so good, it remains unmarked. After a few good hits have been marked as such, the search engine goes to work and examines the marked hits in an effort to identify terms that characterize those hits. If the same word or phrase is found in all of the good hits, that word or phrase becomes a relevant term. The process of identifying useful terms on the basis of good representative documents is a key component of relevance feedback.

The beauty of relevance feedback lies in the utility of a few good documents. Once you point to some good example documents, the system identifies terms that should lead to more good documents. You don't have to think about what terms to use or how to construct a good query because that work is all done automatically. You need only to review some documents and identify the good ones. Relevance feedback is a form of successive query refinement in which the search engine tries to meet you halfway. It can be a very effective and painless way to home in on the documents you want.

A simple form of relevance feedback is found in the Excite and Magellan search engines. If you see a document that is very close to the type of document you want, you can follow a link from that document to similar documents. If one of these documents is also on target, you can ask for more documents just like that one. Each time you select a document and ask for more just like it, the search engine uses that document as a source of additional relevance feedback. If you select a chain of documents that are linked by relevance feedback, the search engine uses all of the documents in that chain each time it searches for more similar documents. You never see the enhanced queries that are generated by relevance feedback, so the whole process feels vaguely magical.

Do-it-yourself Relevance Feedback

AltaVista offers a refine feature that helps you redirect your search by including or excluding specific terms associated with your current hit list. After you conduct an initial search, check the "refine" box and then click "submit." AltaVista will scan the current set of hits and show you the most frequently occurring terms from those documents. This resulting term list might contain terms that you would not think of yourself. You can then mark individual terms as required or excluded, and resubmit your query. This is exactly what a relevance feedback engine does but without any assistance from you. If you try this feature, mark only a small number of suggested terms. You don't need to use all of them. In fact, you will get better results if you use only the most obvious ones. With a little practice, you may find this feature very useful for successive query refinement.

Relevance feedback is particularly effective when paired with intelligent concept extraction. This is because intelligent concept extraction broadens a query, while relevance feedback narrows a query with concrete examples of relevant documents. The result is a very powerful combination of complementary search techniques. You don't even need to generate any explicit queries after the very first one. One initial query gets the ball rolling. Your feedback takes over from there.

Logical Expressions Using Boolean Operators

Almost all search engines give you an opportunity to enter queries in the form of logical expressions. A **Boolean query** is a query that combines keywords and key phrases in logical relations. The logical connectives used to combine terms are called **Boolean operators**. The most commonly used Boolean operators are AND and OR, which can be used to narrow or broaden queries respectively.

```
term1 AND term2   === both term1 and term2
                      must be present (narrower)
term1 OR term2    === either term1 or term2
                      must be present (broader)
```

We will see examples of these operators during our search excursions in this chapter.

Another Boolean operator that comes in handy is the **negation operator**:

```
term1 AND NOT term2   === term1 must be present and
                          term2 must not be present
```

Boolean queries are not hard to create, but there is more to good query generation than having a solid grasp of the Boolean operators. The main difficulty in a Boolean search lies in **term selection**. How do you know what terms to include? How can you know when you've generated the best possible query, or even a moderately acceptable one? These are the truly difficult questions, and the Boolean operators offer no guidance on these matters.

Some people assume that Boolean queries produce the best search results because (a) they are called "advanced" instead of "simple" by the search engines, (b) it takes some effort to learn the Boolean operators, and (c) there are always many variations on a Boolean query and you can make very complicated Boolean queries. Boolean operators probably do win hands down on intellectual snob appeal, but that does not necessarily make them the most effective tool in a Web search. There are some questions that work beautifully with Boolean queries. We will see examples of those in our search expeditions in this chapter. In the meantime, keep in mind this rule that applies to Boolean queries: *If a Boolean query contains more than three terms, it is probably too complicated.* If you use Boolean expressions, plan to use very simple ones. Don't get caught up in dozens of possible variations.

Where Can I Enter a Boolean Query?

Be careful to check online documentation to find out where to conduct a Boolean search. If you enter a Boolean expression where the search engine isn't expecting it, the interface will probably not object. It will conduct a search for you, but it won't interpret the Boolean operators as you had intended. To conduct a Boolean search with HotBot, change the default setting "all of the words" to "the Boolean expression." HotBot always needs to be told what type of search you want to conduct. In AltaVista, you must select the Advanced Search option in order to enter a Boolean query. Infoseek is one of the few engines that does not support Boolean searches.

Query Modes and Search Options

Some search engines have just one input window in which you enter your query, while others have two or three query windows. Many such windows come with one or more pull-down menus from which you can set a variety of preferences. These preferences are called **query modes**, or **search options**. Always consult the search engine's online documentation to learn more about these modes and options. At the very least, *make sure you scan the entries in all of the pull-down menus because these will show you the most important settings.*

It always helps to know what to expect. Although an unfamiliar interface may make everything look strange and initially confusing, there are only a few standard options and you will see the same ones over and over again. Here are some standard scenarios to watch for when you are getting to know a new search engine:

- If there are two separate query windows, one is probably for fuzzy queries and the other is probably for Boolean queries.
- The first query window you see is normally the fuzzy query option.
- A window for fuzzy queries will encourage you to use plain English.
- A Boolean query window is often called an "advanced search" option.
- If there is only one query window, check to see if a pull-down menu controls the query options.
- Watch for a pull-down menu with display preferences for your hit lists. You can usually select from two or three levels of detail for each hit.
- You can usually control the number of hits returned per Web page.

Search engines are not very helpful about mistakes in a given query type. If a query comes back with no hits, you have either asked for something that's not in the database or you are in the wrong query mode. If you can't believe it's the former, consider the latter. Similarly, a query that returns an outrageous number of hits may have been misinterpreted because it's in the wrong query mode. A Boolean query in a search window for fuzzy queries will be interpreted as a fuzzy query and all of the Boolean operators will be ignored.

Some Search Expeditions 7.3

Now that you're familiar with the basic concepts involved in Web searches, let's put these ideas into action and look at some specific examples. We will go on some expeditions in search of specific information, and discuss useful search strategies as we go. Once you've completed these expeditions, you should be ready to venture forth on your own Web searches and get good results.

In summary, there are different types of search features (fuzzy queries, required terms, prohibited terms, exact phrase matching, and Boolean expressions) and different ways to index a database of text documents (selective text and full text). We cannot expect to complete a search on the basis of a single query, but we should not have to review more than the first 20 or 30 document descriptions in a query hit list. If a query generates too many hits, we can try to narrow it to reduce the number of hits. If a query generates too few hits, we can try to broaden it to increase the number of hits. With all of these possibilities, you may find the idea of searching the Web a bit overwhelming. But there are some simple heuristics that work remarkably well. With a little study and a bit of practice, you should be able to find the information you're looking for in a matter of minutes.

Before we start, recall the three types of questions:

1. Voyager: Big, open-ended explorations
2. Deep Thought: Open-ended questions with a specific goal
3. Joe Friday: Fact-finding missions

Each of the following search expeditions will demonstrate a specific search strategy in a concrete search situation. If you try to duplicate any of these search expeditions, don't be surprised if you don't see the same results. These examples were collected in the first half of 1997 and the Web has changed since then. New pages have been added, and some old pages may no longer be available. It is very difficult to replicate a search engine trace on the Web because the Web is such a fast-moving target.

Expedition #1: Improve the Focus for Voyager Questions

Sometimes you don't have a specific question or well-defined information need, but you want to familiarize yourself with the online resources for a particular topic. You just want to explore to see what you can find. A good subject tree will probably point you to relevant resources, but for an even bigger picture, you want to augment those resources with a keyword search.

The major problem with Voyager questions is the proverbial fire hose. It's all too easy to drown in the flood of possibly relevant documents. A fuzzy query on a general topic will bring back thousands, possibly hundreds of thousands, of hits. It is imperative to pare down the offerings and identify the best possible documents that are available to you. Here's an example of how to do this.

Suppose you are generally interested in Colonial America, and you want to see what the Internet has to offer on this topic. This is a very broad topic, so you can easily be overwhelmed by too many documents if you're not careful. An exact match on the phrase "Colonial America" will probably produce more than 1,000 hits, with lots of ties for first place. How can you sift through so many documents in order to find the best ones?

Here are hit counts from some of the most popular search engines:

```
             "Colonial America"

                         Hits

            AltaVista    1245
            Infoseek     1727
            Lycos         212
            Excite       3070
            HotBot       4061
            Magellan      220
            WebCrawler    143
```

The engines that return more than 1,000 hits (AltaVista, Infoseek, Excite, and HotBot) each index 20–50 million documents and use full text indexing. Magellan uses full text indexing but apparently on a much smaller database. Lycos and WebCrawler do not use full text indexing, so while their hit counts are smaller, those hits are sometimes highly relevant. A full text database will produce many irrelevant documents because they retrieve documents that merely mention the phrase anywhere in the body of the document. You need to focus the search and narrow the query.

> Although AltaVista has a larger database than Infoseek, Infoseek often returns more hits for queries on academic topics. This may be because Infoseek covers more .edu pages (about 11 million) than AltaVista (about 4 million). It's not enough to know how many pages a search engine indexes. You also need to know what kinds of pages are indexed.

Bigger Isn't Always Better

A **title search** is one way to tackle a broad topic is by narrowing the search to documents that contain some key phrase in the title of the Web page. This will reduce the number of hits, while retaining those documents that are highly relevant. You may miss a few good ones as well, but that's not a serious problem, since for now, you're exploring.

Not all search engines support title searches, but AltaVista and Infoseek do. To conduct a title search, preface your search term with a title tag as shown on the next page. Any query term can be prefaced by a title tag:

```
                      title:"Colonial America"
```

With this query, Infoseek returned 46 hits:

```
17th c. Colonial America — Bibliography
Section: Colonial America
Living History Organizations, Reenactment of Spanish Colonial America,
Newsletter about Spanish Colonial America Living History, Richard
Colonial America
Hispanic America USA Home Colonial America 1492 -1821 Chronology |
Early Spanish Colonial America The Organization of the Spanish Empire by
Colonial America Quest for Gold Spanish Explorers Follow Their Dreams
Spanish Colonial America (Canada) by P. Cawley The flag of Spain flew on
Colonial America
Cristobal Colon Francisco Vasquez de Coronado Home Colonial America Home
Spanish Colonial America Living History Organizations, Reenacting and
Hispano Romano - Spanish Colonial America & Mexico Period
Colonial America
Ale and Ale brewing in colonial America
10/2/95 ART: How John Singleton Copley became colonial America's best
COLONIAL AMERICA-RELATED COLLECTIONS
[cont.]
```

By viewing just the titles of the hits, you can get a good feel for the most relevant documents in Infoseek's database. To obtain the biggest possible picture, you could think of other possible phrases (e.g., "Early America") and conduct title searches for them, too. In any case, by restricting hits to terms in document titles, you can reduce the number of hits to something manageable that can be quickly scanned. AltaVista, which draws from one of the largest online text databases, returned only 23 hits for this title search.

If a title search is not returning enough hits, broaden your search by thinking of alternative phrases or keywords that can also be used to index relevant Web page titles. A title search is only as good as your ability to predict likely Web page titles. Expect to do some browsing from your search engine hit list, too. You are exploring, so take some time to look around. If you are lucky, you might find a great clearinghouse.

Expedition #2: More Signal and Less Noise for Voyager

Once in a while, a query results in many false hits that are all very similar in some way. For example, you might run into many business pages and advertisements when you have no interest in products or services. When all of your false hits can be characterized by some common denominator, you can usually construct a filter to get rid of them.

For example, suppose you are generally interested in Christmas wreaths. You want to see pictures of wreaths, you wonder if there's any folklore associated with them, and you wouldn't mind seeing some instructions for making them, but you don't want to see ads from companies that sell wreaths. This is a Voyager question, and a fuzzy query like "wreath" or "Christmas wreath" should be a good starting point. But in this case, you will see a very large number of commercial pages advertising Christmas wreathes (try it and see).

Three of the most popular search engines support a **domain search** that makes it possible to remove commercial pages from a hit list. A domain search is much like the title search used in the last example. When you preface a term with a domain tag, that term will be matched against the host name of a document's URL. Most commercial Web pages come from a `.com` domain, so all you have to do is remove any hits that contain ".com" in their domain names. AltaVista, Infoseek, and HotBot each use their own tag type for domain names, but they all do the exact same job:

`host:` (for AltaVista)

`site:` (for Infoseek)

`domain:` (for HotBot)

You use a domain tag as a preface to the name of a Web server's host name or a portion of a Web server's host name. In the example, the hit list will exclude Web pages on the basis of Web page host names as directed:

`-host:.com`	`+wreath`	(for AltaVista)
`-site:.com`	`+wreath`	(for Infoseek)
`-domain:com`	`+wreath`	(for HotBot)

By combining a domain tag with a prohibited marker, you can eliminate all of the Web pages that come from `.com` sites.

If you were very alert, you might have noticed that the suggested prohibited term for HotBot in our wreath example was `-domain:com` (without a period) instead of `-domain:.com` (with a period). HotBot will filter out `.com` sites, but only if you leave out the period. This is just a little idiosyncracy of HotBot that you need to remember.

You may also discover that Infoseek is not very effective at filtering out sites on the basis of prohibited domain terms. I checked with the support staff at Infoseek about this, and was told: "The "-" does not work well on very common words, but should work on rarer terms." If you are having trouble with a prohibited term in a fuzzy query, rework your query using Boolean operators. You might have better luck with a Boolean query. Unfortunately, this is not an option with Infoseek.

DOMAIN SEARCH GLITCHES

Domain tags and title tags are examples of **advanced search constraints**. Not all search engines support advanced search constraints; AltaVista, Infoseek, and HotBot do. Appendix E contains a summary of the advanced search tags available for these. However, it is best to consult the online documentation for each search engine to make sure you are working from up-to-date descriptions. Look for online documentation under "Help," "Tips," or "Search Features."

To work with a search engine that doesn't support search constraints, you can create a very effective advertising filter by prohibiting terms likely to be found in commercial ads, as in this example:

-cash -sale -prices -priced -"order now" -"credit cards" -"for sale"

A list like this is also advantageous because it will filter out ads without blocking any .com pages that are purely informational. Develop your own collection of prohibited terms and save it in a file for future reference. Then when you need to filter out commercial ads, you can just grab and drop your filter onto the end of any fuzzy query.

.com Pages Aren't All Bad

Don't be too eager to filter out .com pages routinely. Many .com pages are purely educational, high-quality, and very valuable. You should filter out .com pages only when your queries are resulting in a flood of advertisements.

The next example shows how domain tags can be used to narrow a search and insert quality control into your hits.

Expedition #3: Two Thumbs Up for Deep Thought

Sometimes quality control is your most important concern. Deep Thought questions are open-ended, but there are times when fewer hits of high quality are preferable to lots of hits of variable quality. This is why some people prefer to search subject trees such as Yahoo!. Another way to insert quality control into your search results is to use a general search engine with a large database of Web pages, but then restrict the search to an archive of Web page reviews. Many online newsletters maintain archives that can be searched using their own specialized search engines, or a domain search. What Siskel and Ebert did for the movies, others have done for the Web. Many people have already taken the time to review a lot of Web pages worth visiting, so all you need to do is match your interests against all of these Web page reviews.

Here are three newsletters that archive Web page reviews on a wide range of topics. Each one has its own site-specific search engine, so they've made it easy for you to conduct a search over a restricted set of Web pages. But if you ever want to search a newsletter archive when there is no search engine for it, just find the host where the archive is stored, and use a domain search to restrict your search to that host.

Netsurfer Digest

Homepage: `http://www.netsurf.com/nsd/`

Search Engine: `http://www.netsurf.com/nsd/search.html`

Or from HotBot, use this domain search:

> `domain:www.netsurf.com AND "Netsurfer Digest"`

The Scout Report

Homepage: `http://wwwscout.cs.wisc.edu/Scout/report/`

Search Engine: `http://www.signpost.org/signpost/`

Or from AltaVista, use this domain search:

> `host:cs.wisc.edu AND "Scout Report"`

Your WebScout — Way Cool Links

Homepage: `http://www.webscout.com/`

Search Engine: `http://www.webscout.com/`

I recommend using the suggested search engines for each archive because these are the engines that appear to index the most Web pages for the resources in question (although the *WebScout* archive was recently moved and did not appear to be indexed by any of the main search engines at this time). It is quite possible for a search engine to index part of an archive without indexing the full archive, so some engines provide more coverage for specific Web servers than do others. Always include the name of the newsletter in your query along with the domain name, because the host machine in question probably houses other documents in addition to the newsletter archives. You don't have to stop with just these three archives. If you find other useful newsletters that review notable Web sites, add them to this list.

When you construct a query for a domain-specific search, remember that you are searching a relatively small document collection (see Figure 7.3). Too many hits are not likely to be a problem, so keep your queries broad.

Let's look at one of these filters in action. Suppose we want to find a good resource page for famous quotations. There are a lot of famous quotation collections on the Web. It will take a lot of time to sift through them all to find the best ones. Wouldn't it be wonderful to insert quality control into our search so that we only see the better page? This is the type of search that benefits from Web page reviews. Let's try a search in *The Scout Report* archives. From AltaVista, we enter the query

> host:cs.wisc.edu AND "scout report" AND quotations

**General
Web Search**

Search space
contains more than
1.2 million Web
servers.

**Domain-Constrained
Web Search**

Search space contains
only one Web server
which contains an
appropriate archive.

This is like looking
at every page
inside 12,000
random books.

This is like using
an index in a book
that probably has
the answer.

FIG. 7.3

Search an Archive
Using a Domain
Constraint

We might have tried the phrase "famous quotations" instead, but this is such a select search space that we shouldn't be too worried about a flood of hits. AltaVista returns four hits, but one is a duplicate, so we really get back only three different hits:

```
The Scout Report - September 27, 1996
        September 27, 1996. A Publication of Net
        Scout Services Computer Science Department,
        University of Wisconsin. A Project of the
        InterNIC. The Scout Report..
        http://wwwscout.cs.wisc.edu/scout/report/archive/
        scout-960927.html - size 21K - 18 Nov 96


Greatest Films of All Time
http://www.filmsite.org/films.html
Greatest Films of All Time is a loving tribute to great
films, provided by Tim Dirks. Here you can find plot
information on hundreds of classic films, arranged by
year, genre, and title. Also, there are sections on
memorable film quotations (which are linked to the movie
they came from), as well as great scenes. Possibly the
best part of the entire site is the large bibliography
of film reference books. The only drawback to the site
is that it is not searchable. Are these the best films
of all time? Half the fun of this site is comparing your
list to Mr. Dirks'.
```

The first hit describes a site dedicated to great films that includes memorable quotations from lots of films. This is probably not what we were really looking for, but it's interesting:

```
The Scout Report - June 28, 1996
        June 28, 1996. A Publication of Net Scout Services
        Computer Science Department, University of
        Wisconsin. A Project of the InterNIC. The Scout
        Report is a..
        http://wwwscout.cs.wisc.edu/scout/report/archive
        /scout-960628.html - size 17K - 18 Nov 96


Quotations Page—updated and redesigned
Sporting a new look and user interface, as well as five
hundred new quotations (and a new URL, so check your
bookmark file!), this site allows the user to search ten
Internet quotation archives for keywords. A new advanced
search page offers the choice to search by the text of
quotations, author or subject, or all fields; users may
search in more than one collection at a time on the
advanced search page. The site also provides links to
other quotation resources on the Internet, organized by
topic. This site is not a replacement for a standard
quotation reference source, but rather a constantly
expanding selection of quotations available on the
Internet.
http://www.starlingtech.com/quotes/
Random quotation page:
http://www.starlingtech.com/quotes/randquote.cgi
```

Bingo! This is exactly what we wanted: a search engine for famous quotations that accesses ten different quotation databases and includes links to other quotation resources.

```
The Scout Report - June 7, 1996
        June 7, 1996. A Publication of Net Scout Services
        Computer Science Department, University of Wisconsin.
        A Project of the InterNIC. The Scout Report is a
        http://wwwscout.cs.wisc.edu/scout/report/archive/
        scout-960607.html - size 21K - 13 Dec 96


Financial Data Finder — Ohio State University
The Ohio State University Department of Finance has made
a Financial Data Finder available on the Web. There are
pointers pages to data providers, including Canadian,
Australian, United Kingdom, and Spanish, as well as U.S.
providers; historical data; free and for-fee current
quotations; market news and analysis; and business
```

```
libraries. "Couch potato" investing tips are also
provided. Most links have brief annotations. There are
also links to other Internet finance resources.
http://www.cob.ohio-state.edu/dept/fin/osudata.htm
```

Financial quotations are off-base, but that's what we get for using a broad search term. With two false hits and one excellent hit, we should be happy.

NO BOOLEAN QUERIES FOR INFOSEEK

Remember that Infoseek does not support Boolean queries, so if you want to run a domain-specific search using Infoseek, mark your domain term with the required (+).

Domain constraints can be used to narrow searches and insert quality control into a search whenever you know of a good resource worth searching. Domain-specific searches can improve hit quality while dramatically reducing hit counts. This is possible only because somebody else took the time to identify sites worth knowing about. Trust their judgment, and benefit from their efforts.

A similar strategy can be used whenever someone else has taken the time to compile an appropriate database of resources. Many specialized search engines are restricted to resources for specific topics. *WebScout* has compiled a list of 100 Specialized Search Engines at

```
http://www.webcom.com/webscout/Search/Engines_Frame.html
```

This site will link you to dozens of special-purpose search engines, including these:

- One that looks exclusively for information related to the 1980s
- One that contains over 3,500 searchable, news-related listings from the American Journalism Review
- One that has reviews of more than 70,000 commercial software products
- One that posts 15,000 biographies for people past and present
- One that is a massive, searchable database of books online
- One that is an environmental news clearinghouse
- One for women
- One that is a searchable database of U. S. Government Web sites

- One that features more than 55,000 e-mail discussion groups
- One that indexes abstracts and articles from the world's major medical sites
- One that searches story archives for a specific topic or for magazines by title
- One that is a database of more than 8,000 music-related Web sites
- One that offers daily news from more than 600 information sources
- One that features Price Watch, the fastest way to find the best street price on a computer product
- One that is a searchable archive of recipes

Whenever you find a collection of search engines like this, scan its offerings and bookmark it for future reference. The next time you need some specific information, your fastest path to the answer may be through a specialized search engine.

Expedition #4: Improve the Focus for Deep Thought Questions

Deep Thought questions are open-ended, so you normally want to see more than one good hit, but you probably don't need more than 10 or 20 good hits. Unfortunately, some Deep Thought questions seem to attract a lot of false hits no matter what you do.

For example, suppose you want to find bibliographies on Colonial America. A fuzzy query is always a good place to start, but you normally need to narrow it in order to see many good hits. Sometimes successive query refinement will reduce the hit list and also pull in good hits to the top of the list, as shown in the chocolate mousse example. Recall how you used successive query refinement in that earlier example:

1. Write an English sentence for a fuzzy query.
2. Quote important phrases from (1) and add required/prohibited tags.

   If the quality of your top hits is still not very good, you can take the refinement one step further:

3. Convert the marked terms from (2) into a Boolean expression.

A Boolean expression tends to narrow queries more than a fuzzy query does. With luck, it will also improve the quality of the top hits. Here's what happens when you look for bibliographies about Colonial America using a Boolean query:

```
"Colonial America" AND bibliography

                    Hits
AltaVista       234
Infoseek         67    ← +"Colonial America" +bibliography
Lycos             1
Excite          350
HotBot          663
Magellan         40
WebCrawler       19
```

Although the number of hits is getting smaller, most are irrelevant because the keyword "bibliography" does not guarantee an online bibliography. A document might just mention a bibliography in passing, as in a review for a textbook or a research monograph. Successive query refinement by itself doesn't always produce good results for Deep Thought questions. If you have narrowed a query to a few hundred hits and you are still having trouble finding enough good hits, you can't really hope to narrow this query any further. It's time to try relevance feedback.

For example, consider the hits returned by Excite on the query `Colonial America` AND `bibliography`. An examination of the first 20 or 30 shows a good hit on the fourteenth: "18th Century Journals Bibliography." With this one good hit, you can just press the More Like This button to find a good collection of good hits:

```
18th Century Native Americans Bibliography
VoS English Literature: 18th Century (a big clearing
   house for 18th Century studies)
18th Century Children's Books Bibliography
18th Century Women Bibliography
18th Century Music Bibliography
```

Relevance feedback is very efficient. If you need additional hits, you can take any of the hits from the first round of relevance feedback and ask for More Like This for each of them. When you start seeing the same documents over and over again, you have either exhausted the database or you need to go back to your initial query and think of some alternate terms.

Seeding a Relevance Feedback Search

Suppose you find a really good hit on a search engine that doesn't support relevance feedback and you'd really like to see if there are more documents like that hit. Go to a large relevance feedback engine and try to locate your hit document in its database (Excite is a good one to try). A long, exact phrase match should do the trick if the document is anywhere in the database. Just pick a phrase

phrase you don't expect to see anywhere else. Once you've located the seed document with a relevance feedback engine, you can then use the relevance feedback feature to locate similar documents.

By the way, Excite and Magellan point to each other and allow you to conduct the same search easily on both engines. If you run a search using one engine, look for the button that says "Run this search on Excite" or "Run this search on Magellan." Those links will take you to the other engine and automatically run your current query as a search there. This makes it very easy to conduct relevance feedback searches on two different databases.

If you are having so much trouble that you can't find even one good hit, go to a search engine that offers intelligent concept extraction (e.g., Excite or Magellan) and see if your luck improves. You may just be working with terms that are not the best.

If you are attempting to gather a comprehensive collection of online documents, never ignore the smaller search engines. They may show you good documents that you can't find in other databases. For example, Magellan returned only 40 hits on the query " 'Colonial America' AND bibliography," but the twenty-third hit was a very good one:

```
Untitled    55%    [find similar]
     Vast electronic catalog transforms research on the
     18th century by Beverly T. Watkins. Education for
     the Research Library Professional, Association of
     Research Libs.
     http://lib-www.ucr.edu/cbs/estcdean.html
```

This document leads to an excellent clearinghouse of literary resources. And since Magellan supports relevance feedback, you can follow its "find similar" link to additional relevant hits. It's a big mistake to think that the larger search engines subsume the smaller ones. Different search engines index different document collections.

Expedition #5: "Just the FAQs, Ma'am. Just the FAQs."

Now we will turn to the final question category. Straight-forward, Joe Friday-style questions are the questions you can answer on the basis of one good hit. For example, suppose you need a fact of the sort found in textbooks or encyclopedias. If you frequently find yourself in this situation, you might want to subscribe to the online version of *Encyclopaedia Britannica*. Many universities have site licenses for this, so if you are a college student, check to see if this resource is already available to you through your school.

If you don't have access to a good online encyclopedia, you will probably find it difficult to locate pedagogical documents using general search queries. For example, suppose you want a definition of ultraviolet-B (UV-B) light. You could try a couple of fuzzy queries:

```
What is the definition of UV-B
UV-B definition introduction elementary
```

But the top 20 hits from both of these queries contain documents aimed at a technical audience. None define UV-B because their intended audience is too knowledgeable for such simple definitions. This problem is often encountered with scientific information because the Web is used by scientists who post technical documents and scientific publications. There may be thousands of documents that mention UV-B, but only a few of them explain what it is. How can you hope to zero in on a definition of UV-B?

Chapter 8 discusses FAQ (Frequently Asked Questions) files at some length. For our purposes here, it is enough to know that FAQ files are pedagogical documents on specific topics that are written for people who are trying to learn about the topic. As luck would have it, there are thousands of FAQ files on the Web. Even better, there are Web sites that collect and archive FAQ files for your convenience. Once you have a URL for a FAQ archive, you can restrict a search to the FAQ files so that all you see are the FAQs. Joe Friday would be right at home.

The following filter will limit HotBot to just the FAQs:

```
domain:www.landfield.com AND NOT "Messages sorted by"
```

You need to filter out documents containing "Messages sorted by" because this particular host also houses a mailing list archive and you don't want to see any hits from the mailing list. Try to find a definition for UV-B using this filter at HotBot with the query:

```
domain:www.landfield.com AND NOT "Messages sorted by"
AND uv-b
```

The first two hits returned are:

```
2.2 IS SUNLIGHT BAD FOR TATTOOS?
    http://www.landfield.com/faqs/bodyart/tattoo-faq/
        part6/section-6.html

sci.environment Newsgroup FAQs
    http://www.landfield.com/faqs/by-newsgroup/sci/sci.
        environment.html
```

The first hit is a section from the Tattoo FAQ. In there, UV is mentioned in a section about skin care and sun screens, but there is no definition of UV-B. The second hit points to a collection of scientific FAQs on environmental topics, including the following:

- fusion-faq/section0-intro/part1-overview
- meteorology/storms-faq/part1
- meteorology/storms-faq/part2
- ozone-depletion/antarctic
- ozone-depletion/intro: Multipart - Single Part
- ozone-depletion/stratcl
- ozone-depletion/uv
- sci/climate-change/basics

The next-to-the-last entry points to "Ozone Depletion FAQ Part IV: UV Radiation and its Effects," which addresses the following questions:

1. What is "UV-B"?
2. How does UV-B vary from place to place?
3. Is UV-B at Earth's surface increasing?
4. What is the relationship between UV and skin cancer?
5. Is ozone loss to blame for the melanoma upsurge?
6. Does UV-B cause cataracts?
7. Are sheep going blind in Chile?
8. What effects does increased UV have upon plant life?
9. What effects does increased UV have on marine life?
10. Is UV-B responsible for the amphibian decline?

Bingo! The very first question leads to a definition of UV-B:

```
"UV-B" refers to UV light having a wavelength between
280 and 320 nm. These wavelengths are on the lower edge
of ozone's UV absorption band, in the so-called "Huggins
bands". They are absorbed by ozone, but less efficiently
than shorter wavelengths ("UV-C"). [continued]
```

Sometimes, factual information is more topical or news-oriented than the enduring facts found in encyclopedias. Then a FAQ archive is less likely to be of use, but a similar trick can be played with newspaper archives. For example, suppose you want to know how to qualify for the Boston Marathon. Runners in the Boston Marathon are required to have completed some other marathon within a certain amount of time in order to qualify for the Boston Marathon. You want to see those qualifying times. If you search for "Boston Marathon" in the FAQ archive, you get only one hit, from a FAQ about the TV show "Mad About You." There might have been a FAQ for the Boston Marathon, but apparently not. It was certainly worth trying.

Whenever the terms relevant to your query are narrow, a Boolean query will narrow the search nicely. Consider this query on AltaVista:

"Boston Marathon" AND qualif*

On many search engines, the asterisk allows you to pick up matches on any terms that begin with "qualif." (Recall from Chapter 6 the **wildcard extender** feature for generalizing a search term.) So "qualif*" will match "qualifying," "qualified," "qualify," "qualification," and "qualifications." On AltaVista, this query returns 337 hits, a lot of which are home pages for regional running clubs and personal home pages by runners. You need to focus your search more.

To get away from all of the personal home pages and club pages, restrict your search to articles in a Boston newspaper, such as the *Boston Globe*, a major Boston newspaper, where you can expect to see a lot of coverage on the Boston Marathon. Its domain name is boston.com. Here's the query when you restrict the search to articles in the *Boston Globe*:

host:boston.com AND "Boston Marathon" AND qualif*

The host: tag narrows the search to only those URLs with the boston.com domain name. The result is only 10 hits. You could stop here, but you can further refine the query by exploiting an additional feature in AltaVista's Advanced Search option: *a date constraint*. In this case, you ask for only those documents that were created or updated in 1997 (this search was conducted in April 1997):

host:boston.com AND "Boston Marathon" AND qualif*
start date: 1/Jan/97

This query produces exactly one hit:

```
Marathon Central on Boston.com
   Transportation | Runners | Spectators | Sports Expo |
   Entertainment. Runners: Transportation: 654 buses
   will carry 38,000 runners from Boston (including...
   http://www.boston.com/sports/marathon/survival.htm
   - size 12K - 3 Mar 97
```

From here, you can follow the link "Runners' Info" and then the link "The Facts" in order to find the qualifying times for the 1997 Boston Marathon:

```
Qualifying Times:

Age Group         Men            Women
18-34         3hrs 10min      3hrs 40min
35-39         3hrs 15min      3hrs 45min
40-44         3hrs 20min      3hrs 50min
45-49         3hrs 25min      3hrs 55min
50-54         3hrs 30min      4hrs 00min
55-59         3hrs 35min      4hrs 05min
60-64         3hrs 40min      4hrs 10min
65-69         3hrs 45min      4hrs 15min
70 & over     3hrs 50min      4hrs 20min
```

This is proof positive that it *is* possible to narrow a search down to exactly one document and have it be the right one! (Just don't expect this to ever happen again.)

Restricting a search to a newspaper or a set of newspapers can be very effective when you need topical information. However, you need to use the right newspapers. Sometimes it's enough to look in the *New York Times* or the *Washington Post*, but regional news requires regional papers. The following Web sites are good indexes for online newspapers in the United States and beyond. Any of these resources will give you domain names for the newspapers listed.

UDKi Index of US newspapers

```
http://www.kansan.com/news/NewspaperIndex/USpaperindex.html
```

News / US Newspapers - MPC

```
http://www.microplus.ca/mpc_inet/newsgrp/us_news.htm
```

Inkpot Inkternational News Links:

```
http://webvisions.com.sg/inkpot/news/usstate.html
```

Some online newspapers maintain archives that are publicly available at no charge. Others restrict access to paid subscribers. If you need to tap newspaper articles on a regular basis, a subscription to one or two online newspapers can be a very good investment. It is also useful to know about these sources that journalists use when they need to research a topic:

Electronic Magazines, Journals, and News

```
http://www.cudenver.edu/public/library/reference/ej.html
```

Dean Tudor's Megasources: Surfing for Information and/or Journalism Resources

`http://www.bowdens.com/msource.htm`

Searches can also be restricted to archives for online magazines. Always be on the lookout for useful archives that you can use in your searches. URL constraints are a very powerful feature when you can target appropriate resources.

Expedition #6: Improve the Focus for Joe Friday Questions

Joe Friday questions often respond very nicely to successive query refinement (remember the chocolate mousse?). In fact, there is one class of Joe Friday questions for which it is actually possible to get an answer after only one query. *If the terms relevant to your query are very specific and not seen very often, then a simple Boolean query is probably all you need.*

For example, suppose you are working on a PC and are having trouble running a piece of software called PKZIP. You have checked with the software company's technical support, and they inform you that the Microsoft's IntelliMouse mouse you are using has a software conflict with PKZIP. That's all they know. You could replace your mouse, or you could search the Internet for more options. This is the type of situation that responds beautifully to a Boolean search because you can characterize your query by using infrequently used terms. Here's a very simple Boolean query and the result:

"Microsoft IntelliMouse" AND PKZIP

```
               Hits

AltaVista       4
Infoseek        0     ←    +"Microsoft IntelliMouse" +PKZIP
Lycos           0
Excite          1
HotBot          3
Magellan        0
Web Crawler     0
```

AltaVista, Excite, and HotBot each return a PKZIP documentation file that acknowledges the software conflict with Microsoft's IntelliMouse and tells you how to fix it. Note that only the full text databases were able to locate this information. There is no point in attempting a query like this with a search engine that does not do full text indexing because you can't hope to find these terms in document titles or link names. Infoseek does full text indexing, so you might have expected it to find it. But the Infoseek database contains fewer `.com` pages than do Altavista and HotBot, and PKZIP is a commercial product with online documentation posted by its commercial vendor. Knowing that Infoseek is weak on `.com` pages, you won't be surprised to see it fail on this query.

For comparison's sake, I attempted to locate this information by also using a fuzzy query on each engine. I couldn't find the relevant document in the top 30 documents using any of them, despite the fact that I knew the document was there for at least three of them. So, when you have infrequently used terms in your query, a Boolean query will take you where you need to go much more effectively than a fuzzy query will.

Some queries lend themselves to obvious Boolean queries, and some do not. The last example was a perfect candidate for a Boolean query. You might not always be quite so lucky. Here's one that is a little less cooperative.

At the time of this writing, World Chess Champion Garry Kasparov was preparing to play the premier chess computer, IBM's Deep Blue. Suppose you want to find out the exact time and place of their planned 1997 confrontation. The obvious terms to use are "Kasparov" and "Deep Blue," but be careful—Kasparov played Deep Blue in 1996 as well, so there are undoubtedly a lot of articles that discuss those 1996 games. Indeed, if you query AltaVista with Kasparov AND "Deep Blue," it finds 1,417 hits. Knowing that most of these documents must describe the 1996 event, you can refine your query in an effort to focus on the 1997 games:

Kasparov AND "Deep Blue" AND rematch

This does reduce the hit count significantly, to 56 documents. You might stop here, but maybe a little additional refinement is possible. So filter out the location of the 1996 games (which can be found by examining almost any of the false hit documents):

Kasparov AND "Deep Blue" AND rematch AND NOT Philadelphia

This query locates only ten hits, and the ninth is this:

```
Press release - Chess challenge rematch to take place in
  New York next spring
  Chess challenge rematch to take place in New York next
  spring.
  Ljubljana, 22. 8. 1996. IBM's Deep Blue and World
  Champion Kasparov To Face Off Once Again..
  http://www.si.ibm.com/news/press/press_29.html -
  size 6K - 6 Jan 97
```

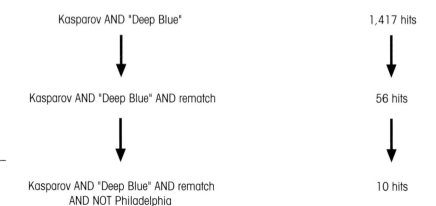

FIG. 7.4

Successive Query
Refinement with a
Boolean Query

This summary sure looks promising, and indeed, when downloaded, it returns

> "New York City, August 20, 1996..IBM and World Chess
> Champion Garry Kasparov today announced that Deep
> Blue, IBM's super-powerful parallel computer, will
> again go head-to-chip with the peerless Kasparov at
> the Millennium off Broadway in New York City from May
> 3 to May 10, 1997."

Bingo! This is exactly what is wanted. The fact that it is in a press release on an IBM server lends credibility to the information found.

When a Boolean query returns too many hits, use successive query refinement to narrow the query (see Figure 7.4). An examination of the false hit documents will often give you ideas and terms you can use to narrow your search. Let the false hits guide you as you go.

Expedition #7: Relaxing with Joe Friday

Sometimes even Joe Friday has to loosen up and relax. If you are working with a Joe Friday question and your query isn't showing any hits remotely close to what you want, you may be dealing with a query that is too narrowly drawn. Most of the time, you'll need to narrow your queries and focus your hits. But once in a while, you need to broaden a query by picking terms that are more general instead of more specific.

For example, suppose you want to know the elevation of Springfield, Massachusetts. You could try a reasonable-looking Boolean query:

(Springfield AND (Massachusetts OR MA)) AND elevation

AltaVista finds 61 hits for this query, including a "Glossary of HIV/AIDS-related Terms." Unfortunately, none of the AltaVista hits contain the information needed. There is no point in refining the query any further, especially since it's not clear how you could. This is one of those times when you need to go in the opposite direction—broaden the query.

If you think about it, you don't really expect to find a Web page out there containing nothing but the geographical profile of Springfield, Massachusetts. If the information is out there, it is probably inside a large database of geographical data for cities all over the United States. If you could find one of those, you could tap it and get the answer to your question. So broaden your query by picking terms that are more general:

+cities +elevation

This is a very simple query. AltaVista's third hit is

```
Geography Web Links
    Geography Web Links. Northern Atlantic Islands
    Programme - information about the islands of the
    North Atlantic. How far is it? - enter two places and
    find.
    http://www.milan.k12.in.us/geog.htm - size 4K -
    22.Jun.96 - English
```

which gives a number of geographical links to check out, including:

```
geo-gw 1.0: Gateway to the Geography Server at UMichigan
```

This turns out to be a specialized keyword search engine based on geographical data about the United States. Looking up "Springfield, MA," you get back

```
Springfield
County: Hampden (25013)
                State: Massachusetts (MA)
                Country: United States (US)
                Remark: county seat
                Feature: Populated place (45)
                Lat/Long: 42 06 05 N 72 35 25 W
                Population (1980): 152319
                Elevation: 70
                ZIP code: 01101 01102 01103 01104 01105 01106
                01107 01108 01109 01111
                ZIP code: 01115 01118 01119 01128 01129 01133
                01138 01139 01144 01151
                ZIP code: 01199
```

Bingo! But why wasn't this page returned when you asked for "Springfield AND (Massachusetts OR MA)) AND elevation"? This is an example of a **fleeting** Web page. A fleeting Web page is a page that is created specifically in response to a request. In this case, the Geography Server created this page just for you in response to your request so that you can see the data. Once you exit the server, the server will throw away this page. The page is not really part of the Web. A spider might pick up a page like this if it happens to visit the server while the page is operational, but the chances of this are remote. Most fleeting pages go away before any spiders see them.

If you can imagine the information you want in a large database of similar information, then rather than creating the specific question you are trying to answer, craft a query that can take you to the database. Some Joe Friday questions can be answered only by relaxing the query and looking for something more general.

Expedition #8: Needles in Haystacks

Every so often, a question seems impossible to answer. The most difficult problems involve information that may be out there in only one or two documents. To make matters worse, there is usually no way of knowing if the information you want is available online. To find something that is not public information or not of general interest to a large number of people, plan to spend some time and summon a lot of patience. When information is especially elusive, you will probably need to conduct your search in three distinct phases:

1. An exploratory search to find useful associations and terms
2. An exhaustive search using all relevant terms
3. Possible follow-up using relevance feedback and browsing

Here's an example of this process. Suppose someone told you about a big project that involves collecting everything known about Henry David Thoreau. The purpose of the project is to include information about all aspects of Thoreau's life, including all of the places he visited, the people he was in contact with, the conveniences and technologies that were available to him, and the books or periodicals he is known to have read. All of this information is supposed to go into a huge hypermedia CD-ROM database so that scholars can study all aspects of Thoreau and the world in which he lived. This undertaking sounds like something you should be able to find on the Web. You want to learn how far this project has progressed, whether it is now available to the general public, and anything else that pertains to the status of the project. This is a Deep Thought question, so you'll start with a fuzzy query and plan to use successive query refinement.

Phase One: An Exploratory Search to Find Useful Associations and Terms

Start, in Phase One, by seeing just how big the search space is for Henry David Thoreau. On AltaVista, an exact phrase match on "Henry David

Thoreau" returns 2,649 documents. HotBot finds 5,015 documents, and Infoseek finds 2,729 documents. Sampling the first few hits based on nothing more than "Henry David Thoreau," you'll see pages dedicated to Thoreau and his writings:

```
The Cambridge Companion to Henry David Thoreau
   The Cambridge Companion to Henry David Thoreau.
   Cambridge Companions to Literature. Edited by Joel
   Myerson University of South Carolina. The Cambridge...
   http://www.cup.cam.ac.uk/titles/3/0521445949.html -
   size 2K - 15 Nov 95

The Henry David Thoreau Room
   The Henry David Thoreau Room. You find yourself
   living beside a pond: "I have thus a tight shingled
   and plastered house, ten feet wide by fifteen
   long,...
   http://levity.com/seabrook/henry.html - size 4K -
   19 Sep 96

From the Journals of Henry David Thoreau
   From The Journals of Henry David Thoreau. How
   indispensable to a correct study of Nature is a
   perception of her true meaning.
   The fact will one day flower.
   http://www.diane.com/readers/thoreau.html - size
   15K - 12 Aug 96
```

Using query refinement, you can add more terms to describe the project, such as "Hypermedia," "CD-ROM," and "scholars." These terms themselves are not very narrow, but when combined with Henry David Thoreau, you should be able to zero in on a relevant document. Try a Boolean query next:

   Henry David Thoreau AND hypermedia AND CD-ROM AND scholars

AltaVista finds three hits for this query, including

```
No Title
   c) copyright Center for Text & Technology,
   Georgetown University, 1993 *** This text may be
   redistributed for not-for-profit uses, but all
   copies must...http://accgopher.georgetown.edu:70/
   0gopher_root%3a[cpet_projects_in_electronic_text.
   digests_disciplines.literature]english.80k - size 64K
   - 28 Feb 97
```

This document is a "Catalog of Projects in Electronic Text" located at the Center for Text & Technology at Georgetown University. The document lists

50 projects and was last updated in February, 1993. One of these projects is listed as the "Thoreau Scholarship Project," which sounds promising:

```
MN Minneapolis/ Thoreau Scholarship Project
   [Educational Technology article (A. Meredith 10/90]
   CPET#319
   1. Thoreau Scholarship Project, Minneapolis, MN
   2. Austin Meredith
         Thoreau Scholarship Project
         2860 Kenwood Isles Drive
         Minneapolis, MN 55408
   3. Henry David Thoreau
   4. Henry David Thoreau
   5. English
   6. Database of the complete works of Henry David
         Thoreau for scholarly use and research.
   8. 256 megabyte disk, soon to be moved to fill a
         1 gigabyte disk. Scanned by either Kurzweil
         character recognition scanner or OmniPage for
         use with a NeXT workstation.
   10. Thoreau, Henry David. complete works. Princeton
         Press.
```

Because the page is dated, you know that this is an old project description. But it is a crucial bit of information because it indicates the project does exist, gives an exact project name, and names a person, Austin Meredith, who is in charge of the project. Now you have two new terms to use in Phase Two of the search: "Thoreau Scholarship Project" and "Austin Meredith." The other two hits on this exploratory query are irrelevant. Although you could try to find more new terms, these two look very promising because they are so specific. So move to Phase Two and see if things work out. (If they don't, you can always drop back to Phase One and work more on the terms.)

Phase Two: An Exhaustive Search Using All Relevant Terms

Start, in Phase Two, with an exact phrase match on "Thoreau Scholarship Project." AltaVista returns three hits, one of which is the Catalog file just seen. The other two are Web pages from Germany:

```
ephtexts.txt
   Electronic Texts in Philosophy. Updated:
   4/21/94: Electronic Texts in Philosophy, 3/ed.
     Date of this version = March 1994.
   Note: This is a HTML-edited...
   http://pollux.zedat.fu-berlin.de/~aporia/ephtexts.
   html - size 64K - 8 Dec 94
```

```
No Title
   Electronic Texts in Philosophy
   ─────────────────────────────────── -

   ── Updated: 4/21/94: Electronic Texts in Philosophy,
   3/ed..
   http://pollux.zedat.fu-berlin.de/~aporia/ephtexts.txt
      - size 57K - 22 Nov 94
```

The December 94 page appears to be an update of the November 94 page, so don't bother to download both of them. Instead, look at the most recent one (which is also the larger one). This file turns out to be another project list. It includes

```
Henry David Thoreau. Complete Works (in
progress, CD-ROM. Contact Austin Meredith,
Thoreau Scholarship Project, 2860 Kenwood Isles
Drive, Minneapolis MN 55408.
```

This doesn't offer any new information, but it is at least consistent with what you already know. Since you are in Phase Two, you'll want to conduct exhaustive searches on the available terms, so try another search engine. HotBot returns two hits for "Thoreau Scholarship Project":

```
1. ephtexts.txt
   99% Electronic Texts in Philosophy Updated: 4/21/94:
      Electronic Texts in Philosophy, 3/ed. Date of this
      version = March 1994. Note: This is a HTML-edited
      version of an ASCII-document. If you want the
      original version (e.g. for download), click here...
      http://pollux.zedat.fu-berlin.de/~aporia/ephtexts.
      html, 65049 bytes,08Dec94

2. (http://pollux.zedat.fu-berlin.de/~aporia/
      ephtexts.txt)
   1% ── Electronic Texts in Philosophy ── Updated: 4/21/94:
      Electronic Texts in Philosophy, 3/ed. Date of this
      version = March 1994. Originally compiled by
      Leslie Burkholder, CDEC, Carnegie Mellon University;
      revised and updated by Eric Palmer...
      http://pollux.zedat.fu-berlin.de/~aporia/
      ephtexts.txt, 58734 bytes, 23Nov94
```

These appear to be the same two `ephtexts.txt` files found with AltaVista. In any case, neither are any newer than December 94, so don't bother to inspect them. Infoseek also finds two 1994 versions of ephtexts.txt, but nothing else. Lycos (beta) and Web Crawler find nothing at all. Excite finds one of the 1994 `ephtexts.txt` files; Magellan returns that same file. So none of the search engines have found anything beyond the three hits that AltaVista originally returned. When seven different search engines can't turn up more than three documents (really just two different documents), you know you are dealing with something that is not very visible.

However, you do have a second term to explore: "Austin Meredith." A preliminary check on AltaVista turns up 47 documents. So next, you'll want to try to narrow the query by adding another phrase, "Henry David Thoreau." Using the Boolean query

"Austin Meredith" AND "Henry David Thoreau"

AltaVista now returns seven documents. The fifth one doesn't look terribly relevant:

```
WEB CONSULTANTS DIGEST 5/21/96
   DIGEST OF THE WEB CONSULTANTS MAILING LIST - 5/21/96.
   TOPICS. INTRODUCTIONS. SUBJECT PREFIX. SURVIVAL AND
   CHANGE. NETSCAPE PROBLEMS. SPEEDING UP GRAPHIC...
   http://just4u.com/webconsultants/dig521.htm - size
   50K - 22 May 96
```

However, when a search turns up so few documents, you can't afford to pass anything up, so take a look at everything that you haven't seen before. This particular document is an archive of messages posted to a mailing list called Web Consultants. This list addresses the interests of Webmasters and others involved in Web page design. The archive was retrieved because it contains an introduction and hello from Austin Meredith:

```
Tue May 21 12:14:57 1996
From: Austin Meredith
Subject: WC: Hi there

Hi there, I'm Austin Meredith of the "Stack of the
Artist of Kouroo" project. We've spent the past seven
years developing the largest hypertext/transclusion mul-
timedia database presently in existence in the humani-
ties, a database which we plan to use not for education
but for purposes of advanced literary research. The
materials focus on the life and times and literary
productions of Henry David Thoreau, but our data ripple
outward from there and, like the ripples on the surface
of Walden Pond, eventually lap against the shores of the
Ganges.

Since the code we have been creating is per Adobe's very
sophisticated FrameMaker application package, it has not
to date been possible for us to put this 20,000,000-link
hypertext "contexture" of Thoreau up on the WWW. Such
code simply does not yet translate into meaningful HTML
because present-day HTML is quite unable to cope with
pull-down menus, reference pages, page backgrounds,
-multiple imbedded frames, transclusion techniques, etc.
```

```
However, we are looking forward to an immediate future
which involves a radically expanded HTML specification,
which _ought to_ allow us at last to go public with
this research literary database. It is for that reason
that we are joining your list — we need to ramp up our
skills so that, as soon as full SGML conversion becomes
feasible, we will be able to go live worldwide.

Henry David Thoreau as every American's kid brother —
Yes!

        Austin Meredith
```

Bingo! This message explains that the project was alive and well in 1996, but is not (yet) available on the Web because the Web isn't technologically ready for it. In the meantime, hypertext development hasn't been hampered by the limitations of the Web. The project is aimed at scholars and researchers rather than the general public, so open public access might not be in the cards. The scope of the project is large, as expected, and it apparently began in 1989, back when hypertext projects were popular but the Web had not yet materialized. This project claims to be the largest hypertext/multimedia database in the humanities.

Note that the project has taken new name, "Stack of the Artist of Kouroo." Now you have a new term for gathering more information, if needed. AltaVista finds 12 different documents that contain the name, but only one other describes the project per se, and that description is less detailed than the one already seen. The rest of the hits merely include the phrase in signature files for Austin Meredith and one other individual affiliated with the project.

Phase 3: Possible Follow-up Using Relevance Feedback and Browsing

This particular example doesn't require a follow-up phase. But you could have followed up if searches on "Stack of the Artist of Kouroo" had turned up a home page for the project. If this project had a Web presence, you might have been able to locate status reports for the project during the follow-up phase.

It helps to think in terms of these three search phases. But don't expect to always follow the phases in order. Sometimes, you'll stumble across new terms in Phase Two and so will need to drop back to Phase One to check them out. For instance, in the previous example, the project name changed. Expect the unexpected, and exploit new terms no matter when they materialize.

Notice that ultimately, you found the information desired in a most unlikely place: an archive for a mailing list about Web page design. While in retrospect this might make sense, it could not have been anticipated. Elusive information often pops up unexpectedly. If you can find the names of individuals who are somehow connected to a project or a problem, be sure to conduct searches for pages involving those people. You might find an informal communication in a mailing list archive or a newsgroup archive that answers your needs. However, resist the impulse to contact directly any person who is likely to have the information you want. When I was preparing this example for the text, I could have tried to contact Austin Meredith as soon as I saw his name in the "Catalog of Electronic Text Projects," but a little extra effort made it unnecessary. Try to be as unobtrusive as possible. Contact strangers with requests for information only after all of your other efforts have failed and only if it is very important for you to get the information. Do not assume familiarity with people you have located through the Internet simply because you found them on the Internet.

Putting It All Together

When you categorize your questions and apply the most effective search strategies to appropriate question types, your Web searches will be more effective and efficient. But don't be afraid to improvise and experiment when a query seems to demand a different approach. For example, I suggested searching an archive of Web page reviews as an appropriate way to narrow a query for a Deep Thought question. But you can use this same technique for Voyager questions, too. Many of these strategies will produce good results for different types of queries. But some strategies are simply more appropriate in certain situations. For example, relevance feedback is less useful for Joe Friday questions because you need one good hit for relevance feedback, and you also need only one good hit to answer a Joe Friday question. Relevance feedback makes more sense when you want to collect at least a few good hits to address an open-ended question. Figure 7.5 shows strategies you can use to adjust your queries when you aren't getting the results you want. Consult this table when you don't know where to begin or your first few queries look like they're going nowhere.

Most searches benefit from successive query refinement, so try to start with a broad query and plan to tighten it as you go. Let false hits suggest useful ways to narrow the query. Query refinement works best if you start fuzzy and slowly move toward a logical expression. Here are the steps to follow when you need to refine a query:

1. Start with a fuzzy query by writing an English sentence.
2. Put double quotation marks around important phrases and mark some terms as required or prohibited.
3. Convert the query to a Boolean query.
4. Add additional terms to increase the focus and shorten the hit list.

	Voyager	**Deep Thought**	**Joe Friday**
Improve the focus	Try a title search	Try relevance feedback	Search a FAQ or newspaper archive
Add quality control	Search archives of Web page reviews	Search archives of Web page reviews	Search a FAQ or newspaper archive
Narrow the query	Use query refinement	Use query refinement	Use query refinement
Relax the query	Try some new terms	Generalize your query	Generalize your query

If you narrow too far, or just start out too narrow, you can always broaden a query like this:

FIG. 7.5

General Strategies for Successful Searching

1. Remove any terms that appear to be overly restrictive.
2. Generalize some terms.
3. Convert a Boolean query to a fuzzy query.
4. Remove some required or prohibited tags.

And if you sense that you are on a dead end and need to start over again, do this:

1. Examine your initial query and see if it really describes what you want.
2. If most of the false hits are very similar, build a filter to get rid of them.
3. Try replacing important terms with synonyms.
4. Try a search engine that uses intelligent concept extraction.
5. Consider looking for a specialized search engine or clearinghouse.

Finally, just because this chapter is devoted to search engines, don't forget that subject trees and clearinghouses are sometimes a much better tool for certain situations. In fact, a subject tree is especially useful for Voyager questions and should probably be checked out first. In the big picture, search engines are just one of your weapons. They are not always the best possible tool for all possible information needs.

7.4

Search Engines and Web Coverage

Many people think the most popular search engines index all or most of the Web pages on the Web. Search engine documentation tends to reinforce this belief. But it's far from true. Currently, there are thought to be about 150 million documents on the Web, although getting an exact count is difficult. At the time of this writing, the largest search engines index at most 50 million documents, no more than about one-third of the Web. Some search engine databases are expanding rapidly, but so is the Web, so it may be a while before anyone can claim to have all of the Web indexed. AltaVista, which is widely believed to offer complete Web coverage, claims to index "31 million pages found on 476,000 servers." That's probably only 20% of the Web. Most users have no idea what they're missing when they use these search engines.

Which documents are visible to the search engines and which aren't? In general, newly created Web pages won't be found by a search engine right away, but that doesn't account for the fact that so much of the Web is not indexed. A search engine can also miss isolated "islands" of Web pages that are not referenced by any hyperlinks outside of the island. If a Web page is not referenced by any other Web pages, it is a good candidate for exclusion.

What the search engines don't reveal is that some of them deliberately ignore portions of the Web because they are already exhausting the capabilities of their current hardware. A hardware upgrade is needed to support additional coverage. These upgrades may not happen any time soon.

It is impossible to know exactly what is missing. If all of the missing Web pages are commercial pages or sleazy sites, then we would at least have some idea what types of pages aren't found by the search engines. But we actually have no idea what types are missing.

There is, nevertheless, evidence that some Web page servers are only partially indexed by specific search engines. For example, John Pike, the Webmaster for the Federation of American Scientists site at `http://www.fas.org/`, reports that he administers a medium-sized Website with some 6,000 Web pages comprising about a half a gigabyte of documents. Let's see how much of this site is indexed by three of the larger search engines. AltaVista, Infoseek, and Hotbot each allow us to collect Web page counts for specific servers using search constraint tags. When we collect counts for `www.fas.org`, we see that none of them index all of the documents on this particular server.

	Domain Constraint	Document Count	Percentage Covered
AltaVista	`host:www.fas.org`	389	6%
Infoseek	`site:www.fas.org`	2,304	38%
HotBot	`domain:www.fas.org`	3,361	56%

None of these large search engines index the entire site, and the best one doesn't index much more than half of it. AltaVista has the worst coverage percentage, with only 6% of the `www.fas.org` documents indexed.

Does this mean that HotBot is the best engine to use when you want to find something on the `www.fas.org server`? Not necessarily. We can't be sure that HotBot indexes all of the same documents as the other two engines. It is possible that different servers have picked up different subsets of the server's pages. We just don't know. This is why it is sometimes very important to conduct a search with more than one search engine.

There is no rhyme or reason when it comes to which URLs make it into a search engine database. Since most pages are collected automatically, URL inclusion is largely random. Some search engine administrators welcome URLs via e-mail, but manual URL processing is slow and expensive, so this pathway is by no means guaranteed. The only practical way to keep up with the Web is through automated spiders. When these methods fail to keep up with everything that's out there, it is difficult to know what is being missed, but isolated instances of missing pages have been verified. In addition to the `www.fas.org example`, the Geocities domain has 300,000 member accounts, but AltaVista sees only 300 Geocities pages. If only 1% of the Geocities accounts have their own Web pages, AltaVista is still missing 90% of them. (See `http://www.melee.com/mica/index.html` for a longer discussion of this problem.)

Some search engines claim to index more of the Web than any other in the hopes of establishing a superior reputation. Unfortunately, search engine superiority is a bit more complicated than that. It does no good to search the largest available index if the information people want isn't included. A larger index is more likely to produce good hits, but there are no guarantees when it comes to a given query. Is it possible to hedge your bets with respect to different search engines? To some extent, yes. With at least some search engines, domain constraints (as described in Section 7.3) can be used to construct a domain profile for each search engine. The following comparison of `.com` and `.edu` page counts is particularly revealing because it says a lot about relative coverage with respect to fundamental content types:

	Total Database	.com Pages	.edu Pages
Infoseek	~25 million	7,148,763	11,047,523
AltaVista	~30 million	10,112,461	4,226,461
HotBot	~50 million	14,032,268	8,559,798

This is an important breakdown if your search activities lean toward academic topics. Although Infoseek has the smallest overall database of the three engines, it has more .edu pages than either of the others, almost three times as many .edu pages as AltaVista. On the other hand, if you are searching for commercial products and services, HotBot appears to provide the most extensive coverage for these pages.

FIG. 7.6

Who Has What

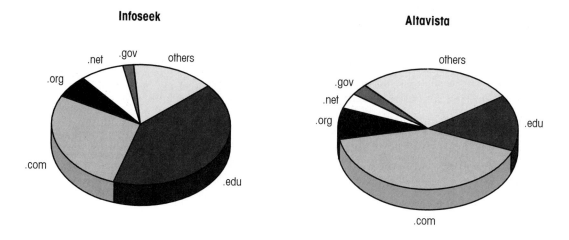

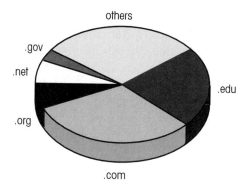

You can collect similar document counts for any host domain that interests you. Figure 7.6 shows a breakdown based on 14 selected domains for three search engines. Remember that the entirety of their databases includes more than these 14 domains, but these domains nevertheless account for a large portion of their total Web coverage.

In each graph shown in Figure 7.6, the category "others" consists of nine host domains (.mil, .ca, .us, .uk, .au, .fr, .de, .jp, and .es). All other host domains are absent from these profiles. If all of the remaining domains were accounted for under "others," that segment of the pie chart would be somewhat larger in each case.

Although it would be interesting to see these breakdowns for all of the most popular search engines, many engines do not support the search constraints that make it possible to collect this data. But it is safe to assume that each search engine has a unique profile with respect to its domain coverage. If you use a few different search engines extensively, you may come to feel that certain engines are likely to be more effective on certain types of queries. This is probably an accurate perception, insofar as domain breakdowns must correlate with content types. A search engine that accesses a database that has 50% of its pages drawn from educational institutions will yield different hits than one that has only 20% of its pages coming from educational sites.

A Comparison of Seven Search Engines

7.5

In this chapter, we've used seven different search engines in our various search expeditions and we've seen how some of them address certain types of situations better than others. It is important to use a variety of search engines to obtain the best possible results, but it also saves time if you can eliminate specific engines from consideration when a disappointing outcome is highly likely. Any truly useful evaluation of search engines must be conducted on a number of dimensions, with the understanding that no one engine is likely to excel on all possible dimensions.

If you use the same search engines extensively, you will eventually learn which ones support which features and you will be able select appropriate engines without much effort. Until then, the summary of different search engines in Figure 7.7 contains will be helpful for fast reference. If you work with a different set of search engines, you will want to work up your own reference table using the features that matter to you. Every effort was made to make this table accurate, but search engines do alter their interfaces and

Key:
- AVss = AltaVista Simple Search
- AVad = AltaVista Advanced Search
- Info1 = Infoseek (UltraSmart)
- Info2 = Infoseek (UltraSeek)
- EX = Excite
- Mag = Magellan
- HB = HotBot
- LYC = Lycos
- WC = WebCrawler

	AVss	AVad	Info1	Info2	Ex	Mag	HB	Lyc	Wc
Fuzzy Searches	X	---	X	X	X	X	X	X	X
Required / Prohibited Terms	X	---	X	X	X	X	X	X	---
Exact Phrase Matching	X	X	X	X	X	X	X	---	X
Boolean Operators	---	X	---	---	X	X	X	X	X
NEAR Operator	---	X	---	---	---	---	---	X	X
Document Ranking Preferences	---	X	---	---	---	---	---	---	---
Title Constraints	X	X	X	X	---	---	---	---	---
Domain Constraints	X	X	X	X	---	---	X	---	---
Other Assorted Constraints	X	X	X	X	---	---	X	---	---
Proper Name Recognition (leading caps in adjacent terms)	---	---	X	X	---	X	---	---	---
Related Topic Suggestions	X	X	X	---	X	X	---	---	X
New Term Suggestions	X	X	---	---	X	---	---	---	---
Subject Tree Searches	X	---	X	---	X	X	---	X	X
Wildcard Matching (*)	X	X	---	---	---	---	---	X	---
Intelligent Concept Extraction	---	---	---	---	X	X	---	---	---
Relevance Feedback	---	---	---	---	X	X	---	---	---
Usenet Newsgroups	X	X	X	X	X	---	X	---	---

FIG. 7.7

Which Search Engine Does What

capabilities from time to time. Always check the online documentation for any search engine that you use to make sure you have an accurate picture of its current capabilities.

Some search engines offer different interfaces and search options. It is important to understand the differences between these options if you want to maximize the utility of the engine. For example, if you enter a Boolean query in AltaVista's Simple Search window, you won't get an error message, but you won't get a Boolean search either. Always take the time to read the online documentation for a search engine found under "Help" or "Tips." Also, some search engines have special features and idiosyncracies. Here are a few worth remembering:

1. In HotBot, you must set an option each time you change your query type. For example, if you want to enter a fuzzy query, make sure the search option says "any of the words" (This is *not* the default setting!).

2. In HotBot, if you include a term that HotBot ignores in a Boolean search or an "all the words" search, it returns no hits.

3. AltaVista's Simple Search shows you approximate term counts and ignored terms.

4. The approximate document count in AltaVista's Simple Search can be very inaccurate. To get an exact document count from AltaVista, go to the Advanced Search option and change the description option to "document count only."

5. AltaVista has a large collection of constraining features. Infoseek has a subset of the AltaVista features. HotBot uses a very different set of constraining features from AltaVista and Infoseek. See Appendix E for more details, or consult online documentation for each of the search engines.

6. Infoseek offers two search options: Ultraseek and Ultrasmart. They are identical as far as their query handling goes, but they return different amounts of information. Ultraseek is a streamlined version of Ultrasmart: it just returns a hit list. Ultrasmart returns the same hit list, but it also gives you Related Topic links into Infoseek's subject tree. Use Ultrasmart if you want to search a subject tree as well as the Web in general. Use Ultraseek when you don't care about the subject tree.

Meta Search Engines and All-In-One Pages

7.6

The various Web excursions in this chapter have demonstrated the importance of working with more than one search engine. If you tap the Web for information on a regular basis, you should be familiar with at least half a dozen search engines. As you may have surmised, it can get tedious carrying a single query around from engine to engine, navigating different interfaces, perusing hit lists, and finding the same false hits over and over again. You may forego the whole process whenever it's not absolutely necessary and you are pressed for time. When something takes more time than it should, a positive outcome may not feel very positive. You have two options, however, to alleviate the tedium: meta search engines and all-in-one pages.

Meta Search Engines

Tapping multiple Web search engines is very repetitive and largely mechanical. For every repetitive and mechanical computer activity, someone has probably written software designed to automate it for you. The automated answer for Web searches is the **meta search engine**. With a meta search engine, you type in your query once and press Enter. The query is then sent by the meta search engine to a number of popular search engines. All you need to do is sift through the hits that come back to you.

Many meta engines are publicly available on the Web. The better ones are careful not to drown you with too many hits or with duplicate copies of the same hits. The meta engine leverages your time and reduces your effort. With a good meta engine, you can streamline your Web searches. But don't delete all of those bookmark entries for your favorite search engines. You'll still need them.

A meta search engine collects the top hits from each of its search engines and decides how to present them to you. It may attempt to interleave them in a single ranked list, or it may let you view them in blocks, one engine at a time. All it does is automate the submission of the query and the assembly of multiple hit lists. It does not add any extra intelligence to your query, beyond making sure that the query makes sense for all of the engines that see it. For some types of queries, this works well. But you should not assume that access to a meta search engine absolves you from all effort. The next section, Dogpile, shows the subtle pitfalls associated with meta search engines.

Dogpile

One meta search engine is called Dogpile (`http://www.dogpile.com/`). Dogpile accesses the following 14 different search engines for the Web, including some engines that are restricted to subject trees:

Yahoo!	PlanetSearch
Lycos's A2Z	WebCrawler
Excite Guide	Infoseek
World WideWeb Worm	Magellan
WWW Yellow Pages	AltaVista
Lycos	Excite
What U Seek	HotBot

To reduce bandwidth consumption and CPU cycles, Dogpile tries three engines at a time and moves on to the next three only if you request more hits. It starts with the narrower databases (the subject trees) and moves to the largest ones. Dogpile queries are limited to a particular syntactic format, including optional Boolean operators. Check the online documentation for a complete description of Dogpile's query options. Figure 7.8 shows Dogpile's home page.

We'll look at just one Dogpile query, so let's use a Joe Friday question. This type of question has the best chance for success on the basis of a single query. Let's see if Dogpile can find out how many people get bitten by fire ants each year in the United States. We'll try the first query we can think of: "fire ants" bitten "each year."

Dogpile shows the exact query submitted to each search engine and it says how many hits were found by each one. The first six engines it tries are Yahoo, Lycos's A2Z, Excite Guide, Lycos, WWW Yellow Pages, and the

FIG. 7.8

The Dogpile Home Page

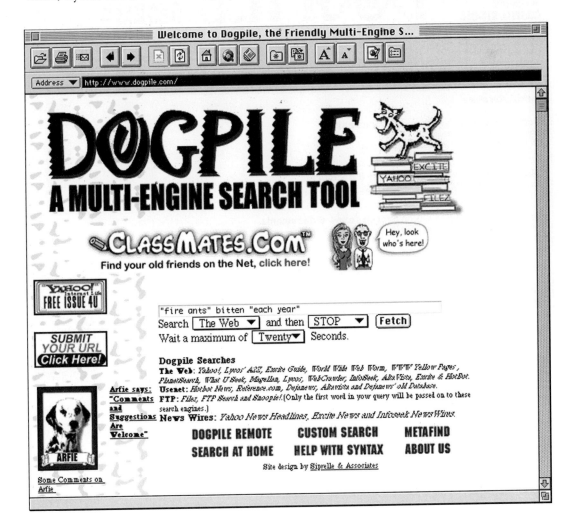

FIG. 7.9

No Hits from the First
Six Engines

World Wide Web Worm. None of these produce any hits. See Figure 7.9. But
we shouldn't be discouraged by the lack of hits just yet. These search engines
have relatively small databases. The first three are subject tree engines. We
also can't feel discouraged if the WWW Yellow Pages doesn't contain information about fire ants.

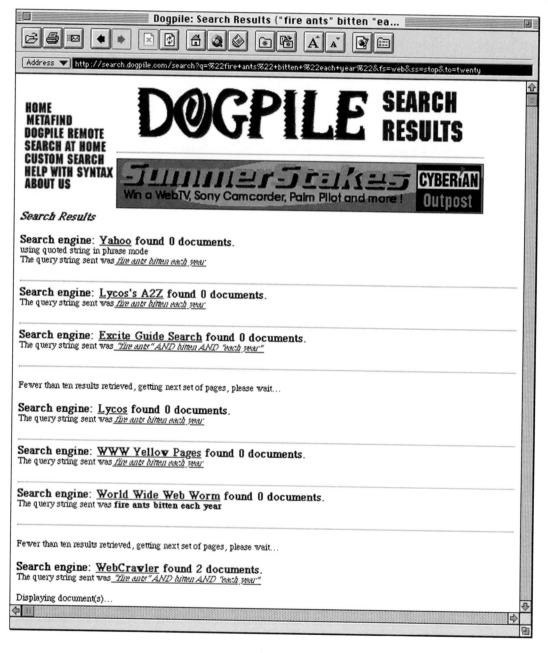

Dogpile sends its query out to three engines at a time. After each block of three, Dogpile checks to see if at least ten hits have been collected. If not, Dogpile automatically moves on to the next three engines. Otherwise Dogpile stops and waits for instructions from the user.

WebCrawler comes up with two hits and PlanetSearch produces ten hits, although most of those are clearly irrelevant. Dogpile shows each hit summary just as the host search engine would display it, so we can see how the different search engines display their documents differently.

Since we've now gathered ten hits, Dogpile gives us the option of going on to more search engines. At this point, we should examine some hits and see if it's necessary to keep going. Figure 7.10 (page 268) shows the results of the first 12 hits returned by Dogpile. hits. In the case of PlanetSearch, we have 69 hits, but Dogpile shows us only the first ten. The rest are available on request. The "Next Set from PlanetSearch" button leads to the next ten hits. However, this doesn't look like a good direction to pursue given how many bad hits popped up in the top ten from PlanetSearch.

Dogpile offers many of the features found at each of the different search engines all in one place. For example, Web Crawler's relevance feedback links are available here just as they are from the Web Crawler server. So if we see a page that might lead to the answer, we can click "Similar Pages." If for some reason we want to visit one of the search engine servers, we can just click the header links that identify the different search engines.

Dogpile is a wonderful meta search engine with a very nice interface. But whenever you find something that looks terribly convenient, look to see what you have to give up in exchange for that convenience. In the case of Dogpile, we lose some control over our query. Since different search engines support different kinds of search features, Dogpile has to rework the initial query to make sure it conforms to the required input format for each search engine. A review of the queries that are sent to each site reveals there are four possible variations:

```
fire ants bitten each year
goes to --> Yahoo, Lycos A2Z, Lycos, World Wide Web
Worm, WWW Yellow Pages

+fire +ants +bitten +each +year
goes to --> PlanetSearch, Infoseek

"fire ants" AND bitten AND "each year"
goes to --> ExiteGuide Search, WebCrawler, AltaVista,
Magellan, Excite

fire AND ants AND bitten AND each AND year
goes to --> HotBot
```

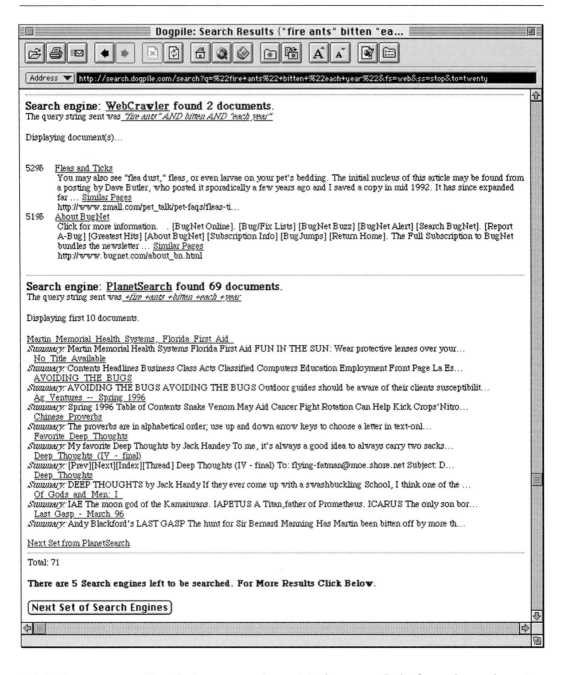

FIG. 7.10

The Results of the First
Twelve Hits

Dogpile has massaged our initial query a little for each search engine. Whenever possible, it generates a Boolean query by inserting AND in between each pair of terms. In the case of HotBot, however, it's not clear why Dogpile does what it does. HotBot does support quoted phrases in its

Boolean queries, so it seems odd for Dogpile to remove all of the quoted phrases. Similarly, Infoseek also accepts quoted phrases, so there was no reason to remove them from that query either. In the case of HotBot, Dogpile queries often return no hits. This is because if your query contains one the words that HotBot doesn't include in its database, HotBot isn't smart enough to remove it from your Boolean query. Hotbot won't return any documents that aren't indexed by such terms, but of course *none* of HotBot's documents are indexed by those terms. Hence, HotBot comes back empty-handed whenever a query contains one of HotBot's ignored terms. Maybe HotBot and Dogpile will learn to get along better in the future. And maybe HotBot will learn to interpret its Boolean queries more reasonably. In the meantime, don't expect much from HotBot via Dogpile.

So, although we need enter an initial query only once, we have to go along with whatever Dogpile sends to each of the search engines. If we agree with Dogpile's actions, then the trade-off is a good one. If we don't like one of Dogpile's actions, there's nothing we can do about it. In some cases, a meta search engine can't be expected to get the query right. For example, if we want to use domain constraints, a meta search engine is no place to go because most search engines don't support domain constraints, and the ones that do require different tags for the constraining terms. On the other hand, for some types of queries a meta search engine can be a real godsend. *If you have a narrow query with infrequently used terms, a meta search engine may save you a lot of time.*

All software interfaces have to balance their ease of operation against powerful features and maximal user control. When an interface is designed to be user-friendly (or maybe even idiot-friendly), it usually does so at the cost of potential power. When an interface offers users maximal control, it is usually more confusing for neophytes. Meta search engines are designed for people in a hurry who want a simple solution to their information needs. They try to deliver maximal return for minimal effort, but they also limit potential power in order to free users from a lot of options and decision making (see Figure 7.11).

Software
Convenience

Software
Control

FIG. 7.11

Balancing
Convenience and
Control

All-In-One Pages

An alternative to the meta search engine is the **all-in-one page**. The all-in-one page allows you to retain complete control over your queries while minimizing the tedium of visiting a lot of different search engines. It is not just a collection of pointers to a lot of different search engines. It is a Web page with windows for entering queries that are then sent to specific search engines. From one page, you can enter your query six times and send it to six different search engines. The advantage is that you retain complete control over all of your queries. You can tune the query for each engine and be confident that the query you type is the query the engine receives. You may have to reenter the query a few times, but this is a small price to pay for total control.

An all-in-one page represents a different solution to the convenience/control trade-off. You retain complete control over your queries while you base all of your operations from a single Web page. You don't waste a lot of time visiting different search engines and negotiating all of their different interfaces, and you don't relinquish any control over your queries. For a knowledgeable user who knows how to adjust a query for different search engines, an all-in-one search page can be a superior alternative to meta engines.

7.7 General Tips to Remember

1. Try a fuzzy query before a Boolean query.

2. Successive query refinement can help you zero in on good hits. Don't give up if the first query fails.

3. Be careful to say exactly what you want, for example, "finding factors for Fermat numbers" is better than just "Fermat numbers."

4. Use different search engines. They each index a different subset of the Web.

5. Be conservative with your use of required and prohibited terms. When you restrict a search with these tags, you might eliminate relevant documents.

6. If you can't find what you want in the first 20 or 30 hits, give up on that hit list.

7. Experiment with different queries and different terms. When you scan a hit list, study those hits to collect additional synonyms and phrases.

8. If you are going around in circles with Boolean searches, try a different search type.

9. If you need a definition, search a FAQ archive.

10. If you need to broaden a search, eliminate required terms with small frequency counts.

11. Use intelligent concept extraction to broaden a search.

12. If you are overwhelmed by too many hits, try a title search to reduce the hit count.

13. Use an appropriate specialized search engine when possible.

14. Require the name of a relevant person or organization as a good way to narrow a search.

15. Collect pointers to site review archives. Search these archives when quality control is your top priority.

16. Plan to browse a bit when you find a document that is not quite relevant but may be connected to something that is. Remember, only a fraction of all available Web pages are indexed by any of the search engines. The one you want may be a link away but invisible to the search engine.

17. Use a filter when you want to get rid of commercial pages—but remember that not all .com pages are advertisements.

18. If you know an exact quotation from a specific document, use exact phrase matching to locate that document.

19. If you know that a document must contain specific terms and phrases, use a Boolean search.

20. If you are not sure of appropriate terms or phrases, try intelligent concept extraction.

21. If you are having trouble finding a good query, go to an engine with relevance feedback and see if one good hit can lead you to more.

22. Don't expect a meta search engine to do your thinking for you. Tossing out a careless query to 14 different search engines is no substitute for sending a few systematic queries to one good one.

23. A meta search engine might save time when you're looking for a needle in a haystack but only if you use infrequently seen terms.

24. An all-in-one page is better than a meta search engine if you need special search features or queries that are carefully tuned for different search engines.

25. Be unobtrusive. Do not contact strangers for information unless doing so is your absolute last resort.

PROBLEMS AND EXERCISES

1. What makes a query "narrow"? What makes a query "broad"?

2. Does successive query refinement increase or decrease the number of hits?

3. Do all search engines support title searches? When are title searches useful?

4. What happens to the number of hits when you add prohibited terms to a query? When you add required terms to a query?

5. What is the difference between a meta engine and an all-in-one page?

6. What is the difference between the term "century" and the term "Century" when used in search queries? How do most search engines treat these terms?

7. When is it better to use a fuzzy query? A Boolean query?

8. What is relevance feedback, and when is it useful?

9. Some large Web sites provide their own keyword search facilities. Is it better to use one of those when it's available or to use a more powerful search engine with a domain constraint?

10. Sometimes you see a Web page that begins by repeating the same word or phrase over and over again (could be a thousand times). Why would a Web page author do this? What's going on?

11. Sometimes a document summary from a search engine displays a description for the document that is not in the document itself. Where do these descriptions come from?

12. If a Web page is returned that does not contain one of your required terms, what probably happened? If a Web page is returned that contains a prohibited term, what probably happened?

13. Do any search engines index the entire Web? If not, how much do the largest databases cover?

14. If one search engine uses a bigger database than another, is it necessarily better? Explain.

15. If you want to shop around for a commercial service or product, would you expect to be better off using Infoseek, AltaVista, or HotBot?

16. If you locate part of a mailing list archive on a given search engine, does that mean the entire archive is indexed by that same engine?

17. What is intelligent concept extraction, and when don't you want to use it?

18. Suppose you are refining a query by adding prohibited terms. You add one last prohibited term, and your hit count drops to 0. Should you remove the last term you added to the query in order to proceed? Explain.

19. Suppose you want to restrict a search to the "Scout Report" archives. Why isn't it enough just to add the term +"Scout Report" to your query?

20. Can a search engine affiliated with a full text database be forced to behave more like a search engine with a selective text database? If so, how? Why would anyone want this?

    Questions 21–30 are sample search questions you can use to practice the techniques described in this chapter. Start by categorizing each question and looking for an example in Section 7.3 that is similar. Try to be systematic in your search activities. Keep some notes describing your queries and results. How many queries did you use for each question? Did you run into dead ends that forced you start all over? Consult Figure 7.5 if you get stuck.

21. [**Hands On**] The "Good Times" virus warning is a legendary Internet phenomenon. When did it first appear?

22. [**Hands On**] What disease can be passed from pet iguanas to people? Is it ever fatal in humans?

23. [**Hands On**] List seven reasons why the Pacific reef systems are in decline.

24. [**Hands On**] Find a ranked list of the ten largest cities in California.

25. [**Hands On**] If you want to remember the signs and symptoms of skin cancer, you can learn the "ABCDE" rule for skin cancer. Can you find a description of the ABCDE rule on the Web? (Don't settle for the ABCD rule. Get the full ABCDE rule).

26. [**Hands On**] Have there ever been any U. S. Presidents who never married? If so, which ones?

27. [**Hands On**] What makes Pele (the legendary soccer player from Brazil) so great? Find some statistics that support his strong reputation.

28. [**Hands On**] What percentage of the American population is functionally illiterate? What does it mean to be functionally illiterate?

29. [**Hands On**] On what date did the Berlin wall go up? On what date did it come down?

30. [**Hands On**] Deep Thought and the number 42 are near and dear to the hearts of all Douglas Adams (*Hitchhiker's Guide to the Galaxy*) fans. What role does the number 42 play in the lives of all dogs?

Usenet Newsgroups

8

THE INTERNET 101 WEB PAGES

- Usenet Information Sites
- How to Find Specific Newsgroups
- Search Engines for Usenet Archives
- News Readers

> The illiterate of the 21st century will not be those who cannot read and write, but those who cannot learn, unlearn, and relearn.
>
> - ALVIN TOFFLER

What Is Usenet?

8.1

In the musical *Guys and Dolls,* Nathan Detroit runs "the oldest established permanent floating crap game in New York." Players come and players go, but the game goes on forever. This is just like the Usenet newsgroups, except that in the case of Usenet, people participate in one long never-ending conversation. In fact, at any one time there are over 18,000 simultaneous conversations taking place under the Usenet umbrella.

Anyone can drop in to listen, ask a question, disagree with a claim, or offer advice. Some people drop by for just a minute, while others are active daily for months or years. Some newsgroups attract serious people who share technical information and help each other solve perplexing problems. Some exist purely for entertainment. And others are national bulletin boards of want ads. There are **moderated newsgroups**, which are run by moderators who approve information before it can be posted, and there are **unmoderated newsgroups**, which allow any message to be posted. Some newsgroups are available to users all over the world, while others are restricted to a particular region. All are associated with a specific topic, and participants are generally intolerant of discussions that stray too far off topic.

Usenet (which is short for User's Network) was first created in 1979. Today, it serves an estimated 10 million users. It is similar to the thousands of bulletin board systems (BBSs) that serve regional users via direct dial-up access, but the scope of Usenet is global rather than local. Because Usenet taps such a large user population, its newsgroups can address very narrow interests and still attract a healthy number of participants. For people with esoteric interests or people who are geographically isolated, access to Usenet is a world of virtual communities that could never exist in any other way.

The term "newsgroup" is a bit misleading, since most newsgroups are not news related. They are really discussion groups, much like an e-mail mailing list, but organized within a large hierarchy and distributed by special news servers dedicated to Usenet communications. Each message that appears on a Usenet newsgroup is called an **article**, and each article contains a header just like an e-mail header. To read and post Usenet articles, you need access to a Usenet news server (ISP services normally include Usenet access) and a special piece of client software called a **news reader**. Many browsers include their own news readers, so if you run Navigator or Internet Explorer, you can use their news readers to get started. If you decide to spend a lot of time working with Usenet, you may want to shop around for a news reader that supports special features. But any news reader will be fine for getting you off the ground.

The Usenet newsgroups are organized hierarchically, with a small number of names that are used to identify broad categories at the highest level. Newsgroup names start with the broadest category on the left and move down through successive subcategories from left to right (unlike host names, which start with a specific host name on the left and end in a general domain name). There are 103 top-level Usenet categories, but most of the traffic occurs in the "Big Eight:"

biz	Business-related topics
comp	Computer-related topics
sci	Scientific topics
misc	Miscellaneous topics
soc	Social issues and topics
talk	Debates and lengthy conversations
news	News and topical subjects
rec	Hobbies and recreational topics

plus another major newsgroup category, alt, an alternative topic hierarchy, which is discussed in more detail shortly.

Newsgroup names are self-explanatory and designed to differentiate closely related groups. The name alone will usually tell you what a newsgroup is about. Here are some examples of Usenet newsgroups:

```
alt.adoption.searching
alt.esperanto.beginner
sci.optics
sci.techniques.mag-resonance
comp.infosystems.www.browsers.misc
misc.health.alternative.diabetes
misc.forsale.computers.mac-specific.cards.misc
```

There are also many newsgroups in which you can get answers to all of your questions about Usenet, including these:

`alt.newbie` (*if you've never seen spam, you'll find it here*)

`news.announce.newusers` (*moderated; informational posts for new users*)

`news.groups.questions` (*a good place to ask where to post specific questions*)

`news.newusers.questions` (*a good place to ask questions about the Internet*)

You'll find many useful articles posted for the edification of new users on the newsgroup news.announce.newusers (see Figure 8.1). Just look for the following titles:

What is Usenet?

What is Usenet? A second opinion.

Answers to Frequently Asked Questions about Usenet

A Primer on How to Work with the Usenet Community

How to Find the Right Place to Post

Rules for Posting to Usenet

Hints for Writing Styles for Usenet

Emily Postnews Answers Your Questions on Netiquette

How to Advertise on Usenet

If you have trouble finding any of these on news.announce.newusers, try an exact phrase search from a Web search engine (as described in Chapter 7).

Like everything else on the Internet, the Usenet newsgroups are constantly evolving. New groups emerge when enough interest in a topic materializes. Old groups can die off if interest in them wanes. Don't expect any published

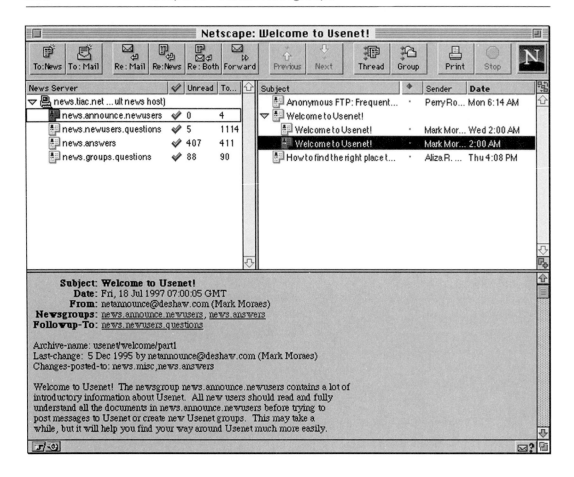

FIG. 8.1

Viewing an Article from
the news.announce
Hierarchy

list of Usenet newsgroups, to be up-to-date. You can find newsgroup lists online that are updated every two months (see the Internet 101 Web pages for pointers).

Despite the large number of newsgroups, it usually is not easy to a create a new one. Newsgroup creation is no small undertaking. It is subject to many bureaucratic requirements. The process requires submitting a "Request For Discussion" (RFD) and a "Call For Votes" (CFV). Votes are collected via e-mail according to a strict voting procedure. If the newsgroup vote passes, then there is a waiting period before the new group is finally created. The entire process takes many months and consumes a lot of time and effort. To get an idea of how much, take a look at the sample RFDs and CFVs that are posted at the newsgroup news.groups.

The alt newsgroups are in a special category because anyone can create an alt newsgroup without RFDs or CFVs. They are sort of an "underground" region of Usenet where the normal Usenet rules do not apply. Because anyone can create one, spurious ones are created every day for the sake of sending a silly newsgroup name out to all Usenet servers. These bogus newsgroups rarely receive any posts. They just clutter up the servers until system administrators remove them.

Once in a while, a silly alt newsgroup actually draws enough of an audience to keep it going. For example, someone was probably just kidding when they created `alt.tv.dinosaurs.barney.die.die.die`, but that newsgroup became moderately active thanks to the popularity of its title and a healthy amount of antagonism towards Barney the dinosaur, a popular children's toy and television show character. A few silly newsgroups acquire a faithful cult-like following, thereby lending credence to the idea that the alt groups represent a countercultural version of Usenet.

Most Netiquette rules that apply to mailing lists apply to Usenet newsgroups, but perhaps more so, because most newsgroups reach more readers than most mailing lists do. Because there are millions of Usenet users worldwide, any one newsgroup can easily be read by thousands of people. Usenet newsgroups are very public and their readership is very fluid. Articles are not visible indefinitely, but they can remain available on Usenet servers for as long as a month. You never know who might read your articles, and no one can limit the readership of a newsgroup unless it is restricted to a regional network. Many Usenet newsgroups are also archived for public access, so articles posted years ago may still be accessible by the public. Never forget that Usenet communications are very visible and very public. It is no place to joke about shooting the President, unless you want to have an interview with the Secret Service.

The Usenet community tolerates commercial advertisements, but only in newsgroups that welcome commercial posts. These newsgroups can be readily identified by the inclusion in the newsgroup's name of keywords, such as "marketplace," "forsale," "wanted," or "biz." Never post a commercial advertisement to a newsgroup unless you are certain doing so is appropriate. Inappropriate Usenet posts are a form of Internet abuse.

Newsgroups are defined by topic, and great care is taken to ensure that each newsgroup is well-delineated with respect to content. If someone, in good faith, posts an inappropriate query to a newsgroup, other Usenet participants may be able to suggest a better newsgroup for the query. It is generally obvious when someone is honestly trying to locate an appropriate Usenet forum. Abusive Usenet posts tend to be inflammatory, insulting, or patently offensive. Usenet abuse is rarely subtle. If someone abuses a newsgroup or engages in inappropriate behavior on a newsgroup, other users are likely to assume a vigilante role and step in to censure the behavior. Public admonitions from random individuals sometimes suffice. But when abusive behavior persists, complaints to an appropriate network administrator can result in a suspension or termination of the originating account.

Get Out Your Asbestos Underwear

Usenet is a perfect medium for people who want to flame, and it seems to attract a lot of cranks, adolescent malcontents, and unpleasant characters with overactive spleens. A perfectly innocent Usenet article can sometimes trigger a vicious attack. If the aggrieved victim decides to fight fire with fire, a flame war can erupt. Some newsgroups seem to condone flame wars, while others try to maintain stronger standards for courteous and civilized communication. Each newsgroup has its own culture and behavioral codes. If you ever get flamed, don't bother to respond. Flames on Usenet that are ignored will usually just die out.

Usenet articles are continuously cycled through each news server. The oldest articles are deleted to make room for new articles, so an article you saw yesterday may not be there today. The life cycle of an article depends on your particular news server. If space is tight on that server, articles will be recycled quickly, within two or three days. On a server with more memory, articles may linger for a week or two. Most news servers carry a subset of the available newsgroups because they don't have enough room for all of them. According to one estimate, one day's worth of Usenet traffic for all newsgroups requires more than 800MB of storage, so memory capacity tends to be limiting a factor. Some newsgroups may be omitted from a server because of space limitations, while other newsgroups may be left out because of administrative policies. A news server in a corporate environment might not carry any recreational newsgroups on the grounds that there is no legitimate need for those in the workplace. If you access Usenet through an ISP or a university and you can't find a newsgroup that you want, just ask tech support if they can add it to their server for you. Most system administrators are happy to honor specific newsgroup requests, unless they violate some policy.

THE ALT.BINARIES NEWSGROUPS

You may have heard conflicting claims about how much pornography is on the Internet. Some people say the concerns about pornography are overblown, while others say the Internet is a cesspool and unfit for children. While it is out there, you have to know where to look for it. On Usenet, you can find entire newsgroups devoted to pornographic images; just look in the alt.binaries subtree. If you are offended by such things, steer clear of the alt.binaries newsgroups. Alternatively, if you want to visit them, please read Chapter 13 so that you will know how to avoid illegal activities. For example, it is a felony in the United States to distribute or own images depicting child pornography. Such activities undoubtedly occur in some of the alt.binaries newsgroups from time to time, and you don't want to get caught in an FBI sting operation. Watch your step.

Usenet communications rely on a text-based protocol, NNTP (Network News Transport Protocol), which does not accept binary files. However, on some newsgroups users can post graphics files or executable programs. This is done by posting a uuencoded version of the file or an attachment in the same way that uuencode and attachments are used for sending binary files through e-mail.

How Does Usenet Work?　　8.2

Your access provider is responsible for making Usenet available to you. Most universities offer Usenet access, as do most ISPs. All Usenet users receive their newsgroups through a local news server. To read Usenet, you need to configure your browser or news reader client with the name of your news server so that it will know where to access Usenet.

Each news server subscribes to a subset of all of the available newsgroups and stores all of the new messages posted to those newsgroups. The decision to add or drop a specific newsgroup is up to the administrators of the news server. It is easy for an administrator to drop an entire newsgroup. It is not easy to monitor all of the articles coming into a newsgroup in order to censor specific Usenet posts. If you access Usenet through a commercial provider, that provider reserves the right to select whatever subset of Usenet they feel is appropriate for their customers. Private companies can practice censorship with impunity. In any case, news server memory limitations typically determine how many newsgroups are available on that server. Someone somewhere has to decide what to carry and what to omit, or nothing will be available to anyone.

When you post an article to a Usenet newsgroup, it is first posted to your local news server. As a result, you can usually see your own articles fairly quickly. But that doesn't mean everyone else is seeing them that quickly on their own news servers. When your news server receives an article, it sends it to one or more of its "nearest neighbors," other news servers nearby on the Internet. As soon as the nearest neighbors receive the article, they post it for their users and then pass it on to all of their nearest neighbors. In this way, articles propagate out across thousands of news servers, moving from neighbor to neighbor much like gossip moving through a grapevine. Eventually, all news servers pick up on the new article and it is visible to everyone who reads Usenet.

Usenet operates automatically, with software continually running on each news server to keep the newsgroups up-to-date. The same software runs at each site, but with different settings for the newsgroups being supported and different expiration policies on those groups. New news servers are added to Usenet and given a feed from a nearby neighbor as long as the new server agrees to act as a feed when one of its nearby neighbors comes on line and requests a Usenet feed.

It is impossible to know exactly when an article will be visible to specific readers. If articles expire quickly on your own news server, your post may be dropped from your own server before it becomes visible to servers far away. Usenet articles ripple outward from each author, and different servers feel the ripples at different times. Don't be surprised if you see a new reply to one of your own Usenet posts a month after you first posted the article. It can sometimes take that long for everyone to see it.

8.3 Frequently Asked Questions (FAQ) Files

There is a lot of user turnover in the Usenet newsgroups, with newcomers always hopping on board to see what they can see. Because each newsgroup targets a specific topic, it is very common to see newcomers asking the same questions over and over again. Someone wants a recommendation for good books on the topic, or someone wants to know how to get started on a new hobby. Someone else wants product recommendations or generic advice of some sort. Each newsgroup generates its own set of frequently asked questions. Newsgroup regulars who want to be helpful find it very tiring to answer the same questions over and over again. Once it becomes clear that there is a fixed set of frequently asked questions, one is strongly tempted to issue a stock reply to each one and recycle these answers for each new user asking the same question. It is good for everyone involved if the frequently asked questions can be answered as quickly and painlessly as possible.

The Usenet phenomena of frequently asked questions led to the idea of a **Frequently Asked Questions File**, called FAQ for short. To create a FAQ file, someone assembles a list of frequently asked questions, answers the questions, and then makes this file publicly available so that anyone new to the newsgroup can easily find it. If all the newbies read the FAQ before posting questions to the newsgroup, then questions covered by the FAQ need never appear in the newsgroup and no one needs to answer the same question a hundred times over. A good FAQ file passes on the institutional memory of an entire newsgroup; some Usenet FAQs are large enough to be books. FAQs became standard fare in the Usenet newsgroups and then spread to other Internet venues. Many mailing lists now have their own affiliated FAQ files, and it is not unusual to find a FAQ for popular software, organizations, or informational Web sites.

From a quality control perspective, FAQ files are generally very reliable information sources. These documents are viewed by so many people that errors and outdated information are highly unlikely. The most knowledgeable people associated with each newsgroup review the newsgroup's FAQ and revise it periodically. Since these documents perform a real service for the resident experts, their content is subject to continual scrutiny. The newsgroup, motivated by self-interest and self-preservation, ensures that information found in a Usenet FAQ file is likely to be as safe as anything you'll find on the Internet. But do be careful to ascertain the status of any document that calls itself a FAQ file. Anyone can call a file a FAQ file. Look for such files on Usenet or in Usenet FAQ archives in order to make sure you are viewing a genuine Usenet FAQ.

The FAQ tradition on Usenet is so established that you can even find writing guides for FAQ authors on the Internet. A well-designed FAQ is formatted as a collection of questions and answers, with a list of all of the questions presented at the front of the file so that users can see if their particular questions are addressed. Some FAQs are very lengthy and come in a number of installments that resemble book chapters. It takes a lot of work to produce a good FAQ. The people who write them are rarely doing it because it is part of their job description. FAQs exemplify the gift economy of the Internet at its best.

If you find a FAQ file that is useful to you, keep in mind that copyright restrictions pertain even if there are no explicit copyright statements in the FAQ. Here is a general notice posted at MIT's FAQ archive describing usage guidelines for FAQ readers:

```
COPYRIGHT NOTICE
~~~~~~~~~~~~~~~~
Nearly all of the files contained in this directory are
copyrighted by their respective maintainers. (Even files
without explicit copyright notices are copyrighted under
the international Berne Convention, in effect in most
countries.) Some of the files, although certainly not
```

```
all, prohibit redistribution for any commercial purposes
without prior approval; other kinds of restrictions may
also be imposed by the maintainers.

Approval for use when there are restrictions imposed
must be obtained from the maintainers of each file,
*NOT* from the maintainers of this archive. If you have
any doubts about whether you may redistribute a particu-
lar file for some particular purpose, contact its
author.

Making a copy for your own personal reading is implic-
itly allowed.
```

If you are new to a newsgroup and are thinking of asking a question, make sure you check the FAQ file before you post. If you ask a question that can be answered by consulting the FAQ, your lack of Netiquette will be obvious to many Usenet regulars. You might even be reprimanded by someone who is tired of newbies who can't be bothered to read the FAQ file.

8.4 ▶ Finding Newsgroups, FAQ Files, and Old Articles

Usenet can be a wonderful resource, but you have to know how to find the groups that best address your information needs. Finding appropriate newsgroups is a relatively straightforward task. Unlike mailing lists, the Usenet newsgroups are catalogued and indexed by Usenet databases. Most of these databases are comprehensive, so if a database is up-to-date, you don't have to worry about what might be missing. Many Web sites offer good search engines for Usenet databases, where a few good keywords will be rewarded with descriptions of potentially relevant newsgroups.

Once you have the name of a newsgroup that addresses your interests, it is a simple hop to the FAQ for that newsgroup, if one exists. Not all newsgroups have FAQs, but the ones that do make them easy to find.

Searching the FAQ Files

A FAQ file archive on the Web is a great place to search for defini-tions, explanations, and factual information. Since FAQ files are highly reliable information sources, a search restricted to a FAQ archive can be very productive (see Chapter 7). Kent Landfield maintains a good Usenet FAQ archive containing over 3,200 FAQs at `http://www.landfield.com/faqs/`. HotBot indexes over 4,000 files at this site (with full text indexing), so this is a good site to search using HotBot. Try this Boolean filter:

domain:www.landfield.com AND NOT "Messages sorted by"

The "Messages sorted by" filter is included because this host also contains a mailing list archive and hits from the mailing list need to be filtered out.

Suppose you are thinking of getting an iguana for a pet and you want to see what wisdom Usenet has to offer on the subject. Start by visiting a Web-based search engine for all of the current Usenet newsgroups. A good one is the **Usenet Info Center Launch Pad** at `http://sunsite.unc.edu/usenet-i/`. At that page, you'll find pointers to a newsgroup search engine, a browsable Usenet hierarchy, and an archive of Usenet FAQ files.

All of the Usenet newsgroups are organized in a hierarchical structure, but that doesn't mean it's easy to find newsgroups by browsing the Usenet hierarchy. No one designed the Usenet hierarchy with browsers in mind. It's fun to browse the hierarchy if you have some time to kill, but whenever you need to locate specific newsgroups, go to a newsgroup search engine.

SEARCH OR BROWSE? WHICH IS BETTER?

Follow the link to the search engine and you'll land on the page shown in Figure 8.2. Now you have to think of good keywords to use to search the database. This particular search engine looks for terms in both newsgroup names and descriptions. Plus, it supports both exact phrase matching and Boolean queries. If you don't know anything about the groups you are looking for, it makes sense to keep your query short and simple. Try a single keyword or maybe two keywords connected with the OR operator (be sure to switch the radio button from AND to OR if you use more than one keyword). Note that this interface wants you to put one term in each input window. Don't try to enter a Boolean expression in the top window—you'll get back nothing.

To find newsgroups that talk about iguanas, start with the single keyword "iguana." Be careful to change the setting on the pull-down menu from Exact Match to Substring Match. In that way, your term will match both "iguana" and "iguanas." Unfortunately, a substring match on "iguana" turns up nothing. It seems that there are no newsgroups specifically dedicated to iguanas at this time (but that could change, since they are so popular). So broaden the query by generalizing—try "reptile."

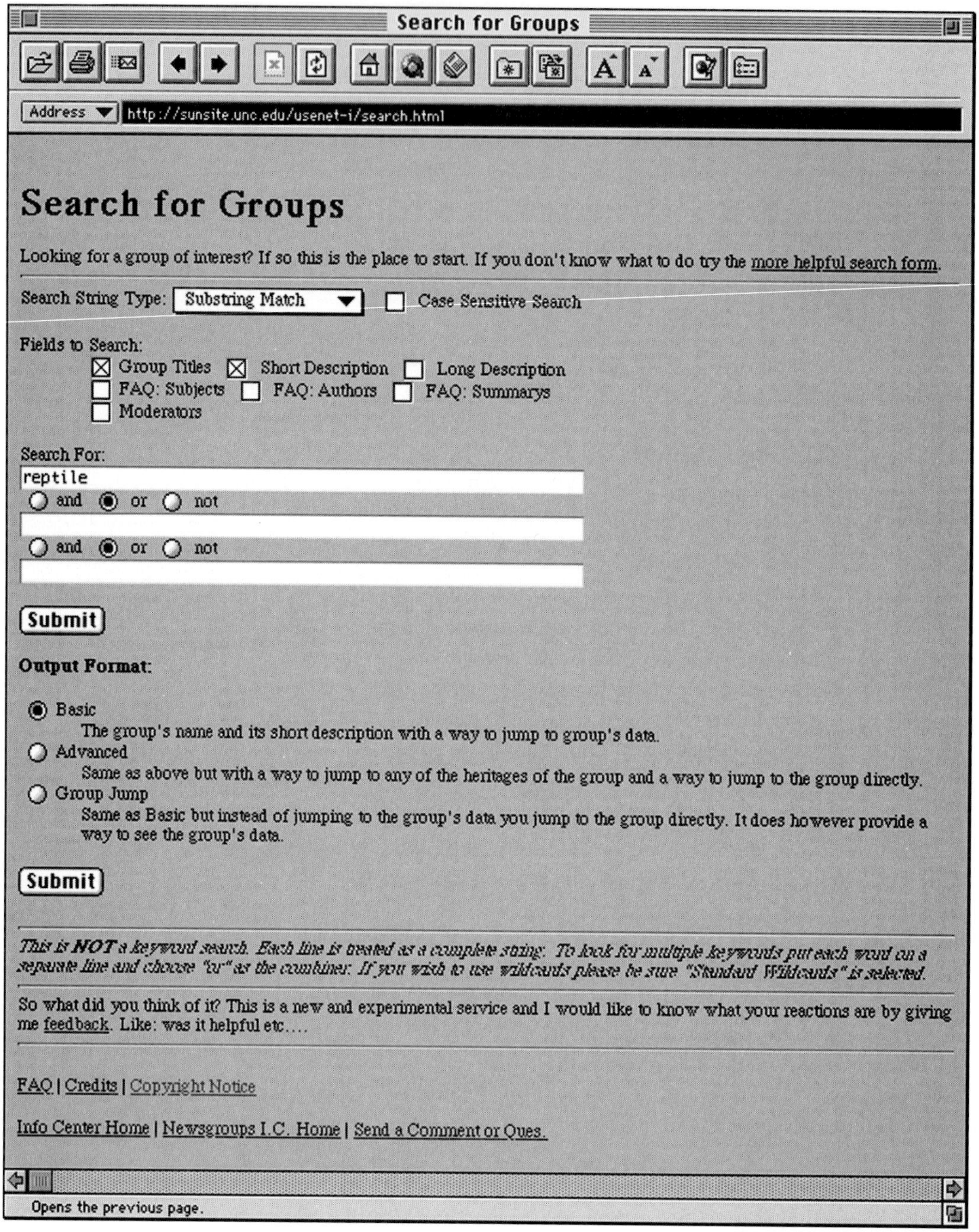

Search for Groups

Looking for a group of interest? If so this is the place to start. If you don't know what to do try the more helpful search form.

Search String Type: [Substring Match ▼]   ☐ Case Sensitive Search

Fields to Search:
☒ Group Titles ☒ Short Description ☐ Long Description
☐ FAQ: Subjects ☐ FAQ: Authors ☐ FAQ: Summarys
☐ Moderators

Search For:
`reptile`
○ and ◉ or ○ not

○ and ◉ or ○ not

[Submit]

Output Format:

◉ Basic
   The group's name and its short description with a way to jump to group's data.
○ Advanced
   Same as above but with a way to jump to any of the heritages of the group and a way to jump to the group directly.
○ Group Jump
   Same as Basic but instead of jumping to the group's data you jump to the group directly. It does however provide a way to see the group's data.

[Submit]

This is NOT a keyword search. Each line is treated as a complete string. To look for multiple keywords put each word on a separate line and choose "or" as the combiner. If you wish to use wildcards please be sure "Standard Wildcards" is selected.

So what did you think of it? This is a new and experimental service and I would like to know what your reactions are by giving me feedback. Like: was it helpful etc....

FAQ | Credits | Copyright Notice

Info Center Home | Newsgroups I.C. Home | Send a Comment or Ques.

Opens the previous page.

FIG. 8.2

Searching for Newsgroups

Sure enough, there are some newsgroups about reptiles (see Figure 8.3). The first one, alt.sex.reptiles, looks bogus (remember that an alt group can be created by anyone without going through the proposal/voting process). The next two—rec.pets.herp and rec.bio.herp—demonstrate the difficulty of finding newsgroups by browsing the Usenet hierarchy of newsgroup names. If all you see are the names, and you don't know that "herp" stands for "herpetology" (How many people are going to know that?) and further that "herpetology" is the study of reptiles (and amphibians), you could easily pass over the herp groups and never know you missed some relevant newsgroups. Search engines that index the newsgroups only by name will be similarly impaired. Notice too that it was important to conduct a substring match (otherwise "reptile" wouldn't match "reptiles") and a search that was not case-sensitive (otherwise "reptile" wouldn't match "Reptile").

Since you are interested in iguanas only as pets, you should follow up on rec.pets.herp rather than rec.bio.herp, as the latter is probably a forum for scientists and veterinarians.

Now that you've located the name of a promising newsgroup, you can either go directly to the newsgroup to see what sorts of articles are being posted or visit the FAQ for that group. From the page shown in Figure 8.3, click the `rec.pets.herp` link; you'll see some traffic and bandwidth

FIG. 8.3

Results from a Case-insensitive Substring Match on "reptile"

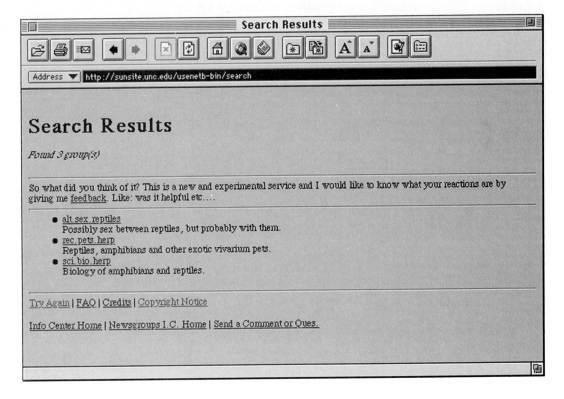

statistics for the newsgroup (see Figure 8.4). From here, you can visit a Web page display of current posts on `rec.pets.herp`.

If your Web browser is properly configured with the name of a news server, you can click Goto Group and see some current `rec.pets.herp` articles. If your Web browser comes bundled with a news reader, clicking a Usenet URL (news:) will automatically fire up the news reader for you.

To go directly to the `rec.pets.herp` FAQ, back up to the home page for the Usenet Info Center Launch Pad and follow the link to the FAQs that are indexed both by topics and by newsgroup names. Enter the name of the newsgroup, and you'll get to the `rec.pets.herp` FAQ (in three parts).

There are many sites on the Web designed to help you locate Usenet newsgroups and Usenet FAQs (see the Internet 101 Web pages for more pointers). News readers themselves are not very helpful when it comes to locating specific newsgroups, unless you already know the name of the newsgroup you want. ***Whenever you need to track down a newsgroup, visit a newsgroup search engine on the Web before you fire up your news reader.***

FIG. 8.4

A Statistical Profile of rec.pets.herp

To locate a Usenet article that is no longer in circulation on the news servers, try one of the public Usenet archives where old Usenet articles are collected and indexed for a search engine. One of the most popular Usenet archives is **DejaNews** at `http://www.dejanews.com/`, which offers "retired" Usenet articles in a searchable full-text database.

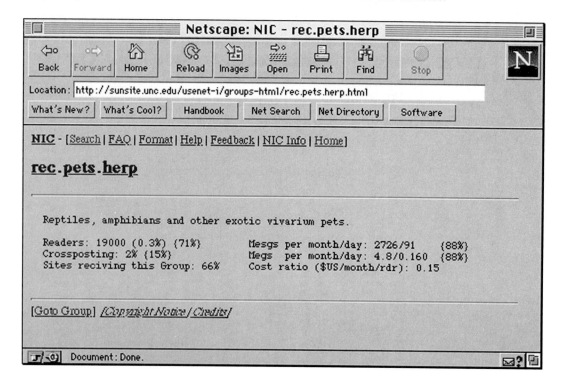

DejaNews also lets you enter topical keywords in a search mode designed to help you locate relevant newsgroups. Because it uses full-text indexing, it can count how many times each keyword appears in each newsgroup. It then ranks the potentially relevant newsgroups based on those frequency counts. For example, if you enter the keyword "twins," DejaNews returns some likely newsgroups. Also included is a confidence rating for each.

99%	`rec.collecting.sport.baseball`
39%	`misc.kids.pregnancy`
28%	`alt.parenting.twins-triplets`
23%	`rec.sport.baseball`

The search engine has no way of knowing if you meant sibling twins or the baseball team, the *Minnesota Twins*. Indeed, it probably has no idea that this keyword is ambiguous. So it faithfully returns hit counts for both types.

Working with News Readers   8.5

As with most popular client/server applications, you have a choice of news reader client software. A graphical Web browser include a news reader already installed and ready to go. You need only configure the news reader with an address for a news server.

News servers are usually not open to the general public, but if you have access to the Internet you probably have access to a particular news server. Ask your ISP for the host address of their news server. To configure the news reader in Navigator:

1. From the Options menu, click "Mail and News Preferences."
2. Click the Servers tab and enter the host address of your news server in the text box marked "News (NNTP) Server."

Once your news reader has been properly configured, fire it up by looking for a Read News command under a Go Menu or a Window Menu.

Three Levels of Usenet

Most graphical news readers are designed to show three levels of Usenet at once in three different windows. The first window lets you navigate the Usenet newsgroups by displaying a set of newsgroups at the **Group Selection Level**. Once a newsgroup has been chosen (just click it) at this level, then the next window displays all of the articles available in that particular newsgroup.

This second window is the **Article Selection Level**. There you can view the headers of specific articles. By your clicking a different newsgroup at the Group Selection Level, a new set of articles will be loaded at the Article Selection Level. The third window displays a single Usenet article at the **Article Level.** This is where you view an article's complete header and message body. Figure 8.5 shows these three levels of Usenet as they are displayed in Navigator's news reader.

FIG. 8.5

The Group Selection, Article Selection, and Article Levels

The display in Figure 8.5 shows the selection of `news.groups.questions` at the Group Selection Level and an article written by Michael Betts at the Article Selection Level. The bottom window displays the selected article, which looks very much like a mail message.

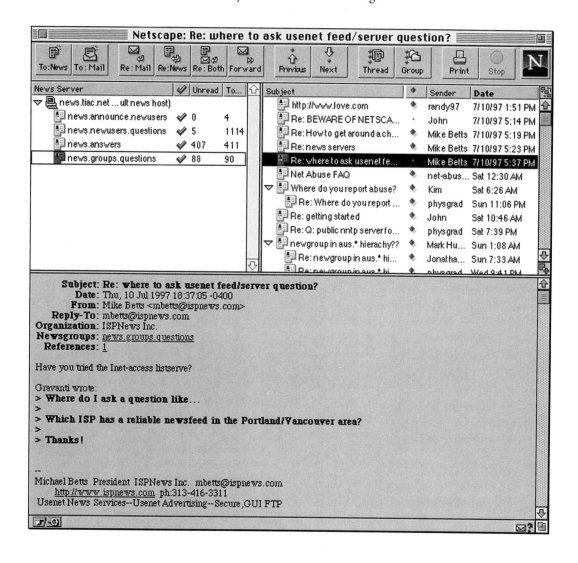

WHAT IF MY GROUP SELECTION LEVEL IS EMPTY?

If you have never used your news reader, there may be no newsgroups in your Group Selection Level. Pick a newsgroup you want to visit (see the last section on how to find newsgroups) and look for a **Load Newsgroup** command. In Navigator's news reader, pull down the File menu and click Add Newsgroup. A dialog box will pop up in which you enter the name of a specific newsgroup. Each time you add a newsgroup, it will appear at the Group Selection Level. You can add as many newsgroups as you want.

At the Group Selection Level, watch for two numbers next to each newsgroup. The larger number indicates how many articles you've downloaded from that newsgroup. The smaller number represents how many of those articles you've read. Some news readers give you a **download limit** that you can set for the number of articles that you want to download at one time for each of your newsgroups. A good default value for this preference setting is 500. To update your Article Selection Level or load more articles than your download limit allows, look for a **Load Messages** command. In Navigator's news reader, pull down the File menu and click Get More Messages. See Figure 8.6.

File
New Web Browser ⌘N
New Mail Message ⌘M
New News Message
Open News Host...
Close ⌘W
Save As...
Remove News Host
Add Newsgroup
Get More Messages
Page Setup...
Print... ⌘P
Quit ⌘Q

FIG. 8.6

Navigator's File Menu (for the news reader)

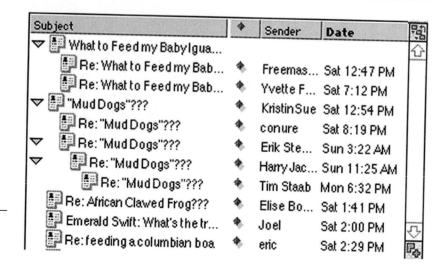

FIG. 8.7

Navigator's Threaded
Display at the Article
Selection Level

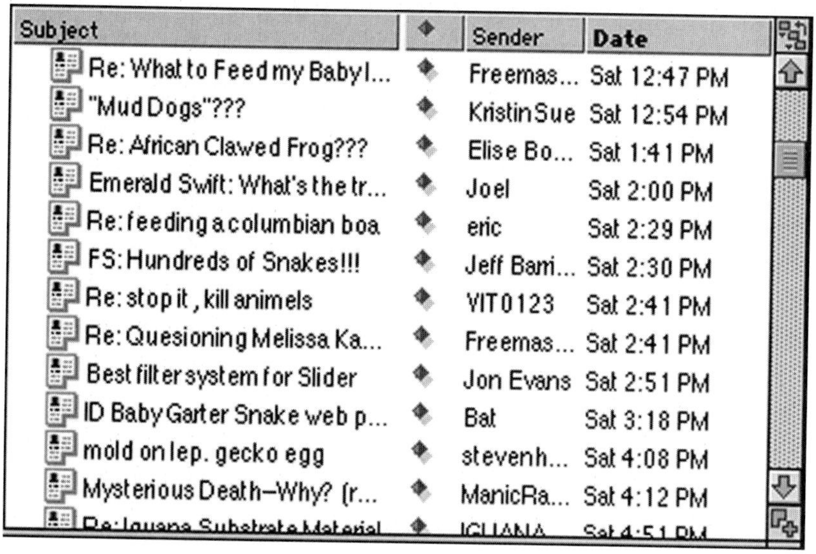

FIG. 8.8

Navigator's Unthreaded
Display at the Article
Selection Level

Most modern news readers are **threaded news readers**. This means that groups of related articles are collected together and displayed in a group, thereby making it easy for you to follow the thread of a conversation. Whenever someone posts a reply to a Usenet article, they start a **thread**. Then if someone else replies to that reply, the thread becomes a chain of three related articles. There is no limit to how long a thread can be. Also, threads don't have to be flat linear chains where each new article replies to only the most recent article in the thread. People can reply to any of the previous posts in a thread, creating entire branches of subthreads in a hierarchical tree structure.

In threaded news readers, look for a **Thread View** or a **Thread Level** that is reachable from the Article Selection Level. In the Thread View, you can see the headers for all of the articles in a thread; you can select any of them for viewing. In Navigator's news reader, a button in the upper right-hand corner of the Article Selection Level lets you toggle between a threaded display and an unthreaded display. Always pick the threaded display.

Figure 8.7 shows a threaded display from `rec.pets.herp`. Figure 8.8 shows the same newsgroup in an unthreaded display. Find the article with the subject header "Mud Dogs"??? in both displays. The threaded display shows that the original Mud Dogs post gathered a thread of four more articles over a three-day period. In the unthreaded view is the initial post, but you'll have to scroll through three days of `rec.pets.herp` articles in order to find the four replies. The threaded view is much more convenient if you want to read the thread about Mud Dogs.

WHAT'S WRONG WITH MY DISPLAY?	The first time you run your graphical news reader, you may find that no newsgroup names appear in your Group Selection Level and no article headers appear in your Article Selection Level. If this happens, simply resize the text display fields for these windows using a simple drag and drop operation. By dragging around the text field boundaries, you should see the text magically appear on any line that contains a newsgroup icon.

Different news readers use different interfaces, but you can always expect to find a Group Selection Level, an Article Selection Level, and an Article Level. A text-based news reader like tin can't show more than one level at a time, but they are all still there. Here is what the Article Selection Level looks like from inside tin:

```
alt.folklore.urban (140T 473A 0K 0H R)                          h=help
    1 +  4   Do CD-ROMs or LPs (remember them?) flow?          Leo G. Simonetta
    2 +  5   Haggis(was:tartan something...                    phill xxxxx
    3 +      Pizza ejaculation                                 Widow
    4 +      Do the French really like Jerry Lewis             James K. xxxxx
    5 +2     QWERTY Myth Refuses to Die                         Steve xxxxx
    6 + 14   Songs to play during the Apocolypse               Mike xxxxx
    7 +  2   Gorilla Suit Mischief                             Loren xxxxx
    8 +      Smilies (emoticons)                               xxx@satlink.com
    9 +      "Darwin" award winner                             Patrick xxxxx
   10 +      102-year-old dies at birthday party               Patrick xxxxx
   11 +  8   Water being scooped up from lake                  Mr. xxxxx
   12 +  3   Two engineer-related stories                      Simon xxxxx
   13 + 29   Year 2000 - leap year (was: 2000 and the comp     Paul J. xxxxx
   14 + 20   Food stereotype origins?                          Heather xxxxx
   15 +  7   True Story-Body in the Basement                   Susan xxxxx
   16 +  5   Greetings from Sunny Aukland, California!          xxx@satlink.com

<n>=set current to n, TAB=next unread, /=search pattern,
^K)ill/select, a)uthor search, c)atchup, j=line down, k=line up,
K=mark read, l)ist thread, |=pipe, m)ail, o=print, q)uit, r=toggle
all/unread, s)ave, t)ag, w=post
```

This screen display summarizes the first 16 articles found in the newsgroup `alt.folklore.urban`, a popular newsgroup dedicated to the origins of pop culture myths. Tin is a threaded news reader, so you can see which articles head threads of related articles. A number that follows the + sign indicates how many articles are included in the thread. The longest thread in this display contains 29 articles (headed by article #13).

To see who has contributed to a specific thread, go to the Thread Level. From the Article Selection Level given previously, you can select a thread and issue the **List Thread command.** Select the first thread (from article #1). The Thread Level looks like this:

```
Thread (Do CD-ROMs or LPs (remember them?) flow?                h=help

    0  +  [  20]  Leo G. Simonetta (1simonetta@gsu.edu)
    1  +  [  35]  Leo G. Simonetta (1simonetta@gsu.edu)
    2  +  [  10]  Andrew xxxxxxxxx (andrewxxxxxxxx@novell.com)
    3  +  [  15]  Lon Stowell (1stowell@pyrtech.mis.pyramid.com)
    4  +  [  19]  RMSpence (ROT13:Enaql.xxxxxx@zfsp.anfn.tbi)
```

From here, you can select the third response in the thread and press Return to open it. Then go to the Article Level, where you'll see this:

```
Tue, 06 May 1997 14:00:20    alt.folklore.urban     Thread    1 of  140
Lines 15  Re: Do CD-ROMs or LPs (remember them?) flow? Response  3 of  4
lstowell@pyrtech.mis.pyramid.com   Lon Stowell at Pyramid Technology
Corporation

In article <336AC794.6DBB@gsu.edu>,
Leo G. Simonetta <lsimonetta@gsu.edu> wrote:
>According to the Kodak website that talks about the lifespan of CDs,
>given reasonable care (keeping out of heat and light) the expected
>lifespan of CDs is a minimum of 50 years.  It does not go into any
>detail about what degrades overtime - I thought it was delamination
>but there was no mention of it at this website or any of the other
>two websites I found using WebCrawler.

   Can't think of anything that would be susceptible to delamination.
   Ordinary CD's are stamped from a master, then the reflective layer
   is applied, then they are usually just lacquered, with the label
   being printed over that lacquer. The reflective layer is extremely
   thin, usually a deposited layer.

    <n>=set current to n, TAB=next unread, /=search pattern, ^K)ill/select,
       a)uthor search, B)ody search, c)atchup, f)ollowup, K=mark read,
       |=pipe, m)ail, o=print, q)uit, r)eply mail, s)ave, t)ag, w=post

                          —More—(99%) [1597/1598]
```

Posting and Saving Messages

You can reply to an article on a newsgroup either publicly by posting your own article to the newsgroup or privately by sending the author a message via e-mail. Most news readers offer both options. In some news readers, a public response to Usenet is called a **follow-up** and a private e-mail response is called a **reply**. In a graphical news reader, the commands for posting Usenet articles and e-mail replies are more intuitive. Figure 8.9 shows the Navigator news reader toolbar containing Follow-up and Reply commands (among others). Watch for a **Quote command** or **Quote option** that loads the current article into the message body for your follow-ups and replies.

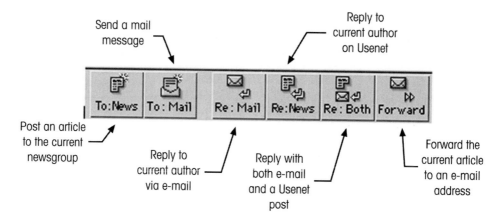

Send a mail
message

Reply to
current author
on Usenet

Post an article
to the current
newsgroup

Reply to
current author
via e-mail

Reply with
both e-mail
and a Usenet
post

Forward the
current article
to an e-mail
address

FIG. 8.9

Navigator's Posting
and Mailing
Commands

To save a copy of an article or a thread for yourself, you select and forward it to your own mailbox. Alternatively, you can use the **Save As command** in the File menu to save directly to a file. If you see a Usenet post you want to save, grab it now because it may be gone tomorrow.

NEWS
READER
CHECKLIST
#1

Study the documentation for your news reader and make sure you know how to do the following:

1. Start up your news reader.
2. Enter the address for your local news server.
3. Scroll through the newsgroups at the Group Selection Level.
4. Open up a specific newsgroup at the Group Selection Level.
5. Post a new article to a newsgroup.
6. Scroll through the articles at the Article Selection Level.
7. See which articles at the Article Selection Level have threads.
8. Open up an article or a thread at the Article Selection Level.
9. Forward a Usenet article to your own mailbox.
10. Send an e-mail reply to an article's author.
11. Post a follow-up article in response to a specific article.
12. Abort an article you wrote without sending it.
13. Exit your news reader.

Keeping Track of Messages

If you monitor several newsgroups regularly, you will want to control the displays at the Group Selection and Article Selection Levels in order to keep track of what's been read and what hasn't. At the Article Selection Level, your display can include either all of the articles currently available on your news server or only the articles you haven't read. In Navigator's news reader, the unread articles are marked with a small diamond, and the articles that you've read are marked with a small dot. Pull down the Options menu (see Figure 8.10), and you'll see a choice of two display options: Show All Messages and Show Only Unread Messages. One of these options must always be selected; you can toggle between the two at any time.

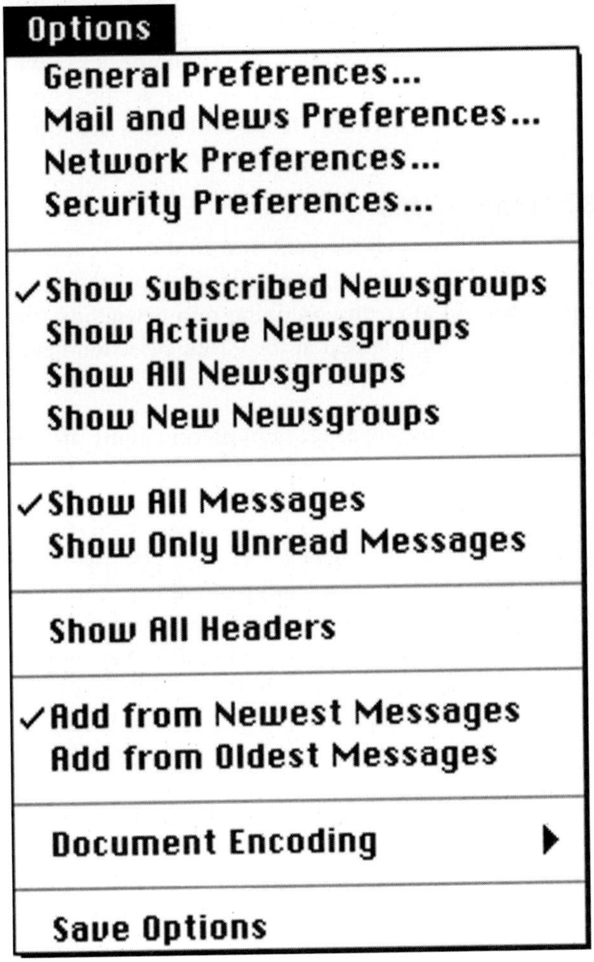

```
┌──────────────────────────────────────┐
│ Options                              │
├──────────────────────────────────────┤
│   General Preferences...             │
│   Mail and News Preferences...       │
│   Network Preferences...             │
│   Security Preferences...            │
├──────────────────────────────────────┤
│ ✓ Show Subscribed Newsgroups         │
│   Show Active Newsgroups             │
│   Show All Newsgroups                │
│   Show New Newsgroups                │
├──────────────────────────────────────┤
│ ✓ Show All Messages                  │
│   Show Only Unread Messages          │
├──────────────────────────────────────┤
│   Show All Headers                   │
├──────────────────────────────────────┤
│ ✓ Add from Newest Messages           │
│   Add from Oldest Messages           │
├──────────────────────────────────────┤
│   Document Encoding          ▶       │
├──────────────────────────────────────┤
│   Save Options                       │
└──────────────────────────────────────┘
```

FIG. 8.10

Navigator's Options Menu (for the News Reader)

Note that reading a Usenet article does not make the article go away. However, it will disappear from your Article Selection Level if you have selected the Show Only Unread Messages option. You can read any article as many times as you want by viewing the Show All Messages display. To override the "read" marker for a specific article, just click the diamond (or the dot) and manually mark an article as read or unread (this is possible only from the Show All Messages display).

Subscribing and Unsubscribing to Newsgroups

Most news readers have some commands that involve the term "subscribe." The term is a little misleading, however, because you don't have to be a subscriber to read or post to a newsgroup. Newsgroups do not have subscribers in the sense that mailing lists do. Being subscribed to a newsgroup means only that you want to see that newsgroup each time you open up your Group Selection Level. All newsreaders give you display options at the Group Selection Level. In the Navigator newsreader, these commands are found under the Options Menu (see Figure 8.10).

Show Subscribed Newsgroups

All newsgroups shown here will have a check mark next to them. To unsubscribe from one, click the check mark to remove it. If you issue the Show Subscribed Newsgroups command after unsubscribing to a newsgroup, the unsubscribed newsgroup will no longer appear at the Group Selection Level.

Show Active Newsgroups

This option displays only those subscribed newsgroups containing articles that you have not yet read.

Show All Newsgroups

Use this if you want all the newsgroups available on your news server to appear in your Group Selection window. This can be useful if you want to subscribe to groups of related newsgroups. Then, when you are ready to select from your set of subscribed newsgroups, use Show Subscribed Newsgroups or Show Active Newsgroups to make the display at the Group Selection Level more manageable.

Show New Newsgroups

This loads all of the new newsgroups that your news server has acquired since the last time you asked for Show All Newsgroups or Show New Newsgroups. This is a largely useless command since it is probably a very long list and it will contain a large number of totally bogus alt newsgroups with silly names.

You can subscribe to new newsgroups either individually or as a group. To add them individually, one at the time, use the Add Newsgroup (or Load Newsgroup) command on the File menu. This will bring up a dialog box where you can type in the name of a specific newsgroup. You must know the exact name of the newsgroup that you want in order to subscribe to it this way. If the newsgroup is not available on your news server, you will get a message to that effect. To add multiple newsgroups at one time, use the Show All Newsgroups command to see a list of *all* of the newsgroups available on your news server. Then navigate this list (it will appear in a hierarchical system of files and folders) and mark the individual groups to which you want to subscribe. This is reasonable if you know exactly what you want and where to find it, but the Usenet newsgroup hierarchy is not well organized for systematic browsing. If you are serious about finding relevant newsgroups, visit the Web and spend some time with a newsgroup search engine.

If You Issue the "Show All Newsgroups" Command, Go Get a Snack

HINT

The first time you issue the Show All Newsgroups command, your news server will have to download entries for all of its newsgroups. This may take a few minutes. After the first time, this process will not take as long. It is possible to spend a lot of time on Usenet without ever needing the Show All Newsgroups or Show New Newsgroups commands.

Adding Signature Files

Another convenience supported by most news readers are signature files (see also Chapter 3). If this feature is available, your news reader will automatically append a designated signature file at the end of all of your Usenet posts. You can use the same signature you use for your e-mail or create a different one just for Usenet. As with mailing list signatures, try not to exceed the standard four-line limit.

To set a signature file in Navigator, click Mail and News Preferences on the Options menus and then click the Identity tab. Click the File: radio button under Signature File and press the Browse button to get a dialog box where you can find your signature file.

Cross-Posting Queries and Messages

Sometimes you may find it useful to post a query or an announcement to more than one newsgroup. If the exact same article can go out to multiple newsgroups, you should **cross-post** the article using the cross-posting header. In this way, only one copy of your article is stored on each news server instead of separate copies for each newsgroup. Cross-posting is more efficient for you and the Internet, as well as for many of the Usenet users who read your article. When an article is cross-posted to different newsgroups, then any follow-up posts are automatically cross-posted as well. This means that a single thread can include participants from any of the cross-posted groups and all articles in the thread will be visible to everyone in the cross-posted groups. The cross-posting on follow-ups is handled automatically by the Follow-up command without any extra effort by the author.

Cross-posting is very convenient and appropriate when more than one newsgroup is relevant for the subject matter at hand. But be careful when you cross-post; you want to avoid cross-posting to inappropriate newsgroups. You can inconvenience a large number of Usenet readers with an irrelevant article, which, if it attracts a discussion, can turn into an irrelevant thread. Think carefully before you post anything to Usenet, and think twice before you cross-post anything.

If an article has been cross-posted to a number of newsgroups and you read it from one, it will be marked as read in all of the other cross-posted groups. This saves you from having to see the same article more than once. Since many Usenet readers monitor multiple newsgroups that are closely related, cross-posting saves time for many people.

Off-line News Readers

If you spend a lot of time in Usenet on a dial-up Internet connection, you can minimize your connect time by using an off-line news reader that allows you to read Usenet articles and write your own Usenet posts off-line (much like Eudora allows you to manage your e-mail largely off-line). However, be careful when you select an off-line reader. Some mangle their article headers and cause substantial problems for news servers. For more information about off-line news readers, consult the FAQ file for `alt.usenet.off-line.readers`.

Killing Articles

No one can be barred from a newsgroup for issuing abusive posts, but many news readers can automatically kill articles from a specific user. When an article is killed by a news reader, it is automatically marked as read so that it is never seen at the Article Selection Level. A **kill file** is a list of users whose posts you don't want to see. You can't control someone's behavior on a Usenet newsgroup, but making that person invisible is probably the next best thing. This type of article filtering is analogous to an e-mail filter, and it can be used to fight spam and other forms of Internet abuse in the same way that e-mail filters can save you from seeing a lot of garbage. Some news readers do not support kill files, so if you feel that this is an important feature, you will want to investigate more powerful news readers.

Experiment First

When you discover a newsgroup that interests you, plan to lurk and read for a week or two before you post any messages. If you want to ask a question, make sure you have first read the relevant FAQ file. When you are posting your first Usenet article, first try an experimental post to make sure you have all of the software commands under control. The newsgroups `misc.test` and `alt.test` are provided for newcomers who want to experiment with their news readers. Use them whenever you need to try out a new news reader or if you want to check a new signature file to see how it looks. Posting test messages to a regular newsgroup is a violation of Netiquette and may attract some harsh words.

If you haven't already posted a test message to `misc.test` or `alt.test`, do it now. Then study the documentation for your news reader and make sure you know how to do the following:

1. Toggle through different displays at the Group Selection Level.
2. Subscribe and unsubscribe to specific newsgroups.
3. Set up a signature file for your news reader.
4. Cross-post an article.
5. Toggle through different displays at the Article Selection Level.
5. Unmark a read article so that it is treated as unread.
7. Make posts from one person invisible (if your browser has a kill feature).

NEWS READER CHECKLIST #2

You can browse Usenet much like you can browse the Web. Some newsgroups are very entertaining, and others may contain interesting conversations about your favorite hobby or sport. If you monitor an informative newsgroup over some period of time, you can learn a lot.

8.6 ▶ Spambots and Cancelbots

If your goal is to reach as many people as possible as cheaply as possible, Usenet probably looks like a gift from God. However, it might become tedious to send out the same ad to 18,000 newsgroups manually. So, thoughtful programmers have written convenient **spambots,** which automate the process. With a spambot, you can post a message to thousands of Usenet newsgroups in a few seconds. Of course, this is Internet abuse, so you'll want to cover your tracks. A few states are experimenting with statutes intended to make spamming illegal, but this is still very murky legal territory.

Great Moments in the History of Spam

In 1994, two attorneys, Laurence A. Canter and Martha S. Siegal, became infamous for hawking their green card services on more than 6,000 newsgroups. Although Usenet spamming was nothing unusual, the popular press picked up on this incident, probably because the perpetrators were attorneys who openly identified themselves and publicly argued that their activities were perfectly legal. Canter and Siegal claimed that the Internet had outgrown its insular academic origins and was now open territory for commercial advertisements. Given the absence of laws and regulations regarding the Internet, Netizens were naive to think that voluntary Netiquette would be an adequate mechanism for regulating behavior on the Internet. This affront to the culture of the Internet symbolized a turning point for the Internet. Some predicted the imminent death of the Internet. Others decided to fight fire with fire.

Usenet articles have an interesting property that makes them very different from e-mail messages. With e-mail, a message that has been posted on the Internet cannot be canceled. But with Usenet, an article that has been posted to a newsgroup can be canceled. The Cancel command was intended to be used only by the original author of an article, in the event that the author notices an egregious error or a disastrous typographical error after the article was posted. Indeed, a news server will not honor a Cancel command unless it is convinced that it comes from the same person who posted the article. When a Cancel command is accepted, it propagates out to all of the other news servers until the article has been removed from all of Usenet.

However, with a little trickery, a person can fool a news server into thinking that someone is the original author of an article when they aren't. This means that anyone can, in principle, cancel anyone else's Usenet article. Unauthorized Usenet cancellations normally represent a serious breach of Netiquette and are dealt with very harshly by system administrators.

Cancelbots

Third-party cancellations represent a technical solution to the problem of Usenet spam. If someone is so inclined, they can monitor a newsgroup for spam and issue an unauthorized cancellation to kill off any offending articles from all of Usenet. Although doing this is controversial, most Usenet users approve of this solution. Worries about censorship and freedom of speech tend to fade in the face of too many unwanted advertisements and emotional diatribes about some pet cause. Programs called **cancelbots** have been designed to detect spam not on the basis of content, but on the basis of multiple postings. If the same article has been cross-posted too many times, a cancelbot will recognize it as spam and issue a Cancel command.

One famous cancelbot operated anonymously under the name **Cancelmoose**. Cancelmoose acted with the utmost sensitivity for the rights of all Internet users. When a spam was canceled, Cancelmoose issued a notice explaining the action and included full copies of all affected spam messages. In this way, no one could argue that their right to see spam had been violated. But now the spam was neatly bundled inside identifiable notices from Cancelmoose. So if you had a kill file, you could add Cancelmoose to your kill file and never be bothered by spam again. In addition, local administrators also had the ability to cancel all Cancel commands issued by Cancelmoose. In that way, each news server could make its own policy decision with respect to Cancelmoose's actions and support it or not.

The war between the spambots and cancelbots is one place where the culture of the Internet has taken matters into its own technological hands. Censorship is a serious threat to open communication, and the use of cancelbots is hotly debated. It seems appropriate to label spam and isolate it, but removing material from Usenet without authorization is a serious offense. Exactly when are unauthorized cancellations defensible?

For example, in 1995 members of the Church of Scientology canceled Usenet articles posted by people who were critical of Scientology. The Scientologists argued that their actions were justified because the canceled posts contained copyrighted material used without permission. Are copyright violations a valid reason for unauthorized cancellations? Who has the right to evaluate a possible copyright violation? Many people feel that the Church was practicing outright censorship. Censorship is a very real danger on Usenet, and you don't even have to be in a position of authority to be a censor.

NoCeM

The most recent solution to the spam problem on Usenet is a piece of software called NoCeM (pronounced "No See 'Em"). At this time, NoCeM is available only for UNIX news readers; however, but it may become an option for other platforms if it catches on in the UNIX community. Here's how it works: People watch for spam on Usenet. When somebody sees spam, they post on a special newsgroup called alt.nocem.misc a notice describing the offending article. When a NoCeM-enabled news reader starts up, it checks `alt.nocem.misc` for spam notices and kills off any targeted articles that it is authorized to kill. Authorization is needed lest random censors place notices on `alt.nocem.misc` in an effort to kill articles they don't like.

To authorize a NoCeM action, each NoCeM user creates a file of authorized signatures representing individuals whom the user trusts to issue spam notifications. Then the NoCeM software acts only on notices posted with authorized signatures. These signatures are encoded using PGP software (see Chapter 12) in order to prevent forgeries. If you have one trusted individual monitoring each newsgroup for spam, then you simply collect the signatures for the spam-monitors who handle the newsgroups you read. This takes some extra effort on the part of the users, who must collect the signatures, and certainly on the part of the monitors, who must post notices to `alt.nocem.misc`. But if the system were used by everyone who read Usenet, the audience for spam would be reduced to zero and there would be no incentive to post spam on Usenet anymore. NoCeM clients could also operate at the level of a local news server, thereby saving everyone on that server from having to manage NoSeM signatures on their own.

Trusted cancelbots could also post to `alt.nocem.misc`. At the time of this writing, one cancelbot was posting notices to alt.nocem.misc whenever the same article was posted to at least 15 newsgroups. During one 24-hour period in May 1997, this cancelbot identified 40 different instances of Usenet spam.

If automated cancelbots could be trusted to identify spam on the basis of frequency counts and news servers implemented NoCeM software at the server level, then individual users would benefit from the actions of the NoCeM system without any extra overhead or inconvenience. A similar NoCeM system is under development for mailing lists. Perhaps these technological solutions can eliminate spam from the Internet without any legalistic intervention. The culture of the Internet may be a stronger force than some Internet newcomers realize.

PROBLEMS AND EXERCISES

1. [**Hands On**] Find three newsgroups that address your three target topics (see Chapter 1) and monitor them for two weeks. If these newsgroups parallel three mailing lists that you found (see Chapter 4), compare and contrast the newsgroups and mailing lists in each case. What differences do you see? Do you feel that one is superior to the other in some respect? Are there any generalizations that apply to the newsgroups on all three topics?

2. [**Hands On**] Browse `news.answers` to see if you can find any FAQs that are posted in more than ten installments. What topics do they address?

3. [**Hands On**] Open up five random FAQs on `news.answers`. Are they all dated? Do they all identify their authors? Are they all affiliated with a specific newsgroup?

4. [**Hands On**] How many Usenet newsgroups are there? Where did you look for the answer to this question?

5. [**Hands On**] Are newsfeeds available via Usenet? If so, where are they?

6. [**Hands On**] Post a test message to `misc.test` or `alt.test` and then watch to see how quickly your test article becomes available on the newsgroup. Does it appear right away? Within an hour? Within three hours? Six hours? Twelve hours? More?

7. [**Hands On**] Can you find a Usenet FAQ about computer viruses? According to the FAQ, roughly how many viruses have been discovered on the PC platform? On the Mac?

8. [**Hands On**] Browse a few random newsgroups and watch for instances of spam. Examine ten different spam messages from different newsgroups. How many are advertisements of some sort? How many are political calls for action? How many are diatribes on controversial social issues? How many have religious content? Have you found any newsgroups that are primarily just "spam magnets"?

9. [**Hands On**] Browse a few random newsgroups and watch for a flame war. How many individuals are involved? How does it end? Is there some sort of reconciliation, or does the war eventually just peter out? Does an impartial party intervene in any useful way?

10. Chapter 7 suggested that searches could be limited to a specific host machine on which a useful archive is stored. When would you want to search a FAQ archive with a Web search engine instead of going to a newsgroup search engine? Are these two options equivalent?

11. While there is a wealth of information associated with Usenet FAQs, it is not always easy to know which FAQ to consult for the answer to a specific question. What newsgroup might be able to help you find the best possible newsgroup for a given question?

12. Newsgroups are more unobtrusive than mailing lists. Explain why and discuss the implication of this for someone in a work environment. When is it better to monitor a newsgroup, and when is it better to subscribe to a mailing list?

13. **[Hands On]** Find a Web search engine with a newsgroup search option. Does this engine index all of the available newsgroups? Does it index Usenet articles that are more than one year old?

14. **[Hands On]** It is possible to post a Usenet article in a way that will keep it out of the DejaNews database. Go to the DejaNews Web page and find out how to make articles invisible to DejaNews. (*Hint:* Check their policy section.)

15. Who can censor Usenet articles? Is anyone legally authorized to censor material on Usenet?

16. What are spambots and cancelbots?

17. How does NoCeM differ from Cancelmoose?

18 **[Hands On]** ROT13 is a feature found on some news readers. What is ROT13? (*Note:* This chapter didn't talk about ROT13. See if you can find it on the Internet.)

19. Name three ways that Usenet newsgroups differ from mailing lists. Are these differences "hard" facts or "soft" generalities?

20. Explain how newsgroups are vulnerable to disintegration over time. How can they disintegrate? Why doesn't this happen to mailing lists?

FTP and Computer Viruses

9

"A professional is someone who can do his best work when he doesn't feel like it."

- ALISTAIR COOKE

THE INTERNET 101 WEB PAGES

- Online FTP Tutorials
- File Formats and File Extensions
- Computer Virus Information Resources
- Software Archives
- Web-Based Archie Resources

What Is FTP?

9.1

The roots of the Internet go back to when computers were all mainframes and the most powerful computers were in great demand. Researchers whose work depended on fast computers had to go where the computers were, and the demand for CPU time far exceeded the supply. ARPA (the Advanced Research Projects Agency) was the funding agency that supported the most innovative computer science. ARPA wanted to find a way to make powerful computers more available to a larger number of researchers, both inside and outside of computer science.

ARPA also knew that research groups involved in software development often invented and reinvented the same software solutions because they weren't talking to each other or trying to share their software. For example, the same program would be written six times by six different groups, each working in isolation and thus reinventing the wheel six times over. All of this duplicated software development represented a serious waste of human resources at the major computer research labs. This was at least as troubling as the problem of too few computers.

ARPA felt that the solution to both problems could be found in computer networks. If a user community had access to many computers on an open network, it would not have to physically cluster itself at specific sites. The balancing act between supply and demand would be mediated by giving all of the users access to all of the machines. In this way, computing cycles could be distributed more effectively. In addition, software duplication could be reduced. A free and open exchange of software within the research community would leverage the work of all computer scientists and minimize redundant effort by eliminating isolated research projects. This sanctioned push toward shared resources was the origin of the so-called gift economy of the Internet. It started with the computer labs supported by ARPA and became an Internet cultural norm.

The free exchange of software required a vehicle. That vehicle was **FTP** (the File Transfer Protocol) for easy file transfers. See Figure 9.1. With FTP in place, files housed on one host machine could be downloaded by any user on any other host machine. Over time, FTP servers accumulated a considerable library of freely available software, and today we have large software archives available for public use. However, not every file on every host machine is available to the public. Most files on most Internet hosts are

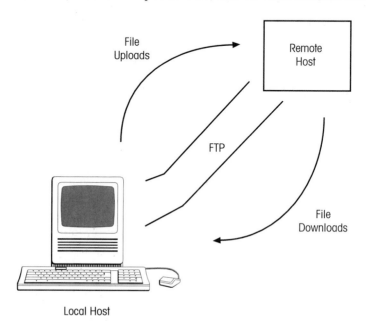

FIG. 9.1

The File Transfer
Protocol (FTP)

private, and a private file cannot be accessed by unauthorized individuals without their using deliberate subterfuge. To make files publicly accessible on the Internet, one must take special steps.

For a collection of files to be available for public consumption, the files must be placed in a public **FTP directory** on an **FTP server**. Then, anyone with an FTP client can download copies of the files on demand via a process called **anonymous FTP**. There are FTP clients for all computer platforms, and Web browsers can also be used to conduct anonymous FTP sessions. To get started with FTP, all you need is a Web browser.

Why Is It Called "Anonymous FTP"?

When you connect to an FTP server with a dedicated FTP client, you are required to log in as a guest on the FTP server. To establish an FTP session, you enter at the login prompt the userid "anonymous" followed at the password prompt by your complete e-mail address. If the server is programmed to accept guest users, these login entries will create a client/server connection.

Before the advent of Web browsers, this was the established procedure for initiating a session with a public FTP server. Hence, the expression "anonymous FTP." But the name is really a misnomer, since all anonymous FTP users identify themselves with their password entries. The programmer who first thought up the anonymous login convention probably had no idea of the legacy that would result from it. If he had told everyone to login as "stranger," then today maybe we'd be talking about "stranger FTP."

FTP in Action

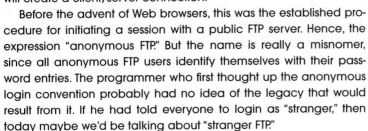

9.2

The University of Michigan maintains a large Mac software archive on an anonymous FTP server. Using Navigator, enter the URL `ftp://mac.archive.umich.edu` just as you would enter a Web page address. Then go to the main file directory of the FTP site as if it were just another Web page. Note, however, that this Web page looks more like a file directory than a normal Web page. You won't see any graphics (beyond perhaps a few icons), and there will be little or no text to read. All you need during an FTP session are directory displays and the ability to navigate a directory hierarchy.

Each page on an FTP server contains two types of links, one that takes you to files and one that takes you to more directory pages. If you have spent any time in Gopher space, you will probably feel right at home visiting an FTP directory.

When displaying a file directory, Navigator uses graphical icons to distinguish files from file directories. Names of files appear next to page icons, and names of directories appear next to folder icons. The subdirectories stand out clearly, thus making it easier to navigate through a directory structure. Not all graphical Web browsers display FTP directories in the same way. Internet Explorer uses a display that is very similar to Navigator's, but without the graphical icons for files and directories. Whatever browser you use, FTP files and directories will all be rendered as hyperlinks. Navigation within an FTP site is just a matter of point and click.

Figure 9.2 shows the main directory for the FTP site at the University of Michigan. Whenever you visit an FTP site, you will be placed in its **main directory**. This directory is also called the FTP site's "home directory," the "root directory," or the "top-level directory." You can visit subdirectories that are beneath the main directory, but you probably won't be allowed to move up to the parent directory of the main directory. An FTP site is like a library or a museum: Some areas are open to the public, and others are off limits.

When you first connect, a brief introductory message is displayed that encourages you to read the readme file `00readme.txt` for useful information. You can locate this file in current directory and click it to see its contents. This readme file turns out to be very detailed and informative. In particular, it explains where all of the site's mirror sites are. A **mirror site** is another server that maintains an exact copy of all the directories at the original site. FTP sites that are very popular tend to have mirror sites so that users can go to alternative locations if the original site is overloaded. Since a mirror site offers the exact same resources, it makes no difference which server you visit. Given a choice of mirror sites, always use the one that is closest to you in order to minimize Internet traffic and download times. If the FTP sites are too busy, you could visit a Gopher archive, where traffic might be lighter.

I Think I Need a Map

If you are exploring a new FTP server and aren't sure where to go, keep your eyes open for files named "index," "welcome," or "readme," as well as subdirectories named "pub" (for "public"). Also, a welcome message printed by the server at the top-level directory might say something useful to aid your navigation. You may also see directory-specific welcome messages when you enter a subdirectory. When you visit an FTP site for the first time, always read everything available that could help you navigate the site.

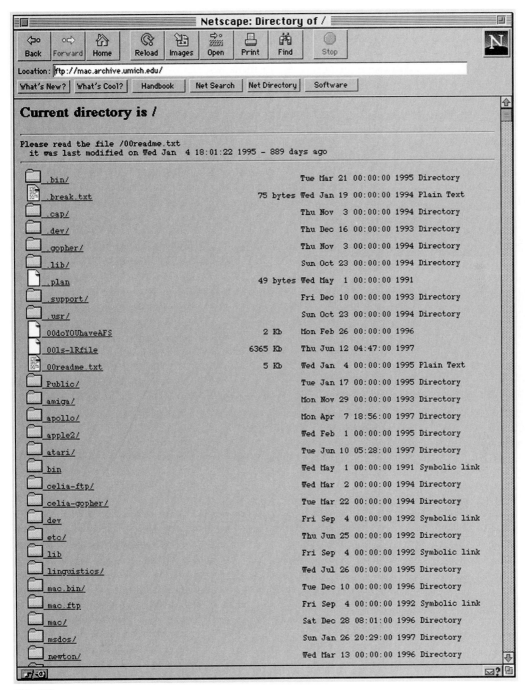

FIG. 9.2

A Software Archive at the University of Michigan

This FTP site is a popular place to find Mac software. You could peruse the offerings by browsing the directory hierarchy, but the readme file indicates there are over 6,000 Mac software files stored there. Chances are you don't want to browse 6,000 filenames, but you can still take a quick look around. Figure 9.3 shows the /mac subdirectory that holds all of the Mac software.

Notice how the address in Navigator's Location: field in Figure 9.2 differs from that shown in Figure 9.3. If you ever get lost in an FTP directory, just look at the current URL in your browser's address window. It will show you the path of all the subdirectories you've followed down from the main directory. Each time you click a subdirectory hyperlink (there are 12 of them in Figure 9.3), you move down one level in the directory hierarchy. You can

FIG. 9.3

The /mac Subdirectory Holds 6,000 Software Files

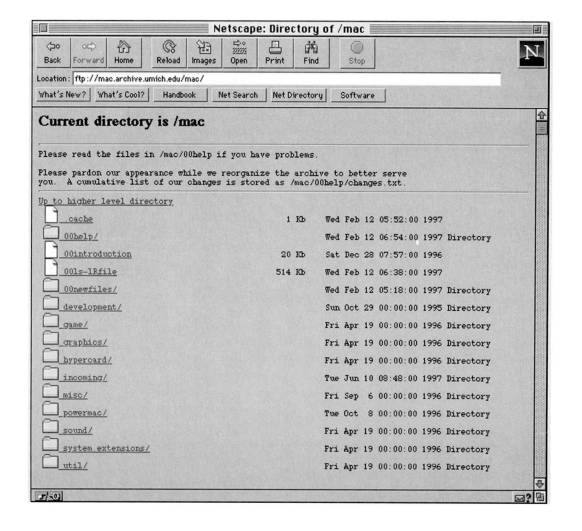

always return to the main directory by using repeated Back commands or with a single bound from your History List. All of the usual Web browser commands and features work here just as they do with any other Web pages.

Navigational Hyperlinks in FTP Directories

In Figure 9.3, the button marked "Up to higher level directory" is a link to the next higher level in the directory tree. Sometimes you see only a cryptic hyperlink containing two periods (**..**). This, too, will take you up to the next level in the directory tree. The two periods are from a directory navigation command for UNIX; the original FTP users could be expected to recognize such a thing as a familiar signpost. Some FTP sites (like the one shown in Figure 9.3) have taken steps to make their navigational links more intelligible for a broader audience. But if you visit many FTP directories, you may still run into those two periods at times.

FTP sites were never designed for easy browsing the way the Web was. The typical FTP user already knows what to look for and where to find it before ever connecting to an FTP server. An FTP server may contain a lot of publicly available files, but it usually offers very minimal documentation. Don't expect to find more than an initial readme file for new users. If you don't know exactly what you are looking for and you just want to look around, feel free to explore. Just don't expect much guidance.

This Is a Busy Signal . . . Please Try Again Later

Sometimes you will click a file in an FTP directory, and your browser won't be able to download it. You might be told something like, "Alert!: Unable to access document." This can happen with a heavily used server during peak periods. It doesn't necessarily mean that the file is permanently unavailable. Try again later. You may be able to get it when the server is less busy.

You can use your Web browser to handle FTP files, with some limitations. Most important, Web browsers let you only download files. A true FTP client supports both downloading and uploading. The advantage of FTP via a Web browser lies in the fact that you already know how your Web browser works and you don't need to learn new software. If you only want to download files, you have no pressing need for an FTP client.

When you visit an FTP site, you are an invited guest on someone else's property. FTP sites are maintained as a community courtesy. Visitors should understand that anonymous FTP is a privilege, not a right. If the site administrators have to field too many questions and complaints, they may decide that the overhead is too great to continue the service. Any FTP server can be shut down at any time for any reason. Remember this and honor any directives or requests that are made of you when you visit an FTP server.

FTP Netiquette

Here is some Netiquette to keep in mind when using an FTP site:

- Try to visit FTP servers during off hours. Late evenings and early mornings are the best times.
- Always read the welcome and readme files for important information.
- Don't contact the tech support staff for an FTP server *unless you have first asked your local tech support staff for help and they advise you to contact staff at the FTP site.*
- If mirror sites are available, use the one that is closest to you.
- Anonymous FTP access is a privilege, not a right. Be a courteous guest.

FTP SESSION #1

Now is a good time for a little hands-on experimentation.

1. Fire up your favorite Web browser and go to
   `ftp://ftp.eff.org/`.
2. Path your way down to
   `pub/Net_culture/Folklore/Dead_Media_Project`.

3. Somewhere in this subdirectory, you can find out what a "chirographer" is. This shouldn't take you more than one minute (unless you get distracted). Search by opening up some files and conducting keyword searches for "chirographer."

4. Find your way back up to the server's main directory.

5. Explore some subdirectories that interest you.

Sometimes a Web site is set up as an interface to an FTP site or multiple FTP sites. For each file of interest on the FTP server, a Web page can offer comments and useful information, in contrast to the FTP directory, which shows only an inscrutable filename. Most of the big software clearinghouses on the Web are friendly interfaces to FTP servers. A full-text search engine indexing all of the commentary helps users locate the files they want. Users never visit the FTP servers themselves until it is time to download a file. Most of the clickable download links you see on the Web are actually pointers to files on FTP servers.

Yes, there is a search tool just for FTP servers, but you probably don't need it. The tool is called Archie, and Archie searches are a fast becoming a lost art. Archie is a search engine that indexes filenames on public FTP servers. It indexes only filenames. So if you know the name of the file that you want, Archie can probably find 100 copies of it on a 100 different FTP servers. If you don't know the filename, Archie cannot help you. Today, with the availability of user-friendly software on the Web and general Web search engines that index URLs for FTP sites, there is little reason to fire up Archie anymore.

Is There a Search Tool Just for FTP Servers?

File Types and File Extensions   ◀ 9.3

There are two basic types of files that matter when you transfer files over the Internet: text and binary. A **text file** contains only the normal display characters that you can type from a keyboard. These are the alphabetic characters (uppercase and lowercase), numeric characters, and some punctuation symbols. Typeable characters are called **ASCII characters**, and text files are sometimes called "plain text files," "ASCII files," or "plain ASCII text files." E-mail message bodies (without MIME attachments) and HTML files on the Web are always ASCII text files.

A **binary file** can contain ASCII characters along with additional characters that are not intended for visual displays. Control characters (those that require two keystrokes on a keyboard to produce) are examples of characters found in binary files that do not occur in text files. Executable computer programs are usually stored as binary files, along with certain types of data files such as those saved by word processing programs. An executable file is not intended for human eyes and cannot be displayed with a text editor. Binary files generated by word processing programs can be displayed, but only by applications that know how to interpret them. Different applications use different formatting conventions for storing information, and there is no universal format that all applications recognize. When one word processor can read files created by another word processor, it is using a translation program that is supplied as a special feature of the software. The world of binary files is a Tower of Babel.

Text Files and Binary Files

Plain text files are normally read by human beings, and binary files are normally read by computers. The ASCII character set is actually a subset of the binary character set, so all text files are technically binary files. Still, it is confusing to call a text file a binary file because the standard usage for these two terms is to treat them as if they were mutually exclusive. It would be more precise if everyone called binary files "binary files that are not text files" or just "nontext files." The usage is a little sloppy, but the convention is well-understood.

Software programs determine a file's type by examining a special file property called the **file type**. People can usually determine a file's type just by looking at its name, specifically its **file extension**. File extensions are a kind of code that reveals the file's type. The file extension is that part of a filename that follows a period. Filenames without periods (called "dots") do not have file extensions. Here are some examples of filenames containing file extensions:

Filename	File Extension
dat10.txt	.txt
sift.exe	.exe
viewer.hqx	.hqx
intro.doc	.doc
received.Z	.Z
bib.html	.html

(We will explain what each of these extensions mean shortly.)

On a DOS-based PC, file extensions can contain no more than three characters. On a UNIX platform, they may contain any number of characters, and you can even nest multiple extensions by putting more than one dot in the filename. Examples of files with multiple extensions will be seen in Section 9.4. In the Mac environment, file extensions are usually avoided in order to make Mac filenames look like plain English. But Macs happily accept filenames with extensions, too. Files found on the Internet almost always use file extensions, even when they are files intended for Macs.

Anyone can name a file using any extension, but some extensions are reserved for specific file types. These are discussed shortly and include .txt, .exe, and .htm. So, when you name or rename your own files, avoid using file extensions that misrepresent the file's type. An incorrectly named file is like naming a boy "Mary." It's not forbidden, but it will cause confusion. Computers are perverse enough without our adding perverted filenames to them.

At first, you may feel overwhelmed by all of the different file extensions you see. But there are only about a dozen file extensions that keep popping up with great regularity. Once you learn to recognize them, you will know everything you need to know about file extensions. For example, here are the most common file extensions for ASCII text:

.txt   An ASCII text file intended for human eyes

.doc   An ASCII documentation file intended for human eyes

.html   A Web page created in a UNIX or MAC environment

.htm   A Web page created in a PC environment

What's Up, Doc?

The PC version of Microsoft Word uses the default file extension .doc when it saves a file in binary format. This would be very confusing if we saw many Word files on the Internet, but people usually don't distribute files publically if they cannot be opened by software that is available to the general public (at no cost). So when you see a public .doc file on the Internet, you are probably looking at a plain ASCII text file rather than a Word file. Text files use the .doc extension to indicate a documentation file. MS WORD presumably adopted the same name because it was short for "document."

HINT

Many network protocols are text-based (SMTP for e-mail; NNTP for Usenet). So programmers have developed software that translates a binary file into an **ASCII-encoded text** equivalent for the purposes of network transfers. These ASCII-encoded files can be safely viewed with text editors and display utilities; however, they will look like gobbledygook, so there's no point in looking at them. To make them usable, you have to reconvert them to their original binary format. Only then will they execute (in the case of computer programs) or be readable by an application (in the case of data files). ASCII text is not always readable text. **Plain ASCII text** is text you can read. Plain ASCII text is also called "plain text," "simple ASCII text," and "simple text." Here are the most common file extensions for ASCII-encoded text:

`.asc`	A text file version of a binary file (probably a PGP file)
`.hqx`	A BinHex text file format
`.uu` or `.uue`	A uuencoded text file format
`.rtf`	Rich Text Format for word processing documents

Figure 9.4 shows all the different categories of files you are likely encounter. As you gain more experience on the Internet, many of these different categories will become familar to you. In the meantime, just remember the major division between text files and binary files.

There are many extensions for binary files. Here are most common:

```
.exe   .com   .zip   .arc   .gz   .Z      .tar  .sit   .cpt  .sea
.bin   .lzh   .ps    .wp    .dd   .gif    .pct  .eps   .jpeg
```

The extensions `.exe` and `.com` are reserved for executable computer programs. All of the other binary file extensions signify different binary file formats. The next section explains some of these formats and why they are good for the Internet.

FIG. 9.4

Computer File Types

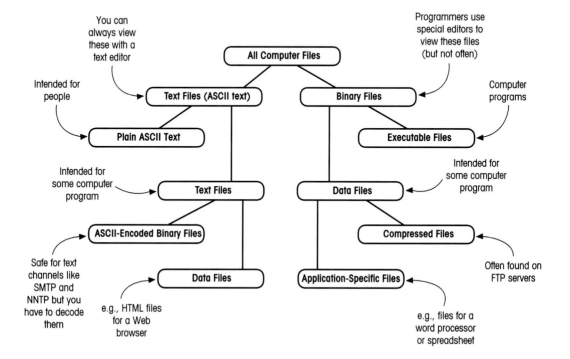

Never try to look at a binary file with a text editor, text display utility, or word processor. All you'll see is gobbledygook. But more important, some of that gook might hang your machine if you try to display it. Viewing a binary file can also produce eeps and dinging sounds, which might raise your heart rate if you are at all jumpy.

NEVER TRY TO VIEW A BINARY FILE—IT MIGHT BITE

File Utilities

9.4

Files can be translated from one format to another with file utilities. A **file utility** is a computer program that does something useful with files, and file utilities are commonly used to translate a file from an unusable format into a usable format. Many of the files available to you on the Internet need to be reformatted before you can use them. For every file format that you find on the Internet, there is probably a free file utility you can use to reformat it. In this section we will explain why Internet files require so much formatting and reformatting, and what you need to do to handle these files.

File Compression/Expansion

On the Internet, bigger is not better. Bigger files mean more waiting for a download, and bigger files consume more bandwidth in transit. If you had a choice between downloading a 200K file or an equivalent 100K file, which to choose should be a no-brainer. Computer files can usually be reduced in size by using more efficient ways to encode the contents of the file. The process of shrinking a file by encoding it differently is called **file compression**. The process of recovering the original file from its compressed version is called **file expansion**. Public files found on the Internet are frequently stored in a compressed file format. Compressed files always need to be uncompressed by an expansion utility before they can be read or executed.

Different compression techniques achieve different results. Large text files in English can usually be reduced by 50–60%. Files with a lot of repeated strings undergo the greatest reductions. For this reason, longer text files tend to compress more than shorter ones. For example, a 25-line text file might shrink 35%, while a 200-line text file may shrink 45% and an 8,000-line file 55%. A file with an unusual amount of repetition can shrink as much as 90%, but such files are not normally encountered in real life.

Something for Nothing?

Have you ever seen software products that claim to double your disk drive's storage capacity? These products don't do anything to change your hard drive. Instead, they double your available storage capacity by running a file compression utility each time you save a file. Then they run a file expansion utility each time you open a file. Aside from a little extra time needed for all this compression and expansion, you never know the difference. You could do it yourself manually and achieve the same effect for free (but with an extra hassle factor that might not be worth it).

People who distribute files over the Internet usually compress the larger files in order to reduce the amount of time needed to download the file. When a group of files go together, it is useful to bundle them into a single unit called a **file archive**. A file archive is one large file that packages a group of smaller files in a way that makes it easy to pull them apart again. Since archives are often very big, archive utilities usually compress everything when packing up an archive. People can then download one big file instead of ten individual smaller files. File archives are often used for computer programs because an executable file can be bundled with data files, documentation files, and licensing information. Then anyone who gets the executable file gets everything else at the same time. Some file archives contain more than 100 files when a large amount of data (usually graphics files) are part of the archive.

A file archive needs to be **unpacked** before its contents can be read or executed. When you open a compressed archive, you both unpack the archive and expand all of its files at the same time. An archive is sometimes called an **exploding file** because it blows up into lots of little pieces when you unpack it.

Some archives are packed so that the archive can unpack itself automatically. An archive that requires no special unpacking software is called a **self-extracting archive**. With a self-extracting archive, you simply execute the file in order to unpack it. In a point-and-click environment, you would do this by double-clicking the archive's icon. Many software installations depend on self-extracting file archives.

Only a few compression utilities are used, and each uses its own extension for the compressed files that result. Visitors to FTP sites are expected to recognize file extensions used by the most popular file compression utilities. One set of file extensions is generally used for Mac files and a different set for PC and UNIX files. Following are the more common extensions and file formats used in these environments.

Common MAC File Formats

`.sit`	A Stuffit Compressed file or file archive
`.cpt`	A Compact Pro file or file archive
`.sea`	A self-extracting file archive
`.hqx`	BinHex format
`.bin`	MacBinary format (an executable file)

Common PC and UNIX File Formats

`.zip`	A zipped file or file archive
`.gz`	A gzipped file or file archive
`.Z`	A UNIX-compressed file
`.uue`	A uuencoded file
`.tar`	A tarred file archive
`.exe`	An executable binary format
`.com`	An executable binary format

Sometimes in UNIX environments, files will have multiple extensions that reveal a history of separate formatting procedures. For example, a file named `datasets.tar.Z.uu` was first archived (`.tar`), next compressed (`.Z`), and then uuencoded (`.uu`). A uuencoded file is a text file, so such files can be sent through e-mail (assuming the recipient knows how to handle it) or over a Usenet newsgroup. To recover the original set of data files from a file named `datasets.tar.Z.uu`, you would first uudecode it (to get `datasets.tar.Z`), then uncompress it (to get `datasets.tar`), and finally untar it (to get `datasets`). The formatting operation applied last must always be the first operation to be reversed, and the first operation that was applied is always the last one to be reversed. Whenever multiple file extensions are seen, you can unravel them by working backwards from the right-most extension to the left-most extension.

UNIX users are generally familiar with file format utilities and the extensions associated with them. PC and Mac users usually learn about such things when they trade files on floppies and find files at FTP sites or electronic bulletin boards. To take advantage of all of the software available to you on the Internet, you will need to handle the different file formats normally encountered. The most popular file utilities are well documented and very easy to use. As an information consumer, you only need to download files, unpack archives, and sometimes uncompress or reformat files. These are the most straightforward file operations. The more complex file utility commands and options are associated with creating archives and compressing files. As long as you are on the receiving end of these transfers, everything is relatively simple.

The better software sites provide documentation that will help you download and handle your files correctly. You can expect to see readme files inside FTP directories and additional readme files included in software packages. If you see any files named readme, always read those files.

File Utility Jargon

In the context of file utilities, the terms "download," "upload," "decode," and "encode" may appear on a pull-down menu. "Download" and "decode" mean the same: expand a file or unpack an archive. "Upload" and "encode" mean the same: compress a file or create an archive.

When you archive an application, you are ready to upload it (put it on a server for Internet access), and when you download an application, you are ready to unpack it and install it. The language is a little sloppy, but the associations make sense.

There are a number of utilities that you can use to handle various file formats. Figures 9.5–9.7 list some popular utilities that are very easy to use. However, PC users most often deal with .zip files, while Mac users deal with mostly .hqx and .sit files. The other utilities listed are given as a general reference; there is no need to memorize any of this. Just remember that there is always a freeware utility to help you unpack or uncompress any of the commonly found file formats you will run into on the Internet.

File Extension	What Is It?	Some Available Utilities
.bin	MacBinary is a binary format for encoding Mac files so they can be safely stored on non-Mac platforms	MacBinary II+ Stuffit Expander
.sit	a compressed file archive created by Stuffit Deluxe	Unstuffit Delux Stuffit Expander
.hqx	Binhex4 is a text format for encoding binary files for text-based protocols	BinHex DeHQX Stuffit Expander
.sea	a self-extracting archive	none needed
.uue	uuencoding is a text format for encoding binary files for text-based protocols	UULite UUundo
.dd	a file compressed with DiskDoubler	Disk Doubler Expander
.cpt	a compressed file archive created by Compact Pro	Extractor Stuffit Expander

FIG. 9.5

Macintosh File
Extensions and Utilities

File Extension	What Is It?	Some Available Utilities
`.zip`	a compressed file or archive	PKUNZIP UNZIP WinZip WizUnZip
`.exe`	usually an executable file but it can also be a self-extracting archive	none needed
`.uue`	uuencoding is a text format for encoding binary files for text-based protocols	uucode xferp wpack
`.ps`	a printable ASCII Postscript file	just send it to a Postscript printer or Postscript viewer
`.wp`	a WordPerfect file	open it with a word processor

FIG. 9.6

PC File Extensions and Utilities

File Extension	What Is It?	Some Available Utilities
`.gz`	a compressed file archive created with gzip	gzip gunzip
`.Z`	a compressed file	uncompress gzip
`.tar`	a file archive (not compressed)	tar detar
`.uue`	uuencoding is a text format for encoding binary files for text-based protocols	uudecode
`.shar`	a self-extracting file archive	sh (but you must be in the UNIX Bourne shell)
`.ps`	a printable ASCII Postscript file	just send it to a Postscript printer or Postscript viewer
`.exe`	usually an executable file but it can also be a self-extracting archive	none needed

`.tZ`
`.tarZ`
`.tar.Z`
	rename it as .tar.Z and handle it in two steps (see above)	(first uncompress it, then untar it)

`.tgz` `.tar.gz`	rename it as tar.gz and handle it in two steps (see above)	(first unzip it, then untar it)

FIG. 9.7

UNIX File Extensions and Utilities

File Utility Helper Applications

If there are more available file extensions and file utilities than you bargained for, don't be discouraged. Don't try to download all possible file utilities on the off chance you might need one someday. Instead, use one big workhorse that will handle 90% of the file conversions you'll ever need. Try WizUnZip for Windows or Stuffit Expander for a Macintosh. Then wait to see if you ever need more. If you run into a problem when you try to download a file, examine its file extension and locate an appropriate file utility from the tables in Figures 9.5–9.7. If you find a file extension not mentioned there, consult the Internet 101 Web pages for a pointer to more comprehensive lists of file extensions and file utilities.

File Decoding Catch-22

If you get on the Internet and look for copies of WizUnZip or Stuffit Expander, you will discover a small Catch-22. Copies of WizUnZip are usually zipped (`.zip`) and need to be unzipped, but you need WizUnZip to unzip them. Copies of Stuffit Expander are usually in BinHex format (`.hqx`) and need to be decoded, but you need Stuffit Expander to decode them. This applies to all file formatting utilities. You need to find a version of these programs that can be executed directly, either an executable binary or an installer version. The best place to get these is straight from the source—the company or organization that distributes the software. Popular software straight from the source is as safe as it gets. Here's where to get it:

If you run Windows 3.x, pick up WizUnZip 3.1 (197K freeware) at

`http://www.cdrom.com/pub/infozip/WIN16/wiz31x.exe`

or you can get PKZIP 2.50 (590K shareware) at

`ftp://ftp.pkware.com/pk250w16.exe`

If you run Windows 95, pick up WizUnZip 3.1 (196K/freeware) at

`http://www.cdrom.com/pub/infozip/WIN32/wiz31xN.exe`

or you can get PKZIP 2.50 (676K shareware) at

`ftp://ftp.pkware.com/pk250w32.exe`

If you run a Mac, pick up Stuffit Expander 4.0 (199K freeware) at

`ftp://ftp.aladdinsys.com/pub/stuffit_exp_40_installer.bin`

Once you have downloaded and installed appropriate file utilities on your computer, you can tell your Web browser to apply these utilities whenever it downloads a file requiring special handling. A good Web browser can automatically invoke helper applications for you on an as-needed basis. A **helper application** or **plug-in** is a utility that your browser can call whenever it encounters files with specific file extensions. Figure 9.8 shows a display from Internet Explorer's Options window. That is where you can add plug-ins to that browser. Start by selecting a file type (for this example, I chose BinHex files) and clicking the Edit button.

Then click the Choose button to bring up a pop-up window in which you can select a file utility to act as the plug-in. Figure 9.9 shows the plug-in set-up window. This utility will be automatically applied to any files encountered by Internet Explorer that have the specified file extension (in this case, all `.hqx` files). You need a properly configured file utility to act as the plug-in. Otherwise, the browser will display an error message when it tries to use the plug-in.

Be careful once you've set up a plug-in for your Web browser or any other application. If you ever rearrange your directories and move the plug-in applications, you will need to update all of the affected plug-ins. When your browser can't find a plug-in, it will complain (see Figure 9.10).

FIG. 9.8

Selecting a File Type for a Plug-in Helper

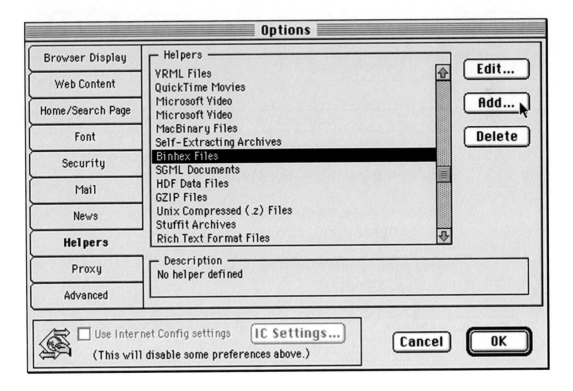

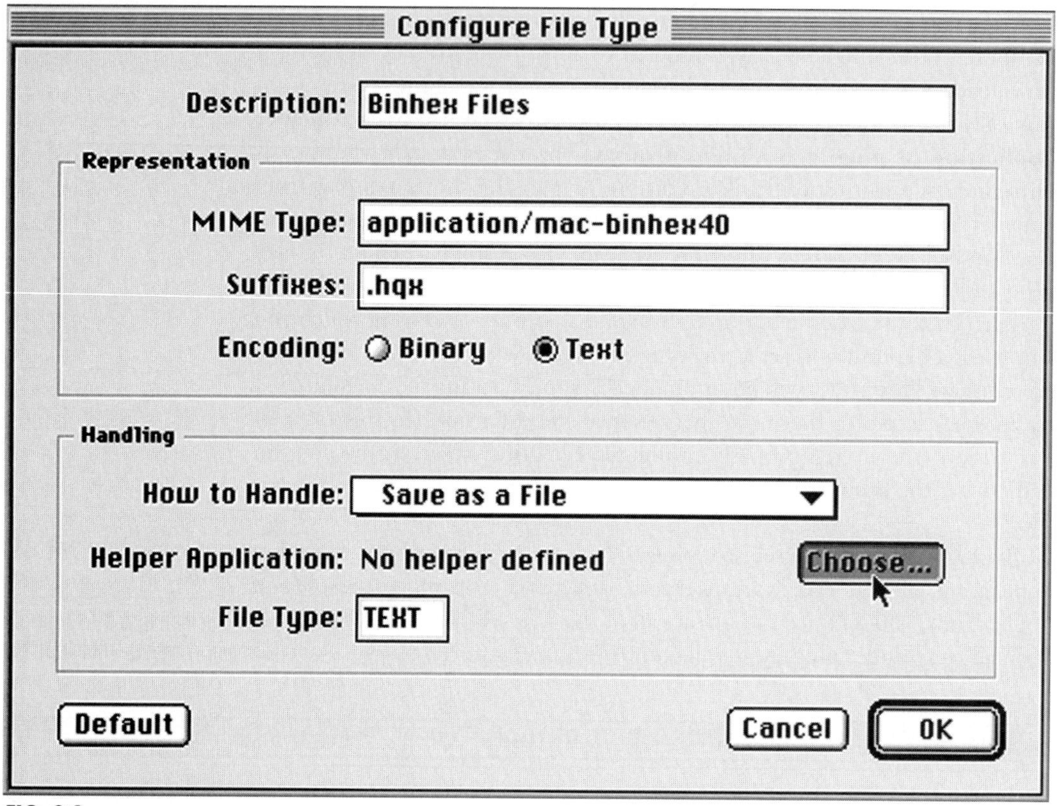

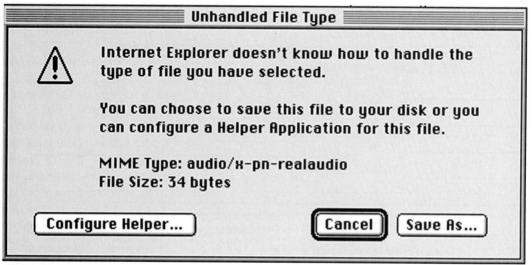

FIG. 9.9

Selecting a Plug-in Utility

FIG. 9.10

Don't Let Your Plug-Ins Get Away from Your Browser

Freeware, Shareware, and Limited Editions

Newcomers to the Internet are usually astonished to find so much free software on the Internet. If you view software as a commodity, it may indeed seem puzzling to see so many people willing to give it away for free. To understand this, one must understand the culture of the Internet and something about computer programming.

Hollywood's image of an iconoclastic programmer who saves the world from nuclear destruction may sell tickets at the box office, but real programmers normally work on narrow problems of limited impact. Programming is mentally demanding, painstakingly slow, and sometimes tedious. Programmers who work on large software projects often answer to managers who not only tell them what to do but exactly how to do it, thereby leaving little room for creative experiments. It nevertheless takes years of education and training to produce a competent programmer. People become programmers because they find the work gratifying in its own right: it is satisfying to produce working code. Professional programmers take pride in their work, and enjoy perfecting complicated creations that incorporate clever code. Some programs are actually pretty (at least to a programmer's eyes).

One of the biggest myths about programming is that programmers are antisocial people who work in total isolation and never interact with other human beings. Programmers do work alone for the most part, but there is also a lot of interaction among programmers. Most programmers are intensely interested in ideas and solutions proposed by other programmers, and good ideas spread quickly throughout the programming community. The Internet was designed to encourage collaboration, and the programming community was, and still is, happy to comply.

The Internet is a perfect medium for programmers who want to talk to other programmers about programming problems. No matter what the problem is, a programmer can find other programmers who are working on the same problem. Moreover, anyone who has a solution can get it out to the larger community by putting it online and making it available to anyone who wants to see it. Once others see it, they can critique it, expand it, refine it, or revise it. Eventually, a result is reached that is often better than anything that one individual could have produced. Programmers are usually quick to acknowledge their intellectual debts, and, when progress is such a public enterprise, credit is readily granted. If you post a solution to a problem that goes out to 100 other people, it's going to be difficult for anyone else to claim credit with those 100 people watching. As a result, small prototype programs are freely shared among members of the programming community.

Programmers share code freely because they know how much benefit is derived from shared resources. Any given programmer probably takes from the Internet more than he or she gives back, so when the opportunity arises to share something that might be of some value to others, programmers are generally happy to make whatever contribution they can. This tradition is firmly in place and is thoroughly self-perpetuating.

Within academic environments, where the Internet was born, questions of intellectual property rights and ownership have traditionally taken a back seat to open communication. In contrast, programmers who work for corporations are usually bound by nondisclosure agreements, so their participation in open forums is likely to be more limited. Good programming ideas undoubtedly emerge from both academic and corporate environments, but an idea that can't be freely shared will not benefit from the widespread scrutiny of programmers all over the world. Proprietary rights and nondisclosure agreements are a necessary fact of life, but they are not compatible with the notion of programming as a community activity.

When software is distributed over the Internet, it is primarily there for the benefit of programmers and hobbyists who know their way around a computer. Now that the mainstream public is on the Internet, commercial software is also being packaged and distributed on the Internet for casual users. But everyone can help themselves to whatever software they can find. The Internet offers freeware and shareware in addition to traditional commercial software, so let's see what makes freeware and shareware different.

Freeware

Freeware is free software. It is made available to anyone at no cost and with no strings attached. Anyone can post freeware on the Internet. It is sometimes written by students who have minimal programming experience. Some freeware is very good, but a lot of it is flawed in some way. Freeware that comes from a reputable software site is less likely to disappoint you, but there are no guarantees. Freeware can carry computer viruses and should be handled with extreme caution (see Section 9.6 for safety tips).

Freeware is not commercial software and *no one assumes responsibility for whatever happens when you use it.* If you don't like something you picked up for free, no one will want to hear you complain about it. If you want to use freeware, start by reading software reviews and looking for software recommendations. There is no quality control on the Internet, but there are plenty of grapevines and newsletters where people offer reviews and recommendations.

File utilities are sometimes a combination of commercial software and freeware. The commercial part is used for encoding (compression or archiving), while the freeware part is used for decoding (expanding or unpacking). Whenever you encounter a file format that requires expansion or unpacking, there is a reliable freeware utility that will handle it.

Shareware

Shareware is not free, but it is available for a free trial period. You can download it and use it at no cost with the understanding that you will pay for it if you like it and want to keep using it, or remove it from your system if you don't. Most shareware agreements ask you to make up your mind within 30 days. If you are still using a piece of shareware after 30 days, you should pay for it.

Shareware is distributed on the honor system. No one will track you down and arrest you if you use shareware without paying for it. What you do with shareware is a matter of conscience. However, some shareware is programmed to let you know when your free trial period is about to end, and some shareware even self-destructs if you haven't registered before your time runs out. Most shareware is modestly priced in the $20–$50 range. Programmers who create shareware don't get rich; few can manage even to make a modest living from it. At best, they cover their development costs and the time they spend helping users who have questions.

Shareware is one step above freeware because someone is willing to accept responsibility for it and listen to complaints and suggestions. Popular shareware is often updated and upgraded. From a quality perspective, shareware is generally better than freeware, but there are exceptions to this rule. The best shareware is found at reputable software sites and should be easy to find.

Software licensing agreements apply to freeware and shareware as well as to commercial software. When you retain a piece of software, you agree to abide by the restrictions described in the license. You have entered into a contractual agreement that is legally binding, even though you never sign a contract. It is a criminal offense to violate the terms of that contract.

ALWAYS READ THE
LICENSING
AGREEMENT

Limited Editions

Some commercial vendors distribute software for free over the Internet in order to attract paying customers. This is analogous to the free snack food tables you sometimes find in supermarkets. These free software packages are commercial quality and subject to licensing restrictions, but they usually support only a subset of the features you can get with the complete version. When software is called "Limited Edition" (LE) or "Special Edition" (SE), it is usually a less powerful version of a more complete software package. Limited editions are a variation on the shareware idea, without the risks of an honor system. Some people are happy to stay with the give-away version and never pay for its more powerful cousin. Others will eventually graduate to the full-fledged version because they need some key feature that was strategically omitted from the limited edition.

Eudora Lite is a good example of a limited edition software package. It is a very popular mail reader for both PCs and Macs. For beginners and people who use e-mail sparingly, Eudora Lite probably meets all of their needs. But anyone who wants to filter and route their e-mail will need to purchase the more powerful commercial version, Eudora Pro.

Software houses hope to hook you on the free version and then reel you in for the more powerful commercial version. This is a very effective strategy because people are more comfortable buying software when they know what they're paying for. If you are thinking of spending big bucks for a software product, look for limited editions on the Internet. You might be able to do some hands-on comparison shopping.

Aggressive Giveaways

Once in a while, a commercial vendor decides it is important to dominate an emerging software market as fast as possible. Software is a cut-throat business, and special tactics are sometimes needed. For example, Netscape Communications gave its Web browser, Navigator, away for free in order to establish a lead in the Web browser market. In fact, there have always been restrictions on the open distribution of Navigator. Commercial users are required to pay for it; the free version is actually an examination copy, which is good only for a limited time. These licensing restrictions depend on the honor system, much like the shareware model. It's not the best way to generate short-term revenues, but Netscape did succeed in establishing itself as the leading web browser company.

Once a market has been cornered by an aggressive giveaway campaign, anyone who wants to compete has to fight fire with fire. So when Microsoft decided to go after the Web browser market, it gave away Internet Explorer in order to compete with Navigator. Aggressive giveaways are the ultimate price war, and consumers are big winners for as long as the giveaways continue. A company has to have deep pockets to play this game, and the ultimate winner may depend more on cash reserves than superior software. When the time comes to pay for some new improved version of previously free software, an educated consumer is more likely to pick the superior product, when all other things, including price, are equal.

Virus Risks and Safeguards

9.6

Computer viruses are a serious problem for everyone online. Just like their medical namesake, some are barely noticeable, while others are hideous killers. If you plan to download software from the Internet, you need to know how to protect yourself. This is one place where you don't want to learn things the hard way. ***You never have to be hurt by a computer virus if you take some simple precautions.***

A **computer virus** is a piece of code someone inserts into an otherwise legitimate computer program for the purpose of causing mischief. Some viruses are just annoying. For example, one may cause a political message or animation display to pop up on your screen, and that's all it does. Other viruses can do considerable damage. A particularly malicious one might erase every file on your hard drive. Viruses are also designed to spread from one machine to another through shared files. A user can unknowingly infect his or her own computer and then spread that virus on to others without realizing it.

Some viruses are visible and obvious, while others are subtle and devious. A virus that quietly operates behind the scenes might cause a gradual slow-down in the performance of your computer over a long period of time. You wouldn't notice anything right away, and you may never figure out what happened to your machine. The only way to know if a virus is present on your computer is with special software designed to detect viruses hiding in your files.

Virus detection software locates known viruses by watching for identifying signatures that give them away. A good detection program will look for thousands of viruses, and periodic software updates are released to keep up with new viruses. The bad news is that there are more computer viruses than ever before, and the number of known viruses will likely only rise. The good news is that computer users have become educated about viruses and are taking appropriate precautions. So the amount of serious virus damage is probably decreasing even as the number of viruses in circulation continues to grow.

A virus can be moved on to your machine, but then stopped before it can cause any damage. In order to cause damage, a virus must first be activated by executing a program or, in some cases, by opening a file. Virus detection software works only if you scan your files for viruses before they have a chance to be activated.

HOW TO AVOID UNSPEAKABLE GRIEF

1. Make sure you use up-to-date virus detection software. Outdated software won't be able to see new viruses.
2. Download software only from large software distribution sites.
3. Stick to popular software that is found on more than one host.
4. Always scan *all* files for viruses as soon as you move them onto your machine and *before* you run them or open them. (I say more about this in the following section, "Macro Viruses").

If you follow these rules and never let a file get by you unscanned, chances are excellent you will never be hurt by a computer virus.

How Viruses Get You

Simply copying an infected file onto your hard drive or floppy disk cannot activate a computer virus. You have to execute a computer program in order to activate a computer virus. Programs are executed when you double-click their desktop icons or filenames (on a Mac or in Windows), or type the name of the file at the command prompt and press Enter (in DOS or UNIX). Also, never leave an unscanned floppy in your computer's drive where it might be read as a start-up disk the next time you turn on your computer. That's another way that files can get executed. See also the following section, "Macro Viruses."

A virus detection package will scan all of your files looking for viruses. You can scan all the files in a given directory, on a hard drive, a floppy diskette, or a CD-ROM. If a virus is located, your virus detection software can remove the virus from your file(s) and advise you of possible damage or additional precautions that you should take. Some virus detectors can be invoked automatically whenever a new file is introduced to your system (via a floppy, CD-ROM, or Internet download). If you have downloaded a file archive or a compressed file, you will need to unpack it or expand it before scanning it.

Do I Have to Spend Money on This?

Some people want to save money even when they are trying to avoid unspeakable grief. It is possible to play it safe without spending big bucks, but you have to be careful. Start by asking technical support for your ISP, company, or school if they have a site license for commercial virus protection software. They often have such site licenses but may not advertise it, so it never hurts to ask. If they do have one, you may be able to legally run it free of charge.

If there are no site licenses, ask tech support for their virus detection recommendations. Do they have a local copy of a freeware program that they recommend? Using a local copy will be safer than pulling one off the Internet because your tech support staff has probably taken precautions to make sure it is safe. If you must download from an external site, then pick software that is popular and well-known and download it from the home page of the company that distributes it. If it's shareware, register it so that you can get notices about updates.

Who Do You Trust?

Hiawatha Bray, a *Boston Globe* columnist, reported that in May 1996 Microsoft sent him a CD-ROM containing demonstration software that included a macro virus (see the following section, "Macro Viruses"). Microsoft found out about the problem and notified everyone who received the CD-ROM one week later, but it's sobering to see a software giant like Microsoft make a mistake like that. Commercial software houses are extremely careful with their final software releases. But one would expect Microsoft to be equally cautious with a CD-ROM of demonstration software. It never hurts to scan everything, no matter where it comes from.

You take the biggest chance when you download a little-known utility from a random Web page (remember the Moldova Scam discussed in Chapter 2) or trade software on floppies with friends. Another risky proposition is the CD-ROM containing 500 free pieces of software included in the back of a magazine. If you scan everything religiously, you can push your luck with potentially risky files and probably get away with it. But if you want to minimize your risk, consider the source whenever you put new software on your machine.

Before you start this exercise, obtain a virus detector and use it on *every* file you download from the Internet during this exercise. If you are a student, ask your professor for instructions on how to obtain a recommended virus detector. If you are not a student, ask your tech support folks for a recommendation. *DO NOT PROCEED WITHOUT VIRUS PROTECTION!*

In this series of exercises, you will use your browser to download some graphics software that will come in handy in Chapter 11.

FTP SESSION #2

Continued on Next Page

Continued from Previous Page

1. Download WizUnZip or Stuffit Expander as described in Section 9.4 (see "File Decoding Catch-22"). ***Scan for viruses.***

2. If you want, install WizUnZip as a browser plug-in for `.zip` files (on a PC) or Stuffit Expander as a browser plug-in for `.hqx` and `.sit` files (on a Mac).

3. If you have a Mac, go to `http://www.shareware.com/` and find clip-to-gif-072.hqx (319K/freeware). Download, unpack, and *scan for viruses*.

   If you have a PC, go to `http://www.winsite.com/` and find gifweb31.zip (333K/$20 shareware) for Win 3.x or gifweb42.zip (1.4M/$15 shareware) for Win 95. Download, unpack, and *scan for viruses*.

4. Note that your downloaded file will be unpacked automatically if you did Step #2. After you have unpacked the file and scanned it for viruses, follow the installation instructions to set up the software (read the readme file). Then wait for Chapter 11.

Unfortunately, no one can ever eliminate all risk associated with computer viruses, unless they (1) never download executable files from the Internet, (2) never use any software freebies distributed on floppies or CD-ROMs, and (3) never use any software passed along by a friend, coworker, or anyone else, including college professors. Commercial software is generally safe, but there have been a few isolated cases of computer viruses turning up in commercial software. So to be 100% safe, you'll have to never use any commercial software. This means you will have to become a computer programmer, write all of your own software, and never accomplish anything else with your life—or else avoid computers altogether and become a Luddite. No life is without some risk.

Macro Viruses

In recent years, the question of what constitutes an executable file has become a little complicated. In 1995, macros for word processors and spreadsheets opened the door for a new class of virus carriers. A macro is a small piece of executable code that can be added to files created by word processors or spreadsheets. This code is then executed when the file is opened. ***This means that anyone opening a spreadsheet file or a word processing file might execute a macro. If the macro is infected with a virus, then the virus is***

activated. A virus inside a macro is called a **macro virus**. Macro viruses are a serious problem because they are fairly new and most people haven't learned how to take proper precautions. All word processing and spreadsheet documents should be treated as if they are executable files just in case they contain an executable macro. However, the only applications that are known to have triggered macro viruses are MS Word and MS Excel, so those are the applications to treat with extra care.

None of this is a problem if the only Word or Excel files you open are ones you've created yourself. When you open a document given to you by someone else is when you have to be careful. People can unknowingly pick up a macro virus and then just as unknowingly pass it on to others. If you are collaborating with someone on a writing project and trading document files via e-mail, FTP, or floppies, it is possible to pick up a virus from a word processing or spreadsheet document even though it comes to you from a trusted friend or coworker.

Macro viruses have become especially prevalent now that mail systems are more sophisticated. Some mailers let you plug in application software in order to display application-specific documents. A mail reader that supports plug-ins opens the door for viruses via e-mail. However, you can prevent an infected macro from ever having a chance to execute before you've had a chance to scan it. Regardless of what mailer you use, the following box gives a simple rule that you can follow to protect yourself from macro viruses when you read e-mail.

Don't tell your mailer where to find Word or Excel as plug-ins (helpers) in order to open a MIME attachment. Instead, whenever you receive a Word or Excel document, instruct your mailer to save it to a file where you can scan it for viruses before you open it. Also apply this rule to all other software packages that support macros. (If in doubt, assume it applies to *all* word processors and spreadsheets.) On a Mac platform, infected Word documents display template icons instead of the normal Word icon. A template icon has a large white arrow on the middle of it. If you ever see one of these in a MIME attachment, it is an infected file. Do not open it: immediately contact technical support for assistance.

HOW TO AVOID EXECUTING A MACRO VIRUS

Note that you have to go out of your way to set up your mailer to launch Word or Excel automatically. But that's easy to do if you're trying to take advantage of all of the MIME-related features. Figure 9.11 shows a helper window in Navigator that will launch Word when its mailer receives a MIME attachment in Rich Text Format.

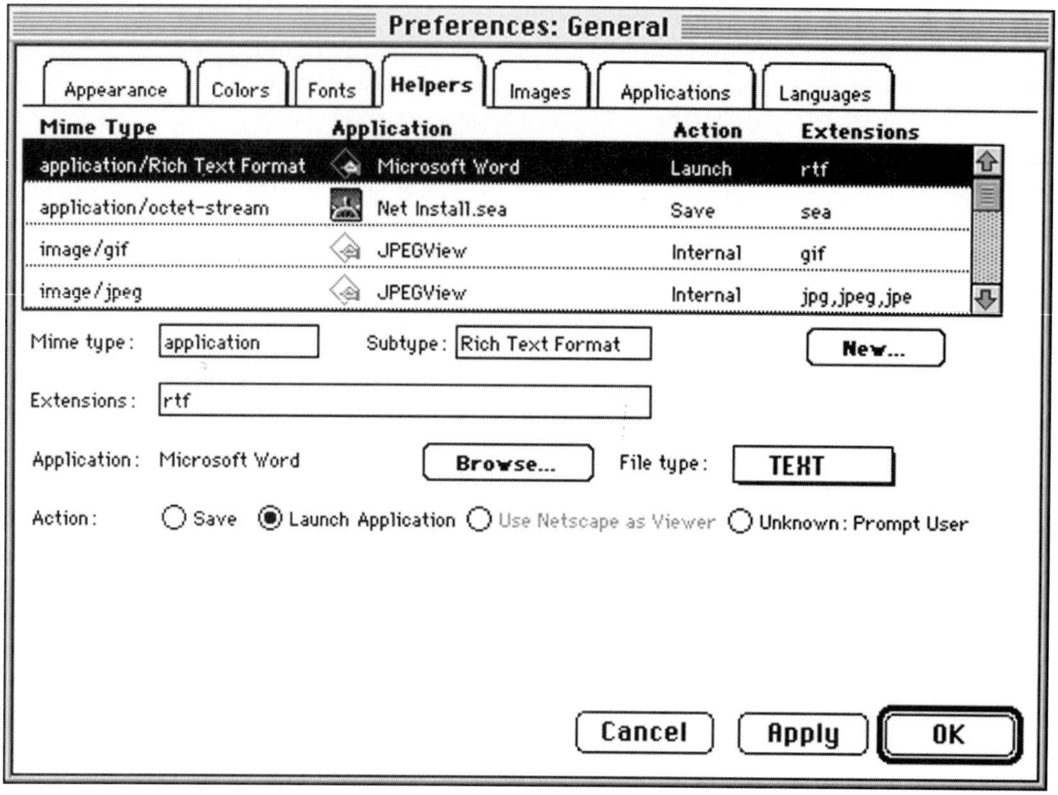

FIG. 9.11

Flirting with Macro
Virus Trouble

Although currently the most frequently encountered macro viruses are associated with MS Word, in particular versions 6.*x* and 7.*x*, there is no reason why macro viruses can't turn up in files generated by any other applications that support macros. Note also that macro viruses can move across platforms. An infected Word file created on a PC can be read on a Mac and can spread the virus to the Mac. If you receive a lot of files with attachments, just remember these three rules:

1. Be careful with your plug-ins.
2. Use virus protection software that has been updated for macro viruses.
3. Before you open any application-specific attachment, scan it.

See the Internet 101 Web pages for more information about computer viruses in general and macro viruses in particular.

FTP Clients

Web browsers all have one major limitation when it comes to FTP. A Web browser is quite adequate for downloading files from the Internet, but no Web browser can upload files if you need to move your own files to a remote host. If you ever want to set up your own home page on the Web, you will need to upload your HTML files to a Web server. That's when many people decide to get an FTP client. People also find it useful to upload files when they collaborate on major projects with coworkers. For example, each chapter of this book was uploaded to an FTP server maintained by Addison Wesley Longman, the publisher of the book. If you rely on computers in a work environment, you will probably need an FTP client.

There are many graphical FTP clients for Mac and PC platforms, and all are very easy to use. Like graphical Web browsers, graphical FTP clients require SLIP or PPP connections. The newer FTP clients support features such as these:

- Simultaneous displays of local and remote directories
- Sorting options for directory displays
- Support for multiple FTP sessions running in parallel
- Support for multiple file transfers
- Intuitive drag-and-drop file transfers
- An address book for automated logins on different servers
- File caching to speed up transfers from pokey servers
- File search facilities

When you use an FTP client to visit an FTP server, you start by specifying the address of the host machine you want to contact. If you don't know which FTP server to visit, your FTP client can't help you.

Figure 9.12 shows the opening window from an FTP client named Fetch. In the Host: window is the DNS address. In this example, you are initiating an anonymous FTP connection, so the User ID: window is filled in as "anonymous" and a complete e-mail address is entered as the password. Leaving the Directory: window blank takes you straight to the main directory. However, if you want to go to a specific subdirectory, enter the appropriate directory path in the window. Next, click OK. Fetch will attempt to make the connection.

```
═══════════════ Open Connection... ═══════════════

  Enter host name, user name, and password
  (or choose from the shortcut menu):

     Host:        ┌──────────────────────────────┐
                  │ uiarchive.cso.uiuc.edu       │
                  └──────────────────────────────┘
     User ID:     ┌──────────────────────────────┐
                  │ anonymous                    │
                  └──────────────────────────────┘
     Password:    ┌──────────────────────────────┐
                  │ •••••••••••••••••••••        │
                  └──────────────────────────────┘
     Directory:   ┌──────────────────────────────┐
                  │ /pub│                         │
                  └──────────────────────────────┘
     Shortcuts:   ┌──┐      ┌──────────┐  ┌──────────┐
                  │▼ │      │ Cancel   │  │  OK  ▶  │
                  └──┘      └──────────┘  └──────────┘
```

FIG. 9.12

Connecting to an FTP
Server, Fetch

If you have a personal computer account on another host, you can initiate a **full-privilege FTP session** in order to move files back and forth
between your two accounts. To create a full privilege session, you use your
actual userid in the User ID: window and your personal password for the
Password: entry.

Will I Ever Need to Use Full-Privilege FTP?

HINT

If you want to set up a home page on the Web, then you will need
to use full-privilege FTP. You will be given a personal account on a
Web server in which you can store your HTML files, but you will want
to develop your Web pages on your home computer. When your
pages are finished, you will need to move your HTML files from your
home computer to your Web server. Uploading files to a remote host
is easy with a full-privilege FTP session running on a SLIP or PPP connection.

Figure 9.13 shows the Fetch window that displays directories on a remote
host once an FTP connection has been established. This window can be navigated using scrolling and point-and-click operations. To download a file,
select the file's name in the remote server and click Get File. A pop-up window will ask you to enter a name for the file and a location for it on your
local machine. To upload a file, display the remote directory in which you

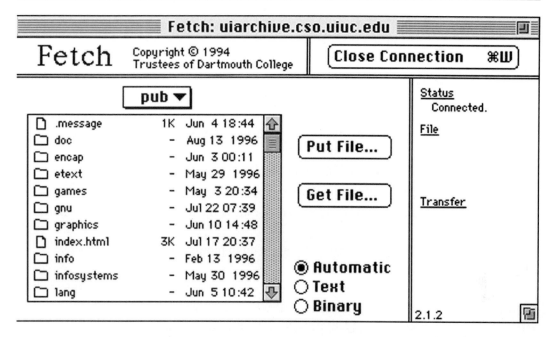

want to deposit your local file and click Put File. A pop-up window will ask you to select a file on your local host for transfer. Once you've done this, the transfer proceeds.

Graphical FTP clients have many convenient features to make FTP fast and painless. For example, Fetch creates a separate window for any welcome messages issued by the remote server, so you can easily refer back to those messages at any time.

All file types can be transferred via FTP, including all binary formats; the speed of the transmission is limited only by the speed of your modem. If your local host is connected directly to the Internet via an Ethernet or T1 line (connections that are faster than phone lines), FTP file transfers are completed in a matter of seconds.

FIG. 9.13

Directory Navigation during an FTP Session

PROBLEMS AND EXERCISES

1. Explain how text files and binary files differ.

2. What makes the main menu of an FTP server special?

3. What is file compression, and why is it important for FTP transfers?

4. How much storage space can you expect to save when you compress a file of English text?

5. Categorize each of the following extensions as a text file format or a binary file format:

   `.hqx`   `.doc`   `.ps`   `.bin`   `.htm`
   `.tar`   `.uue`   `.sit`   `.Z`   `.rtf`

6. What can a "helper application" do for you when you download an FTP file?

7. What is a self-extracting archive? What two file extensions are used for self-extracting archives?

8. How does shareware differ from freeware?

9. Is it illegal to distribute copies of freeware to friends?

10. When is it appropriate to contact the system administrator of an FTP site?

11. What four things can you do to protect yourself from computer viruses?

12. Do you ever have to worry that a virus might be in an ASCII text file?

13. What is a macro virus? Where are they most often found?

14. What can an FTP client do that a Web browser can't?

15. What is the difference between anonymous FTP and full-privilege FTP?

16. [**Hands-on**] Connect to the public FTP server `uiarchive.cso.uiuc`
    `.edu`. How many guests are allowed to access this server at once?

17. [**Hands-on**] Find Project Gutenberg on `uiarchive.cso.uiuc.edu`.
    Browse to see if you can find a file describing the goal of Project Gutenberg. Who is the director of the project?

18. [**Hands-on**] The FTP server at `sunsite.unc.edu` maintains many directories devoted to various academic topics. Try to find a subdirectory devoted to alternative health care and a list of alternative health care resources on the Internet. Consult this list to find out what oxytherapy is.

19. [**Hands-on**] Disinfectant is virus detection software for the Mac. Find a current version of Disinfectant. How old is it? How can you tell if this is the most recent version?

20. [**Hands-on**] Before you begin this exercise, look to see what time it is. Then see if you can locate and download a freeware screensaver for your platform. *Scan it for viruses* and see if it works. If the documentation is not very helpful, look for another screensaver. Report on your experiences. Was it easy to find freeware screensavers? How many did you download? How much time did you spend on this exercise? What did you learn from this exercise?

Telnet

10

"With computers, everything is possible and nothing is easy."

- ALAN PERLIS

THE INTERNET 101 WEB PAGES

- Telnet Resources
- Hytelnet Resources
- Community Networks and Free-Nets
- MUD Servers and MUD Stuff
- Chat Servers

What Is Telnet?

10.1

It is no longer possible to stick your head in the door of a computer lab and surmise anything about the workloads of the machines in front of you. An otherwise empty room containing 20 computers might support the activities of 400 remote users. And each of those people might be running their own Internet applications that take them to additional hosts running servers that are in turn capable of going out to even more servers on demand. Users, data files, computers, and computer programs no longer need to be in close proximity to one another. One's sense of distance is quickly forgotten on the Internet, and some of this magic is accomplished with Telnet.

One way to share computer resources is by giving programmers remote control access, or **remote login** privileges. **Telnet** gives users remote control over other host machines by enabling remote logins over the Internet. The idea of remote login is as old as the original ARPAnet. In 1969, an early version of Telnet was developed. Telnet allows a user on one host to log in to a second host over a network and run programs remotely. Telnet, along with FTP, were thought to be among the most important networking developments of their time.

In a **Telnet session**, the local host acts like a computer terminal connected to another computer that happens to be very far away. A Telnet user establishes a continuous connection to a remote host, and operates software on the remote host. While this sounds like any other client/server interaction, Telnet sessions are distinguished by the fact that there are no restrictions on the software that can be run during a Telnet session. If a user has privileged access to the remote host, a **full-privilege Telnet session** gives that user full command of the remote host's operating system and application software. In addition to full-privilege Telnet access, more restricted Telnet connections can be made available to **anonymous Telnet guests** or, in some cases, **registered Telnet guests**. This chapter looks at all three levels of Telnet privileges.

To establish a Telnet connection, you need to run a Telnet client. The Telnet client can be run alone, or as a plug-in for your Web browser. Here's

FIG. 10.1

Setting Up a Telnet
Plug-In Application

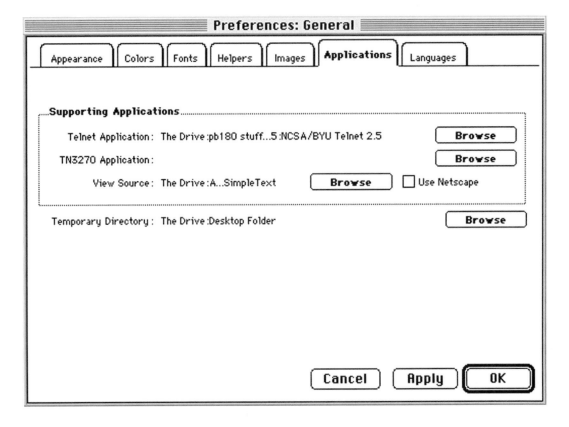

how to plug a Telnet application into Navigator. See also Figure 10.1.

1. From the Options menu, select General Preferences.
2. Go to the Applications tab.
3. Under Telnet Application, use the Browse button to set the application to your Telnet program.
4. Click OK.

That's all there is to it. Telnet is a text-based application, so launching Telnet from a graphical Web browser won't add graphics to your Telnet sessions. But it will allow you to click a hyperlink on a Web page and automatically launch your Telnet client in order to initiate a Telnet session from the Web. Some Web pages contain links to Telnet servers. In order to jump to a Telnet server, your browser needs a Telnet plug-in application.

Full-Privilege Telnet   ◄ 10.2

To initiate a full-privilege Telnet session, you need

1. a Telnet client,
2. the DNS or IP address of a remote host on which you have an account, and
3. your userid and password for the remote account.

Telnet couldn't be much simpler. You log in as if you were connecting to a local host; you do all of the work you want as if you were working on a local host (see Figure 10.2). Then you log off and disconnect from the remote host. Telnet negotiates multiple hardware platforms and different operating systems with apparent ease. Cross-platform compatibility via Telnet is one of the technical achievements that gives the Internet an illusion of effortless connectivity.

Why Would I Ever Want This?   *HINT*

If you never have more than one computer account, you won't need full-privilege Telnet. You may not see any pressing need for two computer accounts, but the situation can arise very naturally. For example, suppose you are a college student and you plan to be off campus during the summer months. If you have an ongoing school account available to you year-round, but you are too far

Continued on Next Page

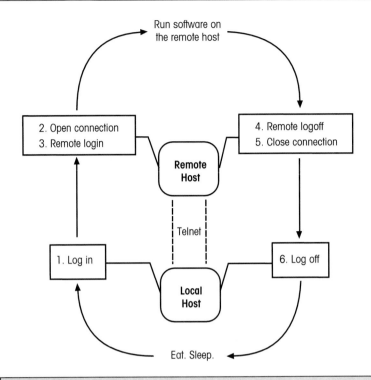

FIG. 10.2

The Circle of Telnet

Continued from Previous Page

away to dial in locally, you might want to subscribe to a local ISP during the summer months in order to use your school account remotely. Then you can dial in to your ISP at local phone rates and connect to your school's host via Telnet. Once you have access to any Internet host, you can always Telnet to your home account in order to manage e-mail and do anything else you would do if you were working locally. With Internet connectivity, you are only keystrokes away from home base no matter where you go.

ONCE IS ENOUGH

Just in case you have six different computer accounts and it occurs to you that you can nest multiple Telnet sessions (as you hop from one host to another and then another, and so on), be warned: Nested Telnet sessions can produce strange behavior. A control character may mean one thing to one Telnet session and something else to a different Telnet session. This can create all sorts of bizarre confusion. The solution is simple: Don't nest Telnet sessions. If you need to visit different hosts, disconnect from each one before you move to another.

Guest Telnet

Some Internet hosts support guest Telnet sessions. Anyone can log in as a guest, but guests are not given the full privileges they would have with their own computer account. Rather, guest Telnet connections are designed for specific purposes. One may deliver regional weather reports, another may give teachers a place to discuss multimedia resources, and a third one may house technical data for microbiologists. Many libraries offer Telnet access to their online card catalog. Public Telnet servers can hook you up to all sorts of information once you know where to look (see the Internet 101 Web pages for pointers).

Telnet Gateways and Web Browsers

You can initiate a Telnet session with your Web browser by clicking a `telnet://` URL. This type of URL is called a **Telnet gateway**. For example, Telnet gateways to online card catalogs in libraries are often encountered on Web pages and Gopher menus. Your Web browser needs a plug-in Telnet client in order to handle these URLs, so if your browser isn't properly configured, it will not be able to link you to a Telnet server. Sometimes Web browsers and Telnet interfaces don't cooperate very well. If you find yourself experiencing a lot of problems with a Telnet URL, grab the Telnet address from the HTML source file and try visiting that same address with just your Telnet client instead of your Web browser. Telnet sessions sometimes behave badly when they are nested inside other applications.

Different Telnet sessions use different interfaces. Commands that work on one Telnet server probably won't work on a different one. If you Telnet to five libraries to look at five online card catalogs, you will probably have to deal with five different interfaces. Always read the welcome message carefully and if you get stuck, look for online help. Poorly documented Telnet sites can be very frustrating. The good ones, however, make it easy to move around and find things.

Since the advent of the Web, many Telnet services have been replaced by Web pages. The Web offers the advantage of a uniform user interface, making it easier to master than the many different Telnet interfaces. As a result, the number of new Telnet servers has undoubtedly declined as system administrators move more and more information services onto the Web. Even so, many Telnet sites are still operating. Someday it may be important for you to know how to use one.

I Know I'm Welcome, But Where's the Door?

Unlike anonymous FTP, which uses the same login convention at all sites, Telnet servers can have idiosyncratic login requirements. Access to a public Telnet server is not restricted, but you have to know how to get onto the server. Whenever you hear about a Telnet server, make sure you get instructions on how to connect to it along with its host address. You need a login name and a password or sometimes just a login name. If you must guess, you can try "guest" at the login prompt. But most Telnet servers require a login sequence that's not easy to guess. If you have trouble connecting to a Telnet server, search for instructions on the Web or ask for help in an appropriate newsgroup. Don't be discouraged if the instructions you find don't work; many online documents describing Telnet sites are out-of-date. Just look for more up-to-date documentation.

Another wrinkle with Telnet concerns **port numbers**. All Telnet connections are made through physical devices called **ports**. A single server normally supports multiple ports, and you may need to specify the correct port when you contact a Telnet server. When no port number is mentioned, Telnet always defaults to port 23. In a point-and-click Telnet client, expect to see a port option in the open connection dialog box. If you type a command line to launch your Telnet client, the proper syntax depends on your operating system. From a UNIX host, you supply the port number right after the host address, separated from the host address by a blank. An example is given below.

Most Internet hosts allow restricted Telnet access on port 13. If you Telnet to port 13 of any Internet host, you will be told the time according to that host machine's internal clock. Here is a port 13 Telnet session from a UNIX host:

```
lehnert:~$ telnet culine.colorado.edu 13
Trying 128.138.129.170...
Connected to CUBoulder.colorado.edu.
Escape character is '^]'.
Wed May 28 13:25:12 1997
Connection closed by foreign host.
lehnert:~$
```

This is about as simple as a Telnet session can be. No login is required, and there is no opportunity for interaction. As soon as the date and time are displayed, the connection is closed.

From inside a Web browser, a port number for a telnet address must be included in the URL. This is done by adding the port number to the end of the host address, separated from the host address by a colon (e.g. `tel-net://culine.colorado.edu:13/`).

As far as I know, port 13 returns the local time on all Internet hosts with the exception of `india.colorado.edu`. When you Telnet to port 13 on that machine, you get the time according to an atomic clock at the National Bureau of Standards. Using port 13 is handy when you want to get a fast sense of how far away a host machine is—just figure out how many time zones you have to cross to get there.

To get a better sense of a host machine's location, you can visit the InterNIC Directory and Database Services and query the netfind database. A netfind query will return the geographical location of a server, and if you have someone's e-mail address, you may also be able to get additional information about that person. For example, suppose you want to know exactly where `msnyder@fsc.edu` is located. Start by making a Telnet connection to `ds.internic.net` (from your Web browser type in the URL `telnet://ds.internic.net/`) and log in as "netfind." The server will connect you without a password. After an initial welcome message, the netfind server presents a top-level menu:

```
Top level choices:
        1. Help
        2. Search
        3. Seed database lookup
        4. Options
        5. Quit (exit server)
->
```

If you're visiting this server for the first time, it makes sense to select #1 and find out how to conduct a search. But to keep this visit short, pretend you know what to do and go directly to #2, entering the information you have about msnyder:

```
-> 2
Enter person and keys (blank to exit) -> msnyder fsc edu
```

The server comes back with four possible domain names for you to check. The server doesn't know which ones to search, so it asks for your favorite choices:

```
Please select at most 3 of the following 4 domains to
search:
        0. fsc.edu (fitchburg state college, fitchburg,
massachusetts, usa)
```

```
        1. fsc.mass.edu (massachusetts regents computer
network, boston)
        2. fsc.psu.edu (pennsylvania state university,
university park, pennsylvania)
        3. fsc.qut.edu.au (queensland university of
technology, australia)
Enter selection (e.g., 2 0 1) ->
```

From this, you can see where fsc.edu is located—at a college in Fitchburg, Massachusetts. Now the server will to look to see if it can find anything about msnyder. To help it along, tell it to look only at fsc.edu:

```
Enter selection (e.g., 2 0 1) -> 0
( 0) SMTP_Finger_Search: checking domain fsc.edu
( 0) do_connect: Finger service not available on host
fsc.edu -> cannot do user lookup

Domain search completed. Proceeding to host search.

PHASE [host search]:

NOTE: Received no responses, and some host or network
failures occurred.
        Maybe try this search again later.
```

Netfind wasn't able to come up with additional information about the user msnyder. But you know more than you did before: msnyder is affiliated with Fitchburg State College in Fitchburg, Massachusetts.

If you are visiting a Telnet server for the first time, don't expect it to be perfectly intuitive and easy to navigate. Telnet sessions are all text-based, so you won't see any graphics (except for maybe some ASCII artwork) and you won't be able to use your mouse. You will have to rely on menus and command lines. Telnet existed before Apple sold the first Mac and before Microsoft sold the first copy of Windows. In those days, few people outside of computer science were trying to do much with computers and no one expected interfaces to be terribly friendly. Try out some commands and see what happens. Experiment. Be patient. Think of it as a puzzle. If you type something that the server can't handle, you will just get an error message, maybe even a little helpful advice. It's perfectly all right to make a mistake when you interact with a Telnet server. No one is watching, and no one will care.

TELNET BEHAVING BADLY

If you fire up a Telnet connection and are rewarded with an unreadable screen or a bunch of crazy characters, you probably have a bad terminal setting. Some Telnet interfaces ask you to set the **terminal emulation mode** at a TERM= prompt. This setting enables different computer platforms to communicate smoothly and effectively. On a UNIX host, a Mac, or a PC running Windows, the correct setting is usually vt100. If asked to provide a TERM= setting, vt100 is probably the right answer. On a DOS-based PC without Windows, the setting is probably ANSI. Disconnect (see the "Help! Get Me Out of Here!" box) and try different settings until you find one that works (another possible setting is vt200). Once you get the right terminal emulation set up, the remote host will be able to speak your computer's language. Bad terminal emulation is a common source of difficulty with Telnet sessions. The other big stumbling block is a badly designed interface with inadequate online documentation. If you can get past the TERM= setting, at least you'll have a fighting chance with the interface.

Some interfaces are easier to learn than others. The friendlier interfaces are menu-based, full of examples, and have helpful command summaries at the bottom of each screen. Read all of the instructions you see. If there are no helpful hints or instructions, try typing "?" or "help" for more information. Don't blame yourself if you don't know what to do right away. Some Telnet servers are designed to operate as business-like components inside other computer programs rather than fuzzy, warm places for people. If you visit a server designed for computers rather than people, you won't see any menus and you'll need to find your own online help. You'll have to meet the machine on its own terms by learning its command set, and you may need to experiment with those commands for a while before you find what you want.

Here's an example of a command-driven Telnet interface that was really designed for other computer programs. The Geographic Name Server at the University of Michigan delivers quick profiles for cities and towns in the United States. To access this server, Telnet to `geoserver.eecs.umich` `.edu:3000` (that's `geoserver.eecs.umich.edu` on port 3000):

```
lehnert:~$ telnet geoserver.eecs.umich.edu 3000
Trying 141.213.11.44...
Connected to martini.eecs.umich.edu.
Escape character is '^]'.
# Geographic Name Server, Copyright 1992 Regents of the
University of Michigan.
# Version 8/19/92. Use "help" or "?" for assistance,
"info" for hints.
```

If you've never been to this server before, type "?" to find out what to do next. If you already know, you can ask for a specific city. Here's a look at Springfield, Massachusetts:

```
Springfield, MA
0 Springfield
1 25013 Hampden
2 MA Massachusetts
3 US United States
R county seat
F 45 Populated place
L 42 06 05 N 72 35 25 W
P 152319
E 70
Z 01101 01102 01103 01104 01105 01106 01107 01108 01109 01111
Z 01115 01118 01119 01128 01129 01133 01138 01139 01144 01151
Z 01199

.
```

This profile tells the county name (1), latitude/longitude (L), population (P), elevation above sea level (E), and all possible zip codes (Z). If you don't want any additional information, terminate the session by typing "quit":

```
quit
Connection closed by foreign host.
```

This interface is so primitive that it doesn't even bother to show a prompt when it's your turn to type something. That is a good tip-off that the server was probably created more for other computers rather than people. People can connect to it and use it, but don't feel overly critical of an interface that was never designed with you in mind.

If this last example seems familiar, you are probably remembering an example in Chapter 7 (Expedition #7) when we visited a "Gateway to the Geography Server at UMichigan" on the Web. This Web page offered a user-friendly interface to the Telnet site just visited. If you are having a lot of trouble with a Telnet server, you might be able to find a friendlier interface to the same server on the Web.

WHEN IT'S TIME TO SAY GOODBYE

When the time comes to say goodbye, you may not know how. Maybe you forgot the instructions on the welcome screen that told you how to quit or you may have never seen any instructions about quitting. Standard Telnet exit commands are "q," "quit," "x," "exit," "stop," "end," "logout," "logoff," and "signoff." You may have to type the command, or you may see an exit option in a menu item that you can select. Sometimes you have to get back to the main menu before you can exit. An exit keyword may take you back to the main menu, where you can make your final exit. If all else fails, see the "Help! Get Me Out of Here!" box.

Most university libraries and many public libraries maintain online card catalogs that are accessible via Telnet. If you are at a university, you can probably connect to your library through a CWIS gateway on the Web or a Gopher menu. Online card catalogs use a combination of menus and keyword searches to give users the information they need. Explore some library catalogs to get a feel for all of the different ways a Telnet interface can operate. Remember that there is no uniformity across Telnet sites, so some sites will be easier to navigate than others.

Many of the most extensive Telnet interfaces are designed to attract regular users to an online community. For example, in 1991 Argonne National Laboratory and the Division of Educational Programs established an electronic bulletin board system for K–12 students and teachers with interests in math, computer, or science education. They called their system "NEW-TON" and made it accessible via Telnet at newton.dep.anl.gov. Here is NEWTON's main menu:

```
Please select one of the following:

   I ... Information Center
   E ... Electronic Mail
   Q ... Quick Mail
   C ... Conference/Chat area
   A ... Ask A Scientist
   F ... Forums (Public Message Bases)
   H ... Homework Assistance
   G ... Gateways
   L ... File Libraries
   R ... Registry of Users
   $ ... Account Display/Edit
   X ... Exit (logoff)

Main System Menu (TOP)
Make your selection (I,E,Q,C,A,F,H,G,L,R,$,? for help,
or X to exit):
```

Each of these choices leads to more menus with more choices and more possible activities. The server supports e-mail, a software library, real-time chat channels where people can talk as fast as they can type, and gateways to additional resources on other servers. NEWTON is an Internet success story in the K–12 community. About 60,000 users have tapped its resources. It incorporates one of the better Telnet interfaces, probably because it was designed to consolidate an online community from a population that was not already online.

If Telnet seems difficult because of Telnet ports, idiosyncratic login requirements, mysterious terminal settings, and problematic user interfaces, you may find yourself wishing that all of the software designers would get together and decide on a uniform interface. Whenever the programming community does not work to establish software standards, a thousand flowers bloom, and end users have to cope with all of them. The Telnet protocol gave rise to a big garden with lots of thriving flowers and a few straggly weeds. Visit ten different Telnet servers and try to remember all of their command sets, and you'll understand why Gopher menus and HTML documents represented major progress in client/server technologies.

HELP! GET ME OUT OF HERE!

Sometimes a Telnet interface dies for no apparent reason. Nothing you type raises a response from the server. It's as if your computer is frozen. When this happens (and it will sooner or later), don't reach for that reset button too fast. Telnet sessions always come with an emergency exit that you should try when all else fails: Ctrl-] (also written as ^]). Hold down the Control key and type the right square bracket at the same time. Telnet will abort your session and transfer control back to the Telnet program on your local host. When you first establish a guest Telnet connection, you may see a welcome message that reminds you about Ctrl-]. This is a standard emergency exit for all Telnet sessions. It is perhaps the only thing that works uniformly across all Telnet connections.

NOTE: Ctrl-] *does not* close your connection to the remote host. ***Always close your session before you quit your Telnet client.*** Otherwise, the connection remains open and you are tying up resources on the remote server. To close the connection, type or select "close" from a pull-down menu and then exit your Telnet client by typing or selecting "quit." Figure 10.3 shows the close command on a pull-down menu from Better Telnet PPP.

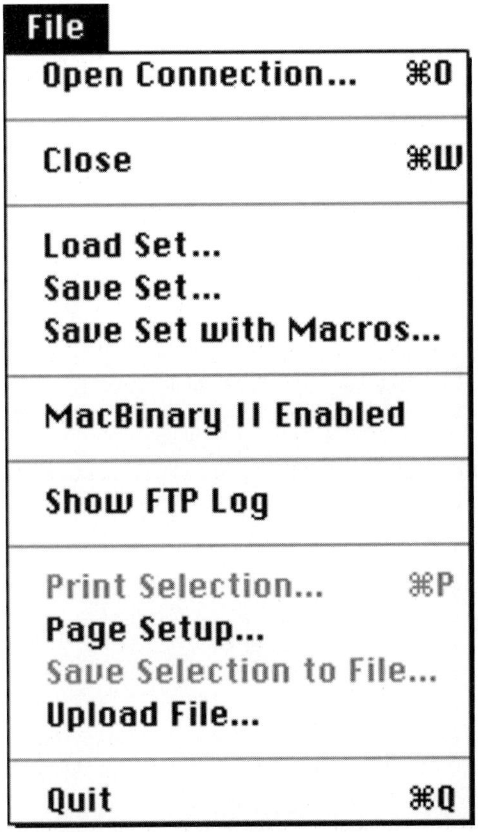

```
┌─────────────────────────────────────┐
│ File                                │
├─────────────────────────────────────┤
│ Open Connection...          ⌘O      │
│                                     │
│ Close                       ⌘W      │
│                                     │
│ Load Set...                         │
│ Save Set...                         │
│ Save Set with Macros...             │
│                                     │
│ MacBinary II Enabled                │
│                                     │
│ Show FTP Log                        │
│                                     │
│ Print Selection...          ⌘P      │
│ Page Setup...                       │
│ Save Selection to File...           │
│ Upload File...                      │
│                                     │
│ Quit                        ⌘Q      │
└─────────────────────────────────────┘
```

FIG. 10.3

All Telnet Sessions
Should Be Closed after
You Exit a Server

What Is Hytelnet?   10.4

Whenever a new client/server application takes off, you can expect to see a new search tool follow in short order. FTP has ARCHIE, Gopher has Veronica, Usenet administrators maintain lists of all of the active newsgroups, and the Web has hundreds of keyword search engines. In the same way, Telnet has clearinghouses of Telnet sites. The most extensive clearinghouse is called **Hytelnet**. Hytelnet is a client program that indexes a master list of Telnet servers. Many people maintain public Hytelnet servers, so there is no reason for you to download a copy of Hytelnet yourself (it has a lot of data files, so a Hytelnet download requires more than 1MB of file space). The Hytelnet database is the largest collection of pointers to Telnet-accessible library catalogs, electronic bulletin boards, and community networks.

Hytelnet's site summaries include host names, port numbers, login instructions, and a brief summary of the site, when available. Its entries are usually based on the opening display of the Telnet connection, so whatever you find in Hytelnet comes straight from site administrators. Some Hytelnet entries are obsolete, but it is still the best place to look for Telnet sites.

Here is a sample Hytelnet entry for a server at `hermes.merit.edu`:

```
TELNET HERMES.MERIT.EDU or 35.1.48.159
Which Host? mdoc-vax
Username: NEWBIZ


                    W E L C O M E     T O     T H E
            M I C H I G A N   D E P A R T M E N T     O F
    C O M M E R C E    I N F O R M A T I O N    N E T W O R K


Welcome to the Business Start-Up Information Database
New Business Info
                Information for New Businesses


    1   Licensing Information for Specific Types of Business
    2   Checklist for Starting a Business
    3   Information for Employers
    4   List of Business Development Centers
    5   Business Financing Information
    6   Help - How to Use NEWBIZ
    EX Exit
```

Unfortunately, this particular Telnet server is no longer operating. When you find a resource in Hytelnet, always check it out before you tell other people about it. Many defunct Telnet servers have not completely gone away; they've just been converted to Web sites. So if a Telnet server is no longer available, conduct a keyword search for the same service on the Web. You might be able to find what you were looking for there.

Even though many Telnet sites are being phased out in favor of Web pages, Hytelnet is still a valuable resource because it has built-in quality control. Telnet sites are sanctioned by institutions and organizations. When you find a resource through Hytelnet, you know that professionals stand behind it. If the site has been moved to the Web, it took its quality control with it. But the Web site may be hard to see in a noisy list of search engine hits. Hytelnet is a noise-free index for officially sanctioned resources.

There are many places where you can access Hytelnet. Some are better maintained than others, and some seem to be more extensive than others. Nowadays, the best Hytelnet sites seem to be on the Web. Several nice ones incorporate keyword search facilities. The best informational site about Hytelnet is maintained by Peter Scott. You can look there for pointers to public Hytelnet servers (see the Internet 101 Web pages for URLs).

Community Networks and Free-Nets

Bigger is not always better. Much has been said about the global nature of the Internet and the ability of computer networks to connect people who live in different regions, countries, and cultures. The ability to communicate with a next-door neighbor is far less challenging from a technological perspective. Indeed, effective communication on a local level is more of a social problem than a technological one. That's why it is easier to drive a rover around Mars than it is to put a telephone in every home. Although 94% of U.S. homes have a telephone and about 33% have a home computer, only 50% of the world's population has ever spoken on a telephone, let alone touched a computer. Computers can leverage an economic advantage in a hundred ways, but it is far less clear how computers help solve problems associated with poverty, disease, and human rights violations.

Difficult problems tend to dodge magic bullets, and people who try to make a difference often face insurmountable odds. Happily, that doesn't stop some people. While ARPA was encouraging computer scientists to connect the world in a global computer network, grassroots efforts were underway to enhance local connectivity. Community bulletin boards attempted to address the information needs of local communities.

Bulletin Board Services

In the early 1980s, private citizens began to set up local **bulletin board systems** (BBSs) using home computers and banks of modems for dial-up access. Anyone within a local calling range (or beyond if they wanted to pay long-distance charges) could dial up and peruse the offerings. Some of these services were offered for free, but the better ones tended to be fee-based in order to cover the expenses of running the BBS. By today's standards (considering ISP subscription rates), the BBSs of the 1980s were relatively expensive. Only a few computer-savvy hobbyists knew about the BBSs, and there was little effort in the way of community outreach. Even so, the number of BBSs mushroomed and *Boardwatch Magazine* chronicled BBS resources and technologies. Each BBS was like a scaled-down version of the Internet, offering newsgroups, freeware, and whatever online resources the board manager wanted to support. The number of BBS systems in the United States was at one time estimated to be over 40,000. Some board managers seemed to have a proclivity for pornography, but others specialized in topics such as amateur radio, games, science fiction, and genealogy. These systems were the seeds for community networking.

In 1984, Case Western Reserve University's Department of Family Medicine set up an Apple II computer as a BBS. The system offered e-mail, file transfers, and message posting in an effort to facilitate communication for medical residents, students, and staff working at different sites throughout Cleveland. The BBS was dubbed St. Silicon and was very successful for two weeks. Then it began to crash on a regular basis. The system was experiencing overloads, and the source of the overloads was quite unexpected. Apparently, the telephone number for the BBS had been leaked, and people were calling in with medical questions in the hopes that a physician might reply.

Thomas Grundner, the creator of St. Silicon, could have changed the phone number or shut down the BBS, but he responded to the situation in a more creative way. He looked at the problem and saw an opportunity to address a community need. He created an online medical clinic called "Doc in the Box," where people could post questions and come back a day later for answers. Case Western Reserve sponsored the project as a community service and an innovative way to deliver health-related information to residents of Cleveland. St. Silicon provided this service on the basis of a single phone line that was continuously in use 18 hours a day. Interest in the service was stronger than anyone ever anticipated. When AT&T heard about Grundner's work, they gave him a UNIX workstation to expand the scope of his BBS.

Free-Nets

In 1986, Grundner launched **Cleveland Free-Net**, the first community BBS open to anyone with a computer and a modem. Cleveland Free-Net offered a variety of services and information resources to its users. Many of these services addressed local events and issues, but others had more general appeal. Users were invited to create their own special-interest groups and act as Free-Net moderators. Grundner also told local organizations about the project and found that open invitations yielded volunteers willing to act as moderators for a variety of special interest groups. Thousands of Cleveland residents have participated in the Cleveland Free-Net, and it has served as a model for Free-Nets in other communities.

Anyone can visit the Cleveland Free-Net and browse for free. Users must register with the BBS before they can post messages or participate in community forums, but registration is also free. Registered users access the BBS with a userid and password, just as with a personal computer account. The two-class user model "read-only" versus "full access" has been adopted by most community networks in order to keep their system loads down. Casual visitors won't bother to register, so requiring user registration is one of the few ways to maintain some quality control in a chat room or a special interest list.

Early BBS systems and Free-Nets could be accessed only over phone lines. Internet access was added later via Telnet, but you can still find some user interfaces that instruct you to "Please hang up now" when you exit the server. These instructions are left over from the pre-Internet days of direct dial-up access. If you are connecting via Telnet, they really just want you to close your Telnet connection. They aren't asking you to hang up the phone on your ISP dial-up connection.

National Public Telecomputing Network

Just as news of St. Silicon leaked out to people in Cleveland, news of the Cleveland Free-Net got out to people all over the Internet. Interest in creating other Free-Nets led Grundner to found the National Public Telecomputing Network (NPTN) to help others create and maintain Free-Nets. NPTN offers newcomers organizing manuals and tips on how to start a Free-Net. Internet communication makes it easy for Free-Net administrators to share experiences and advice with one another, but NPTN also distributes information through off-line channels for people who do not have Internet access. One person can start a Free-Net that will someday touch hundreds or thousands of lives. It is a gratifying way to leverage technology for the public good. If you want to get involved with a Free-Net, check first to see if any already exist in your area. Free-Nets are always looking for volunteers and people with good ideas.

Acceptable Use Policies

To maintain courteous and appropriate communications, Free-Nets and community BBSs ask all participants to respect a code of good behavior. These codes are called **Acceptable Use Policies** (AUPs) and are designed to make community networks pleasant places for everyone. If you visit a community network, take the time to read its AUP and be careful to honor its restrictions. Here is an excerpt from the AUP posted on the NEWTON BBS:

NEWTON Rules

1. Only acceptable language and content will be permitted in all areas.
2. All information (text, files, graphics, etc.) must be educationally appropriate.
3. Users must not abuse their privileges of open and free access to NEWTON. These abuses can occur by having multiple accounts, staying on-line for long periods of time, or not logging off in order to hold a port.
4. All users must provide complete and correct information upon registration, including street address, area codes, postal codes, birth date, etc. Users must sign on with their real name.

5. The user is responsible for the verification of ownership and copyright of all original or altered uploaded/downloaded messages, files, and other information on this system.

The NEWTON Project Management reserves the right to remove any users from the BBS.

NEWTON users are also informed of the BBS's privacy policy, a disclaimer of liability, a disclaimer of endorsement, copyright restrictions, and the criminal consequences of unauthorized system access.

BBS systems strike a balance between open access and civic responsibility. Flame wars and abusive language are not found on a BBS with a restrictive AUP. Since no one is allowed to post to a BBS unless they have registered with the BBS, system administrators have all of the leverage they need to enforce their AUP. Anyone who violates the AUP can be bumped from the BBS. End of problem.

DON'T FORGET YOUR PASSWORD!

Multiple BBS registrations by the same individual are generally prohibited and considered a form of abuse. If you register on a BBS (or any telnet server with a user registration option) and then forget your password, don't reregister and start up a new account. Contact a system administrator and explain your situation. Administrators are always happy to help get you back onto the BBS (unless you make this a regular event).

The amount of traffic in a BBS is usually less overwhelming than on Usenet or a very active mailing list. This can be a problem if you are looking for an immediate reply or some esoteric information. But lower traffic levels also make it easier for system administrators to monitor the BBS for abusive behavior. Since system administrators have the muscle to stop abusive behavior when they see it, BBSs do not have the anarchic quality of the Usenet newsgroups. If you want to avoid offensive language or you don't want to be bothered with spam artists and flame wars, you may find a local BBS more to your liking.

10.6 ▷ Graphical User Interfaces

In 1972, a primitive arcade game named Pong appeared in train stations, college game rooms, and bars all over the United States. Pong was a two-dimensional Ping-Pong game. A green disc bounced off of rectangular paddles against a black background. Each paddle was manipulated by a single controller and could be moved in a straight line along one side of the playing field. You had to position your paddle so that the ball would hit it and bounce back. Each time you missed the ball, your opponent won a point. A generation raised on Nintendo must have trouble imagining a world where Pong was the state-of-the-art in real-time computer graphics. But Telnet predates Pong, and reminds us of an era when computer interfaces were limited to text and command lines.

As computers became more powerful, screen displays gradually began to incorporate graphics into user interfaces. White type on black screens gave way to icons, pull-down menus, and tool bars. Mouse clicks replaced command lines. The term **graphical user interface** (GUI) became widespread the 1980s when high-resolution monitors and the memory needed to support them could be had for less than $10,000. People who worked with Telnet sites began to think about how to make their Telnet sessions look more contemporary. Games have always been a favorite place for computer science students to try out new ideas, and Telnet servers that support interactive games were prime candidates for graphically-enhanced interfaces. So GUIs for game servers began to appear in the 1980s (see Figure 10.4).

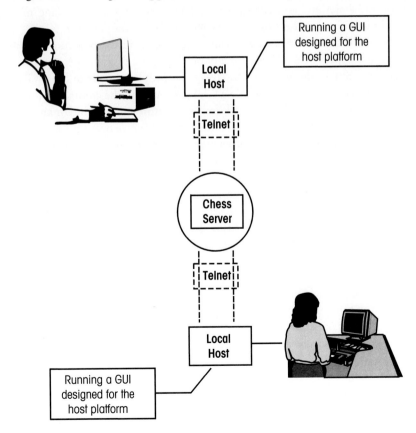

FIG. 10.4

Adding a Graphical User Interface (GUI) to a Telnet Server

Imagine players pairing off to play a game of chess via a chess server. Each new move is sent to the server, which updates a board display and sends the new board out to both players. In a text-based protocol, these board displays have to be crafted from the ASCII character set. No matter how hard you try, you really can't come up with an ASCII chess board that is easy to read. If you had to play chess with such an interface, you would want to set up a physical chess board next to your computer on which you could move real pieces and plan your next move from a real board.

If you are interested, you can Telnet to the Internet Chess Club (ICC) at `chess.1m.com:5000` (see also `http://www.chessclub.com/`) and watch chess games being played in just this way. Using a plain text-based Telnet connection, you can view only the games with ASCII board displays, but that's probably not how the people playing the games are doing it. Almost everyone who plays chess at ICC runs a GUI in order to work with a readable board display in a point-and-click environment. The GUI has to be designed with both a specific server and a specific host platform in mind. For example, there are different GUIs that work with the ICC server on PC, Mac, and UNIX platforms. Most of these are available on the Internet as freeware and shareware, and at least one commercial chess GUI is being marketed for ICC and other compatible chess servers on the Internet.

GUIs for Telnet servers are usually written by skilled programmers who create and support the software as a hobby. They are typically people with a strong interest in the server themselves. The people who write chess GUIs tend to be chess players, too. Once a GUI gets out into the community, users invariably make suggestions and ask for extra features of one kind or another. If the software's author has the time, the GUI will evolve over time and come to reflect the needs and desires of its user community. Telnet GUIs therefore improve over time and incorporate good ideas from many people.

Figure 10.5 shows a chess GUI for the Mac called Fixation. It is acting as an interface to the ICC chess server through a Telnet connection. Fixation is freeware written by Adam Miller. Users wanting to connect to a chess server from a home computer start by firing up the GUI and issuing a dial-up or connect command. Once the local host connection is in place, a Telnet command goes out from the GUI and establishes a connection with the chess server.

When all of the connections are in place, the GUI interprets and renders all information coming back from the chess server. With a good graphical board display, users can play directly from their monitors using a mouse to move pieces. A sophisticated interface will also support additional windows for all of the various things that chess players like to do with their games. One window will display chat channel conversations with other players. A different window might record game outcomes. Whatever people want, the GUI tries to deliver.

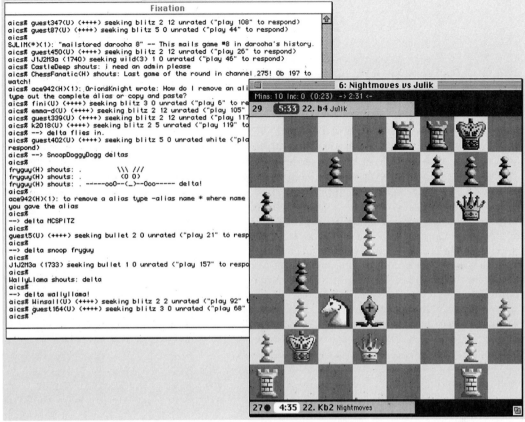

FIG. 10.5

A View from a GUI

Playing chess is a popular Internet pastime. The Internet Chess Club is just one of many chess servers on the Internet. ICC alone averages over 25,000 chess games a day (most are speed chess and last only a few minutes). On May 4, 1997, a club record was set at ICC with 2,266 users logged on simultaneously.

GUI's for Telnet servers are not limited to games. For example, the NEWTON server described in Section 10.3 can also be visited with a point-and-click GUI for easier navigation of NEWTON's offerings. GUIs can display physical landscapes with buildings and locations that correspond to different activities and resources. Information server GUIs make information gathering fun for children and less tedious for adults. However, it does take some time to locate and install a GUI, so you don't want to bother with one unless you plan to visit a specific site regularly. If you are interested in a GUI for a Telnet server, check the server itself for pointers. If there is a compatible GUI available for your computer platform, the server will know about it.

10.7 ▶ MUDs, MOOs, and MUSH

People like to talk to one another over computer networks. Back when ARPA's contractors were preoccupied with FTP and Telnet, e-mail was quietly spreading like wildfire. The Usenet newsgroups were started in 1981 and became extremely popular in no time. Designers of the early chess servers discovered that even chess players like to talk about their games as much as they like to play them. In time, chat capabilities became a standard features on multiuser Telnet servers. The ICC supports no fewer than 300 chat channels, with over 50 standard channels reserved for fixed, special-interest groups. Here's a sampling of what chess players like to talk about at ICC:

```
     1 - Newbie Help Channel:  All guests and new accounts are automati-
cally in channel 1.  Newbies ask questions.  NO chatter in this channel!
Serious questions and answers only, please. "news 403" for details.
     2 - Experienced Help Channel:  for more experienced members to ask
questions and to discuss policies, etc, with admins. Interface/ timestamp
questions here.
     3 - Simul Channel.
     7 - Wild 7 Channel
    10 - Team Game Channel:  For setting up team games.
    11 - Team Game Channel:  For team A.
    12 - Team Game Channel:  For team B.
    14 - Internet Chess for Mac interface help.
    15 - ICC Youth Bunch.  21 and under, meet here.
    16 - ICC Senior Channel.  Socialize with friends over 50.
    17 - Women's channel — female ICC members only.
    24 - BUGHOUSE Channel-partnering and general 'bug' topics.
    33 - Cow Channel-MOO! Go figure.  (Ducks allowed too)
    34 - Sports
    43 - Chess theory — openings, endgames, etc.
    44 - Computer chess-playing programs and chess databases.
    45 - Chess books and magazines. Tell your favorites, ask advice.
    46 - Tomato Channel:  for automated tournaments.  "help Tomato".
    47 - Tomato managers channel.  Managers only, please.
    49 - Flash Channel:  Tomato version for Bullet Tournaments (see 46)
    50 - General unlimited gab.
    55 - Non-chess Software and Hardware discussions.
    64 - Programming and algorithms for chess-playing.
    85 - jimmy/snakeyes Tournament channel.
    89 - The WILD Bunch. - people who like the chess variants.
    90 - The STC Bunch - people who like 30 to 120 minute time controls.
    91 - "Fast Standard Games".  People who like 15 to 30 minute games.
    97 - Politics. (please discuss here, not in shouts!)
    98 - The Zippy channel.
    99 - The Street Corner Where Nothing Happens.
```

```
101 - Music Channel.
102 - TV and Movies Channel.
103 - Religious Discussions/Debates
104 - History Channel.
105 - Literature, books, etc.
106 - Travel Channel:  give/get travel tips, plan to meet people.
166 - Major Chess Events/Chess Politics (such as Kasparov-DeepBlue).
 70 - Greek channel
 71 - Spanish channel
 72 - French channel
 73 - German channel
 74 - Dutch channel
 75 - Russian channel
 76 - Italian Channel
 77 - Japanese channel
 78 - Nordic channel (Denmark,Norway,Sweden,)
 79 - Iceland channel
 80 - Finnish Channel
 81 - Portuguese Channel
 82 - Catalan Channel
```

Chat channels (a.k.a. talk zones, conference rooms, and so on) are one of the most popular activities on community bulletin boards and commercial Internet services. Client software designed to facilitate online conversation has become increasingly sophisticated in response to user interest. For example, if you want to monitor more than one chat channel at a time, it helps to have a separate window for each one. But multiuser interactive software has progressed far beyond different windows for different conversations. As often happens with computers, serious innovations began with a game.

The Birth of MUD

In 1980, two students at Essex University began to collaborate on a version of an earlier game called Adventure. In the original Adventure game, players wandered around a labyrinth of interconnected rooms and locations searching for treasures and dealing with monsters. When Roy Trubshaw and Richard Bartle began their project, they started with an Adventure-like motif and added a multiuser capability that allowed players to talk to each other as they played. The program was called MultiUser Dungeon (MUD), inspired by a popular role-playing game called "Dungeons and Dragons."

In 1984, Bartle and Trubshaw founded a company and released MUD2 as a commercial product. MUD2 incorporated many sophisticated devices, including audiovisual effects and intelligent bots (automated players) that participate in the game just like human players. MUD2 users accessed the game through a dial-up service available only to paying subscribers. Owned by MUSE Ltd., MUD2 was an early client-server experiment that demonstrated the viability of online entertainment as a commercial enterprise.

More MUDs were written by various individuals, and two basic MUD genres emerged. Some MUDs were primarily used for social interactions as a place to meet people and make friends, while others were heavily oriented toward combative, competitive play. Both genres support role-playing, where players assume the persona of a fantasy character. MUDs also contained objects that could be moved around and manipulated by the characters. A number of MUDs were written, primarily in Great Britain, and MUDs became a favorite pastime for college students. MUD habits at the level of 16 hours a day were not unheard of, and more than a few college students dropped out of school as a result of MUD addiction.

Then, in 1989, a small MUD that did not consume much computing power became very popular on the Internet. TinyMud was suitable for Internet use. It also allowed users to create new rooms with links to existing structures. Anyone could add to the collective creation of a TinyMud. Versions of TinyMud expanded into formidable creations. For example, in 1990 a TinyMud installation called Islandia was operating under the collective guidance of 3,000 players, who had constructed a creation containing 14,000 rooms. TinyMud promoted conversation and creativity, rather than competition and simulated violence. Apparently, if you give the public an opportunity to link 14,000 rooms together, people will break down your door to be part of it. MUDs seemed to produce socially compelling watering holes for a large segment of the online community.

Many variations on the MUD idea have evolved, including TinyMUSH (MultiUser Shared Hallucination) and TinyMoo (a MUD that uses object-oriented programming). Role-playing MUDs are managed by system administrators who assign characters to new players via e-mail and mediate occasional disputes among players. Passwords are assigned to players when characters are created, and MUDs are normally available through Telnet connections (see Figure 10.6). MUD characters engage in primitive forms of body language as well as dialogue. Commands for smiling, waving, laughing, and whispering are all standard MUD operations. Even with a point-and-click interface, you still have to learn a lot of commands in order to communicate smoothly in real time.

MUD Clients

Just as GUIs are popular interfaces for game servers on the Internet, several MUD clients have evolved to make mudding easier. With a MUD client, you can "gag" another player who is annoying you. You can also highlight input from designated players or all of the whispers aimed at you so that you don't miss anything by accident. You can create macro commands that allow you to issue long command sequences with one or two keystrokes. This saves time and may also delay the onset of repetitive stress syndrome when you find

```
lehnert:~$ telnet michael.ai.mit.edu
Trying 192.1.100.42...
Connected to michael.ai.mit.edu.
Escape character is '^]'.

Welcome to MuseNet, the Multi-User Science Education Network.

This is michael.musenet.org, your access to Educational Muses.

To use the public TinyFugue client, log in as: guest

MuseNet ULTRIX V4.2 (Rev. 96) (michael)

login: guest
MuseNet, the Multi-User Science Education Network (musenet.org)

MuseNet provides access to participating educational Muse sites
serving the K-12 Education Community.

Guest client systems: guest.musenet.org
======= MuseNet Guest Bulletins =======

Welcome to MuseNet, the Multi-User Science Education Network.

Available Worlds are:

MicroMuse    OceanaMuse    EonMOO    WindsMARE    VirtualChicago and more...

To open a connection to an alternate World, type:  /world <worldname>
To close a connection to a World, switch to it and type:  /dc
To toggle among open Worlds, type:  ESC-B <backward> or ESC-F <forward>
To exit MuseNet, type:  /quit


TinyFugue version 3.4 alpha 10, Copyright (C) 1993, 1994 Ken Keys
Regexp package is Copyright (c) 1986 by University of Toronto.
Type `/help', `/help topics', or `/help intro' for help.

% Loading commands from /winds/guestmgr/guest/tf.lib/stdlib.tf.
---- World MicroMUSE ----
```

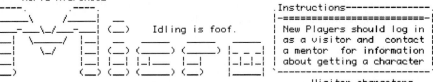

FIG. 10.6

Welcome to a MUD at MIT

yourself typing the same command sequence over and over again. Even better, you can write your own macro triggers so that commands are automatically issued whenever a particular event happens. For example, you might write a trigger that says "Hello" to anyone who says hello to you first.

There are at least half a dozen MUD clients available on the Internet. Some are designed for social MUDs (the TinyMuds) while others are designed for combat-oriented MUDs. One of the most popular clients is TinyFugue for the social MUDs. If you want to experiment with MUDs, start with a good MUD client. You can find out more about MUD clients and MUD servers on the Internet 101 Web pages. But brace yourself for the command sets you might find. When some mudders thought it would be fun to simulate sexual encounters online, new MUD commands materialized to enable virtual sex. TinySex, normally encountered in TinyMuds, is similar to "phone sex" and offers powerful ammunition for the claim that sexual excitement is all in your head (or perhaps your head, plus your MUD client, plus your Internet connection).

Internet Relay Chat

If you aren't quite ready to jump into the complexity of a full-blown MUD, you could start with **Internet Relay Chat** (IRC), which is sort of like preschool for mudders. On an IRC server, you can find channels for all sorts of special-interest groups, depending on who's online and who wants to talk about what. When the O. J. Simpson verdict was announced, dozens of IRC channels were ready to relay the verdict to anyone who wasn't watching CNN. Networks of IRC servers are interconnected so that a channel on one server will appear on all of the other servers. What you type can be read by people worldwide, if they happen to be paying attention.

Some IRC channels are run by people who impose codes of behavior on all participants. On those channels, people can be bumped for bad language or abusive behavior. But IRC is still a public facility, and there are no uniform behavioral codes that apply to all channels. With a few keystrokes, a person can create a new IRC channel on the spot. IRC channels for people who want to trade digital pornography attract FBI sting operations, and anyone can record long log files of chat channel conversations. If you want to have a private conversation with a friend, you can avoid general public scrutiny by creating an "invisible" channel, although someone who really wants to monitor you will find a way to eavesdrop. If you require serious privacy on the Internet, stay away from IRC and read Chapter 12.

IRC is a magnet for college students engaging in avoidance behavior, but it also has had its shining moments. In 1991, news reporters tuned into IRC to get on-site reports from correspondents in the midst of the Gulf War. These satellite-based communications became critical at times when telephones were out of commission. IRC logs from the Gulf War are still available online and make very interesting reading. Another set of IRC logs has been preserved from the Russian coup in 1991. Log documents like these will give future historians a unique "real-time" perspective on world events unlike any other historical records.

IRC becomes an alternative communication channel whenever phone service is disrupted. When the Northridge earthquake struck in 1994, it knocked out phones and overloaded the remaining operational lines out of Los Angeles. People outside of the area turned to the Internet for information about friends and relatives. If you are willing to trust information offered by total strangers, IRC can be a source of eyewitness reports in times of chaos.

IRC servers can be contacted via Telnet, but anyone who plans to spend much time on IRC should use an IRC client. If you access the Internet through an ISP, they may provide an IRC client as part of their service. If you access the Internet via a university or school account, make sure you are familiar with their policy for chat channels and MUDs. Real-time chat consumes a lot of bandwidth and is often prohibited during working hours. Asking tech support for IRC advice is probably a good way to find out about any relevant policies. You can find more information about IRC clients and servers in the Internet 101 Web pages.

IRC is a good place to learn Netspeak, since Netspeak and fast typing skills are highly advantageous during an IRC conversation. If you are new to the Internet, you might want to keep handy a list of Netspeak acronyms to help you keep up with the conversation. You can use IRC to kill time with strangers or to meet a friend at a prearranged time. If an e-mail interaction is too slow for something urgent, you might consider an IRC channel for fast turn-around and more interaction. Then again, sometimes a telephone call is what you really need.

The Future of Telnet   10.8

Telnet and FTP are the two original network applications that complemented each other in a most logical fashion. Telnet made it possible to share CPU's (and executing computer programs) over the Internet; FTP made it possible to share files (and data) over the Internet. Computer programs could be written to perform all sorts of tasks, and any programmer could design a command set or a system of menus as an interface for a Telnet server. There was some burden on the user to negotiate a new interface on each new server, but that was a small price to pay for the computing power of a remote host running what might be a one-of-a-kind computer program.

The only thing that could usurp Telnet's hold on the Internet community was a protocol that could retain all of the power of Telnet while making life easier for users who might not have the time or patience for interface puzzles. The need for easier interfaces became more pronounced when the Internet went mainstream, and two technological advances came into play at just that time to pick up where Telnet left off.

First, the Web gave us intuitive user interfaces expressive enough for any information provider. Second, the **Common Gateway Interface** (CGI) made it possible for Web servers to execute computer programs behind the scenes in order to create fleeting Web pages when a user requires dynamic data. For example, each time you run a Web search engine, the hit list that comes back is displayed on fleeting Web pages generated by a CGI script (the program that maps the indexes in your query to relevant documents in the document database). These hit lists may never be needed again, and they would require constant updating even if we thought they could be recycled. So it makes sense to generate each one only as needed and then discard it afterwards.

When we go to the "Gateway to the Geography Server at UMichigan" on the Web (see Chapter 7), we run a CGI script that taps the same database as the original Telnet Geographic Name Server. Any program run by a Telnet server can also be run by a Web page server, often with very little adjustment. This makes it easy to move existing Telnet services to the Web, and the appeal of the Web makes it the obvious choice for any new information services coming online. Anything you can do with a Telnet server can be done with a Web server and CGI. Since the Web offers graphics and is so much easier to navigate than a Telnet interface, the life expectancy of public Telnet servers is indeed limited.

But let's not jump to any unwarranted conclusions about Telnet in general. Telnet is more than a collection of Telnet servers. Full-privilege Telnet sessions fill a critical need for people with multiple computer accounts, and that need has nothing to do with public Telnet servers. So don't expect full-privilege Telnet to go away anytime soon. Full-privilege Telnet occupies a unique niche on the Internet that appears to fall outside the expanding reach of the Web.

THINGS TO REMEMBER ABOUT TELNET

1. If you don't have any login instructions, try "guest" at the login prompt.

2. Each Telnet server runs its own interface. It takes time to learn a new one.

3. Menu-driven servers are usually easier to learn, but still take some effort.

4. If you get stuck, try typing "?" or "help" for online help.

5. Don't be afraid to experiment with commands. You can't hurt anything.

6. Always close your Telnet connection after you exit a server.

> 7. If you can't exit a session normally, type Ctrl-] to interrupt the session.
>
> 8. Always close your Telnet connection after you use a Ctrl-] interrupt.
>
> 9. If you register with a BBS or a game server, be careful to read their AUP.
>
> 10. If a Telnet server seems to be defunct, search the Web for the same service.

PROBLEMS AND EXERCISES

1. Suppose you are visiting a Telnet site and your screen freezes. Nothing you type raises a response. What should you do?

2. Someone told you about an interesting Telnet site, but when you try to connect, the server won't answer. What can you do next?

3. A book gives an IP address for a Telnet server as 134.129.105.1.385, but you know that this is not a valid IP address (why not?). What do you suppose the correct address might be?

4. What must you always do after you exit from a Telnet server or interrupt a Telnet session?

5. Compare and contrast the NEWTON server and the Geographic Name Server at the University of Michigan. Which one is menu-driven? Which one is command-driven? How else do they differ?

6. A friend tells you that at least half of the entries in the Hytelnet database are out-of-date and no one should bother with Hytelnet anymore. Is this true? Can you make a counterargument even if you concede that your friend's estimate of 50% is possibly too low?

7. [**Hands On**] Telnet to `exnet.iastate.edu` and find out what to do with important documents, photographs, or books that have been damaged in a flood. What one thing should you do with damaged documents as soon as possible?

8. [**Hands On**] Visit the Weather Underground at `downwind.sprl.umich.edu 3000` and find out which four months pose the greatest threat for tornado damage in the United States.

9. [**Hands On**] Telnet to `ttnbbs.rtpnc.epa.gov` to find out what NATICH does and what its help line telephone number is. You will have to supply your name and city/state location in order to browse the site, but you don't have to register (that is, supply additional information) in order to answer this question.

10. **[Hands On]** Section 10.4 talked about a Hytelnet entry for the Michigan Department of Commerce Information Network. The host address in the Hytelnet description is no longer valid, but the database didn't really disappear; it just moved to a new host. Study the Hytelnet entry and see if you can find a pointer to this database on the Web. (*Hint:* Use a full-text search engine.) Then go into the database and find out what kind of license is required to run a pet shop in the state of Michigan.

11. **[Hands On]** Go to the geography server at the University of Michigan and find the population of Homer, Alaska. Then do a netfind search at InterNIC and find out how many businesses in Homer have Internet addresses. (*Hint:* Netfind will match keywords anywhere in the full entry for a DNS name. Set up a query that includes the keywords "Homer" and "Alaska." Read the online help file for netfind to make sure you enter a valid query.)

12. **[Hands On]** Chapter 9 explained that it is good Netiquette to check for FTP mirror sites and work with a site that is nearby. The software archive we visited at the University of Michigan has the following mirror sites:

    ```
    wuarchive.wustl.edu
    grind.isca.uiowa.edu
    sunsite.unc.edu
    archive.orst.edu
    ```

    Use netfind at InterNIC to find out where each of these host machines is located. (*Hint:* Use a bogus person name to head your query. You don't need a valid e-mail address or person name to get the information you want.)

13. **[Hands On]** A good example of a community network is the Youngstown Free-Net at `yfn2.ysu.edu`. Visit this bulletin board and go to the Public Square in order to find a Q/A forum about the Internet. When was the last question posted? Has anyone responded to it? How long was it before an answer appeared? Why might someone want to post questions here instead of on a Usenet newsgroup?

14. **[Hands On]** Use Hytelnet to see if you can find a Free-Net or local community BBS somewhere near you. Visit the site and explore it a bit. Does it contain timely current information about current events? Does this seem to be a healthy, active community network?

15. **[Hands On]** There is a zoo in Peoria, Illinois, that offers free admission one day each week. Which week day is free? *Hint:* Use Hytelnet to find an appropriate community network (Peoria is in Central Illinois) and browse the network for zoo information. What network did you find? What is the name of the zoo?

Web Page Construction

11

Use the talents you possess, for the woods would be a very silent place if no birds sang except the best.

- HENRY VAN DYKE

THE INTERNET 101 WEB PAGES

- Art Resources for Web Pages
- Graphics File Utilities
- HTML Editors and Converters
- HTML Tutorials and Documentation

This chapter is for students who want to go beyond the basics in Chapter 5 and learn more about Web page construction. I do not attempt to present a comprehensive introduction to HTML, but I do cover all of the basics needed to construct attractive Web pages.

Remember the Big Picture

11.1

Before you dive into the details of HTML, it is good to step back and consider the big picture. A good Web page author must try to anticipate the needs and interests of the Web page's readers as much as possible. It is easy to forget this when you are first learning HTML and you are preoccupied with the nuts and bolts of Web page construction. Read this section now to familiarize yourself with the big picture issues, and then review it again as you gain experience and begin to feel at home with the elements of Web page design.

The Three C's of Web Page Design

While developing your Web pages, always remember the three C's of Web page design:

1. Quality Content
2. Reader Convenience
3. Artistic Composition

First and foremost, make sure you have quality content. Check your facts, cite sources if appropriate, and produce a credible document. Next, consider your reader. Construct your Web pages with reader convenience in mind. Make it easy to find things, to move around, and to view the page as you intend it to be viewed. Also, keep download times down to a minimum. Then, and only then, should you concentrate on artistic composition. The look and feel of your Web page will be appreciated only if the first two concerns are adequately met. Beginning Web page authors often are so enamored with the fun of digital graphics that they forget about content and convenience. It's fine to have fun, but make sure the cosmetics aren't getting more attention than the content.

Perfect Your Pages Before You Install Them

All Web pages should be written, viewed, and tested before being installed on a public Web server. You can develop your Web pages on any convenient computer platform (e.g., a home computer). After you are through developing your pages and have uploaded them to a Web server (usually a UNIX host), you check them one last time. But don't experiment with Web page development on a public server. Keep your Web page experiments to yourself.

If you are serious about designing robust Web pages that will look as you intend them to look, you must install more than one Web browser on the machine on which you do your Web page development. Viewing your pages with different browsers will sensitize you to the features that are industry standards and the features that are browser-specific. If half of the population is using Internet Explorer and you are checking your pages with Netscape Navigator only, your pages may look horrible to half your readers.

Life would be easier on Webmasters if everyone used the same browser. A professional Web page designer checks each page using perhaps half a dozen different browsers to make sure the page displays properly in each case. The relatively large number of browsers creates a lot of work for serious Web page designers. You should, at the least, use the two most currently popular browsers (at the time of this writing, Navigator and Internet Explorer) to check all of your pages before posting those pages in public. For maximal convenience, work on a computer with enough RAM—say, a minimum of 32MB—in order to run Netscape and Internet Explorer at the same time. If you can't display your pages with both browsers simultaneously, you will spend a lot of time jumping back and forth between the two.

Remember, too, that there will always be a sizable percentage of the Internet population using a text-based browser, so it is important also to check your pages with lynx on a UNIX platform.

Split Your Site into Multiple Pages

You should split a large Web site into multiple, smaller, self-contained pages unless you expect a lot of your users to copy your entire site to local files (an unusual circumstance). While multiple pages are harder for users to download, they offer several benefits. For example, they allow other Web page authors to reference portions of your site without referencing your entire site. They also are faster to download. It is frustrating to have to wait for a large download when you aren't even sure that the page you are waiting for is something you really want to see. So it is usually better to have a lot of smaller pages than a few large ones. But think about the logic of your Web site organization so that each page makes sense as an identifiable part of the larger whole. Look for categories and associations that will make sense to your readers. Poor Web page organization results in confusing Web sites that are difficult to navigate.

Write Effective Web Page Titles

Keep your Web page titles short but accurate and descriptive. Remember that search engines treat titles with more weight than they do other text elements. Your Web page titles will appear prominently in a list of search engine hits. By selecting your titles carefully, you can enhance your visibility on Web search engines.

Be Kind to "Back Door" Drop-ins

Remember that people can come into your site through "back doors" as well as your main home page. Someone who lands on a page found through a full-text search engine won't know if they are looking at a main document or one small part of a larger Web site. Keep back-door drop-ins in mind and set up navigational aids so that readers can orient themselves no matter where they enter your site.

Keep Download Times Short

Before adding graphics to a Web page, always think about the download times that graphics involve. Readers coming in through a modem may be downloading your page at a rate of 1–2K/second. When conditions are unfavorable, that rate can drop down as low as 100 bytes/second. ***If you are working on an ethernet or other fast connection to the Internet, be careful to remember the readers who connect over telephone modems.*** People working over telephone lines can't see Web pages as quickly as you can, and slow Web pages do not win friends or converts. Avoid large graphics at the top of your main page; visitors will be forced to wait while that image downloads. There are a number of simple techniques that you can use to be courteous to people working with slower Internet access (see Section 11.4, "Tips for Faster Downloads," for more details). Use them.

Make Your Pages Portable

For your own convenience, always create hyperlinks with portability in mind. For example, if you are developing your pages on a Mac, the Mac will forgive you for typing a file name in lowercase when you really meant uppercase. But if you transport your Web pages to a UNIX host, where case sensitivity rules, these same pages may surprise you with bad links that generate unknown file errors. Always copy file names with care, and don't let a platform-specific convenience lull you into a false sense of security. You will save yourself a lot of aggravation by avoiding uppercase characters in your directory names and file names.

If you create subdirectories of Web pages, plan to use the exact same directory structure on your Web page server, with the exact same directory names and file names.

Relative links are always safer than absolute links as far as portability goes. Never use an absolute link unless you are connecting to an external host. For your own pages, use relative links and keep your directory structure stable if you are storing Web pages in multiple file directories (see Section 11.5, "URLs and Pathnames," for more details).

State-of-the-Art or Maximal Access?

If you are determined to learn as much HTML as you can, you will inevitably be tempted to use sophisticated graphics that have audio and video clips. Remember that the most sophisticated Web page displays are also the most computationally intensive pages. Anyone operating an older computer with limited memory and a slow CPU is going to give up on a page designed for state-of-the-art machines. You can create computationally expensive pages if you want. Just don't expect everyone to see them.

Some HTML Tags Aren't Standard

Feel free to steal formatting ideas from Web pages that you admire. However, be aware that some of the tags you find may not be part of the official HTML standard. For example, Netscape has its own extended tag set that is recognized only by Netscape Navigator. When a Web page says something like "This page is best viewed using Netscape Navigator," be on guard for browser-specific tags. On the other hand, if a page doesn't include a browser-specific warning, you cannot assume that it strictly adheres to standard HTML. The only way to know for sure about the status of a tag is to check the HTML standard. A good HTML book will tell you which tags are part of the standard (see Section 11.9, "Where to Learn More").

Web Pages Require Ongoing Maintenance

When your pages are all perfect and installed on a Web server, remember that you're not done. Any Web page on a Web server requires ongoing maintenance. Timely information on your pages should continue to be timely. External hyperlinks should be periodically tested to ensure they aren't obsolete. If you've put your e-mail address on your Web pages, read your e-mail regularly and deal with comments or queries as they arise. If you find your enthusiasm for all of this waning, consider retiring your pages or finding someone else who might want to adopt them and care for them. Being an information provider is a serious responsibility. Many people enjoy the work, but you might not be one of them.

Working with Text

11.2

Web page design will never be like desktop publishing, where the author has absolute control over the final presentation of the text. As long as browsers give users the opportunity to customize preferences on the user's end, Web page displays will always be dependent on input from both the Web page author and the Web page reader.

Control on the part of the reader is essential because any given browser may be operating on any number of hardware platforms. Large complicated screen displays that look great on oversized monitors will be unreadable on the small screen of a laptop computer. For example, a paragraph indentation of 10 characters looks fine in a window that displays 100 characters per line, but it is not so fine in a window that displays only 30 characters per line. Also, browsers wrap text from one line to the next, unless instructed otherwise. Since users can resize their browser's display window, one user may see the text wrap after 70 characters, while another sees it wrap after 60. You have no control over these things and can only hope to create a Web page that will be easy to read for a majority of users. This makes text formatting in HTML inherently more limited than text formatting with a word processor. How much formatting control can you have when you don't even know the dimensions of the window that will display it? These uncontrollable factors make HTML text formatting a challenge.

WYSIWYG Text

WYSIWYG stands for "What You See Is What You Get." A WYSIWYG text editor is one that supports a "preview" feature where you can see exactly how a file will look when it is printed on paper. It would be nice to have WYSIWG web page previews, but the very nature of the Web is largely incompatable with the concept of WYSIWYG page displays.

Web page authors have no control over which Web browsers display their pages or what preference settings will be exercised by those Web browsers. Variable window sizes and variable font sizes make it impossible for a Web page author to know when to break the lines of text in a paragraph. So Web browsers format paragraphs of text as needed, filling each line as much as the window allows and reformatting the text if the window is resized.

While this strategy is usually the right one, there are times when a Web page author wants more control over the appearance of text. For example, the precise placement of line breaks is critical for song lyrics and poetry. If you want a body of text to appear exactly as it is typed, use the preformat tag `<PRE></PRE>`. With it, you mark text segments that should be printed exactly as they appear in the source file. You could insert a break tag `<BR>` at the end of each line to achieve the same effect, but this is tedious for a long body of text. The preformat tag does the job more elegantly by suppressing all line filling and wraparounds. You still can't control the font that will be used to display your text, or the size of that font, but `<PRE>` is as close as you will ever get to WYSIWYG for a Web page.

The preformat tag is often used to display examples of HTML fragments and sample computer programs. These are cases where carefully placed line breaks are needed to make text readable. Text marked with the preformat tag will be rendered in a fixed-width font such as Courier. This makes the text look less attractive than variable-width fonts. Always preview any pages that use `<PRE>` extensively to ensure they are readable.

If you have a large amount of plain ASCII text that you want to move onto the Web fast, encasing the whole file in one big preformatted segment is a quick-and-dirty solution. You can even insert hyperlinks inside a block of preformatted text. However, do not insert HTML formatting elements because they will be ignored.

Controlling the Flow of Text

Here are some tips to keep in mind to control how your text flows:

- To separate blocks of text by a blank line, use the paragraph tag <P>. Note that this will not indent the first line of each paragraph.

- To add the equivalent of a carriage return at the end of a line and no blank line afterward, use <BR>.

- Some people try to insert blank lines into their page by adding multiple paragraph tags to insert "empty" paragraphs. However, most browsers ignore the extra paragraph tags, so this doesn't create any extra blank lines. To insert extra blank lines in your text, use <BR> instead. Browsers don't ignore extra break tags.

- To position a paragraph so that it is left-justified (the default alignment), right-justified, or centered, use one of the following alignment attributes:

<P ALIGN=LEFT>	The default alignment for paragraphs
<P ALIGN=RIGHT>	The most commonly used alignment for a single short line, such as a date
<P ALIGN=CENTER>	Sometimes used to make a list of hyperlinks look nice

- To control the position of headings, use the alignment attribute with heading tags (the default alignment is ALIGN=LEFT):

  <H3 ALIGN=CENTER></H3>

- To control the positioning of text and graphics, you might want text to continue alongside a graphic or you might want to center a graphic with text above and below, but not alongside it (the alignment of text with graphics is discussed in Section 11.3).

Lists

There are three types of lists that you can use:

1. Unordered List (UL)
2. Ordered List (OL)
3. Definition List (DL)

We will describe each of these in detail and show examples.

Unordered Lists

An unordered list can include bullets (or not), and it can include a list header (or not). Use the unordered list tags `<UL></UL>` to mark the start and end of the list, and use the list item tag `<LI>` to mark the start of each list item. You can also include a list heading using the list header tags `<LH></LH>`. The heading will be aligned with the list items, so you will likely want to strengthen (emphasize) the heading to make sure it stands out, for example, by making it a certain level of heading, such as H2 or H3.

Figure 11.1 shows how Navigator renders the following unordered list with a heading and three list items:

```
<UL>
<LH> <H3> The Three C's of Web Page Construction </H3></LH>
<LI> Quality Content
<LI> Reader Convenience
<LI> Artistic Composition
</UL>
```

Unordered lists often appear without list headers when an author wants to draw attention to a collection of items. If you want to use a Netscape extension, you can change the type of bullet used in an unordered list by specifying a `TYPE=` attribute with either of the values square, disc, or circle:

`<UL TYPE=square>`   Netscape displays an open square.

`<UL TYPE=circle>`   Netscape displays an open circle.

`<UL TYPE=disc>`   Netscape displays a filled circle (the default bullet).

FIG. 11.1

An Unordered List

Note that bullet types are not supported by all browsers. Other browsers may default to a filled circle in all cases.

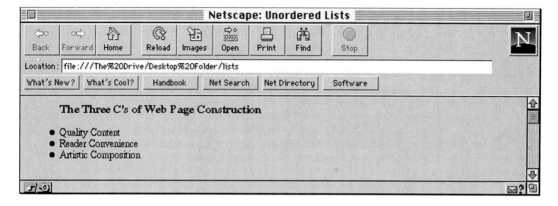

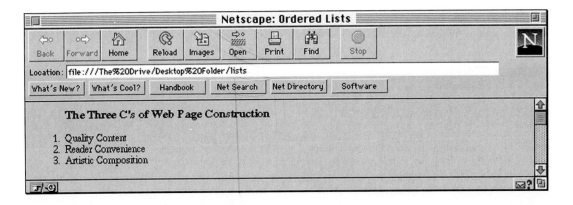

FIG. 11.2

Ordered Lists

An ordered list is like an unordered list, except that the bullets are replaced by numbers, as shown in Figure 11.2.

```
<OL>
<LH> <H3>The Three C's of Web Page Construction </H3></LH>
<LI> Quality Content
<LI> Reader Convenience
<LI> Artistic Composition
</OL>
```

If you want to continue a long list later on, and start the list from a number other than 1, you can specify a VALUE= attribute in the list item tag <LI>. In the following example, the list continues with the item numbered 4 (VALUE=4) (shown in bold):

```
<OL>
<LI VALUE=4> Operational Hyperlinks
<LI> Good Navigational Options
<LI> Descriptive Titles and Links
</OL>
```

Definition Lists

A definition list is useful for glossaries or any list of items that are paired with explanations, annotations, or additional information of any kind. The definition list tag <DL></DL> is used to mark the beginning and end of a definition list. The defining term tag <DT> and the defining definition tag <DD> are used to separate the term being defined from the definition of that term. Figure 11.3 shows the following example:

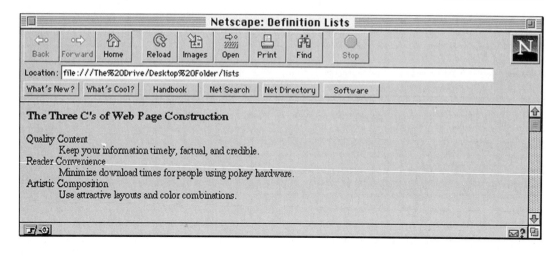

FIG. 11.3

A Definition List

```
<DL>
<LH><H3>The Three C's of Web Page Construction </H3></LH>
<DT> Quality Content <DD> Keep your information timely,
factual, and credible.
<DT> Reader Convenience <DD> Minimize download times for
people using pokey hardware.
<DT> Artistic Composition <DD> Use attractive layouts and
color combinations.
</DL>
```

You can use paragraph tags to add blank lines in between the definitions. Definition lists can be used in a variety of situations. For example, a definition list works very nicely if you want to format dialog from a play. Use <DT> for the names of the characters and <DD> for the actual dialog lines.

Document Visibility

If you care about creating a Web page that will be visible to Web search engines, learn as much as you can about the indexing and ranking strategies of different search engines. Web pages are indexed on the basis of their text, and there are things you can do to make your page highly visible with respect to particular keywords.

Each search engine has its own system for ranking documents; this is a very important component in the engine's interface that Web page authors should know about. Since each search engine may rank documents a little differently, it pays to study available documentation for each of the most popular search engines.

Here is what AltaVista says about its document rankings:

"A document has a higher score if the following hold:

- the query words or phrases are found in the first few words of the document (for example, in the title of a Web page or in the headers of Usenet news articles),

- the query words or phrases are found close to one another in the document,

- the document contains more than one instance of the query word or phrase."

Using this information, you can tune your Web pages so that they will be highly ranked in AltaVista's hit list.

Presentational and Informational Elements

The problem of controlling the final page display is evident even at the lowly level of character formatting. With Netscape, you can use the boldface tag `<B></B>` to create boldface text segments and end up with a document that looks fine under Netscape. Unfortunately, the same document may be very confusing to a lynx user. This is because lynx can't display color (the common way to display hyperlinks in a graphical browser), so it uses boldface to mark hyperlinks. As a result, excessive boldface text can frustrate lynx users who can no longer tell when a text fragment is bold because it is being emphasized, or bold because it indicates a hyperlink. The boldface tag is an example of a **presentational element,** or a **physical element**—a formatting element that is specific, absolute, and nonnegotiable.

In contrast, an **informational element** conveys the intent of the author in terms that are more abstract than specific. For example, you can use the strong tag `<STRONG></STRONG>` to convey your desire that a browser should emphasize a word or phrase in whatever manner the browser sees fit. Although most browsers will convert STRONG-tagged text into boldface, whether it does is up to the browser. For example, lynx ignores the strong tag because lynx is so limited with respect to character formatting. An audio browser designed for blind people might interpret the strong tag in terms of a rise in volume and intonation. No Web page author should have to anticipate the idiosyncrasies of all possible browsers that might display a Web page. By using informational elements instead of presentational elements, you can specify your intent and leave the details of a final presentation to the browser.

If you have been using presentational elements, try using informational elements instead. Here's a translation table that may help:

Informational Element	Approximate Presentational Element Equivalent
STRONG (stand out)	B (boldface)
EM (emphasize)	I (italics)
CODE (monospaced font)	TT (teletype font)
CITE (citation)	U (underline)

Sometimes informational elements are rendered in ways so that they are, to the user, indistinguishable from a presentational element. For example, the citation tag <CITE></CITE> and the definition tag <DFN></DFN> are both likely to produce underlined text. Still, there can be good reason to use two different tags, since other programs may someday scan your documents looking for citations or definitions. If your document is of interest to someone compiling an extensive bibliography, the citation tag will be very useful during an automated citation harvest. HTML 3.0 contains a number of informational elements that are potentially useful to computer programs that scan documents; these same elements are sometimes less useful to Web browsers (or at least today's Web browsers).

11.3 ▶ Working with Graphics

The Web is a compelling medium, in part, because of its graphics. Artwork, color, and photographs can be combined with text to create engaging Web sites. Adding graphical elements to a Web page requires an understanding of inline graphics and a working knowledge of text and image alignment. Traditional elements of graphic design apply to Web pages as well as printed matter, but we will restrict this discussion to the mechanics of graphic elements in HTML.

File Formats

Roughly 50 different file formats are used to store digital images. Luckily, most aren't used on the Web. Browsers are designed to recognize only a few graphical file formats, so those who want people to see their graphics must use the standard formats. Here are the two most commonly seen formats:

GIF - Graphics Interchange Format (.gif files)   for artwork

JPEG - Joint Photographic Experts Group (.jpg files)   for photographs

Some people would like to see GIF replaced by a newer, superior format called PNG (Portable Network Graphics). However, support for PNG is not yet widespread, so stick to GIF for now.

If you find a GIF file on the Web (e.g., in a collection of clip art for the Web), you can download that file by first opening it and then saving it to your local host (see Section 11.4 for more details about opening a graphics file on the Web). Since the file is already in the GIF format, you can use it as is without any further tinkering. But if you have a graphics file that was generated by some other application, you may be dealing with a different file format (e.g., PICT, EPS, or TIFF). In that case, you need to convert the file into the GIF, or JPEG, format before you can add it to your Web page. There are a number of file utilities that convert files from one graphics format to another. If you plan to work with a lot of graphics, you will need at least one file conversion utility (see Section 11.8, "A Webmaster's Toolbox").

To work with graphics, you need to learn about two things. First, you need to familiarize yourself with the HTML elements that handle graphics. Second, you need to know some practical guidelines for keeping your Web page reasonably speedy. A magnificent Web page that takes too long to download will discourage and annoy your users.

Basic Layout Tags and Attributes

The basic layout tags include the following:

- IMG
- BR
- CENTER

while the attributes include:

- ALIGN=
- CLEAR=
- WIDTH=
- HEIGHT=
- ALT=
- BGCOLOR=
- BACKGROUND=

These are discussed in the following subsections.

Embedding an Image

The easiest way to position an image on a Web page is to use the image tag <IMG>. This tag positions the graphic inside the document as if it were simply an oversized character in a text file. This is called an **inline graphic**. The graphic image occupies a rectangular region of indeterminate dimensions, and it is treated as a single text character. Since the image is taller than the characters that surround it, the browser increases the height of the text line to make enough room to display the full graphic. Here's an example (the image tag is in bold), which is illustrated in Figure 11.4:

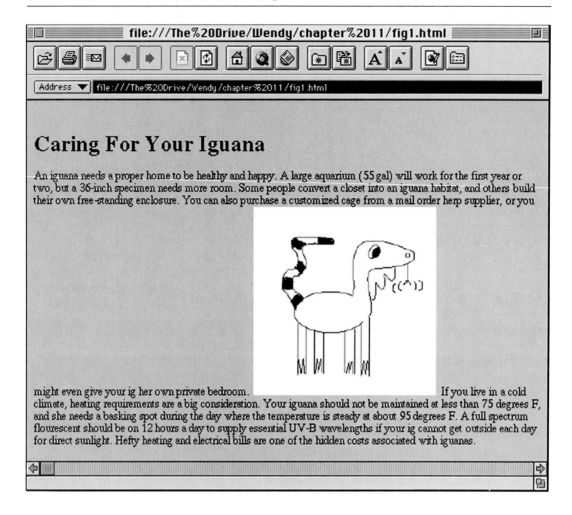

FIG. 11.4

An Inline Graphic

```
<HTML>
<HEAD>
<H1>Caring For Your Iguana</H1>
</HEAD>
<BODY>
<P>An iguana needs a proper home to be healthy and
happy. A large aquarium (55 gal) will work for the first
year or two, but a 36-inch specimen needs more room.
Some people convert a closet into an iguana habitat, and
others build their own free-standing enclosure. You can
also purchase a customized cage from a mail order herp
supplier, or you might even give your ig her own private
bedroom.
<IMG SRC="iggy.gif" WIDTH=200pt HEIGHT=200pt>
```

```
If you live in a cold climate, heating requirements
are a big consideration. Your iguana should not be
maintained at less than 75 degrees F, and she needs a
basking spot during the day where the temperature is
steady at about 95 degrees F. A full spectrum fluores-
cent should be on 12 hours a day to supply essential
UV-B wavelengths if your ig cannot get outside each
day for direct sunlight. Hefty heating and electrical
bills are one of the hidden costs associated with
iguanas.
</BODY>
</HTML>
```

The only required attribute of the image tag is the source file attribute `SRC=`, whose value specifies the graphic file to be inserted. The previous example uses a file named `iggy.gif`. The filename used with a `SRC=` attribute must be within double quotation marks with no spaces between the = and the file-name. Note that this particular image tag also includes `WIDTH=` and `HEIGHT=` attributes, which are used to control the size of the graphic. I talk about those attributes later in the chapter.

Positioning Text Horizontally

You can always insert an image tag inside any text line, but this will not pro-duce the best possible layout. An alternative is to isolate the graphic on its own line, as shown in Figure 11.5. This is easily accomplished with break tags (shown in bold) before and after the image tag:

```
cage from a mail order herp supplier, or you might even
give your ig her own private bedroom.
<BR>
<IMG SRC="iggy.gif" WIDTH=200pt HEIGHT=200pt>
<BR>
If you live in a cold climate, heating requirements
are a big consideration. Your iguana should not be
maintained at less than …
```

Note that the image in Figure 11.5 is left-justified, just as text is normally left-justified (remember that an inline graphic is treated as a text character). If you prefer to center the graphic on its own line as in Figure 11.6 (page 386), use the center tags `<CENTER></CENTER>` around the image tag instead of the break tags, as done here (the center tags are shown in bold):

```
cage from a mail order herp supplier, or you might even
give your ig her own private bedroom.
<CENTER>
```

```
<IMG SRC="iggy.gif" WIDTH=200pt HEIGHT=200pt>
</CENTER>
If you live in a cold climate, heating requirements
are a big consideration. Your iguana should not be
maintained at less than …
```

The center tag keeps the areas to the right and left of an image empty. If you want to run some text alongside the image, you can put an ALIGN= attribute inside the image tag. In the following example, ALIGN=LEFT (shown in bold) results in a left-aligned image with text flowing down along its right side (see Figure 11.7 on page 388):

FIG. 11.5

An Inline Graphic on Its Own Line

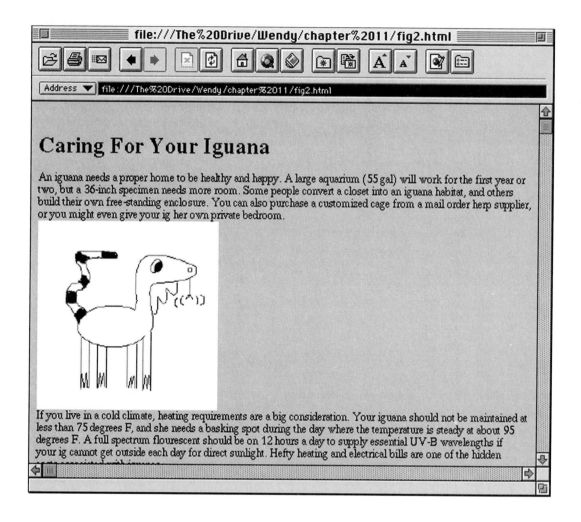

```
cage from a mail order herp supplier, or you might even
give your ig her own private bedroom.
<IMG SRC="iggy.gif" ALIGN=LEFT WIDTH=200pt HEIGHT=200pt>
If you live in a cold climate, heating requirements
are a big consideration. Your iguana should not be
maintained at less than …
```

`ALIGN=RIGHT` will position the graphic on the right side with text running down along its left side. Text flowing around an image creates a nice visual effect. You can alternate left- and right-aligned images on a single screen to break up a page without breaking the natural flow of text.

FIG. 11.6

A Centered Graphic on Its Own Line

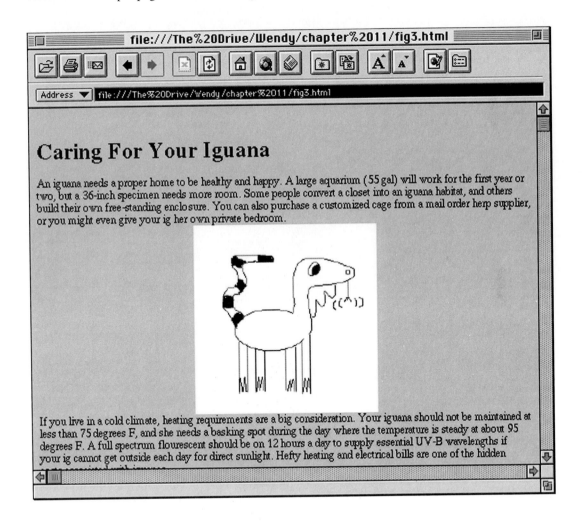

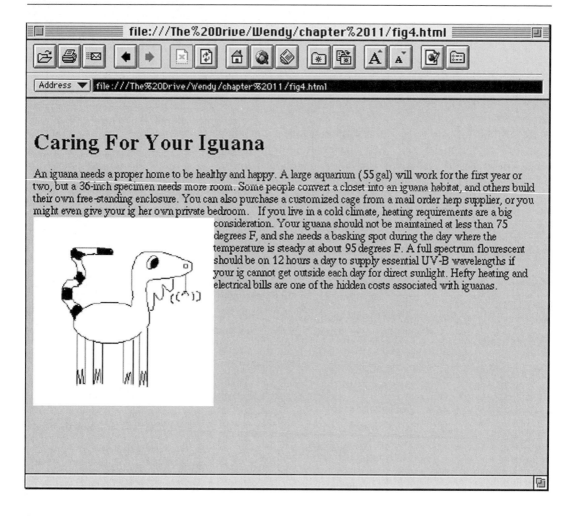

FIG. 11.7

A Left-Aligned Graphic
with Text Flowing
Along Its Right Side

Positioning Text Vertically

The vertical placement of text is controlled relative to text baselines. The **baseline** of a text line is the bottom of the line. All text rests on top of its baseline. As shown in Figure 11.4, the default alignment places the bottom of an inline graphic on the baseline of its text line (so the image sits on top of the baseline). This is equivalent to the ALIGN= attribute value BOTTOM. The attribute value TOP aligns the top of the graphic with the topmost region of its text line (so that the image hangs down from the current line). The MIDDLE value aligns the baseline of the text line with the middle of the image (so that the image is centered halfway up and halfway down from the current line). Here's a summary of these attribute values:

ALIGN=BOTTOM	The image sits on top of the baseline.
ALIGN=TOP	The image hangs down from the highest point in the current line.
ALIGN=MIDDLE	The image rests halfway above and halfway below the baseline.

Resuming Text after a Graphic

About the only thing we haven't done yet is right-justify a graphic *without* having text flow along its left side. This is often desirable when you have two graphics of the same size on the same line, one left-justified and one right-justified. Using ALIGN=LEFT and ALIGN=RIGHT causes text to flow *in between* the two images. To keep the center space blank, you need to use the CLEAR= attribute inside a break tag (see Figure 11.8). Text will flow alongside

FIG. 11.8

The CLEAR= Attribute Can Make a Figure Caption

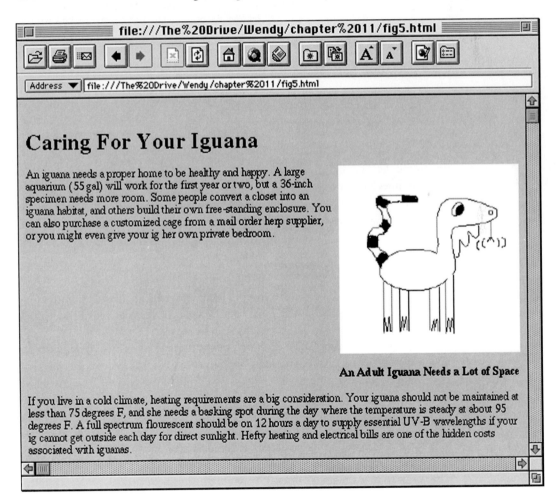

the image until the break tag is encountered. Then, since the CLEAR= attribute has the value RIGHT, the next bit of text will be positioned on the next line that has a clear *right*-hand margin (no elements at the end of the line). Since we have a right-aligned graphic, that means the next text will go beneath the graphic. If we right-justify the text, and format it as a header, we get a caption under the graphic.

```
<P>
<IMG SRC="iggy.gif" ALIGN=TOP ALIGN=RIGHT WIDTH=200pt
HEIGHT=200pt>
An iguana needs a proper home to be healthy and happy. A
large aquarium (55 gal) will work for the first year or
two, but a 36-inch specimen needs more room. Some people
convert a closet into an iguana habitat, and others
build their own free-standing enclosure. You can also
purchase a customized cage from a mail order herp sup-
plier, or you might even give your ig her own private
bedroom.
<BR CLEAR=RIGHT>
<H4 ALIGN=RIGHT> An Adult Iguana Needs a Lot of
Space</H4>
If you live in a cold climate, heating requirements
are a big consideration. Your iguana should not be
maintained at less than …
```

CLEAR=LEFT places the next printable element on the next line with a clear left margin (no elements at the start of the line). CLEAR=CENTER resumes print on the next line that is clear on both margins. Note that the values of the CLEAR= attribute have nothing to do with the alignment of the element about to be displayed. You need a separate ALIGN= attribute to control that.

Scaling Images

The WIDTH= and HEIGHT= attributes in an image tag are useful for both artistic composition and faster downloads. Smaller images download faster than larger ones, so use larger graphics sparingly.

A graphic image can be described by the number of **points** (approximately 72 points = 1 inch) it contains in its horizontal (width) and vertical (height) dimensions. It is important to know the original dimensions of a graphic if you want to scale it up or down. A badly scaled image will come out looking squashed (too short) or squished (to skinny). For example, the image file iggy.gif used in Figures 11.4–8 has the dimensions 247 × 247. For the examples in those figures it was scaled down to 200 × 200. Whenever you change the size of an image, be careful to preserve the original width:height ratio so that the image doesn't look squashed or squished.

```
                    Caring For Your Iguana

[INLINE] An iguana needs a proper home to be healthy and happy. A
large aquarium (55 gal) will work for the first year or two, but a
36-inch specimen needs more room. Some people convert a closet into an
iguana habitat, and others build their own free-standing enclosure.
You can also purchase a customized cage from a mail order herp
supplier, or you might even give your ig her own private bedroom.

                         An Adult Iguana Needs a Lot of Space

If you live in a cold climate, heating requirements are a big
consideration. Your iguana should not be maintained at less than 75
degree F, and she needs a basking spot during the day where the
temperature is steady at about 95 degrees F. A full spectrum
flourescent should be on 12 hours a day to supply essential UV-B
wavelengths if your ig cannot get outside each day for direct
sunlight. Hefty heating and electrical bills are one of the hidden
costs associated with iguanas.
```

FIG. 11.9

Text-Based Browsers
Don't Display Graphics

Image Alternatives for Text-Based Browsers

Now is a good time to remind you that some people view the Web through text-based Web browsers. Web page displays for these browsers never show any graphics. Figure 11.9 shows what the Web page in Figure 11.8 would look like to a lynx user.

If the graphic conveys essential content, this can be a real problem. But if the graphic is purely cosmetic, then a text-based reader isn't missing that much. In either case, it is courteous to say something about what the reader can't see. The ALT= attribute inside an image tag is used for just this purpose. ALT= takes a quoted text string as its value. A text-based browser displays that string in lieu of the graphic image.

Lynx users will see the insert "[INLINE]" whenever an image doesn't include an ALT= attribute. But it is much nicer to have some idea what a missing image depicts. When you add an ALT= attribute, remember to always include square brackets so that the missing image will be readily identifiable as such to all lynx users. Without brackets, an ALT= string looks just like a short text segment. In fact, the best way to make an ALT= string stand out is to use square brackets, start your string with an INLINE: prefix, and use uppercase letters throughout (see Figure 11.10).

```
<IMG SRC="iggy.gif" ALIGN=TOP ALIGN=RIGHT WIDTH=200pt
HEIGHT=200pt
        ALT="[INLINE: A CARTOON IG]">
```

ALT= attributes are not an adequate solution when a Web page is heavily dependent on graphics. Some professionally designed sites deal with this

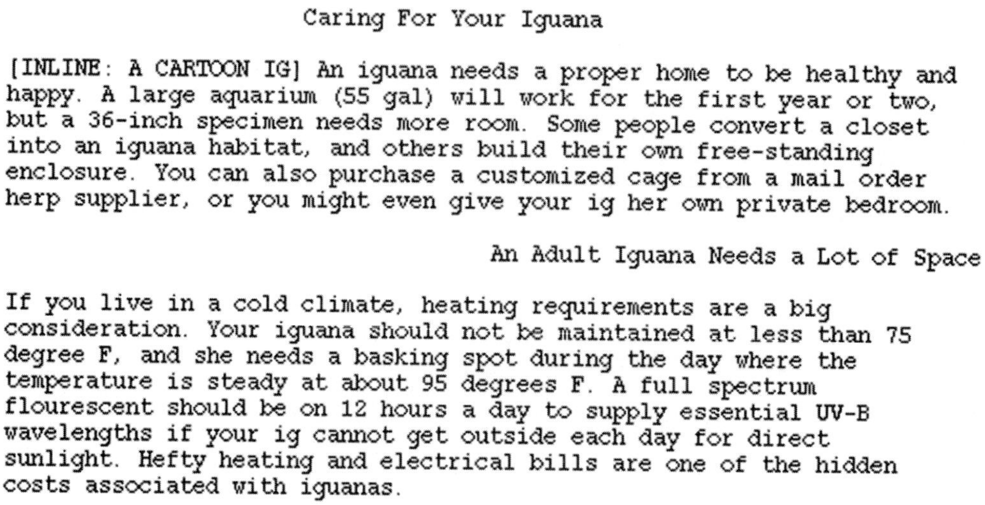

Caring For Your Iguana

[INLINE: A CARTOON IG] An iguana needs a proper home to be healthy and happy. A large aquarium (55 gal) will work for the first year or two, but a 36-inch specimen needs more room. Some people convert a closet into an iguana habitat, and others build their own free-standing enclosure. You can also purchase a customized cage from a mail order herp supplier, or you might even give your ig her own private bedroom.

An Adult Iguana Needs a Lot of Space

If you live in a cold climate, heating requirements are a big consideration. Your iguana should not be maintained at less than 75 degree F, and she needs a basking spot during the day where the temperature is steady at about 95 degrees F. A full spectrum flourescent should be on 12 hours a day to supply essential UV-B wavelengths if your ig cannot get outside each day for direct sunlight. Hefty heating and electrical bills are one of the hidden costs associated with iguanas.

FIG. 11.10

The ALT= Attribute Helps People with Text-Based Browsers

problem by maintaining two separate sets of Web pages: one for graphical browsers and one for text-based browsers. Sometimes you'll see a link at the head of a home page that directs text-based readers to the pages designed just for them.

Creating Transparent GIFs

The GIF file format supports a special property called **transparency** that can be very useful on Web pages. When a file is transparent, its own background blends in with the background of the document in which it is embedded. As a result, the graphic image appears to be drawn directly on the background of the page rather than sitting on top of it. Line drawings and figures with clean foreground/background distinctions are good candidates for transparency. Many GIF file utilities can take a nontransparent GIF and convert it into a transparent GIF. The `iggy.gif` file can be converted into a transparent GIF to make the drawing look like it was drawn right on the page (see Figure 11.11).

Setting Background Colors

The simplest background for a Web page is a plain solid color. Background colors are set with the `BGCOLOR=` attribute inside the body tag; for example:

```
<BODY BGCOLOR="#F8F8FF">
```

The `BGCOLOR=` attribute value is a number written in hexadecimal notation for a specific color. A **hexadecimal number** is an integer represented in base

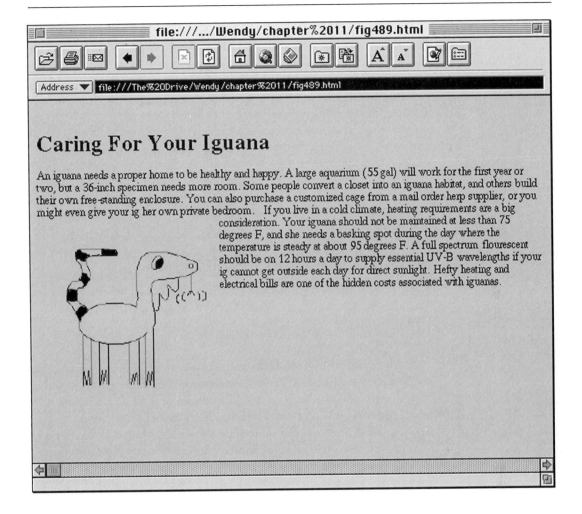

Address ▼ file:///The%20Drive/Wendy/chapter%2011/fig489.html

Caring For Your Iguana

An iguana needs a proper home to be healthy and happy. A large aquarium (55 gal) will work for the first year or two, but a 36-inch specimen needs more room. Some people convert a closet into an iguana habitat, and others build their own free-standing enclosure. You can also purchase a customized cage from a mail order herp supplier, or you might even give your ig her own private bedroom. If you live in a cold climate, heating requirements are a big consideration. Your iguana should not be maintained at less than 75 degrees F, and she needs a basking spot during the day where the temperature is steady at about 95 degrees F. A full spectrum flourescent should be on 12 hours a day to supply essential UV-B wavelengths if your ig cannot get outside each day for direct sunlight. Hefty heating and electrical bills are one of the hidden costs associated with iguanas.

---

16. This means it is written with numerical characters and the letters A–F. The "#" in front of the number indicates a hexadecimal number. In this case, F8F8FF represents GhostWhite, a very light gray. To set a background color, you have to know its hexadecimal representation.

Some graphics applications let you create your own colors on a color wheel. They then show you a code for each color in terms of its RGB (Red-Green-Blue) values; for example, GhostWhite has the RGB value of 248 248 255. Once you have the RGB value for a color, you can translate that value into its hexadecimal representation in order to use that color in a BGCOLOR= attribute. See the Internet 101 Web pages for a URL that will lead you to a list of background colors and their hexadecimal representations.

FIG. 11.11

A Transparent GIF Appears to Have a Transparent Background

Whenever you see a page on the Web with a background color that you like, look at the source file for a BODY tag and see what value is used for BGCOLOR. Note the color code so that you can use that color on your own Web page.

Background colors can serve a useful purpose in your Web pages. For example, a large Web site may color-code its pages in order to help orient readers. Pages containing introductory background materials would be all one color, while pages containing timely updates would be a different color. Technical explanations or examples might be segregated with their own color. If you are building a large site, think about categories for your pages and consider using a color-coding scheme to convey those categories. Web page color coding is a subtle and natural way to reinforce useful information.

Setting Background Patterns

Background patterns are also specified by the BODY tag, but this time with the `BACKGROUND=` attribute, which takes the name of a GIF or JPEG file:

```
<BODY BACKGROUND="wrinkles.gif">
```

Many suitable background files are available on the Internet or you can make your own with a scanner or an artwork application. Some very effective backgrounds are made with three similar shades of a solid color showing a simple pattern in a 3-D base relief. However, it's easy to get carried away with flashy colorful backgrounds; don't pick a background that distracts from what goes on top of the background. A complicated background is appropriate only for an opening title page that doesn't contain much information. Even then, it might not be your best choice. Exercise restraint when you pick background patterns.

11.4 Tips for Faster Downloads

Following are some tips that will help readers download your pages faster.

Place Larger Graphics at the Bottom of the Page

As rule, try to keep all inline graphics no larger than 40K. This will keep your page displays reasonably speedy for most users. If you have a larger graphic, position it further down on the page so that it doesn't need to come up in the very first screen display. In that way, a reader can see the top of your page quickly and spend some time taking it in while the browser is busy downloading graphics for the rest of the page display. Readers don't mind longer downloads when they are occupied with something to read.

Always Use Size Attributes

Always use `WIDTH=` and `HEIGHT=` size attributes even if you are keeping the original dimensions of an image. This is a good idea because Web browsers display pages faster if all inline graphics have explicit size attributes. When a browser sees these settings inside an image tag, it can set aside the necessary space needed for the graphic and continue on with the page layout. When a browser can anticipate the size of all inline graphics, the text appears on a page before the images are added. If the size attributes are left out, then the browser has to download the graphics file to find out how big it is before it can continue with the rest of the page display. This slows down the page display and may leave a reader with nothing to look at while a large image is downloading.

When you want the dimensions of a graphic element to scale up and down as the window is resized, you can specify `WIDTH=` and `HEIGHT=` attributes as a percentage of the full screen. However, be careful to include the percent sign (e.g. `WIDTH=30%`) when you want a percentage. If you do not specify a unit, the browser will default to a unit that does not scale during resizing.

Use Small Files for Backgrounds

A file that is used for a background is automatically repeated in a tiled pattern to fill up the available space. A smaller file results in smaller tiles and a larger file in larger tiles. The number of tiles in your background isn't important, but the time it takes to download the tile graphic is. Smaller files generally download faster than larger ones, although a larger file that compresses nicely can be just as fast as a small file. When in doubt, err on the side of speed.

Use Interlaced GIF Images
for Large GIF Files

One way to make slow downloads less annoying is to use **interlaced** GIF files. When a GIF file is interlaced, the browser displays the file incrementally. The first pass produces a very fuzzy version of the image. The next pass looks a bit better, and eventually the complete file is displayed in full detail. The effect is typically achieved by first displaying every tenth line of pixels. On the second pass, every fifth line is shown. On the third pass, every other line is filled in, and on the fourth pass, the complete image is displayed.

Incremental graphic displays can be interesting to watch and will pacify all but the most harried Web users.

Any GIF file can be converted into an interlaced GIF file as long as the original is consistent with the GIF89 formating standard. Many file utilities and GIF converters support an interlaced GIF option.

INTERLACING AND TRANSPARENCY

If you use one file utility to interlace a GIF file and another to make the GIF a transparent GIF, be careful to interlace the image first and then make it transparent. Otherwise, your image may show some gray ghosts on your Web page.

Use the `<HR>` Tag to Create Horizontal Rules

If you want to insert horizontal dividers to visually separate text or text and graphics, it is more efficient to use the horizontal rule tag `<HR>` than a graphical image. Different browsers render horizontal rule tags differently, but the norm is a shaded and sculptured 3D line. A horizontal rule runs the full width of the page by default, but you can control its width (as a percentage of the window's width), alignment (left, right, center), and thickness (using the `SIZE=` attribute with a positive integer value). See Figure 11.12 for displays of the following horizontal rules:

```
<HR SIZE=6 WIDTH=75% ALIGN=CENTER>
<HR SIZE=5 WIDTH=75% ALIGN=CENTER>
<HR SIZE=4 WIDTH=75% ALIGN=CENTER>
<HR SIZE=3 WIDTH=75% ALIGN=CENTER>
<HR SIZE=2 WIDTH=75% ALIGN=CENTER>
<HR SIZE=1 WIDTH=75% ALIGN=CENTER>
```

You can have some fun with your horizontal rules by filling them with a GIF or JPEG pattern. Just add the `SRC=` attribute to your horizontal rule tag, as in `SRC="wrinkles.gif"`. This is an easy way to add a little extra color to your page.

Use Thumbnail Previews and Other Clickable Graphics

When you have a large graphic image and you don't want to burden your readers with long download times, let your readers decide if the wait is worth

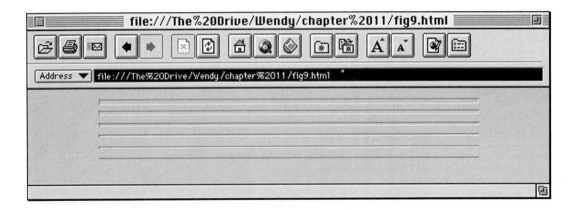

it. The standard way to give your readers a choice is to provide thumbnail previews. A thumbnail preview is a smaller version of a graphic that is placed on the page; the larger version is available only on request. Readers request the larger version by clicking the preview. Including some helpful instructions that explain this convention is always a good idea, since some people are in the habit of clicking everything in sight just to see what happens. If you make the thumbnail graphics very small, experienced Web users will probably understand what's going on, but it never hurts to explain. See Figure 11.13 for the HTML construction of a thumbnail preview.

A thumbnail preview is just a special case of a clickable image, or a hyperlink. Any image can be turned into a hyperlink in much the same way that text segments are designated as hyperlinks. All anchor tags contain an HREF= attribute and a label for the link. Labels can be either text segments or inline images.

FIG. 11.12

Samples of Horizontal Rules

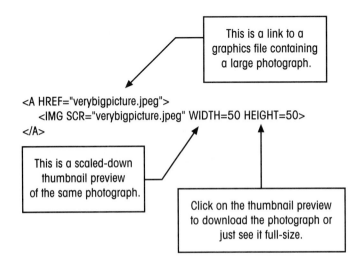

FIG. 11.13

Example Thumbnail Preview

A clickable graphic can point to anything you like. Instead of being a thumbnail preview, you could use it as an entry point to another Web page document. Or, it can point to a completely different graphic, if you want to set up a chain of linked images (e.g., to construct a virtual treasure hunt).

You also don't have to use thumbnail previews to give readers control over large downloads. Any text link can be used to point to a large graphic image. The important point is to set the large graphics aside and isolate them from your main Web pages.

Some Web page authors encourage readers to copy their graphics files by linking all inline graphics to the original graphics files themselves. The reader just points to the inline graphic, clicks to see the original graphic file, and saves it to a local file by issuing a Save As command. The reader can then return to the previous Web page and continue from there. Copying a graphics file can't get much easier than Point, Click, Save As, and Back.

11.5 URLs and Pathnames

When you get involved with Web sites, you have to know something about directory pathnames. There's no way around it. You need to understand pathnames when you set up hyperlinks in your HTML files, when you want to download inline graphics from the Web, and when you move Web pages from one computer to another. I'll begin by reviewing the notion of a hierarchical directory structure.

All computer files are stored in file directories, and all file directories are situated in a hierarchical structure of file directories. When you have a personal account on a large time-sharing computer, your files are stored in a directory that has been assigned to you for your personal use. Suppose your username is `psmith`. Then your directory might be located in a hierarchy like the one depicted in Figure 11.14.

On a Web server, you will probably store all of your Web pages in a directory called `public_html`, which sits directly under your own home directory. Most Web servers store pages in a subdirectory called `public_html` with a home page named `index.html`. In the directory structure shown in Figure 11.14, the full directory pathname to psmith's home page would be

```
/courses/cs100/cs191a/psmith/public_html/index.html
```

The URL for psmith's home page needs a directory path plus the name of the Web server. We will use the host address in Figure 11.14 for our Web server. Happily, URLs do not require a full directory pathname. Web pages

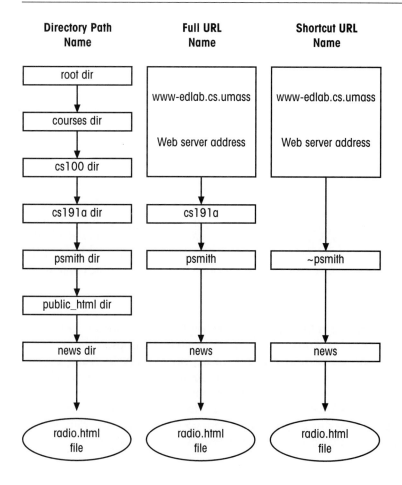

Directory Path Name
/courses/cs100/cs191a/psmith/public_html/news/radio.html

Full URL Name
http://www-edlab.cs.umass/cs191a/psmith/news/radio.html

Shortcut URL Name
http://www-edlab.cs.umass/~psmith/news/radio.html

are typically stored in just one branch of the full directory tree, so the server only needs pathnames within that branch. If `cs100` is the root for all the Web pages, then we can start the URL with the name of the directory immediately beneath `cs100`. At the other end of the pathname, we can assume that any URL which doesn't end in a file name should default to a file named `index.html`. Plus, any URL containing a user's home directory is actually

FIG. 11.14

Directory Paths and Pathnames

referring to that user's `public_html` subdirectory. So all the server really needs to see is

`http://www-edlab.cs.umass/cs191a/psmith/`

In addition, most servers can handle shortcuts to home directories. For example, you will often see URLs such as

`http://www-edlab.cs.umass/~psmith/`

Here the tilde (~) before `psmith` says to search the directory tree for psmith's home directory. The tilde saves you from having to include any of the directories in the path going down to a home directory. This is a shorthand notation used by UNIX. And, finally, there may be a shorter alias for the Web server's host address. Ask tech support if there is a short alias for your particular Web server. It is always good to shorten your URLs as much as possible.

PLATFORM- SPECIFIC ANNOYANCES 	If you are doing your Web page development on a PC and your Web server is a UNIX host, remember that the slashes in a UNIX pathname are *forward* slashes (/), while the slashes in a DOS (or Windows) pathname are *backward* slashes (\). To have your pathnames recognized on the Web server, you must change all of your slashes from the DOS slashes to the UNIX slashes. If you are doing your Web page development on a Mac, you must remove any blank spaces from your filenames and directory names before you move your files to a UNIX Web server.

A URL that contains the name of a Web server and the complete directory pathname to a Web page is called an **absolute link**. You use an absolute link when you create a link to an external Web page (not one of your own). Absolute links tend to be long and hard to type, so for Web pages on your own Web site, you can (and should) avoid absolute links.

The alternative to an absolute link is a **relative link**. Relative links are interpreted in the context of a current directory. When you are viewing a Web page, your **current directory** is the directory that houses the Web page. For example, the current directory for the `radio.html` file in Figure 11.14 is called `news`. When you want to link one Web page to a second Web page in the same directory, you can use a relative link that specifies only the name of the file (see Figure 11.15). When a Web browser needs to locate that file, it will look in the current directory for it. If your Web site has only a few pages in it, keep them all inside the same directory. Then you can always use simple relative links for your own pages.

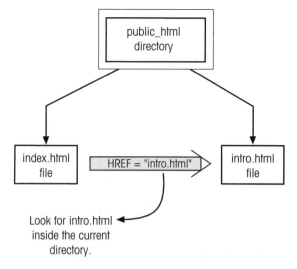

FIG. 11.15

A Relative Link for a
File in the Current
Directory

More complicated Web sites require additional subdirectories in order to keep things nicely organized. When you create a subdirectory for some of your Web pages, relative links to that subdirectory must specify the directory name as well as the filename. But you are still using a relative link because you can locate the new directory as it resides in the local directory hierarchy, in its position relative to the current directory.

Let's look at an example. Suppose you create a subdirectory named `photos` for Web pages containing photographic images and you put this directory directly under your `public_html` directory. If you want a file in `public_html` to link to a file in the photos subdirectory, your relative link has to explain where to look (see Figure 11.16).

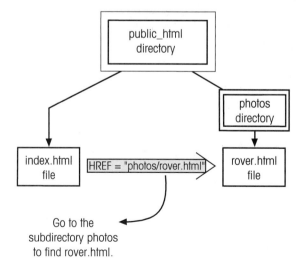

FIG. 11.16

A Relative Link for a
File Beneath the
Current Directory

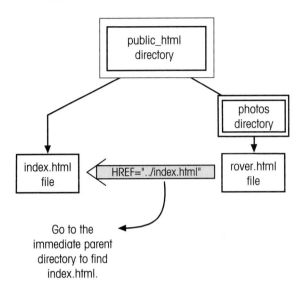

FIG. 11.17

A Relative Link for a
File above the Current
Directory

You can create relative URLs that drop down any number of levels as long
as you specify each subdirectory along the path. So no matter how complicated your directory structure becomes, you can always point to a file's location in terms that are relative to the current file.

Let's see how to make a relative link when you pop back up to a directory
that's higher in the hierarchy than the current directory. Suppose you want to
create a pointer from `rover.html` back to `index.html`. This relative link
only has to say how many levels you want to pop up (see Figure 11.17).

The file `rover.html` is located in the directory `photos`, so any links on
the page `rover.html` will use `photos` as the current directory. If you want
to link to a file in the `public_html` directory, you need to pop up one level
from the current directory. The two periods "`..`" are used in relative pathnames to specify the directory right above the current directory. So
`../index.html` means "pop up to the directory right above the current
directory and then look for a file named `index.html`." You don't have to
explicitly name the directory right above `photos`, because every subdirectory
can have only one parent directory (the directory right above it). It's enough
to reference the parent directory relative to the current directory.

If you need to pop up two levels, just show two parent directories (e.g.,
`../../index.html`). You can move up however many levels you need to go
in this way. Just include a pair of periods followed by a slash for each level.

Now let's look at a tricky path. This example creates a relative path that
goes both up and down in the directory hierarchy (see Figure 11.18). In this
case, there are two subdirectories under `public_html`: `photos` and `refs`.
To link from `rover.html` to the file `books.html` inside `refs`, you first go
up to the `public_html` directory and then down to the `refs` directory. Just

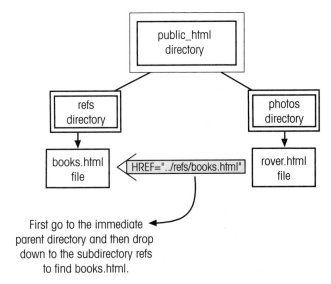

First go to the immediate
parent directory and then drop
down to the subdirectory refs
to find books.html.

FIG. 11.18

A Relative Link for a
File on the Same Level
as the Current
Directory

follow a path from one file to the other through the directory hierarchy. The relative pathname then describes the path. That is, "go up one level `../`, then down to the subdirectory named refs — `../refs` — and finally look for the file named `books.html` — `../refs/books.html`."

When creating complicated relative paths, you may find it helpful to draw a picture of your directory hierarchy and trace a physical path along the picture to help you keep the path name straight.

Once you've created a large Web site with lots of Web pages containing lots of relative links, the worst thing you can do is rearrange all of your files in a new directory hierarchy. As soon as you rename a directory or move a file from one directory to another, you run the risk of creating who knows how many obsolete hyperlinks within your own Web pages (not to mention other links that might be pointing to your pages from the outside). Try to avoid this at all costs. Think hard about your directory structure right from the start so that you won't have to redesign it. If you do find yourself in need of a directory overhaul, look for a utility that will help you locate obsolete links in all of your Web pages.

**DESIGN YOUR
DIRECTORY
STRUCTURE
CAREFULLY**

At this point you might be saying, "Oh well, I think I'll just keep all my Web pages in one directory. Then I won't need to worry about any complicated relative links." As luck would have it, relative paths come in handy for other things in addition to Web page construction. For example, suppose you want to download a graphic image that you find on the Web. You have the

URL for a Web page that contains the graphic you want, but it's an inline graphic using a relative link. To save the graphic to a file on your host, you need to open the graphic's file (not just a page containing the graphic). A Go To command from your browser will take you to the file and open it for you, but only if you can give it an absolute URL. You need to look at the URL for your current page, look at the relative link in the source file for the current page, and figure out an absolute link for the file.

This really isn't so very terrible once you get the hang of it. But it does explain why considerate Web page designers go out of their way to make it easy for users to download their graphics.

WEB PAGE FILE PROTECTION ON UNIX-BASED WEB SERVERS

If you are moving your Web pages to a UNIX server where you have to create new directories for your html files, make sure your new directories and files are visible to the world. UNIX supports a variety of file security attributes that determine who can view a file and who can alter a file. If your new Web pages cannot be viewed on a UNIX server due to a file protection error (the error message may say something about not being privileged for file access), then you need to set your file protection attributes for public access. You can do this with two UNIX commands for each new subdirectory that you have created.

First, go to the *parent* directory of the new subdirectory (suppose the new subdirectory is called newsdir). Next, issue the UNIX command:

```
chmod 711 newsdir
```

Then go into the newsdir subdirectory:

```
cd newsdir
```

And issue another UNIX command:

```
chmod 644 *.*
```

That will make all of your new Web pages visible to the general public.

11.6 ▶ Using Tables and Frames

When most people think of tables, they think of numeric data arranged in a big grid. But tables in HTML are much more general than that. They can be useful for displaying text as well as numeric data. There are times when you want to display columns or blocks of text that can be positioned on your Web page as a unit. Most Web browsers render tables in a shaded base relief that draws attention to the table's contents. Figure 11.19 shows a page of text that has been formatted using tables.

The Web page in the figure was created with five separate tables. The first four appear in base relief, and the last one appears as flat text displayed directly on the background of the page. Tables can contain large bodies of formatted text and hyperlinks, as well as graphical images, so it is possible to format textual Web pages using tables without sacrificing any HTML layout features. In fact, tables also can be used purely for their visual effect. When an image is inserted into a simple table, it appears in a shadowed frame, just like a painting on a wall. Tables can give a professional, polished look to your Web pages.

If you try to master all of the features associated with tables, you may feel overwhelmed. Happily, you can get a lot of mileage out of a few basic features. The more advanced table features will save you time if you create a lot of tables and you want to work more efficiently. But anyone creating only a few Web pages can afford to sacrifice optimal efficiency for the sake of getting something up quickly and easily.

Basic Table Elements

All tables are described in terms of **rows** (which run across the page) and **columns** (which run up and down the page). A data element inside a table occupies a location, or **cell**, that is uniquely determined by its row number and its column number. All of the cells in a given column are the same width and all of the cells in a given row are the same height. Width and height are determined by the largest data element in each column and each row.

Rows and Columns

If you have trouble remembering which are the rows and which are the columns, try a little mnemonic trick. Think of the Parthenon when you think of columns. The Greek columns go up and down, just like the columns in an HTML table. Then think of rows of seats in a theatre and remember that rows run from side to side. If you can remember a movie theatre with many rows of seats and a facade of Greek columns at the entrance, that will help you keep your rows and columns straight.

HINT

The simplest possible table is one that contains one row and one column. This type of table contains only one cell and therefore has room for only one piece of data. However, it is often used to put a frame around a picture or a

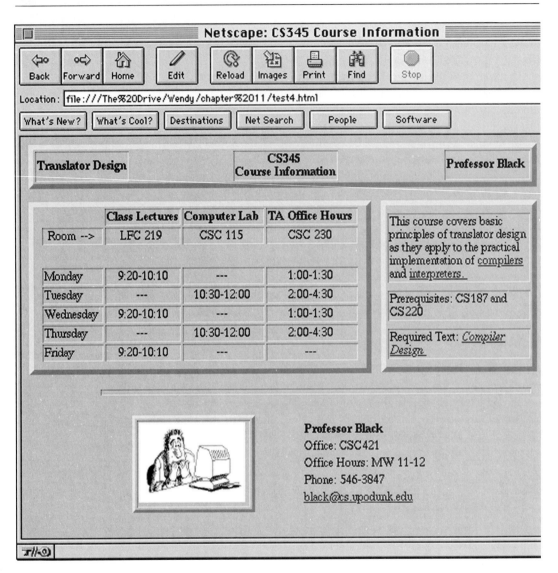

FIG. 11.19

A Web Page Layout
Containing Five Tables

body of text. One of these is in Figure 11.19. The terrified student is a GIF image inside a one-celled table. The HTML for this table looks like this:

```
<TABLE BORDER=3 ALIGN=LEFT>
<TR><TD><IMG SRC="computer.gif" HEIGHT=80pt WIDTH=110pt>
</TABLE>
```

All tables are defined with a table tag <TABLE></TABLE>. The BORDER= attribute is used to specify the thickness of the frame that surrounds the table. The thinnest border has a value of 1, and thicker borders use larger integers.

The ALIGN= attribute is used to position the table on a Web page, just as with IMG tags. In this case, an ALIGN=left has been included so that another table can flow alongside it on the right. If you left out the ALIGN= attribute, your last table would be bumped down to the next baseline.

Inside the table tag are some number of table row tags <TR>. Each <TR> signifies the beginning of a new row in the table (much like <BR> breaks lines of text). The table row tag says to insert a new table row. Each cell entry within a table row must be preceded by a table data tag <TD>. In the case of the previous framed graphic, the row contains only one column, so it is preceded by the image tag with <TR><TD>. After inserting the image into the cell, you close off the table with </TABLE> and you're done. Note that you can control the size of this table by controlling the size of the graphic with HEIGHT= and WIDTH= attributes inside the image tag. These attributes do not describe the size of the table per se. They merely indicate how big the data element inside the table must be. The table then creates a border large enough to accommodate the data. Tables always size themselves to accommodate their data.

You can use any HTML tags inside a <TD> entry. If you want to make the data element a clickable graphic, use the image as a label for an anchor tag. Tables do not place any restrictions on their data elements.

Horizontal Alignment within a Cell

The next simplest table in Figure 11.19 contains the small body of text in the lower right-hand corner. This table contains five textual data elements arranged in a single column. The table contains one column and five rows:

```
<TABLE BORDER=0>
<TR><TD ALIGN=left> <B> Professor Black </B>
<TR><TD ALIGN=left> Office: CSC421
<TR><TD ALIGN=left> Office Hours: MW 11-12
<TR><TD ALIGN=left> Phone: 546-3847
<TR><TD ALIGN=left> <A HREF="mailto:
    black@cs.upodunk.edu"> black@cs.upodunk.edu</A>
</TABLE>
```

This table has no frame around it because the BORDER= attribute is set to 0. In this case, the table's elements look as if they are written directly onto the page's background.

It helps to place each <TR> tag at the beginning of a new text line to help keep the table layout as clear as possible in the HTML source file. Remember that a <TD> tag must preface each new data element inside each table row; for five entries in a table, there will be five <TD> tags inside the table tags. Notice that each table data tag contains an ALIGN= attribute for left alignment. Although you can't see the data cells when the BORDER= is 0, each of these text elements sits inside a rectangular cell and can be aligned to the left, right, or center within that box. In this table, the text elements are all left-justified for a neat alignment of each row on a common left margin. If you don't include an `ALIGN=` attribute, each cell defaults to a left alignment.

BROWSER DEFAULTS

Default values cause many Web page headaches because a default for one browser is not necessarily the default for another. If a certain value is important for the outcome of your layout, explicitly specify the value in your HTML tags and attributes rather than assume the default. Don't rely on a Web browser to give you the one you want.

Controlling Table Sizes

A browser will always try to lay out your tables with cells sized as needed to display all of the data elements. For example, the width of a column is normally determined by the longest data element. This can be a problem if you want to have a large cell of text inside a table. The browser will make that cell as wide as possible (without running outside the display window), which is probably not what you want. You can either control the flow of text inside the cell with break tags, or you can fix a constant width for the entire table using the `WIDTH=` attribute and thereby force the browser to create a display using that assigned width.

The following HTML produces the table in Figure 11.20:

```
<TABLE BORDER=5 WIDTH=160pt>
<TR><TD>
<TR><TD>This course covers basic principles of
translator design as they apply to the practical
implementation of <A HREF="comp.html">compilers</A>
and <A HREF="int.html">interpreters. </A>
<TR><TD>
<TR><TD> Prerequisites: CS187 and CS220
<TR><TD>
<TR><TD> Required Text: <A
HREF="details.html"><I>Compiler Design </I> </A>
<TR><TD>
</TABLE>
```

When the `WIDTH=` attribute is set, the browser will allocate more vertical space in order to fit in all of the data elements. This is a good way to manage large text displays that are subject to change. It's tedious to have to reset line breaks for all of your text every time you make some small change to that text. Setting the table width is much easier and achieves a better result.

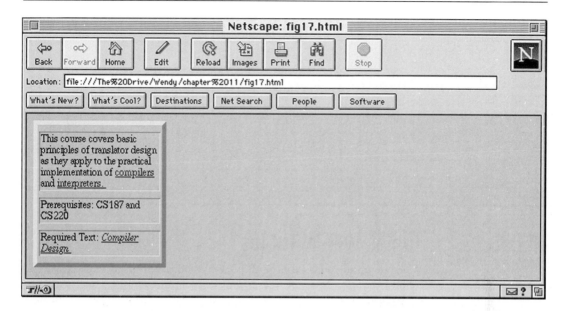

FIG. 11.20

A Fixed-Width Table
with Flowing Text

Note that you can also set the `HEIGHT=` attribute for a table; however, that dimension does not expand to accommodate text unless the width is fixed. Notice how extra space was placed in between the rows of this table by inserting blank rows (rows with empty cells). You can also "pad" a table to add more height to it by making the `HEIGHT=` attribute larger than needed.

Controlling Cell Sizes

The first table in Figure 11.19 acts as a heading for the Web page. To make it fill the top of the page, insert some blank horizontal space to separate the three text elements at the top of the page (see Figure 11.21):

```
<TABLE BORDER=5>
<TR><TD><B>Translator Design</B>
    <TD WIDTH=103pt>
    <TD ALIGN=CENTER><B>CS345 <BR> Course
Information</B>
    <TD WIDTH=103pt>
    <TD><B>Professor Black</B>
</TABLE>
```

Here is a single row (one `<TR>` tag) with five data elements (five `<TD>` tags) inside that row. Three of the data elements contain text, and two are empty. To control the width of the empty cells, use the `WIDTH=` attribute inside the `<TD>` tag with appropriate values (found by experimenting with the page).

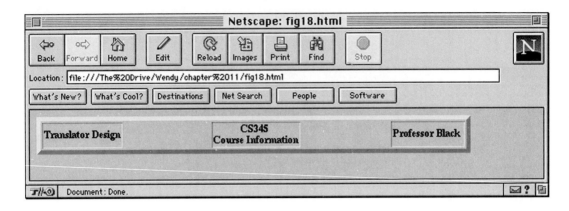

FIG. 11.21

Using Empty Cells to
Control Spacing

Tables within Tables

When designing a layout of multiple tables on a Web page, you can control
the spacing of your tables by putting them inside another table. In Figure
11.19, the last two tables on the page are centered at the bottom of the page
with a little space separating them. This was done by embedding them inside
a simple table with one row and four columns:

```
<TABLE BORDER=0>
<TR> <TD WIDTH=100pt>                          <!- (column 1) ->
     <TD>                                      <!- (column 2) ->
         <TABLE BORDER=3>
         <TR><TD><IMG SRC="computer.gif"
                 HEIGHT=80pt WIDTH=110pt>
         </TABLE>
     <TD WIDTH=40pt>                           <!- (column 3) ->
     <TD>                                      <!- (column 4) ->
         <TABLE BORDER=0>
         <TR><TD ALIGN=left> <B> Professor Black </B>
         <TR><TD ALIGN=left>Office: CSC421
         <TR><TD ALIGN=left>Office Hours: MW 11-12
         <TR><TD ALIGN=left>Phone: 546-3847
         <TR><TD ALIGN=left> <A HREF="black.html">
                             black@cs.upodunk.edu</A>
         </TABLE>
</TABLE>
```

The first cell is empty, but it has a fixed width of 100 points to create an
indentation on the left. The second cell contains the simple table with the
single GIF image. The third cell is another empty cell that is of a fixed width
to give some space between the two table elements. The fourth cell is the text
table with no border. Since the top-level table has no border, everything
about it is invisible except for the two nonempty data cells.

If you ever need to partition your Web page into separate elements, consider using a table to achieve the overall layout. Tables are very good for large layouts because they automatically size their cells to accommodate all data elements. To minimize confusion, first create and review each element to be displayed separately. When you are satisfied with each element, then insert all into a table for the final layout.

Table Captions

Another useful table element is the table caption. Caption tags `<CAPTION></CAPTION>` should be inserted into your table after the `<TABLE>` tag and before the first row of the table. A caption can be situated either above or below a table by specifying an `ALIGN=` attribute with the value `TOP` or `BOTTOM`. The following code aligns the caption (shown in bold) at the top of a table (see Figure 11.22):

```
<TABLE BORDER=1 >
<CAPTION ALIGN=TOP><H4>Leather Dog Collars</H4></CAPTION>
<TR><TD>Item No.<TD>Size<TD>Single<TD>3 or more
<TR><TD>973175<TD>16"<TD ALIGN=RIGHT>$8.29<TD
ALIGN=RIGHT>ea$7.46
<TR><TD>973209<TD>18"<TD ALIGN=RIGHT>$9.29<TD
ALIGN=RIGHT>ea$8.36
<TR><TD>973078<TD>20"<TD ALIGN=RIGHT>$8.39<TD
ALIGN=RIGHT>ea$8.45
<TR><TD>973179<TD>22"<TD ALIGN=RIGHT>$10.79<TD
ALIGN=RIGHT>ea$9.71
</TABLE>
```

FIG. 11.22

A Table with a Caption

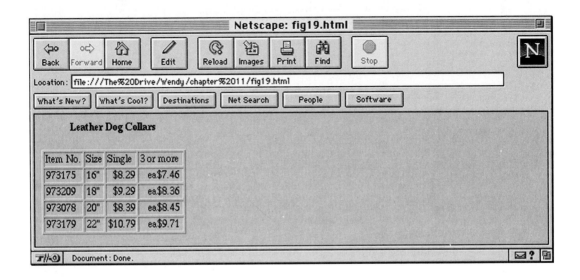

Putting a heading inside the caption tags creates more space between the caption and the table. You can experiment with different formats on your captions to get the look you want. All captions are centered with respect to their tables.

Words of Warning

Some books advise you not to use tables because the standards for tables are not yet widely accepted. It is easy to incorporate browser-specific extensions and end up with a page that is unreadable when viewed by some browsers.

Text-based browsers are even more of a problem because they don't support tables at all. When a text-based browser looks at a table, it ignores all of the tags it doesn't recognize. It effectively deletes those tags and displays the remaining HTML file as is. Here is how the Web page in Figure 11.19 looks under the lynx Web browser:

```
Translator Design CS345
Course Information Professor Black

Class Lectures Computer Lab TA Office Hours
Room LFC 219 CSC 115 CSC 230
Monday 9:20-10:10 1:00-1:30
Tuesday 10:30-12:00 2:00-4:30
Wednesday 9:20-10:10 1:00-1:30
Thursday 10:30-12:00 2:00-4:30
Friday 9:20-10:10
This course covers basic principles of translator
design as they apply to the practical implementation
of compilers and interpreters.
Prerequisites: CS187 and CS220
Required Text: Compiler Design

[INLINE]
Professor Black
Office: CSC421
Office Hours: MW 11-12
Phone: 546-3847
black@cs.upodunk.edu
```

This isn't impossible to read, and most lynx users are used to seeing this sort of thing. But it is clearly not what the Web page author intended to display. People with text-based browsers are very appreciative when alternative Web pages are designed specifically for text-based browsers. You will increase your potential audience by remembering the limitations of text-based browsers.

As long as you understand their limitations, you can use tables effectively without getting too bogged down. You just need to be cautious. Here are some guidelines to keep your tables under control:

1. Always preview your Web pages using the most popular Web browsers to make sure they look the way you want them to.

2. Do not use crowded layouts that include multitudes of tables that depend on a lot of delicate spacing.

3. Always check to see what happens to your layout when you resize the window. Don't worry about windows that are excessively small, but do check to ensure that very large windows don't destroy your display.

4. Text-based browsers don't support tables. Give text-based users an alternative page on which they can view preformatted tables.

Another strategy that works very nicely is to design a page display with tables that look good under one browser and then take a screen snapshot of the display so that your display is captured in a graphic image. Then you can rebuild your page using only the graphic's file instead of table tags. This is an absolutely safe way to make sure your tables look exactly the way you want. There are many freeware and shareware utilities that take snapshots of your computer screen. Until you are very confident about your mastery of tables, the snapshot strategy may be the safest and least time-consuming. However, if you go this route you will need to offer text-based users an alternative page, because the text-based browsers won't be able to see any of your screen shots.

Frames

Another strategy for managing page layouts is to use frames. Frames allow you to partition your Web page into a fixed number of rows and columns, much like a table. However, frames and tables differ in three important ways:

1. A frame layout consumes the entire Web page. That is, everything on the Web page must be placed inside one of the frames.

2. Each frame must contain a link to another Web page or an image file.

3. A frame can be fixed or scrollable.

When you use frames, you effectively divide one Web page into smaller Web pages that can be developed and updated independently. Doing this may give you a convenient way to separate graphical elements and text elements. For example, you could have a string of photographs running down a column on the left side of the page, with a scrollable text window to the right. Since each segment of the page links to a separate file, they each can have a different background.

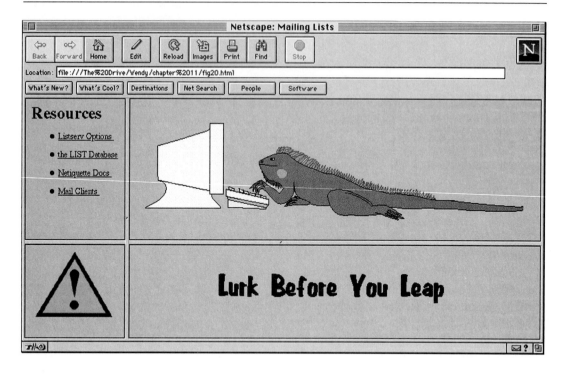

FIG. 11.23

A Web Page with Four
Frames

To create a frame, you insert a ⟨FRAMESET⟩ tag immediately after the HEAD element on your Web page. FRAMESET divides up the Web page using the COLS= attribute, the ROWS= attribute, or both. Each attribute takes as its value a set of percentages separated by commas. For example,

```
<FRAMESET COLS="20%, 80%"
          ROWS="60%, 40%">
```

divides the Web page into four frames (see Figure 11.23). You can have as many rows and columns as you want.

To fill each frame, you use a FRAME tag with a SRC= attribute. If you want the frame to be fixed, set the SCROLLING= attribute to "no." For example, the following construction produces the Web page shown in Figure 11.24:

```
<FRAMESET COLS="70%, 30%">
<FRAME SRC="fig21c.html" SCROLLING="no">
<FRAME SRC="fig21a.html">
</FRAMESET>
```

Frames work very well in certain types of situations. For example, if you have a long scrollable list, it might make sense to isolate it inside a frame instead of giving it a separate Web page.

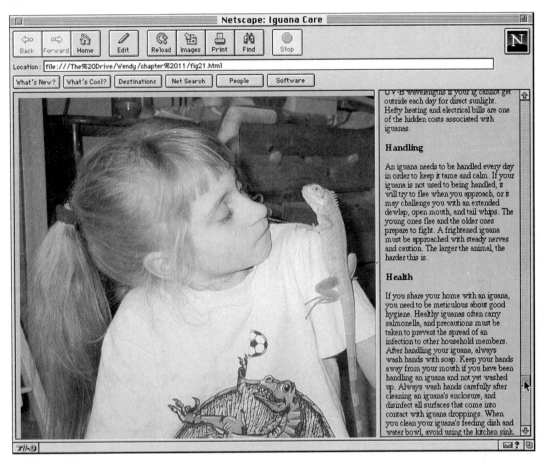

FIG. 11.24

A Web Page with a
Scrollable Frame

HTML Tag Summary   11.7

Following is a summary of the most common HTML tags.

Titles, Backgrounds, and Headers

```
<TITLE>Web Page Title</TITLE>              This goes inside the HEAD
<BODY BGCOLOR="#F8F8FF"                     A background color
<BODY BACKGROUND="wrinkles.gif">            A background pattern
<H1 ALIGN=LEFT|RIGHT|CENTER> </H1>          The largest heading
```

```
<H2>                              .
<H3>                              .
<H4>                              .
<H5>                              .
<H6>                   The smallest heading
```

Presentation Tags

```
<B></B>                Makes type boldface
<I></I>                Makes type italic
<TT></TT>              Makes type a teletype font
<U></U>                Underlines text
```

Informational Tags

```
<STRONG></STRONG>      Makes text stand out
<EM></EM>              Makes text look emphasized
<CODE></CODE>          Makes type a monospaced font
<CITE></CITE>          Marks a citation
```

Text Formatting

```
<PRE></PRE>                       Causes text to be reproduced as is
<BR CLEAR=LEFT|RIGHT|ALL>         Causes text to go to the next clear line
<P ALIGN=LEFT|RIGHT|CENTER>       Starts a new paragraph
```

Lists

Bulleted:

```
<UL>                              Marks the beginning of a bulleted list
<LH><H3>Three Items</H3></LH>     The heading of a list (optional)
<LI> Item X                       Denotes the first of three list items
<LI> Item Y
<LI> Item Z
</UL>
```

Numbered:

```
<OL VALUE=5>                      Marks the beginning of a numbered list
                                     starting at the fifth item
<LI> Item X                       Denotes the list item labeled #5
<LI> Item Y
<LI> Item Z
</OL>
```

Definition:

```
<DL>                                          Marks the beginning of a definition list
<DT> Term X <DD> Definition of Term X         The first term + definition
<DT> Term Y <DD> Definition of Term Y
</DL>
```

Graphics

```
<IMG   SRC="iggy.gif"                         Inserts an inline graphic
       WIDTH=30pt HEIGHT=40pt
       ALIGN= LEFT|RIGHT|BOTTOM|TOP|MIDDLE
       ALT="[INLINE: A CARTOON IG]">          Inserts a text alternative
<HR SIZE=1|2|3                                Inserts a horizontal rule
   WIDTH=25% ALIGN=LEFT|RIGHT|CENTER>
<CENTER></CENTER>                             Centers a graphic element
```

Hypertext Links

```
<A HREF="igtext.html"> Iguana Care </A>       A text link
<A HREF="iggy.gif">                           A thumbnail sketch link
   <IMG SRC="iggy.gif" WIDTH=20pt
       HEIGHT=30pt>
</A>
```

Tables and Frames

```
<TABLE BORDER=0|1|2|3 ...                      A table
   ALIGN=LEFT|RIGHT
   WIDTH=80pt HEIGHT=110pt>                    dimensions are optional
   <CAPTION ALIGN=TOP|BOTTOM> </CAPTION>       A caption (optional)
   <TR><TD  ALIGN=LEFT|RIGHT|CENTER            A row with one data cell
           WIDTH=20pt HEIGHT=20pt>             cell size is optional
      ... text or image element ...           Add more rows/cells here
</TABLE>


<FRAMESET ROWS="30%, 40%, 30%"                 A Web page with 6 frames
       COLS="50%, 50%">
       <FRAME SRC="igpics.html"
           SCROLLING="no">                     A fixed frame
       <FRAME SRC="igtext.html"> ...           A scrollable frame
</FRAMESET>
```

11.8 ▸ A Webmaster's Toolbox

Several useful tools are available for Web page designers. Many are freeware or shareware. Visit the Internet 101 Web pages for pointers to online utilities and other resources.

Commercial products are also available. Web page products compete in a very active commercial market, so watch for new product releases and read some product reviews. But plan to shop around and do some homework before you buy.

Digital Photograph Capabilities

To put your own photographs on the Web, you have many options:

- Use a color scanner (about $200-$400 to buy) to scan in the photos. Alternatively, you can take photographs to a copy shop for color scanning.
- Use a digital camera (about $500 to buy) to bypass film altogether. Alternatively, you can rent a digital camera at a copy shop.
- Use a video frame-grabber that captures images from a camcorder, VCR, or TV (about $200 to buy).
- When you have a roll of film processed, request digital conversion onto floppies (about $5-$10 per roll) or request a PhotoCD ($10 per roll plus $1 per negative).

To digitize an existing photograph, a scanner is always your simplest solution. Color scanners are fairly commonplace these days, so you might be able to borrow one at work or use one belonging to a friend. If you have some money to spend, high-quality scanners are very affordable and fun to have on hand. Anyone who does a lot of Web page design should have a color scanner.

Tools to Manipulate Text and Graphics

The right tool can make ambitious projects possible and routine projects more enjoyable. Good tools can expand your capabilities, save you time, and enhance your creations. If you intend to maintain a Web site or create more than one Web site, you should investigate some of the tools available to Webmasters. Ask friends and colleagues for recommendations, read software reviews, and monitor appropriate newsgroups or mailing lists for timely information. Web page construction is a lot like carpentry: If you have high standards and are serious about quality, you need to outfit a workbench with a selection of helpful tools. Pros tend to use more powerful tools than amateurs, but you don't need to be a professional Webmaster to benefit from good Web authoring tools. Available tools include

- basic HTML editors
- WYSIWYG HTML editors
- HTML syntax checkers
- file converters, including database macros
- audio/video utilities

Basic HTML Editors

A basic HTML editor is essentially an ASCII text editor with some extra buttons for inserting the most frequently used HTML tags. Web page construction goes faster with an HTML editor, but you are still generating all your HTML manually; manual text entry tends to be the biggest bottleneck in Web page development. If you want to crash through the manual HTML bottleneck, you really want a good HTML converter or WYSIWYG editor.

WYSIWYG HTML Editors

WYSIWYG (What You See Is What You Get) editors let you format text and insert graphics on a screen that shows you the final Web page layout as you work while generating the corresponding HTML source file for you behind the scenes. WYSIWYG editors are powerful tools that can produce fast Web pages without your needing any knowledge of HTML. However, all tend to be limited in some respects, so you may not be able to take advantage of certain features in HTML. Also, there can never be a true WYSIWYG Web page display because different browsers will often display the same page differently. Keeping those two caveats in mind, you'll find that a good WYSIWYG editor is great for beginners or anyone who wants to create a simple Web page as fast as possible.

Netscape Navigator Gold 3.0 contains an easy-to-use WYSIWYG HTML editor that is adequate for most people. Special-purpose commercial WYSIWYG HTML editors are also available for Web page authors who need more features. If you need an HTML feature not supported by your WYSIWYG editor, you can always use the editor for a first-pass Web page, and then alter the resulting source file manually to add additional features.

HTML Syntax Checkers

One typo in an HTML tag can produce an empty Web page or a strangely mangled one with large segments of missing text. Sometimes the location of the error is obvious, and sometimes it's not. Fixing a sick Web page can be a time-consuming process that everyone has to grapple with from time to time. An HTML syntax checker can save you a lot of time and is especially recommended for beginners, since they most typically make syntactical errors.

Many HTML editors (WYSIWYG and otherwise) incorporate their own syntax checkers that automatically alert you as soon as you type in a syntactically unacceptable construction. This immediate feedback is very helpful because you can see exactly where an error occurred and can remedy it before it has a chance to interact with additional errors in unexpected ways.

HTML Converters

Many people prefer to design a Web page from scratch using their favorite word processor and then feed it to an HTML converter to bypass all of the tedious HTML tag insertion. You can definitely save yourself a lot of time by avoiding manual HTML generation as much as possible. Some commercial word processors now come with an HTML conversion feature.

Although a good HTML converter can save you a lot of time, it is not likely to produce the best possible Web page for any given document. The output of an HTML converter can get you 90% of what you want. If you are in a rush, that might be good enough. But you will probably want to tinker with the layout to get the best results. So don't throw away your HTML books when you buy an HTML converter; you'll still want to open up the file and do a few things by hand.

Also, remember that a text document that was not written as a Web page will not make a very good Web page without some redesign. Hyperlinks must be inserted, text should be segmented for easy Web page navigation, and lists should be used wherever possible to aid navigation. An HTML converter cannot incorporate any of these high-level Web page features for you.

GIF/JPEG File Converters

With so many graphical file formats, you are bound to find files that aren't in the right format for the Web. This is not a big problem if you have a file conversion tool on hand. Look for a GIF converter that offers a transparency option. If yours doesn't, you can always pick up a special-purpose utility that does. Good freeware and shareware file converters include these:

- For a Mac: GIFConverter, JPEGView, Transparency
- For a PC: LView Pro, Paint Shop Pro, Thumbs Plus, VuePrint, WebImage
- For UNIX: giftrans, pbm plus

Database Macros

Database macros are specialized conversion routines that convert data sheets from database applications into HTML tables. If you don't work with databases or spreadsheets, you will have no use for a database macro. But if your Web pages contain data displays, and especially if they contain data that needs to be updated on a regular basis, you should look for a suitable macro that can automate this part of your Web page. Look for application-specific macros designed for the more popular spreadsheet and database applications.

Audio/Video Utilities

To work with video clips, you need to install a movie viewer, such as one of these:

- For the Mac: QuickTime
- For the PC: QuickTime Player, VMPEG Lite, MPEG Movie Player

Video clip creation is a very involved and memory-intensive undertaking. Commercial software packages are available for digital movie making, but you would be wise to sign up for a course on the subject before you venture off on your own.

To make your own audio clips, you need a microphone and a digital sound recorder. Sound clips are much easier to create than movie videos, but if you want to record professional-quality sound, plan to study the subject first.

An excellent display utility for both audio and video clips is a piece of freeware called RealPlayer (`http://www.real.com/`). Download it, plug it in, and then test it out at National Public Radio (`http://www.npr.org/`).

Where to Learn More   11.9

One chapter on HTML cannot possibly cover the full breadth of HTML. Notable omissions include the use of forms, CGI, Java *applets*, sound, video, PDF files, and HTML style sheets. The intent has been to cover the basics of useful HTML features that might be crucial to anyone working up a personal home page or a small Web site of informational pages. There is much, much more to learn if you plan to create Web pages on a regular basis.

Some HTML elements can help you work more efficiently when creating complex Web sites. For example, if you work with a lot of tables in HTML, you will want to learn all of the design elements specific to tables. To create killer graphics for your Web pages, you will want to learn more about digital artwork and the utilities that help you edit digital images. To create an instructional site, you will want to research organizational strategies for educational Web pages. To use the Web as an entertainment vehicle, you will need to study elements of visual design and ways to keep your interactive Web pages effective and engaging.

If you want to master more HTML or learn about related topics of interest to Web page designers, there are many good books for people with nontechnical backgrounds. For a first book on HTML, I recommend this one:

HTML 3: Electronic Publishing on the World Wide Web, by Dave
Raggett, Jenny Lam, and Ian Alexander. Addison-Wesley, Reading, Mass., 1996, 398 pages.

Written by the lead architect for HTML 3, this book makes it easy to see what's in the HTML 3 standard and what's a browser-specific extension. This is not a comprehensive guide to HTML, but it is easy to read and it covers a lot of ground.

If you want to add a second HTML book to your library, a good companion book is this one:

**Teach Yourself Web Publishing with HTML 3.0 in a Week (Second
Edition),** by Laura Lemay. Sams.net Publishing, Indianapolis, Indiana, 1996, 518 pages.

This book covers some topics that Ragget doesn't (e.g., CGI), and it works well as both a text and a reference book. If you master everything in these two books, you will have a lot of HTML expertise under your belt. Then you can graduate to Java.

PROBLEMS AND EXERCISES

1. What HTML tag will position a date in the upper right-hand corner of a Web page?

2. What tag or tags will insert five blank lines between two blocks of text?

3. What text formatting tag will produce a list of single-spaced hyperlinks, each one centered on its own line?

4. **[Hands On]** Download a small GIF image from the Web and add it to a Web page. Right-justify the image and wrap some text around it. Can you increase the area of your image by about a factor of 4? Explain how. Show your original image tag and the revised image tag for the larger image.

5. **[Hands On]** Set up a Web page that has three graphic images lined up in a row inside three frames. What happens to the frames when you resize the window?

6. What unit is used to set the dimensions of a graphic? What unit is used to set the length of a horizontal rule? How do they differ?

7. [**Hands On**] What colors correspond to the hexadecimal numbers D475A3, 711EE8, and AA5234?

8. [**Hands On**] Locate and download some Web page background files. If you have access to a scanner or an artwork application, try making some backgrounds on your own. View all of your backgrounds with your browser and insert the background behind the page you constructed in Exercise #4 or 5. What two properties should a good background pattern have?

9. Is it better to use relative links or absolute links for the hyperlinks within your own Web pages? Explain. (If you said relative links, find a reason other than their being shorter.)

10. Suppose you are viewing a Web page named `http://www.donut.net/cs/cs101/staff/intro/info/ideas.html` and a relative link inside ideas.html points to `../../../students/jones/projects.html`. Draw a picture of the directory hierarchy and show how `ideas.html` is situated relative to `projects.html`. What absolute link will take you to `projects.html`?

11. Why is it important to preserve all directory structures and directory names when you move a set of Web pages from your development environment to a Web page server?

12. What are thumbnail sketches and why are they useful?

Note: Exercises 13–15 require file utilities. Find and download any utilities you need.

13. [**Hands On**] Take a graphics file in PICT, EPS, or TIFF format and convert it to GIF for the Web.

14. [**Hands On**] Take a suitable GIF file and convert it to a transparent GIF file. Add it to your Web page. What kinds of GIF files are good candidates for transparency?

15. [**Hands On**] Take a large GIF file and convert it into an interlaced GIF file. Set up a thumbnail sketch for this file and add the thumbnail sketch to your Web page.

16. Research how to set up a clickable image that has multiple "hot zones" for multiple hyperlinks. These graphical menus are often a welcome change from a text-based menu. What do you need to make graphical menus? Can you think of any guidelines regarding when to use a graphical menu and when to use a text-based menu?

For exercises 17–20, start with the HTML source for the Web page in Figure 11.19 (you can download it from the Internet 101 Web pages). Make sure you are working with the CS345 Course Information source file for these exercises.

17. **[Hands On]** Remove the border from the first table at the top of the page. Did the layout of the text elements change?

18. **[Hands On]** Remove the WIDTH= attribute from the third table (the one with the short course description). What happens to the table?

19. **[Hands On]** What happens to the layout when you resize your browser window to its largest possible dimensions? Add the attribute WIDTH=100% to the table tag for the first table at the top of the page. How does this change the behavior of the layout when you resize the window?

20. **[Hands On]** Apply the WIDTH= attribute used in Exercise 19 to make the entire page layout expand and contract when you resize the browser window.

Encryption on the Internet

12

> "A martyr or two never hurts a cause, although it's a bit hard on the martyr."
>
> - HERBERT A. SIMON

THE INTERNET 101 WEB PAGES

- PGP Software Sources
- Papers About Encryption
- The PGP FAQ
- Public Key Directories

What Is Cryptography and Why Should I Care?

12.1

Most of us never encounter the word "cryptography" outside of spy movies and espionage novels. It is a fancy word for secret codes associated with classified information and intelligence gathering. You might know something about the important role of cryptography in World War II, but chances are you know only if you went out of your way to read a book about it. And while everyone likely has heard of clandestine operations associated with the Central Intelligence Agency (CIA), many Americans have never heard of the National Security Agency (NSA). It is the NSA that is responsible for developing secure communication technologies.

Cryptography has always been a key component in national security, but the average citizen has little or no knowledge of current technologies or exactly who is developing them. This is likely to change in the next few years. As we move into a new era of digital communication, cryptography is about to touch all our lives.

Cryptography is an issue of great interest to client/server software developers, anyone interested in digital commerce, and all Internet users who want to keep their personal communications private. Sensitive personal communications, legal contracts, valuable data, proprietary documents, insurance records, digital monetary transfers, medical records—all are, in the absence of special safeguards, at risk on the Internet and on any digital medium. Cryptography offers us good options for protecting this information and it will become increasingly commonplace in business environments. It will eventually permeate all digital media as we come to appreciate the importance of secure communication.

When TCP/IP was adopted as the standard communication protocol for global networked communication, secure communication was not a high priority. Open software design, open resource sharing, and public information were the forces driving early network research. The Internet has succeeded as a highly accessible and expandable public network, but our priorities are slowly shifting. As the Internet becomes more commercialized, vendors need to conduct secure business transactions to allay the fears of consumers who are nervous about the risks of online shopping. We have yet to see a high-profile scandal unfold as the result of an Internet "wiretap," but it's probably just a matter of time before some technically inclined investigator figures out how to surreptitiously tap into the e-mail of some unsuspecting individual. Private investigators and lawyers are already examining back-up files as a potential source of legal evidence, but the general public is just beginning to ask about legal protections that pertain to privacy rights.

Companies must insist that sensitive information not be up for grabs just because it is stored on a computer, and citizens should feel reassured that tax returns and other private documents are not available to random individuals for recreational browsing. Online medical records must be handled with care so that employers and insurance companies can't review sensitive information without authorization. Credit records should be safe from the prying eyes of newspaper reporters and private investigators.

With so much public information going online, we've been a little slow to appreciate just how much sensitive personal information has also been going online. The technologies that promote public access were never designed to protect private data. The public has embraced the Internet without fully understanding exactly how it differs from relatively private communication channels, where safeguards for privacy are taken for granted.

The military has always understood that security is a big problem on computer networks. Sensitive military computers are carefully shielded from potentially invasive network connections. Large corporations followed suit by opting for intranet connectivity as an alternative to Internet access. An **intranet** is an internal computer network that is carefully segregated from all external computer networks, such as the Internet. Internet access from an intranet is possible, but only through a secure gateway called a **firewall** that is designed to keep sensitive data within organizational walls. A firewall is like a wall around a castle. As long as the wall works, everyone feels safe and sound. But a wall that is not carefully designed and maintained might be breached so constant vigilance is needed. A castle wall without sentries is probably no better than a wall with a gaping hole in it.

Intranets and firewalls afford good protection and work well for large organizations. But many of our communications are not circumscribed by institutional boundaries. We also want privacy safeguards when we contact friends, acquaintances, and business contacts all over the world. Today's Internet does not have any privacy safeguards built into it. However, as time goes on we will see more and more applications incorporating privacy measures. It is not necessary to understand all of the technical foundations that enable digital privacy, but some understanding of the basic ideas will help you evaluate the available choices.

Single-Key Cryptography   12.2

There was a time in the 1950s when it seemed like every kid in America wore a big purple plastic ring with white and yellow lightning bolts on it. It had a large dial on top covered in letters and symbols. Captain Midnight Decoder Rings were hot, and countless 7-year-olds deftly used these coveted artifacts to unscramble secret messages issued straight from Captain Midnight through the magic of television. Captain Midnight probably never uttered the words "single-key cryptography"; however, it was the use of single-key cryptography that made his code rings work. That is, the rings all contained the same key and anyone with that key could unscramble his coded messages. Figure 12.1 shows the sort of key that could have been on the Captain Midnight code rings.

A --> H	F --> 7	K --> A	P --> 5	U --> E	Z --> ?	5 --> D	/ --> W
B --> C	G --> 0	L --> .	Q --> F	V --> S	1 --> X	6 --> R	. --> Q
C --> 4	H --> B	M --> V	R --> 1	W --> Z	2 --> P	7 --> K	! --> G
D --> I	I --> M	N --> 0	S --> !	X --> J	3 --> L	8 --> Y	? --> U
E --> 6	J --> T	0 --> 3	T --> 9	Y --> 2	4 --> 8	9 --> N	

FIG. 12.1

A Simple
Encryption/Decryption
Key

When you receive a coded message, you map each character to its mate using the key, and you end up with a readable message. For example, suppose your coded message says this:

```
IUUJ IU JNIN66N/ KJ C2I ?95U6 JAU IK23U J6UUL
```

After applying the key to each symbol and writing down the resulting message, you have this:

```
MEET ME TOMORROW AT 4PM UNDER THE MAPLE TREE.
```

The process of creating a coded message is called **encoding** (or **encrypting**). The process of unscrambling a coded message using a key is called **decoding** (or **decrypting**).

Captain Midnight's ring could be used for either decoding or encoding, but it was used for decoding when Captain Midnight's fans unscrambled his secret messages. When the same key is used for both encoding and decoding, the code is called **single-key cryptography**. See Figure 12.2.

If you have the key for a code, it is easy to decode messages. If you don't have the key, you can study some encoded messages and try to figure out the key, but doing this is much harder. If you can discover the key for a code, you have broken the code. A code based on character substitutions, such as the one shown in Figure 12.1, is one way to encrypt information. It is relatively easy to break if you have a lot of encoded messages. The more encoded messages you have, the easier it is to break the code. One way is to identify the most frequently used characters and character sequences in those messages. For example, the letter "e" is the most frequently used letter in the English alphabet. Chances are, one of the more frequently encountered characters in the encoded messages is the encoding for "e." The most frequently used three-letter word is "the." If you see the same three-letter character sequence over and over again, it might be "the." This sort of analysis makes it possible to break simple codes.

Codes designed for military communications must be very difficult to break. The most sophisticated are based on factorizations for very large integers. A branch of mathematics called number theory has useful applications in cryptography, and computers are needed to generate the most complicated

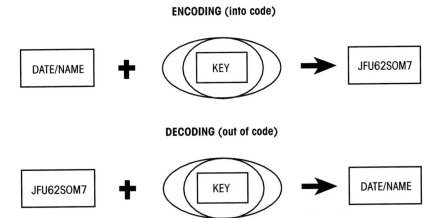

FIG. 12.2

Single-Key
Cryptography

codes. Computers have always been a powerful tool for both code generation and code breaking. In fact, the complexity of today's codes is limited only by the computing power of the machines that generate them.

An effective code transmits messages to its intended recipients—and only its intended recipients. Anyone else should not be able to decode the messages. However, you should assume that coded messages will be intercepted by people who will try to break the code, so every effort must be made to confound the code breakers.

An important problem associated with encryption is the problem of ensuring **key security**. If a code breaker can obtain the key for a code, the code breaker wins. To keep your diary safe from your snoopy big brother, you can use Captain Midnight's Decoder Ring to encode your diary entries. But you better make sure your code ring is safely hidden where big brother can't find it. The most sophisticated code in the world is of no use if the key cannot be held securely. Every precaution must be taken to keep code keys out of the wrong hands.

Single-key cryptographic methods are not very safe, because the same keys have to be shared by too many people. At the very least, the sender needs the key to encode messages, and the receiver needs the key to decode messages. Even when just two people share a key, you could have a problem because the key must be passed from one person to the other person. Each time a key is transferred, you take a chance that it might be intercepted. How can you make sure no one intercepts the key? Should you trust the U.S. mail? Federal Express? A telephone call? An e-mail message? A military courier? Some options are safer than others, but all carry some risk.

If the information you want to encode is not a matter of life and death, you may decide that the risks associated with single-key cryptography are acceptable (it was good enough for Captain Midnight …). But some applications for cryptography are very sensitive and require the best possible safeguards. Military communications come to mind immediately, but now that there is the Internet, many other uses for cryptography have surfaced. For example, when the CEO of a company needs to send a sensitive message over the Internet to corporate offices worldwide, only the best security will do. One way to do this is an intranet with a firewall. Intranets are more secure than the Internet and are routinely used for electronic fund transfers within a corporate environment. But intranets aren't a solution for the general public. To convince a few million consumers that their credit card numbers can be safely sent over the Internet for commercial transactions, you need the best safeguards available. Indeed, concerns about the security of digital funds have been a major stumbling block in the commercialization of the Internet. No one wants to broadcast their credit card number to the world. A popular solution to this dilemma is to use double-key cryptography.

12.3   Double-Key Cryptography

Key security is a problem that can never be completely eliminated, but it can be minimized. The greatest level of key security is achieved when only one person needs to hold the key used to decode messages. This is the advantage of double-key cryptography. Although a little more complicated than single-key cryptography, double-key cryptography does maximize key safety. The basic trick is to use two keys instead of one. One key is used to encode messages, and a second key is used to decode messages. These two keys are generated as a special pair of keys that work only with each other. If one key is lost, the other, by itself, is useless. One key is called the **public key**. A public key can be freely distributed to anyone and everyone. The other key is a **private key**. A private key is held by only one person. Even though the two keys are uniquely connected, having the public key doesn't make it any easier to guess the private key. Let's see how double-key cryptography works by looking at an example.

For me to send you an encrypted message, you first need to create a pair of keys that will enable me to encode the message. You give me a copy of your public key, and you keep your private key to yourself. I then use your public key to encode the message, and you use your private key to decode it. This system is very secure as long as each pair of keys works together as unique partners. Your private key is the only key that can decode messages encoded by your public key. If you are the only person with access to your private key, you are the only person who can read messages encoded for you. It doesn't

ENCODING

key pair
6F94BK33

| DATE/NAME | **+** | PUBLIC KEY | ➡ | FFJKDLSIE:SA |

| FFJKDLSIE:SA | **+** | PRIVATE KEY | ➡ | DATE/NAME |

key pair
6F94BK33

DECODING

matter how many people hold the public key because it is useful only for encoding messages. No one can use the public key to decode messages encoded by the public key. (If the public key could both encode and decode the same message, the cryptographic method would be single-key.) Figure 12.3 shows the concept of double-key cryptography.

For you to send me an encoded message, another pair of keys is needed. I need to create my own pair of keys, with a public key that I can distribute to anyone and a private key that only I can access. I give you a copy of my public key so that you can encode messages for me. Then, when I get an encoded message from you, I use my private key to decode it. You and I can then exchange messages back and forth, using our public keys for all of the encoding and our private keys for all of the decoding.

FIG. 12.3

Double-Key
Cryptography

How Are Keys Broken?

A key is just a string of ones and zeros (that is, a string of bits). A good encryption scheme can be broken only by discovering the key. This means you must try each of all possible strings of ones and zeros until you find the right one. A shorter string is easier to figure out than

Continued on Next Page

Continued from Previous Page

a longer one because there are fewer possibilities. There are 1,024 possible strings containing exactly 10 bits, 1,048,576 possible strings containing exactly 20 bits, and 1,099,511,627,776 possible strings containing exactly 40 bits. In 1995, a graduate student in France demonstrated that a 40-bit key could be cracked in 8 days using 120 workstations and two supercomputers working in parallel. With access to special hardware, a computer with a single special-purpose computer chip can break a 40-bit key in a few hours.

Double-key cryptography is more sophisticated than single-key cryptography, so you may be having some trouble imagining what the keys look like and how they fit together. The code used by Captain Midnight could easily be reversed to both encode and decode. In a double-key cryptography system, the process of encoding is not easily reversible. Someone who can figure out how to reverse the encoding of a public key can crack the code. Double-key cryptography systems can be cracked, but it requires technical expertise and massive computing power. Double keys are effective because a public key cannot (easily) be used to deduce a private key.

Let's consider the implications of double-key cryptography a little further. If everyone on the Internet wanted to communicate with everyone else using double-key cryptography, we would all need to own a personal pair of keys and we would all need to access everyone else's public keys. This may not sound very practical, but all of this key management and key-related bookkeeping could be automated by communications software. For example, a central directory for public keys could be created for the distribution of public keys. Once your public key goes into the directory, anyone can look it up and make a copy for their personal use. If you wanted to send e-mail to someone, your mail program could look up the required key in the public key directory. Then that key would be used to encrypt your mail message before it is sent. If there is no key, the mail would go out unencrypted. The overhead of encoding e-mail could be handled by software behind the scenes, thus requiring no extra effort on the part of the end user.

At the receiving end, your mail program could be smart enough to recognize an encoded message when it sees one, in which case it would apply your private key and decode the message for you automatically. All of this would take place only when you read your e-mail, to maintain maximal security. Everything needed to realize this scenario exists today, including mail programs that automate message encryption and decryption. All of the technical know-how is there to secure our e-mail from prying eyes. **Privacy-enhanced E-Mail** (PEM) is just around the corner and will gradually catch on in the same way that mail attachments became commonplace. No one will distribute their own public keys until they have the proper mail reader in place to decode incoming messages, so people who are slow to jump on the bandwagon won't be inconvenienced in any way. With nothing to lose and everything to gain, what could go wrong?

What Could Go Wrong?   12.4

When people worry about whether they can trust encryption, they generally want to know how hard it is to break the code. If someone can crack your code, that's a catastrophic failure. We know that 40-bit keys can be broken, and broken within a practical time frame using specialized hardware. The amount of time it takes to crack a code is important. Any key that can be broken only after thousands of years of computing time on the world's fastest computers is safe enough. The term **strong cryptography** refers to encryption methods that are safe in this practical sense. A code that can be broken in a practical time frame is called **weak cryptography**.

Anything that can be done using a large number of conventional computers over a period of weeks or months will be reproducible using special-purpose hardware within a period of minutes or hours, so the question of practicality is somewhat fuzzy. A casual hacker with a Pentium PC is in no position to pick off credit card numbers encoded with a 40-bit key. But if someone starts to sell black market "black boxes" designed to crack encryption software, a 40-bit key becomes much more vulnerable. In any case, the federal government would have no trouble decoding messages encrypted with 40-bit keys. So 40-bit encryption is considered to be weak cryptography.

This distinction between strong and weak cryptography is also something of a moving target. As a rule, computer processors double in speed every 18 months. Each time a processor doubles in speed, it can take on one more bit in an encryption key and break a code in the same amount of time. So if 40-bit cryptography was deemed weak cryptography in 1995, then 50-bit cryptography will be weak by the year 2010 and 60-bit cryptography will be weak by 2025. Any dramatic breakthroughs in microchip technologies could completely alter these projections, and it is impossible to say anything about the limitations of future computer technologies with any real confidence.

IS MY CREDIT CARD NUMBER SAFE ON THE INTERNET?

In 1992, the U. S. government placed an export restriction on cryptography software so that U. S. software vendors could not incorporate encryption stronger than 40 bits in their products. In 1996, this restriction was relaxed under certain conditions so that those vendors could go up to 56 bits. Some people argue that 56 bits is adequate for Internet commerce. Others argue that if it is, it won't be for long. It is interesting to note that during the time when the government imposed the 40-bit limitation, it also granted banks and other institutions selective exceptions that allowed them to go up to 56-bit encryption. So, apparently the government felt that the extra safety net of stronger encryption was warranted for certain digital transactions.

If you want to read transcripts from Congressional hearings, you can come to your own conclusions about the adequacy of 40-bit and 56-bit encryption. Alternatively, here's a reasonable rule of thumb for risk assessment. If you (1) feel safe placing a credit card order over the phone or if you (2) allow store clerks to discard your credit card carbons without tearing them up in front of you, then you have no reason to worry about using Netscape Navigator or Internet Explorer for a credit card transaction. There is some amount of risk in all of these scenarios, but most of us live with the risk as a fact of modern life. Commercial transactions on the Internet should be encrypted for your protection, but you shouldn't worry about whether it's 40-bit or 56-bit encryption. In either case, the risks are negligible.

Most clever ideas have a weak spot or two, especially when it comes to computer software. And if there is any way to exploit a weakness, someone will figure out how to do it. Double-key cryptography has two weaknesses other than the possibility of the code being cracked. One has to do with the security of private keys, and the other has to do with forged e-mail. They are both solvable problems, as discussed in the following sections.

Security for Private Keys

The first problem is that of keeping a private key safe and secure. As long as there is even one copy of a private key, there is always the possibility of its being stolen. I am also talking about digital keys that would be stored on computers, in which case you must contend with all of the usual problems of computer security. One effective safeguard is a simple password or pass phrase. If you create a pair of keys, the system creating your keys can ask you to enter a password or phrase. Then, whenever anyone tries to use your private key, the software asks for your password or phrase. If the correct word or phrase is not entered, the software refuses to decode anything. Privacy-enhanced e-mail would require you to enter your password or phrase each time you read e-mail, but entering it once per e-mail session is probably a small price to pay for secure communication.

The security of your private key now depends on the security of your password or phrase. To maintain optimal security, you need only ensure that you never give your word or phrase to another person and that you never write it down. As long as you can remember your word or phrase and you are the only one who knows it, your private key is useless to everyone but you. But wait. Isn't your password or phrase stored on your computer, too? What if someone steals it from your computer? This would be a problem if it were stored without safeguards. But it can be stored in an encoded form so that a stolen word or phrase would have to be decoded to be of any use. Cracking an encrypted password or phrase is no easier than cracking your private key in the first place. So using a password or phrase is a simple and powerful way to keep a private key safe and secure.

Safeguards against Counterfeit Keys

This problem is a little more devious. You have to think like a criminal to grasp it. Suppose for a moment that you have no scruples and suppose further that you want to read John's e-mail. Intercepting John's e-mail is fairly easy for someone who knows their way around computers, so while we're at it, pretend you also know all about computers. You could grab John's mail before it ever gets to him by using snooping software called a **packet sniffer**. All you need is access to John's host machine or any of the hosts that feed mail to his host machine. You might need to gain access to one of these machines illegally, but that wouldn't deter someone with criminal tendencies. If John's e-mail is not encrypted, access to a host that sees his mail is all you need. But suppose the e-mail you want to read is encrypted with John's public key and John is using strong encryption. Then you need to work a little harder.

It's too hard to break a strong encryption code, so you'll have to find a way to stop people from using John's public key in the first place. This might sound impossible, but this is where a devious imagination comes in handy. All you need to do is plant a counterfeit key wherever John's key has been posted for public consumption. For example, suppose John has posted his public key in a public directory. Then you have to break into that directory and replace John's public key with a public key of your own (which is paired with a private key that you own). Leaving aside the question of exactly how you might manage this, assume that you somehow manage to plant your counterfeit key under John's name in the key directory. Then anyone looking up John's key will have no way of knowing that a counterfeit key has been substituted for his legitimate key. Hang on to a copy of John's real public key—you'll need it later.

Now suppose someone decides to send John an encoded message. They (or their mail client) look up John in the key directory and unknowingly grab a copy of the counterfeit key. They use the counterfeit key to encode a message, and then they mail the message to John. You have a packet sniffer set up to intercept all of John's incoming e-mail, so you get this message before it reaches John. Since you have the private key that decodes messages encoded by the counterfeit key, you can decode the message and see what it says. If that's all you care about, then you're done.

Chances are, however, you really want to monitor all of John's incoming e-mail for a while. So you need to ensure John thinks everything is normal. In particular, you have to ensure John gets all of his mail. So you will take the decoded message that was intended for John and encode it using John's real public key (this is why you saved a copy of that key). Now all you have to do is send the newly encoded message on to John, with a forged e-mail header so that it looks like it came from the original sender. When John finally receives the message, he will decode it with his private key and everything will appear to be as it should be. John won't have a clue that his e-mail has been tampered with. Figure 12.4 illustrates how all this is done.

You can now monitor all of John's incoming e-mail and never cause any suspicion. Once the packet sniffer has been set up and the counterfeit key has been planted, everything else you need to do can be totally automated so that no significant delays slow down the delivery of John's incoming mail. John will have no way of knowing that his privacy has been violated unless he realizes that the key in the public directory has been altered.

The interception of encrypted e-mail is no small undertaking. It requires somewhat sophisticated expertise as well as security breaches that are illegal under various state and/or federal laws. So the scenario described here is highly unlikely. However, it *is* feasible, and feasibility is all it takes to make a security problem.

The solution to this problem lies in the integrity of public key directories. Adding a key to one of these directories or changing an existing key in a directory must be done only when legitimate and authorized by the appropriate person. For that matter, any public keys that can be exchanged privately should also be subject to careful scrutiny. Since e-mail is not secure, anyone can intercept public keys that are distributed through e-mail and then substitute counterfeit keys, all without arousing suspicion. You need to know who really owns all of these keys.

The process of identifying a person as the legitimate owner of a public key is called **key authentication**. A lot of thought has gone into this process. Different levels of authentication have been identified, ranging from risky

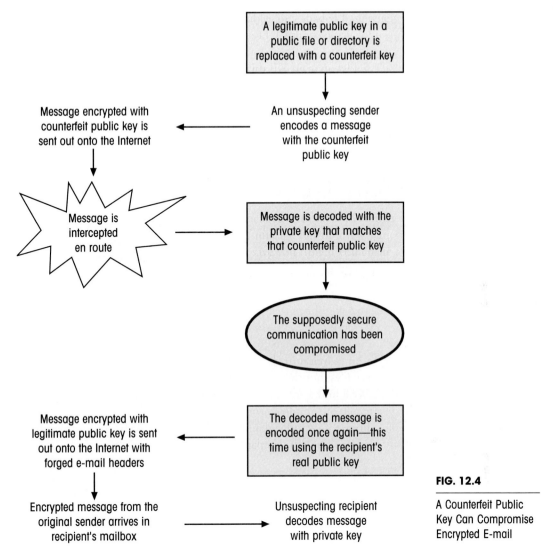

FIG. 12.4

A Counterfeit Public Key Can Compromise Encrypted E-mail

(unprotected) digital distributions to highly secure distributions made at public meetings in the presence of colleagues and associates who are willing to vouch for the identity of anyone distributing a public key. Many rituals have been proposed for secure key exchanges.

Key authentication is a special case of a more general problem related to digital signatures. When you send a letter on paper, you guard against forgeries by including a written signature that is recognizable to at least those correspondents who know you well enough to know your signature. It is an imperfect system, but it does offer some degree of security. If more security is needed, you can sign papers in the presence of a notary public, who stamps the paper with a unique impression and signs off on the document as well. This is a good system, as long as no one steals the stamp. Most reasonable systems can be breached if someone really wants to.

When someone accepts a public key and uses it for encoding a message, they need to understand the level of risk associated with that key. If the level of risk is too great, the key shouldn't be used. Everyone should decide for themselves how much risk they are willing to assume.

12.5 ▶ "Pretty Good Privacy"

Double-key cryptography is more than a theoretical pipe dream. It's a reality. A very popular implementation of double-key cryptography is available in a computer program called **Pretty Good Privacy** (**PGP**). There is a good chance that PGP will creep into your e-mail client sooner or later, so I'll demystify it a bit here.

The actual algorithm that generates key pairs and makes it so difficult to crack a PGP code is rather technical and requires some familiarity with mathematics. But you don't have to understand the technical underpinnings of PGP in order to feel at home with its operation. PGP-encoded files are normally binary files, but they also can be encoded as ASCII files for easy e-mail transfers. We'll look here at some ASCII output for the sake of seeing something printable.

Some people advertise their public key on the Web, so you may have already seen one. Here is what a PGP public key looks like:

```
——-BEGIN PGP PUBLIC KEY BLOCK——-
Version: 2.6.2

mQBNAzKwvR4AAAECANN071G1RrvXfdtd5Ay1OsST4A+72Y1p1H1vIfp2C
JPPc1ESKzw00ItB7dxF3KtjI2vYYe12/Lpu8136i4LXOzkABRG0CG1hbm
R1cnNv
=MxBA
——-END PGP PUBLIC KEY BLOCK——-
```

If you were to copy a public key like this from a Web page, PGP could add it to a **virtual key ring** where PGP collects copies of public keys for your convenience. A virtual key ring is just a file that contains encryption keys. To add a key to your key ring file, you need to know the name of the person associated with the key and his or her e-mail address. A properly created PGP key already contains all of this information bundled with the key itself.

Here's an example message that's been encoded with a PGP key:

```
—-BEGIN PGP MESSAGE—-
Version: 2.6.2

hEwD8136i4LX0zkBAf4q261Umb4Wgx8758C2r14EsQUA3fQLoc3CQEYpr
weaQP3NJPguCEvhf+1VxzTok8NdiU+SENMfz0xk5U6GbeW0pgAAAN30a1
zKWvoXIPWid6rz+pn4KqY0Q+s4kNSDXZPWSn26Y/iG77MxIYwcxmt/uwe
+FqB99avYcPN6rJkUZMvcOJuB1VKNTTXdJQoH149rE8Y1u9603pFs1mv7
QHG27i7Yew/oj9VXnwaCOsjnjwwGBAdLLJgQ5hGMYPKDMfbcFIFP04ftG
CP94UdsqiY4UNs7ImL2y5yLJ+EOIz6xxbriWe2uWNGj63Ka3BgdNnw05b
T1ZDxF0p55vRaDiHGz14BU21hF0LJ5bumga6U23j50Ex+nw/+Qula6+gW
blFefjA==
=6d5D
—-END PGP MESSAGE—-
```

If this were a message encoded with your public key, it could be decoded only with your private key. If it were encoded with someone else's public key, you couldn't decode it.

Once PGP software has been installed, it is very easy to set up a key pair for yourself and a key ring for other people's public keys.

Figure 12.5 shows the most commonly used PGP commands (for Pretty Good Privacy™ 2.6.2 operating on a UNIX host). The command for generating a key pair asks you to enter a password or phrase for your private key. It also asks you to specify a level of security. PGP lets you create keys at various complexity levels. Longer keys produce codes that are harder to crack. For example, a 1,024-bit PGP key is suitable for military communications. A long key takes a little more time to generate (a 1,024-bit key might take about 5 minutes on a Mac), but longer keys do not slow encoding and decoding operations, so there is no serious overhead associated with the highest security levels. Here is a trace of PGP creating a key pair on a UNIX platform:

```
e118:~> pgp -kg
No configuration file found.
Pretty Good Privacy(tm) 2.6.2 - Public-key encryption
for the masses.(c) 1990-1994 Philip Zimmermann, Phil's
Pretty Good Software. 11 Oct 94 Uses the RSAREF(tm)
Toolkit, which is copyright RSA Data Security, Inc.
Distributed by the Massachusetts Institute of
Technology.
Export of this software may be restricted by the U.S.
government. Current time: 1997/05/16 12:45 GMT
Pick your RSA key size:
    1)    512 bits- Low commercial grade, fast but less
          secure
```

```
    2)  768 bits- High commercial grade, medium speed,
        good security
    3)  1024 bits- "Military" grade, slow, highest
        security
Choose 1, 2, or 3, or enter desired number of bits: 2
Generating an RSA key with a 768-bit modulus.

You need a user ID for your public key.  The desired
form for this user ID is your name, followed by your
E-mail address enclosed in <angle brackets>, if you
have an E-mail address.
```

Getting Started

To generate your own unique public/private key pair: **pgp -kg**

To add a public key to your key ring: **pgp -ka filename**
where the file you specify contains a PGP key.

For help on other key management functions: **pgp -k**

Encrypting a File

To encrypt a plain text file with the recipient's public key, first make sure you have the recipient's public key on your key ring. Then, make sure you know the correct userid for your recipient. You can use the command **pgp -kc** to review all the keys (and userids) on your key ring.

  pgp -e filename userid   (creates the binary file filename.pgp)
  pgp -ea filename userid   (creates the ASCII file filename.asc)

Signing a File

To clear sign a plaintext file with your private key:
            pgp -sat +clearsig=on filename

To sign a plaintext file with your private key, and then encrypt it with a recipient's public key:
            pgp -es filename userid (for a binary file)
            pgp -esa filename userid (for an ASCII file)

Decoding a Document or Verifying a Signature

For signature verification you will first need the necessary public key on your key ring.

            pgp filename

FIG. 12.5

The Most Commonly-
Used PGP Commands

```
For example:  John Q. Smith <12345.6789@compuserve.com>
Enter a user ID for your public key:
Lee Cunningham <lcunning@elux3.cs.umass.edu>

You need a pass phrase to protect your RSA secret key.
Your pass phrase can be any sentence or phrase and may
have many words, spaces, punctuation, or any other
printable characters.

Enter pass phrase:
Enter same pass phrase again:
Note that key generation is a lengthy process.

We need to generate 337 random bits.  This is done by
measuring the time intervals between your keystrokes.
Please enter some random text on your keyboard until you
hear the beep:
   0 * -Enough, thank you.
h.....................................****  .........****
Key generation completed.
```

Note that the user can specify the level of desired security. A 512-bit key is probably good enough for anyone not involved in espionage, but most PGP users opt for 1,024 bits.

PGP Signatures

12.6

One of the most useful features of PGP is the ability to generate a **PGP signature**. A PGP signature is a document validation device that operates as a safeguard against forgeries and alterations to an original document. A PGP signature is used by an author when distributing important information to reassure receivers that the information is authentic, untouched by intermediate hands, and authored by the identified author. You may see one in an e-mail message, a Usenet article, or on a Web page. The inclusion of a PGP signature enables the receiver to verify the integrity of a document that has gone out over the Internet.

A PGP signature differs from its handwritten namesake in one important way: It changes from document to document. A PGP signature contains information about the person who signed it, *as well as information about the document being signed*. This makes it impossible to forge a PGP signature by taking a signature from one document and inserting it into a different document. A transplanted PGP signature won't fit any document except its original one. A PGP-signed document can also safeguard against the possibility of counterfeit keys, as long as the recipient bothers to verify the signature.

If you don't need to encode the document, you can put a PGP signature on a plain text file and distribute the text as a readable document. A PGP signature attached to a plain text file is called a **clear signature**, and a file signed with a clear signature is called **clear-signed**. Here is what a clear-signed text file looks like:

```
—-BEGIN PGP SIGNED MESSAGE—-

5/12/97 voting results

Smith 27
Jones 23
Fox    16
Webb   12

—-BEGIN PGP SIGNATURE—-
Version: 2.6.2

iQBVAwUBM3en5sY2EipHoMxpAQGLXgH/ahfFSW/7uwBGHsloz1DiLQWC2
3gNm2S7B6kIusLnYH2v/BkIAKUu5+ULTLb3QBRMNmLC1DD31d1Fxs1sYY
uyHQ==
=p1dn
—-END PGP SIGNATURE—-
```

The body of the text that was present at the time of the signing is marked "BEGIN PGP SIGNED MESSAGE"; the PGP signature appears at the bottom. If this message went out via e-mail to 100 people, each could verify the authenticity of its contents by running a PGP signature check using the author's public PGP key. For example, I would generate PGP signatures with my private PGP key and then anyone can verify my clear-signed documents with a copy of my public PGP key.

Let's see how someone on the receiving end could verify this message by checking my signature. Assume that the receiver already has a copy of my public PGP key on his or her virtual key ring. If the signed message resides in a file called comm.txt.asc, a single PGP command can check my signature and verify the message:

```
e119:~/.pgp> pgp comm.txt.asc
No configuration file found.
Pretty Good Privacy(tm) 2.6.2 - Public-key encryption
for the masses. (c) 1990-1994 Philip Zimmermann, Phil's
Pretty Good Software. 11 Oct 94 Uses the RSAREF(tm)
Toolkit, which is copyright RSA Data Security, Inc.
Distributed by the Massachusetts Institute of
Technology.
Export of this software may be restricted by the U.S.
government.
Current time: 1997/05/12 23:32 GMT
```

```
File has signature. Public key is required to check
signature. .
Good signature from user "Prof. Lehnert
<lehnert@elux3.cs.umass.edu>".
Signature made 1997/05/12 23:30 GMT
```

PGP not only identifies the signature as mine but also ensures that the body of the message was not altered after I signed it. Here's what happens if I edit `comm.txt.asc` and then try to verify the message. I'll change the vote count for Smith from 27 to 20, changing nothing in the file but the 7 in 27. After that one minor edit, we'll try to verify the document to see if everything is still okay:

```
e119:~/.pgp> pgp comm.txt.asc
No configuration file found.
Pretty Good Privacy(tm) 2.6.2 - Public-key encryption
for the masses. (c) 1990-1994 Philip Zimmermann, Phil's
Pretty Good Software. 11 Oct 94 Uses the RSAREF(tm)
Toolkit, which is copyright RSA Data Security, Inc.
Distributed by the Massachusetts Institute of
Technology.
Export of this software may be restricted by the U.S.
government.
Current time: 1997/05/12 23:36 GMT

File has signature. Public key is required to check
signature. . WARNING: Bad signature, doesn't match file
contents!

Bad signature from user "Prof. Lehnert
<lehnert@elux3.cs.umass.edu>".
Signature made 1997/05/12 23:30 GMT
```

PGP warns us that the signature does not match the file's contents. This tells us that the file checked is not the file signed. Clear signatures are a good way to make sure that information moves across the Internet untouched and unscathed.

Note that a clear signature is created by one person with the expectation that anyone should be able to verify it. An encrypted document can be created by anyone with the expectation that only one person can read it. Clear-signed documents are like an inverse of encrypted documents. You use a private key to create a signature, and a public key to verify it. You use a public key to create an encrypted document, and a private key to decode it. When you have a PGP key pair, either key can be used to unravel an encoding created by the other key, so the same key pair can be used for both signatures and encryption. This makes PGP an elegant solution to the dual demands of document encryption and digital signatures. See Figure 12.6.

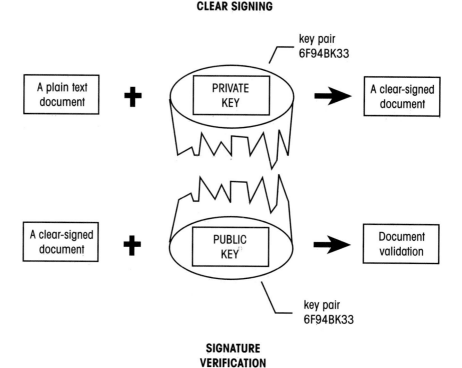

CLEAR SIGNING

key pair
6F94BK33

A plain text
document

+

PRIVATE
KEY

A clear-signed
document

A clear-signed
document

+

PUBLIC
KEY

Document
validation

key pair
6F94BK33

**SIGNATURE
VERIFICATION**

FIG. 12.6

Clear Signing and
Signature Verification

When I place a clear signature on a document, PGP asks me for my password or phrase before it applies my private key. As long as I am the only person who knows my word or phrase, my PGP signature is secure. No one else will be able to generate PGP signatures using my private key, even if they somehow get their hands on my private key. For maximal security, I could clear-sign a document and then encode it using my recipient's public key. Then my recipient would use his or her private key to decode the message and a copy of my public key to verify my signature. PGP makes it possible for my recipient to do all of this with a single command. A communication that is both signed and encrypted using PGP is very secure.

Utah and Wyoming recently passed laws that make digital signatures legally binding for certain kinds of transactions. To use a PGP signature for legal purposes, you should consult a lawyer to see if a PGP signature will be recognized as a valid form of identification.

PGP signatures are also used for **key certification**. Key certification is the process of attaching a PGP signature to a key along with a claim for its authenticity. Whenever you add a public key to your public key ring, you need to guard against counterfeit keys. So PGP asks a lot of questions whenever you add a new key to your key ring. Following is a trace of PGP accepting a new public key. For this example, assume that Lee Cunningham has a public key for Ann Rodak in a file named arodak.key.pgp. Here is what happens when Lee adds this new key to his key ring:

```
e118:~> pgp -ka arodak.key.pgp
No configuration file found.
Pretty Good Privacy(tm) 2.6.2 - Public-key encryption
for the masses. (c) 1990-1994 Philip Zimmermann, Phil's
Pretty Good Software. 11 Oct 94 Uses the RSAREF(tm)
Toolkit, which is copyright RSA Data Security, Inc.
Distributed by the Massachusetts Institute of Technology.
Export of this software may be restricted by the U.S.
government.
Current time: 1997/05/16 13:02 GMT


Looking for new keys...
pub   512/80B7AF61 1996/12/03   Ann Rodak <arodak@edlab
.cs.umass.edu>

Checking signatures...


Keyfile contains:
   1 new key(s)

One or more of the new keys are not fully certified.
Do you want to certify any of these keys yourself
(y/N)? y

Key for user ID: Ann Rodak <arodak@edlab.cs.umass.edu>
512-bit key, Key ID 80B7AF61, created 1996/12/03
Key fingerprint =  38 57 B7 43 D8 46 FB 33  76 44 13 11
CE 72 FA A0
This key/userID association is not certified.
```

At this point Lee could call Ann on the phone and verify the key's fingerprint in order to make sure this is a valid key. A counterfeit key won't have the same fingerprint as Ann's key. If Lee doesn't want to go to that much trouble, and he certifies the key anyway, he must be absolutely certain that this is a legitimate key:

```
Do you want to certify this key yourself (y/N)? y

Looking for key for user 'Ann Rodak':

Key for user ID: Ann Rodak <arodak@edlab.cs.umass.edu>
512-bit key, Key ID 80B7AF61, created 1996/12/03
Key fingerprint = 38 57 B7 43 D8 46 FB 33 76 44 13 11
CE 72 FA A0
```

```
READ CAREFULLY: Based on your own direct first-hand
knowledge, are you absolutely certain that you are
prepared to solemnly certify that the above public key
actually belongs to the user specified by the
above user ID (y/N)? y
```

When Lee answers "yes," he is indicating his willingness to **certify** this key and put his own PGP signature on it. Lee's signature has now been added to this copy of Ann's key and will be there if Lee ever passes the key to someone else. Lee should think carefully before putting his signature on the key. Lee's private PGP key is used to generate Lee's signature. So Lee needs to enter his password or phrase before his signature can go on the key:

```
You need a pass phrase to unlock your RSA secret key.
Key for user ID "Lee Cunningham <lcunning@elux3.cs
.umass.edu>"

Enter pass phrase: Pass phrase is good. Just a moment...
Key signature certificate added.

Make a determination in your own mind whether this key
actually belongs to the person whom you think it belongs
to, based on available evidence. If you think it does,
then based on your estimate of that person's integrity
and competence in key management, answer the following
question:

Would you trust "Ann Rodak"
to act as an introducer and certify other people's
public keys to you?
(1=I don't know. 2=No. 3=Usually. 4=Yes, always.) ? 1
```

In answering this last question, Lee has to decide how meaningful Ann's signature is when it appears on other public keys. If Lee ever picks up another public key signed by Ann, PGP will check to see if Lee considers Ann a trustworthy key certifier.

All this care is taken because key integrity is a potential weak spot in PGP. As long as all the keys we use are valid, strong PGP keys are impossible to crack. If a PGP failure ever occurs, it is likely to happen as a breach in key authentication.

When you view the contents of a key ring, you can see all of the signatures associated with each key and what level of security applies to each signature (in the opinion of the key ring owner):

```
el18:~> pgp -kc
No configuration file found.
Pretty Good Privacy(tm) 2.6.2 - Public-key encryption
for the masses. (c) 1990-1994 Philip Zimmermann, Phil's
```

```
Pretty Good Software. 11 Oct 94 Uses the RSAREF(tm)
Toolkit, which is copyright RSA Data Security, Inc.
Distributed by the Massachusetts Institute of
Technology.
Export of this software may be restricted by the U.S.
government.
Current time: 1997/05/16 13:05 GMT

Key ring: '/users/users3/fac/lehnert/.pgp/pubring.pgp'
Type   bits/keyID   Date       User ID
pub    512/80B7AF61 1996/12/03 Ann Rodak <arodak@edlab.cs
.umass.edu>
sig!       C2309975 1997/05/16 Lee Cunningham
<lcunning@elux3.cs.umass.edu>
pub    768/C2309975 1997/05/16 Lee Cunningham
<lcunning@elux3.cs.umass.edu>

   KeyID      Trust      Validity       User ID
   80B7AF61   unknown    complete    Ann Rodak
<arodak@edlab.cs.umass.edu>
c             ultimate               Lee Cunningham
<lcunning@elux3.cs.umass.edu>
* C2309975    ultimate   complete Lee Cunningham
<lcunning@elux3.cs.umass.edu>
```

An ultimate level of trust is given to any keys signed by the owner of the key ring. ***Never certify a PGP key unless you are absolutely confident that the key is valid.*** If you transfer your copy of the key to another person, your PGP signature and reputation for credibility automatically goes with it. A PGP key that passes through many hands can accumulate a number of signatures with different authentication values. Then each new user can examine the available signatures and decide whether the key seems to be a good risk.

Why Is PGP Available to Everyone?

12.7

Some software is written by professional programmers because they are paid to write it. Other software is written by students who are playing around and having fun. Programmers learn their craft by experimenting and playing with ideas that interest them; some highly innovative programs take shape when programmers are just playing around. So a lot of wonderful software is not created within corporate environments as a part of someone's job description.

When software is created by programmers working on their own time and their own equipment, those individuals own the resulting creations and can sell them or give them away as they wish.

If all of your software has come from your neighborhood computer store, you may wonder why on earth programmers would ever give away their software. The answer lies in the origins of the Internet and the culture of the programming community.

In the Internet culture, software is never truly finished. Powerful software lives, evolves, and benefits from the contributions of multiple caretakers. One person codes up a nice tool and then passes it on to anyone who wants it, for free. A second person picks it up, adds some nice features to it and then makes this newer version available to anyone who wants it. Then a third person . . . you get the idea. This tradition of freestyle software development makes perfect sense in academic environments, where ideas are freely shared and no one is being paid to produce off-the-shelf software.

Freestyle software development is not consistent with corporate models for productivity, but it does explain why so much progress on the Internet seems to have happened by accident. Some of the best ideas on the Internet (e.g., e-mail, Usenet, and the Web) were never anticipated by anyone in a position to authorize projects and set deadlines. Some software is available simply because somebody had an idea that was good enough to catch on. This can happen only in a community that shares all of its ideas openly.

It helps to keep this cultural Zeitgeist in mind when considering Phil Zimmermann. Phil was a software specialist with an interest in cryptography and privacy, and he gave away the most powerful encryption technology ever developed: PGP. He wrote PGP and gave it to the Internet community just as thousands of programmers have written programs and handed them off to anyone who wanted them. But before I tell the story of Phil Zimmermann, first consider why government officials have a vested interest in cryptography software.

12.8   Strong Encryption and Law Enforcement

Suppose that strong cryptography is available for general use. Anyone can generate his or her own pair of keys, post a public key in a public directory, and exchange encrypted e-mail with anyone else. The codes for these keys cannot be cracked. This means that terrorists can safely communicate with one another and say anything without fear of discovery. Criminals can plan robberies and plot murders. Right-wing militia leaders can debate the best way to stage a retaliation for the attack on the Branch Davidians in Waco, Texas. Religious extremists can talk about which abortion clinic to bomb next. A plot to assassinate the President can be fine-tuned. In short, communications that used to require face-to-face meetings in very private settings can now be conducted with blinding speed over unimaginable distances. Material that wouldn't be trusted to a phone conversation or a mail service is perfectly safe on the Internet, because powerful cryptography is available to anyone who wants it.

Even before the advent of computer-based communications, law enforcement agencies had technological capabilities that enabled them to eavesdrop on certain conversations. With a court order, the police can tap a phone line or a local postmaster can open a piece of mail. The FBI has a variety of surveillance techniques used to listen in on private conversations. Although these powers can and have been abused on occasion, they also provide law enforcement personnel with legitimate weapons for combating crime and terrorism. Some people believe that the loss of these powers would be tantamount to pulling the plug on law enforcement.

Powerful cryptography on the Internet pulls the law enforcement plug in a big way. As long as the codes can't be cracked, there is no way for the FBI to monitor an encrypted e-mail conversation between suspected criminals. Encrypted communications would make it much harder for the police to collect evidence in a criminal investigation. Drug dealers, organized crime, terrorist organizations, and random criminals can all use strong encryption to great advantage. So the government has a strong vested interest in cryptography. Digital communications and strong encryption open the door for problems unlike anything seen before. The distribution of PGP over the Internet has brought strong encryption into the hands of the masses, good and bad alike. People who use PGP today routinely create 1,024-bit private keys, thereby ensuring a level of security like that of top-secret military communications.

What can the government hope to do about this technology? One possibility is to outlaw the use of strong cryptography. Cryptography software would be restricted and distributed only to authorized personnel, probably through some sort of government licensing. The good guys could have it, but the bad guys couldn't (or at least shouldn't). This is the only scenario that gives law enforcement agencies a fighting chance against strong cryptography.

There are problems with this, however. Some people would oppose laws outlawing strong cryptography based, at least in part, on the First Amendment. Another problem is the global nature of the Internet. A law that applies to U.S. citizens would not be enforceable for messages exchanged by non-U.S. citizens. We might be able to prohibit our own citizens from using strong cryptography, but how can we hope to control the rest of the world's population?

In a preemptive strike, the U.S. government has made a highly controversial attempt to limit the spread of strong cryptography by making it illegal to export it outside of the United States and Canada. Cryptographic software has been categorized as "munitions," and hence the unregulated export of encryption programs is prohibited under the International Traffic in Arms Regulations, a set of laws usually used against illegal arms dealers. Advocates of free speech aren't the only ones who find fault with this restriction. Commercial software vendors claim that it ties their hands with respect to all software development involving encryption. Other countries are selling products with strong encryption (128 bits and more), but U.S. companies can sell only products that use inferior encryption (40 bits, or 56 bits under certain circumstances), provided they want to steer clear of possible export violations. No laws have been passed to limit the use of strong cryptography *within* the United States, but steps have been taken by the government to insert classified encryption software into all digital communication devices manufactured in this country.

Governmental control of digital communications could be quietly accomplished with the cooperation of major hardware manufacturers in the absence of legislation and public debate. Here's how it would work: Double-key cryptography would be hard-wired into all computer chips inserted into modems, telephones, and other network communication devices. Then any computer communication over the Internet would have to pass through a government-approved encryption chip. Files going onto the Internet would automatically be encoded using strong cryptography approved by the government, and files coming off the Internet would be automatically decoded using the same technology. Everything would be handled behind the scenes by ubiquitous encryption chips. A casual user wouldn't even have to know that any of this was going on.

Each encryption chip would be programmed with its own unique key pair. To give law enforcement the power to monitor encrypted communications, the government would need access to all of the private keys in all of the encryption chips. This would be done by a **key escrow** system. Under a key escrow system, whenever an encryption chip was manufactured, a copy of its private key would be handed to the government for safekeeping and indexed by its serial number. No one would have access to any of these private keys except under a court order authorizing a digital wire tap. Then the serial numbers of the relevant devices would be used to retrieve the necessary private keys for the proper authorities. This would effectively give law enforcement personnel a "back door" into all Internet communications.

A key escrow system is the government's best bet for digital wiretapping. Unfortunately, anyone who wanted to defy an authorized wiretap could get their hands on their own cryptography software and encode messages using keys that aren't held in escrow. This would sabotage the whole key escrow system. A key escrow system can work only if powerful encryption software is not available to the general public. Law enforcement would be needed to restrict the activities of computer programmers and other technical people who might be inclined to play around with cryptography. But how many programmers could do what Phil Zimmermann did? How many people could implement and release powerful encryption software into the software underground? A war on encryption software seems unlikely to stem the tide of grassroots encryption.

Strong Encryption and the Internet Culture

12.9

What goes on between a programmer and his or her hard drive is a very private matter. Programmers are intensely loyal to favorite programming languages, and their fascination with particular problems leads them to identify with specific programming techniques. They embrace projects with intensity and experience a gamut of emotions when engaged in long-term projects. Frustration, excitement, pride, and euphoria are all part of the programming experience. Practicing members of the programming community support and help one another by sharing tips, tricks, and tools. There is a very strong sense of community among programmers, and shared software is the lifeblood of this community. So the idea of some government bureaucrat decreeing certain software off-limits raises the hackles of most computer programmers. Software is closer to the world of ideas than the world of things, so any move to outlaw a category of software seems downright fascist to most programmers. To them, it is only one small step away from thought control.

At one time, government officials hoped to suppress the spread of strong cryptography by pressuring software manufacturers to avoid it. With strong cryptography categorized as a munitions and a munitions export restriction in place, anyone responsible for letting strong cryptography slip into the wrong hands could be prosecuted for violating an export regulation. This was reason enough to dissuade the software houses from getting heavily involved in cryptography. Software is a tough enough business without risking prison simply for the sake of a sale. The resulting "moratorium" on strong commercial cryptography has been very effective.

But prohibitions that apply to software companies can't touch the lone programmer who writes software for other reasons. Thousands of programmers write software just for the fun of it. A few write software because they actually believe their efforts will make the world a slightly better place. Phil Zimmermann was one of those programmers.

Phil was profoundly bothered by the possibility that privacy might become the property of a federal agency. He read some theoretical papers on cryptography and pieced together the techniques he needed to implement a strong cryptography package. The resulting PGP package made it possible for users to generate key pairs for strong encryption. It also gave them a lot of convenient utilities for encoding, decoding, and managing collections of PGP keys on virtual key rings. PGP was strong encryption bundled in a neat little box, ready for the masses (or at least the masses on the Internet). It also represented a law enforcement nightmare.

Phil believes that strong cryptography belongs in the hands of the people. A copy of PGP was posted to a Usenet newsgroup in June of 1991, although Phil didn't post it himself. After a few news reader keystrokes, the PGP genie was out of the bottle and could never be stuffed back into the theoretical journals from whence it came. Most of the fallout landed on Phil, but he did not stand alone. Phil may have acted alone when he released PGP, but his actions were widely supported by the Internet community.

Phil was the object of a Grand Jury investigation for three years, during which time messages were circulated on the Internet soliciting support for his defense fund. Phil was very good at handling interviews, and his lucid descriptions of PGP attracted an even broader audience to his cause. News pertaining to the Grand Jury investigation was posted on the Internet, and the on-line community braced itself for an indictment. In the meantime, PGP slowly attracted more attention and support. People found that PGP was well documented and easy to use. Public key directories were created and technical folk began to post their public PGP key in their signature files and on their Web pages. Respected authorities on computer security used PGP to clear-sign documents so as to prevent e-mail forgeries. PGP interfaces and add-ons were written for existing mail programs in order to create privacy-enhanced e-mail capabilities. While commercial vendors have steered clear of PGP because of the export laws, the programming community is openly creating and sharing code using PGP outside of the commercial sector.

Massachusetts Institute of Technology (MIT) is the official distribution site for PGP. Downloading PGP from MIT involves the most complicated downloading procedure on the Internet. You have to answer a set of questions and swear to answer them truthfully. If you are not a U.S. or Canadian citizen, you cannot legally download it. If you give PGP to someone who is not a U.S. or Canadian citizen, you can be prosecuted for violating U.S. export regulations. If you lie or misrepresent yourself, you can be prosecuted for fraud. MIT does not police the distribution of PGP, but they do what they need to do to distribute PGP without violating the law. This presumably includes maintaining a record of all Internet addresses receiving PGP downloads. Although the original PGP software was written for UNIX, MIT now distributes versions for Mac's and DOS platforms as well. Other sources distribute PGP for PC Windows (see the Internet 101 Web pages for pointers).

No one knows how many computers house a copy of PGP and how many of those copies are illegal or pirated from secondary sources. As has been emphasized time and time again, the technology of the Internet makes it very easy to do things that may not be legal.

What's Next?   12.10

Phil Zimmermann often explains PGP via an analogy involving letters and postcards. He argues that encrypted e-mail is like a letter in an envelope. A letter in an envelope is a private communication, and everyone takes that privacy for granted. An e-mail message that is not encrypted is like a message on a postcard. Anyone can read what you write on the back of a postcard, so people don't put a lot of sensitive personal information on postcards.

No one needs to defend their right to put a letter in an envelope. No one assumes that you are engaged in an illegal activity just because you choose to put a letter in an envelope. In the same way, no one should assume that you are up to something suspect if you prefer to encrypt your e-mail. You are just asking for the same level of privacy that an envelope affords you. If someone denies you that level of privacy, they are effectively saying you must put everything you write on postcards for all the world to see.

The letter/postcard analogy is provocative for anyone who thought that e-mail communications were private or secure. Phil is right about the lack of security inherent in unencrypted e-mail. If you wouldn't want to write something on a postcard, you shouldn't put it in unencrypted e-mail. But the postcard analogy is not quite accurate when you consider that the Postmaster General can open envelopes containing letters when authorized by a court order. PGP is not like a letter in an envelope because no one can inspect a PGP file unless they hold the one and only private key that can decode the file. The analogy breaks down when you realize that the U.S. Post Office never has to cope with anything analogous to private PGP keys.

PGP is still a toy for the technically inclined. It hasn't trickled down to the AOLers, and in its current form, it never will. But countless programmers and computer specialists are using it now. It will be very difficult to convince those people to delete their PGP files if a law is ever passed that makes PGP illegal.

In January 1996, Phil Zimmermann's Grand Jury was disbanded—no indictment was issued. The case against Phil was either too precarious or otherwise inadvisable to pursue. This makes some people think that grassroots cryptography is here to stay. As soon as the commercial vendors feel that it's safe to build PGP into their products, strong encryption is likely to be integrated into all network communication packages. Phil appears to be betting on the eventual commercialization of PGP. Shortly after the Grand Jury halted its investigation, he founded his own company to develop enhanced versions of PGP with easy-to-use GUIs.

In the meantime, the federal government has not abandoned its key escrow idea. Digital wiretap legislation is periodically reviewed by Congress, and its proponents show no signs of giving up. President Clinton supports the development of a digital communications standard from which to construct a government-controlled key escrow system. Only time will tell if the digital world will some day be permeated by trap doors. In the meantime, PGP is still subject to export restrictions and one is well-advised to honor the legal restrictions that pertain to PGP.

12.11   Where to Learn More

There are numerous online resources on the Internet 101 Web pages. Also available are published books that describe the programming culture, cryptography in general, and PGP in particular, including these:

Hackers: Heroes of the Computer Revolution, Steven Levy, Dell Publishing, New York, NY, 1994.

> An engaging description of the early (1960s) programming community, with insights into current Internet attitudes toward privacy, open communication, and administrative authority.

The Codebreakers: The Story of Secret Writing, David Kahn, Macmillan, New York, NY, 1967.

> The story of encryption and the research effort conducted during World War II.

The Puzzle Palace: A Report on America's Most Secret Agency, James Bamford, Houghton Mifflin Company, Boston, MA, 1982.

> All about the National Security Agency and its national security mission.

The Official PGP User's Guide, Phil Zimmermann, MIT Press, Cambridge, MA, 1995.

PGP: Source Code and Internals, Phil Zimmermann, MIT Press, Cambridge, MA, 1995.

PGP: Pretty Good Privacy, Simson Garfinkel, O'Reilly & Associates, Sebastopol, CA, 1994.

Protect Your Privacy—A Guide for PGP Users, William Stallings, Prentice-Hall, Englewood Cliffs, NJ, 1994.

PROBLEMS AND EXERCISES

1. Explain why double-key cryptography is superior to single-key cryptography.
2. Where can people post public PGP keys?
3. Why hasn't PGP been incorporated into commercial e-mail programs?
4. When was PGP posted on a Usenet newsgroup?
5. Who can legally download PGP from the MIT site?
6. How can someone intercept and read encrypted e-mail?
7. What is a PGP signature, and what do you need to verify it?
8. Describe a situation in which you would want to use a clear signature.
9. Under what conditions should you certify a public PGP key?
10. **[Hands-on]** Phil Zimmermann posted a signed statement to the Cypherpunks mailing list on October 21, 1994. Locate a copy of this post on the Web. From it, find out who is trying to develop a version of PGP in Europe.

The following exercises are for people who want to install PGP and use it. If possible, work with a partner who is also learning PGP. If you know someone who already uses PGP, you can ask that person to act as your partner for these exercises.

11. **[Hands-on]** Download and install PGP. Read any short instructions or brief introductions that come with your installation. Make sure you are not breaking any laws and make sure you have an official version of PGP. A long, two-part user's guide written by Phil Zimmermann should be part of your package. If it is not, you do not have an official version and you should look for one.

12. **[Hands-on]** Create a test key pair. Don't plan to post this public key anywhere; it's only for these exercises. Select a 1,024-bit key and time the key generation process. How long does it take to generate your keys? Pick a password or phrase you won't forget.

13. **[Hands-on]** Encrypt a text file using your public key. Make sure you generate an ASCII version of the encrypted file. Look at your encrypted file. Is it longer than the original file?

14. **[Hands-on]** Decode the file you created in Problem 13 using your private key. Check this new file to see if it looks like the original.

15. **[Hands-on]** Exchange public keys with your partner. To send your partner your public key, you must first copy it from your key ring to a file. If you create an ASCII version of the key, you can send it to your partner via plain e-mail. To add your friend's public key to your key ring, you first must put it in a file (or select it if you are in a point-and-click PGP environment).

16. **[Hands-on]** Display your public key ring and make sure your partner's key is there. How many bits are in your partner's key? How many signatures are in your partner's key?

17. **[Hands-on]** Create a text file that you want to send to your partner. Sign it with your private key and encrypt it with your partner's public key. Make sure you generate an ASCII version of the encrypted file. Then mail it to your partner. Ask your partner to do the same for you.

18. **[Hands-on]** Decode the encrypted message you receive from your partner. Check the signature and make sure it's valid. Check with your partner to see if your message came through ok.

19. **[Hands-on]** Create a text file and add a clear signature to it using your private key. Send this file to your partner and see if he or she can validate your signature with your public key. You might want to edit your file after you sign it and see if your partner reports a problem with the signature. Ask your partner to send you a file with a clear signature on it so that you can try to verify the signature.

Social Issues

13

"The future belongs to those who believe in the beauty of their dreams."

- ELEANOR ROOSEVELT

THE INTERNET 101 WEB PAGES

- Internet Watchdog Organizations
- Computer Crime Laws
- Articles about Copyright Issues
- Surfer Beware (an EPIC Report on Privacy)

Illegal Activities: How to Stay Out of Trouble

13.1

A number of illegal activities can be conducted online, some by people who don't even realize they are breaking the law. Many offenses won't attract the attention of the police, but they nevertheless will jeopardize your Internet access privileges. Ignorance is never an acceptable defense, so it's important to understand your responsibilities as a good Netizen.

Computer technologies and public networks make it easy to copy and distribute lots of information that originated elsewhere. ***Just because something may be easy to do doesn't make doing it ethical or legal.*** And don't count on software to regulate your behavior or keep you on the right side of the law. Computers and software can't do anything illegal. It takes a person to commit a crime.

Q: What Sorts of Things Are Illegal?

The thought of illegal activities on the Internet invokes images of caffeine-crazed hackers who break into Pentagon computers at 3 A.M. Computer break-ins are indeed illegal. But there are many other illegal activities that require no great expertise with computers or computer security, including these:

- The unauthorized distribution of copyrighted materials
- The possession of child pornography
- Software piracy
- Chain letters for profit (Ponzi or pyramid schemes)
- Fraudulent advertising or business practices
- The distribution of certain software to parties outside of the United States
- Threatened acts of violence

Each of these activities is illegal both on and off the Internet; there is nothing specific to the Internet here. However, all of them are easier to commit and easier to execute on a grander scale when the perpetrator has Internet access. For example, software files can be easily moved from one Internet host to another. Someone on the Internet saying, "Take it, it's free" might just be issuing an invitation to software piracy.

Q: What Is Software Piracy?

Software piracy is a felony punishable by a jail term and a fine. You are guilty of software piracy if you make or distribute ten or more unauthorized copies of commercial software worth $2,500 or more. Penalties also apply to lesser offenses. Always read the licensing agreement that accompanies commercial software. Whenever you use commercial software, it is your responsibility to understand applicable licensing restrictions. If you find undocumented software on the Internet that seems too good to be true, it probably is. *Legitimate software is always accompanied by a licensing agreement, even when it's freeware.* If you download any software that is not bundled with a licensing agreement, discard the software.

Q: Is It Illegal to "Trash" a Person or a Company Online?

You can get into trouble for posting libelous statements on the Internet. **Libel** is any written or pictorial statement that is damaging to a person or organization. Libel is not a criminal offense, so you can't be sent to jail for it, but you can be sued for damages in a civil court. No one knows how many large corporations monitor online discussions in public forums. However, there have been cases in which an individual was sued when a company representative stumbled across questionable and potentially damaging statements about corporate services or products.

Libelous statements about individuals constitute potential fodder for lawsuits, although individuals are less likely to initiate lawsuits. If you pick on a public figure, you are probably safe. In 1988, a Supreme Court decision established that public figures can be publicly ridiculed, even if that ridicule borders on libel. For example, Bill Gates is a public figure and therefore a fairly safe target. If Bill Gates won a civil suit each time someone said something nasty about him on the Internet, he could probably collect enough money to buy out all of his shareholders. But be careful what you say about people who are less famous. A private individual who has not opted for public life has stronger rights in a libel dispute.

If you must broadcast critical comments about a large corporation, you might want to run it by a lawyer first. Statements about a company's products or services are grounds for libel if they result in lost revenues for the company. The Internet offers ample opportunities for people to make damaging misrepresentations that could have widespread negative consequences. *You can be sued for disseminating information that is deemed harmful to a company, even if the information is accurate.* For example, in 1994 a company named EPS (Electronic Postal Service) began to circulate messages offering free Internet access and cash payments to anyone who was willing to receive commercial e-mail messages. Brock Meeks, the author of an online newsletter, investigated this operation and determined that EPS was operated by SCI (Suarez Corporations Industries). SCI had been involved with a number of direct mail operations that had attracted the interest of state and federal law enforcement agencies in the past. Meeks discovered that SCI was creating mailing lists out of responses to the EPS announcements and using these mailing lists for unsolicited direct mailing campaigns. Meeks described these activities in *Cyberwire Dispatch* and was sued for libel by SCI. The lawsuit was eventually settled out of court, but after considerable expense and inconvenience to Meeks. A private individual or small business owner can probably not compete with the legal resources of a large company. Having truth and right on your side is slim consolation if your financial resources have been drained by a lengthy legal dispute.

Information is difficult to contain on the Internet. All digital communications can be easily reproduced and distributed without your permission, so you can't be sure that a private e-mail communication will remain private. Something you send to a friend today could end up on a Usenet newsgroup tomorrow. Before you send anything out onto the Internet, ask yourself how you would feel if your message turned up on the front page of the local newspaper. If that thought makes you sweat, think again before you post your message. You never know where a digital communication is going to show up.

As far as I know, no "flame wars" have ever resulted in a libel suit, but there's always a first test for everything. I suspect it hasn't happened for two reasons. First, in a typical flame war the person being attacked has ample opportunity to respond in a timely manner and before the same audience. So no one has the upper hand in terms of media access. Second, the people who participate in flame wars are generally very young (probably students) who would find it difficult to establish a basis for damages in the absence of a professional or income-related reputation. There is also often a tongue-in-cheek undercurrent to the more erudite flame wars (check out `alt.folk-lore.urban` for some relatively high-class flames). This presumably renders otherwise damaging statements null and void. A savvy defense lawyer might even try to argue that this tongue-in-cheek undercurrent is universally implicit in the culture of the Internet.

Q: Can I Go to Jail for Using Indecent Language Online?

At the time of this writing, the answer is no. This question was first raised when the Telecommunications Act was approved by Congress in 1995. Part of this legislation was the Communications Decency Act (CDA). The CDA attempted to make the Internet safe for children by outlawing objectionable language on the Internet. President Clinton signed the CDA into law on February 8, 1996. According to the CDA, it was a federal crime to use indecent language on the Internet, punishable by up to two years in jail and a fine of up to $250,000. However, the CDA was worded so vaguely and so broadly that it appeared to be a blatant violation of the First Amendment.

The American Civil Liberties Union (ACLU) challenged the legality of the CDA, slapping U.S. Attorney General Janet Reno with a lawsuit as soon as President Clinton signed it into law. On June 12, 1996, a panel of federal judges ruled, in a unanimous vote of 3 to 0, that the CDA was unconstitutional. According to Judge Dolores K. Sloviter, "[t]he CDA is patently a government-imposed content-based restriction on speech, and the speech at issue, whether denominated 'indecent' or 'patently offensive,' is entitled to constitutional protection." The Court went on to say that, "the evidence and our Findings of Fact based thereon show that Internet communication, while unique, is more akin to telephone communication, at issue in Sable, than to broadcasting, at issue in Pacifica, because, as with the telephone, an Internet user must act affirmatively and deliberately to retrieve specific information online." In other words, no one is going to stumble across offensive material on the Internet without first taking steps to find it.

On June 26, 1997, the U.S. Supreme Court upheld the lower court's ruling, and the CDA was ruled unconstitutional. This decision was viewed as a big victory for freedom of speech and an endorsement of a "hands-off" relationship between the U.S. government and the Internet.

So what defines indecent language? A few specific words have been identified by the Supreme Court as "indecent speech," but those same words are protected by the First Amendment in the context of radio broadcasts. So it seems unlikely that words allowed on the airwaves for public broadcast could be prohibited on the Internet. However, it is up to the court system to examine such questions and render new rulings. We will discuss in greater detail the question of indecent language and its legal status in Section 13.3, "Free Speech and the First Amendment."

Q: Can I Get into Trouble for Simply Having a File?

Sure. If the file is valuable or sensitive and there is no legitimate reason why you should have it, you could be prosecuted for theft. If you're not a thief, this is not likely to happen, but it is possible. People with limited computer skills can still get their hands on files that might incriminate them. For example, pirated software might be freely available to you on the Internet. If you download such software, those files become incriminating evidence if your hard drive happens to be confiscated under a search warrant.

A hacker might post a stolen file to a mailing list or a Usenet newsgroup. If you then save that file to your hard disk, you possess stolen property. If you see something online that looks odd or suspicious, you are advised to leave it alone. If you are concerned about something that looks suspicious, you should report it to your ISP's technical support personnel. Let them decide what, if any, action should be taken.

It is also a felony to possess child pornography. The FBI has conducted sting operations on the Internet to trap people who violate child pornography laws. A pornographic photograph involving a minor could make you a felon if it is found on your computer.

Q: What Things Could Result in the Suspension of My Computer Account?

Now you're talking about activities that might be not illegal in the eyes of the law but which are forbidden by other codes of conduct. For example, suppose you are a student and you have an educational account on a university computer. Most educational computing environments have an Acceptable Use Policy (AUP) (see Chapter 10, Section 10.5, for more about AUPs) that describes legitimate and illegitimate activities for computer users. It is your responsibility to know the AUP for your environment. For example, university AUPs typically prohibit the use of educational facilities for profit, activities that constitute harassment, or anything associated with academic dishonesty.

Good Netizens also know that certain communications on the Internet are frowned upon by system administrators and will not be tolerated by the folks who control computer accounts. So whether you are in an educational environment, in a work environment, or using a commercial ISP, you should know that it is improper to do the following:

- Spam a mailing list or a Usenet news group
- Mail bomb a spammer in retaliation for their spamming activities
- Send unsolicited e-mail of a commercial nature (electronic junk mail)
- Forge an e-mail message or otherwise misrepresent your true identity
- Initiate an electronic chain letter of any kind
- Misuse broadcast e-mail for inappropriate announcements

Offenses of these types may result in a stern warning or the suspension of your computer privileges, depending on the policy of your system administrators.

Q: Can a Lowly Newbie Attract the Attention of the FBI?

Yes. As mentioned earlier, you don't have to be a computer expert to get into big trouble. The FBI watches for the illegal transport of stolen or illegal materials across state lines. Pornography rings that operate over the Internet are obvious targets. Pyramid schemes over the Internet or any other money-making scams that cross state lines are also magnets for FBI attention.

One offense that is very specific to the Internet concerns the distribution of powerful cryptography software outside the United States. As a U.S. citizen, you have legitimate access to the PGP cryptographic software (see Chapter 12). However, export restrictions on powerful cryptography prohibit the transfer of PGP to foreign countries—according to the law, it is munitions. So if you hand off a copy of PGP to someone outside the United States or Canada, you conceivably could be charged with a crime normally reserved for gun runners and arms dealers.

However, the chances of being arrested for a PGP export violation appeared to diminish in 1996 when a grand jury dropped its investigation of Phil Zimmermann, author of PGP (see Chapter 12 for a discussion of the government lawsuit against Phil). If the government decided not to go after Phil, it would be strange for them to pick on someone less instrumental in the worldwide distribution of PGP. Then again, the federal government is full of surprises, so you never know.

Even if you never touch cryptography software, you could still attract the interest of the FBI. There has been at least one case in which a high school student made a casual threat against President Clinton on a Usenet newsgroup (presumably without serious intent) and was subsequently interviewed by FBI agents. It's hard to know on the Internet when someone is kidding. When it comes to threats against the President of the United States, even a smilee emoticon might appear sinister.

Aside from these special cases, it is probably difficult to get into really big trouble if you don't know you're doing something wrong. Law and order in cyberspace is very much a work in progress and is experiencing growing pains. Nevertheless, ignorance of the law and good intentions are a poor defense if you are unlucky enough to be in the wrong place at the wrong time. Think before you leap.

Copyright Law and the Internet　　13.2

Copyright laws protect the creative and economic interests of writers, musicians, and artists. In a free society, creative works should be freely distributed, but with some restrictions. No one should be allowed to steal a creative work, either by taking credit for its creation or assuming the ownership of any resulting revenues.

If you have created a work and wish to distribute it over the Internet, you will want to learn more about copyright law than this book is prepared to teach. You can start by consulting the online references in the Internet 101 Web pages. However, before placing your work online, you also should talk to legal counsel. Make sure you understand the consequences of placing your work online *before* you post anything. For example, if you intend to publish a written work, you should know that some publishers will not publish a work if it has been distributed digitally. Make sure you understand the consequences of placing your work online *before* you post it. Once something has been made available online, you can't take it back.

Chances are you aren't worried about a work of your own creation. Rather, you want to know what you can and can't do with all of the text and graphics that you find online. Web browsers have made it easy to create personal copies of files from all over the world. But what restrictions apply to those files? You need to find the answers to such questions as these:

• Do I have a right to incorporate files found elsewhere on my own Web pages?

- Do I have a right to alter files and make those altered files available online?
- Do I have a right to excerpt material and distribute those excerpts online?
- Do I have a right to print copies of online materials?
- Do I have a right to store on my own personal computer files that I find elsewhere?
- Do I have a right to forward a personal e-mail message to a friend?
- Do I have a right to forward a personal e-mail message to a newsgroup?
- Do I have a right to download a Web page and mail it to a friend?

Popular software makes doing all of these things so easy that you might have assumed it is perfectly okay. Maybe you never gave it any thought. But are these actions legal? Before answering, I'll first discuss the general concept of a copyright. Then I'll return to address each of these questions in detail.

Q: What Is a Copyright?

The foundation for copyright and patent law is found in the U.S. Constitution (Article I, Section 8, Clause 8):

> "The Congress shall have Power ... To promote the Progress of Science and useful Arts, by securing for limited Times to Authors and Inventors the exclusive Right to their respective Writing and Discoveries."

A copyright confers certain rights and privileges to its owner. Copyright privileges are normally granted to the author of a written work (or artist or musician, or similar), but they can be transferred to another individual or company in a contractual agreement. For example, the author of a book typically transfers his or her copyright to a book publisher in exchange for a publishing contract. Sometimes copyright privileges are automatically granted to an individual's employer when a work has been generated in the service of one's job.

A copyright protects not only the creator's economic interests but also the integrity of a work. It does this by authenticating its originality. No one can copyright a work that has prior copyright protection, although someone may challenge the validity of an original copyright if he or she can prove that a work was stolen, plagiarized, or adopted from an existing work and modified in minor ways (an argument most often applied to musical creations). Authors normally want to facilitate a widespread readership, but they also want recognition for their work, as well as compensation for the sale of books, magazine articles, or whatever print distributions take place.

A copyright is a form of intellectual property rights, which is a broader category of legal protections that include patents and trademarks. Written documents are normally protected by copyrights, while artifacts (inventions) are protected by patents. Patents are obtained after a complicated legal procedure, but copyrights are automatically associated with all written documents that contain original material.

Q: Does an Author Renounce Copyright Privileges When a Work Appears Online?

No. An author can relinquish copyright privileges only by putting a work into the public domain. For a work to be placed in the public domain, the author has to include a statement that says, "I grant this to the public domain" (or words to that effect). ***Placing a work online is not equivalent to putting it into the public domain.*** An author can transfer copyright privileges to a specific recipient only through a contractual agreement. Copyright privileges cannot be surrendered in the absence of a contractual agreement.

Q: Aren't All Posts to Mailing Lists and Usenet Newsgroups in the Public Domain?

No. Posts to mailing lists and Usenet newsgroups are all copyrighted and subject to copyright restrictions unless the author expressly places it in the public domain.

Q: Aren't All Older Written Works in the Public Domain? How Can I Tell If Something Is in the Public Domain?

An author is allowed to maintain copyrights on his or her works for life. After the death of an author, the author's heirs or publisher may renew the copyrights for another 50 years. If an author has been dead for 50 years, any materials by that author are considered to be in the public domain. If something is in the public domain, you may distribute it freely in both electronic and print form. For example, all of the electronic texts found in Project Gutenberg (`http://jg.cso.uiuc.edu/PG/welcome.html`) are works in the public domain (see Problem #17 in Chapter 9). However, it is dangerous to assume that a work is in the public domain simply because it is popular or ubiquitous. For example, the song "Happy Birthday" is not in the public domain.

Q: Doesn't an Author Have to Mark a Document with a Copyright Notice in Order for It to Be Protected?

No. An explicit copyright declaration used to be required in the United States. Then the law was changed so that works created after April 1, 1989 are copyrighted and protected whether or not they contain a copyright notice. *If you see a document that has no copyright notice, you should always assume that copyright protections apply.*

Q: Can an Author License Specific Rights to the General Public by Including a Statement Describing What Rights and Privileges Are Being Granted?

Yes. For example, a Web page might include the following statement:

> "Permission is granted to freely copy (unmodified) this document in electronic form or in print as long as you're not selling it. On the WWW, however, you must link here rather than put it up on your own page."

This effectively allows anyone to reproduce and post an exact copy of the document online in almost any fashion. However, mirrored Web pages are explicitly prohibited.

Another commonly encountered copyright provision reads as follows:

> "This work may be redistributed freely, in whole or in part, but cannot be sold or used for profit or as part of a product or service that is sold for profit."

If no such statement is included, then you must assume that no such privileges have been extended. *When a copyright provision allows for redistribution without permission, it is still necessary to identify the author, source, and publisher (if there is one) in all distributions of the original work.*

Q: Can I Go to Jail for Violating a Copyright?

Yes, but it is unusual. Most copyright violations are treated as a civil offense rather than a criminal offense. In a civil court, you can be sued for damages but not sent to jail. There are some criminal copyright penalties, which include both large fines and jail terms, but only the federal government can instigate a criminal copyright action. The next time you rent a videotape, read the FBI warning at the beginning of the tape for a description of criminal copyright violations.

Q: If I Don't Make any Money from a Copyright Violation, Can I Still Be Sued for Damages?

Yes. If you distribute a document online, you might undermine a potential for-profit print distribution, which could be assessed in terms of lost income to the copyright owner. The fact that you didn't profit yourself is irrelevant.

Q: If a Photograph or Cartoon Has Been Published in a Newspaper or Magazine, Can I Scan It and Put It Online?

No, unless you track down the owner of the copyright and secure written permission from them to do so. The copyright owner might be the photographer or artist, a wire service (in the case of a photograph), or the publication in which the work appeared. Photographs and drawings are protected by default copyright restrictions just like written text. For example, Playboy Enterprises sued the Event Horizons bulletin board for distributing unauthorized digital copies of *Playboy* photographs. It received $500,000 in a settlement. *Photographs and artwork often have greater revenue potential than text documents and must therefore be handled with extreme caution.*

Q: Copyright Violations Are So Common on the Internet that No One Can Keep Track of Them All. What Difference Will It Make If I Add One More Violation?

Even if you don't get pulled into court for a copyright infringement, your actions can affect other people and may result in a loss of online resources. For example, there used to be a Dave Barry mailing list on which columns by humorist Dave Barry were posted to the list each morning. Mr. Barry's publisher asked everyone to respect the copyright by not redistributing the columns. The Dave Barry mailing list worked for a while until someone chose to ignore the restriction, and one of the columns showed up on another mailing list. When the publisher found out that the copyright restriction had been violated, it shut down the Dave Barry mailing list. They didn't sue the individual responsible for the copyright violation. But by pulling the column off of the mailing list, thousands of people who had enjoyed reading Dave Barry online were denied that privilege. So the actions of one thoughtless individual affected thousands of other people. Old Dave Barry columns can be found online in some Web archives, but no one can read new Dave Barry columns via e-mail anymore.

Q: What If I Just Want to Include an Excerpt from a Larger Document? Can I Freely Distribute an Excerpt as Long as I Identify It and Acknowledge My Source?

This is normally okay as long as you conform to the **doctrine of fair use**. The doctrine of fair use allows writers and scholars to refer to other works by quoting excerpts from those works. This is typically done to argue a point, to present evidence, or for the sake of illustration. To quote from a copyrighted work, you must follow the rules of thumb listed under "Guidelines for Fair Use."

GUIDELINES FOR FAIR USE

You may quote 300 words from a book or 150 words from a magazine or newspaper article as long as you observe the following guidelines:

1. The excerpt is not a complete unit in the larger work (for example, a complete poem, a complete article, or a complete list of rules from a manual).
2. The excerpt consists of less than 20% of the original work.
3. The excerpt is integrated into your own writing and does not stand alone as a header or chapter opening.
4. You give full credit to the author, source, and publisher.

If you excerpt a series of quotations from a single work, the total sum of those word counts should not exceed 300 words from a book or 150 words from a magazine or newspaper article.

If you want to quote a personal e-mail message, a Usenet newsgroup article, or an unpublished document, you must always obtain permission from the author.

When the fair use guidelines do not apply, copyright permission must be secured for exact quotations from the works of others. Note that ideas cannot be copyrighted; it is the specific arrangement of words used to express an idea that is the object of copyright protections. You are always free to summarize or restate the content of any work in your own writings. However, a summarization of someone else's work without proper acknowledgment constitutes an act of plagiarism. **Plagiarism** occurs when you adopt the substance of someone else's work, rewrite it in your own words, and fail to give proper credit to the original source. Always be careful to acknowledge a source if you are drawing information from that source in detail.

If an explicit statement prohibits the distribution of a text excerpt that normally would be justified under the fair use guidelines, then the fair use doctrine cannot be applied. For example, suppose the following prohibition appears on an online document:

> "No part of this electronic publication may be reproduced or retransmitted without the prior written permission of the publisher."

In this case, no excerpts can be reproduced without prior consent.

Or suppose someone distributes a document with a notation that says, "Do Not Quote." If you see that annotation, you can't distribute any excerpts. Explicit restrictions always override default conventions.

Q: Suppose I'm Teaching a Class and I Want to Distribute Hard Copies of an Online Document to My Students. Is that Protected by the Fair Use Doctrine?

The fair use doctrine is commonly invoked by teachers and professors who distribute copies of journal articles, newspaper articles, and magazine articles to students in classes as a part of their educational practice. The fact that these activities are nonprofit is commonly thought to protect them under the fair use doctrine. However, there have been some recent court cases associated with the creation of "coursepacks" by copying services that suggest that the application of the fair use doctrine is far from straightforward in these situations.

If you are a teacher, you should investigate these controversies and find out what practices have been adopted by your local institution. For a timely discussion of this issue, see "University Copy Centers: Do They Pass The Fair Use Test?" (you will find a pointer to this document in the Internet 101 Web pages). If an online document explicitly states that redistribution is permitted, then there is no problem. The question is more problematic for documents that grant no explicit permission, in which case it is prudent to obtain the permission of the author or the publisher (who may ask for a royalty).

Having discussed some of the basic ideas associated with copyright restrictions, I return to the Internet-specific questions posed at the beginning of this section.

Q: Do I Have a Right to Incorporate Files Found Elsewhere in My Own Web Pages?

Yes, as long as you observe some restrictions. ***Most important, you must not make a copy of someone else's Web page and then create a pointer to that copy. If you want to reference another Web page, create a pointer to the original page.*** In that way, the author of the page retains control over the material. If the author wants to update it, make a correction to it, or modify it in any manner, you will automatically benefit from those efforts. If the author decides to remove a page from public distribution, your pointer will become obsolete, but removing the page is the rightful prerogative of the author.

If you find some graphics on someone else's Web page and you want to incorporate them in one of your own Web pages, the same rule applies. You shouldn't copy the file and then create a pointer to your copy, but you can create a pointer to the original file. A professional Web page designer would go one step further. Because graphics files are commonly copied and redistributed across the Web without proper copyright permissions, there is an excellent chance that any graphic you find on someone else's Web page has already been bootlegged and is being used illegally. This is especially true of professional photographs. A responsible Web page author will attempt to locate the rightful owner of the graphic and secure permission to link to that graphic at the site where it legally resides. Unfortunately, it may be difficult to locate the legal owner of an online graphic, especially if the image is popular and found on a number of different Web pages. As a result, many Web page authors don't bother to locate the rightful owner and a legitimate linking site. Indeed, many Web page authors probably don't think about copyright laws at all, opting instead to simply do whatever their software allows. This is why copyright violations are so prevalent on the Web.

Some Web page authors ask that you reference their pages at some "top-level" entry point. They do not want you to set up a link to a secondary page if that page was not designed to be a self-contained, stand-alone page. When an author explicitly makes such a request, you should respect it. It is good to link to main entry points for large Web sites for practical reasons as well. The people who maintain large Web sites rearrange their pages and rename files from time to time. If you reference a secondary page directly, your link may become obsolete when the site undergoes a file reorganization. If you reference the main entry to a Web site and explain what links to traverse to get to a secondary page, your citation is more likely to survive the test of time and require fewer updates.

Keeping Web page pointers current and operational is one of the overhead costs associated with Web page design and maintenance. But anything you can do to avoid obsolete pointers will be greatly appreciated by your readers.

Q: Do I Have a Right to Alter Files and Make those Altered Files Available Online?

When you alter a document that is not your own, you must be extremely careful to acknowledge the extent of your alterations and the source of the original document. Some authors explain the situation by identifying the altered file as a "heavily edited modification of an original source document by so-and-so, which can be found at such-and-such a location." If you alter someone else's file and present it as your own, you may or may not be violating copyright laws (depending on how much original material survives verbatim), but you are probably guilty of plagiarism. If you present the substance of someone else's words, be sure to identify and acknowledge the original source. ***In an academic environment, plagiarism is a form of academic dishonesty and grounds for serious disciplinary actions.***

There is one notable exception to this general document modification scenario. If you download the HTML-version of a Web page because you like the format of the page, you may retain all of the HTML commands and substitute your own content into the HTML framework without permission or acknowledgments. An HTML format is purely stylistic. ***The "look and feel" of a computer display is not protected by copyrights or patents and can be freely duplicated without permission.*** As long as you substitute your own content, you are not violating any copyright restrictions and you are not engaged in plagiarism. Indeed, this is an easy way to create a sophisticated Web page, as well as an honorable way to learn HTML.

Q: Do I Have a Right to Excerpt Material and Distribute those Excerpts Online?

Yes, if you adhere to the fair use guidelines described previously. If you want to use more material than can be justified under fair use, then you should obtain permission from the author or whoever owns the copyright.

Q: Do I Have a Right to Print Hard Copies of Online Materials?

If you print one copy for your own personal use, there is no problem. If you want to print copies for friends and the material does not contain an explicit statement about allowable distributions, then you should obtain permission from the author or whoever owns the copyright.

Q: Do I Have a Right to Store on My Own Personal Computer Files that I Find Elsewhere?

Yes, provided you do not distribute those files to others or make them publicly available. Just keep in mind that the author of the work no longer controls the copy. If you want to reference the file or quote from it later, you should locate a current version in case the author has changed it.

Q: Do I Have a Right to Forward a Personal E-mail Message to a Friend?

You do not have a right to forward e-mail without the author's permission. However, as an e-mail author, you should assume that people reading your e-mail probably violate this rule all of the time. This is one place where good Netiquette is violated a million times a day. Personal e-mail messages are technically protected by copyright laws, although it would be hard to sue for damages if no loss of revenue can be established (which is highly unlikely in the case of an e-mail message). Regardless of the e-mail's legal status, you violate an author's privacy when you forward e-mail without prior permission. It is similar to taping a phone conversation and replaying the tape for a third party. If you don't want someone to violate the privacy of your messages, don't violate the privacy of other people's messages.

Q: Do I Have a Right to Distribute a Personal E-mail Message to a Newsgroup?

Only with permission from the author (see previous answer).

Q: Do I Have a Right to Download a Web Page and Mail it to a Friend?

This amounts to duplication and distribution. If the Web page does not explicitly grant you permission to freely distribute it, then you need permission from the author. In the case of a Web page, it is easier just to send your friend the URL. This is the correct way to share Web pages without violating the rights of a Web page author.

When you consider the rights and restrictions that apply to online text, think about how easily a text document can be spread in digital form. If someone grabs a document and posts it to a newsgroup or mailing list, it may be accessible through an archive for years to come. Copies of the document may be mirrored at countless Web sites and redistributed via e-mail over and over again. If the original author wants to correct an error in the original document or revise it with important updates, recalling all of the copies of the original version will be impossible. The author no longer controls the document in the same way that a publisher can control print editions of a book. Everyone benefits when authors retain maximal control over the digital distribution of their documents. This is the only way to minimize the propagation of misinformation or outdated information, and it gives all of us access to the best quality information online. In the interest of effective online communication, we must be sensitive to the rights of authors, no matter where a document was originally posted or how limited the potential scope of the document may be. With 50 million people online, it is impossible for anyone to predict the digital trajectory of an online document.

The body of law that establishes precedents for copyright law is always challenged when new technologies emerge. Important precedents are being established right now on the issue of data collections. For example, can the contents of a database be copyrighted? Can someone own the data that describes the human genome? Can someone own the DNA sequences associated with a specific gene? As soon as a technology makes it possible to ask a thorny question about new forms of intellectual property, court cases attempt to sort out the relevant precedents that apply. For example, in 1991 the U.S. Supreme Court decided that no one can copyright the information contained in a telephone directory's white pages (*Feist vs. Rural Telephone*). According to the court, no copyright can be granted for a compilation of facts unless the compilation entails some original "selection, coordination, or arrangement" of those facts. Some databases are compiled at great expense and represent an investment that could give a company a clear commercial advantage. Exactly when do the criteria of "selection, coordination, or arrangement" apply? This issue has implications for the intellectual property rights associated with online data collections such as subject trees, clearing houses, and file archives.

In 1993, the Clinton administration created a Working Group on Intellectual Property Rights as part of the Information Infrastructure Task Force to resolve concerns about intellectual property and the digital distribution of text, images, videos, and audio recordings. A proposal advocating a revision of copyright law was released in 1994, but there has been substantial resistance to this proposal because it would interfere with free and open communication among the scientists and educators for whom the Internet was originally designed. There is tension between opportunities for commercial profit and policies designed to protect the public good. New legislation is probably needed to protect both ends of this spectrum.

In a digital environment, questions of ownership and control need to be carefully reexamined. When text was restricted to physical print, it was relatively easy to control the distribution of that text. The advent of copying machines eroded that control and forced us to rely to a greater extent on voluntary compliance with copyright laws. Now the rapidly growing body of digital text has upset the balance yet again, forcing us to assume even greater responsibility for voluntary compliance with existing laws. New technologies have a tendency to defy existing laws. During periods of swift technological change, we all need to stay abreast of major court decisions, new legislation, and public policy debates. These are the forces that shape new behavioral codes and social responsibilities in our increasingly technological society.

13.3 Free Speech and the First Amendment

Americans are an individualistic lot. We value individualism, respect personal freedom, and romanticize loners. For all of our passionate feelings, we are often ignorant about the true nature of our constitutional rights. One of our most important rights, periodically invoked in the context of the Internet, is the right of free speech.

Q: Why Is Free Speech so Important?

Free speech is a cornerstone for a free and open democracy. It encourages people to participate in public discussions and debates. These, in turn, produce better-educated voters. By protecting free speech, society encourages an individual's right to learn and grow. This is crucial for a nation that values individual freedoms as much as we do. In countries in which individual freedoms are not respected, censors assume tremendous powers and severe penalties are instituted to suppress free speech. Feelings of oppression thrive under such conditions, thereby leading to clandestine meetings and surreptitious communications. Sooner or later, politically motivated acts of violence assume a symbolic status and become ideological statements. Free speech gives everyone an opportunity to express themselves without having to resort to acts of violence or civil disobedience.

The American tradition of public schools is another cornerstone for a democratic society. Thomas Jefferson founded the University of Virginia because of a profound appreciation for public higher education. These words of his appear above an archway in Cabell Hall at the University:

"This institution will be based on the illimitable freedom of the human mind. For here we are not afraid to follow truth wherever it may lead, nor to tolerate any error so long as reason is left free to combat it."

Any institution that honors freedom of speech furthers people in the their pursuit of truth. Thomas Jefferson believed that a free and democratic society would thrive and prosper because its people would pursue knowledge and truth. He would be gratified to know that strong respect for freedom of speech is being championed today by many Internet technologists.

Q: How Does the Internet Encourage Free Speech?

The very architecture of the Internet supports freedom of speech by defying hierarchical control. Information is relatively easy to manage in a hierarchical social organization. Authorized information trickles down from the top of the hierarchy. Unauthorized information originating at the bottom can be suppressed or censored whenever it tries to edge upward. But the Internet is organized heterarchically (see Chapter 2) so there are always multiple pathways from one node to another. If someone attempts to censor information by monitoring and sanitizing everything that moves through a specific gateway, pathways around that gateway can always be found. Censorship operating at one entry point can always be bypassed by going to a different entry point.

Oppressive governments in countries like Singapore and China are attracted to the economic opportunities of the Internet but threatened by a technology that supports highly interactive communication on a massive and global scale. The Internet does not recognize national boundaries. There is no class system for host machines that confers special privileges on some machines while restricting the communication potential of others. On the Internet, a machine is limited only by memory and bandwidth. Every day gigabytes of new information are available on the Intrnet making it impossible for anyone to control the content that moves freely among 19 million host machines, just as it is impossible to monitor millions of private conversations on an hourly basis. With its origins in American universities, the Internet embraces a culture of unrestricted communication. As Americans, we may take this for granted, but unrestricted communication is far from the norm in many other countries.

Q: What Does the First Amendment Say?

Many people know that the First Amendment protects free speech in the United States, but most people don't know exactly what is and is not protected. The First Amendment does not grant everyone the right to say anything at any time and any place. Here is the actual text of the First Amendment:

> "Congress shall make no law respecting an establishment of religion, or prohibiting the free exercise thereof; or abridging the freedom of speech, or of the press; or the right of the people peacefully to assemble, and to petition the government for a redress of grievances."

This amendment was designed to restrict the powers of government. The reference to "Congress" is actually a reference to all legislative bodies, either federal or state. In matters of religious freedom and freedom of speech, the First Amendment says that it is better to err on the side of individual rights and to curb the power of government. Our founding fathers were worried about oppressive governments. They wrote the First Amendment with those concerns in mind.

Q: How Powerful Is the First Amendment?

The First Amendment protects freedom of speech, but it does not defend all manner of communication. In particular, it was designed to curb government powers. Private companies and institutions not connected to the government are still free to impose their own rules and standards on individuals. If a restaurant employee is fired for discussing unsanitary kitchen practices, the First Amendment can do nothing for that employee. If a teacher at a private school is given a mandatory leave of absence for writing a book about creationism (or evolution, for that matter), the First Amendment cannot protect that teacher. The First Amendment would apply only if the restaurant were a government facility or if the school were a public school instead of a private school. Then the restaurant worker and the teacher would be dealing with potential censorship by state or federal government. That's when First Amendment protections apply.

The First Amendment is also restricted by specific exclusions established by the courts. There are two basic types of exclusion to the First Amendment: content-specific and content-neutral.

Content-Specific Exclusions

Following are the content-specific exclusions to the First Amendment:

- Obscene material
- Libel (written falsehoods) and slander (verbal falsehoods)
- Harassment
- "Fighting words" (intended to incite a riot or violent behaviors)

Defining Obscenity Note that obscene material is not protected under the First Amendment, but indecent materials and pornographic materials are protected. What's the difference? The line between indecency and obscenity is tested periodically in the courts. In 1982, the Federal Communications Commission (FCC) argued that seven words used by comedian George Carlin in his "Filthy Words" comedy monologue were sufficiently offensive to be a violation of FCC broadcasting restrictions (*the FCC vs. Pacifica Radio*). Pacifica Radio maintained that any penalties imposed by the FCC would violate the First Amendment. The case went to the Supreme Court. You can find the full text of the Supreme Court decision on the Web, including the full text of Mr. Carlin's monologue (see the Internet 101 Web pages for a pointer).

The upshot of the case is that the seven words used by George Carlin were deemed indecent but not obscene. As such, they are protected by the First Amendment. However, indecent language is precisely what the CDA sought to make a felony offense on the Internet. When the Supreme Court overturned the CDA, it struck an important blow for free speech on the Internet.

Content-Neutral Exclusions

The second class of exceptions to the First Amendment are the content-neutral exceptions. These exceptions do not target a particular type of content. Rather, they seek to establish restrictions that depend on time, place, and manner. Some objectionable things can be said, but only in certain places at certain times in certain contexts. Context is the deciding factor.

For example, a town governing board might pass a local ordinance that prohibits people from playing music too loudly in a residential neighborhood after 11 P.M. This is a content-neutral exception to the First Amendment. No one will win a court case against the ordinance by claiming that their First Amendment rights have been violated. In another example, a municipality can restrict "adult theaters" to a certain section of town in an effort to segregate some types of businesses (similar to a zoning restriction). While no one can prevent the establishment of an adult theater in a town, the town can dictate where one is allowed to set up shop.

"Time and Place" on the Internet What is "time and place" on the Internet? That's a very good question. Community standards play a big role in content-neutral regulations and are an interesting issue for communications on the Internet. Are there community standards that apply to the Internet? Whose community? How can time and place restrictions apply to a medium that crosses all time zones and creates mirror sites worldwide?

Place restrictions might be useful on the Internet if we can abandon the concept of geographical locations and adopt a sense of location based on something else. For example, some organizations have been manually reviewing Web sites in an effort to identify the ones that are safe for children to visit.

The idea is to stamp something like the "Good Webkeeping Seal of Approval" on sites that have won approval from the site reviewers. Any Web site that has not been rated would be considered unsafe, as a precautionary default. A Web browser could then check for the seal of approval whenever it visited a new Web page. If the browser was operating in "smut avoidance mode," it would block access to any site that has not been approved.

The ability to identify child-friendly places on the Web safeguards freedom of speech for all Web authors, while offering practical parental controls when children get on the Web. Indeed, if Web sites are profiled with category ratings for violence, sex, drugs, and so on, then a parent could configure a Web page filter based on a customized definition of "unacceptable for children." This more detailed profiling obviates the problem of a monolithic rating system that may or may not agree with everyone's sense of what is acceptable for children. Web page rating services and rating-driven Web page filters represent workable technological solutions to new technological problems. If such a technological solution proves workable, there will be no need for governmental regulations on the Internet. But it all depends on finding new ways to look at the concept of place.

Time is even more problematic because instantaneous communications on the Internet span the globe. When a television station broadcasts a show late at night because it is inappropriate for prime-time viewing, that schedule can be imposed on each time zone where the show is offered. Even news broadcasts can be "blacked out" in specific time zones if need be, as in the case of early East coast election results that might affect voting patterns in the Western states. These broadcasting restrictions are easily enforced for television because television is hierarchically controlled. Everything we see on television has been authorized by programming executives. The advent of VCRs freed us from the tyranny of television programming schedules: a late-night show can now be viewed in prime time if we are willing to see it the next day. But VCRs do not reproduce broadcasts beyond the reach of one television set at a time.

The Internet gives us the freedom to distribute information heterarchically and this makes it very difficult to stop information from hopping across time zones. If someone is broadcasting news on a chat channel, there is no central authority who decides which hosts are allowed to tune in and which are not. Even if that authority existed, the Internet would make any such restrictions very difficult to enforce. Indeed, now that audio signals can be digitized, radio stations all over the world are broadcasting live on the Internet and expanding their reach to a global scale. And if you aren't able to hear a broadcast live, a recording may be available for replay at your convenience. Time and place on the Internet is basically "all the time" and "any place with Internet access."

There are many questions about the First Amendment and how it can be applied to the Internet. Because the Internet crosses international boundaries, what governmental powers pertain to the Internet? There are no global or international jurisdictions that transcend national boundaries as easily as the Internet. Is the physical location of an online computer at all meaningful with respect to the Internet? Everything we thought we understood about time and place needs to be reconsidered with the Internet in mind.

Privacy Issues   13.4

Some concepts are so entrenched in our culture that we rarely think about them, examine them, or question them. As long as our lungs are full of air, we don't have to think about respiration. As long as our supremacy in the food chain is secure, we don't have to think about predators. As long as life moves along in a predictable fashion, we try not to dwell on potential catastrophes. Then, when the unexpected happens, we cope first and reflect later.

The concept of privacy has been a dormant assumption in the lives of most Americans. We know the difference between public and private activities, and we keep a safe social distance from people we don't know or don't want to know. We all have information that we share only with trusted friends. Most of us do not have to elude paparazzi or worry about being the next hot item in the tabloids. So we drop the shades at night and feel safe from the eyes of the world. As social causes go, privacy issues have yet to make much of a dent in our collective consciousness.

If you think you are relatively aware and informed about your privacy rights, test yourself to see how much you really know. Here's a little true/false quiz on privacy in the United States:

1. U.S. citizens have a right to privacy that is protected by the U.S. Constitution.

2. Employers can legally monitor many employee activities in the workplace without prior notification.

3. It is illegal to send junk mail (unsolicited materials) to someone else's fax machine.

4. It is illegal to send junk mail (unsolicited materials) to someone else's e-mail address.

5. It is illegal to collect and sell personal data without the permission of the people being described.

6. It is illegal for an ISP to monitor the online activities of its subscribers and to sell user profiles based on subscribers' data.

7. An ISP can legally have the right to inspect the e-mail of any sub-scriber for any reason as a term of its service agreement.

8. Anyone with a radio scanner can legally eavesdrop on cordless phone calls.

9. It is legal for a credit bureau to disclose to a third party your finan-cial history without your prior permission.

10. The U.S. Post Office sells the information on completed Change of Address forms it receives to direct mail marketing companies.

Do you feel confident that you know the answers to more than five of these? If so, congratulate yourself for being an informed citizen. If not, you are not alone. Go to the "Discussion Questions" at the end of this chapter to check your answers.

Q: What Laws Are Designed to Protect My Privacy?

There is nothing in the U.S. Constitution that protects privacy rights for U.S. citizens. Most laws related to privacy are state laws, so your rights may vary depending on where you live. Even so, the laws that exist tend to be very narrowly drawn. For example, in 1988 Congress passed a law protecting video-tape rental records. And in 1997, it passed a law making it illegal for Internal Revenue Service employees to view random tax returns for their entertainment. However, we have no federal laws at this time which regulate the privacy of medical records or consumer data in general.

There is no legislative body in the United States that studies privacy or works toward a systematic legal code for privacy rights. The privacy laws we do have are the result of isolated crusades. They protect us like a crazy quilt, with a patch here and a patch there. For example, the videotape rental law came into being after the Supreme Court confirmation hearings for Judge Robert Bork, at which time some enterprising reporter dug up information about Judge Bork's video viewing habits. The incident scared our elected offi-cials, and they quickly crafted legislation to make sure nothing like that could ever happen again.

Q: How Does the Internet Figure into All of This?

A lot of publicly available information has always been there for the taking, but only with some effort. Before the Internet, a court record from a divorce proceeding was public but available only if you visited the courthouse at which it was stored. Copies of old newspapers might have been available on microfiche, but you had to travel to the newspaper publisher or to a regional library and spend time in front of a microfiche reader. Private investigators doing background checks know their way around all of the public resources, as well as a few back door tricks of the trade. Whatever sources they pumped, it was always a job involving some amount of footwork. Hence, information that was technically free extracted a very real price in terms of time and energy.

The Internet is changing many of the hidden costs associated with "free" information. When a court places its records online, no one has to travel to the courthouse to see them. When phone listings for the entire United States are available online, you can research ten cities as easily as one. The Internet isn't giving us anything we couldn't get before; it simply makes many information-gathering tasks almost effortless. The convenience factor is shifting. In a legal sense, nothing has changed with respect to the availability of information. But in a practical sense, nothing will ever be the same. Not only is the work of the private investigator facilitated, but people who would never have taken the time to learn about resources in a public library are now surfing the Web and learning about all sorts of information sources online. Rank amateurs are barging in where only professionals used to tread.

Computer technologies are also altering the line between transient information and archival information. Articles in newspapers and magazines used to have a limited shelf life. A 10-year-old newspaper article could easily vanish from the face of the earth and be gone forever. Now, as more and more newspapers put their content online, newspaper stories become part of the permanent record. Literally anyone can create a massive digital library for anything online. Hook it up to a search engine, post it on the Web, and the world has instant access to an archival resource. Items that used to fade and die natural deaths can now assume the technological equivalent of eternal life.

Digital records also make it easier for people to assemble information from disparate sources. If you want to pull up an instant profile for someone who is active online, it takes less than a minute to type a name into a Web search engine and be rewarded with hits from Web pages, Usenet newsgroups, and mailing list archives. All of the legwork of looking in different places and all of the brainwork of figuring out where to look in the first place has been solved by the indexing capability of a search engine that operates in the space of seconds. When it comes to assembling bits of data about people, the whole is always greater than the sum of the parts. No one piece of information may be particularly threatening or worrisome. But when a hundred pieces of information can be pulled together, we begin to see the big picture. Big Brother didn't materialize as the result of a massive totalitarian government, but it seems to be emerging from what amounts to technological serendipity. Nobody really planned it this way. Like so many things on the Internet, forces were simply set into motion, and now the consequences require our careful consideration.

Q: Is Anything Private on the Internet?

People are used to thinking about degrees of privacy. Absolute privacy is difficult to attain, but relative privacy may be a reasonable goal. For example, a message posted to a mailing list is public relative to that list but private with respect to the world at large. Most e-mail messages are read and discarded or sometimes just discarded without even being read. Even when mailing lists are archived by listservs, the business of locating and searching a mailing list archive is not so terribly easy (see Chapter 4). As long as the convenience factor is low, mailing list participants enjoy some degree of privacy.

But with computers, tasks that used to be difficult often become effortless. The Web is a case in point. All those difficult-to-read mailing list archives can now be placed on Web pages, where they are suddenly fairly easy to find. Before you know it, search engines are pointing to e-mail messages sent seven years ago. Archives that were relatively private in 1990 can suddenly pop up in hit lists for all the world to see. Just because something was inconvenient at one time doesn't mean it's going to stay inconvenient forever. If it's digital, it has unimaginable potential for public distribution.

Digital environments and low-cost memory are also making it easy to create massive archives of information. If you mail a message, you have no control over its digital life span. You may expect it to be deleted and die, but you really have no control over its longevity. Any recipient can save it. Or it could get caught on a backup tape, where it can sit indefinitely. Or it might be passed on to additional readers, thereby creating even more possibilities for digital perseverance. Every piece of e-mail you've ever sent can be trapped and kept for digital perpetuity.

Consider the online chat channels. Surely all of the conversations taking place in MUDs and on IRC go away when the conversations end. Chances are, that's true. But anyone can monitor a chat channel and record every last word in a log file. Most Telnet clients include a log file option that makes it easy to record chat conversations. On a public channel, anyone can lurk and record. No one is creating IRC archives yet (to my knowledge), but the technology is there. All you need is massive amounts of memory, or what seems massive by today's standards.

To be realistic, all online interactions should be considered public communications. It doesn't matter if you write to one person or a thousand. Everything you do online can be made public. Even an encrypted message to a single recipient can be decrypted, saved in a readable format, and caught on a backup tape.

Everyone needs to think about whether the benefits of the Internet outweigh the possible indignities of reduced privacy. For some people, the ability to communicate freely and openly on a global scale is well worth it. For others, any loss of privacy is an unsettling prospect requiring careful consideration.

Q: Can I Do Anything to Protect My Privacy on the Internet?

At this point, you might be thinking, "Well, I'll just keep a low profile. I'll never post to a mailing list, I'll never post to a newsgroup, and I'll never mail anything to anybody. I'll never register myself on a Telnet server, and I'll never fill out a user survey for anyone. Then I'll be invisible." This would certainly reduce your privacy risks, but it won't eliminate them altogether.

The next time you visit a search engine on the Web, watch the ad banners that pop up each time you conduct a search. If you ask a question about cars, you see an ad for a car dealer. If you ask a question about books in print, you get an ad for a bookstore. Web advertisers know you are more likely to click an ad related to your queries than a random ad that is of no interest to you. So commercial search engines "sell" keywords to their advertisers. If you type in a keyword that belongs to an advertiser, you'll get an ad from that advertiser. Web servers are capable of watching you when you visit a Web site, and of learning something about you in the process.

Web servers are in a good position to collect information about you and your interests. They can ask you to fill out forms as well as track the pages you visit, the amount of time you spend on each one, and the links you click. All of this data is potentially valuable for marketing purposes and could be sold to data brokers who specialize in online data collection.

The good news is that you don't have to avoid online services in order to preserve your privacy. Whenever you visit a Web site that is in a position to collect marketable data, look for a statement of policy concerning data collection. For example, you might see a statement like this:

> "Occasionally, we share the e-mail addresses of our subscribers with providers of quality goods and services. If you would prefer not to receive such mailings, make this change to your subscription file by . . . ."

or

> "We consider the information regarding your membership, orders, and the products you purchase to be personal and confidential . . . . We will use the information to communicate special news, promotions, and product deals to you on a regular basis, unless you indicate that you do not wish to receive the messages . . . ."

Many online services have adopted a privacy policy based on **notice and consent**. They post a statement explaining what data is being collected and how it is being used. Users then have the option of denying them the right to resell personal data. As long as you know that it is up to you to look for these policy statements and communicate your wishes to the company, then you can stop the distribution of personal data from those sources. If you cannot find any such policy statement or if the policy statement does not give you an opportunity to block any undesirable use of your personal data, then you should assume the worst. Note that these policies are always set up so that you have to explicitly deny permission to use your data. If you do nothing, they do what they want with it.

Q: How Much Data Is Being Collected Surreptitiously?

This is hard to say, but many companies seem to be changing their data collection practices so that users have more control.

One of the most controversial data collections practices on the Web involves something called cookies. A **cookie** is a file created by a Web server and stored on your host machine. It's a small file that sits around waiting until the next time you visit the Web. Any Web server can check to see if you have a cookie file and check it for useful information about you. For example, suppose that the last time you visited a particular site, you spent all of your time on two particular pages. A cookie can record this information so that the next time you visit the site, the server might greet you with a page display that makes it especially easy to navigate to those pages again. The Web server is using its knowledge about you and your prior activities. Some of this knowledge may have been collected with your assistance (you have to tell it your name if you want a personal greeting). Some is automatically derived from your online activities.

How can you tell if you've got a cookie on your computer? Just search your hard drive for a file involving the string "cookie." It might be called `cookies.txt` or `MagicCookie`. It will be in a subdirectory where your browser is stored. You can look at this file—it's just a text file. It will contain separate entries from different Web sites. Here's an example of a short cookie file with three entries from two different Web sites:

```
MCOM-HTTP-Cookie-file-1
www.kids.com   FALSE / FALSE 946713299 voi-webwatch
30f15eb4-000b3cc7-0000268e
.infoseek.com   TRUE / FALSE 826467213 InfoseekUserId
BCF59DF42114EDD38C7D7AD0411683AF
.infoseek.com   TRUE / FALSE 826467213 InfoseekLook tables
```

The names of the sites responsible are given, so I can always tell where the cookies came from. Each of these sites will check for a cookie file the next time I drop by. If they find the file with their entry in it, they can handle my visit a little differently than they would if nothing were known about me.

Cookie files can be used to make life nicer for a Web user. Suppose I visit a site in order to find books of interest. If a Web page associated with a bookstore can keep a profile of my reading preferences, it won't have to ask me the same questions about my reading preferences each time I visit. It would be better to be greeted with a customized book recommendation each time I visit the site.

Mostly, cookies are used to target banner ads at probable customers. For example, if you visit the Netly News at `pathfinder.com`, the site will record any mouse clicks that reveal an interest in specific technologies. A resulting cookie will be used the next time you visit Pathfinder in order to show you an ad about a product that reflects your interests.

You might feel that cookies provide a useful service. Maybe you would like to hear about products and promotions that might interest you. On the other hand, you might also like to be reassured that all of this information about your reading habits, consumer spending, recreational activities, and so on, is not being sold to information brokers and marketing companies. At the very least, you might want to be informed if a Web site is going to put a cookie on your hard drive.

In a 1997 survey conducted by the Electronic Privacy Information Center, 24 of the Internet's one hundred most popular Web sites were programmed to create cookies. (No one knows how many Web sites are doing it in total.) In an effort to respect privacy rights, some Web browsers are now asking their users for permission to have a cookie (e.g., the most recent versions of Navigator and Internet Explorer are now "cookie-correct"). Here is the cookie query that lynx generates when it visits InfoSeek:

```
www.infoseek.com cookie:
Infosee=FE382B6CA3C25793F1 Allow? (Y/N/Always/neVer)
```

This query is asking for permission to create a cookie file or add an entry to your existing cookie file. You can answer yes (Y) or no (N), and the browser will respect your wishes. If you answer always (A) or never (V), you are instructing the browser not to bother you with any more cookie requests during this visit to this host. This is appropriate when more than one Web page is prepared to generate a cookie. Each time you return to the Web site, you'll have to respond to an initial cookie query all over again, but this inconvenience is there to protect your privacy.

If your browser isn't asking permission for cookies, you can always check for a cookie file to see who is adding information to it. Deleting this file before each session on the Web will prevent Web sites from using any information collected during a previous visit. It will also prevent the site from creating an extensive profile about you based on multiple visits.

Q: Do We Need Federal Regulations to Protect Privacy on the Internet?

This question was raised by the Federal Trade Commission (FTC) in 1997. The FTC held a hearing to explore the issue of privacy on the Internet and to determine whether governmental regulation was needed. There were arguments on both sides. At the close of the hearings, FTC Chairman Robert Pitofsky commented:

> "There has been some talk, especially in the last hour or so, about whether voluntary guidelines ever work . . . . Believe it or not, there are some people who think government regulation doesn't work all that well either. And in an era in which all of government must do more with less, we cannot afford to ignore the possibility that cooperation and collaboration will lead to the appropriate result."

So it appears that the FTC is not eager to impose federal regulations to protect the privacy of U.S. citizens on the Internet. At the very least, voluntary compliance with industry guidelines has not been rejected as a viable solution.

Q: Is Voluntary Compliance on the Part of Business Enough of a Safeguard?

People who view governmental regulations as intrusive would prefer to see industry adopt self-regulating standards. Indeed, the desire to avoid federal privacy regulation is so great that Microsoft Corp. and Netscape Communications Corp., bitter rivals on the Internet market, pledged to work together on voluntary industry standards.

There also have been notable instances in which industry has demonstrated that it can be responsive to public opinion on the matter of personal privacy. For example, in 1990, Lotus Development Corp. teamed with the Equifax credit bureau to produce a database of 120 million consumer profiles. The Marketplace database would contain names, marital status, estimated incomes, and purchasing habits. Lotus planned to market the data on a CD-ROM for $700. Word of this got out on the Internet and a letter-writing campaign was initiated by privacy rights advocates. In no time, Lotus received 30,000 angry letters from Internet users who objected to the project. Sensing a public relations disaster, Lotus quietly backed off and dropped the project. A company with less concern for consumer opinion could have easily ignored the outcry.

Privacy ripples were felt after the Marketplace fiasco. For example, two of the three big credit report brokers, Equifax and TRW, agreed to stop selling consumer credit data to direct marketing vendors. These were voluntary actions on their part. Trans Union did not concur. Also, the state of California created the Privacy Rights Clearinghouse and the first privacy hotline in the nation. More recently, in 1997, AOL reversed itself concerning a plan to sell subscriber telephone numbers. AOL does reserve the right to sell personal information about its subscribers to direct marketers, and it was about to add telephone numbers to their data sales. Word got out, the media voiced widespread criticism of the plan, and AOL quietly backed down.

So at least some companies are sensitive to public opinion and would very likely comply with industry standards on a voluntary basis. On the other hand, voluntary self-regulation could be easily side-stepped by smaller companies struggling to survive, any company that maintains a low public profile, or very large corporations that are simply not worried about public opinion. Whenever an industry relies on voluntary compliance, there will inevitably be those who violate the guidelines to gain a competitive advantage.

Q: Are There Other Possible Solutions?

Some people argue that existing laws pertaining to fraudulent and deceptive practices are adequate and simply need to be applied. For example, the Center for Media Education (CME) brought a complaint before the FTC in 1996 concerning the data collection practices of the Web site KidsCom. Many Web sites designed for children had been set up to collect personal information as the "price of admission" to games and other online activities. This data was then sold, without parental permission, to third parties for marketing purposes. The complaint by CME argued that data collection from children in the absence of parental consent amounted to an unfair and deceptive trade practice. The FTC agreed and issued guidelines for responsible practices with respect to online marketing aimed at children.

Still other privacy advocates believe that technological solutions are the only acceptable solutions. NoCem (see Chapter 8) and PGP (see Chapter 12) are grassroots responses to specific privacy soft spots that can be adopted by end users, system administrators, or software designers.

Regardless of how the problem is resolved, one thing is certain: Public awareness of privacy issues is bound to increase, and people will have to decide for themselves what their privacy is worth. Personal data is a commodity, and some fundamental questions have to be answered about who can own that data, who can sell it, and who can broadcast it and under what circumstances. This is one problem that is not going to go away or sort itself out without a concerted effort.

The Future of the Internet

The Internet is a synergistic blend of the technologies that enable it and the people who use it. Predictions about technology are almost always embarrassing in retrospect, and predictions about computer technology are especially perilous. With that caveat in place, let's talk about the future.

Q: What Lessons from the Past Might Help Us Predict the Future?

New technologies often blindside people. The Internet is no exception. Indeed, the evolutionary path to today's Internet can be said to rest, in part, on a series of fortuitous events that no one saw coming.

First, there was the unanticipated popularity of e-mail. In 1972, ARPA's leadership was preoccupied with scientific advancement and therefore concentrated on the use of networks to transfer files and enable remote logins. No one saw a pressing need for casual communication over networked computers. People had telephones for that, and typing out messages on a keyboard probably seemed like a step backwards from spoken communication. Even when the appeal of e-mail was apparent, ARPA was not eager to be associated with it.

Next, there was the so-called "computer revolution," which brought affordable computers into the hands of the general public. Although the commercialization of microcomputers was well underway during the 1970s, the personal computer finally went mainstream in 1981 with the release of the first IBM PC (with 64K RAM). It is interesting that this didn't happen earlier. Established computer manufacturers with strong track records in mainframes and minicomputers were relatively slow to appreciate the potential market and long-term impact of low-cost personal computers.

Then, in 1984, Apple Computer released the first Macintosh computer (with 128K RAM) and established itself as the leader in graphical interface design. The computer "For the Rest of Us" was based on simple point-and-click operations instead of typed commands. Although the Mac received a lot of media attention, the challenges of user-friendly interface design failed to generate much interest on the part of the programming community, perhaps because programmers have always been fundamentally more interested in computers themselves than in the people who use them.

In 1992, New York City had two ISPs. In 1993, the number grew to seven. By that time, the commercialization of the Internet and the appearance of the Mosaic Web browser had begun to bring the Internet into people's living rooms. The three threads of (1) networked communication, (2) affordable home computers, and (3) easy-to-use graphical interfaces were coming together. In retrospect, the Web seems inevitable, yet no one saw it coming. Even the community of researchers and system developers specializing in hypertext/hypermedia never anticipated the marriage of their technology to the Internet.

Each of these events holds an important key to understanding the forces that are likely to shape the Internet of tomorrow. The popularity of e-mail taught us that people are drawn to the Internet as a communication medium as much as an information resource. The delayed entry of IBM into the microcomputer market taught us that revolutionary technologies do not always originate within the laboratories of Fortune 500 companies. The popularity of the Web shows us that people are eager to act as both information consumers and information providers.

Finally, the fact that user interfaces have not changed much since the introduction of the Mac tells us that the computer industry is not taking the problem of user interfaces very seriously, which itself reflects a fundamental lack of interest in the real needs of end users. It is not surprising to see that AOL led the initial drive toward easy Internet access (as opposed to IBM or Microsoft). It seems that we are overdue for some serious advances in interface technologies—and we should not be surprised if these advances come from unexpected places.

Q: What Role Will the Government Play in Regulating the Internet?

First, there are indications that the government is taking a hands-off attitude toward many aspects of the Internet. For example, consider strong encryption. After seven years of debate, Congress may have begun to sense that strong encryption is too valuable and too inevitable to be sacrificed on the alter of law enforcement. Earlier restrictions on commercial encryption have been loosened, and support for key escrow systems appears to be softening. The matter is far from settled, but the wind seems to be shifting.

Similarly, proposals for revised copyright laws to better address the Internet have apparently stalled in the face of massive protests from scientific societies, library associations, and major telecommunications companies. At the same time, the Supreme Court upheld freedom of speech on the Internet by ruling the CDA unconstitutional. In both of these areas, proposed government interventions have been successfully challenged and subjected to in-depth review.

There is, nevertheless, an important role for the government with respect to telecommunications cost structuring in the regulation of telephone company charges for Internet usage. FCC rulings over telephone billing practices will continue to play a crucial role in the accessibility of the Internet. But beyond issues of infrastructure, the government seems reluctant to pass laws specific to the Internet. Congress and the public at large are both beginning to appreciate some of the complexities that characterize digital communications. Laws may be forthcoming, but they need to be crafted with great care and considerable concern for their consequences.

Q: Which Parts of the Internet Are Not Long for this World?

The Darwinian forces of the Internet are fast, furious, and irrevocable. As the Internet grows up, parts of it mature and thrive, while other parts show signs of old age and imminent death. For example, the rise of the Web became a death sentence for Gopher. Computer technologies are like sharks: They must constantly propel themselves forward or be doomed. Sometimes you stumble across a corner of the Internet that is so quiet that you feel like you've fallen into the ancient catacombs beneath the city of Paris. Some of these places are still operational in the sense that servers respond and software executes, but it's hard to imagine who is using them.

There are many servers on the Internet that have seen happier days, but my best candidate for Longevity Past the Call of Duty is FTP by e-mail. Before the Web explosion (1994), mail servers were set up to handle FTP requests for users whose only access to the Internet was via e-mail. Although this is still a sizable user population, FTP by e-mail appears to be in a state of serious decline. The first indication is the number of retired servers. If you look in old books (before 1996) that give addresses for FTP mail servers, you will find that most of those servers no longer operate.

While I was working on this book, I did manage to find one at `ftpmail@publ.pa.vix.com` that was operational. On May 26, 1997, I sent a query to it for a file on the server `wiretap.spies.com`. I instructed the server to go to the directory `Library/Media/Misc` and retrieve a file called `fair.lis`. About 10 minutes later, I received a confirmation from the server informing me that my request had been received and that there were 643 jobs ahead of mine. I expected the process of fetching the file to take a day or two, maybe a week or two at the most—FTP mail servers are known to be pokey. They tend to be run at a low priority (the host takes care of other jobs before getting around to the FTP requests), and they are sometimes down for a week or more. However, after a month had passed without a response, I assumed that my request had failed in some way and the server hadn't bothered to inform me. Imagine my surprise when the `fair.lis` file did arrive in my mail box—on August 18, 1997. It took 84 days, but the server eventually delivered.

Here's something to ponder the next time you grow fidgety waiting for a Web page to download: Who were those other 643 people with FTP requests ahead of me? How long did they each wait for their files? Were they primarily curiosity seekers like me, or were they serious Internet users whose only access to FTP files was via e-mail? If even one of those jobs fell into the latter category, I regret consuming any amount of CPU time on the part of that FTP mail server. It is important to remember how wide-ranging the world population of Internet users is. Some of us are cursing a chess server because of lag time during a chess game with someone 3,000 miles away, while less fortunate people may have to wait weeks to get a single file from an FTP server.

Q: Computers and the Internet Are Supposed to Make People More Productive, But I Don't See It. Is that Ever Going to Change?

Whenever a new technology surfaces, there is a lot of talk about how it will change our lives, our work, and sometimes our very thought processes. Computer technologies are typically impressive for their processing speed and memory capacity. As a result, we all feel pressured to work with increasingly larger amounts of data but with less preparation time and less time for reflection. The time-saving potential of these high-speed technologies has somehow produced a population of workers who feel more stressed for time and less capable of staying on top of it all.

Perhaps we are merely undergoing a period of adjustment. We all need to learn how to deal with "creeping featurism" (Chapter 1), flooded mail boxes (Chapter 3), and the millions of documents that comprise the Web (Chapter 7). We also need to become more objective and disciplined about the time we spend online. How much time spent online is justifiable in terms of greater productivity at work? How much is enriching life at a personal level? How much is simple avoidance behavior or escapism? We all need to think about what we're really doing online. As the novelty of the Internet wears off, people will be more realistic about what to expect from the Internet.

This is not to say that the Internet does not pose unique risks. It is credited with the destruction of at least a few marriages. More than a few grade-point averages have suffered as a direct result of Internet access. In fact, the possibility of "Internet addiction" is being studied by psychologists who suspect that the pull of the Internet is simply too strong for some people. There are those who prefer online life to real-time life, and the consequences of this preference are not clear.

But if someone wants to end a marriage, self-destruct, or withdraw from society, chances are they will succeed with or without the Internet. Anyone who is firmly plugged into the real world will probably accept the Internet as one more ball to juggle in the daily mix of work, family, and the pursuit of happiness.

Q: Is the Internet Really Going to Make the World a Better Place?

Vinton G. Cerf, who created TCP/IP (with Robert Kahn) and has been a guiding force behind the Internet from the beginning, wrote a short piece on the question of whether the Internet holds some intrinsic value for humankind. He suggests that the answer is yes, but only if we rise to the challenge of pursuing truth and substance over wishful thinking and expedient answers.

Truth and the Internet

"Truth is a powerful solvent. Stone walls melt before its relentless might. The Internet is one of the most powerful agents of freedom. It exposes truth to those who wish to see it. It is no wonder that some governments and organizations fear the Internet and its ability to make the truth known.

"But the power of the Internet is like a two-edged sword. It can also deliver misinformation and uncorroborated opinion with equal ease. The thoughtful and the thoughtless co-exist side by side in the Internet's electronic universe. What's to be done?

"There are no electronic filters that separate truth from fiction. No cognitive "V-chip" to sort the gold from the lead. We have but one tool to apply: critical thinking. This truth applies as well to all other communication media, not only the Internet. Perhaps the World Wide Web merely forces us to see this more clearly than other media. The stark juxtaposition of valuable and valueless content sets one to thinking. Here is an opportunity to educate us all. We truly must think about what we see and hear. We must evaluate and select. We must choose our guides. What better lesson than this to teach our young children to prepare them for a new century of social, economic and technological change?

"Let us make a new Century resolution to teach our children to think more deeply about what they see and hear. That, more than any filter, will build a foundation upon which truth can stand."

DISCUSSION QUESTIONS

Here are the answers to the privacy quiz in Section 13.4:

1) F   2) T   3) T   4) F   5) F   6) F   7) T   8) F   9) T   10) T

If any of these answers surprise you, get on the Web and research them. A good place to find discussions pertaining to most of these questions is the Privacy Rights Clearinghouse at `http://www.privacyrights.org/`

1. What can happen to you if you start a chain letter on the Internet that asks its participants to mail $5 to each of the last ten people listed in the chain letter? What can happen to you if you start a chain letter on the Internet that says nothing about sending anyone money?

2. What will happen to you if you post an article to a newsgroup describing one hundred fictitious bugs that you claim to have found in popular Microsoft software products?

3. If you send an e-mail message to a friend about your ex-wife's sordid private life and that message somehow turns up on a Usenet newsgroup, can your ex-wife sue you for damages?

4. If you find some child pornography on the Internet, can you download it without fear of legal repercussions? If you find pornography that doesn't involve children, does that change the situation? Can you post pornographic images on a Web page without fear of reprisals? Does it matter if your Web server is run by a private university? What about a public university?

5. Can someone who forges an e-mail message be arrested? Can someone scan a newspaper article and post it to a mailing list without the publisher's permission and be arrested for doing so? Can that person be sued? Can someone quote a paragraph from a newspaper article without the publisher's permission and be arrested for doing so? Can that person be sued?

6. If you set up a link from your Web page to someone else's Web page that contains a photograph, can you be sued for copyright infringement? What if you copy the file and set up a link from your page to your own copy of the photograph? What if the owner of the other Web site grants you permission to make and use a copy of the image, but that person does not have a copyright for the photograph? Are you legally at fault for having trusted that person and used the photograph?

7. Why aren't more publishers suing thousands of Internet users for copyright violations?

8. If you want to post a message to a mailing list and encourage people to redistribute it freely, what should you do?

9. Can you be sued for libel if you reveal damaging, but true, statements about a company? Who decides if a statement is damaging?

10. Can someone advocate rioting on behalf of a political cause and be protected by the First Amendment?

Appendix A

Internet Service Providers

Once you have a home computer with a modem, you can sign up with an ISP. Most ISPs will give you options for different types of accounts. To run a graphical Web browser such as Netscape Navigator or Internet Explorer, you will need a SLIP or PPP account. Most people are getting onto the Internet in order to browse the Web, so SLIP/PPP accounts are a popular service.

You may also hear about a POP (Post Office Protocol) service. You need this to move e-mail smoothly back and forth between your ISP account and your home computer. Having this is a good idea because it enables you to read and answer your e-mail remotely on your home computer without being connected, thus minimizing connect time.

As far as the ISPs themselves go, your options will vary depending on where you live. Heavily populated areas will offer more choices than rural settings. However, even remote regions of the United States often are covered by more than one ISP. If you are able pick and choose your ISP, here are five things to consider before you select one:

1. How much do they charge?
2. Do they offer a free trial period?
3. Is their modem pool reliable and adequate for their customer base?
4. How good is their technical support?
5. Do they offer any extra services?

I discuss each of these questions in some detail in this appendix so that you will understand exactly what they mean and what you need to do to get an answer to each. Questions 1, 2, and 5 are the only ones you can answer without trying out the service. To answer the others, you need to actually try out the ISP. That's why most ISPs will offer you a free evaluation period.

1. How Much Do They Charge?

You have various options: If you live in an urban area, you should be able to find a service offering unlimited connect time for $20–30/month. You might pay $20/month as a baseline access charge with no connect-time charges. Or, you might pay a baseline charge, with additional connect-time charges for each hour after the first 10 or 20 or 40 hours. In the latter case, the best deals have a ceiling on those connect-time charges so that you know you'll never spend more than a fixed amount each month no matter how much time you spend online. Connect-time ceilings may range from $20 to $60 per month, depending on what the market will bear. Most ISPs also charge a one-shot set-up fee to cover the cost of creating a new account.

What do you get for your money? Look for these features:

- Either a PPP or SLIP account
- An e-mail address with POP e-mail service
- Access to at least 10,000 Usenet newsgroups
- 5MB or 10MB storage space for a personal Web page
- Additional Web page space for an extra charge

Keep in mind that you also pay for your telephone charges whenever you dial into an ISP, so make sure you find an ISP with local dial-up access. Otherwise, your phone bills will probably overwhelm all other expenses. Always look for a service that can be reached with a local phone call.

2. Will They Let You Try Them Out Free for a Week?

Most ISPs will give you a free account for one or two weeks. This is important because so many questions can't be answered without first-hand experience. Your neighbors may have no problem with busy signals, but they may not be dialing in at the same times you'll want to dial in. A friend may say the technical support is great, but your friend may have very different needs than you do. Some things you have to check out for yourself.

Any ISP should be able to help you with the necessary software installations so that you can dial up your account and establish a working connection. This is one place where you should be able to get fast and courteous help from technical support. If you have trouble getting connected, call them for help. It's their job to get you up and running, and they should help you with this during your free trial period.

If you sign up for a free week, pick a time when you can be online as much as possible. Try to connect frequently and see if you get any busy signals. If you get a busy signal on the first try, can you get through on a second or third try? Install some software (e.g., a Web browser) to see if it goes smoothly. Use your news reader to read messages on the subscribers' newsgroups and see what people are saying about customer support. If an ISP is going down the tubes, you'll see complaints from disgruntled customers. Look for problems that you can take to tech support. How quickly do they respond? Do they treat you courteously? Do they help you solve your problem? Don't feel embarrassed to ask for help. They are in the business of helping people get underway with Internet access. If they make you feel like you are wasting their time, look for another ISP.

3. Is Their Modem Pool Reliable and Adequate for Their Customer Base?

The answer to this question determines whether you can connect whenever you want and then stay connected as long as you want. There is nothing more frustrating than a busy signal from your ISP when you really need to get online. To find out how often busy signals occur, you have to try out the service for a few days and see what happens each time you dial in.

A **modem pool** is a large bank of modems that your ISP uses to handle hundreds or thousands of incoming phone calls. Each subscriber relies on the modem pool for an available phone line into his or her ISP account and a reliable connection that won't disconnect. If a modem pool is not large enough for the subscriber population, some callers will get a busy signal when they try to connect. If the hardware in the modem pool is not good quality, subscribers may experience frequent disconnects.

Unfortunately, the adequacy of a modem pool is one of the more unstable aspects of ISP service. An ISP may be doing fine in January, experience a spurt of dramatic growth, and then in March, you start getting busy signals. Successful ISPs sometimes have trouble growing as fast as their customer base. This is one reason why recommendations for ISPs must be current. *If someone recommends an ISP, make sure that person is a currently active customer.*

4. How Good Is Their Technical Support?

Even the most self-sufficient computer user needs high-quality technical support. You may need to report a problem over which you have no control. You may hit a snag with software that isn't working. You may want to request a specific Usenet newsgroup. You shouldn't need to interact with technical support on a regular basis, but when you need them, it's usually for some important reason.

Here are some signs that technical support is up to speed:

- They have their own PC installation package for a graphical Web browser.
- They have a person who works specifically with Mac users.
- They have a 24-hour support line that's available 7 days a week, including holidays.
- They have multiple e-mail addresses for user queries (e.g., billing versus tech support).

- They help you promptly with any problems during your free trial period.
- They maintain local newsgroups on which subscribers can discuss questions and problems.

Once again, you need a trial period in order to assess the situation. ISPs experiencing explosive growth rates often have trouble keeping up with customer support. Services that are excellent one month can be completely unsatisfactory only a few months later.

5. Do They Offer Any Extra Services?

To maintain a competitive edge, some ISPs offer special services. Watch for these and weigh their value to you when deciding on the ISP. Here are two specific options you can ask about:

Space for a Personal or Business Web Page

Most ISPs will offer you space for Web pages that will be accessible by the rest of the world. These can be personal pages or pages for a business. They may be pages of your own creation, or pages that were created for you by a professional Web page designer. If you expect to set up your own Web site, find out what your ISP can offer you. Many ISPs provide 10MB of space for Web pages as part of their standard service. Additional space should be available for an extra charge.

Ability to Forward E-mail If You Change ISPs

It is also reasonable to think about what happens if you need to change ISPs. Chances are, you would like to have e-mail forwarded to your new address, just like the U.S. Post Office forwards mail for you when you change your street address. Most local ISPs will forward your e-mail for a charge. But some do not offer mail forwarding. If you expect to deal with a lot of e-mail that is important to you, then when you shop around for an ISP ask about forwarding mail. This is especially important if you ever want to use an ISP for business communications.

As you can see, many of the criteria may be difficult to assess without some experience. Even with a trial period, beginners may find that they haven't been able to do much more than establish a connection. If you have a number of ISPs in your area and you are not certain that you've picked the best one, don't worry about it too much. The relative merits of your local ISPs will probably all change six months from now anyway, thus making it virtually impossible to be certain that your ISP is the best one available in the long run. Prices, the quality of technical support, and modem pool reliability can all change without warning. ISPs live in the fast lane and rise or fall accordingly. If you find one whose service seems reasonable to you, be happy and turn your attention to other matters.

Appendix B

Dial-Up Access

If you have a PC or a Mac with a modem, you should be able to dial in either to your university's LAN or to your local ISP. If you want to transfer set-up software over a phone line, you need to have your computer account set up beforehand. You also need some crucial information when you first set up your account, including this:

- Your userid
- Your password
- The phone number(s) for the modem pool
- The DNS name for your remote host[†]
- IP numbers for your remote host and gateway host[†]

Next, you need to initialize settings in the telecommunications software that you'll be using to dial in. The software you run depends on both the type of computer you have and the type of account to which you are connecting. Different software is needed for SLIP/PPP accounts and shell accounts. The ISP who provides you with a remote account should also give you the telecommunications software you need, as well as assist you with its proper installation. Each installation has its own procedures for getting connected, so ask for the instructions that apply to you.

To Run Graphical Applications

If you have a PPP or SLIP account you can run graphical Internet applications. You just need some software for handling TCP/IP (see Chapter 2). Windows 3.XX users can use a Trumpet Winsock interface, Windows 95 users have Dial-Up Networking, and Mac users can use MacTCP. An Internet application can then activate your modem, dial out, and create a connection over the phone line to your remote host. Once a connection has been established, you can run any Internet application, including graphical Web browsers, graphical FTP clients, Telnet clients, and GUIs for specific Internet servers. You can quit one Internet application and start up a different one on the same connection. All of

[†] For SLIP/PPP accounts only.

this software is designed for point-and-click environments, so you can get everything underway with a few simple mouse clicks.

To Run Text-Based Applications

PPP and SLIP accounts make Internet access over a phone line relatively painless. But you may someday find yourself trying to access the Internet under less favorable conditions. If you have access to a time-sharing host that doesn't offer PPP or SLIP support, then your home computer assumes the role of a remote terminal and you communicate with your host computer via typed command lines. If you are running Windows 3.XX, you should have an application called Terminal (look for it in the "Accessories" folder). If you are running Windows 95, you have an application called HyperTerminal (from "Start" choose "Programs" and then "Accessories"). If you are on a Mac, you may need to obtain ZTerm or some other terminal emulator..

There are four telecommunications settings that need to be set correctly for things to work properly. These are shown next, along with their most common values:

stop bits = **1**

data bits = **8**

parity = **none**

flow control = **hardware** (although Xon/Xoff may also work)

Look for these under a "telecommunications" menu. If you are still experiencing difficulties, talk to a technical support person and ask if these settings are correct.

Different hosts and host gateways require different command sequences. For example, following is the procedure for students at the University of Massachusetts at Amherst who connect to a UNIX shell account in the Computer Science Department's EdLab. (*Note:* This procedure won't work unless you have an account with the Computer Science Department at UMass-Amherst.)

1. Dial-up on **545-3700.**

2. Select menu item **#1 (Computer Science).**

3. At the prompt, type

   ```
   conn elxx.cs.umass.edu
   ```

   where *xx* is a number between 1 and 20.

4. Enter your userid at the prompt login: **xxxxxxxx.**

5. Enter your password at the prompt password: **xxxxxxxx.**

Once you are connected, you can enter commands for the remote operating system (e.g., UNIX or VMS) as if you were on a terminal directly connected to that host.

If You Have Trouble

If you cannot make a connection, contact the technical support staff responsible for the machine to which you are trying to contact. Ask them to give you all of the correct settings for your telecommunications software and change the settings on your machine as needed. If there is still a problem, ask tech support for advice.

If you can connect, but you are experiencing frequent disconnects, try replacing your telephone/modem cable. The cable that runs between your modem to your phone jack can become damaged, yet show no signs of wear. A cable may appear to be working insofar as you can establish your connection, but it may cause frequent drop-outs due to signal degradation. You can prevent cable problems by keeping your cable where it won't get stepped on or tripped over.

If the problem is not your cable, there may be a problem with hardware at the receiving end. Try dialing into a different computer (perhaps a local ISP) to see if the problem is site-specific. If the problem occurs with more than one dial-in connection, you might have a problem with your phone line that the phone company can fix. Or it might be a problem with your own modem. To solve a persistent problem, you may need to talk to technical support staff affiliated with your modem, support staff associated with the computer installation you are trying to contact, and a telephone company representative. When all else fails, replace your modem.

It is possible to have flawless components operating at each step along the way, yet still have problems because the hardware and software just don't get along with one another. If your modem insists on a connection at 56Kbps and you are trying to connect to a receiving a modem that can't cope with that speed, neither side is at fault; it's the combination of components that doesn't work. For this reason, experienced computer users consider carefully before purchasing new high-speed modems that may not be compatible with older hardware at a remote installation. When you place yourself on the cutting edge, you might discover that it's more trouble than it's worth.

Appendix C

When to Talk to Tech Support

Technical support staff are paid to assist users of computing facilities so that they can work more efficiently and effectively. Increasingly, technical support staff are also helping people who have questions about the Internet. However, one staff member may be responsible for dozens, if not hundreds, of computer users. So it is not realistic to expect intensive hand-holding, especially on a regular basis. It also is a mistake to assume that the only people who can help you are technical support staff.

If you are a beginner, it is relatively easy to find people who can help you; there are usually a lot of people who are one jump ahead of you. In fact, someone who is only a little bit more experienced may be more helpful than someone who has moved on to more sophisticated problems. If you ask around, you will probably find someone who is willing and able to help, if only because most people love it when someone asks them for advice.

Here are some possible resources that often are available to college students:

- Friends and acquaintances who are experienced with computers
- Other students who use the same computer and software
- Any online help files or local discussion groups for beginners

In the case of a commercial ISP, where you are a paying customer, the rules for technical support are somewhat different. There you have a right to ask for all sorts of help, whenever you need it, and the ISP ideally will deliver good technical support as a part of their contracted service to you. Then, once you get off the ground, you can peruse online bulletin boards on which fellow subscribers post questions and ask other subscribers for help with problems. Sometimes this works and sometimes it doesn't, but it's always worth a try, especially if you can't get a fast response from technical support.

In general, a good tech support person is a precious resource and should be treated accordingly. If you are lucky enough to have good tech support people available to you, remember that they are handling many problems in addition to yours. Don't take up more time than is absolutely necessary. Many problems are easily solved, while others require extra effort and patience. There also are some truly nasty problems that defy solution no matter how many people give it their best effort. Happily, most problems can be solved.

If you have decided to approach a tech support person with a question, take some time to collect relevant information beforehand. For example, suppose you keep getting the same error message each time you try to start up a new piece of software. You can save yourself and tech support a lot of time if you do the following:

- Copy down exactly what the error message said.
- Know the name of the software you are using, including its version number.
- Know what operating system you are running, including its version number.
- Know whether this problem happens consistently or sporadically.

If the error happens only sporadically, try to identify any conditions that are always in place when the error occurs. For example, is there another application open at the time? Does the error happen only after you've been using your computer for a while? The more information you can provide, the easier it will be to identify the likely problem. As you gain more experience with tech support interactions, you will learn what sorts of things are likely to be relevant. The better prepared you are for your conversation with tech support, the better the outcome is likely to be.

Appendix D

Commands for Mailing Lists

The following commands are not case-sensitive. Angle-brackets are used to indicate entries that you need to replace with appropriate names and identifiers. Do not include the angle brackets in your own commands.

Listserv

All of the following commands should be sent to

```
listserv@<the.host.address>
```

with the listserv command in the message body.

To subscribe:

```
subscribe <listname> <your-first-name> <your-last-name>
```

To unsubscribe:

```
signoff <listname>
```

or

```
unsubscribe <listname>
```

To get an informational file describing available list options and commands:

```
info <listname>
```

To get a list of all unconcealed subscribers:

```
review <listname>
```

To remove yourself from the list of unconcealed subscribers:

```
set <listname> conceal
```

To place yourself on the list of unconcealed subscribers:

```
set <listname> noconceal
```

To get a list of all archived files:

```
index <listname>
```

To get a specific archived file (normally used after reviewing the archive index):

```
get <filename>
```

To receive all list messages in digest format:
```
set <listname> digest
```

To receive all list messages individually:
```
set <listname> nodigest
```

To receive a daily index of all messages posted that day with instructions for how to retrieve specific messages:
```
set <listname> index
```

To turn off the daily index and resume receipt of all messages:
```
set <listname> noindex
```

To temporarily halt all list messages:
```
set <listname> nomail
```

To resume receipt of all list messages:
```
set <listname> mail
```

To receive copies of your own messages to the list:
```
set <listname> repro
```

To turn off copies of your own messages to the list:
```
set <listname> norepro
```

To receive acknowledgments each time you post a message to the list:
```
set <listname> ack
```

To turn off acknowledgments each time you post a message to the list:
```
set <listname> noack
```

To receive a list of all listserv settings currently active for your subscription:
```
query <listname>
```

To find out who owns the list:
```
review <listname> short
```

To receive online documentation:
```
help
```

Listproc

All of the following commands should be sent to
```
listproc@<the.host.address>
```
with the listproc command in the message body.

To subscribe:
```
subscribe <listname> <your-first-name> <your-last-name>
```

To unsubscribe:
```
unsubscribe <listname>
```

To get a list of all archived files:
```
index <listname>
```

To get a specific archived file (normally used after reviewing the archive index):
```
get <listname> <filename>
```

To receive all list messages in digest format:
```
set <listname> mail digest
```

To receive all list messages individually:
```
set <listname> mail ack
```

To temporarily halt all mail messages:
```
set <listname> mail postpone
```

To resume receipt of all list messages:
```
set <listname> mail ack
```

To receive a list of all listproc settings currently active for your subscription:
```
set <listname>
```

To get a list of all unconcealed list subscribers and to find out who owns the list:
```
review <listname>
```
(The e-mail address of the list owner will appear in the `cc: field of the reply.`)

To receive online documentation:
```
help
```

To receive copies of your own posts:
```
set <listname> mail ack
```

To turn off copies of your own posts:
```
set <listname> mail noack
```

To remove yourself from your list of unconcealed subscribers:
```
set <listname> conceal yes
```

To place yourself on the list of unconcealed subscribers:
```
set <listname> conceal no
```

Majordomo

All of the following commands should be sent to

```
majordomo@the.host.address
```

with the majordomo command in the message body.

To subscribe:
```
subscribe <listname>
```

To unsubscribe:
```
unsubscribe <listname>
```

To get a list of all archived files:
```
index <listname>
```

To get a specific archived file (normally used after reviewing the archive index):
```
get <listname> <filename>
```

To find out who owns the list:
```
info <listname>
```

To receive online documentation:
```
help
```

Appendix   **E**

Advanced Search Features

The following descriptions of advanced search features are taken from the online documentation for each of three popular search engines: AltaVista, Infoseek, and HotBot. Note that some of these same search engines incorporate an interface in which you can enter optional search constraints (e.g., a domain name or a start date) into additional input windows. This makes it possible to exploit the tag functionality described here, without needing any knowledge of the tag set being used.

    Search engines are often upgraded and updated with new features. Please consult online documentation for the most accurate information on the search engines you use.

AltaVista's Constraining Features

`title:"The Wall Street Journal"`
Matches pages with the phrase *The Wall Street Journal* in the title.

`anchor:click-here`
Matches pages with the phrase *click here* in the text of a hyperlink.

`text:algo168`
Matches pages that contain the word *algo168* in any part of the visible text of a page. (ie, the word is not in a link or an image, for example.)

`applet:NervousText`
Matches pages containing the name of the Java applet class found in an applet tag; in this case, *NervousText*.

`object:Marquee`
Matches pages containing the name of the ActiveX object found in an object tag; in this case, *Marquee*.

`link:thomas.gov`
Matches pages that contain at least one link to a page with *thomas.gov* in its URL.

`image:comet.jpg`
Matches pages with *comet.jpg* in an image tag.

`url:home.html`

Matches pages with the words *home* and *html* together in the page's URL. Equivalent to `url:`"home html".

Trick: use the term `url:http` to get a count of all the pages in the DB.

`host:digital.com`

Matches pages with the phrase *digital.com* in the host name portion of the URL.

`domain:fr`

Matches pages from the domain `.fr`. There are few domain names: `.com`, `.edu`, `.net`, country codes (`.fr` is for France), and a few others.

Constraining Searches in Usenet News Articles

`from:napoleon@elba.com`

Matches news articles with the words *napoleon@elba.com* in the `From:` field.

`subject:`"for sale"

Matches news articles with the phrase *for sale* in the `Subject:` field. You can combine this with a word or phrase. For example, `subject:`"for sale" "victorian chamber pots".

`newsgroups:rec.humor`

Matches news articles posted (or crossposted) in news groups with *rec.humor* in the name.

`summary:invest`

Matches news articles with the word *invest*, *investment*, *investiture*, etc., in the summary.

`keywords:NASA`

Matches news articles with the word *NASA* in all caps in the keyword list.

Infoseek

Advanced Searching Using Field Searches

You can restrict searches to certain portions of Web documents by using Infoseek's field syntax. This allows you to search for Web pages' titles, urls, and embedded hypertext links. The field name (either link, site, url, or title) should be in lowercase, and immediately followed by a colon. There should be no spaces after the colon and before the search terms.

Examples

`link:infoseek.com`
Matches pages that contain at least one link to a page with infoseek.com in its URL. For example, you can use *+link:infoseek.com -url:infoseek.com* to see how many external links point to Infoseek. Note that unlike other search engines, Infoseek gives you exact counts, not approximations. Some search engines call this feature *searching backwards*.

`site:sun.com`
Finds pages on the Web site sun.com. The site field search examines the "site" part of the URL only. Therefore, *site:sun.com* will find such sites as `java.sun.com`, `www.sun.com` and `playground.sun.com`, but won't match any site that ends in *sun.co.uk*. You can use the site field search to bring up all pages at a particular Web site.

`url:science`
Returns pages with the word *science* anywhere in the page's URL.
This will find pages with URLs such as

`http://www.discovery.com/DCO/doc/1012/world/science/science.html`.

You can also use the url: field selection to find out the exact number of pages currently in Infoseek's database. Just type *url:http*. This number is updated as pages are added and removed from the database.

`title:"The New York Times"`
Finds pages with the phrase *The New York Times* in the title portion of the document.

HotBot

Meta Words

Meta words are shortcuts that allow experienced searchers to use HotBot's non-text search features from the main text box. A **meta word** is a keyword:value pair, separated by a colon (with no spaces). For example: the title keyword finds values in the titles of web pages, so a search containing the meta word *title:president* will return documents with the word *president* in their titles.

It is important to understand that HotBot treats Meta words as words, not as commands that effect the entire search. So the search *title:president Nixon* will return documents with *president* in the title and *Nixon* in the body of the document. Furthermore, all of the advanced search modifiers can be used with meta words. For example,

```
-feature:image +title:president Nixon
```

will return pages that must not contain images, do have *president* in their title and may have the word *Nixon* in them.

These special search words can be added to queries to restrict search results in a number of ways. Most of these effects can also be achieved by using the controls on the HotBot page.

domain: [name]

Restricts a search to the domain selected. Domains can be specified up to three levels deep (*.com*, *intel.com*, or *support.intel.com*).

depth: [number]

Restricts the depth of pages retrieved.

feature: [name]

Limits your query to pages containing the specified feature. Most of these controls are also available under the Media Type panel. The name can be any of the following:

feature:acrobat
Detects Acrobat files

feature:applet
Detects embedded Java applets

feature:activex
Detects ActiveX controls

feature:audio
Detects a range of audio formats

feature:embed
Detects plugins

feature:flash
Detects the Flash plugin in HTML

feature:form
Detects the use of forms in HTML

feature:frame
Detects the use of frames in HTML

feature:image
Detects image files (GIF, JPEG, etc.)

feature:script
Detects embedded scripts

feature:shockwave
Detects Shockwave files

feature:table
Detects the use of tables in HTML

`feature:video`
> Detects a range of video formats

`feature:vrml`
> Detects VRML files

`linkdomain:[name]`

Restricts a search to pages containing links to the specified domain. For example, `linkdomain:hotbot.com` finds pages that point to HotBot.

`linkext:[extension]`

Restricts a search to pages containing embedded files with the specified extension. For example, `linkext:ra` finds pages containing RealAudio files.

`newsgroup:[full newsgroup name]`

Restricts Usenet searches to articles that have been posted to the specified newsgroup.

`scriptlanguage:[language]`

Searches for pages containing JavaScript or VBScript.

`title:[word]`

Searches for pages containing the given word in their titles.

Date Meta Words

Restricts query results to pages modified within a specific range of dates by using date meta words. Currently, they are special cases in the search engine and will only function correctly if used as a single term within a Boolean clause, without any pluses or minuses. So (`+cloning -sheep`) and `within:8/months` is okay, but `+cloning -sheep +within:8/months` will not work.

`after:[day]/[month]/[year]`

Restricts a search to documents created or modified after the specified date (e.g., `currents` AND `after:30/6/96`).

`before:[day]/[month]/[year]`

Restricts a search to documents created or modified before the specified date (e.g., `cyber crime` AND `before:30/6/96`).

`within:number/unit`

Restricts a search to documents created or modified within the last specified time period (e.g., (`pet +care`) AND `within:3/months`). Units can be days, months, or years.

Hint: The terminally curious can use View Source in their browsers to examine the query comment near the top of the results page. This shows how the query specified with the HotBot forms interface has been mapped to meta words.

Bibliography

Barrett, Daniel J., *NetResearch: Finding Information On-line*, Songline Studios, Inc. and O'Reilly & Associates, Inc., Sebastopol, Calif., 1997 (186 pages).

Campbell, Dave and Mary Campbell, *A Student's Guide to Doing Research on the Internet*, Addison-Wesley, Reading, Mass., 1995 (349 pages).

Clark, Carol Lea, *A Student's Guide to the Internet*, Prentice-Hall, Upper Saddle River, N.J., 1996 (184 pages).

Comer, Douglas E., *The Internet Book: Everything You Need to Know about Computer Networking and How the Internet Works*, Prentice Hall, Englewood Cliffs, N.J., 1995 (312 pages).

Computerization and Controversy: Value Conflicts and Social Choices (Second Edition), Rob Kling (Ed.), Academic Press, San Diego, Calif., 1996 (961 pages).

Crump, Eric and Nick Carbone, *English On-line: A Student's Guide to the Internet and World Wide Web*, Houghton Mifflin Company, Boston, Mass., 1997 (244 pages).

Gilster, Paul, *Digital Literacy*, John Wiley & Sons, New York, N.Y., 1997 (276 pages).

Gilster, Paul, *Finding It On the Internet* (Second Edition), John Wiley & Sons, Inc., New York, N.Y., 1996 (379 pages).

Grauer, Robert T. and Gretchen Marx, *Essentials of Netscape*, Prentice-Hall, Upper Saddle River, N.J., 1997 (111 pages).

Hafner, Katie and Matthew Lyon, *Where Wizards Stay Up Late*, Simon and Schuster, New York, N.Y., 1996 (304 pages).

Hahn, Harley and Rick Stout, *The Internet Complete Reference*, Osborne McGraw-Hill, Berkeley, Calif., 1994 (817 pages).

Hauben, Michael and Ronda Hauben, *Netizens: On the History and Impact of Usenet and the Internet*, IEEE Computer Press, 1997 (384 pages). Also available on the Web at `http://www.columbia.edu/~hauben/netbook/`

Heslop, Brent and David Angell, *The Instant Internet Guide*, Addison-Wesley, Reading, Mass., 1994 (209 pages).

Kehoe, Brendan P., *Zen and the Art of the Internet* (Fourth Edition), Prentice-Hall, Upper Saddle River, N.J., 1996 (255 pages).

Lemay, Laura, *Teach Yourself Web Publishing with HTML 3.0 in a Week* (Second Edition), Sams.net Publishing, Indianapolis, Ind., 1996 (518 pages).

Leshin, Cynthia B., *Netscape Adventures: Step-by-Step Guide to Netscape Navigator and the World Wide Web*, Prentice-Hall, Upper Saddle River, N.J., 1997 (316 pages).

Levy, Steven, *Hackers: Heroes of the Computer Revolution*, Dell Publishing, New York, N.Y., 1984 (458 pages).

Mitchell, William J., *City of Bits: Space, Place, and the Infobahn*, MIT Press, Cambridge, Mass., 1995 (225 pages).

Negroponte, Nicholas, *Being Digital*, Vintage Books (Random House), New York, N.Y., 1995 (255 pages).

Pitter, Keiko, Sara Amato, John Callahan, Nigel Kerr, and Eric Tilton, *Every Student's Guide to the Internet*, McGraw-Hill, Inc., New York, N.Y., 1995 (183 pages).

Raggett, Dave, Jenny Lam, and Ian Alexander, *HTML 3: Electronic Publishing on the World Wide Web*, Addison-Wesley, Reading, Mass., 1996 (398 pages).

Rose, Donald, *Internet Chat Quick Tour*, Ventana Press, Chapel Hill, N.C., 1995 (174 pages).

Salkind, Neil J., *Hands-On Internet*, Boyd & Frasier Publishing Co., Danvers, Mass., 1995 (198 pages).

The Internet 1997 Unleashed, Jill Ellsworth and Billy Baron (Eds.), Sams.net Publishing, Indianapolis, Ind., 1996 (1,269 pages).

"The Next 50 Years: Special Anniversary Issue," *Communications of the Association of Computing Machinery*, February 1997, Vol. 40, No. 2.

Tolhurst, William A., Mary Ann Pike, Keith A. Blanton, and John R. Harris, *Using the Internet, Special Edition*, Que Corp., Indianapolis, Ind., 1994 (1,188 pages).

Wyatt, Allen L., *Success with Internet*, Boyd & Frasier Publishing Co., Danvers, Mass., 1995 (443 pages).

Zimmermann, Phil, *The Official PGP User's Guide*, MIT Press, Cambridge, Mass., 1995 (216 pages).

Credits

I am grateful to the following individuals and organizations for providing valuable information and granting copyright permissions for reproduction.

Numerous screen shots throughout the book were taken with Netscape Navigator 2.01. Each figure containing a screen shot of Netscape Navigator is subject to the following restriction: "Copyright 1996 Netscape Communications Corp. Used with permission. All Rights Reserved. This electronic file or page may not be reprinted or copied without the express written permission of Netscape." In addition, Netscape Communications Corporation has not authorized, sponsored, endorsed, or approved this publication and is not responsible for its content. Netscape and the Netscape Communications Corporate Logos, are trademarks and trade names of Netscape Communications Corporation. All other product names and/or logos are trademarks of their respective owners.

Additional screen shots were taken with Internet Explorer 2.1. Screen shots reprinted by permission from Microsoft Corporation.

Chapter 1

- The Unofficial Netscape FAQ (`http://www.sousystems.com/faq/`) was designed and programmed by Jay Garcia, with significant contributions from Kevin Hecht, and is currently maintained by Frank Tabor. The UFAQ screen shot has been reproduced here with permission from Jay Garcia.
- Permission to use the FreePPP screen shot was granted by Adam C. Engst, who is also the publisher of TidBITS (an online newsletter for Mac users) and many books about the Internet (see `http://www.tidbits.com/adam/`).
- The command counts for Microsoft Word in "Creeping Featurism" came from "Creating the People's Computer," by Michael Dertouzos, *Technology Review*, April 1997.

Chapter 2

- "Who Uses the Internet?" was based on data from the GVU's 6th WWW User Survey conducted by the Graphics, Visualization and Usability Center at the Georgia Institute of Technology, (originally available at `http://www.gvu.gatech.edu/user_surveys/survey-10-1996/`).

- The data for Figure 2.1 was collected by Network Wizards (and is available at `http://www.nw.com/`).
- The data for Figure 2.4 was collected by the Merit, Inc. and is found at `nic.merit.edu` in the FTP file `/nsfnet/statistics/history.packets` (and is also available at `http://www.merit.net/statistics/nsfnet`).
- "How Reliable Are Computer Networks?" was based on the article, "Moment's downtime kills thousands of messages," *Communications News*, February 1996.
- The description of Internet administration was derived primarily from *The Internet Unleashed (second edition)*, Sams.net Publishing, 1995.
- "Regulating Internet Access Costs" contains an excerpt from The Internet Tourbus (U. S. Library of Congress ISSN #1094-2238), copyright 1995–97, Rankin & Crispen. All rights reserved. (Archives for The Internet Tourbus are available at `http://www.TOURBUS.com`)
- "Digital Scam Artists" contains an excerpt from the Internet Fraud newsletter distributed by the Consumers League Project through the National Fraud Information Center (originally available at `http://www.fraud.org/february97.htm`) and an excerpt from the CNET Internet newsletter distributed by CNET, Inc. (originally available at `http://news.com/NEWS/Item/0,4,8077,00.html`).
- The source for "Boon or Bust for the Baby Bells?" was an article "Phone Hogs or Good Customers?", Catherine Arnst, *Business Week*, February 17, 1997 (page 8).

Chapter 3

- Text displays associated with the elm mail client were generated by Elm 2.4 PL25, of November 11, 1995 (©) Copyright 1988–1992 USENET Community Trust Based on Elm 2.0, (©) Copyright 1986,1987 Dave Taylor.
- Eudora Pro 3.1 is the property of 1997 QUALCOMM Inc. (Eudora Division). All rights reserved. (See `http://www.eudora.com`)
- Figure 3.1 contains selected signatures from a sig file collection compiled by Hugh Satow (originally available at `http://www.bilpin.co.uk/sims/hs/sigs`).
- "An Hour a Day" contains survey data from NUA Internet Surveys: 1996 Review of the Year, by Nua Ltd. (originally available at `http://www.nua.ie/surveys/1996review.html#email`).
- "Generation Gaps" includes an excerpt from "Libraries: A Critical Lane on the Information Superhighway," a speech by Susan Ness delivered on February 16, 1997, at the American Library Association. (originally available at `http://www.fcc.gov/Speeches/Ness/spsn704.html`).
- The excerpt from AOL's autoreply ("Postmaster Mail Receipt Notification") received on Dec. 8, 1996, was reproduced without alteration. The e-mail follow-up on Dec. 13, 1996, from Michael Truman, Assistant Postmaster at America Online, was reproduced here in its entirety. Copyright 1996–1997 America Online, Inc. All Rights Reserved.

Chapter 4:

- AWAD mailing data was compiled by Anu Garg, creator of A.Word.A.Day (see `http://www.wordsmith.org/awad/`).
- The instructions for creating a mail filter rule in Eudora were adapted from instructions written by Adam Boettinger (originally available at `http://www.exposure-usa.com/email/spam.html`).
- "Do Not Post Irrelevant Material to a Mailing List" quotes an excerpt from the welcome message for the "golden" mailing list (`listserv@hobbes.ucsd.edu`), written by Wade Blomgren and reproduced here with permission from Wade Blomgren.
- "Just How Good Is a Spam Filter?" used a version of Adam Boettinger's personal filter rules list (originally available at `http://www.exposure-usa.com/email/filters.html?`).

Chapter 5

- The Internet Archive Project was described in "The Next 50 Years: Special Anniversary Issue," *Communications of the Association of Computing Machinery*, February 1997, Vol. 40, No. 2. (See also `http://www.archive.org/`).
- The origin of hypertext and the Web was based in part on *Hypertext and Hypermedia*, Jakob Nielsen, Academic Press, Inc., (1990) and *The Internet Unleashed (Second Edition)*, Sams.net Publishing,. Indianapolis, Ind., (1995).
- The home page for the Yahoo! subject tree (`http://www.yahoo.com/`), owned by Yahoo! Inc., was reproduced without alteration.

Chapter 6

- Numerous examples throughout this chapter were taken from Gopher pages supported by the University of Minnesota and the University of Massachusetts at Amherst (the latter's Gopher server has since been retired).
- The data for Figure 6.3 was collected by Merit, Inc. (originally available at `ftp://ftp.isoc.org/isoc/charts2/growth/90s-www.txt`).

Chapter 7

- Numerous examples throughout this chapter are based on search engine output from Infoseek, AltaVista, Hotbot, Excite, and Magellan.

  Infoseek, Copyright 1995–1997, Infoseek Corporation. All rights reserved.
  AltaVista output has been reproduced with the permission of Digital Equipment Corporation. AltaVista, the AltaVista logo and the Digital logo are trademarks of the Digital Equipment Corporation.
  Hotbot Copyright 1996–97 Wired Digital, Inc. All rights reserved.
  Excite, Excite Search, and the Excite Logo are trademarks of Excite, Inc. and

may be registered in various jurisdictions. Excite screen display copyright 1995–1997 Excite, Inc.

Magellan Internet Guide and the Magellan logo are trademarks of The McKinley Group, Inc., a subsidiary of Excite, Inc., and may be registered in various jurisdictions. Magellan screen display copyright 1997 of The McKinley Group, Inc., a subsidiary of Excite, Inc.

- The three excerpts from the Scout Report have been reproduced with permission. The Scout Report (Sept 27, 1996; June 28, 1996; June 7, 1996) is a publication of the Internet Scout Project, Computer Sciences Department, University of Wisconsin–Madison, sponsored by the National Science Foundation.

- The elevation of Springfield, Massachusetts was found in output from the Geography Server (geo-gw 1.0) at the University of Michigan (originally available at `http://www-iwi.unisg.ch/~dlincke/geo-gw/index.html`).

- The e-mail message describing "The Stack of the Artist of Kouroo" project was reproduced here in its entirety with permission from Austin Meredith.

- The example of search engine coverage for the Federation of American Scientists Web site was brought to my attention by John Pike, director of the Space Policy Project at the Federation of American Scientists, and reproduced here with his permission. (see also `http://www.fas.org/spp/`).

- The data in Figure 7.7 was collected using advanced search features and resulting document counts from the search engines themselves. I do not assume responsibility for any errors associated with the document counts provided by these search engines.

- The screen shot of the Dogpile home page and the output pages from Dogpile have been reproduced with permission from Aaron Flin.

- The unexpected behavior of Infoseek during a -site:.com search as described in "Domain Search Glitches" was confirmed in a personal communication from Infoseek's support staff on July 21, 1997.

Chapter 8

- Screen shots of the Usenet in action were taken with the Netscape Navigator news reader.

- Output traces of the tin news reader (version 1.2 for UNIX, Copyright 1991–93, Iain Lea) were reproduced with permission from Iain Lea. The tin news reader is available at `ftp://ftp.ecrc.de/pub/news/clients/tin-unoff/`.

- The copyright notice from the RTFM FAQ archive at MIT (`rtfm.mit.edu`) has been reproduced with permission.

- Screen shots from the Usenet Info Center Launch Pad were made possible by SunSITE USA, which is sponsored by Sun Microsystems, Inc ., Cisco Systems, Inc. , and the University of North Carolina at Chapel Hill (originally available at `http://sunsite.unc.edu/usenet-i/`).

- Output from DejaNews demonstrating a search for Usenet newsgroups was generated by the Interest Finder at `http://www.dejanews.com/`
- Excerpts from Usenet posts written by Leo G. Simonetta and Ceylon Stowell were reproduced here with their permission.

Chapter 9

- The Macintosh Software Archive is maintained by the University of Michigan.
- Screen shots of Fetch were reproduced with permission from Dartmouth College.

Chapter 10

- The netfind server is maintained by the InterNIC Directory and Database Services provided by AT&T and partially supported through a cooperative agreement with the National Science Foundation.
- The Telnet server at `geoserver.eecs.umich.edu` is maintained by the University of Michigan.
- The main menu for the NEWTON BBS server was reproduced here in its entirety. The NEWTON BBS server was developed by and is maintained by Argonne National Laboratory.
- The screen shot of Better Telnet PPP was reproduced with permission from Rolf Braun. Better Telnet is available from `http://www.cstone.net/~rbraun/`
- The Telnet site maintained by the Michigan Department of Commerce Information Network (at `hermes.merit.edu`) is no longer in operation (but see problem #10).
- The discussion of Freenets is based primarily on a description in *The Internet Unleashed (second edition)*, Sams.net Publishing,. Indianapolis, Ind., 1995.
- The excerpt from NEWTON's Acceptable Use Policy was reproduced here with permission. The NEWTON BBS server was developed and is maintained by Argonne National Laboratory.
- The screen shot of Fixation in action was reproduced with permission from Adam Miller.
- The list of chat channels at the Internet Chess Club was reproduced with permission from Sleator Games, Inc.
- The MicroMUSE opening screen was reproduced courtesy of the MicroMUSE Operations Council: `chezmoto.ai.mit.edu` 4201.

Chapter 11

- The iguana graphic (Cyber-ig 1997, Copyright Marian Briones) in Figure 11.23 was reproduced with permission from Marian Briones.

Chapter 12

- Portions of this text are copyrighted and reprinted with the permission of Pretty Good Privacy, Inc., 1990–1994. All rights reserved.

Chapter 13

- The fair use criteria in "Guidelines for Fair Use" are a slightly modified version of those presented in *English Online: A Student's Guide to the Internet and World Wide Web*, Eric Crump and Nick Carbone. Houghton Mifflin Company, Boston, Mass. (1997), pages 152–153.
- The discussion of copyright issues was inspired by the article "10 Big Myths About Copyright Explained," Brad Templeton (originally available at `http://www.clarinet.com/brad/copymyths.html`).
- The discussion of the First Amendment was based on a guest lecture delivered to CompSci 191a at the University of Massachusetts in fall 1995 by Professor Ethan Katsh of the Legal Studies Department at the University of Massachusetts at Amherst.
- "Truth and the Internet" was reproduced here in its entirety with the permission of Vint Cerf, senior vice president, MCI Communications.

Appendices

- Appendix E contains on-line documentation from the following:

  Infoseek (`http://www.infoseek.com/`)
  AltaVista (`http://www.altavista.digital.com/`)
  Hotbot (`http://www.hotbot.com/`)

Index

O